22nd EDITION

GUNS
ILLUSTRATED®

1990

Edited by Harold A. Murtz
and the Editors of Gun Digest

MEMBER OF THE
NATIONAL
SHOOTING
SPORTS
FOUNDATION
INC.

DBI BOOKS, INC.

About Our Covers

Springfield Armory, of Geneseo, Illinois, has become a major force in the firearms industry. Beginning as basically a one-gun company, their product line has blossomed considerably, with myriad offerings for nearly every shooting need and style.

Our front cover shows two of Springfield's latest goodies for pistol shooters. On the left is the 9mm Parabellum P9 automatic, based directly on the Czech CZ-75. This standard model has a frame-mounted thumb safety, Commander-style hammer, low-profile sights, serrated front and rear frame straps, and a 16-round magazine. The barrel length is 4.72 inches and the gun weighs 35.3 oz. It's also available in a compact model with 3.66-inch barrel, weight of 32.1 oz., and 10-shot magazine. Both versions are available in polished blue or satin nickel finish.

On the right is the Springfield Master Grade Competition "B" 45 ACP with all the "bells and whistles." Included are fully-adjustable low-profile sights, ambidextrous thumb safety, tuned speed trigger, Commander hammer, National Match barrel and bushing, checkering on rear of slide, lowered and flared ejection port, special compensator unit, and more. The "Pin Gun" is just the ticket for USPSA/IPSC competition or bowling pin shooters.

On the back cover, the excellent Springfield M1A is shown with walnut stock and handguard. This is the premium quality civilian version of the military M-14 rifle and it can be had chambered for either 308 Win. or 243 Win. and in three styles—Standard, Match or Bush Rifle. The Standard version weighs about 8 lbs., 15 oz., measures 44½ inches overall, and has a 22-inch barrel (without flash suppressor).

To the right of the M1A is the Springfield Armory SAR-3 Standard model that includes all the features of the German-made G3 rifle. It's chambered for the popular 308 Win. cartridge, weighs 8.7 lbs., has an 18-inch barrel, and comes with two magazines, leather sling, tech manual and cleaning kit. As with the G3, the SAR-3 uses the proven delayed roller-lock locking system.

See page 20 for a report on these guns.
Photos by John Hanusin.

GUNS ILLUSTRATED STAFF

EDITOR
Harold A. Murtz

ASSISTANT TO THE EDITOR
Lilo Anderson

EDITORIAL/PRODUCTION ASSISTANT
Jamie L. McCoy

CONTRIBUTING EDITOR
Clay Harvey

GRAPHIC DESIGN
James P. Billy
Steve Johnson
Mary MacDonald

MANAGING EDITOR
Pamela J. Johnson

PUBLISHER
Sheldon L. Factor

DBI BOOKS, INC.

PRESIDENT
Charles T. Hartigan

VICE PRESIDENT & PUBLISHER
Sheldon L. Factor

VICE PRESIDENT—SALES
John G. Strauss

TREASURER
Frank R. Serpone

ISBN 0-87349-039-8 Library of Congress Catalog #69-11342

CONTENTS

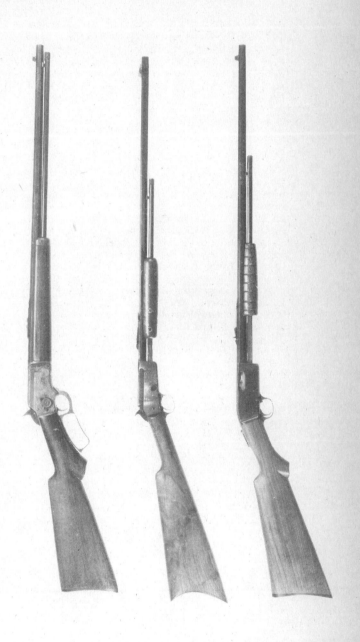

FEATURES

My Favorite Shooting
A.B. Swan **4**

Product Liability Suits—Opportunity Unlimited
Bill Holmes **10**

All Dressed Up to go Shooting
Rick Hacker **14**

Springfield's P9 and Master Grade "B" Pistols
Clay Harvey **20**

You Don't HAVE to Use a Scope!
Michael Thomas **25**

Whitetales—Fun Yarns from the Deer Fields
Clay Harvey **30**

Antique from Antietam
Joseph W. Byers **36**

Requiem for the Benelli Pistol Family
Donald Maclaren **42**

Oehler's New Model 35P Chronograph
Dick Eades **52**

Firearms Ads of the 1930s
Kenneth L. Kieser **56**

Marlin's Model 1894 Classic
Sam Fadala **61**

The Bolt-Action Shotgun
J. Rakusan **65**

Shooting Heavy-Barrel Rifles
Wilf E. Pyle **68**

The Sharps and the Buffalo
Norman Wiltsey **75**

Wilson Neck Sizing Dies
Jon Leu **80**

On the Firing Line
Clay Harvey **83**

The 16 Gauge—Coming or Going?
John Haviland **93**

A Gun for All Seasons: T/C's New Englander
William Josephs **98**

DEPARTMENTS

GUNDEX **104**
Handguns—U.S. & Imported **112**
Rifles—U.S. & Imported **160**
Drillings, Combos, Double Rifles **195**
Shotguns—U.S. & Imported **215**
Blackpowder Guns **246**
Air Guns **265**
Metallic Sights **281**
Scopes & Mounts **285**
Directory of the Arms Trade **295**

Plinking with a 22 rimfire is not only enjoyable, it is also educational. The good shot with a 22 rifle is generally a good shot with a big bore. The 22 offers the kind of practice which transfers to the big game rifle.

My Favorite Shooting

A good 22, a box or two of ammo and a few hours of time are all you need to enjoy yourself and get away from things. Here're one shooter's thoughts on the subject.

by **A.B. SWAN**

Much of the author's small game is taken with the 22 Short hollowpoint round, which is available nearly everywhere. It's accurate and reliable.

THE MOST IMPORTANT shooting I do is with the big game rifle, harvesting "cholesterol free" meat for my freezers and filling my trophy hunting book of memories with priceless experiences. I live in a game-rich region, where "putting meat in for the winter" is much more fact than a cliche. So the big game rifle is my most *important* shooting instrument. But the 22 rimfire is my *favorite*. I like its manners — quiet and mild. I like its style — reliable and accurate. And I like the fact that you don't have to plunk down a wad of green cabbage thick enough to choke a mule in order to buy a box or two of 22 fodder.

In this land alone, about three billion — that's billion, not million — 22 rimfire rounds are popped per annum. I think you can chalk up another several million to billion worldwide. The 22 rimfire is found all over the globe, from Russia to Australia, Africa to China, where the sun shines hot or the wind blows cold. Twenty-two ammo is manufactured in Canada, Brazil, Mexico, Argentina, Yugoslavia, Korea, Finland, Italy, Germany and a great many other countries. Reloading certain centerfire rounds renders them the most versatile ammo of all, of course; however, you can accomplish myriad shooting tasks with the everyday 22 rimfire, with the lavish luxury of expelling the tiny brass case instead of salvaging it. Because of this broad service at modest expense, the 22 holds the record for rounds fired, and it's been doing so for a very long time. 1987 marked the 22 Long Rifle's centennial year, and the 22 Short dates back to at least 1857.

Twenty-two rimfire history is rich in diversity, from the 22 BB Cap through the 22 Winchester Magnum Rimfire, with more wrinkles in it than an elephant's hide. There have been so many different brands and loads over the years that I doubt anyone could now produce a totally reliable chronology of 22 rimfire growth from Flobert's parlor round to current specialized 22 target ammo. Twenty-two handgun history is also replete, but if I were to become a gun collector, my major interest would be 22 rifles, everything from 2-pound single shots given away to kids who peddled enough salve or soap, to special target

Cottontails for supper, taken with a bolt-action 22 rifle, the author's favorite small-game getter. This kind of hunting also sharpens a hunter's skills.

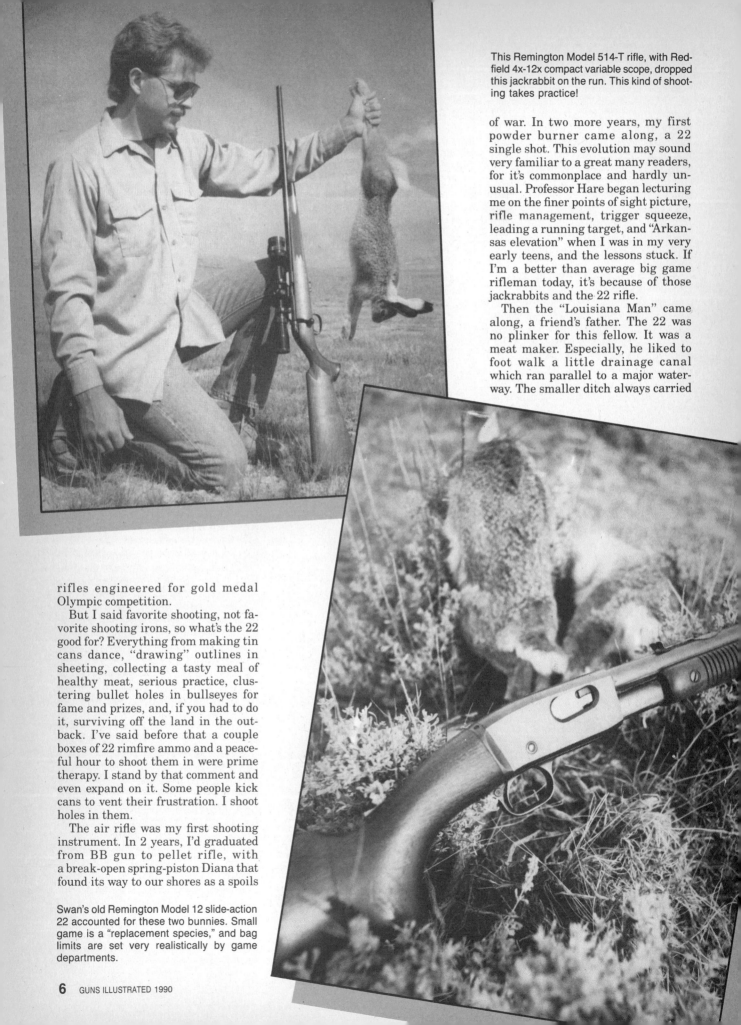

This Remington Model 514-T rifle, with Redfield 4x-12x compact variable scope, dropped this jackrabbit on the run. This kind of shooting takes practice!

of war. In two more years, my first powder burner came along, a 22 single shot. This evolution may sound very familiar to a great many readers, for it's commonplace and hardly unusual. Professor Hare began lecturing me on the finer points of sight picture, rifle management, trigger squeeze, leading a running target, and "Arkansas elevation" when I was in my very early teens, and the lessons stuck. If I'm a better than average big game rifleman today, it's because of those jackrabbits and the 22 rifle.

Then the "Louisiana Man" came along, a friend's father. The 22 was no plinker for this fellow. It was a meat maker. Especially, he liked to foot walk a little drainage canal which ran parallel to a major waterway. The smaller ditch always carried

rifles engineered for gold medal Olympic competition.

But I said favorite shooting, not favorite shooting irons, so what's the 22 good for? Everything from making tin cans dance, "drawing" outlines in sheeting, collecting a tasty meal of healthy meat, serious practice, clustering bullet holes in bullseyes for fame and prizes, and, if you had to do it, surviving off the land in the outback. I've said before that a couple boxes of 22 rimfire ammo and a peaceful hour to shoot them in were prime therapy. I stand by that comment and even expand on it. Some people kick cans to vent their frustration. I shoot holes in them.

The air rifle was my first shooting instrument. In 2 years, I'd graduated from BB gun to pellet rifle, with a break-open spring-piston Diana that found its way to our shores as a spoils

Swan's old Remington Model 12 slide-action 22 accounted for these two bunnies. Small game is a "replacement species," and bag limits are set very realistically by game departments.

water and a good supply of bullfrogs. You could shoot downward into the water because the bullets would never ricochet, and so my mentor would lean over the steep bank, holding a "fine bead" on the head of a bullfrog (it was legal to collect bullfrogs with a 22), and at the crack of his tiny Remington rolling block rifle, my buddy or I would scramble down the bank and into the water to collect dinner before it sank. At the close of a good day, a frog leg dinner was certain, and it was a poor hunt when to go with it there were fewer than a half-dozen cottontail rabbits.

He used the 22 Short exclusively in the rolling block, considering the Long Rifle more than necessary for small game collecting at close range. I still use the 22 Short, in the hollow-point version, for my own small game harvesting when the range doesn't exceed 50 yards. The head shot's the rule, and the 22 Short high-speed hollowpoint is more than sufficiently accurate to count on it centering the 2-inch wide target presented by the sedentary cottontail rabbit. No season goes by when I don't collect white-meat dinners with my 22. Properly cared for and cooked, the rabbit represents delicious fat-free high protein meat.

I realize that where I hunt out west, the bunnies aren't sophisticated, and you may have to use a shotgun to collect your powder-puff tails. However, stillhunting along, slowly—there's no hurry; save the hurry for something else — I usually get a sitting shot at my rabbits at an average of about 20 paces. Running shots? If the opportunity is close and clear, sure. The Short hollowpoint plunked into the chest cavity at close range will cleanly drop a rabbit with one shot. I carry a 22 rifle, broken down, on my big game jaunts, too. It always pays off.

One season, two out-of-state friends and I dropped off a big plateau and down to the banks of the Platte River where we located a camping spot of rich grasses and trees. We fished for trout in between filling three antelope tags. And we ate a couple of fine cottontail dinners gathered up by my little rimfire rifle. Everybody knows that the cottontail is number one in the world of small game hunting. But number two is just as important, and even more heavily hunted in certain specific locales. He's the tree squirrel. Chances are, you have better squirrel hunting than I do. I have to drive for mine, quite a distance. But it's always worth it.

On squirrels, I usually switch ammo, from the 22 Short high velocity hollowpoint to a Long Rifle of the same type. In some areas, I know I can get shots at only a few yards' distance, and I know, too, that I can call a head shot every time (or a clean miss). And I've used the 22 Short hollowpoint on these treks, or the standard velocity Long Rifle. But the high velocity LR hollowpoint will do a much better job if a squirrel is chest struck. Squirrels are tough. Where I hunt 'em, they're out all season long, denned up only when wind or rain drive them inside. You can hunt bushytails many ways, but in my favorite spot, the best way is to walk along quietly, keeping a sharp eye out for movement, especially on the forest floor.

When the squirrel dashes for his tree, you dash after him. Up he climbs, and by the time you get there, it's an eye-hunt for the rodent, who can turn himself into a chunk of tree bark in a split second. I've found the excellent, modern, compact binocular (I like B&L's 7x24 Discoverers) just right for such squirreling, because these glasses can optically separate a squirrel from a tree limb with their good resolution. And they close-focus to a couple yards. You crane your neck,

The Marlin Model 25M in 22 WMR proves to be a fun and effective prairie dog rifle out to about 125 yards. It has plenty of punch for such varmints.

The hyper-velocity 22 Long Rifle is a good one for varmint hunting. These Federal Spitfires come in a round can holding 50 rounds and it fits nicely in a shirt pocket.

glass every inch of the tree over your head, and rely on patience and clear optics to find your supper for you, which you harvest with a perfect head shot.

Incidentally, never regret taking your lawful bag limit of small game animals. These animals cycle anyway, and hunting has precious little to do with population dynamics. When a population does drop off due to hunter harvest, there are always sufficient breeding stock left behind for the closed season mating and gestation periods. The mathematics of hunter success on small game fall into the low numbers as there are fewer animals, for your odds of getting shots become poorer and poorer. Disease, winter and normal cycling make the major inroads in small game numbers. For example, my local cottontail spot is in the down ebb of its cycle. Shot out? I hardly think so. The place is privately owned and seldom sees three hunters a year on it, and there were so many cottontails there a few years ago that a 10-limit bag didn't take 1 hour of hunting time. Then . . . crash! It's typical. And typically, the population will work its way back up. And then cycle again.

Small game hunting offers many valuable transfer lessons to big game hunting. Obviously, your shooting eye is sharpened on small game or varmints. But you also learn to spot wild-

life from experience in the small game field. And you can even find out how well various hunting gear works for you, from apparel to shellholders, to trying new items before the big game season arrives. About those varmints, I'm more than aware that under many circumstances, the 22 rimfire is not the best choice for these animals. If you intend to shoot woodchucks or rockchucks at long range, for example, grab a hotshot 22, such as the 22-250 or similar loading, and go for it. But if you want to *hunt* varmints with a 22 rimfire, go ahead. I hunt prairie dogs on ranchlands which have too many of these little rodents burrowing

into the earth to leave horse-tripping holes and pasture-destroying land erosion in their wake. These rodents are not hunter wise, and they are stalkable. I would say my average shot is from 50 yards. I aim for the head and only the head, and one 22 Long Rifle hollowpoint, in either the high velocity or hyper-velocity loading, will quickly and cleanly dispatch these fellows on the spot from such close range.

When I have to shoot at over 75 yards, I switch to a 22 WMR. I realize that the 22 Magnum, as it's commonly called, catches a lot of flack from a lot of folks, but turn a deaf ear to much of this disparagement. I shoot quite a number of 22 WMR rounds annually, and I'll guarantee that it's very useful ammo, deadly on varmints to 125 yards, far more accurate than I can hold the rifle in the gamefield, and deadly, too, for a couple of big game-style creatures — the wild turkey and the javelina, on which the 22 WMR is legal where I hunt. Make no mistake, gobblers are tough, and if you may have to take a moving shot, use the hollowpoint version of the 22 WMR.

But if you can get close, or call 'em in, or if you hunt from a blind, the full metal jacket version will do a good job on Ben's bird, especially if the bullet is placed in the pinion area, where wing joins body. Or, if the bird is going away, the spinal area, low, or the

Small pests such as ground squirrels and prairie dogs can often be "controlled" with the 22 rimfire, such as this old Winchester Model 69A. Such shooting sharpens your eye!

This Remington 514-T with Redfield 4-12x compact scope accounted for several prairie dogs at modest range.

head/neck shot will, obviously, drop the turkey quickly. As for javelina, the little "wild pig" of the Southwest and Mexico, use the hollowpoint 22 WMR, and get close, which is easy to do. A javelina can't tell you from a lamp post at 50 yards if you don't move too much. But he can tell what brand of after-shave you use from a half mile, and he can hear you snap a twig even farther away. Be quiet. Keep the wind in your favor. And stalk for a 30- or 40-yard shot, where good bullet placement will make the 22 WMR very effective.

Once a year, a buddy and I take off for the backcountry when the small game and grouse season opens up. We call the trek our "survival hunt," though it's no such thing. We take along essentials in our backpacks, and if we got no game at all the worst that would happen is a modest loss of weight. So far, no weight has been lost because we've never had to go hungry, thanks to the 22 rimfire rifles we pack. This *constitutional* outing is made for the 22 rifle. Packing 50 to 100 rounds of ammo is no problem, and the rifles aren't heavy to tote either. Mountain grouse are open season to the 22 rimfire, as are cottontails. Delicious fare. Camp time, the fire is going. We cook with grate and grill, a grate for broiling meat, a grill for frying. Condiments lend good flavor. Oleo margerine keeps the meat moist as it broils over the coals. The mountain grouse are especially tasty, be they blues or ruffed.

But *what* 22 rifle for all of this fun, the plinking, 22 games, silhouette shooting, targets, small game, grouse, varmints, 22 WMR hunting of wild turkeys and javelina? That question is as easily answered as "What car's best for driving from coast to coast in summertime America?" The answer is, "Lots of different ones." My favorite rifle style seemed to grow with me. I had little to do with the choice. After well over 3 decades of 22 rimfire shooting, it turns out that the bolt-action model gets the most attention from me. I really don't know why. Chambering a 22 rimfire in a bolt-action rifle is like bashing a mosquito with a 2x4 plank. It's a classic case of overkill. However, this past week my son and I embarked on a couple of 22 shootfests. I used four rifles: my old Winchester Model 75 Sporter with 4x scope, my even older Remington Model 12 pumpgun with iron sights, a new Remington Model 514-T with 4x-12x variable and a Marlin Model 25M with a 6x scope. Three bolt actions and a pump.

My son carried his Model 69A Winchester with 4x scope and 10-shot clip (from Lodewick's of Portland), another bolt-action model, for most of his shooting. He also had a Browning lever action along, with 4x scope, which did a beautiful job for him. All the rifles worked perfectly.

I've run across very few 22 rimfire rifles which weren't satisfactory. I believe we gravitate to a certain rifle style by sheer personal preference. Among my 22 rifles, I have two semi-autos, a Marlin and a little Explorer which goes just about everywhere I go. A couple slide actions. A single shot. And several bolt actions. Sometimes I set up a bevy of tin cans on a sandy flat at 200 paces. Then I'll use something like my Remington 514-T with its high-power scope. It's fascinating to shoot that far with a 22 rimfire; it's also educational. Every aspect of riflery is magnified. Drop is terrible. Wind drift is discouraging. However, you find yourself "homing in" after several shots, and the dirt-filled cans begin to topple with surprising frequency.

Unreliable and illegal for big game hunting, lousy for long range shooting in the slightest breeze, whipped handily by benchrest centerfire rifles for supremely tight 100 yard groups, yet the little rimfire serves the shooter in a vast number of worthwhile ways, from the simplest of dirt-bank plinking to the most serious competition. I find the 22 rimfire round and its rifles, as well as its handguns, not only interesting, but also indispensable in my personal world of shooting. The little 22 may not be the most important round or rifle in my shooting life, but it's certainly given me the most pleasure. I intend to do my part in keeping the simple 22 rimfire the most fired round in the world. ●

Product Liability Suits...

Opportunity Unlimited

by BILL HOLMES

Looking back on a few of life's more "memorable" happenings, the author can't help but think of all the money he's lost just by being honest.

FOR THE PAST DECADE or so, it almost seems as if one of the easiest paths to riches has been product liability suits. We find instances where one young boy points an air rifle at another and pulls the trigger, shooting him in the eye. The boy's parents promptly file suit against the manufacturer for building an unsafe product, and are awarded several million dollars.

Another person shoots himself in the foot with a six-gun and collects from the manufacturer for building an unsafe product. Still other cases come to mind whereby a firearm was used in the commission of a crime and someone was killed or wounded. The injured parties, or their survivors, immediately file suits against not only the dealer who sold the gun, the distributor who sold the gun to the dealer, but the manufacturer as well, and more often than not manage to collect. It goes on and on with no end in sight, with the lawyers getting richer and the firearms manufacturers getting poorer. It's no wonder that gun prices continue

to rise, what with the makers having to spend ridiculous sums in attempts to defend themselves. And just think what those insurance premiums cost!

It hasn't always been that way. I remember back in 1941. I was 12 years old at the time and World War II was just about to get going. My father took me aside one day and presented me with an old Colt "Lightning" 38 double-action revolver. Of course, I wasn't to have any ammunition, or so he said. But they were considerably more lax in those days concerning who could buy shells. In fact, if you were tall enough to put your money on the counter you were considered old enough to buy just about anything you had money to pay for. So the following Saturday I made my way into a hardware store and bought a box of shells, no questions asked.

Now, it happened that we lived on a farm at the time, several miles from town. There was no electricity to the rural areas until after the war. Consequently, there was no running water

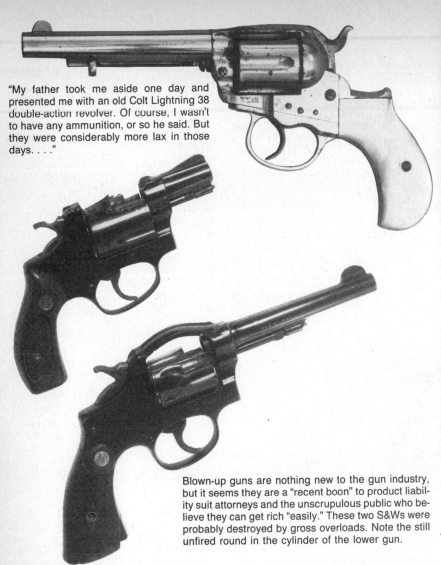

"My father took me aside one day and presented me with an old Colt Lightning 38 double-action revolver. Of course, I wasn't to have any ammunition, or so he said. But they were considerably more lax in those days. . . ."

Blown-up guns are nothing new to the gun industry, but it seems they are a "recent boon" to product liability suit attorneys and the unscrupulous public who believe they can get rich "easily." These two S&Ws were probably destroyed by gross overloads. Note the still unfired round in the cylinder of the lower gun.

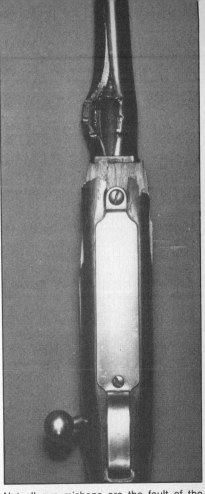

Not all gun mishaps are the fault of the shooter/reloader—sometimes the equipment can be at fault. This Remington Model 721 barrel blew at the chamber and the experts weren't able to conclusively pin down the cause—either high pressure (an overload) or a barrel defect.

and, therefore, no indoor toilets. In fact, the only lights we had were kerosene lamps. Our heat came from a woodburning stove and a fireplace, and we were required to trek to an outdoor toilet some 50 yards from the house when the need arose. Since this was quite an inconvenience, especially on a cold winter night, I had fallen into the habit of simply raising the bedroom window a few inches and urinating thru the screen when I had the need.

I also had a bad habit of reading the pulp detective magazines which usually cost a dime a copy and were frowned on by my mother and grandmother as being a "bad influence" on a young boy. So these were kept hidden, as well as my ammunition.

So, it happened that on this one particular night, with the covers pulled up over my head, my trusty Colt under my pillow, its cylinder stuffed with six rounds, I was reading, illuminated by my five-cell flashlight, an especially exciting story about a group of Nazi spies who were lurking outside the home of an American scientist. They were pre-

paring to break in and kidnap him.

Suddenly, there was a loud scraping noise at my window. They were here, coming for me!

I wasn't having any of that, however. Out came my Colt. Pointing it at the window, I yelled, "Get away or I'll shoot!" The only response was another scraping noise. They were tearing the screen off. "They'll never take me without a fight," I vowed silently. I thumbed back the hammer on my old pistol and gave them one last chance. "Get back or I'll shoot. This is your last chance," I said in what I thought was a particularly menacing voice.

The only response was another noise. They were almost inside now and I couldn't wait any longer. I let fly all six rounds right through the window.

My parents burst into the room as I quickly reloaded the Colt.

"Don't go near the window," I screamed, "there's a bunch of Nazi spies out there!"

However, an examination of the premises revealed that there probably hadn't been any Nazis out there at all,

or if there were, they had used a cow as a shield, because that's what lay dead just outside the window—one of my parents' milk cows.

It was later determined that my repeated pissing through the screen had left a salt deposit which the cow had discovered and started licking, thus creating the noise I heard.

As for me, I received the most cruel and unusual punishment possible. My gun and ammunition were confiscated as well as my magazines and flashlight, and any money that I might come up with for several months following was taken as partial payment for the cow. No law suits were filed.

Unfortunately (?) the legal climate was different then. If it was like it is now, my parents could have brought suit against Colt, the hardware store and clerk that sold me the ammo, and the ammo maker for, at least, loss of the cow, loss of use of the cow and the trauma my folks suffered from the incident as well as the trauma I suffered from having taken the life of the cow. So we missed our first opportunity at

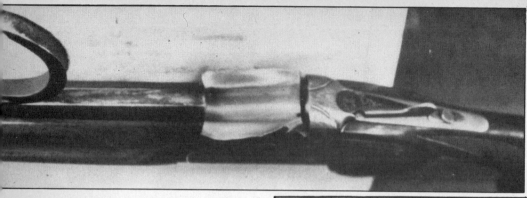

The Weatherby Regency over/under the author finally got had changed in appearance. The entire breech area of the upper barrel was blown open (right) and the rib was curled up forward over the barrel (above).

Below—The "restored" Weatherby after Holmes finished with it. He made up an adjustable-impact, truss-type rib which can shift the point of impact some 20 inches, ported the barrel, and installed a choke tube.

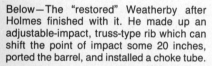

becoming wealthy.

Another incident comes to mind which happened during my basic training period in the Army back during the Korean War. As happens in every outfit, we had one particular "know it all" who was an expert on about any subject one could name. This dude was one of the worst. I mean, any subject that came up this S.O.B. knew all about it and insisted on telling everything that he knew.

Sooner or later, as is normal among a group of men, the conversation turned to guns, and, as usual, our boy was right there. He dominated the discussion with some of the most lopsided ideas about what guns would and wouldn't do that I ever heard in my life. However, also as usual, I kept my own mouth shut and simply let him talk. I kept quiet, that is, until he finally went too far and then I had to speak up.

He had rambled on for several minutes about just how puny a 22 rimfire cartridge was.

"Why," he said, "you can hold your thumb real tight over the muzzle of a 22 rifle, and if you hold it tight enough the bullet won't come out of the barrel when the gun is fired."

Now about this time I had all I could stand and I had to tell him that I didn't believe his statement was entirely accurate.

"What do you know about it?" he snorted. "I have experience with these things. I'm going to be a deputy sheriff when I get out of the army."

So, of course, I had to go and ask him if he had the guts to prove it. Well, one thing led to another and pretty soon several bets were made, and the following weekend several of us met in a secluded area off the post. Our self-proclaimed expert grasped the barrel of the single shot 22 rifle that someone in the group had come up with, placed his thumb firmly against the muzzle, and wrapped his other hand around the hand holding the barrel and asked for someone to pull the trigger. Someone in the group pulled it and the gun fired. But he apparently didn't hold his thumb on it tight enough because the

bullet came out and blew a nice little round hole through his thumb, nail and all.

Everyone kept their mouths shut about what actually happened. Our boy told the doctor and the authorities that he was hunting on the weekend and shot himself accidently. Nobody got in any trouble over it, but the braggart almost lost his thumb as well as his willingness to talk so much.

Here again we should have filed suits against the gunmaker, the owner of the gun and the ammo maker for not forseeing such a thing happening and not inscribing a written warning both on the barrel of the gun and on the ammunition box. There was also pain and suffering, trauma, etc., enough to make any court in the land award us a generous settlement

The time I really missed the boat though, happened just a couple of years ago. A friend of mine, an avid reloader, owned an almost new Weatherby Regency trap gun. He didn't like the gun. Said it kicked too hard. At the time, I was into building high-rib trap guns

After getting hit in the forehead with the clay bird, Holmes figured he was "already ugly as mud," and another scar didn't make much difference, so he let another "opportunity" get away from him. Too bad more folks don't think this way!

the cause of the blow up.

Now it happened the next afternoon, as was usual on most Saturday afternoons, that a couple of my buddies came over and we proceeded to spend the afternoon shooting practice rounds, since I also had a trap field and an automatic trap out in front of my shop.

On this particular Saturday afternoon, however, things didn't go quite right. All of a sudden targets quit coming out of the trap house when we mashed the button. And, since it was my trap and my trap house, naturally I was the one expected to fix it.

I never did figure out exactly what happened. Maybe someone mashed the firing button again. Or, maybe, whatever hung the trap up simply let go, but just as I started to climb down into the trap house, *Whack!*, the trap fired and a clay bird hit me right in the face, breaking my glasses and laying a gash open in my forehead clear to the bone.

Here now was my golden opportunity, and I had two ways to go. All I had to do was claim that the Weatherby shotgun blew up and disfigured me and surely a jury would award me just about any amount I asked for. Or, I could go after the trap maker, claiming it had a faulty release mechanism, and similarly demand princely sums of money.

But, once more, I let it get away from me. I was already ugly as mud, so another scar didn't make much difference. So I was too dumb to file any lawsuit, or maybe I just didn't want to lie. Whatever, anyway, everything worked out.

I removed what was left of the upper barrel and sawed it apart lengthwise. There was no sign of any obstruction which might have been in the bore, not a blemish of any kind. It was my conclusion, with which several other semi-experts concurred, that the blowup was caused by an overloaded shell.

I milled the top of the monoblock flat, dovetailed a chunk of steel into it and machined it back to approximately the outside contour of the original. The muzzle end of the barrel was expanded slightly and machined to accept screw-in choke tubes. I also made up an adjustable-impact truss-type rib which was 1 inch higher than the original and built up the stock comb to match. I also ported the remaining barrel.

So I wound up with another "Unsingle" shotgun which only kicks about half as much as it did originally. Fred uses considerably more care in his reloading now. And the only way Weatherby will even know about this happening will be if they read it here.

But think what could have been. ●

and I wanted this gun to convert to an "Unsingle," or a lower-barrel-only single shot. Fred, the owner of the Weatherby, said that if I would come up with a Browning BT-99 in decent shape he would trade for it. I agreed to try to find one and we left it at that.

The following Friday evening Fred called and asked if I still wanted the Weatherby. I replied that I did, but hadn't found a suitable gun to trade him yet.

"Forget the trade," he said. "Come on over here and get it. I'll just give you the damned thing."

Since he only lived a couple of miles away, I drove right over to his home whereupon he handed me the shotgun. Except now it had changed somewhat. The entire breech area of the upper barrel was blown open—the upper portion of the breechblock or monoblock, or whatever you want to call it, was demolished and the rib was curled up resembling a stinging scorpion's tail.

"What happened?" I inquired.

He said he was shooting a practice round of doubles and on his fifth pair the upper barrel simply blew.

"What kind of shells were you using?" I asked.

"Factory-loaded 3 dram Winchester double As," was his reply.

Of course, that wasn't true. This guy has never used factory-loaded ammo to shoot practice rounds in his life. But then, who wants to admit to possibly loading a shell that would demolish a gun?

"Aw, come on Fred," I said, "you know you didn't use factory loads to shoot practice."

"No you didn't, Fred," his wife chimed in. It turned out she was pulling for him at the time. (They had a trap of their own in their back yard.) "You were using reloads."

"I guess I probably was," he admitted, "but there wasn't anything wrong with my shells."

I took the gun back to my shop with the intention of looking further into

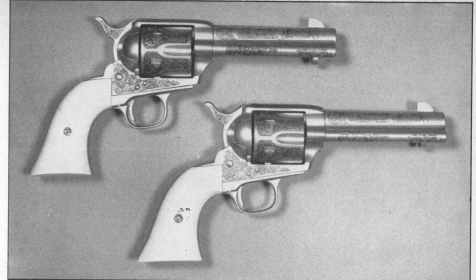

These two Cimarron Arms replica single actions were "dressed up" by Baron Technology. First they were etched with matching patterns and then given an "antiqued" nickel plating and fitted with polymer-ivory grips, also from Cimarron. The result gives them a look of guns costing four times as much.

All Dressed Up to go Shooting

All guns have some beauty all of their own, but there's nothing wrong at all with making them just a bit prettier, maybe even personalized. Hacker shows how he's dressed up a few of his favorite shootin' irons to suit his tastes.

by RICK HACKER

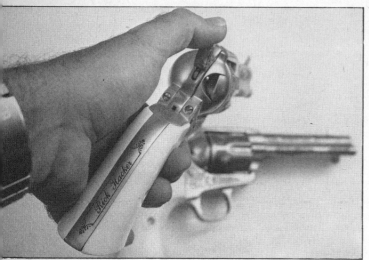

Baron Technology can etch a gun owner's name and even his signature on the backstrap or barrel of any firearm. It's a nice, personalized touch for favorite guns.

IT'S A PRETTY SAFE BET to say that anyone reading this article would consider most guns to be things of beauty. Whether it is the sculpted Victorian lines of a Henry repeater or the harsh, black, stoic look of an HK-91, all firearms have some artistic integrity to their designs that bespeak their purpose. Yet, these basic wood and metal testimonials to the gunsmith's art can almost, without exception, be improved upon by adding even the slightest visual embellishment.

In the case of Sam Colt's cap and ball revolvers, for example, these finely crafted "working guns" suddenly became museum-quality pieces of art by the simple addition of engraving and ivory grips. Unfortunately, this artistic adornment usually took these guns out of the shooting class and put them in display cases, where they rarely saw the inside of a holster. The same thing happened with many of the engraved Winchesters and earlier 17th and 18th century firearms of European nobility —exquisite hunting arms that were not used for hunting at all. It's a shame that these guns, by virtue of their embellishments, were never allowed to fulfill the purpose for which they were

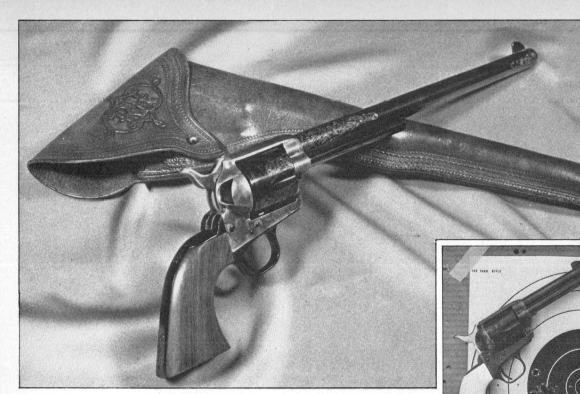

Hacker took an already impressive Colt Buntline Special and made it even more so, with special engraving by Bernie Wolfe and a custom "antiqued" Buntline holster crafted by Wild Bill Cleaver, who ages his leatherwork so it looks like an original. Author's initials are carved into the holster flap.

Hacker's theory that guns that look better shoot better is shown by this Colt SAA fitted with ivory, monogrammed grips from Eagle.

originally created. I'll never forget a visit to the castle of King Frederik VII of Denmark, where I saw a magnificent set of cased, gold inlaid and engraved Colt 1860 Armys that had been presented to the king by Abraham Lincoln. "Alas!" I thought, looking at the mint condition guns, "they have never been fired. What a pity." The good king never realized what superb shooting revolvers he had.

But, fortunately, such was not always the case. Noted lawman Bat Masterson used to mesmerize local townsfolk by regularly shooting his special-order, factory-engraved, nickel-plated Colt Single Action Army and "walking" a tin can down the main street of Dodge City. And a young dude rancher in Dakota named Theodore Roosevelt regularly packed a fully-engraved Colt 44-40 with specially carved ivory grips, a gun that gave him much stature among the rough and ready cowmen he associated with. A similarly-embellished SAA in 45 caliber was kept in reserve. These men were indicative of a very special breed of shootist who realized that firearms were meant to be used, no matter how much tinsel they had hanging on them. The mere fact that Masterson and Roosevelt, for example, had guns that were a little bit fancier than the com-

mon store-bought variety merely made a statement about what the man thought of himself. I often wonder whether Masterson would have shot as straight with a standard blued-and-case-hardened Colt. Or if TR would have felt just as "bully" with a plainer six-shooter in the handcarved holster that he wore slung over his sheepskin chaps.

Today, the same observation still holds true. I have long had a theory that we shoot better with guns that look better. Yet, with all the modern collectible firearms and specially engraved, limited edition commemoratives on the market, it becomes very difficult for many people to test this theory out, for the minute you fire a commemorative, you blow about half its value out the barrel. And even on custom guns, how many people today actually take that $1,000 factory engraved Smith & Wesson Model 29 out and shoot it? Not many, and what a shame. Like King Frederik, they will never know just what a great gun they have, a gun made even greater by virtue of the fact that it is special. It stands out on the firing line. And so would you, if only you would take it there.

Yet, there is hope. Today, thanks to a very select group of fine craftsmen,

it is possible to take an existing gun that you own and actually create an artistic masterpiece that you can shoot. I'm not talking about an after-market extravaganza, where extra clips and re-arranged stocks are slapped onto the basic chassis of a standard firearm. I'm referring to the creation of an artistic exterior that transforms a regular firearm into a personal "commemorative" for the owner. And, if my theory is correct (which it is, as I have already proven it to myself with thousands of rounds), you will actually shoot *better* with your dressed-up gun. Not only will you be proud of your shooting ability, but you'll be proud of your gun. And chances are you won't be hurting its value any either, especially if it is a little bit shopworn to begin with.

I'll give you an excellent example. I owned a badly battered Colt Government 45 Series 70 that could shoot the center out of a 10-ring at 50 yards, but looked like it had been dragged through a couple of wars tied to the

Collectible guns that are still shooters can be given even greater value and beauty simply by adding special grips. The ivory on the Colt New Service (top) and pearl on the S&W Model 24 (bottom) were done by Eagle Grips.

driveshaft of a jeep. The gun had once been reblued and now even that had worn off. The replacement grips were fat, ugly plastic and the sights were accurate but battered. In short, the Colt was too good a shooter to get rid of, but it hurt just to look at it. So I decided to dress it up. The first step was to send the 45 to Baron Technology, the firm that does the excellent gold and silver etching and plating on many of the limited edition commemoratives offered by the major gun companies. Baron Technology has recently started offering their services to individuals, so I decided to take advantage of it. My stripped-down 45 Government was sent to the firm, which first chemically cleaned the gun. Then, using line artwork that I supplied, along with their own scroll patterns, they literally created a gold-etched-and-blued masterpiece out of the old warhorse. Now the gun looked better than it shot, so I had the well-known accurizing firm of Kings Gun Works perform one of their special "trigger and sight" magic numbers on the Colt. Not wanting to go the expense of real ivory grips, which I was afraid might crack under the recoil of the semi-automatic, ivory-polymer grips from Altamont were used to finish the newly created one-of-a-kind "treasure" that now shoots cloverleafs, much to the awe of bystanders, who try to figure out which Colt commemorative it is that I am shooting. Then they ask themselves why I'm shooting it! In its attractive

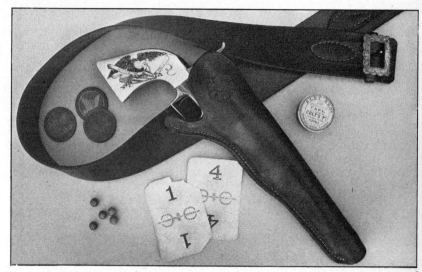

A well-used replica Colt Navy also becomes a historical showpiece when it's outfitted with scrimshawed ivory grips, and fitted in an authentic 1850s-period holster.

new package, the Colt Government is now worth far more than it was when it was new, even though it has had hundreds of rounds put through it.

Another rags-to-riches story centers around a holster-worn second generation Colt single-action 45 that had been my companion on many a hunt, until only about 60 percent of its finish remained. Deciding to put some new life into the old Peacemaker, I sent it to one of the top gun engravers in Texas, a chap named Jim Riggs, who does much of the engraving on the stainless steel guns carried by many of the Texas Rangers who want something

just a little bit special. I told Jim I still wanted to pack the Colt, but I wanted to dress it up a bit, frontier-style. It took about 6 months, but the gun I got back was akin to a factory-engraved Colt done by Nimschke, complete with antiqued nickel finish and gold-plated cylinder, ejector rod and hammer! It is indeed a Western showpiece that looks as if I ordered it right out of the 1910 catalog. Only the gun's serial numbers give it away. And yes, shooting the Peacemaker has blown some of the soft gold right off the cylinder face, but like Jim says, any gun that can be shot can be replated.

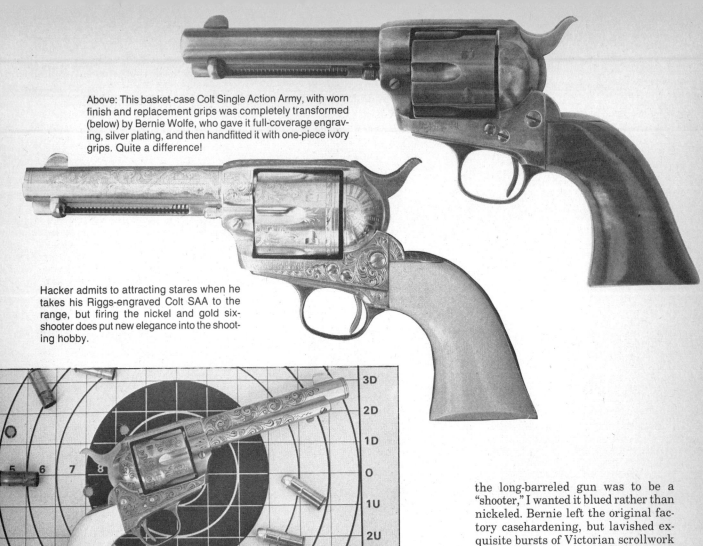

Above: This basket-case Colt Single Action Army, with worn finish and replacement grips was completely transformed (below) by Bernie Wolfe, who gave it full-coverage engraving, silver plating, and then handfitted it with one-piece ivory grips. Quite a difference!

Hacker admits to attracting stares when he takes his Riggs-engraved Colt SAA to the range, but firing the nickel and gold six-shooter does put new elegance into the shooting hobby.

Bernie Wolfe is another Texas gun engraver whose work is so exacting and authentic, it is only the minute presence of his signature that keeps many of the SAAs he has engraved from being identified as Helfricht or Young factory originals. Like Jim, Bernie's work is about half the price you would pay a factory custom shop to create the same artistic perfection— a rather pleasant discovery that I made by accident. As a writer and Western history buff, I had long been fascinated with the lore of the Colt SAA Buntline Special, the long-barreled sixgun that writer Ned Buntline supposedly special ordered for some select Western characters. What better gun for a gun-writer to have, I reasoned. So I began saving the meager amounts I got paid for writing about my favorite hobby, planning to someday purchase a customized Colt Buntline with special

engraving, just as if Ned Buntline himself had ordered it. Alas, by the time I was ready to order, the old Model P had been discontinued by the factory and at that time, special orders were out of the question. Undaunted, I began scouring local gun shows, where I eventually acquired a mint-condition 45 Buntline and sent it to Bernie to have it suitably adorned. A history buff himself, Bernie suggested that with a single action as unique as a 12-inch Buntline, full "D" coverage was not in order and, in fact, would border on the gaudy. This type of honest input from a man who was motivated more by "what's right" than by "how much money can I make" is what separates a good engraver from one who is a true artist in his profession. Bernie created a classic Buntline pattern, featuring "B" engraving in the style of L.D. Nimschke. Because

the long-barreled gun was to be a "shooter," I wanted it blued rather than nickeled. Bernie left the original factory casehardening, but lavished exquisite bursts of Victorian scrollwork along the barrel, cylinder and trigger guard, even engraving my name on the backstrap in the exact Colt scrollwork of the 1880s. As a final touch, he also case-hardened the hammer, just as they did in Ned Buntline's day. The cost for the complete masterpiece, including my purchase price of the gun, was half of what I had planned to pay for a factory original!

But engraving is not the only way to dress up a gun that you already own. Simply adding nickel plating can do wonders for a gun's appearance, and in addition to the standard shiny appearance, all three firms listed above have their own special "antiqued" finishes that give a semi-matte look to the gun. Baron Technology will even gold plate your gun for you (the ideal "lady's" gun that you might want to give someone special for Christmas!). Of course, having a special sentiment or name engraved along the backstrap is a time-honored method of dressing up a gun, and with Baron Technology's patented etching process, they can duplicate your exact signature along the backstrap or barrel.

Adding special grips to a handgun is perhaps the simplest, quickest and

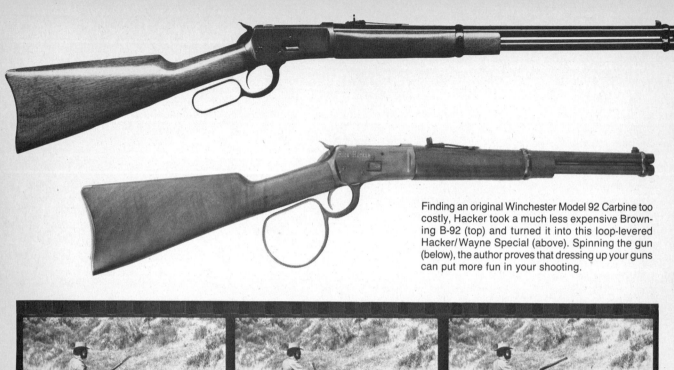

Finding an original Winchester Model 92 Carbine too costly, Hacker took a much less expensive Browning B-92 (top) and turned it into this loop-levered Hacker/Wayne Special (above). Spinning the gun (below), the author proves that dressing up your guns can put more fun in your shooting.

least costly way to give it a new look. In fact, very few of my guns still have their original factory grips. I tend to use staghorn for most of my hunting guns, as this natural material is both rugged and picturesque. I put ivory on some of the guns that "demand" it, such as the nickel and gold Colt that Jim Riggs engraved. But the Wolfe-engraved Buntline, with its deeply blued and casehardened finish, seemed to go best with the rich color of rosewood.

Needless to say, there are many companies making many styles of grips nowadays, but one of the most prolific and expert in this service is Eagle Grips. This one firm is the nation's largest source of stag, ivory, rosewood and pearl grips. They hand carve grips from horn and ebony as well. Eagle Grips are made for virtually every gun on the market and their prices are among the lowest, costing less than the mass-produced synthetics in many cases. In addition to their regular designs, they will custom make any grip and for an additional $25, their experts will even handfit their grips to your specific gun . . . I recently had Eagle Grips make a duplicate set of grips for my Colt New Service so that I could

shoot the gun without worrying about cracking the original factory hard rubber, which is difficult to replace.

Other methods of dressing up your gun for shooting can become more elaborate. For example, when Browning brought out their B92 replica of the 1892 Winchester carbine, and with original Winchester Model 1892 carbines becoming much too scarce and costly, I reasoned that here was the perfect shootin' iron to recreate that classic Winchester John Wayne first used in the movie, *Red River* (the same style of '92 modification was later used by Chuck Connors in the old *Rifleman* TV series). Thus, armed with a studio still of the "Duke" and his loop-lever saddle gun, I had King's Gun Works create an exact duplicate. All that was really necessary was to reshape the lever, cut back the barrel to 16¼ inches so that it would clear my armpits while spinning, and shorten the forend for visual appeal. Conners' Model 92 also had a special retainer to keep his shells in the gun while spinning, but as spinning a loaded carbine with a chambered round is a foolhardy thing to do, I omitted this feature. I have since taken my Hacker/Wayne Special on a number of coyote and turkey hunts and

it has become a much favored, fast handling little brush gun. Wherever I go with it, I am always asked where I got it; now you know. Kings will still do this custom work, using your gun or theirs. Write to them for the latest quote.

Handgunners can add a special aura to their sixguns with special holsters; in fact, a revolver fitted with special finish or grips *deserves* to be carried in leather that is just a little bit out of the ordinary. Even factory-plain guns get a custom look in a custom holster. Unfortunately, with today's escalating labor costs, there are very few holstermakers who still want to take the time to do something out of the ordinary. The George Lawrence company is one. El Paso Saddlery is another old-time company that will put special carvings on any of their rigs. Perhaps one of the most talented holstermakers to come along recently is "Wild" Bill Cleaver, a fellow who handcrafts holsters that are not only styled authentically, but actually *look* authentic, right on down to the worn leather and tarnished buckles. Bill Cleaver's creations are usually snapped up by museums and motion picture companies as well as collectors of western Americana. After

Right: Hacker's Government Model 45 auto shot well, but had seen much abuse. Below: The transformed 45, with its new "commemorative" image. Special target sights and trigger from Kings Gun Works keep it shooting as good as it looks. The work was done by Baron Technology.

Jim Riggs can turn standard replica cap and balls into 19th century-styled presentation pieces. He regularly packs this nickel-engraved Navy.

seeing his work (which I initially mistook for being a 19th century original), I commissioned him to create an "authentic" rig for my custom Buntline; the resulting holster, designed for a left-hand crossdraw and complete with protective flap and handcarved Victorian initials, is ample testimony to the exactness of his work. He can make holsters for virtually any frontier-era firearm. And what is most important, his holsters are designed to be *users*, not just lookers.

Though many gun companies now have their own custom departments, many of us can't afford the money or the time it takes to treat ourselves to this luxury. In addition, we may want to customize a gun that is no longer being made. That's where the ability to dress up our own shooting irons comes into play. After all, the artisans are out there, and adding to the visual appeal of a favorite firearm can put a whole new dimension of individuality into our sport. Besides, when your gun is all dressed up, you know you'll be shooting in style!

●

Sources

Baron Technology
62 Spring Hill Rd.
Trumbull, CT 06611
203/452-0515
(Chemical etching, plating)

Jim Riggs
206 Azalea Trail
Boerne, TX 78006
512/249-8567
(Custom engraving, plating)

Bernie Wolfe
900 Tony Lama
El Paso, TX 79915
915/594-3962
(Custom engraving, plating, scrimshawing)

Wild Bill Cleaver
Rt. 4, Box 462
Vashon, WA 98070
206/463-9325
(Custom holster maker)

Eagle Grips
Art Jewel Enterprises
460 Randy Rd.
Carol Stream, IL 60188
800/323-6144
(Ivory, pearl, rosewood, staghorn, ebony grips)

Kings Gun Works
1837 Glenoaks Blvd.
Glendale, CA 91202
818/956-6010
(Custom gunsmiths)

Altamont Grips
510 N. Commercial St.
P.O. Box 309
Thomasboro, IL 61878
217/643-3125
(Polymer, ivory, rosewood grips)

El Paso Saddlery
P.O. Box 27914
El Paso, TX 79926
915/544-2233
(Holsters, leather goods)

Springfield Armory Model P9 Pistol.

Springfield Armory's P9 Auto and Master Grade 1911A1 Pistol

With a family lineage like these guns have, it's hard to go wrong when you want one for totin' and one for targets—they're both winners!

by CLAY HARVEY

Springfield Armory Master Grade Competition B.

YOU MAY HAVE deduced from our cover photo that there's a new CZ 75-type 9mm on the market, brought to you by the friendly faces in Geneseo, Illinois. The 9mm cover gun is finished in satin nickel which is relatively impervious to corrosion from sweaty palms, rain, or rice pudding. Standard finish is blued, of course, and the new handgun—dubbed the Springfield P9—is offered in both full-size and compact renditions.

My sample full-bore "standard" edition featured a drift-adjustable rear sight and serrated-blade front, both dovetailed into a full-length serrated rib. Catalog weight is 35.3 ounces, barrel length 4.72 inches with a one-in-10-inch right-hand twist. Magazine capacity is 16 rounds; with one in the chamber that means you have a whole lot of bullets to sling at something in a hurry.

The P9 is one of the few double-action 9mm autos to offer selective double/single-action attitudes. Like the original and widely heralded CZ 75, it can be carried cocked and locked. The safety lever is frame-mounted, and down is "fire," just as on Model 1911 semi-automatics. The reach is a tad long for short thumbs, but the manipulation is oily slick and positive.

The second option is to carry the P9 hammer down; then a long tug on the trigger will fire the piece, just as with other double-action autos. Since the gun is large, and the staggered-column magazine a real handful, the trigger reach is better suited to large hands if a "correct" grip is to be taken. Still, we short-fingered folk can get by nicely simply by easing our mitt around to the side a mite; the DA pull is so light and sweet that it's a cinch to control, even

Function firing provided only one miscue in 312 rounds, a failure to eject. Shooting the big P9 rapidly was a piece of cake. Despite my short digits I found I could draw and fire the gun for two shots (DA first, SA follow-up) about as quickly as I can other DA autos with grip frames more my size. With my best-fitting DA—the Ruger P-85—my average time to draw and dump a pair of shots into the kill zone at 7 yards is 1.72 seconds. A Beretta B-92F requires 1.82 seconds for the same feat, with my SIG-Sauer P226 taking 1.78 seconds for the drill. The P9, big grip and all, showed a 1.76-second aggregate for six tries, faster than all but the small-

gripped Ruger. Surprised? I was. How, you ponder, did I manage it if the P9 is really too bulky for my dainty hands? The light DA pull, that's how; it makes up to a large extent for the long trigger reach.

Locked onto the target, gun tight as my version of the Weaver method could make it, I fired a trio of shots (first round DA, second and third SA, of course) into a 7-yard silhouette in 1.11 seconds. I did it again in 1.06, then in 1.14, for an average of 1.10 seconds.

With the P-85, the time ran to 1.06; the B-92F took up 1.10; the SIG-Sauer required 1.23 seconds, due to its heavy, grating DA pull, I'm sure. The point of

Harvey's test P9 was the standard model with satin nickel finish which is resistant to corrosion. Safety lever, slide and magazine releases, and sights are blued.

The new Springfield P9 is an Italian-built clone of the famed CZ 75 9mm. Author's test gun shot well throughout his tests. It's also available in a Compact model.

with an "improper" grip.

Single-action release is equally smooth and lighter yet, although as on all CZ clones it suffers from too much sear engagement. The pull is spongy. Still, my shooting has never been noticeably hampered by the trigger on any CZ type. (My cronies claim my skill level is at such an inconsequential level that it is unhamperable.)

The front of the grip frame is serrated vertically to assist a slippery hand during rapid fire. It works. The slide articulates within the frame rails, not outside as on the various Browning systems. The magazine release button is located just aft of the trigger guard, on the left side, as with the M1911.

Unless you're trying to marry a small hand to the large grip, the P9 is ergonomically pleasing. All the controls are in the right places, work with a gratifying snick-snick feel, and the sights are large and quick to pick up. Quality of fabrication is as good as any CZ-type pistol I have examined, with sharp edges notable for their lack. The only faux pas on my test gun was an overabundance of tool marks at the sides of the slide rib.

Shooter Jim Giles tries his hand with the P9 auto. In over 300 rounds only one miscue was noted—a failure to eject. Gun handles well for most shooters, though the grip is a bit large for Harvey's hands.

Shooting Blazer 115-grain JHP ammo in the P9 (its favored load) gave an average of 2.74 inches for four five-shot groups at 25 yards. This 2.39-inch target was one of the better efforts.

The Springfield Armory Master Grade B has all the bells and whistles: skeletonized hammer, checkered walnut stocks, checkered frontstrap, modified ejection port, Bo-Mar adjustable sights, beavertail grip safety, ambidextrous safety, compensator, and more. It's expensive but performance shows.

Harvey used the Master Grade 45 to good effect on the Springfield Armory Writer's Shoot-Out, killing this pig with the gun.

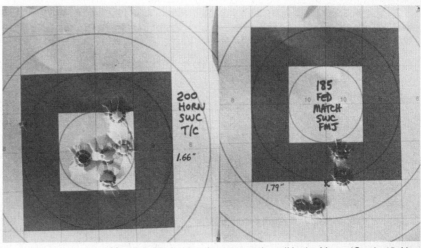

Match-grade fodder shot extremely well in the Master Grade 45. Hornady 200-grain truncated cone ammo (left) shot into 1.66 inches, Federal 185-grain SWC FMJ went 1.79 inches, both at 25 yards.

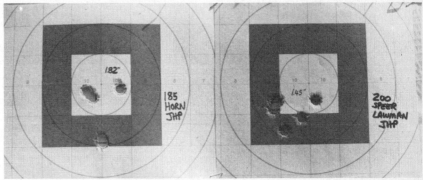

Hot hollowpoint hunting ammunition printed and fed well in the Master Grade gun: Hornady 185-grain JHP (left) shot into 1.82 inches, Speer Lawman 200-grain JHPs slipped into 1.45 inches, both at 25 yards.

the foregoing is not to show what a gee-whiz speed demon I am with a pistol, but simply to provide you with a base for comparison.

Lest you suspect that the person doing the timing might have let human error creep into his use of the stopwatch, I'll head you off. An excellent PACT timer provided the numbers (all of which, incidentally, *include reaction time*), handling all the electronic chores with accuracy, convenience, and style. I would not be happy without my PACT

unit, no sir.

So, the Springfield P9 is well made, probably as durable as a John Deere, affordable at $454 retail ($82 extra for nickel), reliable, and—to my eyes, at least—quite handsome. But how does it group? Like so: Blazer 115 JHP went into 2.74 inches from a rest at 25 yards, averaging four five-shot strings; Blazer 124 JSP gave 2.99 inches; Blazer 124

TMJ, 5.40; Federal 115 JHP, 3.01; Federal 124 Match, 3.44; Federal 125 Nyclad, 4.48; Federal 147 Hydra-Shok, 3.98; CCI Lawman 115 JHP, 3.09; Black Hills Shooting Supply 115 JHP, 2.99; Hornady 115 JHP, 3.10.

Its best ammo, as you can see, prints a bit under 3 inches, which I consider par for a service auto. How does that compare to some other 9mms? Well, the

The various "battle rifles" such as these produced by Springfield Armory make fine hunting arms. They're quick to field strip for cleaning after a day's hunt in the rain, they're reliable, accurate and rugged. The assembled writers found the guns effective.

Gun writer Finn Aagaard (*American Rifleman*) slew this pig with the short SAR-48 Bush Rifle in 308.

various SIG-Sauers that I have tested would print around 2 to 2¼ inches with their pet loads; my Berettas have gone into from 2⅛ to 2½ inches, on average, with their best stuff; the Ruger P-85s and Smith & Wesson 9mms were all in the same arena as the Springfield, around 2¾ inches, though an occasional S&W has shaded that slightly. My original CZ 75 grouped under 2 inches with three loads, going 1.67 inches with the super-precise Blazer JHP. My chrome TZ 75 (by Tanfoglio of Italy) averaged exactly 2.5 inches from its pet handload, much worse with factory stuff, with some groups as large as 6½–7 inches. A similar blued version showed an aggregate of 1.93 inches with the always-good Blazer 115 JHP, and went into 2.74 with 90-grain Hornady hollowpoints.

The upshot of all these numbers is: Tanfoglio-built guns will shoot; my sample P9 scored a passing grade – not as accurate as some examples of its competitors, but as good or better than others; the Springfield has all the precision *required* in a home-defense/police pistol.

The all-steel P9 works; you can afford one without having your kids suffer at Christmas; it'll hit what you aim at if you squeeze and hold properly; its quality is comparable to most anything in its price range. A fie on anyone who expects more.

Springfield Master Grade B

Springfield offers from its custom shop quite a range of modified 1911s, including the Custom Carry Gun, the Competition Grade, the National Match, the Master Grade Competition versions A and B. My test gun is the B, top of the line. At $1943 out the door, it ain't cheap, but oh is it good.

Comparably equipped guns built on Springfield frames run from around $1400 to $2000 or better, and none I've seen from *any* smith has been better crafted than my test pistol.

So what was added to my gun to justify all that loot, aside from hours of skilled labor provided by a long-suffering craftsman? Fully adjustable Bo-Mar sight at the aft end with a serrated blade forward; ambidextrous safety lever; "speed" trigger, lengthened, lightened and crisp, with no backlash; National Match barrel and bushing; 40 lpi serrations at the rear of the slide; lowered and flared ejection port; funneled magazine well; polished feed ramp; throated barrel; polished and adjusted extractor; long recoil spring guide; compensator up front to reduce recoil and muzzle rise; checkered frontstrap, 20 lpi; checkered walnut grip panels; special hollowed-out hammer; two stainless magazines.

And the execution? Just fine, thanks. Oh, the trigger pull was a bit heavy at about 6 pounds, but what do you expect in these litigious times? It was crisp as could be, with no discernible movement after sear release. All the serrating and checkering was faultless, the grip panels nicely figured wood; all flats were flat, the curves symmetrical and clean, the finish nigh perfection.

Functioning was flawless with such high-performance ammo as Speer's deadly 200-grain JHP, the notorious "Flying Ashtray" that works so well on impact but is so hard for many 45 autos to feed. The 200-grain Blazer TMJ and similar Hornady offering failed to make the trip from magazine to chamber about 20 percent of the time; the gun felt a bit undersprung. But Hornady's JHP 185 and the short-nosed Federal 185 full-jacketed semi-wadcutter match stuff functioned perfectly, all the time.

And accuracy? Best aggregate of four strings, by a hair, came from the 200 Hornady truncated cone semi-wad, a tidy 1.85 inches, with one group an incredible 1.11 inches at 25 yards. The Federal Match 185-grain FMJ semi-wadcutter was just off the pace at 1.87 for a quartet of groups. Hornady's 230-grain flat-nose ball came next at 2.00 on the button. Most precise of the hunting/defense ammo was Hornady's 185 JHP at 2.09, then the 200 Speer lawman JHP at 2.19. Other results went thus: Hansen 230 ball at 2.23; Samson 185 full-patch semi-wadcutter, 2.24 inches; 185 Black Hills Shooting Supply at 2¼ inches; Blazer 200 TMJ Combat Match at 2.26; Federal 230 Hydra Shok at 2.58 inches. Note that all loads tried shot pretty well; this gun is anything but finicky.

I have tested only two other 45 autos that would shade my test 1911A1. One, a Gold Cup I owned 20 years ago, would group from 1½ to 2 inches. The other, a Browning BDA I tested for *Handloader* magazine more than a decade ago went 1.65 with its pet handload, and under 2 inches with a few other loads. Of the many, many SIG-Sauers, standard and accurized Colts, and perhaps a half-dozen S&Ws I have tested, none has equaled my Springfield. Most wouldn't come close.

I have punctured nary a bowling pin with my Master Grade B, but I did take it on a wild pig hunt. I was easing along a creekbed when a black, smallish hog strolled out of a patch of trees, stopped, peered myopically in my direction, decided I was neither edible nor dangerous, and ambled on toward me. He drew up at perhaps 40 yards and reassessed

Harvey's second porker fell to the SAR-48 Bush Rifle, basically a clone of the well-respected FN-FAL autoloader.

his first impression. As he stood pondering, I shot him in the left shoulder, high up, too high up, and he departed.

There was a blood trail. Followed it for quite a distance. No pig. I sought canine assistance. The pooch found the hog soaking his injury in a muddy bottom and bayed the message back to me.

"Here he is, Mack," he barked, "but I ain't sure for how long."

I managed to arrive at the scene, slip a 200 Blazer TMJ slug betwixt two trees without hitting the dog, and broke the porker's neck, all without falling down. Natty Bumpo personified.

For such work at modest distances, the 45 is capable if the proper bullet is placed in a tender zone. I can't think of a better hunting 45 than this Springfield. We plan to do it again, Master Grade B and I.   •

Springfield Armory 27, Porkers 0

Bob Grueskin, honcho of the Unsavory Character department at Springfield Armory, called me up a few months ago to see if I owed him money. During the resulting conversation, he asked if I could come up with an idea for a hunt of some kind, one suited to the use of so-called "Battle Rifles," one that could be arranged on short notice, one that might prove enjoyable to a sordid coterie of gun scribes, and one that might possibly even be successful, assuming said journalists could be cajoled out of bed of a morning. I knew just the thing.

In lovely Stanfield, North Carolina, there resides the premier Hawg Guide amongst hawg guides, Gerald Almond, a bewhiskered gent, though affable. Gerald's outfit, Goldmine Hunting Preserve (Route 2, Box 95C, Stanfield, NC 28163, phone 704/786-0619), has ample acreage, lots of game, caters to nimrods year round at reasonable prices, and specializes in guiding inexperienced hunters, which meant Rick Jamison could come along. I called Gerald. After hearing my plan, he allowed as how a gaggle of gun writers shouldn't tarnish his reputation irreparably, and promised he wouldn't let anyone get gored by no pigs. Well, at least not too badly, anyway.

I called Mr. Grueskin—soon to be dubbed "Killer Bob" by his contemporaries, but I'm getting ahead of myself—and we parlayed a spell. Directly a guest list was made up, including only two or three writers that were likely to get lost. A date was set, details were ironed out, and directly everyone was sequestered in Gerald's lodge deep within the forbidding western Carolina forests.

Former African guide Finn Aagaard of the *American Rifleman* was along, as was Burt Carey of *Gun World,* the aforementioned Mr. Jamison, Al Miller from *Rifle,* Charles Petty of *Guns,* Ross Seyfried representing *Guns & Ammo,* and yours truly.

I do not plan to steal my pals' thunder by telling all their stories here. I will drop a few hints, however. When the smoke had cleared after 2 days of hunting in typical North Carolina bluesky spring weather, 27 hogs had been slain. Only three bona fide charges had ensued. The recipients were Ross Seyfried, who disrupted a porcine snooze, Rick Jamison, who popped a well-toothed blue pig in a not-immediately-lethal area (which on a

hog is *anywhere* except the brain or spine!), and finally, ah . . . Ross and Pat Squire and me. But that's another story.

Everyone got a pig. Or two. Killer Bob Grueskin slew enough to fill a coal barge, though Ross had to finish one and I another. No reflection on Bob, who can shoot with the best of 'em.

My first hog had been bayed by Gerald's bitch, Bird Dog. I snuck up, planted a 150-grain Winchester Power Point in his boiler room, and another, and another. He died then. My rifle was the new SAR 3, a copy of the famed Heckler & Koch HK-91, reamed to 308. Issue iron sights were used to good effect in the dense brush.

The following day Rick Jamison and I were sitting on a stand overlooking a goodly expanse of grass when three hogs came to drink from a bordering creek. I waylaid one with a 165-grain Federal softpoint boattail to its chest. It hollered, swapped ends, headed north. My buddy Don Beamon was supposedly snapping the shutter on his Nikon like crazy, capturing this for posterity, as I sent another round after the departing pig, which fell into the creek, complaining vociferously of my manners, lineage, and company. I showed him; I ran over and turned him off with one in the neck.

Rick congratulated me, as well he should since I hadn't fallen down or let him get eaten by a boar. Don, alas, had been taken by surprise by the abruptness of the melee, and had nothing on film. He did better later.

I have hunted with various battle rifles before, including the SAR 48 with which I took the second pig. Aside from being a bit weighty, there are no flies on this type of armament for hunting. They are sufficiently accurate; they work; they are affordable; they are easy to field strip should they take an unexpected plunge into a mud hole or get caught in a downpour; and they are scopable. I do prefer a five-round magazine, as the longer 20-round jobs get in the way. Besides, all those cartridges simply make the guns heavier. (Springfield offers five-round mags for all of their rifles.)

Ross hunted with the handy 18½-inch barreled M1A-A1 Bush Rifle. Worked for him. I believe that Finn Aagaard commandeered the same carbine later.

Everyone had a good time and no one told any lies except Jamison. Which is okay. Nobody believes him anyway. •

You Don't HAVE to Use A Scope!

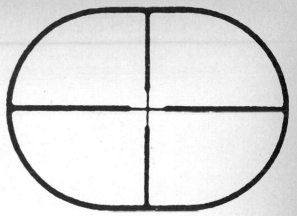

In this age of sophistication, all that's glittery and glass may not be the best way to go. Some guns don't *need* a scope sight to be effective. In fact, a glass sight can be a case of "overkill!"

A FEW YEARS AGO, every centerfire rifle in my gun cabinet was equipped with a scope sight. Many of us have grown up in the age of the telescopic sight and have had no experience with non-scope-sighted rifles, save the rimfire 22s that we learned to shoot with years ago.

Scope sights have been around since before the turn of the century, but didn't come into their own until the post-WWII years. During this time, technological advances and manufacturing techniques led to the production of glass sights that were both extremely dependable and easily affordable. In short, they became a "must have" item for centerfire hunting rifles.

Open sights and aperture sights did not just take a back seat to the new contraptions; they were practically forced into total obsolescence. As a result, few of us today give more than a passing thought to any sort of sighting device that contains no glass.

Some time back, the author bought a 90-year-old Model 1885 Winchester single shot rifle at an auction. This piece, commonly known as a "low wall," had a long, relatively heavy octagon barrel. Chambered for the 32 WCF (Winchester Center Fire) or as it is more commonly known, the 32-20, the rifle appeared to be nothing more

After being sure the rifle is zeroed from the benchrest, the prudent shooter will do considerable offhand shooting as well, and at varying distances. Iron sights are effective if you'll take the time to practice with them.

by MICHAEL THOMAS

This sporterized 30-40 Krag is equipped with a Lyman #57 peep sight, one of the most popular and useful of its type ever marketed.

A coarse front sight blade (below left) is fine for short-range snap shooting, but the wide blade covers too much target as the distance increases. A fine bead front sight (below) is the most versatile type for use with either open or peep rear, particularly if ranges extend to 100 yards or more.

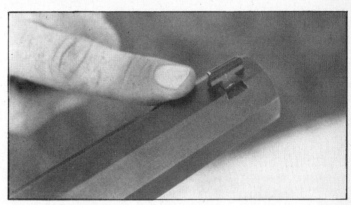

than a 25- or 30-yard plinker. The rifling was only in fair condition and the entire bore was interspersed with light pitting. In fact, it was downright rough. Of course, the gun only had iron sights (open rear plus a tang-mounted aperture).

Factory loads barely hit the target paper at 25 yards, but lead bullet handloads (115-grain bullet at 1230 fps) were a different story. I shot several very small 25-yard groups which caught my attention. When I backed up to 100 yards and shot groups measuring 2 to 2½ inches, I decided there must be something to this open and aperture sight business after all. The tightest groups were made using the aperture sight, but even the open sight was good for 3½- to 4-inch groups! Not bad for a rifle with a bore that looked like the inside of a stovepipe.

Within 2 years, I found myself working with a variety of other scopeless centerfire rifles and carbines, mostly lever actions. Included were the following: a '94 Winchester rifle in 25-35 WCF, two 30-30 '94 carbines, a '94 rifle in 7-30 Waters, a Rossi 92 357 Magnum carbine, another Rossi carbine in 44 Magnum, a Marlin 1895 (new model) rifle in 45-70 Gov't., a Navy Arms Rolling Block reproduction, also

in 45-70, and a sporterized Krag rifle in 30-40.

Virtually all of the guns shot well at 100 yards, but several were capable of very outstanding accuracy once suitable handloads had been stumbled upon. All loads used cast bullets at or near comparable jacketed bullet velocities. No exceedingly light loads were used. As cantankerous as cast bullets are, I think it reasonable to say that most jacketed bullets would at least equal the accuracy I obtained with my bullets.

Let's get back to the sights themselves. Why use open or aperture sights on any hunting rifle in this day and age? There are a number of perfectly valid reasons, some of which have been largely ignored in past treatments of the subject.

Open and aperture sights are the least expensive sighting "systems" available. They are also very durable. Once adjusted for a particular load, they need no further adjustments, checks, sighting shots, etc. Set and forget! Such sights work well in snowy and rainy conditions and don't require constant wiping or cleaning. They are lightweight. For all practical purposes, they equal the effectiveness of a scope sight out to 100 to 150 yards for hunt-

ing deer-size (or larger) game. It's no secret that the vast majority of our 200- to 300-yard game shots are actually only 75 to 150 yards at best. Few are longer.

With all this praise, could there possibly be any drawbacks to open and aperture sights? You bet. They are somewhat slower to get into operation than scope sights, but not appreciably so. I have found that considerably more range time must be spent in order to shoot well with these sights. However, once familiarity has been established and mastered, proper usage becomes second nature and the hard part is over. There is an added bonus for the extra work. You'd be quite amazed at how your marksmanship improves when you return to using a scoped rifle.

It is certainly not my intention to criticize or condemn modern rifle scopes. They have their place, certainly. Just as it would be asinine to use open or aperture sights on a bolt-action 22-250 intended for long-range varmint hunting, so is it absurd to scope a lever-action 45-70 intended for 50- or 75-yard deer hunting.

Sighting equipment should be compatible with the capabilities of a particular rifle/cartridge combination. That's a fundamental point but one

Due to the limitations of some cartridges, open or peep sights are just right for the application. Rifles chambered for (left to right) 25-35 WCF, 7-30 Waters, 30-30, 30-40 Krag, 32-20, and 45-70 don't really need scopes to be effective.

New open rear sights such as these from Williams (top) and Marble Arms (above) can be had at relatively low cost, and in many styles from modern to "old timey" looks. Many rifles come from the factory already drilled and tapped for installation.

that is often ignored. It makes little sense to use an expensive luxury car for hauling hay to the cows when a much cheaper farm truck would be far more functional. That same truck would probably be dismally lacking on a cross-country trip. So it is with sights.

With open or aperture sights, and shots limited to about 150 yards, a practiced marksman can expect to shoot groups that are only slightly larger than he could were he using a rifle equipped with a low-powered scope. That may be surprising to many, but it's true. A 50 or even 100 percent group size enlargement (say 5 inches) is an academic point when we're talking of game the size of whitetail or mule deer. Most often, much of the enlargement can be attributed to open sights. Aperture, or peep sights will sometimes allow a shooter to *equal* group sizes fired from rifles equipped with low-powered scopes at 100 yards.

Lyman, Williams, and Marble (open sights only) still make quality, affordable sights; all are proven for effectiveness through many decades of use by hunters. No better candidates for open or peep sights exist than the Winchester and Marlin lever-action carbines. These were designed as hunting guns. Period. They are not in the same

league, accuracy or power-wise, as many bolt-action and single-shot rifles. Most any of these guns, however, will keep all their shots within 2½ to 4 inches at 100 yards with compatible loads (and a compatible shooter).

Many firearms enthusiasts have read time and again how the open rear sight with front blade (or bead) combination is very difficult to use well. Gun writers tell of how the target, front sight, and the open rear sight must all be brought into perfect alignment before such devices can be used effectively. What the writers have preached is basically correct, but with practice, the difficulty decreases until the process becomes automatic. When shooting with the open sight, particularly in a split-second hunting situation, the unpracticed shooter will often fail to pull the front sight down into its rightful place. If the front sight is not pulled into proper position with the rear notch, overshooting invariably results, even at close range—an extremely important point to remember.

'Tis a fact that the aperture sight is superior to the open sight as the range increases. The superiority factor is of little significance until the range increases to 75 yards and beyond. With open or aperture sights, a fine bead

front sight is generally easier to use than a coarse bead or a blade except in low-light situations. Even at that, the coarse front sight covers a lot of target should the range become extended, and the margin for error is greatly increased when sighting-in.

I have found all open rear sights to be equally easy to use, comparatively speaking, with two important exceptions: the shallow "V" notch and the full buckhorn. Why these were designed and marketed is something of a mystery. The shallow "V" allows only for the crudest form of short-range sighting and the sides of the full buckhorn sight will block out far too much of a deer-sized animal's silhouette at 100 yards.

The aperture sight may appear to be rather crude and awkward at first glance. After adequate familiarization, however, many shooters (myself included) begin to think of this sight as a scope without glass, since the two work similarly. The eye will naturally center the front sight in the seemingly small aperture. Some rather amazing shooting can be done using the aperture sight. Again, a fine front bead is best for distant shooting. Some shooters recommend removing the small aperture from its threaded hole

An excellent example (left) of an early tang sight is this Ideal peep on a 32-30 Winchester low-wall single shot. Very fine vertical adjustments can be made with this sight, but there is no provision for windage—that must be done by drifting the front sight left or right.

Tang sights are very effective for long-range shooting, but are rarely seen today. Shown is a fully adjustable tang sight on a Navy Arms 45-70 Rolling Block rifle. The open rear sight has been removed.

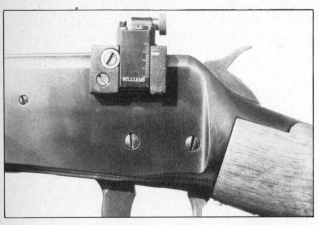

The Williams 5D peep sight is easily attached to this Model 94 Winchester and adjustments are rather straightforward. Elevation gradations are seen on the left side, windage reference marks are on the top.

and sighting only through the "ghost ring" (actually a very large aperture) after the rifle has been zeroed. This procedure works well for snap shots in heavy brush and it attendant short ranges and allows quick target acquisition. If it does, fine.

Many lever-action carbines and some bolt-action rifles come from the factory drilled and tapped for aperture sights. Installation is usually a 5-minute job, except where stock wood must be relieved (as on some bolt guns). For rifles not drilled and tapped, the work can be done by a gunsmith at minimal expense.

There is one problem area that exists with many front sights that needs addressing. Often, particularly in bright-light conditions, an "imaginary bead" will appear on the part of the bead that has the greatest amount of light. The shooter will try to compensate for it as a natural reaction. In doing so, he will hold away from the brightest area of the sight. Depending on the particular sight, the author has found that what seems to be reasonable compensation will often change the point-of-impact up to several inches at 100 yards. Hooded front sights will help to alleviate the problem. With sufficient practice in varying light conditions, the

perplexities of the imaginary bead can be recognized and overcome without subconscious compensation.

Proper eye relief with open and aperture sights is hardly worth mention because it comes so naturally to shooters. Unlike a number of high-magnification scopes, eye relief is generous and not critical.

At this point, it is fitting to mention a little about aperture tang sights. These are somewhat specialized and not often seen sighting pieces these days and enjoy the least popularity. They are excellent sights, however. Fundamentally, a tang sight and an aperture work in exactly the same manner despite the fact that their appearances are dissimilar. Theoretically, more accurate shooting should be possible with a tang-mounted aperture because of the longer sighting plane; something of little consequence when hunting, however. Tang sights are usually used today on reproduction single-shot rifles. For very long-range work these sights have no peers. Just as in the old buffalo hunting days, enthusiasts are now doing some impressive shooting with tang sight-equipped rifles at distances up to 500 yards. Apertures are quite small and some of the sights are awkward and bulky.

For stand hunting in good light they should work fine. Because of the specialized nature of these flip-up wonders, hunters will often remove the tang sight for use on game and rely solely on auxiliary open sights.

After firing several thousand rounds through my open-sighted and aperture-sighted rifles, I have made a number of fact-based comparisons. I believe the following figures to be reasonably correct for most people who have the impetus to shoot well with these sights.

Maximum Effective Ranges

Open rear, coarse blade
or coarse bead front   –100 yds.
Open rear, fine bead front –125 yds.
Aperture rear, coarse blade
or coarse bead front   –125 yds.
Aperture rear, fine bead
front   –150 yds.

These figures may seem conservative to some. Perhaps they are. Exceptional shooters can likely extend the range on each line by as much as 50 yards. Past 200 yards, however, trajectory becomes a problem. Such shots on game are seldom taken by the prudent hunter, and 200-yard distances should really be considered the territory of scope sights only.

The sighting-in procedure for open-

These two Rossi carbines, chambered for 357 and 44 Magnum, have open sights that may seem crude at first, but the guns can easily be set for the desired zero with minimal trial and error work. These are short-range hunting guns, to be sure.

As with sighting-in any rifle, open or aperture-sighted guns are best zeroed from a suitable rest. Initial shooting is done at 50 yards, then at 100 for fine tuning.

and aperture-sighted rifles is not at all similar to performing the same task using a scope. Following is what I've found to be an effective way of doing the job with the fewest attendant headaches.

Many "standard" targets will not work well. A slow-fire pistol target is fine, but it's very easy for the shooter to make an adequately large target. Using typing paper, draw a 6-inch diameter bull with a Magic-Marker. Blacken the entire inner circle. Make up several of these or run off duplicates on a copy machine. Unless you have a very light background on which to affix the target to a target frame, surround the target with additional sheets of blank white paper. This is important in that while using a 6 o'clock hold for sighting-in, a white background will greatly enhance the bull itself. Far less eye strain, too. Post the target initially at 50 yards.

Pay particular attention to the bead or blade in the bottom of the notch or "V" with open sights. If you completely "bottom" the front sight (where the very top can just be seen), that's fine, but hold it in the same position for each shot. Don't make the mistake of trying to put the bead or blade in the center of the black bull. That's okay for hunt-

ing or offhand practice, but not for sighting. We are only concerned with establishing a proper zero at this point. Aim at exactly 6 o'clock and fire three rounds. Let the barrel cool between three-shot strings.

I find that for full-power and near-full-power 30-30 loads with 160-170-grain bullets, it is best to get the point-of-impact 1 inch high at 50 yards. Drift the rear sight so that the group is perfectly centered. A 50-yard error should theoretically double at 100 yards, but it often appears to quadruple. When all is set, fire a couple of three-shot strings from the benchrest for the sake of confidence. With step-adjustable rear sights, vertical adjustment can usually be set to within 1 or 2 inches of the desired impact point at 100 yards. Sometimes it will be right on. The sight notch can be filed slightly, if necessary, for an exact vertical zero. Now do some 100-yard shooting. Using the 30-30 as an example again, shots should print to point of aim: the very bottom center of the bull. My suggestion for a 100-yard zero is based on the premise that a center hold on a deer, even at 150 yards, will plant a bullet in the killing zone without worrying about holdover. Again, it's far easier to sight on the target instinctively

while hunting, so forget the 6 o'clock hold except for zeroing.

The process for zeroing aperture-sighted rifles is even easier due to their finer adjustments. As mentioned earlier, the eye will automatically do much of the work, so adjust the sights and shoot several groups at both 50 and 100 yards. At the longer distance, groups should average much less in size than the diameter of the 6-inch bull.

Now is the time for some shooting without the aid of the benchrest. If you can stand, sit, kneel, or get into the prone position and keep all shots somewhere in the bull at 100 yards, you've passed with an A+. Many people can't brag of such shooting when using a scope.

That's all there is to it. Again, I don't advocate junking the scope that's mounted on a favorite 30-06 in favor of an open or aperture sight setup. But for short- to medium-range hunting, scopes are all too often too much of a good thing. These sights may be a little more trouble to learn to use properly, but the shooting practice will pay dividends in the game fields. Simple but effective, inexpensive yet rugged—that says it all for open and aperture sights. ●

Harvey's super eight-point Missouri buck scored 152 Boone & Crockett points. He used his Ultra Light 358 Win. Mag. rifle.

Whitetales

Fun Yarns From the Deer Fields

Hunting by itself is enjoyable, but there's also a lot of fun involved in the sport. Here's a lighthearted look at some humorous happenings of recent note.

by CLAY HARVEY

JAMISON was droning on about something, perhaps rhino hunting in Cleveland. Our host Gerald Ryals, manager of Pamlico Manor's Western holdings, appeared to be listening attentively. Probably sleeping behind open lids.

I was comfortably ensconced on Gerald's settee, coffee at hand, mesmerized by Rick's mellifluous narrative and the magnificent horns on the wall above me. Two identical sets of perfectly symmetrical, long tined, heavily beaded whitetail deer antlers reposed side by side. They were flawlessly matched, of course, because they had been shed by the *same* huge buck, 2 years running. Gerald had rescued them from the ravages of sun, pestilence, and porcupines, then had taxidermist Bill Farley mount them on throwaway capes.

Their splendor was breathtaking. What a deer this must be! Gerald saw the huge buck several times a year, but usually at a considerable distance. Once, he had gotten close enough to snap a color photo. He had shown it to me. And thus had I been hooked.

To Missouri I went, for a chance at the old boy before his horns began to wane. Bobby Rupert, owner of Pamlico Manor, had set up the hunt. I'd brought Rick Jamison along to teach him how to shoot, hunt deer, and lie about rhinos in Cleveland. So far, he was catching on quickly.

We retired about midnight, swapped deer stories and off-color jokes in the dark, giggling and goading and boasting like school boys playing hookey. Rick and I don't get together often enough. Or maybe too often, the way some of our hunting compadres tell it. We ignore them. Eventually, we lulled each other to sleep.

Mr. Ryals woke us about 5 minutes later. Coffee on, aromatic and enticing; eggs piled in a steaming heap; bacon chuckling happily on the griddle. Rick even let me eat some.

At first light, Gerald dropped us amid his 320 acres of overgrown Missouri farmland, wished us luck, then trucked off into the dim light, taillights evanescent in the gloom. Jamison admonished me against getting lost; I suggested he perform an unnatural act with a guppy. On that note, we separated.

Before his departure, Gerald had informed us of the presence of a pair of concupiscent bulk elk in our vicinity — the rut being in full swing at the time — suggesting that it might be prudent to avoid them. I allowed as how he was probably right. (Alas, I didn't manage to circumambulate said wapiti entirely, but that's another story.)

After still-hunting all morning, I

This view of author's huge Missouri buck shows the height of the horns, length of the tines and eye guards. What a buck!

joined Rick and Gerald for a noon repast, spending my postprandial hours once again in the woods. I passed up many a deer that day, including at least four bucks better than any I had previously slain. Ever. All were impressive, within range, unspooked, mine for the taking. None was the Big Guy. I let 'em pass.

On and on I walked, circuitously, silently, Natty Bumpo personified. Of course, the gusting wind might have helped a little in quelling the leafy crunch of my footfalls, but I prefer to remember my progress as being wraithlike. After all, I'm a professional.

I only fell down once

Rick and I had made plans to meet at last light beneath the one Texas-style elevated stand on the property, an edifice 40 feet high if an inch. One spindly ladder led upward, disappearing from view as it neared the shadowed floor of the aerie. Mr. Jamison is not exactly enamored of heights. Neither am I. We prodded and insulted each other to the top, whereupon we dived through the trapdoor, clutched something (anything) solid, and strove

to ease our pulse rates back below 200.

Eventually, we grew accustomed to the place, so much so that we ignored (for the most part) its wind-initiated vacillations. Rick kept watch toward the descending sun; I glassed a creekbed to eastward. Before long, a deer or two came out of the woods on my side, and Rick espied a couple of does and a six-point buck feeding along in his venue. No Big Guy. We waited.

I was peering intently into the darkening forest when Rick hissed, "There's a couple bucks. Big bucks. One is *real* big!"

During this fervent appraisal, I had pussyfooted to his side of the tower, plucked my rifle from its corner, and was now peeping through its scope. He was right. There were two bucks on the horizon, and both of them were big. One of them was *real* big.

The Big Guy himself.

I recognized those massive horns instantly. Stopped breathing. He stood there glaring at me . . . straight into the objective bell of my scope, or so it seemed. His deep-chested crony ambled over to the small herd, rudely shoul-

Gerald Ryals, manager of Pamlico Manor's Western operation in Missouri, shooting Harvey's Ultra Light Arms Model 20 in 358 Win. The author feels this is the ultimate whitetail rig for all terrain.

dered the little six-point out of his way, dipped his snoot for a mouthful of whatever it was on which they supped.

The Big Guy just stood there. Looking at me. Looking *through* me. Into my intent. I hammered him, hard, before he could bolt.

Rick yelled, "Good shot!" as I wracked the knob. The liquid "plop" of a solid hit floated back. I saw the buck stagger, right himself, go into a blind run. Followed him through the scope, swinging right along, holding my breath, taking up the pounds of pressure needed for sear release. An instant before a second "boom" could rend the air, he crashed headfirst into a tree, collapsed, entangling his rack in its trunk. The tree trembled from his death throes. Then all was quiet, save for the tintinabular after effects of my shot.

"You really busted him!" shouted Mr. Jay, pumping my hand like a Nebraska pump handle. He was as joyous as I, the sure sign of a true and selfless friend. Neither of us had killed a buck that day, and not only had Rick spotted the two big ones, but they were on his side of the tower. There was never any question who would shoot, either. Merely a quick and simple mental exchange, without the need to verbalize.

And to this day, Rick has never killed a whitetail buck that big.

Thanks, Buddy.

Long Range and the 10mm Buck

Last year, Master Jamison joined me in North Carolina for a go at the monstrous coastal bruins indigenous to the state. While we were there, he expressed a desire to down a deer using an experimental 30-caliber bullet. He had some with him, of course, loaded into ammo for one of his everpresent 300 Winchester Magnums. The bullet maker was back home, Rick swore,

champing at the bit to find out how well his nascent projectile would work on flesh and bone.

Furthermore, R.J. had brought along a Colt Delta Elite, 10mm persuasion, stuffed to the gills with a fresh batch of Hornady's new 170-grain jacketed hollowpoints. We had handloaded same on *my* Big Max press, at *my* house, using *my* powder. And had Steve Hornady sent *me* any of his spanking new projectiles? He had *not*. I brooded apace; if it fretted Rick any, I couldn't tell it.

One day, not long after Rick had embarrassed me irreparably in a local restaurant by ordering "one *chicken* egg" for breakfast, we got our chance at a buck. (When I queried Jamison about his unusual breakfast request, he simply shrugged, opined that he didn't know what all kinds of eggs might be

served adjacent to a North Carolina tidewater swamp, and he wanted there to be no misunderstanding about the kind of egg he intended to wash down with his coffee. I've never been so mortified.) We were gliding along the edge of a plowed-under soybean field when I espied a little "cow horn" buck at the far side, watching us tool along in my four-by-four. I braked; Rick's size elevens hit the turf; his elbows clumped down on my hood. Putting my binoculars on the buck, I watched the show.

POW! spoke Rick's Big Thirty. *Zip* went the bullet across 300 yards of space, sunlight and humidity conspiring to make visible to me the projectile as it homed in on the unwary buck. Well, almost homed in. It slipped over his neck by an inch or three.

The buck didn't move. Nor even duck. Just watched us placidly. This guy was so dumb he *needed* culling before his genes got passed on to the herd!

I felt Rick jack his bolt, heard the clink of the case as it rattled off my hood, was concussed by the reverberation of his follow-up shot. I watched this one also as it wended its way across 900 feet of agriculture, just like the first one had, seemingly in slow motion, as if in an old Peckinpah movie.

Whap! That one was no miss. The buck fell over. Tried to get up. Couldn't manage. Crawled off into the bushes.

We followed it up. Rick closed the gap, popped it with a finisher. From his 10mm. And thus did he become, for-

Rick Jamison softened up this North Carolina buck with his 300 Win. Mag. at 300 yards, then finished it off with his 10mm Colt Delta Elite. This is, officially, the first animal ever slain with Hornady's 170-grain, 10mm bullet.

ever, the first person to kill an animal with a Hornady 10mm handgun bullet. Never liked Jamison much.

On Changing Stands and Recalcitrant Safeties

My old school chum Fred Ritter each year hunts a real whitetail hotspot in Alabama. Naturally, he never invites me, but that's okay. He snores.

Last January he was easing along the soggy edge of a 70-acre grown-over field, trying to keep his feet dry and his mind on what he was about. Neither comes easy to Fred. The back end of the field had always seemed enticing from a distance, but since he had enjoyed considerable success at its upper end—taking two fine eight-pointers there the previous year—he hadn't found it necessary to examine the back side meticulously. This season his intent was to remedy that situation.

The rainfall in mid-January had been heavy; water in the neglected field had pooled waist-deep to an ostrich. Fred wisely skirted the deeper puddles while searching for just the right spot to erect his stand. Buck sign was everywhere; large rubs on the smaller pines, fresh fewmet, tracks of all sizes heading in every direction. No question about it; this was a major deer thoroughfare.

But where were the intersections?

Ritter stopped beside a sizable pine, was scrutinizing it closely for its treestand potential, when he glanced around to check visibility and field of fire. Not 60 yards away a heavy-horned

Rick Jamison is shown caping out his nice 10-pointer taken at Pamlico Manor West.

buck was tippy-toeing through the broomstraw, enroute from a small thicket to a sheltering woodlot at Fred's right. It didn't make it.

The deer was ambling along nose to the ground, likely following a doe, when it was intercepted by a Ritter bullet. The 140-grain slug sliced through its chest, invoking a 20-yard death run. And that was that.

Not content to rest on his laurels (greedy, in other words), Fred dressed the buck, deposited it in a handy spot, then went about setting up his ambush site for the following morning.

The next day's first dim light found our hero up the big pine, secure in his stand and probably half asleep, though he denies it. A buck similar in size to the one he'd greased the day before sashayed out of a thicket on the far

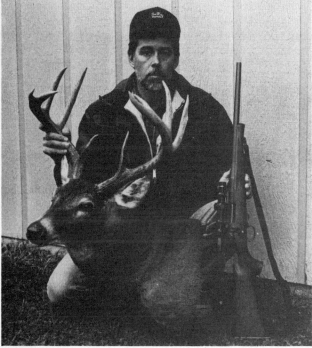

Fred Ritter is shown with a monster Alabama buck he took with a modified Remington Model Seven in 7mm-08. One shot, one buck that scored just under 150 B&C points, measured green.

side of the field, pawed briefly at a scrape, and quit the scene. No chance for a shot.

Depressed at the missed opportunity, Fred climbed out of his nest just before noon, gave the area a careful once-over, then relocated his stand. Fickle Fred. Back to camp he strode to fill his larder with victuals. That done, he elevated himself once more and settled in, prepared to waylay the shifty mossyhorn.

Nigh dark, a different buck—every bit as large as the one seen that morning—slipped from the woods, pushing a doe ahead of him. He passed right under the large pine wherein Mr. Ritter had spent his early hours. Once again, no clear shot was proffered.

"Beelzebub!" muttered our intrepid nimrod, or something more suitable but less quotable. Down the tree. Move the stand. Back where it was originally. Pant! Huff!

The following morn, ever eager, Fred sought his perch earlier than before, up even whilst the beavers slept. Persistant. Vigilant.

About 10:30, another fine buck materialized from the sheltering thicket, skirted wide a puddle of rain water, and stopped right under Fred's stand. Aha! Venison on the hoof. Fred eased off his safety. Put his crosswires on the deer. Squeezed the trigger. Squeezed some more.

The deer stood its ground, unconcerned. (Perhaps it had seen Fred shoot?) Ritter shoved forward on the safety lever. No good. It was stuck, half on and half off.

Fumbling out his skinning knife, Fred sat in the tree poking at his safety, trying to be quietly unobtrusive, while a big fat horny buck posed 'neath his boots. Does that not present a frustrating but amusing picture? Eventually, the deer meandered off, obviously having lost patience with its would-be assailant.

Fred invented several cuss words. A bit puerile, perhaps, but of considerable assistance in venting one's spleen and staving off the effects of stress.

Back to camp; switch rifles; return to the woods. For a few hours, Fred watched the birds play and the squirrels sing, or whatever. A smallish six-point waltzed out of the obviously overcrowded thicket to feast on acorns. Fred passed him up. Frying pan size. No challenge.

At lunchtime, Ritter fetched his original 7mm-08 rifle, fixed its safety, and went back on stand. The wind had shifted, running now from his hiding spot to the magic thicket. No good. Leaving his stand in place, he moved to a more favorable location to spend the afternoon.

Late that evening, Fred "felt" the presence of another being. Turning slowly in his stand, he espied a monster buck directly aft, standing on a knoll watching him. At his movement, the huge whitetail evaporated.

More creative cussing.

Back at camp that night, Fred's claque ridiculed his plight, suggesting that he was given to mendacity. Questioned, in fact, whether he had seen any deer at all, let alone a trio of enviable bucks. Fred sulked himself to sleep. He'd show *them*, by golly!

With the first hazy light of dawn, a flight of woodies whispered in on the wind, lit in the sopping field, began to breakfast on the abundant mast crop. Fred watched morosely as they fed, envying their easy camaraderie.

A movement caught his eye, 80 yards away. He snicked off the safety. Checked again; it was indeed off this time.

The movement he'd spotted proved to be a deer's back. Its head and neck were hidden behind a tree. No hurry, thought Fred, the wind is right. So there he sat, primed, waiting.

Abruptly the deer swung its head into full view. Wow! Even under the prevailing early-morning low-light conditions, it was easy to discern that this was no ordinary buck! The deer took three or four steps and stopped. Looked around. This one ain't going nowhere but down, thought my pal, then pulled the trigger. And that's exactly what happened.

Wood ducks scattered to the four winds, quacking and flapping and raising a ruckus. Then all was silent. *Absolutely* silent. No movement either, from Fred or the buck. Death had come to the forest.

And the silent woods creatures waited and watched and bided their time.

After a half-hour, Fred shimmied down, walked over to commune with the fallen monarch. At such moments, the paradoxical amalgam of remorse and accomplishment combines to bring a lump to the throat, a misty coating to the eye of the compassionate hunter. Fred is such a hunter; for him it was no different. Part of him wished the buck back to life, so it could fulfill forever its role as suzerain of this forest. Another part swelled with pride at the singular accomplishment, the fair-game taking of a patriarchal, trophy-quality whitetail buck. And thus will it always be, for many of us.

Unveilin' the Whelen

I couldn't stand it; I had to go back to Missouri for another go at Gerald Ryals' deer herd. Now, Gerald's place is special. He allows the culling of only 10 or 12 whitetails a year, and gets $1500 for each one. But his hunter-success ratio is 100 percent, his hospitality unmatched, his 320 acres wonderful to roam around on. (He also offers the hunting of exotic sika deer, and probably has the nicest heads to be found anywhere, in abundance. They cost even more to hunt than whitetails.) The best way to reach Mr. Ryals for information is by phone: 816/947-2624.

Arrangements were made for me to head west. So what gun to take? For years, I've intended to have a rifle built around the wildcat 35 Whelen, but have never gotten around to it. This was as good a time as any.

Chris Latta, ramrod of The Base Camp (2407 West 5th St., Washington, NC, 27889, 919/946-3113), had offered to build for me any kind of rig I wanted, and at a very affordable price. We conspired to make the following modifications to a Yugoslavian Mark X Mauser action from Interarms: AA fancy walnut stock, very slender, with a rosewood forend tip; checkered-steel grip cap; recoil pad; sling swivel studs; Jaeger front sight, with a Remington open rear unit to complete the emergency sighting system; Douglas air-gauged barrel, sporter contour, 24 inches in length. We agreed to forego checkering to keep the total cost under a thousand bucks (retail), but I insisted Chris apply one of his gorgeous color case-hardening jobs to the receiver, bolt, floorplate and trigger guard, even the Redfield all-steel mounts. To top the outfit I chose a Redfield 4x Tracker scope; at the bottom was to be installed an adjustable Timney trigger, set to 3 crisp pounds. Chris normally glass beds his rifles, so I concurred.

The result is a delight to shoot, tote, and look at. Only two handloads have been tried, with one quickly settled on for hunting use. Remington legitimized the cartridge just last year; I secured a sampling of both bullet weights. With either the factory 250-grain round nose or my reloads featuring the same bullet (by Hornady), five-shot 100-yard groups run between 1¼ and 1.35 inches. I suspect that a limited amount of load development will yield groups in the 1-inch neighborhood.

I sighted my handsome new rig to impact 2⅜ inches high at 100 yards and boarded the plane to Missouri. I hunted for two days before spotting the buck I wanted. When I did, he was only some 125 or 130 yards out, walking along bent on chow, a nice eight-pointer, sleek and symmetrical. As I was swinging along with him, he stopped, turned to face me head-on. I

Rick Jamison is posing with the author's eight-point buck, taken with the custom Mark X in 35 Whelen. Another one-shot kill.

Guido Anoon Byrd with Harvey's nine-point North Carolina lovelorn buck. Estimated weight was 165 pounds on the hoof.

sunk one low center in his chest, taking out his heart. The 250 Hornady soft point put him on the ground after a gallop of 15 or 20 yards. Although we looked hard for the bullet, we didn't find it. It was likely dumped inadvertently with the entrails.

I'm having him mounted as I type this, by famed Bill Farley, taxidermist nonpareil. Bill has something special in mind, and I hope to get it back in time to include a photo in a future piece. We'll see.

Soft Heart, Empty Head

I had been up in my stand for several hours when I saw Anson Byrd swing his dilapidated old pickup onto the access road beside which I was sequestered. He motored along in my direction, slowly, often obscured from my view by treetops.

I stayed where I was simply for the lack of anything better to do. One thing was certain: With him trundling down the road, no self-respecting deer would be in sight.

Wrong.

The rut, which I'd neglected to consider, was in full swing. Two does crossed the road between my stand and the approaching vehicle, although I didn't know it at the time; I couldn't cover that section of road from my vantage point. But Anson could.

Abruptly he stood on his brakes, slewed to a halt, piled out of the truck. Then disappeared from sight.

Boom! went his rifle. Then Boom! again. Then silence. After a few minutes, I heard him slam the truck's door, put it in gear. On he came.

Stopping 50 yards to my front, on the verge of the road, he stepped out of the cab, shoved his cap to the back of

his head, and peered back the way he had come.

"Did you see that buck?" he queried.

"Nope," I replied, trying to abandon the tree stand with a modicum of dignity, and particularly without falling out of it. I managed, but it wasn't easy.

"Man," quoth Anson, "that was some buck for these parts. He was following a couple of does. Didn't even notice me."

Now there's a dumb animal, thought I, if he walked onto a dirt road right in front of a truck. I know that buck deer go a bit off their rocker during the rut, but had no idea that even the most tumescent of bucks would be that heedless.

Wrong again.

"Let's go eat," said Mr. Byrd, loquacious as ever.

"Okay," I responded, following suit.

Anson U-turned the truck, started back the way he had come. Zip! Zip! Two does pranced across in front of us and disappeared into the foliage beside the road. Hot on their heels stepped a buck. A very nice buck, especially for coastal North Carolina. He stopped in the middle of the road.

Anson peered at him, spat out the window, said, "Might's well pop him. I'm outa ammo." Laconic even when staring at a buck most anyone would be proud to pose beside. Amazing.

So excited I was about to irrigate my camos, and striving desperately not to appear so, I drawled, "Yep. Maybe I oughta shoot him. Help with the gene pool. He's so dumb you can smell it on him."

Anson looked askance at me, divested himself of another mouthful of liquid, wiped his beard, said, "You gonna do it *today*?"

I got out of the truck.

The buck was confused. The objects

of his desire were no longer in sight, although I'm certain his keen nose apprised him of their whereabouts. Years of experience dodging hunters were speaking urgently into his inner ear that something was seriously amiss. But his tumid neck bespoke a glandular priority that overrode said mental tocsins.

He stood statue-like and watched me quit the vehicle, withdraw my Ultra Light Arms 6.5x55, chamber a round, assume a steady position, and find him in my scope. One-hundred-fifty yards or so. No problem. I applied pressure to the trigger, gently, holding my breath, until the rifle roared and bucked and sent a 125 Nosler Partition on its way. The bullet's strike sounded like swatting a pony in the rump with a tennis racket.

He humped up, galloped across the road full tilt, changed his mind, circled, retracing his route. Meanwhile, I was recharging the barrel, following his progress through my scope, pressing the trigger. The little gun spoke again, sending its muzzle skyward from recoil. In an instant I was back on him, watched him slide in a heap to the side of the road, dead as a fire hydrant.

My first bullet had blown a chunk of his heart out onto the ground; the amorous fud had been dead on his feet. My finisher had been unnecessary, but directed to a lethal spot at least. Good for me.

Anson opined that my performance had been adequate, congratulated me, acquiesced to sit still long enough for a photo or two. After I was finished, I noticed him standing over the carcass, musing.

"Wish I hadn't run out of bullets. That's a right nice buck."

Praise from Caesar. ●

Antique from Antietam

Neglected for years, and even abused, the author tried to bring this heirloom Civil War veteran back to usefulness with lots of tender loving care. It shoots again, but . . .

by JOSEPH W. BYERS

THE HEAVY BEARDED turkey gobbler stepped out from behind the tree, offering a clear shot. With extreme care, and being as quiet as possible, the lock was clicked into the ready position, and the trigger finger began to tighten with as much calmness as the moment would allow. In an instant, the hammer flew forward, exploding the cap on the nipple, generating a spark and a mild "pop" that was barely audible through the closed den door.

"Okay, it's my turn," said cousin Lynn, and with all the adventure that fills the imagination of two 8-year-old boys, the old musket was recocked, a paper cup placed over the nipple, and another imaginary hunt began. The room was wallpapered in a print that contained birds and animals, making it, literally, wall-to-wall adventure for two young lads. For years, each visit to Grandma's house, sooner or later, ended up with a fanciful hunt with the old muzzleloader.

The "musket," as it was called, was actually a rifle built in 1861 by the London Arms Company in England. Whether it had been bought, shipped, and assigned to a Union soldier, or smuggled through the Union blockades by daring rebel captains, one can only guess. As it was, the British made and sold arms to both the North and South during the Civil War, making it very difficult to determine if the arm was used by the one side or the other.

Most assuredly, the piece saw action in the Battle of Antietam, or Sharpsburg as it is known in the South, and if its battered muzzle could speak in language other than fire, smoke, and hot lead, its tale would be legend indeed. The scratches on its stock, like wrinkles on the face of an aging general, are marks of experience and hardship, remnants of life and death, the hell of war, and the fingerprints of care and abuse.

On the solemn day of September 16, 1863, the arm glistened with the care that a man gives a weapon upon which his life depends. Less than a year old, it was surely held with great respect. By sunset of this day of carnage, the

Byers took the London Arms rifle to Jim Culler, a blackpowder-only gunsmith, to have it brought up to snuff for shooting. The gun needed quite a bit of work.

Barrel inspection revealed a noticeable dent near the muzzle that needed to be removed. The gun would probably be safe to shoot shot, but not a ball.

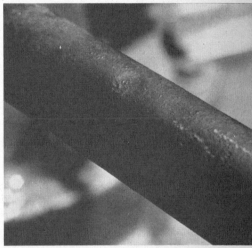

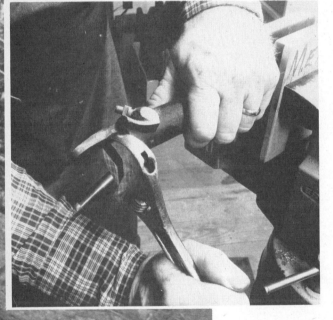

After determining the gun was not loaded (don't laugh—some Civil War guns have been found to be fully loaded!), the breech plug was drilled out and replaced with a reproduction plug and new nipple.

arm would survive, unlike several thousand brave men in blue and gray who would perish on the battlefield as part of 23,000 casualties on both sides.

Perhaps it belonged to a Reb standing in ranks in the thick cornfield along the Hagerstown Pike. The tall, mature stalks were a good disguise until the rising sun glinted from Confederate bayonets and gun barrels. Hooker, the Union general, focused the full effort of his artillery on the field and mowed the corn as if by a knife, slaying the soldiers exactly where they stood.

Possibly the piece belonged to Union soldiers who would learn first hand the obsolescence of Napoleani's tactics with rifled guns. Toward midday,

McClellan directed the Union army to attack the Confederate center, which was awaiting the advance and hidden in a natural rifle trench known as the "sunken road." Union troops, like band members at half-time of a football game, marched in straight columns toward the well-concealed Rebel line. Holding their fire until at point-blank range, the blackpowder rifles devastated the Union troops in wave after wave.

Could it have belonged to both sides at one time, as could have happened in the western movie-like ending of the battle?

General Burnside, near day's end, had finally succeeded in crossing the lower bridge of the Antietam Creek, outflanking Lee and his men. With the Union army now on three sides of the greatly outnumbered Confederate forces, Lee's army seemed doomed to destruction. But, just as Burnside's men were making a final advance, A. P. Hill, who had driven his men

Right—Culler's dent removal tool was a piece of tool steel turned to a few thousandths under bore diameter with a tapered end. It fit snugly into the barrel. Above—The taper on the rod was long enough to go just past the dent, indicated by the pencil.

By rotating the rod and rapping the outside of the barrel with a hammer, the dent was removed in minutes. There is very little sign of this work being performed.

Through years of kicking around and being more of a toy than a real gun, Byers' Civil War rifle became a bit battered. The muzzle was dented and, in an effort to renew accuracy, it was re-crowned. Sadly, it didn't help.

relentlessly, arrived at Sharpsburg in time to launch a counterattack, ending the fighting for the day. His men had just captured the federal arsenal at Harper's Ferry, and certainly confiscated many Union arms.

Whatever its origin, the Civil War piece moved from Shephardstown, West Virginia, (located across the Potomac river from Sharpsburg) to Maryland in 1902, along with the Byers family. For the next 80 years, it would stand in a corner, activate the imagination of generations of young boys, be shown with pride to visitors, but otherwise remain out of mind and out of sight.

Enter the young boy, now 30 years beyond his cap shooting days, who seems to be displaying the ever-spreading symptoms of Blackpowder Fever! You guessed it. The Enfield rifle suddenly came out of the closet. Friends who shot blackpowder were asked about the possibility of shooting an antique. As irresistible as the urge is to shoot the century-old piece, good sense prevails enough to take it to someone who knows enough about the subject to give a valid answer—a blackpowder gunsmith.

Many gun collectors, as well as shooting enthusiasts, have Civil War or other period antique arms that are hanging over a fireplace (a terrible place to put a gun, by the way), in a gun cabinet, or other place of honor. As interesting as these arms are to own and research, they are also fun to shoot and, if given proper care, can make effective hunting rifles as well. Much pleasure is derived from a favorite deer rifle, but taking an antique afield, especially if it has historical significance, can open up a whole new world of enjoyment.

Blackpowder gunsmiths aren't common in most areas, but by asking friends at local sporting goods stores, Jim Culler's name was mentioned several times. He owns the Fort Chambers Gun Shop (blackpowder only) in Chambersburg, Pennsylvania, and would be the source of new life for the antique from Antietam. A graduate of the Colorado School of Trades, Culler has been doing blackpowder work for 20 years and knows his business well, as he was soon to demonstrate.

After giving the rifle a thorough going over, it became clear that some repair was in order. Oddly enough, the first order of business was to determine if the gun was loaded. The breech plug was hopelessly seized to the barrel, and had to be drilled out. With the replacement of the plug and a new nipple, the gun was fireable, with one major exception. It was safe to shoot shot, but a noticeable dent was found in the barrel.

"It's not safe to shoot a ball," was Culler's assessment. Dented barrels are nothing new to shotgun buffs, and are fairly simple to remove. Unfortunately, a hydraulic dent remover was not available in .575 caliber, and even if one could be located, it was doubtful it would reshape this heavy barrel.

The actual removal of the dent was such a simple process that it took less than 5 minutes, and left no mark in the barrel, even though a metal hammer was used. The techique utilized was a special process that may be of use to shooters with a similar problem.

Guns may have dented barrels without the knowledge of the owner. Three signs of danger are when the ramrod or patch suddenly gets tight, or won't go smoothly down the barrel. A second indication of a dent is to look down the barrel, holding it up to a light, and seeing a high spot or shadow. Perhaps the easiest way to detect a dent is to carefully rub the barrel with fingers, noting carefully any bumps or recesses, and then checking the bore with a light.

If a problem is found, there is one sure way to eliminate it. "Move from the dent toward the breech ½-inch and saw off the barrel," Culler says with a chuckle. Although very effective, this method plays havoc with trivial things such as accuracy, value, and aesthet-

The beauty and the beast! The original 1861 London Arms Co. rifle lays on a Civil War blanket next to a modern reproduction. The differences are slight.

ics. The most common way is to use a hydraulic dent remover as mentioned previously, but if this is not workable, a third method is advised.

First, carefully measure the bore with an inside micrometer—.575-in. in this case. Next, a piece of tool steel drill rod is cut on a lathe to a slightly smaller diameter, and polished. The length of the rod is determined by how far the dent is from the muzzle. It should be long enough to surpass the dent by ½-inch and still protrude from the bore by about an inch.

One end of the rod is cut with flats to be turned with a wrench, while the other end is cut on a flat taper.

Grease the rod to prevent seizing, and tap it into the barrel so that the taper snugs under the dent. Using a small hammer, tap the outside of the dent.

At first this may seem to be exactly

the wrong thing to do, and will appear to make the indentation deeper. However, the force of the steel rod stretches the barrel, and it goes back to its original shape. When the rod will rotate completely under the spot where the dent was, the barrel is repaired.

Once my gun was shootable, it was "Katie bar the door" to get to the range. Although this gun was made in England, it is almost an exact duplicate of the Springfield Rifle Musket of 1855, '61, '63. The rifles performed similarly down range. The parts are not interchangeable, but the rifle was built with the same concept in mind. Surprisingly enough, the Springfield and other similar arms were designed upon much research and experimentation.

The rifle was designed to shoot a 500-grain bullet with 60 grains of powder, generating a muzzle velocity of about 950 feet per second. The accuracy that

Considering its age and history, the original gun compares quite well with the shiny new reproduction gun. The antique was carried on many youthful "safaris."

The ramrod on the original gun had been lost over the years and long ago was replaced with one from another gun. The reproduction gun has the original-style rammer.

was projected at the time was astounding, and could reportedly hit a target the size of a man on horseback at 600 yards, and penetrate 4 inches of pine board at 1,000 yards.

At lesser ranges the rifled musket was expected to put 10 consecutive shots in a:

4-inch bullseye at 100 yards;
9-inch bullseye at 200 yards;
11-inch bullseye at 300 yards;
18½-inch bullseye at 400 yards;
27-inch bullseye at 500 yards.

When discussing accuracy of military weapons of this period, one must keep in mind the style of fighting that occurred up until this time. Europeans traditionally fought in well-disciplined lines of soldiers marching shoulder-to-shoulder toward each other in parade fashion. In the mid-19th century a military rifle was considered accurate if it could hit a military target 6 feet high and 20 feet wide (a column of advancing troops). Obviously, this is a few thousandths more than today's marksmen are satisfied with.

The London Arms Co. rifle was designed to shoot a Minié bullet. In fact, this arm and others in .575 caliber had three choices of projectiles. The patched round ball was the most accurate bullet; however, it was slow to load and was unsatisfactory for military use. During the Revolutionary War, for example, a soldier could load about one round per minute vs. the Hessians with their smooth-bore muskets who could get off four to five rounds per minute.

The Minié bullet, a 500-grain conical-shaped projectile with built-in grease grooves, was the state of the art bullet of the time for several reasons. Without having to use a patch, a soldier could get off three rounds per minute. Secondly, the Minié bullets shot accurately, almost as well as the Kentucky rifles of the time, and finally, the heavy mass of the projectile carried energy farther down range.

Owning a historical rifle is somewhat like owning a classic sports car—the lines, form, and heritage may be of excellent quality; but, how does it perform?

Unfortunately, 125 years of age would have been kind if the rifling in the barrel had only developed wrinkles instead of pits and rust. Trying as many loads as I could, keeping a group on an 8 × 11-inch sheet of paper at 25 yards was impossible with patched round ball. Accuracy seemed to improve at 70 grains of powder with an occasional hit close to center.

Discussing this disappointing performance with Rich Jaggers, a gunsmith from Ohio, he anxiously asked to be able to give the gun a try. He's a recent graduate of the Trinidad Gunsmithing School in Trinidad, Colorado, and has a special interest in long rifles.

Unfortunately, his report a month later was not encouraging. "I tried three or four different types of Minié balls but couldn't get them to shoot at all. If they'd pick up just a hair of the rifling, I thought they might work but I couldn't keep them on a 4-foot square target at 50 yards. Round balls on top of paper weren't much better. I used a target board wad, with a paper patch (.570-in. roundball and a .015-in. patch). Next, I tried a folded 4-inch square of newspaper on top of the powder and then a lubed patch. This brought the group down to about 18 inches at 50 yards."

The problem, Jaggers summarized, is that the bore is so pitted and rough that the fire and heat of the charge consumes the patch before it leaves the barrel. "Even if you can make the patch last during the shot by continued experimenting you may only bring

Hunting with an original gun like the 1861 rifle adds enjoyment to the challenge. As of yet the author has not found a load that will group under 18 inches at 50 yards.

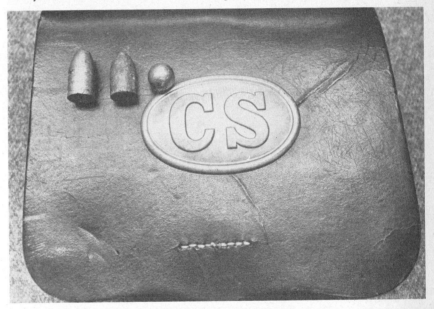

Caliber 575 Civil War projectiles on a Confederate cartridge box, left to right: Minié bullet, British Pritchette bullet, and round ball.

your groups down to about 12 inches at 50 yards, not enough to be a satisfactory hunting rifle. One option is to have the barrel bored out to a smooth bore, but this would reduce the value of the rifle."

As this indicates, my antique is not a match rifle. One of the dilemmas the owner of an old gun will face is how much to shoot it and under what conditions. For best accuracy, a rifle should be test fired at 5-grain powder increments, with variations in patch-

ing and projectiles to reach the optimum load. In my case this "perfect combination" of lead and powder may be a long time coming and could be impossible without a major overhaul. However, the value of the gun to me is in its history and its importance to the family and the area. Owning an original is a thrilling experience, and being able to shoot it is just icing on the cake.

Well, if balls won't work there's always buckshot! ●

REQUIEM
for the BENELLI
PISTOL FAMILY

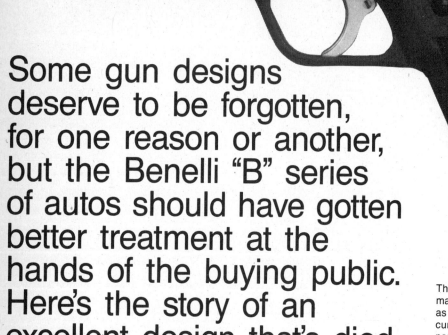

This prototype Benelli Model B76 shows many differences from its later brothers, such as the bottom magazine release, tightly curved trigger guard, rear sight, dull grip panels. Serial number is 12.

Some gun designs deserve to be forgotten, for one reason or another, but the Benelli "B" series of autos should have gotten better treatment at the hands of the buying public. Here's the story of an excellent design that's died an early death.

by DONALD MACLAREN

Right side view of a very early Benelli Model B77 chambered for 32 ACP. The tight trigger guard curve (arrow) was still in production and the rear sight was changed from the number 12 gun. It was imported by Sile Distributors, sold through Mandall's.

Left-side view of serial 1428 (still early production) shows relocation of the magazine release, addition of glossy finish on grips. The rear sight is, again, different, slide contours have been changed, but the trigger guard curve is the same.

THE AVERAGE AMERICAN is brought up to think that if you build a better mousetrap, the world will beat a path to your door. In the fickle field of firearms design, this is not always the route followed by the public; better guns come and go almost without even a footpath to that portal.

Some 20 years ago, the advanced Whitney 22 automatic pistol suffered the same treatment as the Benelli family of pistols was about to go through. These excellent Benelli arms were first offered to the American public in 1976/77, more than 10 years ago, and their arrival didn't cause a ripple on a rural dirt road, let alone on an interstate. Unfortunately for Benelli, the first ones sold here were their Model 77s, a rather robust automatic in 32 Automatic Colt Pistol (ACP), generally thought to be a pocket-pistol chambering. These pistols weigh over 35 ounces empty and are 7⅞ inches long by 5⅜ inches high, hardly what one would call a pocket automatic pistol. As an example in contrast, the Colt Mustang in 380 ACP weighs only 18.3 ounces, or just over half as much. No, a pocket pistol the Benelli ain't.

In the early days of the Benelli pistols in America, only 200 of these heavyweight 32 autos were imported by Sile Distributors, Inc. of New York City. The Benelli 32 ACP was as unpopular as the Hi-Standard G-380, another giant pistol in a pocket pistol caliber, 380 ACP. The Hi-Standard

auto preceded the Benelli by a few years.

What's wrong? Doesn't anyone in the United States want a big full-size pistol which shoots the impotent 32 ACP? The answer is, *nobody*! So, back to the drawing board for the designers at Benelli. This time they were sure that they knew what the shooting public wanted and they were going to give it to them. The Benelli exhibits some extremely modern design concepts. For example, the much more secure roll pins are found instead of the time honored solid pins. Snap rings are used to hold assemblies together. Yet, strangely, almost no plastic parts are used. To avoid the possibility of a separation of the shell casing on pistols with high chamber pressure, small grooves running parallel to the axis of the barrel are engraved into the forward neck of the chamber. These grooves allow a small amount of gas to float the shell casing at the moment of high pressure and make its extraction much easier. When fired cases are examined, they show no permanent creases caused by these grooves. Thus

the ammo can be sized and reloaded. The gun's serial number is found in three different places: on the left side of the frame over the trigger guard, the left side of the slide, and the barrel under the slide, but, strangely, the bolt is not numbered.

The Benelli pistol is patented in the U.S.A., with patent number 3,893,369 issued July 8, 1975. It was also patented in Italy, patent number 44012/72, issued February 29, 1972. The patents are in the name of the inventor, Sen. Giovanni Benelli, of Urbino, Italy. In 1983 the Benelli firm was united with Beretta and Breda in a cooperative relationship which involved those companies' participation in Benelli's capital.

Here is a list of what Benelli was to offer the shooting public:

1. Rigid non-recoiling barrel.

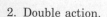

2. Double action.
3. Hard chromium-plated parts.
4. Pressed steel frame.
5. Caliber 9mm Parabellum.
6. A Luger-like slant to the grip.
7. Checkered walnut grips.
8. Magazine catch at the rear of the trigger guard.
9. Excellent sights.
10. Adjustable trigger over-travel stop.
11. Recoil buffer system.
12. No-tool takedown.
13. Easy to load magazine.
14. Loaded chamber indicator.
15. An excellent instruction manual.
16. Adjustable hammer tension.

That's a pretty impressive list of features for any pistol, so let's look at them in detail first and then discuss the few things that the Benelli pistol didn't have that made it so unsaleable.

1. Rigid Non-recoiling Barrel

The Benelli locked breech has been called a hesitation blowback, which is really not true. Its action is really locked at the moment of firing and yet its barrel is rigid, not recoiling like that of the Colt-Browning automatic pistol. Recoil-operated pistols heretofore have had moving barrels, which move in some direction as the slide unlocks from the barrel. In the Browning

A very late import Model B80, but not from Sile, serial number 2288C. This example has the more graceful trigger guard (arrow), different slide machining and coarser slide pull serrations. Gun is chambered for 7.65 Luger.

system, the barrel drops slightly to unlock. In the Walther P.38 system, the barrel moves directly backward to unlock the slide. In the Steyr and Roth-Steyr system, the barrel rotates to unlock. In the Benelli pistol, the barrel doesn't move in any direction, but the bolt of the slide is locked to the barrel at the discharge of the firearm. The slide assembly is in two separate pieces, the lightweight bolt and the much heavier slide. The bolt has, at its rear, a moveable toggle that also bears on the slide, and the breech closure assembly. This engagement is such that when the slide is in its fully closed position, it bears on the toggle which in turn pushes the bolt downward, locking it to a notch in the subframe. At the instant of firing, the bolt is locked. Next, the slide starts to move back-

ward from inertia; at this moment the bolt, through the action of the toggle, cams itself out of the locked position and recoils rearward, locked in its up position in the slide by its control stud. The biggest difference shown in the patent as compared to the actual gun is that the patent shows that the bolt locks in semi-circular grooves in the subframe. Does this system work? It sure does and since the barrel is rigid, the pistol is inherently more accurate. In the past, I tried firing the Benelli without its locking toggle and found that the bolt was violently blown rearward, shearing off its control stud and the extractor. Though this caused no damage to me, it didn't help the pistol any, and it had to be repaired. The other much easier way to convince yourself that the Benelli has a locked breech, is to examine a bottle-necked case like the ones fired from the pistol in 7.65mm Luger. If the Benelli's action were blowback, these highly bottle-necked shells would exhibit no neck after firing and would be ruptured in that area. This is not so; the cases show only the slightest amount of setback and have absolutely no tendency to rupture.

2. Double Action

The ability of an automatic pistol to fire its first shot from the trigger cocking mode has been pooh-poohed by some, but we can safely say it's a feature that is here to stay. For safety's

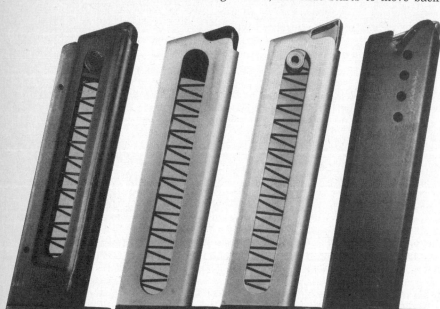

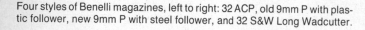

Four styles of Benelli magazines, left to right: 32 ACP, old 9mm P with plastic follower, new 9mm P with steel follower, and 32 S&W Long Wadcutter.

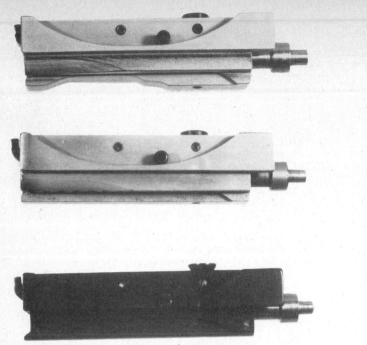

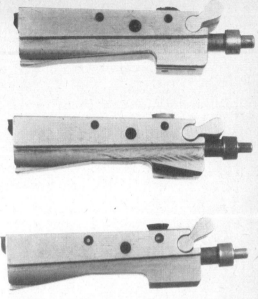

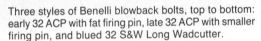

Three styles of Benelli blowback bolts, top to bottom: early 32 ACP with fat firing pin, late 32 ACP with smaller firing pin, and blued 32 S&W Long Wadcutter.

Benelli's locked-breech bolts also varied through production, top to bottom: early 9mm P, later 9mm P, and a late 7.65 Luger.

sake, we are told not to carry a live round in the chamber, but many whose lives depend on speed of firing ignore this warning and do so. If you do keep the chamber loaded, then for first-shot speed you must have trigger cocking and firing of the pistol. This single eventuality has made the double-action pistol popular. Also, if a round fails to fire at the first pull of the trigger, this gives the shooter a quick second chance.

3. Hard Chromium-Plated Parts

Those who served in the recent Vietnam War can best testify to the ability of Chinese chromium-plated parts to resist rust, corrosion and wear. In the Benelli, all the parts that come in contact with powder gases are hard chrome plated, and the firing pin is stainless steel. In order to prove to myself the corrosion resistance of chrome-plated steel, I fired some of the grungiest, corrosive primed ammo through a 9mm Parabellum Benelli and left it two weeks in a moist climate and two weeks in an arid one without any attempt at cleaning it. The results were amazing—absolutely no rust or corrosion, in either case, to be seen at the end of the month. As a further testimony to chrome plating, look at the beaten up Chinese SKSs that have been coming into the United States the last few years. Most of these guns look like shot out pieces of junk, but the

bores appear brand new, and yet the Chinese ammo also available is corrosive as sin. The only exception to Benelli's practice of chrome plating their pistols are the very recently made MP3S 9mm and 32 S&W Long target models. All that I've seen have had all their parts blued that would normally have been chrome, except the barrels.

4. Pressed Steel Frame

Bill Ruger, back in the 1940s, made a pistol's frame out of two steel stampings welded together. The 22 automatic pistol thus formed was Ruger's beginning in the firearms world and has led to the great success of Sturm, Ruger & Company. A frame made out of pressed steel is basically cheap to fabricate, but at the same time it is strong. The steel used in making the Benelli's frame is .075-inch thick. After forming, the left and right halves are welded together and the external junction lines of the weld are carefully ground off, so that to all appearances there is no junction at all. In those places where more strength is needed, steel inserts are welded in. Where screws will hold items like the grip pieces to the frame, the steel is embossed to give more depth to the threads. Where the magazine enters the frame at the bottom of the grip, there are two inward dimples in each half of the frame to insure that the magazine fits tightly in the frame. But

the restriction comes only after the magazine has been partially inserted so as not to make the initial insertion of the magazine too slow. Pressed steel in firearms design has an advantage over today's almost universally used investment casting, in that pressed steel is much more like a forging and there is no danger of voids and weak spots in the finished product.

5. Caliber 9mm Parabellum

The bulk of the Benelli guns imported here are 9mm Parabellum caliber. This now being our nation's military cartridge for handguns, it has become popular and in the future it will be even more of a favorite. The Benelli is also available in 7.65 Luger, the already mentioned 32 ACP, and the unusual caliber of 32 Smith & Wesson Long wadcutters. Overseas, the pistol has been made in 9mm Ultra, which is a cross between our 380 ACP and the 9mm Parabellum. Lastly, it has been made in the popular Spanish caliber of 9mm Bergmann-Bayard or Largo. In prototype form, the Benelli has been made in 38 Super. The pistols in which the chamber pressure is relatively low are blowback, with no attempt to lock the breech. These are the 32 ACP, 32 Smith & Wesson Long WC, and the 9mm Ultra. In these guns, they have a bolt which is longer and lighter than normal and has no toggle to interact with the slide. In other words, the slide

These five slides show variations of interest to the collector, top to bottom: early B77 in 32 ACP, early B76 9mm P, late B76 9mm P, very late MP3S in 32 S&W Wadcutter (Target, no front sight), and late B80 in 7.65 Luger.

and the bolt act as one piece. Test Benellis have been fired with cartridges as hot as 1320 fps, firing a bullet weighing as much as 130 grains. It seems that the greater the chamber pressure, the mose positive the locking action.

6. A Luger-like Grip Angle

On a Benelli, the angle that the grip makes with the axis of the bore is 65 degrees, which is similar to the well-loved P.08 Luger 59-degree grip angle. Though this laid back angle is very comfortable for the shooter, it can cause feeding problems and there are frequent jams with the Luger. The Benelli does not suffer from these feeding jams. Also, the front and rear grip straps are serrated to give the hand a good grip. The front of the trigger guard is not serrated.

7. Checkered Walnut Grips

Most of today's automatic pistols, as a matter of economy, have gone to plastic grips. This is not true of the Benelli which sports a set of hand-checkered walnut grips. On most Benellis, these grips are treated with a clear plastic coating for durability.

8. Magazine Catch at the Rear of the Trigger Guard

One of the most unchanging requirements of the U.S. service pistol is that the magazine release catch can be operated with the shooting hand. This requirement has spilled over to the civilian shooting population, and you will find that most American pistols have the magazine release on the left side directly behind the trigger guard. Conventionally, the release is pushed inward to drop the magazine, but in the Benelli it is pushed forward so that it is much less likely to be operated by accident. Also, the magazine is forcefully ejected so that a loaded unit can be instantly inserted. In prototype Benellis, the magazine catch was found in the usual European position at the bottom and rear of the frame's grip.

9. Excellent Sights

The ability of a pistol's sights to be seen in failing or bad light seems so basic that it usually goes without saying. Yet for years in this country, sights were blued with the rest of the gun and

Various recoil spring assemblies, top to bottom: 32 ACP, early 9mm P (without Belleville washers), late 9mm P (with washers), and 32 S&W Long Wadcutter (no washers).

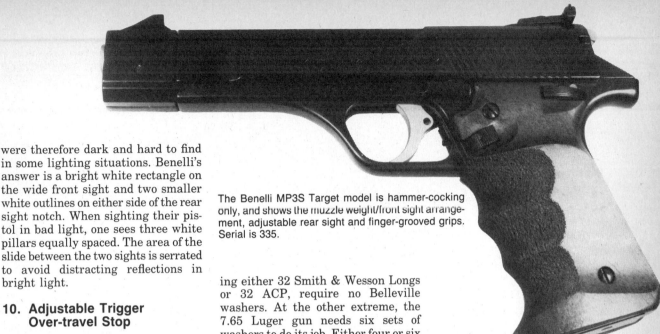

The Benelli MP3S Target model is hammer-cocking only, and shows the muzzle weight/front sight arrangement, adjustable rear sight and finger-grooved grips. Serial is 335.

were therefore dark and hard to find in some lighting situations. Benelli's answer is a bright white rectangle on the wide front sight and two smaller white outlines on either side of the rear sight notch. When sighting their pistol in bad light, one sees three white pillars equally spaced. The area of the slide between the two sights is serrated to avoid distracting reflections in bright light.

10. Adjustable Trigger Over-travel Stop

When the trigger is pulled to fire a pistol, there is a tendency, especially when trigger-cocking the hammer, to jerk the gun off target because of trigger over-travel. For this reason, some expensive target pistols have an adjustable trigger stop. The Benelli has such a stop which is an Allen set-screw behind the trigger. The small wrench which is used to turn the screw out or in is shipped with every pistol. The use of a trigger stop on a double-action pistol does pose some problems, however, since the hammer's point of release is rarely the same in the trigger-cocking and hammer-cocking modes. The best you can end up with is a compromise, but that is a lot better than nothing. The front face of the trigger is serrated to prevent slippage.

11. Recoil Buffer System

One of the design problems facing an automatic pistol manufacturer is to reduce the weight of the gun but only to the point that recoil isn't excessive. Enter here a buffer system, and the Benelli has a very ingenious one that is reminiscent of the one Browning designed for the Remington Model 8 and 81 autoloading high powered rifles. As the slide flies backward, the recoil spring collapses into a steel tube which prevents the spring from over stressing. The remaining backward motion is absorbed by pairs of tough saucer-like Belleville washers. Depending on the cartridge being fired and on the amount of snubbing needed, more or fewer sets of washers can be assembled, still using the same recoil spring. This buffer assembly is mounted on the recoil spring guide and captured by a snap ring. The buffer assembly in the blowback Benellis, shoot-

ing either 32 Smith & Wesson Longs or 32 ACP, require no Belleville washers. At the other extreme, the 7.65 Luger gun needs six sets of washers to do its job. Either four or six sets are used in the 9mm Parabellum guns.

In the earliest Benellis, the buffer tube was a weldment on the frame, and the Belleville washers are found on the rear of the assembly. Every Benelli pistol, be it blowback or locked breech, has a small rubber buffer mounted in the rear overhang of the frame to cushion the hammer in its maximum rearward position.

12. No-tool Takedown

Gun writers in the past have more or less laughed at the fact that no special tools are required to field strip a firearm, but this is either because they never take any gun apart or because the only one they feel at home with is the 45 Government Model. The Benelli automatic can be taken down for a thorough cleaning without anything more specialized than the tip of a pencil. This is because the pencil is required to ease the breech closure assembly out of the slide. Because the bolt is not an integral part of the slide, it can have its working face easily cleaned. So, too, with the slide, because with the bolt removed, the slide is just a U-shaped piece of steel. The hammer, even if the trigger is pulled, will not strike the firing pin, in the unlikely event that on reassembly the owner might forget to close the two little lock pieces on the breech closure assembly. This is because the open lock pieces won't let it past.

13. Easy to Load Magazine

Like most Italian magazines, the one found on the Benelli is extremely easy to load. This is because the follower has finger gripping "ears" on both sides and

slots on both sides of the magazine's wall. The loader's fingers can depress the follower as each cartridge is inserted, which makes the whole job of loading a lot more simple.

14. Loaded Chamber Indicator

I'm almost loathe to mention this next "safety" feature found in the Benelli line of automatic pistols. It is so important and so often overlooked by designers that I feel as though I'm getting up on my soap box when I start to preach how important it can be. If it weren't for the number of "I didn't know it was loaded" accidental deaths each year by people who should know better, I wouldn't mention it. The use of the microscopic movement of the extractor when a round is in the chamber does not, to my mind, constitute an adequate warning device to the unpracticed gun handler. It is just this type of loaded chamber indicator that the Benelli pistol is damned with. Worse, in a way, on the Benelli, in order to see the red warning on the extractor's head, you practically have to look down the pistol's barrel. Not really a "safe" device!

15. Excellent Instruction Manual

The Benelli pistol comes not only with a numbered certificate of guarantee but also with a 50-page, four-language instruction manual which really has sufficient and clear enough photos to completely understand the pistol. The phantom views of the pistol are outstanding, and extremely helpful.

Factory cased Benelli Model B76S in 9mm P is an early gun, showing serial number 95. The optional case was covered in leather, the interior done up in velour. The "S" in the model designation means the gun is a double-action type. All Target models are rare.

16. Adjustable Hammer Tension

The Benellis coming to the U.S.A. were mostly 9mm Parabellums and had their hammer tension set at the factory for the relatively hard NATO primers. However, hammer tension is adjustable on the Benelli so that the user can adjust it to the type of ammo that he expects to be using.

So, the above are all the "plus" features that the Benelli line of automatic pistols had to offer. What went wrong? Why didn't the public rush out to buy them? One factor was that the squareness of the slide's cross-section gave the pistol a boxy look, but the single biggest factor in the lack of acceptance is the sinking value of the American dollar on the European money market. The following table shows the 1988 list prices of the last of various Benellis imported recently by Sile. They are not what you would call give away prices, yet the Benellis are fine pistols offering many things not found on domestic handguns. Price is only one of the deterrents. Below are other "minus" items.

Model	Caliber	Price
B-76	9mm Para.	$427.50
B-76S (Target)	9mm Para.	$713.50
B-77	32 ACP	$399.00
B-80	7.65 Luger	$384.50
B-80S (Target)	7.65 Luger	$571.50
MP3S (Target)	32 S&W Long WC	$785.00

Here is the list of the other things that the Benelli line should have had to make it more saleable in the fickle American marketplace.
1. High magazine capacity.
2. Ambidextrous controls.
3. Firing pin and hammer drop safeties.
4. More rounded appearance.

1. High Magazine Capacity

The next Benelli mistake was not taking the U.S. government's testing for our service pistol seriously enough. The MX-9 program should have warned Benelli that their magazine capacity was too low for modern thinking. For years, the public was able to live or die with five or six shots in a revolver and six to eight shots in an automatic pistol. But with the popularity of the 13-round Browning High Power after World War II, the cry went up from the military for more magazine capacity, with less emphasis on

Benelli Models

Model	Caliber	Comments	Action
B 77	32 ACP	Earliest	DA
B 76	9mm P	Most common	DA
B 76T	9mm P	Target sight only added	
B 76S	9mm P	Full target model	DA
B 76S	9mm P	Full target model in leather case	DA
B 80	7.65	Fairly common	DA
B 80S	7.65	Full target model	DA
B 80S	7.65	Full target model in leather case	DA
MP3S	9mm P	Full target model in leather case	SA
MP3S	32 S&W Long	Full target model	SA
MP3S	32 S&W Long	Full target model in leather case	SA
?	9mm Ultra*	Never seen in the U.S.	DA
?	9mm B-B*	Never seen in the U.S.	DA

*These overseas variations may also be available in target models.

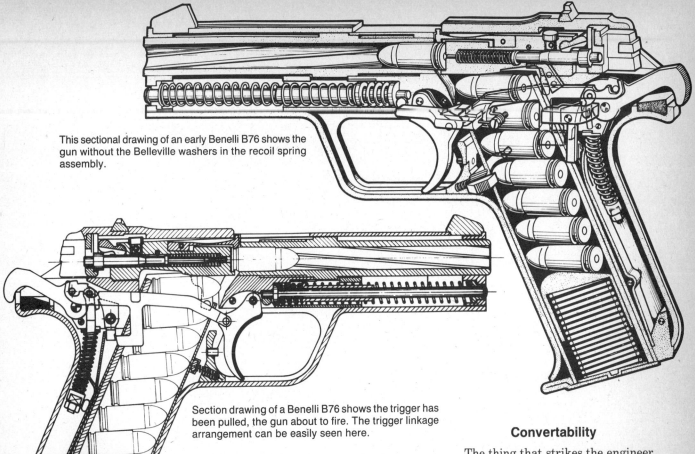

This sectional drawing of an early Benelli B76 shows the gun without the Belleville washers in the recoil spring assembly.

Section drawing of a Benelli B76 shows the trigger has been pulled, the gun about to fire. The trigger linkage arrangement can be easily seen here.

accuracy and marksmanship training. Benelli's eight-round magazine, right or wrong, had gone the way of the dodo bird.

2. Ambidextrous Controls

Also covered in our government's testing for a pistol to replace the venerable Model 1911-A1, was the desirability of having a pistol that could be fired and operated by both right- and left-handed people. This feature is not to be taken lightly and many guns today are designed for handgun shooters using either hand. Some pistols come with this sublime feature already built in, while others have to be modified slightly by the shooter. However, Benelli ignored this two handedness and has been, in turn, ignored itself.

3. Firing Pin and Hammer Drop Safeties

The last big feature that Benelli should have had was the almost God-like worshipped hammer drop safety.

If a shooter wants to lower the hammer from its cocked position, he must hold it with his thumb while pulling the trigger. This is dangerous and accidents can happen. Now to the firing pin lock. Although we struggled for years with the inertia firing pin given us by that design genius John Browning, we have found that if a loaded pistol, even if it was on safety, fell from high enough and it should strike a hard enough object muzzle or hammer first, it might accidentally fire. This set of rather rare coincidences was countered by having a lock on the firing pin that was only deactivated when the gun's trigger was pulled fully rearward. The Benelli just had only the time-proven inertia firing pin type safety.

4. More Rounded Appearance

There is no doubt that the Benelli pistols are a little boxy looking, but every effort has been made to give them a pleasant outward appearance. Contrasting colors, high gloss walnut grips, etc. all appeal to my eyes, but apparently not to many other shooters.

Most of these "minus" features made the Benelli unacceptable to our government and that, in turn, made it of doubtful acceptability to American shooters in general.

Convertability

The thing that strikes the engineer first when he examines the entire Benelli family of pistols is the ease with which the factory can convert from caliber to caliber, plain model to target, and from locked breech to blowback. This ease is not something that came by accident; the first Benelli handgun must have been designed with convertability in the designer's mind.

For example, to change the caliber from 9mm Parabellum to 7.65 Luger, a new barrel is screwed into the subframe. The number of Belleville washer pairs on the recoil spring guide assembly seems to be up to the mood of the assembler. There are two cosmetic changes required—the left side of the slide has its model identification changed and the correct caliber, in most cases, can then be stamped on the subframe chamber area as viewed through the ejection port in the slide. That's all there is to it.

The target models have a 5½-inch barrel while the standard guns have a 4¼-inch barrel. So, to go to a target model, a longer barrel is screwed into the subframe. A combination weight and front sight is added to the muzzle of the longer barrel, and held in place by an Allen screw. The metric wrench for the weight's Allen screw is also supplied in the shipping box with each target model. The holes in the slide, where the standard front sight would have

The early Benelli B76 (serial number 25) is shown taken down into its basic assemblies for normal maintenance.

been, are plugged and polished so that they are invisible from the outside. A fully adjustable rear sight is added to the old fixed rear sight's dovetail in the slide. In the most recently made target Benellis the trigger cocking knob is ground from the trigger bar, making the target pistol hammer-cocking only. Large finger-grooved target grips are added to the grip frame, but there is also available a blank walnut grip that the user can carve to exactly fit his hand. A new larger shipping box is used, although the regular ones have a provision in the styrene liner for a 5½-inch barrel without the front sight weight assembly. A special target Benelli manual is also added.

The most difficult conversion is to make a blowback-operated pistol from a locked breech type. A special non-toggle-equipped bolt (which is also much lighter, but longer than a locked-breech style) is added. Then, of course, a subframe with no locking notch is used, as is a recoil spring assembly without the Belleville washers. Special magazines are added in the case of 32 ACP and 32 S&W Long, the latter with a block to make its capacity five rounds.

Collectability

The thing that will interest the gun collector now, and more so in the fu-ture, is that there haven't been very many Benellis made. Total production seems to be in the neighborhood of 10,000 pistols and the future looks very dim for any great quantity more to be manufactured. So we are left with the bulk of the guns in 9mm Parabellum, with some as target models; a very few prototypes; a smattering of 32 ACPs; and some unusual calibers like 32 S&W Long wadcutters in target models only. Then there are the 9mm Ultra and the 9mm Bergmann-Bayard, which we never find here since ammo is unavailable, and lastly the 7.65 Lugers and their target models. These guns were probably originally made for South America where that caliber is still popular. The tabular form for these models is nearby.

Variations

For a gun on the market so few years, the Benelli shows a remarkable number of variations as well as models, all of which delights the gun collector. The variations noted by this author in their chronological order are as follows:

The early 32 ACP and 9mm Ps have a different firing pin. The end closest to the hammer has a diameter of .147 inches and the boss immediately behind it has a diameter of .273 inches. In all later guns these diameters are .116 and .255 inches respectively. The early hammers have no lightening cut at the web under the spur and the shape of the spur is a good deal sharper. None of the 32 ACPs that I've seen have those little serrations on the back of the breech closure piece to help in sliding it off the slide. There seems to be two serial number ranges for the 32: the first is 1001 to 1200, the second is in the 2100s. There are some 9mm pistols between the two sets of numbers. Collector Howard Resnick has a consecutive pair of Benellis, one in 32 ACP and the other, one digit higher in 9mm P. Even more strange, they were proofed in a different year!

The external machining on the sides of the slide, more cosmetic than functional, was reduced as production got under way. The original pistol had 30 sawtooth slide pulls on each side of the slide, but later this was reduced to 15, flat-bottomed grooves. Very late, the

This early Benelli B80 Target model is chambered for 7.65 Luger and was shipped without the special target-type grips. Note the high front sight.

angle of the slide pulls was increased.

In very early pistols, the pressed sheet form of the forward upper edge of the trigger guard had a very small radius. This radius was later increased to give the entire pistol a more pleasing contour. It also reduced strain marks from the forming of too tight a curve in the steel.

The extractors on early 32s and 9mms in the 1000 to 2000 serial number range were self-springing and of one piece. Later, probably because of breakage, the extractor was changed and a standard coil compression spring was used to activate its motion.

The bolt control stud on the blowback 32s, even where there was no need to control the bolt motion, was just a .255-inch constant-diameter stud. On the locked-breech pistols, this stud is undercut giving it a mushroom-like appearance. The undercut stud locks the bolt in a slot on the slide during the slide's recoiling cycle, when the bolt is in the upper position.

Very late target Benellis have a wider rear sight bar which has no white highlighting.

At some point in the pistol's production, the plastic magazine follower of the 9mms must have been giving trouble and a formed steel metal type was introduced, still with the finger "ears" on each side. The 32 S&W Long target models have a metal follower with no ears, and no slots on each side of the magazine's tube for the ears.

The high gloss plastic coating given to the grips of early pistols was deleted in the middle run of 9mm P pistols and on all target pistols, but very late standard pistols do have the coating. To my mind, the natural walnut wood is much more attractive than the coated type.

Somewhere between serial numbers 3100 and 4800, the disassembly cut at the back of the right hand side of the slide was first reduced in size, and then between serial numbers 4800 and 5600, it was deleted since it served no

purpose and the breech closure during disassembly is always slid rearward out of the slide. Lastly, the slide finishes vary. The earliest 32 ACP pistols had highly polished flats on both sides where the logo is found. On very late pistols, the entire slide is more deeply blued and polished than found on mid-production guns. The finish on mid-production slides and frames is exactly alike, usually called gray matte finish, or "Pakerizing" in the service.

The last place that variations are found is in the legends stamped on either side of the slide. The earliest Benelli in my collection is a Model B 77, 32 ACP. It is serial numbered 001107, or the 107th imported. It is marked "SILE DISTRIBUTORS, N.Y.-N.Y." on the right side, which is unusual for a Sile import. Also, the pistol has the dealer's name pantographed underneath: "Mandall's Scottsdale, AZ." On the left side is found the universal Benelli stamping: the serial number over "BENELLI ARMA S.P.A.-URBINO-ITALY,"over the model number. A later 9mm P Benelli, Model B 76, has stamped on the right side: "SILE INC. N.Y.-N.Y." over "U.S. PAT. NO. 3,893,369," and the standard left side stamping. If the pistol wasn't imported by Sile, then the right side logo is deleted, and the left side is as above.

Target pistols can be separated into three types, all of which are rare. The first type has a much higher front sight and a fully adjustable rear sight. These are the only changes from a standard pistol. They are all 9mm parabellum to my knowledge. Their model number has a "T" added to it. These might have been made up in New York by Sile because the model number on the slide has no "T" added. The second type has

the 5½-inch barrel and a weight added with the front sight. The grips are "target" style. These target pistols could be had originally in 9mm Parabellum or 32 Smith & Wesson Long wadcutter; at a later date, the 7.65 Luger was added as a model. If they are double action, an "S" is added to the model number. If the pistol is hammer-cocking only, the model changes to MP3S. The third type is extremely rare and is exactly the same as the above target pistol except that it comes in an optional, Benelli-marked, fitted leather case. This makes a very attractive combination, and few have been seen on this side of the Atlantic.

This then, is the story of the Benelli automatic pistol to date and it is the end of a sad story. The Benelli Armi Co. tells me by letter that the B 76 and its spin-offs are no longer in production and that the next handgun to be offered by them will be a target 22 Long Rifle automatic pistol followed by target 32 S&W Long and 22 Short pistols. They will continue to manufacture their excellent 12 gauge automatic shotgun in the Super 90, the M1 Super 90, and the new Raffaello 121.

The demise of the Benelli pistol is a great shame because the gun deserved much better treatment than it was given. Apparently the U.S. Navy Seals and the Russian KGB knew quality when they saw it and adopted the Benelli. So let it rest in peace—we will be a long time seeing its likes again.

●

The Oehler Model 35P is shown ready to use. Note the reading of "---0" indicating it is ready to accept another shot. There is no on/off switch—removal of the Start screen plug turns the unit off, plugging it in turns it on.

Oehler's New Model 35P Chronograph

Ever the innovator, Ken Oehler has devised a new and better chronograph system that makes his previous excellent machine obsolete!

by DICK EADES

THE OEHLER MODEL 33 has, for several yers, been the outstanding ballistic chronograph for individual use. During a recent telephone conversation with Ken Oehler, I was shocked when he told me I should retire my trusty Model 33 since it was, in his terminology, obsolete. I couldn't imagine how that machine could be obsolete since it included all the functions any handloader could desire. It even tallied a string of rounds, displayed the highest velocity, the lowest velocity, the average for all rounds fired and then threw in the standard deviation, just for good measure. And, the mea-

surable range is from 100 fps to over 5000 fps. Obsolete, indeed!

Ken explained that he had just developed a new chronograph which combines all the desirable features of the Model 33 with a couple of new items he felt all serious shooters would want. First, the new chrono, dubbed Model 35P, includes a built-in printer, relieving the shooter of the chore of writing down his results on the range. Next, it has a "proof" channel to verify that the readings obtained are reasonable and not the result of a skyscreen malfunction.

Users of skyscreens will, from time to time, experience a reading which is obviously in error. This is usually the result of lighting conditions which cause a "glint" or reflection from the bullet nose. Obvious errors are not particularly a problem, but Ken wanted to eliminate those which are not so obvious. His first suggestion was that users employ two chronographs in tandem, using one to check the readings of the other. But, of course, the cost of two machines for a single user would be, for most shooters, prohibitive.

The Model 35P is exactly what Ken originally suggested—two chronographs in one box. The difference in screen spacing prevents identical readings but the two chronographs resident in the M35P should furnish velocity figures very close to one another.

If the variation in velocity readings is great enough to make the machine believe an error may have occurred, it simply prints an asterisk (*) beside the

gle set of figures instead of two for each shot. Every shot leaves you with an uncomfortable feeling of, "was that reading *really* accurate?"

In use, the M35P is as simple to set up and operate as any other chronograph. The complete kit consists of the chronograph, two tripod stands, a marked, 4-foot pipe and a set of three screens and cables with sunscreens.

To ready the M35P for use, simply set up the tripod stands, insert the pipe through the hole in each skyscreen and align each by sighting through the shooting triangle, and tighten the retaining screws. Then plug each of the cables into its marked socket on the chronograph and start shooting. There is no on-off switch—the chronograph

comes on automatically when the start screen is plugged in and shuts off when the plug is removed. The machine is powered by a single 9-volt battery that gives about 25 hours of operation.

A large LCD display on the front of the chronograph will produce a reading of "---0," indicating it is ready to accept a round. As soon as the shot is fired, the velocity is displayed on the screen and, at the same time, the printer comes to life and produces a written record of the velocity for both the primary and proof channels. It also prints the round number between the two velocity readings. As soon as the printer is finished, the chronograph is automatically reset and ready for the next round.

At any time during the string, a summary may be printed by pressing a but-

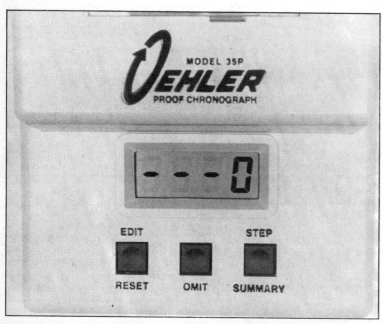

The control panel of the Oehler Model 35P is straightforward and easy to read. Each key is marked with its function. The LCD display is easily read under normal range conditions.

reading on its tape and waits for the operator to decide whether or not he wants to include or delete it from his string. As you may gather, this is a smart machine, but a polite one which won't make a decision on its own. It only suggests you might want to look at the results it thinks are strange.

Although some chronograph users may see little advantage to a double reading, it doesn't take much time to become accustomed to the comfortable feeling brought on by the second, or confirmation, reading. If you think it's not for you, I have a suggestion. Try the M35P with the three screens active for a few shooting sessions. Then, remove the center screen and shoot with just two. The chronograph will work normally, except you will have a sin-

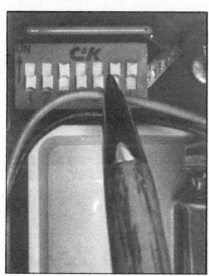

Oehler's new machine comes with three Skyscreen IIIs with cables and plugs. Not shown is the sunscreen assembly which shades the receptor from direct sunlight.

Seven DIP switches (indicated by the ballpoint pen) which alter functions of the chronograph are easily accessible through the battery compartment opening. The unit runs for about 25 hours on one 9-volt battery.

Because airgun projectiles are difficult for most chronographs to detect, author thought this would be a good test for the Model 35P. The machine passed with flying colors! BBs must be fired very close to the screens to be recorded effectively.

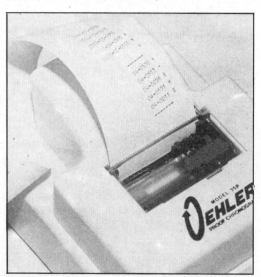

The Model 35P is shown with a run of tape printed with several shot strings. When checking loads from several guns, simply note the type of gun on the tape, tear it off and go on to the next gun/string.

With the sunscreens in place on the skyscreens, this shooter is checking velocities of a favorite slug gun while shooting for accuracy. The Model 35P is compact and doesn't clutter the shooting bench.

ton marked "Step/Summary." Results will be printed in this order: Highest Velocity, Lowest Velocity, Extreme Spread (Difference between High and Low), Median Velocity (Average) and Standard Deviation.

After the summary is printed, a dash line is displayed and shooting may continue. Additional shots are considered part of the original string and will be added to the averages and considered for High and Low velocity as if the summary had never been printed. To start a new string, simply press the "Edit/Reset" button twice. A new "---0" will be displayed and each shot will become part of a new string.

The central button on the panel is marked "Omit," and that's just what it does. In Edit mode, the button simply deletes a single shot from the string for its calculations. The velocity is still on your tape and may be used later for whatever purpose you choose but, the chronograph, at your command, has discounted it from the string calculation.

The user may elect to use the M35P in a Proof or non-Edit mode instead of the Edit mode. An internal DIP switch (very easily accessible) permits the selection of either mode. In the Edit mode, each string is limited to 20 shots. In the Proof mode, a string can consist of as many as 255 rounds. Personally, I prefer the Edit mode and can't recall ever firing a single string of more than 20 rounds.

To test the M35P, we decided to start with the tough item first. Most chronographs don't do well in the extremely low velocity ranges, so we elected to start by measuring velocity of a few arrows. A compound bow set for a pull weight of approximately 60 pounds was used, along with field pointed arrows and a few broadheads.

Since we didn't have to worry about muzzle blast, we moved much closer to the screens than is normal for a firearm. Screen spacing was left at the standard 4-foot distance recommended by Oehler. The archer, a friend who is also a bowhunter, was particularly interested in performance of his broadheads but, at my insistence, we first chronographed the field points.

Velocity of the field pointed arrows was remarkably consistent. Careful drawing of the bow to the same point each time resulted in a string averaging 183 feet per second (fps) with the Standard Deviation printing out as 1 foot per second! This was accomplished by shooting a string of eight arrows.

Next, we shifted to broadheads and obtained similar velocity readings. Again, velocities were extremely consistent and the SD for broadheads registered only 2 feet per second. Average velocity was 181 fps.

One distinction was noted in using the broadheads. Apparently, the brightly polished arrowhead blades reflect light almost like a mirror since we frequently got readings that differed widely from the primary to the proof channel. Velocities were, however, remarkably similar to those for the field points. The archer explained that although the broadheads were physically much larger than the field points, they were precisely the same weight.

We shifted next to an air rifle and measured the velocities of its BBs at an average of 521 fps, with a high of 539 and a low of 513 fps. Standard deviation for the BBs was calculated at a mere 11 fps.

BBs, like arrows, are one of the more difficult projectiles to chronograph. Due to their small size, they must be fired closer to the screens than most bullets. Many chronograph screens will not react to the passage of a BB but the Oehler M35P has no such problems. After we decided where to place the diminutive projectiles, each reading was recorded faithfully.

Our next test was conducted with a 22-caliber revolver, using standard velocity ammo from its 3-inch barrel. Variation in velocities was greater from the 22 than from the arrows or the air rifle. A five-shot string averaged 914 fps with a high of 935 and a low of 898 fps. The standard deviation for this string was computed as 18 fps.

Deciding it was time to get serious about the accuracy of this chronograph, I next set up the screens to clock an old loading from a 225 Winchester. Although this time we were dealing with velocities topping the 3,000 fps mark, the M35P performed flawlessly. Care was taken to back away from the screens so the machine wouldn't read the muzzle blast, but each shot and confirmation reading were registered with very small variations.

Setting up the new Oehler chronograph takes only a few minutes. The screens are placed on a piece of thin walled tubing and tightened with the fingers. An extension of the securing bolts is dropped into the hollow center post of the stand, and the sunscreens are then inserted into the "U" shaped openings in the sides of the skyscreens. All that's left to do is plug in the screens and start shooting. Plug-in locations are clearly marked on the body of the chronograph so mix-ups should be minimal. A plug in the wrong socket won't damage anything, but readings

will be wrong.

There's also an optional tripod adapter for only $5 if you don't like using two separate stands to support your skyscreens. The adapter makes it easy to set up and take down the screens since it simply allows you to bolt the rail to any camera tripod. If you plan to shoot at a target while measuring velocities, the two stands at each end of the rail make more sense. If you are simply measuring velocity without regard to where the bullets hit, the tripod adapter can save some space and set-up time.

Although I'll admit it is with some reluctance, I do plan to retire my old Model 33 Oehler chronograph in favor of the new Model 35P. It has all the features of the older chronograph with the added proof channel and built-in

printer. Best yet, the new M35P won't bankrupt the average handloader/shooter. The chronograph and printer are priced at $345, including three Skyscreens III. You can opt for mounting stands and a rail for $50. Full details can be had from Oehler Research, Inc., P.O. Box 9135, Austin, TX 78766, phone 512/327-6900.

If you are in the market for a chronograph, don't buy until you see the new Oehler M35P. •

Author's bowhunting friend wanted to compare velocities of his field points against broadheads. Careful drawing of the bow each time resulted in velocities of 183 and 181 fps, respectively. The chronograph is shown on the ground next to the first screen stand.

Eades also tried a handgun in his tests, shooting for velocity and accuracy at the same time. He found it comfortable to have the "proof" channel included and will soon be retiring his older Oehler Model 33 chronograph.

Firearms Ads of the

1930s

STOPS ANY GAME
ON THE AMERICAN CONTINENT

COLT
Super .38
AUTOMATIC PISTOL

FROM the Everglades to Hudson Bay, knowing sportsmen depend on this rugged, hard-hitting, straight-shooting Colt Super .38 Automatic Pistol—chambered to shoot the powerful, high velocity .38 Automatic cartridge.

A Thoroughbred Big Game Gun

Built on the .45 frame and identical, except for caliber, with the famous Government Model .45 Automatic, the Colt Super .38 is made to withstand the hard knocks of travel, camping and the gruelling abuse of big game hunting. Hundreds of inspections and tests are made that not a single flaw of material and workmanship shall mar its smooth and positive operation. A truly big game gun of great shocking power with grip, feel and action that command confidence.

POWERFUL—FAST—ACCURATE—U—

The Super .38 comes equipped with both manual and automatic safety locks — and is always ready for that instant emergency when only a Colt will do. Big game hunters, trappers, explorers . . . . . everyone who requires a powerful arm of proven accuracy and dependability find the Colt Super .38 without equal. The coupon will bring you detailed specifications and price.

SPECIAL FEATURES

Shoots the New with velocity of

COLT'S PATENT FIRE ARMS MFG. Co
Hartford, Connecticut
I am interested in your Sup
send me catalog containing full part

Name

Street

City

COLT'S PATENT FIRE ARMS MFG. CO. HARTFORD CONNECTICUT
Phil B. Bekeart Co., Pacific Coast Representative, 731 Market Street, San Francisco, California

Yes, those were the "good old days" of what we now think of as cheap prices, but we all tend to forget about the dollar-a-day wages most workers were earning. Here's a fun look back at what was available as well as the advertising jargon that was so freely used.

by KENNETH L. KIESER

$26.75 **SENSATIONAL GUN SALE!!!**
GUARANTEED BRAND-NEW FACTORY GOODS

SAVAGE
Model 45 Super-Sporter

Selected Walnut Stock; checkered grip and forestock; Lyman rear peep sight with elevation and windgauge adjustments; folding leaf middle sight; white metal bead front sight. CALIBERS: .30/30 only. Price $26.75. SAVAGE MODEL 40.—Same style as above, without checkered pi.tol grip and forearm. Open rear sight, raised ramp front. CALIBERS: .250/3000 .30/30 only. Price $21.75.

Remington Rep. Pump Model 29................$26.95	Colt Model 1917, .45 Auto. Ctge...............$21.95
Rem. Auto. Rifle, 24A Mod., .22 Short or L. R. $17.85	Winchester Rep. Shotgun, Mod. 97...............$24.95
Stevens Rep. H'mless .22 Cal. Mod. 75..........$11.95	Marlin Repeater, Mod. 39, .22 Cal..............$18.95

HUDSON SPORTING GOODS CO., (Write for folder No. 75 on special priced guns.) **F-52 Warren St., New York**

Hunting & Fishing, 1933

"BRONCO" 25 Cal. AUTOMATIC

Fires 7 shots in 3 seconds; $7.45
accurate; powerful; will
not miss or jam; double
safety; flat model; perfect
grip; blued. 25 Cal. 10 Shot........$7.95
Holster, 60c; Cartridges, 65c box
32 Cal. 8 Shot Automatic............$8.45
Mil. & Police D. A. Revolver 5" Blued 32/20; & 38..$10.95
$2 Deposit on C.O.D.s. Send stamp for Catalog
K. LEE SALES CO., 35 West 32nd St., New York

Hunting & Fishing, 1933

WHEN WAS THE last time you found yourself wishing for the "Good Old Days" as you walked out of a gun shop with a lighter billfold?

Though the firearm prices of the 1930s are gone forever, so are the $1.00 per day wages. Even so, those gun prices are extremely attractive by today's standards. Let's step back in time and take a look at some of the advertisements and prices from the 1930s magazines — they may make you weep.

In 1933 the *Hunting and Fishing* magazine advertised the H&R Single Gun for $13.00. This breakopen single shot came in 12, 16, 20, and 410 gauge. The 410 was designed to handle the then-new 3-inch shell. The Western Long-Range company sold a double-barrel shotgun for $17.50, and for an additional $3.50 they would install a single trigger.

Winchester offered Super-Speed long range shotshells in 1933. The sensational new 3-inch 410 shells with double shot charge were said to be good for kills at 35 yards and farther. One of their lines in the ad reads: "Controlled Shot String—That is the name it is loaded under. But out where it gets in its work it is WHAT PUTS MEAT IN THE POT."

Colt also had a 1933 ad that claimed their "Super .38 Automatic Pistol would stop any game on the North American Continent." This 38 was built on a Government 45 frame and was said to be "Truly a big game gun." For those after smaller game, the K. Lee Sales Co. offered a "Bronco" 25 ACP pocket pistol. This was said to fire 7 shots in 3 seconds and for an additional 60 cents you could get a holster with the gun.

The Hudson Company ran an advertisement in 1934 magazines that offered a Marlin Model 39 lever-action 22 repeater for $16.95. This featured a 24-inch octagonal barrel and a magazine that would hold more cartridges than any other 22. The same ad also offered Winchester 44-caliber carbines with 14-, 16-, and 20-inch barrels for $19.65.

H&R's 1934 ad featured a 12¼-inch barrel chambered for 22 Long Rifle and 32-20. This pistol had a detachable stock and combination peep and open rear sight, screw adjustable for windage and elevation. This was also offered in 410 and 28 gauge. A special holster carried both the stock and gun.

Other 1934 bargains included a Mossberg 22-caliber repeater for $12.95 and a single shot for $7.25. The Francis Bannerman Company sold a "Springfield Rifle, Model 1903" for $16.50. This 30-caliber rifle was offered without bayonet, but for $3.50 you could buy 100 rounds of ammo.

The December, 1935 *Fur-Fish-Game* ran a Colt advertisement that read, "Half a ton of moose bows to Colt Woodsman 22 caliber." This ad described how "Jim Waddell, famous Alaskan Guide" had taken the mea-

Hunting & Fishing, 1934

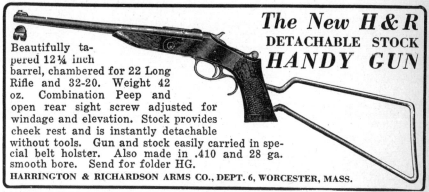
Hunting & Fishing, 1934

Hunting & Fishing, 1934

Hunting & Fishing, 1934

Hunting & Fishing, 1933

sure of two moose with his Colt Woodsman. The ad said, "A thousand pounds of moose is quite an order for a .22 pistol. But a Colt Woodsman is no ordinary .22."

Remington also used celebrities in their advertisements in 1935. In an ad featuring the Model 12 repeater and Model 24 autloader, Columbia star Jack Holt and his son were shown with rifles. Also shown in the ad were actors George Breakstrom, Jackie Searl, and Jimmy Butler, who starred in the movie *No Greater Glory.* All were pictured with new Remingtons.

Other 1935 bargains included a 44-40 Colt Service Model for $14.85, a Marlin 30-30 carbine for $21.75, Winchester Model 97 shotguns for $27.50, and Remington 20-gauge automatic for $38.50. The New York Gun Company's ad included a "No. 34" Remington 22 repeater for $12.00, and a 22 Winchester "No. 67" rifle for $5.50. This ad offered a free pair of binoculars with any firearm sold.

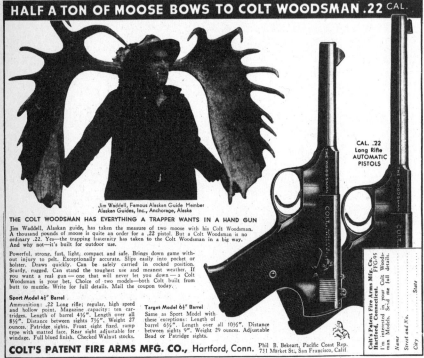
The July, 1936 *Hunting and Fishing* had an ad that read: "Here's real news for shotgun shooters! A new one-turn Poly Choke with each degree of choke plainly marked from the Poly Choke Company." The Lyman Gun Sight Company also had a new innovation, the Compensator. This was a tube designed for shotguns to show a remarkably even spread and true pattern on every shot. Pattern control tubes for all game shooting were advertised as being quickly interchangeable.

The Weaver Company advertised the Model 344 scope in 1936 for $8.00. This had micrometer eyepiece focus and ½-minute internal click adjustments. Weaver's complete line was priced from $4.75 to $11.70.

Ithaca's 1936 ad claimed: "Seven Grand American Handicaps, America's greatest shooting classic won with Ithacas in 17 years." Ithacas were priced from $43.00 to $900.00. Fox Sterlingworth double barrel shotguns were priced from $42.85 to $500.00. Marlin offered an over/under shotgun for $38.40 and was sold for Skeet, field, and trap use.

The 1936 Lefever Arms Company ad read: "U.S. Battleships carry Lefevers for sailors to hunt with in foreign countries. The navy wants guns for sport and war which give the best service. .410, 20, 16, and 12 gauge, singles $17.50, doubles $28.90.'"

In 1937 the grinning face of movie star Tom Mix said, "Every boy should know how to handle a gun." The Marlin Model 100 bolt action 22 rifle was advertised to sell for 10 cents per day,

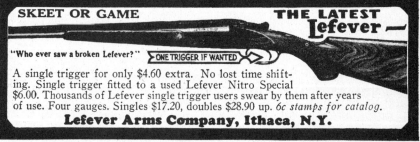

payable weekly at dealers. Mix was listed as the owner and featured star of his own circus-shoots, exclusively using Marlin guns. A simulated gold military-type bullseye ring and book by the National Rifle Association was also offered for 10 cents.

A Winchester ad read: "$5.00 will hold a Winchester Carbine until Sept. 1, 1937. Either 30/30 or .32 special — $27.50." Savage Arms Corp. advertised their Model 420 over/under 12 and 20 gauge Skeet guns for $35.00. The deluxe Model 430 sold for $39.50.

The May, 1938 edition of *The National Sportsman* carried "The Sultan of Swat, Babe Ruth" advertising for Remington. The ad read: "Looks like we're all three Remington shooters. When I hunt small game or pests, I want a cartridge that shoots straight and hits hard, says Babe Ruth, who knows plenty about hard hitting . . . and about all kinds of shooting too."

Remington also featured Bob Bartlett, famous adventurer and explorer. "His favorite gun for the seal, walrus, narwhal, bear, and musk-ox he brings back for museum groups is a Remington M/30 in a .30-06 caliber. For ducks and geese Captain Bartlett uses a M/31 pump gun." The ad included a picture of Bartlett's ship, the "Morrisey," on her latest trip to the Arctic.

Winchester's 1938 celebrity was Grant Ilseng who had just shattered the world's 28-gauge long run record of 110 straight Skeet birds with an amazing run of 257 straight birds using a Winchester Model 12. He later broke another world record with a Model 12 by breaking 506 targets. The advertisement also noted: "The .410 gauge, ½-ounce world's record of 136 straight shot with a Winchester Model 42 skeet gun by Bobby Parker, phenomenal junior shooter at Tulsa, Okla."

Other 1938 ads priced Stevens 22-caliber rifles at $12.50, Winchester 30-30s for $27.50, Hi-Standard 22 automatic pistols for $28.50 to $40.00, and Fox Sterlingworth double barrel shotguns for $35.00. Ithaca Featherlight pump shotguns went from $42.95 to $87.35, L.C. Smith double barrel shotguns from $25.00 to $43.20, and the Winchester Brushmaster Model 92 Carbine in 44-40 caliber for $26.95.

Magazines of the 1930s also had some interesting personal ads. Before the demise of the market hunter, you often found advertisements like: "Guaranteed live decoys, trained to give real sport. Calls geese, mallards, also pheasants, quail." You could also purchase domestic gray mallard

National Sportsman, 1938

National Sportsman, 1938

National Sportsman, 1938

ducks for decoys, $3.00 each. Another ad that would interest game officials today reads: "Wanted — Eagle tails, claws, good prices for undamaged feathers."

Todays collectors would have loved this next ad from the January, 1935 edition of *Hunter-Trader-Trapper* magazine: "War relics for clubhouse or den. Vickers aircraft machine guns; cost Government $700.00. Rendered unserviceable without marring, only $7.75 each. Sent C.O.D. on payment of $1.00. Weight 33 pounds." The same edition also included an ad that read: "New Rifle Muffler—Makes the 22 sound like a air rifle. Stops flinching, improves accuracy. $3.50."

Other miscellaneous ads read: "U.S. Springfield Rifles, 45/70 caliber, 32" barrels with bayonet and scabbard, good used condition, $3.95 each. 45/70 cartridges—60-cents per box." "Duck Stamps — 1934 and 1935 issue, good specimens, 60 cents each or two for $1.00."

No personal ad section would be complete without land ads: "Ozarks — 10 acres White River Frontage — unimproved, $150.00, $5.00 down, $5.00 monthly." Or, how about "30-acre farm — $450.00, dandy trout stream, 1800-foot elevation, good road, 4-room house; good deer and small game country."

The 1930s offered excellent prices, but remember that most people were lucky to earn $2.00 per day. Still, if anyone ever invents a time machine I'll be first in line. ●

National Sportsman, 1938

Marlin's Model 1894 Classic

Return of the Native

After more than a half-century hiatus, Marlin has reintroduced the Model 1894 Carbine and they've chambered it for two still popular old-timey cartridges. It's a handsome and neat little gun.

by SAM FADALA

SOMETIMES a cartridge is too good to die—and sometimes it is too popular. Although both the 25-20 WCF (Winchester Center Fire) and 32-20 WCF, sometimes called the 32 Winchester in older literature, have been ballistically superceded multifold by numerous cartridges, the pair has been factory loaded for about 100 years. The 32-20 dates back to 1882. It was offered in the Model 1873 Winchester lever-action rifle, as well as many revolvers. The 25-20 was born in 1893 (some experts date the cartridge's appearance as 1895) for Winchester's Model 1892 lever-action rifle. It isn't that either round is indispensable in the world of shooting—then, what cartridge is? The 25-20 and 32-20 have survived the erosion of time because shooters *like* them. There is an audience which continues to clap hands over these diminutive performers. When a cartridge remains in factory production after firearms cease to be made for it, such longevity begs a question: Why is there no current firearm for this round? No production rifle has been chambered for either 25-20 or 32-20 for some time. Yet neither has turned toes up. Thompson/Center has recently chambered its Contender pistol in 32-20, however, and there is to be a limited edition Ruger revolver in the same caliber. But where's the rifle?

Now there *is* a rifle for both 25-20 and 32-20. The gun is based on an old native, Marlin's Model 1894, which they brought out in that year. The rifle was chambered in calibers 25-20 and 32-20 and, according to *Flayderman's*

Guide (DBI Books), sold about a quarter-million copies from its birth-date to 1935, when it was discontinued. The Model 1894 was also chambered for the 38-40 Winchester and 44-40 Winchester. Incidentally, ammo for these last two cartridges has also remained available. The new Marlin Model 1894 is called the CL for Classic, a title based upon the fact that the 25-20 and 32-20 Winchester rounds are considered "classic" cartridges. The return of the 1894 has been greeted with signs of approval from the shooting community. My sample of the rifle is chambered in 32-20, which I selected because I have a 32-20 pistol, and not necessarily in deference to its ballistic utility over the 25-20. Historically, the 32-20 has often been considered the more accurate of the pair. That this is the case in the new Marlin, I cannot say.

Putting the horse properly before the cart, let's talk about the 25-20 and 32-20 rounds in terms of modern usage. I think it is very important to see where these two oldtimers fit into the scheme of things before discussing the

new rifle. What in the world is either good for? If shooters selected all cartridges on the basis of common sense and application, the list of factory offerings would dwindle to a handful. So I am not going to suggest that either of these rounds is a can't-live-without-it number. Is there such a cartridge? My favorite all-round big game cartridge for the west is a properly loaded 7mm Remington Magnum. One of my sons chose to follow Pop's lead and he shoots a Zollinger custom 7mm Remington Magnum. The other, however, carries a Bishop 300 Magnum. Neither has a complaint. So don't buy the Marlin CL because you need a ballistic niche to fill. Buy one or the other for reasons of shooting enjoyment.

On the other hand, these two gnomes of the centerfire world do have worthwhile applications. The first is informal shooting—plinking, if you will. By casting his own bullets, a shooter can fire 25-20 or 32-20 ammunition at low cost. Both rounds make very satisfying tin can poppers. They give more plink to plinking than the 22 rimfire, although the latter shall remain king

Shooting from the offhand position, the little 32-20 Marlin 1894 CL handled beautifully. It proved to be quite accurate and a lot of fun to shoot. The half magazine tube is quite handsome, too.

Marlin's new 1894 CL compares favorably with this original carbine model. Easily discernible differences are the barrel band and buttplate. Original chamberings were 25-20, 32-20, 38-40 and 44-40. About 250,000 Model 1894s were made between 1894 and 1935.

The author's Model 1894 CL is chambered for the 32-20 cartridge (right), and is shown here compared to the 30-30. The 32-20 may seem like a real "pip-squeak" to some, but it's great for plinking and small game hunting.

of the sand hill backstop at least for the remainder of our lifetimes. However, the heavier bullets of these little centerfires satisfyingly shatter clay pigeons and send mobile targets into orbit in front of the bullet backstop. So the two midgets serve nicely for target practice. "This rifle is fun to shoot," one of my friends declared, as he plinked away. Yes, the 25-20 and 32-20 are fun to shoot.

Then there's small game. I'm not going to pin a blue ribbon on either of these little rounds as small game winners. They aren't. But think about them as combination cartridges, good for more than one application. And then they become very worthwhile small game takers. Remember, you can handload, either with cast or jacketed bullets, to deliver projectiles at tortoise-like velocities from either round. Recoil isn't a word in the ballistic vocabulary when you talk about the 25-20 and 32-20. And both are very soft-spoken. That's important when you hunt on ranch or farm lands. The cow won't stop giving milk and the chickens won't refuse to lay eggs when you shoot either of these on the back forty. I'm not going to vote for either of these over the 22 rimfire where I hunt cottontails and tree squirrels. But if you go for the head shot, clean harvests result. Both are legal in many western areas for mountain grouse, too. And the accuracy of the Marlin rifle is well within the bounds of head-shooting these edible birds. But their usefulness does not end with small game.

Wild turkey hunting. Now the 25-20 and 32-20 shine, both working admirably at 100 to 150 yards, commensurate with the shooter's marksmanship. I've put a Thanksgiving bird in the oven with the 32-20 firing a lead bullet at about 1200 feet per second muzzle velocity. You couldn't ask for a nicer harvest. Are the 25-20 and 32-20 cartridges better than the 22 Hornet or 22 Winchester Magnum Rimfire for turkeys? Hard to say. The Hornet is considered ideal by some gobbler hunters. But I can't see where it could be any better than a 25-20 or 32-20 out to 150 yards. Low velocity loads promote meat-saving. But trajectory is improved when the bullet's velocity is boosted. If the turkey hunter needs the extended range, he can handload the 25-20 or 32-20 to give a sufficiently flat trajectory for 150-yard work. But there's no free lunch. Higher velocity will set up a broader shock wave, even with the jacketed bullet, and that shock wave will create a larger wound channel which means more ruined meat. My own Marlin 32-20 will use a Remington jacketed 100-grain bullet for turkeys. This bullet is available as a reloading component from Midway Arms, 7450-F Old Highway 40 West, Columbia, MO 65201.

The 25-20 was once considered a varmint cartridge. Before the days of the true high-velocity 22 centerfire varmint round, the no-kick 25-20 was thought quite effective on non-game animals. Eventually, the high-velocity version of the 25-20 developed over 2000 fps. That was pretty good speed. An old-timer defining long-range varminting might have said, "Why, he was so far out there, he looked like a fly speck on a window pane," which translated: "The varmint was 200 yards away." Three hundred yard-plus shooting with consistency on small targets with high-speed bullets fired from precision bolt-action rifles topped with high power scopes was down the pike

There are now four guns in the Model 1894 spotlight, including the CL version: Model 1894M (22 WMR), Model 1894 CS (38/357 Magnum), and the Model 1894 S (41 Magnum, 44 Special/44 Magnum, 45 Colt).

a distance when the 25-20 was prince of varmint rounds. All the same, the 25-20, and the 32-20 as well, do make perfectly adequate varmint cartridges. All varmints are not taken at 300-plus yards. Many are encountered at 30 yards, or 100 or 150. Jackrabbits, for example, are often jumped from their forms—the little Marlin lever-action rifle in either of our two calibers will get the job done in that theater. Sometimes I prefer hunting varmints with stalking in mind, too. Again, the little Marlin will fill the bill. So the lever action rifle in 25-20 or 32-20 will serve the casual varminter.

There is one heavier duty function for both cartridges, however—javelina. The little Southwestern peccary only dresses in the 30 to 40 pound range, and though plenty tough for his size, a well-placed bullet from the 25-20 or 32-20 will put a porker in the pot. The 32-20 with a 100-grain jacketed bullet handload is just about ideal for javelina, and there's nothing wrong with the 25-20's 86-grain bullet at 1750 fps, or a 60-grain pill at 2200 fps. The light Marlin rifle will be super in javelina country. Shots at musk hogs, for that is what javelina truly are, generally take place at close range. These little porkers can hear well and their sense of smell is highly developed. But they see no better than the near-sighted Mr. Magoo. A careful stalker, keeping the wind in his favor and his boots quiet, can get a 25-yard shot without a problem. I've taken many of these little pigs at such ranges, and even closer.

Pet loads for these two cartridges are many. Both were widely handloaded in the early days. *Do keep in mind that the magazine of the new Marlin is tubular—bullets with blunt noses, not sharp points, are called for.* I have an *Ideal Handbook of Useful Information for Shooters*, Ideal Manufacturing Company (The Marlin Firearms Co., Successor). The old booklet is not dated, but reference to a "new" Model 27 Marlin on the back cover (The 27 was offered in 25-20 and 32-20, by the way), suggests the early 1900s. The pump-action Model 27 was introduced in 1910. The little manual clearly shows that there was sincere interest in reloading for the two little rounds, especially with cast bullets. The following is supplied mainly for reader interest, however, and to show that both rounds enjoy a certain degree of versatility. A good plinking load, for example, includes a lead bullet and a modest powder charge. A load that shoots well in the new Marlin (not recommended for old blackpowder firearms) is the #257312 Lyman cast bullet, 88 grains weight, in front of 5.0 grains of Unique for about 1500 fps. Here is a neat little plinker load. The 32-20 using a #311419 91-grain cast bullet propelled by 5.5 grains of Unique will also achieve around 1500 fps. Marlin's new 1894 CL has a .311-inch bore diameter, by the way, not .308-inch as found in the Thompson/Center Contender pistol. Choose your bullets accordingly.

The light cast bullet target loads can be used for small game hunting and mountain grouse. Depending upon the hunting conditions, such loads are also good for wild turkeys. They would be ideal where I hunt Ben's Bird, because I go for gobblers on the streambottoms of my home state. Lead bullets at modest velocity save meat, while effec-

tively anchoring these big birds. Shots are often at 20 to 30 yards. However, a Hornady .257-inch 60-grain jacketed bullet, blunt nosed, can be scooted away at about 2200 fps out of the 25-20 Winchester using 11.5 grains of Hercules 2400 powder. The 86-grain jacketed soft point bullet from Remington, also available from Midway Arms, will take off at about 1750 fps with 13.0 grains of IMR-4198. The 100-grain Remington bullet can be propelled at almost 2000 fps in the 32-20 with 15.0 grains of IMR-4227. These loads are for the new Marlin rifle, not for old-time firearms.

On javelina, the byword is maximum power from the two Lilliputians. The last three loads mentioned make fine javelina-getters. This means the 60-grain jacketed bullet at about 2200 fps, or an 86-grain jacketed bullet at about 1750 fps from the 25-20, and a 100-grain jacketed bullet at about 2000 fps from the 32-20. Factory ammo will suffice, of course. Winchester and Remington both offer an 86-grain bullet at about 1500 fps from the 25-20, and a 100-grain lead or 100-grain jacketed bullet from the 32-20 at about the same velocity. Remember that the javelina is stalkable. Glass a lot. Find your quarry before it spots you. Then get close. The javelina is taken successfully with the 22 Winchester Magnum Rimfire cartridge, which does not deliver the authority of either the 25-20 or 32-20. In spite of their vintage, the loading manuals are replete with good information on these two cartridges. Be mindful of the exact components listed in the manuals. Do not alter those components. The small rifle primer is used for both rounds. The loads suggested above were built around the *standard* small rifle primer. Cases happened to be Winchester brand. With the high velocity loads, the CL in either 25-20 or 32-20 can be sighted in about 2 inches high at 100 yards. Bullets will drop only about 2 inches below line of sight at 150 yards.

Having looked into the pigeon hole ballistically occupied by these two classic rounds, Marlin's decision to chamber its new Model 1894 CL rifle for them becomes, perhaps, more plausible. Now about that rifle. Beginning with the exterior, all metalwork, which is nicely polished, wears the standard blue finish. The black walnut stock is finished with Marlin's trademarked "Mar-Shield." The CL can be fitted with a sling or carrying strap. There is a metal forend cap, attached with two screws, and the half-magazine is attached via a small bolt entering a dovetail blank resting in a dovetail

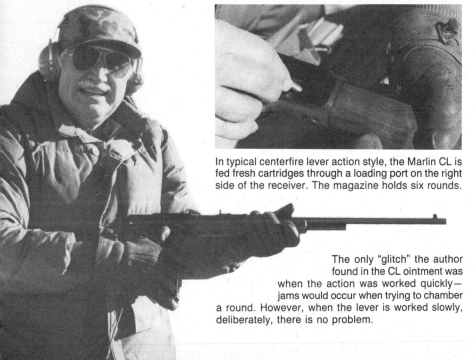

In typical centerfire lever action style, the Marlin CL is fed fresh cartridges through a loading port on the right side of the receiver. The magazine holds six rounds.

The only "glitch" the author found in the CL ointment was when the action was worked quickly— jams would occur when trying to chamber a round. However, when the lever is worked slowly, deliberately, there is no problem.

The bead front sight is held in a dovetail notch and can be drifted for windage adjustment. Move it to the left to move the bullet impact right, and drift the sight right to cause the bullet to impact to the left.

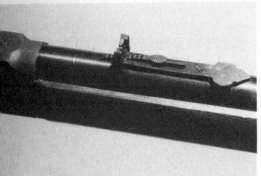

The semi-buckhorn open rear sight is adjustable for elevation via an elevator bar, but also can be drifted left or right for windage.

The action is shown open, lever down. At this point, a cartridge has been moved from the magazine to the carrier. When the lever is closed, the round will be chambered. The wood to metal fit on the CL is excellent.

All Marlin lever actions now have this hammer-block safety, which is simply pushed inward to activate and release. It's a worthwhile system.

notch on the underbarrel. The receiver is nicely polished and blued on the sideplates, but the flat top of the receiver and upper tang are of matte finish, as is the lower plate and tang. The hammer spur is serrated. My test rifle in 32-20 tipped the balance at just a shade over 6¼ pounds. I measured the overall length of the rifle at 38.5 inches. The six-groove barrel is 22 inches long.

Functionally, the CL feeds rounds from a tubular magazine onto a carrier when the lever is dropped. The uplifting of the lever elevates the carrier and aligns the cartridge with the breech. The forward thrust of the breech bolt drives the cartridge into the chamber. Meanwhile, the hammer has been cocked by the rearward action of the breech bolt. And the rifle is ready to fire. I did not have success in working the action rapidly. When the action was worked snappily, feeding of the rounds was inefficient. Conversely, when the lever was operated smoothly and without haste (deliberately), cartridge feeding was perfect. The tubular magazine, meant for blunt-nosed projectiles only, holds six rounds. These cartridges are fed through a loading port on the right-hand side of the rifle. With one in the chamber, the CL is a seven-shot rifle.

The safety aspect of the Marlin 1894 CL is unique in that there is the usual half-cock position of the hammer, but there is also a hammer-block safety which functions just as its name implies. This is a cross-bolt rod which slides into position to prevent the fall of the hammer. The hammer can still be drawn to full cock and released; however, the hammer nose cannot make contact with the firing pin when this safety is activated. Initially I wasn't certain that I liked this aspect of the rifle. However, the large head of the safety is easy to get to and its function is fast and smooth.

The Model 1894 CL is factory equipped with iron sights. I found these sights very functional. The front sight is mounted in a dovetail notch—no ramp. The gold bead is round. It rests optically in a U-notch rear sight of the semi-buckhorn style. Buckhorn sights have long been considered obstructive of the shooter's view of the target. I have never found them so, nor did this model obliterate my target. The sight picture was very clear. For shooting up to 100 yards, I doubt that I will mount a scope on the rifle; however, should I put the CL to work as an incidental varminting rifle, as well as wild turkey tool, I may indeed attach a scope to its flat-topped receiver, which is already drilled and tapped for mounts. Remember that this is a side-ejection design, and the scope can be mounted very low on the receiver. There is no bolt uplift to demand high mounts, nor does the hammer spur require a lot of clearance, but a spur extension is provided. It attaches directly to the hammer, allowing a scope to ride low on the receiver. Without the exten-

sion, a shooter's thumb might pinch between hammer spur and the ocular bell of the scope. The rifle balances well. I suspect that the addition of a scope will do nothing to negate that good balance.

Accuracy was tested rather informally. My major interest was function of the CL as a hunting rifle with iron sights. I set up targets at 50 yards, and with iron sights only, kept all of the bullet holes in the bullseye, five-shots grouping into about 2 to 2½ inches. My informal shooting with the rifle was very worthwhile. Using the iron sights only, empty 12 gauge shotshells were zinged away one by one at 25 yards. I am confident that the same sort of field accuracy will pertain on small game, mountain grouse, wild turkeys and javelina. But the shooter interested in refining his aimpoint will, of course, add a scope sight. Some rifles are easy to hit with, and the Marlin 1894 CL seems to be one of those rifles. It fits the left hander, too, who will not have to play switchover games with this gun. My trigger pull gauge showed a release of 4.5 pounds.

Suggested retail price of Marlin's Model 1894 CL in either 25-20 or 32-20 is $383.95. Ammo runs about $17 per box for lead bullet loads and close to $25 a box for jacketed bullets, 50 cartridges to the container.

This lever action native of early American shooting is returned in two classic calibers, either of which will bring the shooter a great deal of enjoyment. But don't try to justify the comeback of the 25-20 or 32-20 Winchester cartridges. The more logic you stir into the subject, the muddier the waters. Simply enjoy the rounds and the new rifle for basic target shooting, small game hunting, wild turkeys and javelina. All without bothersome recoil or disconcerting muzzle blast.

You'll love it, too. ●

THE BOLT-ACTION SHOTGUN

Introduced to the "gun-hungry" shooting public in the early post-war years, the bolt-action shotgun had a relatively short life, as guns go. The design served thousands of shooters well, and probably soldiers on in many hands today.

by J. RAKUSAN

THE LATE 1940s were turbulent times for many of the U.S. gunmakers. Those who had military contracts during the war had to retool for sporting arms production. They all faced the problem of deciding what the postwar firearms buyers wanted. Several things were certain: they could use the old tooling to make the models they had offered before the war, and there would be a ready market for just about anything they produced.

The gunmakers discovered that the bolt-action rifle would retain its prewar popularity, and even grow stronger in the post-war years. Yes, offering bolt

action rifles would be a safe bet. But what about shotguns? Certainly the slide action would remain popular, in spite of the growing strength of the self loader in the marketplace. The real question was, "What can we offer the low-priced market?" Single-barrel break-open shotguns would satisfy a portion of this market, but what of those who wanted repeating shotguns but couldn't afford them?

I suppose it was then that someone in the industry remembered that after WWI, a gunmaker in Suhl took a great many surplus '98 Mausers and converted them to two-shot repeating

shotguns. They were made in 12, 16 and 20 gauge, and most bore trade names such as Remo and Geha.

In his book, *Mauser Bolt Rifles,* author Ludwig Olson writes that in most of these guns only the safety lug at the rear of the action locked the bolt. Olson says, "There have been rumors that these shotguns are dangerous to fire because they have only one locking lug, but the author has never heard of an actual instance where the locking system failed."

So it came to be in the U.S. that a proliferation of bolt-action shotguns began to appear on the market, and

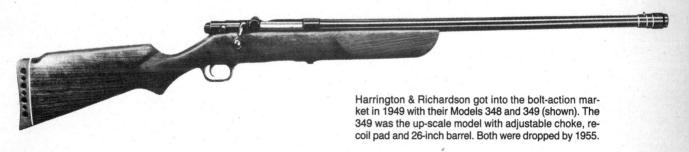

Harrington & Richardson got into the bolt-action market in 1949 with their Models 348 and 349 (shown). The 349 was the up-scale model with adjustable choke, recoil pad and 26-inch barrel. Both were dropped by 1955.

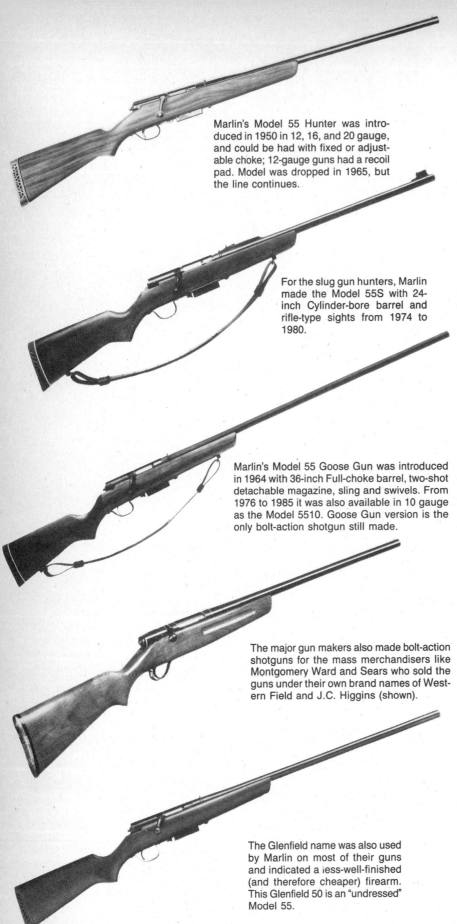

Marlin's Model 55 Hunter was introduced in 1950 in 12, 16, and 20 gauge, and could be had with fixed or adjustable choke; 12-gauge guns had a recoil pad. Model was dropped in 1965, but the line continues.

For the slug gun hunters, Marlin made the Model 55S with 24-inch Cylinder-bore barrel and rifle-type sights from 1974 to 1980.

Marlin's Model 55 Goose Gun was introduced in 1964 with 36-inch Full-choke barrel, two-shot detachable magazine, sling and swivels. From 1976 to 1985 it was also available in 10 gauge as the Model 5510. Goose Gun version is the only bolt-action shotgun still made.

The major gun makers also made bolt-action shotguns for the mass merchandisers like Montgomery Ward and Sears who sold the guns under their own brand names of Western Field and J.C. Higgins (shown).

The Glenfield name was also used by Marlin on most of their guns and indicated a less-well-finished (and therefore cheaper) firearm. This Glenfield 50 is an "undressed" Model 55.

most, if not all of them emulated the reworked Mausers in that they had no front locking lugs. Their detractors called them "junk," but they sold by the thousands. Many youngsters graduated from the slow single-barrel shotgun to the faster bolt-action repeater. During their heyday they were the bread and butter guns for many American gunmakers.

Pre-WWII Models

The earliest U.S.-made bolt-action shotgun I can find is the Winchester Model 41, a single shot 410 with 24-inch Full choke barrel. This was, of course, a pre-WWII offering that never got to be involved in the big bolt action push of the 1950s and '60s. The Model 41 was introduced in 1920, and discontinued in 1934. It is interesting that the last retail price of the Model 41 was under $10. Its current collector value would be over $200.

Introduced in 1933, the Stevens Model 58 was a true repeater. This bolt-action 410 had a three-shot detachable magazine. In later years the Stevens line included the Model 59, a five-shot 410 tubular magazine repeater, the Model 258 in 20 gauge, and the Model 51 in 410.

Post War Boom

It was the period of the early 1950s that I recall as the great boom of the bolt action shotgun. I sold many of them myself—most to the fathers who had promised their sons a repeating shotgun.

One demonstration with dummy rounds, working the long, sloppy bolt and ejecting one, two, three shells in only a few seconds, was enough to make the kid's eyes bug out. Forget that in some cases he might have to use two hands to pull the trigger, or that the chances of the ill-fitting stock cracking from the recoil were better than 40 to one.

I remember the Kessler shotguns. Not because I sold so many of them, but because they were the most likely to need repair. Kessler, a short-lived outfit from New York, offered their bolt action in 12, 16 and 20 gauge. The detachable box magazine held two rounds, and if you were brave enough to carry a round in the chamber, you could have a three-shot repeater. The Kessler had a short and rather unhappy life span from 1951 to 1953. During this period Kessler also offered a lever-action shotgun, also short-lived.

Marlin also offered bolt shotguns, beginning with their Model 55 in 1950. This was possibly the first one to offer an adjustable choke as an option. The Model 55 was made in 12, 16 and 20 gauge. This model continues in the line today as the Model 55 Goose Gun, a 12-gauge bolt shotgun with a 36-inch Full-choke barrel. A Super Goose in 10 gauge was made by Marlin from 1976 to 1985. The Marlin line also included the Model 59 Olympic, a single-shot 410. Other bolt-action shotguns were produced by Marlin under the Glenfield name.

Perhaps the most prolific of the bolt-action shotgun makers would have to be Mossberg. It began for Mossberg with the Model 83D. This two-shot 410 had a fixed magazine, loaded from the top. Introduced in 1940, it had interchangeable choke tubes, a 23-inch barrel, and a one-piece stock with the distinctive Mossberg finger grooves on the pistol grip that also formed the trigger guard.

Mossberg introduced a 20-gauge gun at the same time, in 1940, known as the Model 85D. The "D" models were followed by the "K" models with adjustable choke devices—the Mossberg C-Lect-Choke. In 1963, Mossberg introduced their 385K, 390K and 395K models. All had detachable two-round magazines, and the Mossberg C-Lect-Choke. These were to be the last of the breed, Mossberg having discovered that they could survive almost solely on their competitively priced slide-action shotguns.

The bolt-action shotgun has all but left the scene today, the Marlin being the only one offered in 1989. There are many speculations why this action type went the way of the dinosaur. Many feel that they were not safe, and would not have survived today's onslaught of product liability actions. Others claim that as pump shotguns grabbed the lion's share of the low-to-medium price market, the bolt-action guns couldn't maintain the price differential they once had. And, there are others who are certain that the shotgun shooters didn't really want a bolt-action shotgun, and that they survived as long as they did because the bulk of the consumers were not knowledgeable enough to really know what was the best gun for their needs. After all, in those post-war years there was a scramble for nearly anything new on the market and people would buy what they could.

Whatever the reason, it is unlikely that we will ever see a resurgence of popularity for the bolt-action smoothbores. For those who like to look into the future, the question is, "Will the slide-action shotgun go the way of the bolt action?" Considering the ever-increasing popularity of the autoloaders, who knows? ●

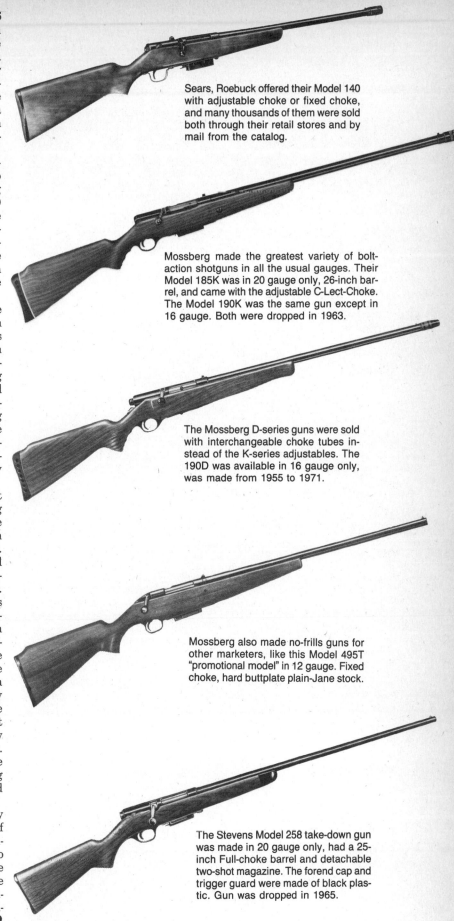

Sears, Roebuck offered their Model 140 with adjustable choke or fixed choke, and many thousands of them were sold both through their retail stores and by mail from the catalog.

Mossberg made the greatest variety of bolt-action shotguns in all the usual gauges. Their Model 185K was in 20 gauge only, 26-inch barrel, and came with the adjustable C-Lect-Choke. The Model 190K was the same gun except in 16 gauge. Both were dropped in 1963.

The Mossberg D-series guns were sold with interchangeable choke tubes instead of the K-series adjustables. The 190D was available in 16 gauge only, was made from 1955 to 1971.

Mossberg also made no-frills guns for other marketers, like this Model 495T "promotional model" in 12 gauge. Fixed choke, hard buttplate plain-Jane stock.

The Stevens Model 258 take-down gun was made in 20 gauge only, had a 25-inch Full-choke barrel and detachable two-shot magazine. The forend cap and trigger guard were made of black plastic. Gun was dropped in 1965.

Shooting
HEAVY-BARREL
Rifles

Are those lightweight guns the best way to go for hunting? Not according to this shooter who likes his weight out front where it counts.

by **WILF E. PYLE**

Heavy-barrel rifles in mid-size centerfire calibers are fun to shoot, and people owning them are often highly motivated to shoot. They use them all year round, taking whatever small game is available and expending a lot of ammunition in doing so.

Four heavy-barrel rifles in the author's battery are, left to right: Winchester Model '86, Parker-Hale 1200V, Remington Model 700, and Sako AI. All are long range tack-drivers.

a major undertaking. Lighter rifles fit well into these kinds of demands and pressures. As well, right now weight of any kind—be it on our bellies or our rifles—is decidedly unpopular. Weight is out and light is in vogue.

While the hardy among us would never openly admit that rifle design follows fads and fashions, it appears to be the case in our current love affair with the lightweights. Yet, heavy-barrel rifles offer several advantages currently overshadowed by the light-weights.

Let's take a proactive look at the advantages heavy-barrel rifles offer the hunter and shooter. Perhaps these benefits will be rediscovered in a few years, and hailed with the vim and vigor that only a trained marketer can bring. On the other hand, heavy-barrel rifles exist for reasons that produce results useful in the field. These advantages are never out of vogue.

Let's begin by qualifying what a heavy-barrel rifle is and is not. The term "heavy-barrel rifle" has become a generic name for any rifle carrying a

HOW ABOUT A heavy barrel rifle? You know the kind. They're often called varmint, target weight or bull-barrel. What advantages do these offer over others and is there a place for such heavy, cumbersome rifles in modern day small-game hunting? Should the average hunter choose one for all of his shooting needs? Does this type of rifle deliver any real benefits? These questions, and many others are legitimate given recent thinking in rifle design.

Lightweight rifles—with pencil thin barrels—now dominate the consumer market and have pretty much pushed heavy barrel numbers onto the back burner. Trends in rifle design often reflect changes in hunting styles. Over the last 20 years hunting has moved from a sport pursued from the back steps of rural America to something that now has to be planned and de-tailed with almost military-style pre-cision and at about the same cost. For some, just getting to the rifle range is

The benchrest shooter's quest for accuracy has driven barrel weight upward until a stiff, oversized mass of unwieldy steel has resulted. Heavyweight barrels for hunting are lighter than these specialized tubes.

At one time, heavy barrels were a necessary fact of life because steel was softer and a lot of it was needed to contain the pressures of even blackpowder cartridges.

barrel that is larger, thicker, heavier and sometimes longer than the sporting version in the same rifle line. It is, however, not a competition, match or silhouette rifle with the accompanying exaggerated stock. Generally, a heavy-barrel rifle used for hunting will carry a slightly modified sporter-style stock.

In recent years, the benchrest shooter's search for accuracy has driven barrel weight upward until a stiff, oversized mass of unwieldy steel has resulted. Sporting-weight barrels, however, have not changed greatly in nearly three decades. Heavy-barrel rifles lie somewhere in between. They are often referred to as varmint-weight barrels, bull barrels or simply just heavy barrels. No specific weight is implied or intended by the use of these terms. Any rifle with a barrel heavier than what is common to the sporting version is considered a heavy-barrel rifle.

Where did heavy-barrel rifles come from? It's a fair question and one not particularly vexing. Much is discovered from our shooting and hunting history. It is a history covering many years, reflecting much change in shooting conditions, manufacturing techniques, shooter tastes and subtle shifts in shooter preferences. The correct question is, where did light-weight barrels originate, and the answer is from heavier barrels.

At one time, heavier barrels were a necessary fact of life. Thick barrels were needed in the manufacturing process. Steel was soft, often unfairly compared to butter, and a lot of it was needed to contain the pressure of even old blackpowder cartridges. Without great gobs of steel old time gun barrels couldn't contain the available operating pressures. Thinner barrels would have burst, so it was necessary to use lots of steel.

This manufacturing conundrum soon produced its own brand of tradition. There was a long time period where the composition of barrel steel didn't improve significantly. Advances in metallurgy were few and those that did occur were not readily applied to rifle barrel technology.

This changed when high powered, smokeless cartridges came onto the scene. Better steels allowed greater chamber pressure and therefore faster moving bullets. They also permitted development of lighter weight barrels.

However, shooters found the combination too much. The fast stepping lightweights were harder to hold steady and barrels heated quickly during extended shooting.

Besides, the new smokeless cartridges had vastly improved mid-range trajectories and many shooters misjudged intermediate shots. Initially, this produced much missed game, and in the minds of our forefathers the blame sat squarely on the weight of the barrel. They could see the barrel was thinner and little logic was needed to conclude that missed shots were the result of different barrel designs. Soon, heavy barrels became associated with better accuracy. Demand for heavy barrels returned and found a strong following among dedicated shooters.

The 1886 Winchester represents the classic example of this mentality in action. It was one of the first highly popular repeating rifles that successfully transcended from blackpowder cartridges to high intensity smokeless types. Its heavy barrel styling was borrowed from the Winchester, Browning and especially the Sharps single shot rifles that had proceeded decades before. Accuracy in these rifles was well established and largely attributed to the heavy and often long barrels that accompanied their short actions.

While the 1894 Winchester, available in the then-new 30-30, was making inroads with a new breed of hunters, the old '86 hung on and refused to die. It successfully competed head to head with the 1894 for over 30 years. Old-time back woodsmen and sophisticated Eastern hunters continued to select the heavy barrel '86 well into the 1920s. They simply wanted the most accurate repeating hunting rifle they could buy, and this was thought to be one with a heavy barrel. Sales of special order heavy-barrel '86s actually improved during the time that both the '94 and the '86 were jointly available. By the way, these same observations apply to the Marlin Model 1895.

By the mid-1930s, preferences for heavy-barrel guns declined. However, demand was sufficient that manufacturers continued to cover all their bases and they still offered heavy-barrel rifles. The Winchester Model 54, the first bolt action rifle made especially for hunters, was regularly cataloged in heavy-barrel version. Although few were ordered, dedicated long range shooters demanded these rifles.

The traditional relationship between accuracy and barrel weight still exists. Today, the heavy barrel is largely considered an option chosen by accuracy

By the mid-1930s preferences for heavy barrels declined, but the gunmakers continued offering them. The Model 54 Winchester was regularly cataloged in heavy versions and these guns made excellent varminters.

There are five practical advantages for hunters using heavy or target-weight barrels. First is the familiarity that develops between shooter and rifle. Heavy-barrel rifles, usually in mild mid-sized centerfire cartridges, are fun to shoot and tend to be shot more frequently. As well, people owning these kinds of rifles are often highly motivated to shoot. They use them all year round, taking whatever small game is available and expending much ammo checking their rifle's zero. These shooters are frequently more familiar with their rifles and routinely fire much ammunition.

The weight of the rifle means different shooting styles must be learned. A heavy rifle demands better muscle control, solid stance and revamped tactics from the shooter. Any rifle weighing 10 pounds requires good fit and firm support so thought has to be given to stance. Shooting off-hand is more difficult, while using a sitting position is actually easier. These factors make the hunter think about his shooting and in doing so serve a major advantage. The hunter becomes more refined in his shooting.

As well, using a rest is almost always required. Improvised shooting rests are a must. The slightly straighter stock found on heavy-barrel rifles is used to advantage when shooting is done with the rifle's forend supported in some manner. This all combines to make the hunter careful, more considerate of circumstances and alert to the potentials and handicaps of his particular rifle and cartridge combination. These demands really make the shooter a better hunter and leave him with a major advantage over others—he *thinks* about his shooting.

Reduced nervousness is a third advantage. While drawing a bead, everybody shakes. This is because the human body is a quivering mass of flesh with the heart pumping blood through miles of veins and arteries, lungs exchanging air and the brain consuming energy while making thousands of split second decisions and overseeing other organs. All this activity physically makes the body shake. Add to this the adrenalin let loose by inexperience or hunt tensions, and it's a physiological wonder that man can stand, let alone execute a clear shot.

The solid feel of a heavy-barrel rifle

conscious shooters.

Tradition alone does not fully account for the continued demand for heavy-barrel rifles. Dedicated shooters will quickly point to the physical characteristics of varmint rifles. Going from breech to muzzle, varmint barrels have little taper. This gives the barrel extra stiffness and vibration resistance. These physical features are at the heart and soul of the improved accuracy produced by heavy-barrel rifles.

The physical differences do not stop there. Heavy-barrel rifles are offered today without sights. This contributes to better accuracy as there no gadgets interfere with the barrel's sine wave created during firing. Ballisticians and physicists believe the barrel, free to vibrate unencumbered, is more likely to repeat its pattern in the same manner shot after shot. As well, greater attention is paid to action bedding and barrel fit in the stock. All models feature free floating barrels. For the hunter-shooter, these physical differences translate into tighter groups.

Heavy barrels are associated with better accuracy for a variety of reasons, as noted in the text. Top to bottom are the author's personal favorites: Sako AI, Winchester Model 54, Remington 700, Parker-Hale 1200V.

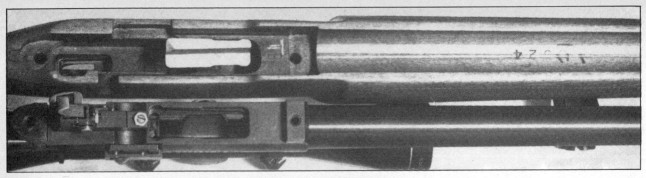

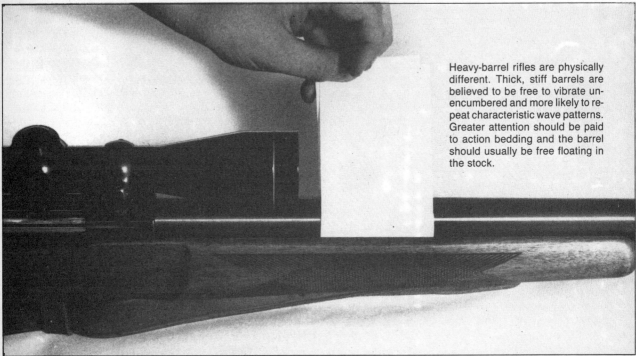

Heavy-barrel rifles are physically different. Thick, stiff barrels are believed to be free to vibrate unencumbered and more likely to repeat characteristic wave patterns. Greater attention should be paid to action bedding and the barrel should usually be free floating in the stock.

reduces these built-in shooter stresses. It settles into position easier than a lightweight version, and is harder to move off target. Physiologically, more muscle bundles are utilized while holding a heavy gun than a light rifle. The added weight seems to telegraph the body, saying it means business, and the body responds by diverting energy into the effort. Nearly every hunter can tell you about this very characteristic feeling, and indeed, it's a necessity for success with these kinds of rifles.

A major advantage of heavy-barrel rifles is the reduction in felt recoil. Along with this is the near elimination of muzzle jump. These are real aids to shooting and will, quite independent of other factors, have positive influences on accuracy and marksmanship.

This fact was well established in early military rifles, many weighing in at over 9 pounds when fully loaded. Routinely fired from the prone in the field, or from parapet or parados in

fixed positions, recoil from powerful cartridges like the 30-06, 8 x 57 or 303 British rarely became a factor in extended shooting sessions.

The same holds true today. Long shooting sessions, firing hundreds of rounds at targets like prairie dogs or various ground squirrels is pleasant, even when done with 25-06s or hot-loaded 110-grain bullets stuffed into the 30-06. Remember, too, the effect of recoil is cumulative and even mild jarring firearms can become disconcerting after several rounds. After all other shooting skills are learned, recoil is still the single greatest deterrent to good marksmanship. Heavy barrels reduce apparent recoil and when combined with mild powered cartridges virtually eliminate the problem, freeing the hunter to concentrate on his shooting.

Heavy-barrel rifles handle heat better than their lightweight counterparts. Heat generated during firing becomes a shooting problem when

several rounds are rapidly fired without leaving time between shots for the barrel to cool. Undissipated heat, both from the sun and shooting, causes a barrel to change the bullet's point of impact. Heavy barrels are not as susceptible to this because of their rigidity and their ability to transfer heat uniformly along their length. As well, their sheer size and weight allow more heat to be absorbed and redistributed throughout the steel. This not only contributes to better accuracy, but allows that accuracy to be maintained during extended shooting. This is a real plus, and one any shooter must consider if restricting shooting opportunities to a few heavy sessions per season.

Heavy barrels have another benefit: They hold on target better due to their added weight. This means less movement when shooting from a camouflaged position, and less difficulty returning to or relocating the target. As well, the shooter doesn't become as tired of the actual shooting. Shooting

Pyle feels that heavy-barrel rifles are capable of accurately digesting a number of load variations. Heavy barrels are at their best in the following accurate cartridges, left to right: 223, 222 Rem., 222 Rem. Mag., 22-250, 225 Win., 220 Swift, 6mm PPC, 243, 6mm Rem., 250 Savage, 25-06, and 270 Win.

Most shooters usually find that heavy-barrel rifles hold on target better due to the added weight. This translates to less movement before the shot and easier target acquisition after the trigger is pulled for follow-up shots.

is an exhausting activity, requiring good concentration and coordination and this places unique demands on the body, unlike those of other sports or athletic endeavors. While these may seem unimportant benefits, their significance increases during long-range shooting, particularly at small targets like ground squirrels or gophers.

In general, heavy-barrel rifles are capable of accurately digesting a divergence of ammunition. Combinations of closely related powder types, similar bullet weights, and equivalent primers tend to shoot to like points of impact. My heavy-barrel, factory Sako AI in 222 Remington is a gem. It will shoot the 55-grain Hornady and Speer 55-grain spitzer to nearly identical points with the same load—24.7 grains of IMR 4320. Though this certainly is not *always* true, I've found that heavy-

barrel rifles tend to be less load specific than their lightweight cousins. Many shooters know that top performance in most rifles is only reached with one particular load, often achieved after much experimentation and field testing. Heavy barrels tend not to be restricted in this way, and will frequently shoot extremely well with several different loads. At times the same point of impact can be attained with widely different bullet weights.

In the field, hollowpoint ammunition can be interchanged with spire point, or, depending on the shooting application, FMJ ammo. There is some freedom to assemble loads from a variety of components knowing there will be little change in end performance. At times, same or familiar reloading components are not readily available, especially when traveling or having to

reload in the field. The heavy-barrel rifle allows a certain amount of reloading flexibility unavailable with the lightweights.

There are good reasons for choosing a heavy-barrel gun over lightweight types or even sporting weights. Where these advantages are needed, heavies are the way to go. However, there is also a downside, and it is encapsulated in one word—heavy. Heavy-barrel rifles are heavy.

All popular models in production today weigh in excess of 9 pounds, and when outfitted with scope, mounts and sling will tip the scale at over 10 pounds, with several going to 11 pounds when big variable scopes are part of the package.

Another issue is carrying the big rifle. Aside from sheer weight, heavy-barrel rifles are cumbersome to carry. That heavy barrel moves the balance point forward compared to a standard rifle. When slung over the shoulder, the extra weight pulls the barrel back and pushes the stock more forward, resulting in an awkward carry. This is mitigated somewhat by slinging the firearm barrel down, but many hunters don't like this carrying method, simply because the longer barrel is easy to accidently drive into the ground.

Military rifles avoided this by hav-

ing front swivels well forward. Some hunters move the front swivel onto the barrel by using shotgun-type swivels, but this is not recommended as the tinkering will interfere with barrel performance. However, the move does change the balance point, allowing the hunter to carry in traditional fashion.

Much of the carrying problem is academic. Holding the barrel and placing the stock over your shoulder is a good carrying method, and no changes need be made to the rifle. Traditionally, heavy guns were carried across the front of the body in the crotch of the arm and few were slung. Practically speaking, any hunting rifle should be carried at "quarter port" position, using both hands so that it can quickly be brought into action.

The rifle sling delivers other benefits. Heavy rifles benefit from the sling more as a shooting aid and less so as a carrying device. In the sitting posi-

tion, a quick-set sling or a more formal military style set will keep groups on small game acceptable out to maybe 200 yards.

There is one last complaint. It is alleged that heavy-barrel rifles are difficult to snap into shooting position, especially when shooting offhand. Stocks on these rifles have higher combs, wider forends and thicker butts, as well as being designed to favor prone or rest shooting rather than offhand use. The shooter must become familiar with these slightly different stock dimensions through dry fire practive. And with practice, shouldering the heavy-barrel rifle is no more difficult than a sporter-weight gun.

It may be unnecessary to mention, but scopes are a must. The scope lets shooters approach the rifle's limits of accuracy. Pick the best you can afford. Rifles used on small game and varmints are best outfitted with 8x to 12x

An improvised rest is important no matter what rifle you are shooting in the hunting field. In order to squeeze the most out of your rifle, learn to find rests wherever your shooting takes place.

scopes.

Using a rest ensures better accuracy, easy handling and more long range hits with any rifle. With a rest the rifle is capable of delivering its full potential as a specialized long-range shooting tool. Small game shooters use rests whenever possible and heavy barrel shooters should consider a rifle rest mandatory before taking a shot. Some shooters feel the necessity to suitably rest heavy-barrel rifles inhibits shooting. That's doubtful, but it does focus the shooter on accuracy. The extra attention will produce more and better downrange hits allowing the shooter to take full advantage of any heavy-barrel rifle. ●

Huge herds of buffalo roamed the Western prairies in the late 1800s and their destruction was considered one of the keys to bringing the Indians to their knees. This J. H. Moser painting of 1888 depicts a lone hide hunter shooting a heavy-barrel Sharps rifle from a bluff. He has four skinning knives in a large belt sheath and a bandolier of ammunition next to him.

The Sharps and the Buffalo

The powerful and accurate Sharps rifle served admirably in the Civil War, but it also was the tool that proved quite effective in opening the late 1800s West to white settlement.

by NORMAN WILTSEY

IN 1848 CHRISTIAN SHARPS developed the first of his famous breechloading rifles, an epochal gunmaking event that was to directly and drastically influence the course of Western American history. For the final, crushing defeat of the Plains Indians and the subsequent opening of the West to unobstructed white settlement, depended solely upon the destruction of the vast buffalo herds that comprised the Indians' commissary. The powerful Sharps rifle was precisely the weapon buffalo hunters needed to do this monumental job of wholesale butchery. So it was that the booming roar of the first Sharps on the buffalo plains signaled ultimate tragedy for the wild red nomads of the prairie; the Sioux, Cheyennes, Comanches, Arapahoes, and all their brother tribesmen.

Although previously used in limited numbers against Indians in the West by both cavalrymen and settlers, the Sharps received its greatest impetus through its excellent combat record in the Civil War. Nearly 90,000 Sharps rifles and carbines were used by Federal troops during the colossal 4-year struggle. Colonel Berdan's Sharpshooters—the apt title appears to have been purely coincidental—were the scourge of the Confederate Army. Many of Berdan's carefully trained marksmen carried 54-caliber Sharps rifles equipped with telescope sights. Officers and artillerymen were the prime targets of the Sharpshooters, who brought down their human prey at incredible ranges with all the cool, impersonal efficiency of pioneer riflemen at a turkey shoot.

The Civil War Sharps rifles were of the percussion type, designed to handle linen cartridges ranging from 36 to 54 caliber. In 1869, 30,000 Model 1859 and 1863 52-caliber Sharps guns were converted to take metallic cartridges.

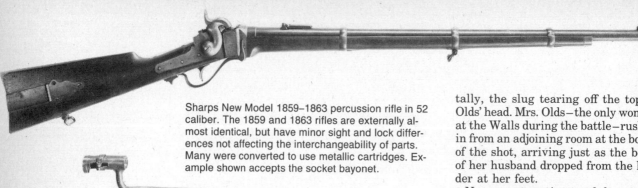

Sharps New Model 1859–1863 percussion rifle in 52 caliber. The 1859 and 1863 rifles are externally almost identical, but have minor sight and lock differences not affecting the interchangeability of parts. Many were converted to use metallic cartridges. Example shown accepts the socket bayonet.

Added modernization was a new vertically sliding breechblock. The barrels were bored oversize with a liner inserted. The liner was then rifled to 50-caliber size and chambered to take the 50-70 metal centerfire Army cartridge. Known as the "Big Fifties," along with a later rifle using 50-90 cartridges, these long-range hard-hitting rifles were favored by most buffalo hide hunters.

Continuous shooting made the hide hunters the best rifle shots in America, as the Indians discovered on numerous bitter occasions, notably in the Second Battle of Adobe Walls in late June of 1874 in the Texas Panhandle. There—holed up in three sod buildings, a saloon and two stores—28 buffalo hunters held off an estimated 600 warriors of the Kiowa, Comanche, Cheyenne and Arapahoe tribes in a three-day battle that went down in frontier history as one of the greatest Indian fights against tremendous odds ever fought on the plains.

By the third day of the siege, the Indian head chief, half-breed Quanah Parker, convinced his fellow chiefs that further attack was hopeless. Scout and hide-hunter Billy Dixon hastened the wavering chiefs' decision to withdraw by dropping a mounted warrior with a miraculously lucky shot with his Sharps. A small party of braves appeared on a bluff nearly a mile off. From a window in Rath's store, Billy tried a shot with his "Big Fifty." Lacking an elevation-adjustable rear sight on his rifle, he held high to allow for the inevitable drop in the trajectory of the heavy bullet and carefully squeezed off a shot. An Indian fell from his horse following the report, and his companions picked him up and raced away. It was the last shot of the fight.

Shortly after Billy's coup, all the Indians pulled out for good. Venturing cautiously out from behind their barricaded doors, the victors found 13 dead warriors and 56 deads horses. Ten of these slain horses had belonged to the hunters. Only three hunters had been killed; two in the first dawn attack, and the third in a tragic accident two days after the main body of Indians had withdrawn. On this fifth day of the waning siege, a lookout spotted a party of 25 to 30 Indians coming down the valley of Adobe Walls Creek, heading east. He shouted the alarm, and Bill Olds started to descend the ladder from his post atop Rath's store, rifle in hand. A second later the gun fired accidentally, the slug tearing off the top of Olds' head. Mrs. Olds—the only woman at the Walls during the battle—rushed in from an adjoining room at the boom of the shot, arriving just as the body of her husband dropped from the ladder at her feet.

No accurate estimate of the enemy casualties could be made, since the defeated warriors carried away most of their dead and wounded. The toll must have been staggering, for the allied tribes never again mustered such a powerful force to throw against the whites in the Southwest.

A 22-year-old Frank Mayer was probably the best known exponent of the Sharps rifle on the buffalo plains. A wierd assortment of gun-toters were busy hunting buffalo when Mayer arrived in Texas in the spring of 1872 to try his hand at making a quick fortune in "buffalo dollars." None knew better than Frank that the ruthless slaughter of the great bison herds was an ugly business at best, but he needed money and this seemed the quickest way to acquire it. Young Mayer became an object of curiosity to the hide hunters, for he carried with him a fine 10x German-made telescope sight, an unheard of accessory on the buffalo plains.

Mayer found the world's greatest slaughter of wildlife literally booming around him, the thunder of gunfire resounding daily from sunrise to sunset on the rolling Texas plains. Veterans of both the Union and Confederate armies were banging away at the sluggish beasts with old army muskets; Eastern "sportsmen" were shooting the big buffs with light deer rifles and shotguns loaded with slugs; some few hunters, endowed with more guts than

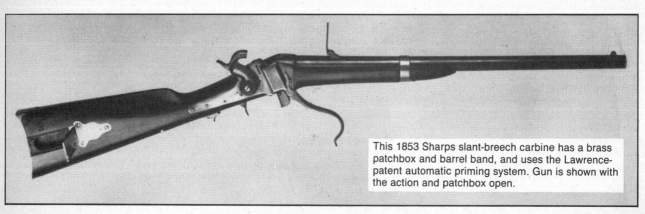

This 1853 Sharps slant-breech carbine has a brass patchbox and barrel band, and uses the Lawrence-patent automatic priming system. Gun is shown with the action and patchbox open.

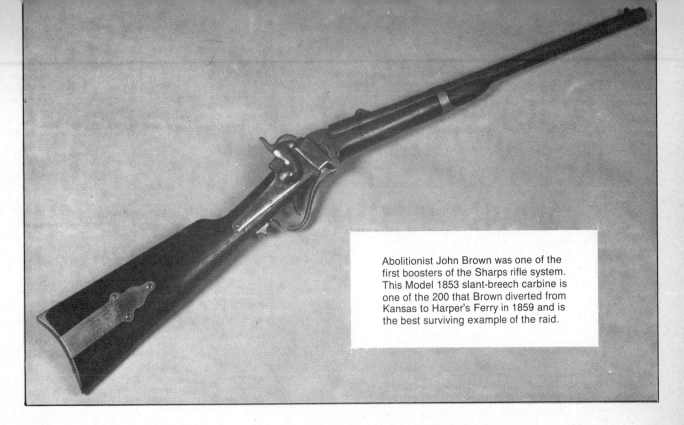

Abolitionist John Brown was one of the first boosters of the Sharps rifle system. This Model 1853 slant-breech carbine is one of the 200 that Brown diverted from Kansas to Harper's Ferry in 1859 and is the best surviving example of the raid.

brains, were using Colt and Remington sixguns at ranges of 6 to 10 yards. As an inevitable result of this clumsy barrage, more buffalo were being wounded than killed outright, a fact which disgusted and angered the true professional hunters, who performed the grim job of destroying the great buffalo herds in sober, business-like fashion.

Methodically, the youthful Mayer went about assembling his outfit in Texas. He had made a stake working and adventuring in Mexico, and now he spent it freely but shrewdly to acquire his hunting equipment.

Reasoning, logically, that guns are of primary importance to a professional hunter, Frank bought the best rifles obtainable. He had his precious telescope sight fitted to a 45-120-550 Sharps, weighing 16 pounds and sighted in at 200 yards. For alternate rifles—an absolute must in those days of blackpowder ammunition and excessive fouling of barrels—he selected a 40-70 and a 40-90 Sharps. Wisely, he spent a lot of money for a complete reloading outfit. Thousands of hides were lost when hunters ran out of ammo in the fields, and Frank didn't intend to lose a single skin playing the fool that way.

Next in importance to proper shooting irons was the careful selection of an experienced partner. Here Mayer was lucky, teaming up with Bob McCrea who had already put in 3 profitable years at hide hunting. They made an improbable pair; the lanky, rawhide-lean Texan and the soft-spoken university-educated Mayer, but they hit it off together from their first meeting. McCrea was a "savvy hombre" in the parlance of the oldtimers. He was an invaluable aid to Frank in putting an outfit together, buying horses, wagons, tents and supplies, and hiring a cook and skinners.

"We made quite an impressive appearance when all was assembled and ready for the hunt," wrote Mayer in his journal. "I doubt that any but a large band of Indians would have the nerve to attack us."

Nevertheless, the Indians challenged Mayer's outfit on his very first hunt. The Kiowas and Comanches were wasp-mean that hectic spring of 1872, knowing surely that their nomadic way of life and their very existence were threatened by the hordes of hide hunters encroaching ruthlessly on their ancestral hunting grounds. A number of whites were killed and their wagons burned before most of the hide men decided to try their luck in Kansas, beyond "bad Injun" country. Mayer and McCrea talked the situation over and decided to work the north Texas plains in spite of the Indian menace.

Six days out from base camp a band of Comanches made a pass at the expedition. "The lookout warned us in plenty of time," recalled Mayer. "Nobody got rattled, not even the cook. Cookie grabbed his old shotgun and loaded both barrels with buckshot—he was ready for 'em! We placed our two wagons about 20 feet apart, parallel with each other, and tied our horses securely between them. We stacked supplies and buffalo hides we had managed to gather across the openings at both ends for breastworks. We knew they'd circle us at the start of the attack, so we put one man with two rifles on each at both ends of the barricade and two men behind the wagon wheels on each side. All sides were covered, so we just sat tight and waited for 'em to make their move. We counted strongly on the fact that Indians are the world's most practical fighters—they will never make an all-out attack on an armed and alerted foe unless the odds are heavily in their favor. Indians are smart tacticians in warfare; they calculate their chances of success beforehand. Well, right off I aimed to let them know that cleaning up our outfit would prove too costly in casualties for them to turn a profit on the deal. I had a plan in mind that might throw a chill into them before they got well started on the attack."

Riding fast and strung out to present a difficult target, the Comanches started their famous and dreaded wheel formation around the barricaded wagons at about 500 yards distance and began gradually to close in.

"The poor devils got the shock of their lives," remembered Mayer years later. "At about 400 yards I picked out the chief by spotting the *coup* feathers in his hair through the 'scope. I led him maybe 30 feet—his pony was on a dead run—and swung that 16-pound Sharps

Fanciful depiction of shooting buffalo with a revolver, and in the company of Indians. The Indians realized the value of the buffalo for food and clothing and soon took to protecting their natural resource with a vengeance —which means they killed many hide hunters who ventured onto Indian land.

This slant-breech Sharps rifle has full-coverage engraving, double set triggers and a tang sight, the latter two features highly desirable for long-range shooting. This is an excellent example of a high grade gun.

broad area "as far as a horse can run in three days."

"What made it such a bargain," said Mayer, "was the fact that no other hide hunting outfits were allowed in that area by the Indians without a hell of a fight. We cleaned up $5000 worth of prime hides in three weeks before moving on. The Indians took what meat they wanted from the carcasses, and I must admit it was a sorry bargain from their standpoint. Still, if we hadn't taken the hides somebody else would, and I salved my conscience with that thought and the realization that many men, both red and white, would have died in the fighting that would inevitably have followed. It is curious to what lengths a man will go to justify his actions, no matter how wrong they are."

An expert marksman, Mayer seldom

like I was leading a duck with a shotgun. The bullet hit him plumb center and knocked him spinning off his horse. Lucky shot? Sure it was a lucky shot, yet only a heap of practice with that big rifle made it possible."

"That one shot broke up the Comanche wheel. When the chief went down, the warriors clustered their horses around him on the prairie. They made a fat target bunched up like that, but we were hunting buffaloes, not Indians. We watched and waited, rifles ready but damned willing to call it quits. Pretty soon four braves picked up the dead chief, two on a side, and carried him off a-wailing as they rode. We were mighty happy to see them go. We never had any more trouble with the Comanches. Hell, I could understand their bitter feelings about us hide hunters, and if I had been in their place I'm sure I would have reacted the same way to the invasion of my territory and the wholesale destruction of my food supply."

The Comanches were so impressed with Mayer's "Spirit Eye" rifle that a chief known as Medicine Arrow sold Frank what was probably the first hunting license ever issued in the

Buffalo were fairly easy targets because of their sheer size and the fact that they didn't spook terribly easy. They were no match for heavy-caliber rifles, repeating or not, and were slaughtered by the thousands.

West. The fee was pretty high—10 silver dollars and 10 Mexican blankets—but Mayer considered it the best buy he ever made. Armed with his license—a stiff piece of buffalo hide 6 inches long and 3 wide, carrying a message in picture writing—Frank was thereby entitled to shoot buffalo in a

required more than one shot per buffalo, ranking in skill with his partner McCrea. He never went "hog wild" with the lust for killing, like some hunters. (Tom Nixon, for example, burned out the barrel of a new Sharps killing 120 buffs in an hour of practically constant shooting.) Every detail

Buffalo Bill Cody, Teddy Roosevelt and other hunters took to the various Winchester repeaters in such a way that the Sharps single shot was doomed to "extinction." Cody is shown on the cover of this 1891 issue of "Beadle's Dime Library" with a stylized lever action rifle.

of Mayer's operation was meticulously planned to ensure a steady profit. He took only 30 buffalos a day on average, as that was the maximum number of hides his three skinners could skin and peg out, working by hand. Many outfits used horses to pull the hides off the carcasses, thereby stretching the skins out of shape, often tearing them, and always leaving pieces of flesh on the inside—flesh which quickly turned putrescent to rot the hide beneath. Mayer paid his crew well, emphasizing to them that he preferred fewer hides of high quality to rolling up a big score. He had only contempt for hunters like Brick Bond—so-called "Champion of the Hide Hunters—who averaged 97 kills a day in the bloody fall and winter of 1875–76, for a record one-man bag of 5,855 buffalo.

Mayer was a careful craftsman with his 'scope-sighted 45-120 Sharps. Using a steel bipod shooting stick made specially for him, Frank could drop a buff at ranges up to 500 yards when necessary. His preference as to range, however, was under 200 yards to be virtually certain of clean one-shot kills with a minimum of suffering for the buffalo. His best string was 50 clean kills out of 62 shots. The other three animals were mortally hit, but did not die within the 10 to 15 seconds considered by Frank to comprise a clean kill. His favorite target was always the neck, since the heart was a much more difficult mark to hit precisely.

Yet, fine marksman that he was, Mayer never quite equalled the record set by Bob McCrea. Hunting alone along the Brazos River, McCrea spotted a small herd of buffalo grazing the bottomlands. Approaching under the crests of the low hills, Bob rode within 300 yards and there made his stand. Setting up a rest of crossed sticks secured with a rawhide knot, McCrea dropped the buffs one by one with a single well-placed bullet apiece from his 44-90-400 Remington. Each shot struck the neck or the heart, the only target on a buffalo vulnerable to a clean kill. In all, 54 shots resulted in 54 dead buffalo.

McCrea's feat of unerring marksmanship precipitated much good-natured ribbing of Mayer by the lanky Texan on the superiority of the Rem-

ington 44-90 over the Sharps 45-120. Mayer never conceded that the Remington was more accurate than his own Sharps, insisting that it was "the man behind the gun that made the difference."

Mayer abruptly quit the hide hunting business late in 1875 with a hefty bankroll. "Too many hunters and too few buffalo," he expained to his partner and employees. Those who knew him best declared that Frank was just sick of the endless slaughter and the consequent vast waste of meat.

A Civil Var veteran from the last year of the great conflict—he had enlisted at the age of 15—Mayer re-enlisted in the Army after renouncing hide hunting and served through the military mop-up of the Sioux after the Custer debacle at the Little Big Horn in June of '76, and in the later Apache wars. In all, he served 37 years, retiring in 1915 with the rank of lieutenant

colonel. He remained a "Sharps man" until his death in 1953 at the age of 103.

The virtual destruction of the buffalo herds and the advent of heavy-caliber repeating rifles on the Plains were the two major factors that combined to eliminate the Sharps from its position as the top rifle on the frontier. Sales dwindled and the Sharps factory stopped operation in 1881. By that time, Winchester's improved Model 1876, handling the 45-75 cartridge, and a companion gun using the powerful 50-95 Express load, were the Western hunter's favorite rifles. Buffalo Bill Cody and Theodore Roosevelt took up these guns, and Winchester assumed the lead in the sporting rifle race. A whole colorful era in Western history passed out of existence with the passing of the Sharps Rifle. ●

The Wilson neck sizing die is a simple instrument of precision. These neck dies are available for most benchrest and varmint calibers, as well as for a number of the more popular hunting cartridges.

Wilson Neck Sizing Dies

Precision tools make precision handloads, and this neck sizing die will help things along considerably.

by JON LEU

Shooters interested in wringing the best possible accuracy out of a favorite rifle would be well advised to take a long and careful look at a neck sizing die from L. E. Wilson, Inc.

The all-steel Wilson neck sizing die was introduced early in 1983 in a variety of benchrest calibers. Since then, the number of calibers for which it is available has been expanded to include most of the more popular varmint hunting calibers as well as a number of big game cartridges.

Like many of the reloading tools produced by the Wilson firm, their neck sizing die is designed with precision and portability in mind. This is a hand die—devoid of the usual ⅞-14 threads—designed to be used either by tapping the case into the die with a mallet or pushing the case in with a small arbor press. Combined with the justly famous Wilson straight line seater, the

The Wilson neck sizing die is broken down into its component parts by removing the two screws which hold the cap of the die onto the die body. The decapping punch/knockout rod is captured in the cap of the die by two fiber-tipped screws. The Wilson sizing bushings, one of which is sitting beside the two screws (opposite), are available in increments of .001″.

The interchangeable sizing bushings are held in a cavity at the top of the die body. To change sizing bushings, the user needs merely remove the top of the die, slide out the old bushing, and replace it with one of the required size. The bushings are a very close fit with the die body.

shooter who desires to do his loading "on the spot" is well equipped.

Though there have been Wilson neck sizing dies in the past, this is the first of the Wilson dies to feature interchangeable sizing bushings which allow the shooter to match the die precisely to his cases and the neck diameter of his chamber. Sizing bushings for the new die are available in increments of .001″.

Dies of the same general type as the Wilson have long been used by benchrest shooters but, to the best of my knowledge, this is the first time a die of this type has been produced by a major manufacturer of reloading equipment for sale to the general shooting public.

Unlike some of the other sizing dies of this type, the sizing bushing of the Wilson die does not "float" from side to side within the die body to allow it to align itself with the neck of the case to be sized. Too, the die body is chambered rather than being bored straight through at maximum case body dimension. Both of these features, according to Wilson, result in improved die performance.

Changing sizing bushings is accomplished by removing two cap screws which secure the two parts of the die together. A wrench of the proper size is provided with the die. This same wrench fits the two horizontal screws which apply friction pressure to the decapping rod to keep it from falling out of the die body. Pressure on the decapping rod can be adjusted to suit the user's desires, and Wilson thoughtfully provides an extra set of pads which keep the pressure screws from actually making contact with the decapping rod.

Unlike most dies of this type, the sizing bushings made for the Wilson die have a .001″ internal taper. As cases become work hardened from repeated reloading, they frequently require a bushing somewhat smaller to maintain a proper grip on the bullet. The .001″ taper in the Wilson bushings allows the reloader an "emergency fix" for work hardened brass by simply reversing the bushing in the die.

Two tests were conducted to check the function of the Wilson dies. In the first of these (see Table One), 10 cases which had been fired in a 6mm PPC

benchrest rifle were checked for neck runout using a concentricity fixture fitted with a .0001″ dial indicator. The *average* neck runout for these 10 cases was .00032″.

These same 10 cases were then sized in a Wilson die fitted with a .261″ bushing. Checked again with the concentricity fixture, the average neck runout was calculated to be .00034″, an increase of only .00002″. The same die was then refitted with a .260″ bushing, and the entire test was repeated. After sizing with the .260″ bushing, the average neck runout for the 10 cases was calculated at .00036″.

The die was then fitted with a .259″ bushing, and the same 10 cases were neck sized for a third time. On this trial, the average calculated neck runout after sizing was .00044″. It should be noted, however, the runout figure for a single case (#7) was abnormally large. Removing this case from the calculations, the average runout after sizing with the .259″ bushing would be .00039″.

In all, 10 cases were sized three times each with three different sizing bushings fitted to a single die. Neck runout

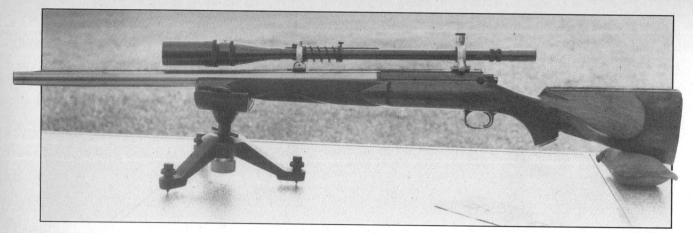

Both benchresters and varmint hunters are interested in getting the best possible accuracy from their rifles and the Wilson neck sizing die may be just the ticket to shrink group sizes.

which could be attributed to the die at the end of three separate sizing operations amounted, on the average, to .00012″. This is exceptionally good performance for any sizing die—all the more so when you consider the use of three different bushings.

In the second test, 50 cases which had been fired in a different 6mm PPC benchrest rifle were divided into five groups of 10 cases each (see Table Two). Each of five Wilson dies was fitted with a .259″ sizing bushing. For the five groups of fired cases, average runout was calculated at .00025″, .00023″, .00024″, .00034″, and .00028″—.000268″ average for the entire lot of 50 cases.

Each group of cases was then sized in one of the five Wilson dies. After sizing, average runout for the five groups of cases was calculated at .00036″,

.00033″, .00026″, .00077″, and .00050″. The average runout for the entire lot of 50 cases—sized in five different dies—was .000444″, an average increase of .000176″ for 50 cases sized in five dies.

For both tests, the cases were driven into the die(s) with a rawhide mallet. In the second test, some of the cases (Die #1, Die #2, and Die #3) were driven into the dies with a series of very light hammer blows. For Die #4 and Die #5, the cases were driven in with a lesser number of heavier blows. For the first three dies, average change was .00011″, .00010″, and .00002″. For the final two dies, average change was .00043″ and .00022″—an indication that those who choose a mallet rather than an arbor press would do well to apply caution as well as muscle.

Wilson neck dies are presently available for the 222 Remington, 223 Remington, 222 Remington Magnum, 22 PPC, 22 BR Remington, 22-250, 220 Swift, 6 x 47, 6mm PPC, 6mm BR Remington, 243 Winchester, 6mm Remington, 257 Roberts, 25-06 Rem-

ington, 6.5 x 55, 264 Winchester Magnum, 270 Winchester, 7mm TC/U, 7mm BR Remington, 7mm IHMSA, 7mm-08 Remington, 7mm Remington Magnum, 308 Winchester, 30-06, and 300 Winchester Magnum. With a retail price of about $40, for the die with one bushing, the Wilson die is not cheap. But its relatively high price is certainly not out of line when one considers the quality and accuracy potential of the die.

My only criticism of the tool—and this applies to many Wilson products—is that the well-machined steel die is totally devoid of any protective finish. If you live in a high-humidity environment or—like me—are blessed with hands which can rust plastic, you'll be in a constant battle with red rot on the die's surface. Some sort of a rust preventive finish would make an otherwise excellent die even better.

If accuracy is what you're looking for in your reloading tools, the Wilson neck sizing die is a piece of equipment worthy of your consideration. ●

Table One

Case #	Fired	.261″	.260″	.259″
1	.0004	.0005	.0004	.0005
2	.0002	.0003	.0003	.0004
3	.0004	.0003	.0003	.0004
4	.0005	.0005	.0005	.0004
5	.0003	.0003	.0003	.0003
6	.0004	.0004	.0004	.0004
7	.0003	.0003	.0004	.0009
8	.0002	.0002	.0002	.0003
9	.0003	.0003	.0004	.0004
10	.0002	.0003	.0004	.0004
Avg.	.00032″	.00034″	.00036″	.00044″

Table Two

Case No.	Die #1 Fired	Die #1 Sized	Die #2 Fired	Die #2 Sized	Die #3 Fired	Die #3 Sized	Die #4 Fired	Die #4 Sized	Die #5 Fired	Die #5 Sized
1	.0002	.0002	.0002	.0003	.0003	.0002	.0004	.0003	.0002	.0004
2	.0003	.0006	.0002	.0004	.0002	.0005	.0002	.0006	.0002	.0003
3	.0003	.0004	.0003	.0001	.0002	.0003	.0004	.0009	.0002	.0005
4	.0004	.0003	.0002	.0004	.0003	.0003	.0002	.0009	.0003	.0002
5	.0003	.0003	.0002	.0003	.0004	.0002	.0003	.0005	.0002	.0006
6	.0002	.0002	.0003	.0004	.0002	.0002	.0002	.0008	.0003	.0005
7	.0002	.0003	.0003	.0004	.0002	.0001	.0004	.0011	.0005	.0009
8	.0002	.0006	.0001	.0003	.0002	.0004	.0007	.0011	.0002	.0005
9	.0002	.0005	.0003	.0005	.0002	.0002	.0002	.0004	.0003	.0006
10	.0002	.0002	.0002	.0002	.0002	.0002	.0004	.0011	.0002	.0005
Avg.	.00025	.00036	.00023	.00033	.00024	.00026	.00034	.00077	.00028	.00050
Change:	+ .00011″		+ .00010″		+ .00002″		+ .00043″		+ .00022″	

Average runout for 50 fired cases = .000268″
Average runout for 50 sized cases = .000444″
Average sizing change for 50 cases = .000176″

Line On The Firing

Line

by CLAY HARVEY

- Anschutz Bavarian and Achiever
- Browning Composite Stalker, Micro-Medallion
- Coonan 357 Magnum
- Dakota Arms Model 76
- Desert Eagle 41 Magnum
- Franchi Auto Shotguns
- L.A.R. Grizzly 45 Win Mag
- Marlin 336 LTS, 39 TDS 1894 CL
- Ruger M77 Mark II, 77/22 AW, SP 101

Here's a look at some things new, and others not so fresh. Over a dozen guns get Harvey's thorough going-over this time around.

Anschutz Bavarian uses the 1700-series target rifle action. Harvey's rifle was chambered for 22 Hornet.

Anschutz Bavarian and Achiever

Anschutz has been making the Model 54 for a long, long time, in both 22 rimfire and centerfire versions. Recently the company added a new rendition to their queue, although the changes are purely cosmetic. Dubbed the Bavarian, the nascent item offers these features: select European walnut stock, Monte Carlo comb and European-style angular cheekpiece; fully curved pistol grip; extensive cut checkering; matte finished woodwork; schnabel forend treatment.

The action is the famous 1700 series, one that has figured in more target shooting championships than you can shake a divining rod at. It's strong, reliable, has a superlative adjustable trigger, and it is oily slick.

I chose my sample in 22 Hornet. I'm glad I did; it has turned in the finest ac-

curacy of any Hornet I ever tested, and that's been more than a couple, I assure you. So how accurate is it? Like so: a 1.02-inch 100-yard average for five five-shot groups with Norma 45-grain factory ammunition. That's just under 1 minute of angle; no other Hornet in my experience has come very close to that performance. Remington's 45-grain hollowpoints printed 1.86 for three groups, with the same company's softpoints going 2.35 inches.

For any small critters I find within the Hornet's effective range – say 150 yards or a step more – my Bavarian will handle its end of the chore.

Anschutz recently introduced what they bill as the "ideal first rifle for starting young shooters." They may well be right. The Achiever is a 5-pound semi-target rifle that is less than 37 inches in overall length, comes with an adjustable length of pull (11⅞ to 13 inches), a match-grade two-stage trigger pull that is factory set at a claimed

2.6 pounds, standard folding-leaf rear sight and hooded-ramp front (true target aperture sights are available as an option), and a receiver grooved for scope mounting.

The bolt-action repeater has a single-shot adapter that fits into the magazine well, making things safer for the beginning gunner. The buttstock is stippled at the pistol grip for good purchase; the forend has three elongated cutouts per side just below the upper forend line. The barrel is moderately heavy and free floated.

Accuracy of my test rifle was not competition quality, but for the neophyte it was more than sufficient. Winchester Mark III Match ammo gave a .683-inch average, with Eley Match just to the rear at .818. CCI Green Tag came next at .809, plenty good and inexpensive to boot.

All in all, the Achiever is quite a package. Most youngsters would swap 50 Garbage Pail Kids cards for one, easy.

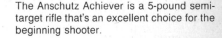

The Anschutz Achiever is a 5-pound semi-target rifle that's an excellent choice for the beginning shooter.

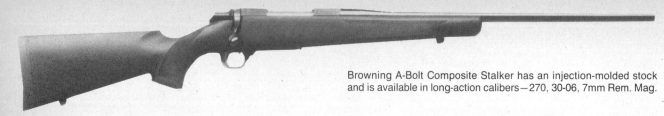

Browning A-Bolt Composite Stalker has an injection-molded stock and is available in long-action calibers—270, 30-06, 7mm Rem. Mag.

Browning Synthetic and Micro-Medallion A-Bolts

Browning has finally brought out their long-awaited synthetic-stocked rifles, and they're doozies! There are two versions, one whose steel parts are stainless (the Stainless Stalker) and a similar matte-blued permutation (the Composite Stalker). Both are clothed in an injection-molded composite graphite/fiberglass stock. The color (non-glare black) is impregnated, not painted on, so there is none to wear off. Hooray! The stock is checkered, wears a recoil pad and sling swivel studs. In addition to being impervious to the vagaries of weather and temperature, the composite handle is nigh unbreakable, well fitted, handsomely shaped, and light in weight. The only sour note is too much drop at the comb, which makes the rifles difficult to shoot well off-hand since one's face doesn't make firm contact with the stock unless one is a mite lantern jawed.

Available only in long-action calibers at this time (270 Winchester, 7mm Remington Mag., and 30-06), every synthetic-stocked A-Bolt I have examined has been very well fabricated, as is usual with Browning. Barrels are floated, and exhibit no excessive gappiness.

The same two maladies that afflict almost all A-Bolts crop up on the synthetics as well. Foremost is creepy trigger pulls that most gunsmiths claim little can be done about. Second, the floorplates wiggle and wobble, which is more annoying than seriously hindering.

Good points are the scissors-like magazine follower, smooth bolt articulation (and through only a 60-degree arc), fine attention to detail, the hinged floorplate with its detachable-box magazine, gas baffles a la the Savage 110, and accuracy. Let's talk about accuracy for a spell.

I have, to date, fired a dozen standard-sized A-Bolt rifles in nine chamberings (only one a 22 centerfire), and *all* of them grouped under 1½ inches at 100 yards for an average of three or more five-shot strings. Of those 12 rifles, three would print under 1 inch (a 270, a 7mm-08, and a 7mm magnum), and one would do so with *factory ammo!* In my experience, such precision is unprecedented among popular-priced rifles.

So how did my synthetic perform? Just fine, thanks. A Stainless Stalker printed 1.16 inches for the mean with my current favorite 30-06 varminting load: 55.0 grains of IMR 4064 and the new 125 Nosler Ballistic Tip. Not only will this load group, but its speed (3208 fps instrumental velocity) spells death on woodchucks. It will do a whitetail no good either if heavy bones are avoided.

Runner-up in the accuracy sweepstakes was Federal's 150 softpoint at 1.30 inches for the aggregate, with the same firm's 165-grain softpoint boattail vying for third slot with 1.43 inches. Tieing it was the 150 Speer softpoint boattail over 58.0 grains of Hodgdon's H414, yielding not only a 1.43 average for four groups, but slightly in excess of 3000 fps at the muzzle.

I borrowed pal Grady Shields' Composite Stalker and fired a few rounds through it with my pet Big Seven recipe—72.2 grains of IMR 4831 and the 115 Speer hollowpoint; it printed 1.25 inches for three strings. Grady has since coaxed it under 1 inch with his own favorite varmint load. Reckon A-Bolt synthetics will shoot?

Functioning is fine, as I've come to expect of A-Bolts. Feeding is extra slick thanks to a patented cartridge depressor riding 'neath the bolt.

I've killed naught with my composite A-Bolt so far, but Mr. Shields hied off to eastern North Carolina to hunt whitetails with Edwin "Booger" Harris (Pungo Acres Hunting Lodge, P.O. Box 55, Pantego, NC 27860, phone 919/935-5415). Took two fat bucks on the last day of the season, the first at roughly 240 yards, the second around 100 yards. His 7mm Magnum let the air out of them nicely, one shot each. Grady is happy with his synthetic A-Bolt.

And I'm happy with mine.

The new Micro-Medallion is specifically aimed at the youth and/or feminine market. The stock is a scaled-down number of European walnut with a 13⁵⁄₁₆-inch length of pull (as opposed to 13⅜ on all other A-Bolts); weight is a scant 1 ounce over 6 pounds according to Browning; magazine capacity is reduced by one (to three rounds); only short-action chamberings are offered (223 Remington, 22-250, 243 Winchester, 257 Roberts, 7mm-08 Remington, and 308 Winchester); barrel length is 20 inches.

My main complaint with the Mirco is the placement of its forward sling swivel stud. Due to the extremely short forend, the stud protrudes right where a full-sized shooter positions his forward hand. The punishment said hand takes under recoil is no fun. Better in my view would by the Pachmayr recessed swivel receptacles that Browning once offered on their turnbolts. Perhaps a gunner of small stature might not reach so far forward, thereby negating the foregoing caveat. I dunno. And it matters little; I still think the Pachmayr system is the best solution—and one which should pose no problem on a rifle in this price range. (The Medallion series are not bargain-basement specials.) But then no one asked me.

Aside from this flaw, and the aforementioned mediocre trigger pull indigenous to the A-Bolt breed (which would hinder a tyro much more than an experienced gunner), the little Micro-Medallion is a giant step in the right direction. I doff my cap to Browning for acknowledging the distaff and budding shootist as viable markets by producing a rifle intended solely for them. More companies should follow this lead.

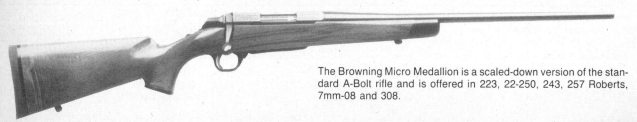

The Browning Micro Medallion is a scaled-down version of the standard A-Bolt rifle and is offered in 223, 22-250, 243, 257 Roberts, 7mm-08 and 308.

Coonan 357 Magnum

The Coonan Arms 357 autoloader has been around for some years, but I wanted to wait until its continued success and production were assured before wringing it out. It is and I have.

Basically, the Coonan is a locked-breech auto similar to the 45 Government Model in profile, operation, size (only ¼-inch longer overall, and ½-inch deeper in the grip area), and takedown. Its slide and frame are stainless steel. It has a "stud" at the rear of the barrel to help insure consistent lockup for accuracy. There is no frame-mounted feed ramp but extended magazine lips that enable a near straightline feed. (The result of this latter item is very reliable feeding indeed.)

My test gun wears screw-adjustable Millett sights that are void of any coloring–simply black on black. This works fine when the light is good; not so well when visibility could be better. For bullseye gunning, no better irons are available.

The extraction system is more akin to Smith & Wesson than Colt, being pivoted at the rear and coil-spring powered. My Coonan failed to extract empty cases from its chamber five times out of perhaps 125 rounds, more frequently with Blazer aluminum-cased ammo than with other brands, but nothing was totally immune. No other malfunctions reared their heads.

The shape of the grip safety precludes any biting of the web of the hand, at least for me. There is an obligatory and nicely done extended safety lever, plus an extended slide stop. The hammer is bobbed Commander style, complete with hole. (This part is plated chrome-moly, not stainless. Neither is the barrel built from stainless, which I view to the good.) Barrel length is just under 5 inches; weight is 42 ounces unloaded. Overall, the pistol goes 9 inches in length, actually measured. At this size and heft, it is the lightest and most compact of the "magnum" autos.

Fabrication is commensurate with its $680 price tag. Aside from a few tool marks at the bottom edge of the slide and a casting mark or two on the trigger, the Coonan is first rate. Trigger pull is light at 3 pounds, 14 ounces, albeit a bit soft and mushy, but it is easy to control.

For example, earlier this week Gerald Almond of Goldmine Hunting Preserve (Route 2, Box 95C, Standfield, NC 28163, phone 704/786-0619) suggested that I relieve him of a fine Corsican ram. I allowed as how I just might.

After hunting most of the day, I finally located the ram I wanted amid a small band of Barbarossa sheep and

Coonan 357 Magnum auto is accurate, handles well, got Harvey a ram.

The author slew this Corsican ram with the Coonan at a paced 43 yards. Ammo was Winchester 158-grain JHP. One shot, one ram.

three decidedly antsy Spanish goats. One of the goats–a black devil with very long horns–had spotted me earlier. He kept running around the herd, peering this way and that, looking for me. Putting one over on him was not going to be easy.

Slipping around a knoll and down to a creek bottom, I secreted myself behind a huge tree trunk. Gerald gave me time to get in position, then came through the woods from the opposite direction. The animals were 'twixt me and him. He raised some ruckus, tossing rocks and limbs, rattling the forest litter. My ram and his protective entourage slowly walked into view.

Alas, one of his cohorts espied my handsome visage peeping out from behind the tree. The group stopped. Milled around. Changed their minds, began to move back from whence they came. Not good.

Good old Gerald spotted this change of plans and instituted a ploy. He started throwing dead branches *at* the sheep. They didn't like that much. They knew very well where I was, but at least I wasn't tossing things at them. Yet.

The herd piled up again at 45 yards or so. Pooled suspiciously. A large Barbarossa stood on the other side of my Corsican. I didn't want to risk shooting

through and killing (or wounding) a second animal, so I waited.

After a week or so the Barbarossa shifted a mite, then came on around the hindquarters of my Corsican and stopped, blocking my view of the shoulder. I had the Coonan up, looking at them both over its sights, my arm rested solidly against a tree trunk. The Barbarossa backed up a step, exposing the chest area of my Corsican.

BOOM! went the gun. WHAP! struck the bullet. PLOP! went the ram.

Forty-three yards. Paced. One 158-grain Winchester hollowpoint, in the neck. Dead Corsican.

To provide such results in the field, a handgun has to have the requisite accuracy, and my Coonan does. With 125-grain Blazer JHP ammo, it grouped 2.44 inches from a rest at 25 yards. The Winchester load I hunted with went into 2.54 inches. Although this may not be up to revolver standards, the Coonan makes up for it by being very fast on repeat shots. Besides, this autoloader is accurate *enough*. The 357 is a 50-yard cartridge (at best) on deer-sized game (the Corsican weighed about 150 pounds, more than most whitetail bucks on the hoof). Fifty-yard groups of 6 inches or less are plenty good.

And that's what the Coonan is. Plenty good.

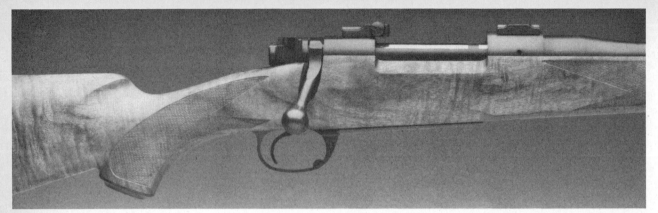

Close view of the Dakota 76 rifle shows the crisp lines and excellent workmanship. It has a Model 70-type three-position safety.

Dakota Arms Model 76

The pre-1964 Model 70 Winchester is held in such high esteem, it was inevitable that some outfit or other would bring it back in one form or another. Kimber has been working on a turnbolt design for years that combines many features of the old Model 70 and the even older Mauser Model 98. Guns are said to be "at your dealer's soon." But then they said that 3 years ago.

Dakota Arms, Inc., of Sturgis, South Dakota is actually *producing* bolt-action Model 70 look-alikes as I write this. Actually, the Dakota Model 76 is said to be an improvement on the revered Model 70, boasting as it does such features as: a flush-mounted bolt release at the left rear of the receiver bridge; improved gas handling capability; a two-screw action (the Model 70 carries a third action screw); a lack of a "coned breech" at the aft end of the barrel (having instead a recessed barrel that accepts the nose of the bolt, which is constructed like the Mauser with its locking lugs back a bit from the snout); a one-piece trigger guard/floorplate assembly; and a unique (to my knowledge) "Reverse Round Follower" which accepts the first round (in a right-hand rifle—both right and left versions are available) under the *left* receiver rail instead of the right, making loading the magazine much easier.

The original Model 70 trigger, long side-spring extractor, rear-located pivoting ejector, three-position safety riding on the bolt sleeve, and striker weight and lock time were retained. The Dakota 76 boasts an all-steel action containing no forgings or castings, according to its makers. All parts are fabricated by computer-controlled machining centers from solid bar stock, which method provides very smooth work and close tolerances.

Considering all the foregoing, the Dakota 76 may well be the finest controlled-round feed rifle currently produced. Maybe *ever* produced.

The handle is hewn from select walnut (although composite versions are available, set in Brent Clifton's superb stocks) in the classic pattern. The standard rifle is bereft of a forend tip or cheekpiece, but these items (and many others) are available for a fee. Barrel length on the standard gun is 23 inches. The wood is very handsome and extensive checkering is provided; the hinged-steel floorplate has its release in the graceful guard bow; a steel grip cap is in evidence; a recoil pad is affixed. Weight is cataloged at 7½ pounds. Nice gun, constructed of high-quality materials by dedicated craftsmen. But does it work? And shoot? And look good? Yep.

I betook myself to the range with all the 270 ammo I could dig out of my ammo locker. Ten rounds (all I had left) of Federal's 150-grain round-nose softpoint printed two groups averaging 1.33 inches at 100 yards, from the bench of course. That was the top performance of the loads tested. Runner-up was the 150 Norma semi-pointed softpoint, which turned in a three five-shot group mean of 1.44 inches.

The rest of the loads went like so: 130 Norma semi-pointed, 2.20 inches; 130 Federal Premium softpoint boattail, 2.25; 140 Hornady softpoint boattail, 1.97; 150 Federal Premium Partition, 2.05; 150 Federal Premium softpoint boattail, 2.05.

Feeding was reasonably smooth, although two or three cartridges popped out from under the right rail without feeding up underneath the extractor claw, something that is never supposed to happen in a controlled-round feed rifle. In addition, the extractor did not ride over a cartridge's rim easily when single-loading the chamber (bypassing the magazine). Aside from these minor annoyances, there were no further

The bolt release of the Dakota 76 is nicely inletted and out of the way. The rear surface is even checkered—nice touch!

functional miscues.

So far as looks, feel, fit, finish, and quality were concerned, the Dakota got an A-Plus. Everything from the wasp-waisted pistol grip to the superlative wood-to-metal joining bespoke quality. Two tiny chips of wood broke loose at the juncture of stock to tang as my testing proceeded; there was absolutely zero clearance there, so I half expected as much to happen. There were a few barely noticeable overruns in the borderless checkering pattern, but only a paid nitpicker would uncover them. I've seen worse on $5,000 custom rifles!

The Dakota Arms 76 retails for $1,950.00 in standard mode. There is a costlier Safari grade, plus a nifty new short-action rendition in both the classic and a lightweight Alpine model featuring a stock from which more wood has been whittled, a 21-inch barrel of exiguous heft, and a blind magazine. This little hummer scales only 6½ pounds according to the friendly folks in South Dakota. I faunch for one reamed to 250-3000 so severely I salivate.

Desert Eagle 41 Magnum

Magnum Research Inc. has finally brought forth a 41 Magnum version of their excellent and popular Desert Eagle semi-automatic handgun. It is exactly like the 44 magnum version; in fact the receiver is marked "41/44 Magnum Pistol." Magazine capacity is eight rounds; with one up the spout that makes for nine hard-hitting loads on tap.

Various finishes are available, such as satin nickel, bright nickel, high-polish blue, matte hard chrome, polished hard chrome, and brushed chrome. The standard item comes in matte black (blue?). Although I have not examined a satin-nickel iteration, the standard finish is my pick of what I have seen.

Barrel lengths are 6, 10, and 14 inches. Standard sights are drift-adjustable plain black rear and a similar front. Available are the excellent Millett fully adjustable (rear element) units, in either red or white up front. When you've used these sights in the field—*actually hunting, not shooting holes in paper*—you will never be happy with anything else short of a scope. Yes, they are that good. A detachable scope base and rings can be had for a price, and they work nicely, holding a scope in place as if it were welded. To my notion, any Desert Eagle purchaser should consider buying a 6-inch tube with Millett sights for close-range hunting or self defense, adding an extra 10-inch barrel with scope mounted for hunting only.

The Desert Eagle has a few drawbacks, none of them the gun's fault. When scoped (unless the glass is mounted very far forward) the slide is quite difficult to grasp with sufficient control to rack it to the rear. Unscoped, the problem in nonexistent.

The slide release does not protrude adequately to yield enough leverage to enable depressing the cartridges in the magazine, thus releasing the slide forward. Most users just grab the rear of the slide, pull it a bit rearward, and let go.

The guns are very heavy: 62.4 ounces (3.9 pounds) in 6-inch persuasion, unloaded, steel frame; 51.9 (3.2 pounds) in the 6-inch aluminum-framed version. Folks, that is *damned* heavy for a handgun. Keep adding barrel length and the weight keeps climbing. A 14-inch, steel-frame 44 wearing a 1-pound glass, 6 ounces of scope mount, and 8 ounces of ammo would heft at an incredible 6 pounds, 3½ ounces! That's more than my scoped, loaded, and slung 22-250 Ultra Light bolt-action rifle.

The grip frame is necessarily large; small fingers do not often encircle it well. But there is little that can be done about any of the above, except maybe extending the slide release and design thinner stocks.

Now that I have seemingly lambasted the Desert Eagle unmercifully, let me hit the good points. Every one I ever shot *worked*. I can say that about *very* few centerfire autoloaders, believe me. And I have fired at least a half-dozen Desert Eagles, in all three chamberings—357, 41, and 44 Magnums.

Desert Eagles are well made. The

The 41 Magnum Desert Eagle is exactly like the 44 Magnum version, except for caliber. Receiver is marked "41/44 Magnum Pistol."

workmanship is stellar, positively. Everything is robust, well designed, long-lived, and properly thought out. (Except maybe the slide release.)

And every DE I have fired has been accurate. All of them would group five shots at 25 yards under 2 inches with their best loads. Many high-dollar magnum revolvers can't equal such a record.

My sample 41 was no exception. With 210-grain Winchester JHP ammo, three strings went 1.98 inches. The 210 Remington softpoint was next at 2.26 inches, and the 210 Federal JHP came in at 2.56. Good? With careful handloading, I expect groups to shrink to 1½ inches, maybe better. My 10-inch 44 will print 6.7 inches at 100 yards with an excellent Burris 1x scope on the

bridge, from a rest of course. At 25 yards, the same gun goes into 1.36 inches with its favored factory load—the 220 Federal MCP—and will group under 1½ inches with several others. And that's with its 6-inch barrel in place. Are Desert Eagles accurate?!

One word of advice. Always spring the extra money it takes to have your DE come with the optional adjustable trigger. The standard appendage is heavy, mushy, generally undistinguished. The adjustable unit is brilliant—crisp, two-stage, light, predictable. Don't buy yours without it.

Harvey's shootin' buddy Booger Harris found the 41 Desert Eagle to be a fine whitetail taker with the 10-inch barrel.

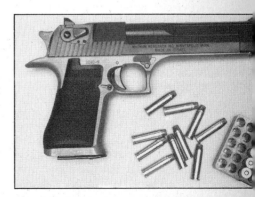

The Desert Eagle is a big gun, make no mistake. It weighs just under 4 pounds in the steel-frame version, a little over 3 in aluminum.

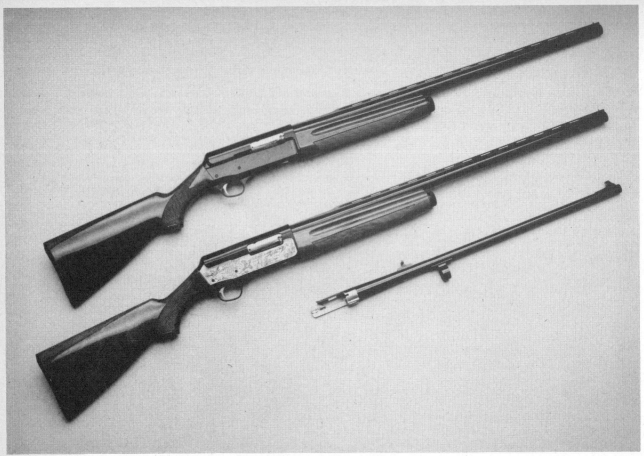

Franchi's gas-operated shotgun comes in the two grades shown — the Prestige (blued receiver) and Elite with engraved receiver.

Franchi Shotguns

F.I.E. of Hialeah, Florida, imports Franchi sporting shotguns, as well as the Franchi-built SPAS, SAS, and LAW military/police line of scatterguns. In case you aren't familiar with Franchi products, they are first rate in every respect.

There is a gas-operated pair that claims superior recoil attenuation over other gas autos by means of "specially designed barrel cones" and "double cocking slides." Only 12 gauge is offered, though in two grades—the Prestige model and the more expensive Elite. The less costly version boasts extensive cut checkering and an unadorned aluminum receiver, whereas the Elite wears complete-coverage engraving on its receiver and stippling instead of checkering of its buttstock and forend.

Both models have 2¾-inch chambers, a five-round capacity (without plug, of course), and catalog heft is a tad under 7½ pounds depending on wood density. Gas pistons are fabricated of stainless steel and the sleeve is hard chromed for durability and rust prevention. Stock material is a good grade of European walnut. Both models offer as standard

Grady Shields waits for a chance at a fast-flying dove with the Franchi Elite. The gun performed without a hitch during the hunt, even using varied loads.

a 7mm-wide ventilated rib, except, of course, on the slug barrels.

Also available is the Model 48/AL, a recoil-operated hump-backed-profile shotgun in either 12 or 20 gauge persuasion. Aluminum receivers come in black or "white" finish, with the latter being engraved as was the case on the Elite gas-operated gun. The 48/AL permutations hold five rounds, are 47½ inches long with 28-inch tubes, have chrome-lined bores, vent ribs, and both models sport cut-checkered European walnut. Listed weight is 6 pounds, 4 ounces in 12 gauge, 5 pounds, 2 ounces for the 20-bore. Alarmingly, none of the Franchis is fitted with a recoil pad, and the super light, recoil-operated 48/AL sorely (pardon the pun) needs same!

Grady Shields, Mike Holloway, and I took various iterations to the dove fields and beat ourselves up all day filling the sky with lead—even bagging an occasional dove. The Franchis worked fine, malfunctioning not once despite a rather eclectic mixture of shells, both in shot size, dram equivalent, and country of origin. The temperature rose; birds fell; the feathery smoothbores perked happily along. Nice guns.

LAR Grizzly Win Mag in 45 Win Mag with the compensator installed.

Harvey and the Grizzly teamed up on this hog. The pig did his best to upset the upstart duo, and came close to doing it.

LAR Grizzly 45 Winchester Magnum

LAR's Grizzly semi-auto pistol is a big—53 ounces, loaded, 10⅝-inch overall length—handsome 1911 look-alike that nearly everyone wants to see and handle. It comes in 5.4- and 6.5-inch barrel lengths as standard, with 8- and 10-inch versions available. A "Grizzly Comp" is offered, and reduced the felt recoil markedly on my test gun, a 45 Winchester Magnum. (Factory specs show a 230-grain full-patch slug getting 1400 fps at the muzzle; that's a handful.) Also cataloged are the 357 Magnum, 357/45 Grizzly (a wildcat based on the 45 Win. Mag. necked down), 10mm, and 45 ACP. All chamberings are built on the same frame; conversion kits for any and all are listed. Actually, I think the 10mm and the 45 ACP should be built on different frames, being much shorter cartridges.

The big gun uses the Browning-type short-recoil system of operation, and is composed of 4140 steel in the slide and receiver. The front sight is a fixed, ramped blade with bright red vertical coloring; rear element is fully adjustable Millett unit with a white outline and vertical stripe. These are my favorite iron sights for handgun use.

Magazine capacity is seven rounds. Trigger reach is quite long. Quoted as 3⅛ inches in factory literature, my test sample went 3⅜ inches, measured with a steel tape. For contrast, the big Desert Eagle auto goes 3⅜ inches, with the Coonan 357 measuring the same as the DE. Thus, for short fingers, the Grizzly grip is not ideal.

But it is manageable. When testing the gun for accuracy and zero at the range, I noted no difficulty in controlling the piece. That may have been due as much to the compensator and the excellent gripping surface provided by the Pachmayr grips as to the fact that my fingers managed to make the long reach.

Further proof of recoil controllability came on a boar hunt. I tackled a hog that weighed 250 pounds with the Grizzly. My first shot blew a hole in both lungs. He spun on me, seemed to consider charging, decided against it and lunged into the woods. I circled ahead of him, spotted him again, poked another hole in him. That was the final straw. With both lungs leaking air and fluid, he brought the fight to me.

I whacked him in the chest. The hulking 225 Speer hollowpoint didn't even slow his charge. Again the big pistol bucked in my hand; this one absolutely pulped his right shoulder joint at 30 yards. Down he went. Shot to doll rags, he still showed fight, tried to heave himself to his feet. One more through the bellows did the trick.

Yes, the compensated Grizzly is quite controllable. And reliable. Not once has it failed to feed, fire, and eject on schedule, either at the range or in the woods.

Accuracy is no problem either. The 230-grain Winchester factory load groups 2.18 inches at 25 yards. My hunting handload—16.8 grains of Blue Dot under the 225 Speer—prints 2.01.

This gun is not only for hunting, although that is its forte. For combat shooters there is a beveled magazine well for rapid reloading, a flat checkered-rubber mainspring housing, a lowered and rear-chamfered ejection port to take it easy on brass, and a polished feed ramp to handle sharp-shouldered lead semi-wadcutters. All standard. There is also a smooth-working ambidextrous safety, Colt style, plus the ubiquitous grip safety indigenous to the 1911 and its copies. The slide release is lengthened to the rear, making it quick and easy to find when you're in a hurry. With a shorter trigger reach (read smaller grip, front to back), this gun would be a fine, fine combat item in 10mm or 45 ACP.

Quality control is excellent. There were a few casting bubbles just under the left safety lever, and some minor tool marks on one side of the trigger and one side of the frame. No big deal. Everything else was shipshape. In fact, admirable. The gun is built strong like a tank, getting much of its heft from that strength. For instance, there is an integral rib running the full length of the slide, on top, into which the rear sight is nicely inletted and to which the front sight is affixed. It is ⅝-inch wide, smoothly scalloped along the sides to blend smoothly with the slide.

The trigger pull is just fine. It weighs a bit over 5 pounds, and had a tiny glitch in its takeup when I received it; the latter has cured itself upon repeated use.

Heavier than the Coonan 357, the Grizzly is not as pleasant to tote all day, although doing so is not out of the question. It is much lighter than the Desert Eagle, and I have carried one of those for many an hour. Besides, I'd not want to fire a 45 Magnum that weighed much less than the Grizzly, even with the excellent and effective comp on the slide. No, I think all three of the above mentioned autos are just right in heft for their respective calibers.

The Grizzly, like its kin in the magnum autoloader arena, is well made, reliable, and priced competitively. I do not plan to send mine back.

Marlin Model 336 LTS in 30-30.

Marlin

The Marlin Firearms Co. has several new variations on their normal theme of high-quality, affordable lever actions. Bowing to the industry trend toward lighter weight, the North Haven firm recently introduced the 336 LTS, a five-shot 30-30 carbine scaling but 6½ pounds according to the catalog, and only 34⅜ inches in length. Sacrifices attendant to the weight-loss plan include slimmer woodwork and a scant 16¼ inches of barrel. Since the 30-30 is no long-distance dialer to begin with, such abbreviation by no means renders it useless for brush-country deer, black bear to 150 yards or so, and a superior javelina rifle probably doesn't exist.

My sample LTS boasted nice wood, a crisp but moderately heavy trigger pull, fine wood-to-metal fit, and subnormal 30-30 precision. With open sights, groups ran 3½ inches on average, for five-shot strings. The gun was not fastidious in its taste; it grouped everything about the same. Still, that is sufficient accuracy for a 150-yard deer gun, although it was not up to normal Marlin snuff. (Marlins are without question the most accurate of the traditional lever actions on a gun to gun basis.)

Functioning, as is usual with Marlin, was faultless. When paired with the gun we are about to discuss, the little LTS makes a lot of sense.

The Model 39 TDS is to the 39 Mountie what the LTS is to the standard-configuration 336—shorter of barrel, thinner of lumber, lighter in heft. It comes with a handy carrying case of floatable (in case you overturn your canoe), padded Cordura. The whole rig is short, since the 39 can be taken down in seconds without tools, and stores the gun in two pieces.

Sights are the same on the 39 TDS as on the centerfire Marlins—open rear, hooded bead front. On any Marlin, mounting a scope is as simple as turning a screwdriver.

Although the bitty TDS is amply accurate (.8-inch 50-yard groups with Eley Club ammo) for any kind of small

Marlin Model 39 TDS in 22 Long Rifle comes with this handy floatable carrying case of padded Cordura.

game pursuit, and sufficiently quick-firing for high-speed plinking sessions, and heavy enough for a grown man to hold steadily, the gun's forte is as a trainer for a distaff or youthful gunner. Most of its feathery heft is biased toward the rear so it balances nicely to the slight of build. It feels very much like its larger bore sibling (mentioned above), so the training acquired through its use would carry over well should an aspiring deer hunter seek to move up in power. As companion guns for the teenage gunner, no better pair is available.

The jewel in the Marlin firmament is the dandy little 1894 CL, offered in 25-20 Winchester and 32-20 Winchester. The rifle sports a 22-inch barrel, weighs 6¼ pounds, has slender, graceful stocks, holds six rounds in its half magazine, and does not have Micro-Groove rifling (which means it should handle lead bullets like gangbusters). I have shot nothing but Winchester 100-grain lead bullets in my 32-20; it pops them into 2-inch five-shot clusters at 50 yards with the regularity of a dowager on prune juice.

Rick Jamison has handloaded extensively for his similar rifle and reports energy levels in the 700-foot-pound range. There are at least five component bullets on the market useful in the 32-20. Most of them will achieve accuracy on the order of 1½ inches at 50 yards, which is minute-of-bunny-noggin for certain. Although I would not advise someone else to use a properly handloaded 32-20 Marlin on deer, I would not hesitate to do so myself. I'd simply restrict my range severely, place my shots carefully, and have little doubt of the consequences. For coyotes, bobcats, and suchlike, the 1894 CL would be the berries. (Not, however, in 25-20. To the best of my knowledge, there are no suitable component bullets available commercially to the reloader, although that may change.)

As with the 39 TDS, the 1894 makes a fine training rifle. A handloader who casts his own bullets could shoot one quite cheaply, get really good with it, then switch to his heavy-caliber Marlin with amazing effectiveness. Plus, he could make life tough for prairie dogs and groundhogs clear out to maybe 125 yards or so if he could judge range and read the wind a mite.

Do I like the handy 32-20 Marlin? You bet!

Marlin Model 1894 CL in 32-20.

Ruger's M-77 Mark II is available in 223 Rem. with 20-inch barrel. Weight is about 6.7 pounds.

Ruger

Sturm, Ruger and Co. is one of the busiest gun makers in the business. Every year they bring out one or more new items, oftimes something really newsworthy. This year has been no exception. Let's look at them.

First there is the Model 77 Mark II, a dandy little centerfire that combines many of the best design elements of both the M77/22 rimfire and the 21-year-old M77 centerfire. The bolt of the new gun is crafted entirely of 400-series stainless steel to minimize corrosion. The safety is the three-position type pioneered on the 77/22. When in the forward position, the gun will fire if a cartridge is in the chamber; when moved halfway to the rear it enables loaded rounds to be cycled through the action with the safety "on"; all the way to the rear has the safety "on" and the bolt handle locked down. The system is similar to that offered by Winchester on the Model 70 for 50 years; there is none better.

The Mark II comes only in short-action calibers as this is written, although in the future a true magnum-sized action will be built along the same lines, one that will house such gargantua as the 416 Rigby. The 223 was the first round housed in the new carbine.

The stock is very slender, similar to that of the M77 Ultra Light but without the contrasting forend tip. There are the traditional Ruger hinged floorplate (albeit with a new latching system and a steel trigger guard) with forward-angling front action screw, plastic grip cap inset with the Ruger eagle (heraldic falcon, phoenix – choose one), red rubber recoil pad, and wonderful Ruger scope mounting system. Catalog heft is a bit shy of 6½ pounds. As with the trigger found on the rimfire 77, the new version is not adjustable. A step backward.

The thin, whippy barrel is 20 inches long and of identical contour to that of the M77 Ultra Light – which is to say very, very light. I can't follow the reasoning here. A turnbolt 223 is not a brush-country rifle of any sort, so a 22-inch (or even 24) is apropos, and a medium-sporter contour would be even more in keeping with its *raison d' etre* without adding much to the avoir-

dupois. Obviously someone at Ruger is of the same bent; a recent press release foretold the coming of a 22-inch heavier-barreled iteration.

My test gun weighed in at 6 pounds, 8 ounces. It worked just fine, and man did it shoot. It is the first popular-priced flyweight rifle I have ever fired that would average under 1 MOA (1.047 inches) at 100 yards. Using 25.5 grains of Hodgdon's H4895 under the excellent 52-grain Berger match hollowpoint, the tiny rifle turned in a five-group aggregate of 1.01 inches. My trusty Oehler Model 35 chronotach read 3090 fps instrumental, which means a foot-second or two over 3100 at the nozzle. Pretty quick. The same powder charge provided a 1.095-inch average with Watson match bullets, and 28 grains of Hodgdon BL-C(2) pushed the Berger hollowpoints to nearly 3300 fps and 1.55-inch clusters.

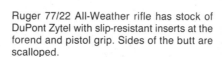

Ruger 77/22 All-Weather rifle has stock of DuPont Zytel with slip-resistant inserts at the forend and pistol grip. Sides of the butt are scalloped.

Federal's superb 40-grain Blitz turned in a 1.12-inch mean, with the Israeli-made Samson 63-grain softpoint next best at just over 1½ inches. Is this abbreviated Ruger accurate or what?

Also new and interesting in the Ruger long-gun lineup is the All-Weather 77/22 (a trademarked monniker, by the way) in 22 Long Rifle. It sports an injection-molded stock of DuPont Zytel (super tough 6/6 glass-fiber reinforced nylon) that has screwed-on panels (of G.E. Xenoy 6123, a material that is both chemical and impact resistant) where checkering normally is found (at the pistol grip and forend) and a large hollowed-out section on each side of the buttstock. There is a ribbed buttpad,

sling swivels, and the standard Ruger integral scope mounting system. The major metal components are of heat-treated ordnance-quality 400-series stainless steel. What this all means is that neither rain nor shine nor gloom of night will have much effect on this rifle, one way or the other.

The AW 77/22 hefts about 6 pounds, uses a 10-round rotary magazine similar to that of the 10/22 autoloader, has a trigger guard formed as part of the stock, a 20-inch barrel, and comes either without sights or with a bead front and folding rear sighting system, at the buyer's option.

My sample rifle is very smooth in operation, more so than many much

Young shooter Joel Simon found the Ruger 77/22 All-Weather to his liking, but the squirrels didn't. It's great to see young shooters like Joel getting involved in the sport.

more expensive rimfire rifles. It feeds from the magazine with nary a hitch; the safety is slick and reasonably silent in operation; the trigger pull is crisp and almost light enough at 4 pounds, 14 ounces.

From the bench at 50 yards, the following results: Eley Club, .779 inch (1.49 MOA) for five five-shot strings; Eley Match, .83 inch (1.59 MOA); Winchester hollowpoints, .96 (1.84 MOA); Winchester Hi-Velocity solids, 1.10 (2.11 MOA); Winchester Mark III Match, 1.06 (2.03 MOA); Remington Hi-Speed solid, 1.30 (2.48 MOA); and Federal Champion, 1.20 (2.30 MOA). I used the Winchester hollowpoints on squirrels. Worked fine when I managed to squeeze off correctly.

This is one excellent hunting rig. It does not engender tears in the eye of a purist who dotes on fine walnut, indefectible checkering, classic stocks, and such foofooraw. However, it is with little doubt the finest hunting rimfire ever produced when *all* factors are considered.

The cute little SP101 38 Special five-shot revolvers are out at the dealers now, in 2¼- and 3-inch-barreled versions. At 25 ounces (for the shorter tube), these are the smallest and lightest revolvers I know of designed specifically for +P 38 ammo usage on an indefinite basis. (That's one reason they hold only five cartridges.)

SP101s are all stainless. The frames are wide where they should be to withstand the high pressures attendant to +P loads. There is considerable steel surrounding the chambers, along with offset locking notches. The cylinder is locked fore and aft by the normal Ruger method—spring-loaded cylinder pin at the standing breech, a large spring-loaded latch at the crane. Construction is modular, as on all Ruger double actions; the works can be removed quite easily through the bottom of the solid frame. Even a hamhanded gun writer can get the SP101 apart and back together correctly. I know. I did it.

The grip is of the trendy one-piece design that attaches to the gun by means of a tenon at the bottom rear of the mainframe. Grip material is soft and pliable and recoil-absorbing Monsanto Santoprene with either wood or Xenoy inserts to add a dash of color. They feel good, definitely make the little gun more comfortable to shoot, and the method of attachment offers unlimited room for creative experimentation by the various aftermarket grip manufacturers. Recoil attenuation is so pronounced that even with Samson 110-grain +P+ ammunition, rapid-fire strings went right where they

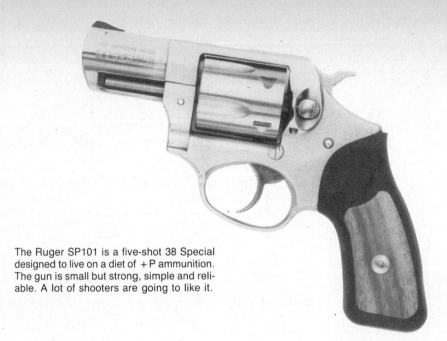

The Ruger SP101 is a five-shot 38 Special designed to live on a diet of +P ammunition. The gun is small but strong, simple and reliable. A lot of shooters are going to like it.

were supposed to go on target, using one hand or two.

I obtained test guns in both barrel lengths. One was quite accurate; the other much less so. The 3-inch gun did thus: 110 Samson JHP +P+, 3.07 inch average for three five-shot groups at 25 yards, from a rest; everything else—of five loads tried—printed between 4.17 inches (125 Hornady JHP) and 4.95 inches (148 Samson Match wadcutters).

Much better was the shorty. To wit: 2.22-inch aggregate for a trio of groups with Blazer 158-grain lead hollowpoint +P stuff; 3.63 inches with 140 Hornady +P JHPs; 3.69 with 125 Hornady JHP (not +P); 5.38 inches for Samson 158 lead hollowpoint +P. In conjunction with a test for another publication, I fired the 2¼-inch SP101 at 100 yards, from a rest of course. Two five-shot strings went just over 15 inches for the average. Not bad, huh?

The SP101 is a timely, high-quality addition to the 38 snubby ranks. I'll have to test several more guns before I make a definitive judgment on the question of accuracy, but for now I'd not hesitate to recommend the bitty, burly five-shooters to anyone considering a purchase from this market segment. Quite frankly, for the shooter who intends to use *only* high-performance ammunition in his snub, the Ruger has *no* competitors in its size and weight class. If normal-pressure 38 Special fare is on the agenda, other viable choices exist. It's up to the buyer to decide. ●

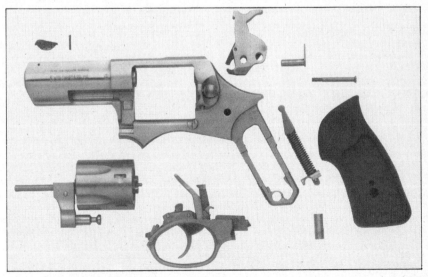

Field-stripping the SP101 is easy and neat.

THE

16 GAUGE

by JOHN HAVILAND

Gail Haviland holds a couple of blue grouse taken on a recent hunt. A 16 gauge is all she uses for duck and grouse hunting and it serves the purpose very well.

Coming or Going?

It seems that the death knell has been sounded for the lonely 16-gauge shotshell, but its lights haven't yet gone out. With a new steel shot loading this old gal still has a lot of life left in her.

Patterning a shotgun can be pretty dull work, but it pays big dividends. Only by patterning did the author discover that his 16-gauge gun shot No. 6s better than 4s.

CAUGHT BETWEEN the 12 and 20 gauge, the 16-gauge shotgun is slowly being squeezed out of the market. All that has prevented the 16 from being choked off completely is a loyal following of traditionalists.

I was raised in that tradition. The first duck I ever shot was with a Mossberg bolt-action 16 gauge. I don't know if the duck or I bled more. I had only shot a 410 shotgun a few times before and had no idea what recoil really was. I wrapped my hand around the pistol grip of the shotgun and put my nose at the front of the comb, right behind my thumb. The recoil punched my thumb back into my nose. After the nose stopped bleeding I looked out on the pond. The duck was floating, feet up.

Twenty years ago, almost every shotgun manufacturer made a 16 gauge. The 1969 *Gun Digest* listed 13 compa-

nies that sold 16-gauge shotguns in automatic, pump, side-by-side double barrels, single shots and bolt actions. Today, no 16 gauge shotguns are made in America. The Japanese-made Browning "Sweet Sixteen" automatic is the only repeating shotgun made in 16 gauge. However, there are six or seven different Spanish side-by-side 16s imported into America, and Browning now makes its over/under Citori in 16.

Browning stopped making the 16 gauge in 1976 after production of the Auto-5 ceased in Belgium. According to Paul Thompson, of Browning, the reason the 16 gauge was not continued in production in Japan was because of the drop in demand and the development of better performing 20 gauge shells.

Although there was no rush to buy 16-gauge shotguns, enough shotgun-

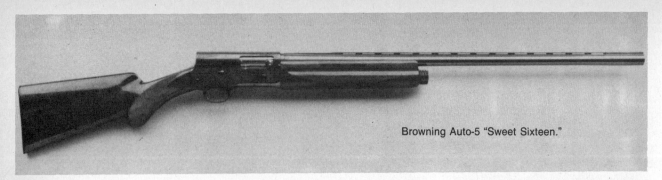

Browning Auto-5 "Sweet Sixteen."

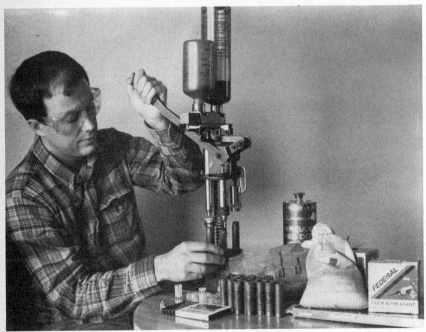

Reloading expands the number of loads available for the lonely 16, but even then wads are becoming hard to find for this shell. Most shotshell press makers offer equipment to load the 16 gauge.

With the mandatory use of steel shot, the 16 will have to fight it out with the 20 gauge as an upland gun. The author finds the 16 gauge just right for sharptail on the prairie.

ners kept asking for new 16s that Browning finally heard the noise. By reintroducing the 16, Browning is "trying to accommodate those people . . . with the option of buying a current production gun in an over/under or a semi-automatic design," Thompson said.

However, not everyone is as optimistic as Thompson.

Dick Dietz of Remington says the number of 16-gauge guns in use have been declining every year. "The demand dropped to such a point about 6 years ago that it was uneconomical to make 16 gauge shotguns and we made a decision to drop the 16," Dietz said. "We were the last American manufacturer to make repeating shotguns in the 16."

The 12 and 20 gauge have done the same thing to the 16 gauge that the 16 once did to the 14 gauge.

Before World War I the 14 gauge used to have a modest following. But 14-gauge guns were just as heavy as 12s. Anyone who wanted a lighter weight gun chose a 16. Empty brass

and paper shells for the 14 were sold into the 1920s, but the more useful 16 gauge finally buried the 14. About the only place you will see a 14-gauge shell now is in a collection.

For the next 40 years the 16 held its own against the 12 and 20 gauges along river bottom sloughs for ducks and in stands of quaking aspen for ruffed grouse.

In *The Shotgun Book*, first published in the early 1960s, Jack O'Connor noted a gradual shift away from the 12 gauge toward the smaller gauges. The 16 and the 3-inch 20 gauge could both be loaded with 1¼ ounces of shot and to O'Connor that was plenty of shot for an all-round shotgun. "Actually, the 16 is a fine choice as an all-round gun, as it patterns about as well as the 12, kicks less, handles enough shot for most purposes, and makes up into a trimmer gun," he wrote.

When lighter 12-gauge repeating guns such as the Ithaca "Featherlight" were introduced, the 16 lost one of its few advantages. I blame my father's

12-gauge Ithaca Model 37 for my thinning hair. Shooting magnum duck loads in that 6½-pound Model 37 would give me a headache down to my follicles.

Over the last 10 years, sales of 16-gauge ammunition have not increased as compared to the 12 and 20 gauges. Hunters are not shooting their 16s less, but fewer new 16-gauge guns are sold. According to the Federal Cartridge Co., sales are not drastically expanding or declining.

Dietz says there is nothing wrong with the 16. "Versatility is the reason the 12 is so much more popular," he said. "But the 3-inch 20 gauge did in the 16. The 20 gauge matches every load the 16 has, but the 16 doesn't offer anything beyond the 20 gauge."

The 20 can also be made into a trimmer automatic or pump gun than the 16. The head of a 12-gauge shell is .88-inch wide. The head of the 16 is .82-inch, only .06-inch smaller. So 16-gauge pump and automatic shotguns were made with the same size receiv-

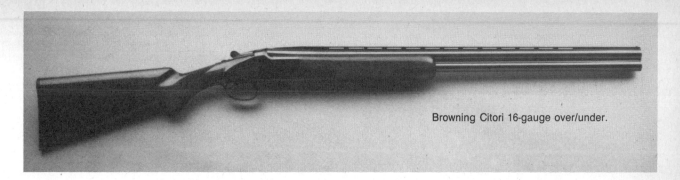

Browning Citori 16-gauge over/under.

ers as the 12 gauge. The slimmer barrel of the 16 is the only reason a 16 was lighter than 12 gauge in the same model. The head of a 20 gauge, though, is .76-inch wide and can fit in a smaller and trimmer receiver.

John Falk, of the Winchester division of Olin Corp., put it bluntly. "There is really no advantage or need for the 16 gauge. The 16 is not as good as the 12 and some say not even as good as the 20."

Falk sees a bleak future for the 16. "What can I say, it's just laying there like a dead fish in the bowl," he said.

Dietz says he has recently seen new interest in the 16 gauge. "I may be seeing a niche that needs to be filled," he said. In some areas, like western New York and the South, the 16 is the preferred gauge. "There are pockets of 16-gauge users," Dietz said. Tradition plays a big role with 16-gauge users. "If dad hunted with one, then he goes out and buys one for his son."

After that bolt-action Mossberg, my next 16 was a Remington 870 pump. My older brothers had out-grown it and bought a 12-gauge.

When my cousin and I were teenagers, we went duck hunting every weekend of the season. One Saturday we were standing in the willows along a muddy creek watching mallards fly high over us and on down the creek. The ducks looked out of range. A geeenhead came over and Rich put his 12 gauge to his shoulder and said, "Watch this!" He shot and the duck fell out of the air at an angle. Rich ran out and brought the duck back.

Another mallard was flying down the creek. "Give him lots of lead," Rich said. I swung the barrel of the 16 out in front of the duck and shot. The hen fell in almost the same spot as Rich's greenhead.

Another mallard flew over and Rich dropped it with one shot. A greenhead flew over and I did the same thing. Then Rich killed another. It was my turn when a hen came over. The hen faltered when I shot, but started its wings again and flew on.

"That's too far away to shoot," I said.

"If you had a 12 it wouldn't be," Rich said.

Rich was shooting 1¼ ounces of No. 4 shot. I was shooting 1⅛ ounces of No. 6 shot. The ducks were about 50 yards from the willows we were standing in. That is a long shot for any gauge, especially on fast flying birds. But I agreed with Rich. I couldn't wait to buy a 12 gauge.

But over the next 5 years my gun buying tastes leaned toward big game rifles. I finally bought a 12 gauge, 2¾-inch Browning Automatic. I quickly found I couldn't kill ducks any farther with the 12 than the 16. My 16 gauge had a Full choke which threw 85 percent, and sometimes more, of its shot in a 30-inch circle at 40 yards. The Browning 12 gauge has a Modified choke and printed 65 percent of its pattern in the circle. The few extra ducks I scratched down with that tight choke on the 16 did not make up for all the misses I made on blue grouse sliding through the fir trees at 20 yards. An open Modified choke would make a better all-round gun of the 16.

The 12 does have more factory loads and reloading information available. In the third edition of the *Lyman Shotshell Handbook* there are 93 pages of loads for the 12 gauge and 11 pages for the 16. The 20 gauge has 41 pages. Federal Cartridge lists 19 different loads for the 16 gauge, from 1 ounce of No. 8 shot to 1¼ ounces of No. 2.

Remington and Winchester will continue to make a variety of 16 gauge loads. "We have not reduced the number of 16 gauge loads and we'll probably make 16 ammunition forever," Dietz said. There are plenty of loads for the 16 on sporting goods dealer's shelves but not reloading supplies. It is difficult to find wads for the 16, so when I do, I stock up.

I learned long ago a gun will only shoot one load at a time. Like most hunters, I select one load for my shotgun and use it for everything from ruffed grouse to mallards. In the 16, I load 1⅛ ounces of No. 6 or 7½ shot for everything. That load is enough shot for even high flying ducks.

Is the 12 gauge that much more ver-

Like his father did with him, the author has introduced his 12-year-old daughter to the 16-gauge shotgun, and it looks like that's the only thing that will keep this gauge alive—tradition.

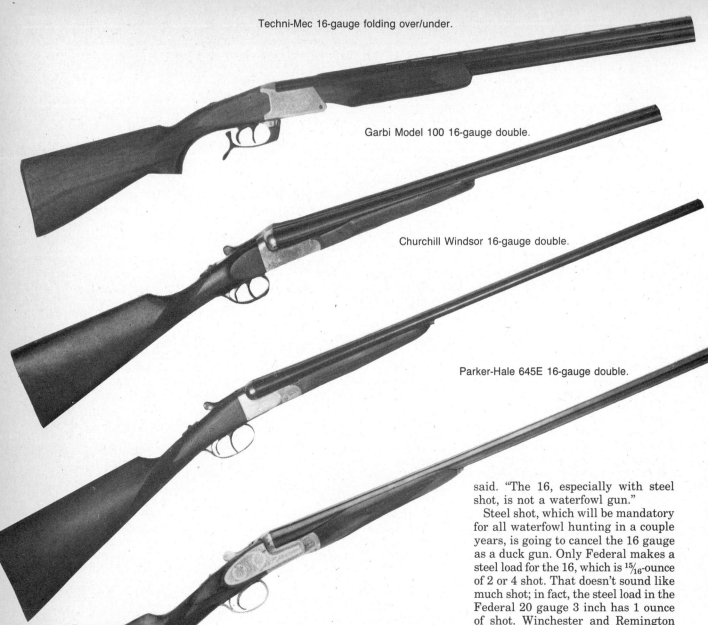

Techni-Mec 16-gauge folding over/under.

Garbi Model 100 16-gauge double.

Churchill Windsor 16-gauge double.

Parker-Hale 645E 16-gauge double.

satile a duck gun that I needed to put the 16 in the back of the gun cabinet? The standard 12-gauge duck load is 1¼ ounces of No. 4 or 5 shot. A 16 gauge will handle that much shot. The line about the 12s shorter shot column deforming fewer pellets as it grates down the barrel and printing a better pattern is not true. The 16 will pattern just as well as the 12.

If I wanted to hunt bigger birds than

ducks, I would be better off with a bigger gauge than the 16. My brother, Allan, though, has shot dozens of greater Canada geese with 1¼ ounces of No. 6 shot. However, that is the heaviest load the 16 will take. If I wanted to hunt spring gobblers, I would prefer a 12 gauge and 1½ ounces of No. 6 and if my 12 was chambered for 3-inch shells I could load up to 1⅞ ounces.

This versatility with heavier loads is why the 12 gauge has run over the 16, then knocked it flat again when it backed up to see what it hit. The 12s greater shot volume is also an important consideration for steel shot. According to Remington's Dick Dietz, shotshell development is toward more case capacity such as the 3- and 3½-inch 12 gauge, and even the 10 gauge. "The problem with steel shot is finding enough capacity for the shot," Dietz

said. "The 16, especially with steel shot, is not a waterfowl gun."

Steel shot, which will be mandatory for all waterfowl hunting in a couple years, is going to cancel the 16 gauge as a duck gun. Only Federal makes a steel load for the 16, which is $^{15}/_{16}$-ounce of 2 or 4 shot. That doesn't sound like much shot; in fact, the steel load in the Federal 20 gauge 3 inch has 1 ounce of shot. Winchester and Remington don't have plans for a steel shot load for the 16 gauge, but they are considering it.

The 20 gauge is also going to suffer as a waterfowl gun because of steel shot. That leaves it as an upland bird gun and in direct competition with what little niche the 16 gauge has left.

Practically all 20-gauge shotguns sold these days have a 3-inch chamber and will shoot from ⅞ to 1¼ ounces of shot. That covers everything the 16 can do. The 20 is so popular as an upland bird gun that Ruger introduced its over/under shotgun first in 20 gauge and not 12.

My brother David has both a Ruger over/under and an old Remington Model 11 automatic in 20 gauge. He uses either gun for hunting blue grouse. Both shotguns are easy to carry in the mountains all day during the

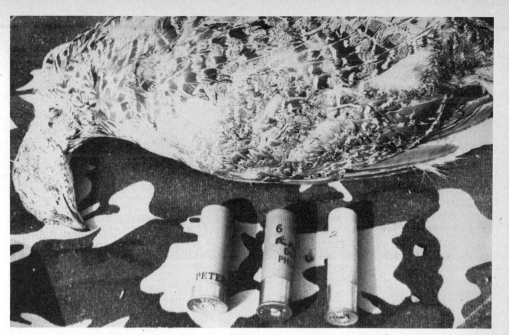

The 12 gauge (left) and 20 gauge (right) have put a strangle hold on the 16 (center), but the loads still available for the 16 make it a good grouse gun.

September blue grouse season. Both of the 20s are quick on blues twisting and turning through the fir trees.

In October, David takes his 20 gauge and 250-3000 with him when he hunts antelope in eastern Montana. After the antelope hunt is done, the 20 gauge comes out for sharptail and sage grouse on the prairie, and pheasants along the Yellowstone River. A sage grouse is twice the size of a pheasant, but a 20 gauge has no problem knocking them down as they fly out of the sagebrush. If David had a 16 gauge instead of that 20 he would never notice the difference. And that is the 16s problem. It does not do any more than the 20. Nobody is going to limit themselves to the few models available in 16 gauge when 20 gauge guns are available in every make and style. A used 16 gauge, even at a good price, will sit on the rack for a long time.

Dietz says he wouldn't buy a 16 gauge and in the future the 16 will slip even further in popularity. "It wouldn't be worth trying to bring back the 16," he said. "Although, we do make what people want to buy and if enough people wanted a 16, Remington would make them."

The only way hunters can vote to bring back the 16 is by shooting their 16s more. But, I am afraid the 16 is going down like a sinking ship, slowly at first and then all of a sudden it will be gone.

When I was 14 I was duck hunting along a creek of slack water. Tall brush grew along both banks. At every opening in the brush I snuck up to the bank to look up and down the creek for ducks. As I walked up to one thin spot in the brush, a greenhead mallard

squawked as he flew off the creek. The duck flew straight up to clear the brush and I shot when the blur of the 16s barrel covered half the duck. The duck dropped, another greenhead flew up, and I pumped in another shell and killed that one. A third duck flew up and the 16 knocked it down. A fourth greenhead flew up, and the firing pin snapped on an empty chamber. The three mallards lay dead on the other side of the creek in an area no bigger than a kitchen table.

That is the best shooting I have ever done. And I did it with a 16-gauge. When my sons start hunting I'm going to hand them that same 16-gauge gun.   ●

Federal's ¹⁵⁄₁₆-ounce steel shot load is the only one of its type available for the 16 gauge but, hopefully, other makers will follow suit.

16 Gauge Loads

Shot Charge (ozs.)	Shot Size	Wad	Powder/Wgt. (grs.)	Velocity (fps)
1	6	SP16	SR4756/23	1182
1	7½	SP16	Red Dot/16	1105
1⅛	4	SP16	SR4756/21	951
1⅛	6	SP16	Unique/18	1056
1⅛	6	SP16	Unique/21	1198
1⅛	7½	SP16	Unique/21	1239
1⅛	6	SP16	SR4756/22	1046
1⅛	6	Federal Factory Load		1223
1¼	6	SP16*	SR4756/21	973
1¼	4	Alcan PGS & Win. ½" Fiber Wad	SR4756/21	1105

All loads shot from a Full-choke, 16-gauge Remington 870 with 27-inch barrel and Remington SP plastic cases. Chronograph was an Oehler Model 33, 5 feet between sky screens. Velocities are an average of five shots.
*Wings cut off the SP16 wad.

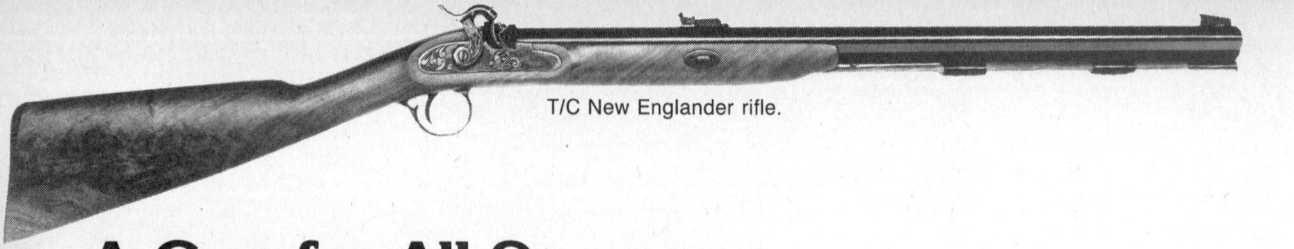

T/C New Englander rifle.

A Gun for All Seasons:
T/C's New Englander

by WILLIAM JOSEPHS

*It's a rifle!
It's a shotgun!
Thompson/Center's
New Englander
combines front-
loading fun in
a package that
will bring home
the game all
year long.*

T/C New Englander shotgun.

QUESTION: Which gun comes with one stock and three barrels? Can be used for shooting birds on the fly, bucks in the brush, or elk on the run? And, can provide blackpowder excitement in all four seasons of the year? The answer is the "New Englander," a blackpowder rifle-shotgun offered by Thompson/Center that provides more shooting possibilities than most shooters will have items in their possibles bag. In fact, whether a fellow is looking for a specific rifle to meet a particular need, or just wants to buy a front loader to explore the many thrills of blackpowder shooting and hunting, the T/C New Englander has it all.

For the past year I've been field testing the rifle-shotgun combo and found it to be a real performer. In fact, it is one of the most enjoyable firearms I've owned and I find it hard to take any of my "old faithfuls" along on a hunt anymore.

Is there a new blackpowder rifle in your future? Perhaps you've always wanted to try a blackpowder shotgun. Or maybe, like an increasing number of sportsmenn each year, you've been smitten by the "blackpowder and white smoke" virus and are looking for a cure. In any event, these characteris-

tics of the New Englander are worth considering:

Versatility

This was the feature that first caught my eye about the New Englander. A gun to use for both shotgun hunting and rifle shooting as well? It sounded interesting and is one of the setups' strongest features. The New Englander comes from the factory with one of three barrels: either a 50-caliber rifle, a 54-caliber rifle, or with a 12-gauge shotgun tube. For the person who has a need or a wish for more than one setup, the extra barrels can be ordered and interchanged easily with the same stock and percussion firing mechanism. To paraphrase an old expression, you get "lock, stock and barrels," depending upon the variety you choose.

The barrels are changed easily with a tap of the wedge pin which frees the barrel and ramrod from the stock. The ramrod stays with the barrel which means if the change is from rifle to shotgun, or vice versa, the rods won't get mixed up. The switch is very easy and is the same process used to dismount and clean the barrel after a day of shooting. The fact that the same cap is used for all three barrels helps to

Fig. 1 on next page).

An additional item that makes the shotgun easy to use, especially for beginners, is the optional T/C shotgun accessory pack. It includes all the basic ingredients a shooter will need to get started except safety items such as eye and ear protection. The directions in the T/C "Shooting Black Powder Guns" manual take the loading and firing process from start to finish, including data on various loads and the game they are recommended for.

If all of this sounds surprisingly easy and fun, that's because it is. Don't let the open choke discourage you. Even though this choke (or lack of it) is most suited for doves or quail, I found the gun to give good performance out to 30 yards on gobblers with the heavier loads. Of course, you will want to pattern your gun using various charges and shot sizes, but "loading your own" is half the fun.

50 Caliber Rifle

My field test of the New Englander began last year just a few days before Christmas. I barely had a chance to sight the rifle in when the deer season opened. On the last day of the blackpowder season, I got my big chance which resulted in one of the strangest deer stories ever told. Hunting from a tree stand, I caught sight of a spike buck that broke from a deer drive and passed my stand at a reasonable 30 yards. Swinging on the buck, I touched off the shot but my aim appeared high. As white smoke filled the air, the buck was bowled over but got up and escaped before I could reload. A shot a few minutes later signaled that another hunter's aim was more on the mark. However, as I examined the vicinity of the hit, there were traces of blood and a most unexpected find—both spikes sticking in the ground. The 50-caliber round ball missed the vital organs, but hit with such impact that the buck was knocked down and both antlers stuck in the soft ground and separated from the skull, the same as "shed" antlers do.

The rifle had performed well, but the hunter had not, primarily because of a lack of experience with the gun. To remedy this, I have spent more time on the range since then, as well as getting in some summer hunting as well. One day, after testing a powder load, I put the gun over my shoulder and headed

keep things standard and simple. Being able to use the same stock and supplies for a variety of shooting situations is a plus, but let's look at each one individually.

The Shotgun

With the shotgun barrel in place, the New Englander operates as a short, reasonably lightweight, single shot shotgun. It comes only in 12 gauge, but this isn't that important since it can be loaded for a variety of circumstances. In fact, experimenting with various loads is half the fun of this version of the gun. By varying the size of the shot used and the weight of the powder charge, the gun can be loaded for anything from clay pigeons to upland game, to turkeys. Now some folks may scoff at using an Improved Cylinder blackpowder load for the seemingly armor-clad wild turkey. After all, don't fellows generally use 3-inch magnums and even 10 gauges for these wary birds? Certainly, many hunters prefer Full-choke magnum shotguns, especially in the spring, yet my experience speaks for itself.

Last spring, while hunting at the White Oak Plantation in Alabama with guide Bo Pittman, a long bearded old gobbler pushing 23 pounds took on the challenge and lost. The shot was from 22 yards and, once the smoke cleared, the tom went down for the count as well as any I've ever taken. Even using No. 6 shot, the gun wasn't using the heaviest load possible.

Thompson/Center recommends using powder-shot combinations ranging from 70 grains of FF powder and 1 ounce of shot up to 100 grains of FF and 1⅜ ounce of shot for their heaviest load (two medium mixes inbetween). Although playing with these combinations may sound a bit tricky, actually it is quite simple. The rule of thumb for a blackpowder shotgun is to use one measure of powder and the same measure of shot. For example, if the measure is set for a charge of 70 grains of powder, fill it up with shot and use that amount. If the powder measure is set to yield a larger load, the number of shot pellets required to fill the measure increases proportionally, yielding more shot in the pattern but traveling at approximately the same rate of speed. In fact, using this "equal measure" philosophy, pellets only increase by 60 feet per second even though the charge is increased from 70 grains to 100 grains (see

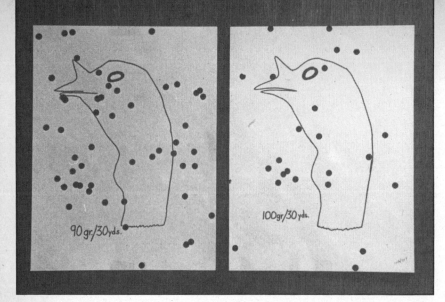

Patterning any shotgun before a hunt is necessary to determine which load gives the best performance. The 90-grain load (left) showed better pellet coverage than the 100-grain payload (right).

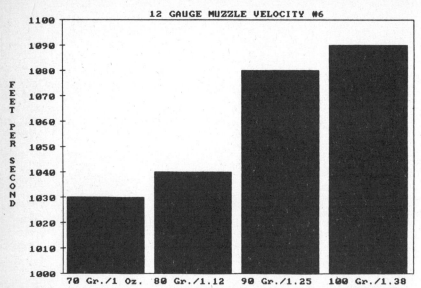

Fig. 1—By using the "equal measure" principle, although powder charges increase, the shot velocity does not rise appreciably, due to the increased weight of the heavier load.

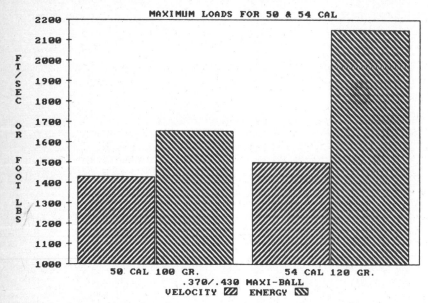

Fig. 2—The 54-caliber Maxi-Ball does not travel much faster than the maximum load for the 50-caliber bullet, but there is a great difference in down-range energy.

for a fence row that had numerous groundhog burrows. I hadn't gone far when a big one ran to his den but stopped for one last peek at the danger. When the hammer fell and the smoke cleared, a very dead woodchuck lay on the ground. My aim was a few inches left of the shoulder, taking the chuck squarely in the head. Although not the shoulder hit anticipated, that 75-yard off-hand shot could be well within the vitals of a spike buck, should one cruise by this year.

The New Englander rifle is a relatively short, light gun and is handy to take for groundhogs or other pests in the spring and summer. Using 175-grain round balls and .010-inch pre-lubed patches, it consistently grouped well on the shooting bench or with any rest that was available such as a nearby tree or log. Generally, with several loads the horizontal spacing of three shots overlapped—the group would not exceed the width of the ball at 50 yards. The vertical grouping was not as good but usually was less than 2 inches. This difference, I believe, is due to the fact that charges were measured, rather than weighed, and all of them were not *exactly* alike. My plan was to use the New Englander "as is," using the same measures and loads that most hunters would use, rather than equipment that probably would not be available in the field.

The sights on the New Englander are my one area of criticism, although if I could find a way to cook those spike horns, my opinion may change. The front sight is a very thick rectangle which makes it difficult to use at longer distances. Likewise, the rear sight did not have enough vertical adjustment to yield a true military sight picture with the top of the post even with the top of the rear sight. On the other hand, the rear sight is adjustable for both windage and elevation, and these changes are easily made. Also, the sights are ruggedly made and not

At the target range, the New Englander front stuffer handled very well on clay targets and milk jugs thrown by author's companion. The gun weighs only a bit over 5 pounds, barrel length is 28 inches.

Each barrel of the New Englander comes with its own ramrod, so you don't need to worry about getting them mixed up when changing from one caliber/gauge to another—a thoughtful touch by T/C.

Blackpowder hunting isn't just for the cold weather months. Getting in some hunting practice on ground hogs in the summer can pay big dividends in better shooting skills and familiarity with the gun when deer season opens.

Above—The low luster finish and large trigger guard are two features that deer hunters will appreciate. This "whistle pig" was toppled by a 75-yard shot using the 50-caliber barrel.

Below—This 50-yard group attests to the New Englander's accuracy potential with the rifle barrels. Head shots at this range on woodchucks shouldn't be a problem.

likely to get jarred loose by rough handling. The rear sight even comes with a lock screw to assure it doesn't change settings.

54 Caliber Rifle

Many sportsmen, motivated by "The Longhunter Society" (a record book for blackpowder shooters), will be going for bigger than deer-size game and will be searching for all the power they can get. For these folks or any hunter looking for heavy-hitting power, the 54-caliber option will be of interest. Is the .04-inch difference really significant, a person may wonder, over the 50-caliber load?

Fig. 2 points out that the answer to this question is definitely "yes." The 54 not only is a larger slug, but it is designed to be shot with a heavier powder charge. Note that although velocity only increases by less than 100 fps, the difference in energy is substantial, generating more than a ton of knockdown power with the maximum load, a full third more than the top load with a 50-caliber Maxi-Ball. Whether a person is looking for a bullet for big game, or just a little extra stopping power for deer hunting, the 54 caliber is a good choice. Another benefit is the greater availability of balls at local shops. When my New Englander arrived just

prior to deer season, there wasn't a 50-caliber Maxi-Ball within 50 miles. I shot a patched round ball because virtually everything in ½-inch size was sold out, although the dealers were sufficiently stocked with the 54 size goodies.

To Have and to Hold

Because the New Englander offers such shooting versatility, most of the information presented so far has been performance oriented. Let's look at the piece in general to get a feel for it as a whole.

"That's a good-looking gun" was the consistent comment from hunting and

Above—Hunter Rich Norkunas took this large doe with a single shot at 90 yards using a patched round ball with the 54-caliber barrel.

Below—Thompson/Center's optional Accessory Packs include everything but powder and caps for rifle and shotgun shooters: wads, powder measure, extra nipple, wedge pin puller, ramrod extension, cleaning patches for shotguns, Maxi-Balls, measure, bullet starter, nipple wrench, extra nipple and Maxi Lube for rifles.

shooting companions. The New Englander comes with an American walnut stock and round barrels, both of which have a matte finish that will cut down on reflective glare in the woods. The rifle barrels are 26 inches long with a 1-in-48-inch twist for accuracy. The shotgun barrel is slightly longer, measuring 28 inches. Both rifle and shotgun come in either right or left-handed models and weigh a moderate 7 pounds, 15 ounces. Designed for use in cold weather, the single trigger has a large guard so that the gun can be shot with gloves. Also, by holding the trigger back (very carefully) the hammer can be brought to full cock with-

out the characteristic "click" that has alerted a legion of deer over the years.

Thompson/Center puts a lot of faith in this gun and provides a lifetime warranty, which is a far cry from what a person gets with some modern guns. Furthermore, for the person who wants to do some of the finishing, a kit is available at a reduced price—a very affordable price, actually. It is always risky to discuss the price of a gun because the numbers tend to escalate with time. However, the versatility of this rifle/shotgun is such a plus that the price tag will come as quite a surprise. At the time of this writing, I've seen the New Englander selling for

$180.00, and the kit for $140.00. Add the shotgun barrel for $100.00 and a fellow can add four seasons of shooting fun to his calendar for a very reasonable sum.

For many sportsmen, blackpowder deer season is something looked forward to for many months. However, the New Englander can transpose a one-season hunter into a four-season shooter by taking advantage of the wide range of shooting possibilities it offers. Whether it's gobblers in the spring, deer in the fall and winter, or chucks in the summer, with the New Englander, blackpowder fun is always in season! ●

GUNDEX®

A listing of all the guns in the catalog, by name and model, alphabetically and numerically.

Auto Handguns—Service & Sport . . .112-133
Competition Handguns 134-140
Revolvers—Service & Sport 140-149
Single-Action Revolvers 150-156
Miscellaneous Handguns 156-160
Centerfire Military Auto Rifles 160-168
Centerfire Sporting Auto Rifles 168-169
Centerfire Lever, Slide & Misc 170-174
Centerfire Bolt Actions 174-192
Centerfire Single Shots 192-194
Drillings, Combos, Double Rifles 195-198
Rimfire Auto Rifles 198-203
Rimfire Lever & Slide Actions 203-204
Rimfire Bolt Actions & Single Shots . .205-209

Competition Rifles 210-215
Auto Shotguns 215-219
Pump Shotguns 219-222
Over/Under Shotguns 223-233
Side-By-Side Shotguns 233-239
Bolt-Action & Single Shot Shotguns .239-243
Military & Police Shotguns 243-245
Blackpowder Pistols 246-249
Blackpowder Revolvers 250-253
Blackpowder Muskets, Rifles 254-263
Blackpowder Shotguns 263-264
Air Pistols .265-270
Air Rifles 270-280

A

AA Arms AP9 Pistol, 112
AMAC Long Range Rifle, 160
AMAC Targetmaster Pump, 203
AMAC Wagonmaster Lever, 203
AMT Automag II Pistol, 112
AMT Lightning Small Game, 198
AMT Lightning 25/22 Rifle, 198
AMT 45 Hardballer, 112
AMT 45 Hardballer Long Slide, 112
ARS/Farco Air Shotgun, 271
Action Arms AT-88S, 88P, 88H, 112
Action Arms Timber Wolf Rifle, 170
Air Arms Bora Air Rifle, 270
Air Arms Camargue Air Rifle, 270
Air Arms Firepower Air Rifle, 270
Air Arms Firepower K-Carbine, 270
Air Arms Khamsin Air Rifle, 270
Air Arms Mistral Air Rifle, 270
Air Arms Shamal Air Rifle, 271
Air Arms Shamal Match, 271

Alpine Bolt Action, 174
American Arms AKC 47 Rifle, 160
American Arms AKY39, AKF39 Rifles, 160
American Arms Brittany, 233
American Arms Camper Special, 240
American Arms Combo Single, 240
American Arms Commando, 271
American Arms Derby, 233
American Arms EP380 Pistol, 113
American Arms EXP-64 Rifle, 199
American Arms Gentry, 233
American Arms Grulla #2, 234
American Arms Ideal #83 Air Pistol, 265
American Arms Jet, 271
American Arms Jet Jr. #56, 271
American Arms PK22 Pistol, 112
American Arms PX-22 Pistol, 113
American Arms RS Combo, 195
American Arms Silver I, II, 223
American Arms Single Barrel, 239

American Arms Slugger Single, 239
American Arms Sterling, 223
American Arms TT9MM Pistol, 113
American Arms Turkey Special Double, 234
American Arms Turkey Special O/U, 223
American Arms Turkey Special Single, 240
American Arms Waterfowl Special Double, 234
American Arms Waterfowl Special O/U, 223
American Arms Waterfowl Special Single, 240
American Arms Waterfowl 12-Ga. Spec., 223
American Arms ZC380 Pistol, 113
American Arms/Franchi Black Magic Game, 223
American Arms/Franchi Black Magic Skeet, 223

American Arms/Franchi Black Magic Trap, 223
American Derringer Model DA 38, 157
American Derringer Model 1, 156
American Derringer Model 3, 157
American Derringer Model 4, 157
American Derringer Model 6, 157
American Derringer Model 7, 157
American Derringer Model 10, 156
American Derringer Semmerling LM-4, 157
American Derringer Texas Commemorative, 156
Anschutz Achiever Rifle, 205
Anschutz Bavarian CF Rifle, 175
Anschutz Bavarian RF Rifle, 205
Anschutz Classic 1700 RF, 205
Anschutz Custom 1700 RF, 205
Anschutz Deluxe 525 Auto, 199
Anschutz Exemplar Pistol, 157
Anschutz 54.18 MS, 54.18 MSL Silhouette Rifles, 210
Anschutz 64-MS, 64-MS Left, 210
Anschutz 1403D Match Rifle, 211
Anschutz 1416/1516 Deluxe Rifles, 205
Anschutz 1418D/1518D Deluxe Rifles, 205
Anschutz 1700 Classic CF, 175
Anschutz 1700 Custom CF, 175
Anschutz 1700 FWT RF, 205
Anschutz 1803D Match, 210
Anschutz 1808ED, 1808 EDL Super Running Target, 211
Anschutz 1827B Biathlon, 211
Anschutz 1907, 1907-L Match Rifles, 210
Anschutz 1910 Super Match II, 210
Anschutz 1911, 1911-L Match Rifles, 210
Anschutz 1913, 1913-L Super Match, 210
Anschutz 2001, DRT Match Air Rifle, 271
Arizaga Model 31 Double, 234
Armoury R140 Hawkin Rifle, 113
Armscor AK22 Auto Rifle, 199
Armscor Model 14P Rifle, 206
Armscor Model 20P Rifle, 199
Armscor Model 30 Pump Shotgun, 219
Armscor Model 30R Riot Shotgun, 243
Armscor Model 200SE Revolver, 140
Armscor Model 1500 Rifle, 206
Armscor Model 1600 Auto Rifle, 199
Armsport Single Barrel, 240
Armsport 1050 Double, 234
Armsport 2700 O/U, 223
Armsport 2700 O/U Goose Gun, 224
Armsport 2751 Gas Auto, 215
Armsport 2755 Pump Shotgun, 219
Armsport 2783 Combo, Turkey, 195
Armsport 2801 Bolt Action, 175
Armsport 2900 Tri-Barrel Shotgun, 224
Army 1851 Revolver, 251
Army 1860 Revolver, 252
A-Square Caesar Rifle, 174
A-Square Hannibal Rifle, 174
Astra A-60 Pistol, 113
Astra A-90 Auto Pistol, 114
Astra Constable Pistol, 113
Astra Model 44, 45 Revolvers, 140
Astra 357/9mm Revolver, 140
Auto-Ordnance Model 27A-1, 161
Auto-Ordnance Model 1927A-3, 199
Auto-Ordnance Thompson M1, 161
Auto-Ordnance ZG-51 Pit Bull, 114
Auto-Ordnance 1911A1 Pistol, 114

B

BF Arms Single Shot Pistol, 134
BGJ Magnum Double, 234
BRI Special Rifled Shotgun, 220
BRI/Benelli 123-SL-80 Shotgun, 216

BRNO CZ 75 Pistol, 116
BRNO CZ 83 DA Pistol, 116
BRNO CZ 85 Pistol, 116
BRNO CZ 58I O/U, 225
BRNO Model ZH 301 O/U, 225
BRNO Model 500 O/U, 225
BRNO Super Express O/U, 195
BRNO Super O/U, 225
BRNO ZH Series 300 Combo, 195
BRNO ZKB 680 Fox Bolt Action, 176
BRNO ZKK 600, 601, 602 Bolt Actions, 176
BRNO ZKM 452 Rifle, 206
BRNO ZP149, ZP349 Doubles, 235
Baby Bretton O/U Shotgun, 225
Baby Dragoon Model 1848, 1849 Pocket Wells Fargo Revolvers, 251
Barrett Light-Fifty Model 82A-1, 161
Beeman Carbine Model C1, 273
Beeman FX-1, FX-2 Air Rifles, 275
Beeman Mini P-08 Pistol, 114
Beeman Model P-08 Pistol, 114
Beeman P1 Magnum Air Pistol, 265
Beeman R1 Air Rifle, 273
Beeman R1 Air Carbine, 274
Beeman R1 Laser Air Rifle, 274
Beeman R7 Air Rifle, 274
Beeman R8 Air Rifle, 274
Beeman R10 Air Rifle, 274
Beeman/Feinwerkbau C10 Pistol, 265
Beeman/Feinwerkbau C60 Rifle, 272
Beeman/Feinwerkbau FWB 65 Mk.I, 121
Beeman/Feinwerkbau FWB 65 Mk.II, 121
Beeman/Feinwerkbau F300-S Running Boar, 272
Beeman/Feinwerkbau 100 Pistol, 265
Beeman/Feinwerkbau 124/127 Magnum, 271
Beeman/Feinwerkbau 300-S Match, 272
Beeman/Feinwerkbau 300-S Mini-Match, 272
Beeman/Feinwerkbau 300-S Universal Match, 272
Beeman/Feinwerkbau 601 Air Rifle, 272
Beeman/Feinwerkbau 601 Running Target, 272
Beeman/Feinwerkbau 2600 Target, 211
Beeman/HW Model 60J Rifle, 175
Beeman/HW Model 60J-ST Rifle, 206
Beeman/HW Model 660 Match Rifle, 211
Beeman/HW 55SM, 55MM, 55T Rifles, 273
Beeman/HW 77 Rifle, Carbine, 273
Beeman/Harper Aircane, 273
Beeman/Krico Model 400 Rifle, 175
Beeman/Krico Model 600/700 Rifle, 175
Beeman/Krico Model 720 Rifle, 175
Beeman/Unique D.E.S. 69 Target, 134
Beeman/Unique 2000-U Match, 134
Beeman/Webley Hurricane Pistol, 265
Beeman/Webley Omega Air Rifle, 273
Beeman/Webley Tempest Pistol, 265
Beeman/Webley Vulcan II Deluxe, 273
Beeman/Weihrauch HW-60 Target, 211
Beeman/Weihrauch HW-70 Pistol, 121
Benelli Black Eagle Shotgun, 215
Benelli M1 Super 90 Defense, 243
Benelli M1 Super 90 Field, Super Field Autos, 215
Benelli M3 Super 90, 243
Benelli Montefeltro Super 90 Hunter, Left, Turkey, Uplander, 215
Benjamin 242/247 Air Pistols, 121
Benjamin 342/347 Air Rifles, 274
Beretta A-303, Trap, Slug, Youth, Clays, 216
Beretta A-303 Upland, 216
Beretta AR70 Rifle, 161

Beretta Express S689, SSO Double Rifles, 195
Beretta Field 686, 687 Shotguns, 224
Beretta Model 21 Pistol, 116
Beretta Model 84F/85F Pistols, 115
Beretta Model 86 Pistol, 115
Beretta Model 92F, 92FC Pistols, 115
Beretta Model 950BS Pistol, 115
Beretta Series 80 Pistols, 116
Beretta Series 682, 687 Shotguns, 224
Beretta SO5, SO6, SO9 Shotguns, 224
Beretta 500 Series Bolt Actions, 176
Beretta 626, 627 Doubles, 235
Beretta 682, 687 Sporting Clays Shotguns, 224
Beretta 1200F Shotgun, 216
Beretta 1200FP Shotgun, 243
Bernardelli Model AMR Pistol, 114
Bernardelli Model USA, 114
Bernardelli Model 69 Target Pistol, 134
Bernardelli PO10 Target Pistol, 134
Bernardelli PO18, Combat Pistols, 115
Bernardelli Series Roma Doubles, 234
Bernardelli Series S. Uberto Doubles, 234
Bernardelli System Holland H., 234
Bersa Model 23 Pistol, 116
Bersa Model 83, 85 Pistols, 116
Black Watch Scotch Pistol, 246
Blaser K77A Rifle, 192
Blaser R84 Rifle, 176
Browning A-Bolt Camo Stalker, 176
Browning A-Bolt Gold Medallion, 177
Browning A-Bolt Left Hand, 176
Browning A-Bolt Micro Medallion, 177
Browning A-Bolt Pronghorn Antelope, 177
Browning A-Bolt Rifle, 176
Browning A-Bolt Short Action, 177
Browning A-Bolt Stainless Stalker, 176
Browning A-Bolt 22 Gold Medallion, 206
Browning A-Bolt 22 Rifle, 206
Browning A-500 Auto Shotgun, 216
Browning Auto-5 Gold Classic, 216
Browning Auto-5 Light 12, 20, Sweet 16, 216
Browning Auto-5 Magnum 12, 216
Browning Auto-5 Magnum 20, 216
Browning Auto-22 Grade VI, 199
Browning Auto-22 Rifle, 199
Browning BDA-380 DA Pistol, 117
Browning BL-22 Lever Action, 203
Browning BLR Model 81 Lever Action, 170
Browning BPS Ladies, Youth Shotguns, 220
Browning BPS Shotgun, 220
Browning BPS Stalker, 220
Browning BT-99 PLUS, 240
Browning BT-99 Trap, 240
Browning Big Game BAR, 168
Browning Buck Mark Silhouette, 116
Browning Buck Mark Varmint, 117
Browning Buck Mark 22, Plus Pistols, 116
Browning Citori GTI Clays, 226
Browning Citori O/U, 225
Browning Citori O/U Trap, 226
Browning Citori PLUS Trap, 225
Browning Citori Skeet, 225
Browning Citori Superlight, 226
Browning Gold Classic O/U, 226
Browning High-Power Auto Rifle, 168
Browning Hi-Power Pistol, 117
Browning Lightning Sporting Clays, 225
Browning Limited Edition Waterfowl Superposed, 226
Browning Magnum Auto Rifle, 168
Browning Model 12 Shotgun, 220
Browning Model 65 Rifle, 170
Browning Model 71 Rifle, 170

Browning Model 1885, 192,
Browning Special Sporting Clays, 225
Bryco Model 38 Pistol, 117
Bryco Model 48 Pistol, 117
Bushmaster Auto Pistol, 118
Bushmaster Auto Rifle, 161

C

CVA Blazer Rifle, 263
CVA Brittany II Shotgun, 263
CVA Colonial Pistol, 247
CVA Express Rifle, 262
CVA Frontier Carbine, 113
CVA Hawken Pistol, 247
CVA Hawken Rifle, Combo, 113
CVA Kentucky Rifle, 256
CVA Mountain Rifle, 113
CVA O/U Carbine-Rifle, 262
CVA Pennsylvania Long Rifle, 255
CVA Philadelphia Percussion Derringer, 248
CVA Pocket Remington, 252
CVA Remington Bison, 252
CVA Siber Pistol, 248
CVA Squirrel Rifle, 255
CVA Third Model Colt Dragoon, 250
CVA Trapper Shotgun, 264
CVA Vest Pocket Derringer, 249
CVA Wells Fargo, 252
CVA 1858 Remington Target, 251
Cabanas Espronceda IV, 206
Cabanas Laser Rifle, 206
Cabanas Leyre Rifle, 206
Cabanas Master, Varmint Rifles, 206
Calico Model 100 Carbine, 199
Calico Model 105 Sporter, 199
Calico Model 110-P Pistol, 118
Calico Model 900 Carbine, 168
Calico Model 950 Pistol, 118
Century Centurion 14 Sporter, 177
Century Enfield Jungle Sporter, 177
Century Enfield Sporter #4, 177
Century Swedish Sporter #38, 177
Century Mfg. Model 100 SA, 150
Chapuis RGExpress Model 89, 195
Chapuis RG Progress, 235
Charleville Flintlock Pistol, 246
Charter AR-7 Explorer, 200
Charter Arms Bonnie, Clyde Revolvers, 140
Charter Arms Bulldog, 141
Charter Arms Bulldog Pug, 141
Charter Arms Bulldog Tracker, 141
Charter Arms Off-Duty, 141
Charter Arms Pathfinder, 141
Charter Arms Pit Bull, 141
Charter Arms Police Bulldog, 141
Charter Arms Target Bulldog, 141
Charter Arms Undercover, 141
Charter Arms Undercover Police
  Spec., 140
Cheney Plains Rifle, 256
Chipmunk Silhouette Pistol, 134
Chipmunk Single Shot Rifle, 207
Churchill Highlander, Regent Bolt
  Actions, 178
Churchill Monarch O/U, 226
Churchill Regent Combo, 195
Churchill Regent O/U, 226
Churchill Regent Trap, Skeet, 226
Churchill Royal Double, 235
Churchill Windsor I Double, 235
Churchill Windsor O/U, 226
Cimarron Artillery Model SA, 150
Cimarron Sheriff Model SA, 150
Cimarron U.S. Cavalry Revolver, 150

Cimarron 1873 Button Half-Magazine, 171
Cimarron 1873 Peacemaker Repro, 150
Cimarron 1873 Short Rifle, 170
Cimarron 1873 30″ Express Rifle, 171
Cimarron 1875 Remington Repro, 150
Cimarron 1890 Remington SA, 150
Classic Doubles Model 101 Field I, II,
  Waterfowler, 227
Classic Doubles Model 101 Sporter, 227
Classic Doubles Model 101 Trap,
  Skeet, 227
Classic Doubles Model 201 Double, 235
Colt AR-15A2 Delta H-BAR, 162
Colt AR-15A2 Gov't. Model Carbine, 162
Colt AR-15A2 Gov't. Model Rifle, 161
Colt AR-15A2 H-BAR, 162
Colt AR-15A2 Sporter II, 162
Colt Combat Commander Pistol, 118
Colt Combat Elite Mk IV/Series 80, 119
Colt Delta Elite 10mm Pistol, 118
Colt Delta Gold Cup, 135
Colt Gold Cup Nat'l. Match, 135
Colt Gov't. Model Mk IV/Series 80, 118
Colt King Cobra, 142
Colt Lightweight Commander Mk IV/Series
  80, 118
Colt Mustang Plus II, Mustang 380, Mustang Pocket Lite, 119
Colt Officer's ACP Mk IV/Series 80,
  L.W., 119
Colt Python, 142
Colt Series 90 Double Eagle Pistol, 118
Colt Single Action Army, 151
Colt 380 Gov't. Model, 119
Competitor Single Shot Pistol, 135
Confederate Tucker & Sherrard, 250
Cook & Brother Confederate Carbine, 260
Coonan 357 Magnum Pistol, 119
Cosmi Auto Shotgun, 217
Crosman AIR 17 Rifle, 275
Crosman Model 66 Powermaster, 275
Crosman Model 84 CO$_2$ Match Rifle, 275
Crosman Model 338 Air Pistol, 121
Crosman Model 357, 1357 Air Pistols, 121
Crosman Model 760 Pumpmaster, 274
Crosman Model 781 Single Pump, 275
Crosman Model 788 BB Scout, 275
Crosman Model 1322, 1377 Air Pistols, 267
Crosman Model 1389 Backpacker, 275
Crosman Model 1600 BB Pistol, 267
Crosman Model 2100 Classic, 275
Crosman Model 2200 Magnum, 275
Crosman Model 3100 Rifle, 275
Crosman Model 3357 Spot Marker Pistol, 121
Crosman SSP 250, 121
Crosman/Skanaker Match Pistol, 267
Crucelegui Hermanos Model 150, 235

D

Daewoo AR100 Auto Rifle, 162
Daewoo AR110C Auto Carbine, 162
Daisy Legacy 2201, 207
Daisy Legacy 2202, 207
Daisy Legacy 2203, 2213 Auto Rifles, 200
Daisy Legacy 2211, 207
Daisy Legacy 2212, 207
Daisy Model 188 BB Pistol, 267
Daisy Power Line 44 Air Revolver, 267
Daisy Power Line 92 Pistol, 268
Daisy Power Line 717, 747 Air Pistols, 267
Daisy Power Line 753 Target, 276
Daisy Power Line 777 Pellet Pistol, 268

Daisy Power Line 814, 914 Rifles, 276
Daisy Power Line 840 Rifle, 276
Daisy Power Line 856 Pump-Up Rifle, 276
Daisy Power Line 860 Pump-Up, 276
Daisy Power Line 880 Pump-Up, 276
Daisy Power Line 900 Pellet Repeater, 276
Daisy Power Line 922, 970, 920, 277
Daisy Power Line 953, 277
Daisy Power Line 1200 Pistol, 267
Daisy Youth Line 95,105, 111, 277
Daisy Youth Line 1500 Air Pistol, 268
Daisy 1938 Red Ryder Classic, 277
Dakota Bisley SA, 151
Dakota Single Action Revolvers, 151
Dakota 1875 Outlaw, 151
Dakota 1890 Police, 151
Dakota Arms 76 Classic Rifle, 178
Dakota Arms 76 Safari Rifle, 178
Dakota Arms 76 Short Action, 178
Dakota Arms 416 Rigby African, 178
Charles Daly Hawken, Wilderness
  Hawken, 113
Charles Daly Field Grade, 226
Charles Daly Lux O/U, 226
Davis Derringer, 157
Davis P-32 Auto Pistol, 119
Desert Eagle 357 Pistol, 120
Detonics Combat Master MC I, 120
Detonics Combat Master Mk VI, 120
Detonics Janus Scoremaster Pistol, 135
Detonics Scoremaster Target, 135
Detonics Servicemaster Pistol, 120
Dixie Abilene Derringer, 248
Dixie Brass Frame Derringer, 248
Dixie Delux Cub Rifle, 257
Dixie Hawken Rifle, 259
Dixie Indian Gun, 254
Dixie LePage Dueller, 249
Dixie Lincoln Derringer, 248
Dixie Magnum Percussion Shotgun, 263
Dixie Model 1863 Springfield Musket, 261
Dixie Model 1873 Lever Action, 171
Dixie Overcoat Pistol, 247
Dixie Pennsylvania Pistol, 246
Dixie Percussion Wesson Rifle, 259
Dixie Philadelphia Derringer, 248
Dixie Queen Anne Flintlock, 246
Dixie Screw-Barrel Pistol, 249
Dixie Squirrel Rifle, 254
Dixie Tennessee Mountain Rifle, 254
Dixie Third Model Dragoon, 250
Dixie Tornado Target Pistol, 249
Dixie U.S. Model 1861 Springfield, 260
Dixie W. Parker Pistol, 247
Dixie Wyatt Earp Revolver, 253
DuBiel Bolt Actions, 178

E

E.M.F. Henry Carbine, 171
El Gamo 126 Super Match, 278
Elgin Cutlass Pistol, 249
Encom Mk. IV Pistol, 120
Encom MP-9, MP-45 Pistols, 120
Erma ER Match Revolvers, 135
Erma ER-777 Revolver, 142
Erma Model ESP 85A Pistol, 120

F

FAMAS Air Rifle, 277
FAS Model 601 Match Pistol, 135
FAS Model 602 Match Pistol, 135
F.I.E. Arminius Revolvers, 142
F.I.E. Buffalo Scout SA, 151
F.I.E. Cowboy SA, 151
F.I.E. D-86 Derringer, 158

F.I.E. Hombre SA, 152
F.I.E. Little Ranger SA, 152
F.I.E. Series '88 TZ-75 Pistol, 121
F.I.E. Spectre Auto Carbine, 163
F.I.E. Spectre Auto Pistol, 121
F.I.E. S.S.S. Single, 240
F.I.E. Standard Revolver, 142
F.I.E. Super Titan II Pistol, 120
F.I.E. Texas Ranger SA, 152
F.I.E. Titan Tiger, 142
F.I.E. Titan Tigress Lady 25, 121
F.I.E. Titan II Pistol, 121
F.I.E. Titan 25 Pistol, 121
F.I.E. Yellow Rose Revolver, 152
F.I.E./Franchi Alcion S, 227
F.I.E./Franchi LAW 12, 244
F.I.E./Franchi Prestige, Elite Autos, 217
F.I.E./Franchi SAS l2, 244
F.I.E./Franchi Slug Gun, 217
F.I.E./Franchi SPAS 12 Pump/Auto, 243
F.I.E./Franchi 48/AL, Hunter, 217
Feather AT-9 Auto Carbine, 162
Feather AT-22 Auto Carbine, 200
Feather Guardian Angel Pistol, 158
Feather SAR-180 Carbine, 200
Federal XC-220 Carbine, 200
Federal XC-900/XC-450 Carbines, 162
Federal Ordnance M14SA Target, 211
Ferlib Model F VII Double, 235
Finnish Lion Target Rifle, 211
Auguste Francotte Bolt-Action Rifle, 178
Auguste Francotte Double Rifles, 195
Auguste Francotte Doubles, 236
Freedom Arms Boot Gun, 152
Freedom Arms Mini Revolver, 152
Freedom Arms Percussion Mini Revolver, 253
Freedom Arms 454 Casull, 152
French-Style Dueling Pistol, 248

G

Galil Hadar II Rifle, 163
Galil Model AR Rifle, 163
Galil Model ARM Rifle, 163
Galil Sniper Rifle, 163
Garbi Model 100, 236
Garbi Model 101, 236
Garbi Model 103A, 103B, 236
Garbi Model 200, 236
GAT Air Pistol, 268
GAT Air Rifle, 277
Glock 17 Auto Pistol, 121
Glock 19 Auto Pistol, 121
Gonic GA-85 Rifle, 263
Grendel Model P-10 Pistol, 122
Grendel SRT, SRT-20F Compact Rifles, 179
Griswold & Gunnison Revolver, 253

H

Hammerli Model 150, 152 Free Pistols, 136
Hammerli Model 208s Pistol, 136
Hammerli Model 232 Rapid Fire, 136
Hammerli Standard 208, 211, 215 Pistols, 136
Harper's Ferry 1803 Rifle, 254
Harper's Ferry 1806 Pistol, 247
Hatfield Squirrel Rifle, 255
Hatfield Uplander Shotgun, 236
Hawken Rifle, Hawken Hunter, 113
Heckler & Koch HK-91A2, A3, 163
Heckler & Koch HK-93A2, A3, 163
Heckler & Koch HK-94 Pistol, 122
Heckler & Koch HK-94A2, A3, 164
Heckler & Koch HK-300 Rifle, 200

Heckler & Koch HK-770 Rifle, 169
Heckler & Koch PSG-1 Marksman, 211
Heckler & Koch P7-K3 Pistol, 122
Heckler & Koch P7-M8, P7-M13 Pistols, 122
Heckler & Koch SL-6 Rifle, 169
Helwan Brigadier Pistol, 122
Heym Magnum Express Rifle, 179
Heym Model 22S Safety Combo, 196
Heym Model 33 Drilling, 196
Heym Model 37 Sidelock Drilling, 196
Heym Model 37B Drilling, 196
Heym Model 55B, 55SS Double, 196
Heym Model 55BF Combo, 196
Heym Model 88B Double, 196
Heym SR 20 Alpine Series, 179
Heym SR 20 Classic Safari, 179
Heym SR 20 Classic Sportsman, 179
Heym SR 20 Trophy Series, 179
Heym 88B Safari Double Rifle, 196
Heym-Ruger Model HR 30/38, 192
Holmes Model 88 Shotgun, 244
Holmes MP-22 Assault Pistol, 122
Holmes MP-83 Assault Pistol, 122
Howa Heavy Barrel Varmint, 179
Howa Lightning Rifle, 180
Howa Model 1500 Rifle, 180
Howa Model 1500 Trophy Rifle, 179

I

IAI Automag III Pistol, 123
IAI Backup Pistol, 123
IAI Javelina 10mm Pistol, 123
Interarms Model 22 ATD Rifle, 201
Intratec TEC-9, TEC-9S Pistols, 123
Intratec TEC-9M, TEC-9MS Pistols, 123
Intratec TEC-22T, TEC-22TN, TEC-22, 123
Ithaca Deerslayer II Rifled Shotgun, 220
Ithaca Model 5E Trap Single, 240
Ithaca Model 87 Deerslayer, 220
Ithaca Model 87 Deluxe Pump, 220
Ithaca Model 87 DSPS M&P, 244
Ithaca Model 87 Hand Grip, 244
Ithaca Model 87 Supreme, 220
Ithaca Model 87 Ultra Field, 220
Ithaca X-Caliber Pistol, 158
Ithaca-Navy Hawken Rifle, 113

J

Jaeger African Rifle, 180
Jaeger Alaskan Rifle, 180
Jaeger Hunter Rifle, 180
Jennings J-22, J-25 Pistols, 124
Iver Johnson Enforcer Pistol, 123
Iver Johnson Li'l Champ Rifle, 207
Iver Johnson PM30HB Carbine, 164
Iver Johnson TP22, TP25 Pistols, 124

K

Kentuckian Rifle, Carbine, 254
Kentucky Flintlock Pistol, 247
Kentucky Flintlock Rifle, 254
Kentucky Percussion Pistol, 247
Kentucky Percussion Rifle, 254
Kimber Big Game Rifle, 180
Kimber Model 82, 84 CF Super Grades, 181
Kimber Model 82, 84 Super Grade RF, 207
Kimber Model 82 Government, 212
Kimber Model 82B, Continental RF, 207
Kimber Model 84 CF Sporter, 180
Kimber Model 89 African, 181

Knight MK-85 Hunter, Stalker, Predator, 263
Kodiak Mk. IV Double Rifle, 196
Kodiak Mk. IV Perc. Double Rifle, 262
Krieghoff K-80 International Skeet, 227
Krieghoff K-80 Pigeon, 227
Krieghoff K-80 Single Barrel Trap, 241
Krieghoff K-80 Skeet Set, 227
Krieghoff K-80 Sporting Clays, 228
Krieghoff K-80 Trap, Skeet, 227
Krieghoff KS-5 Trap, 241
Krieghoff Teck, Ulm Combos, 197
Krieghoff Trumpf, Neptune Drilling, 197

L

L.A.R. Grizzly Win Mag Mk I Pistol, 124
L.A.R. Grizzly Win Mag 8″, 10″ Pistol, 124
Laurona Silhouette 300 Clays, 228
Laurona Silhouette 300 Trap, 228
Laurona Super 82G, 82S, 83MG, 84S, 85 Game, 228
Laurona Super 85MS Super Trap, Pigeon, 85S, Skeet, 85MS Sporting, 228
LeMat Army Model Revolver, 253
LeMat Cavalry Model Revolver, 253
LeMat Naval Style Revolver, 253
Ljutic LTX Super Deluxe, 241
Ljutic Mono Gun, 241
Ljutic Recoilless Space Shotgun, 241
Ljutic Skeet Set, 228
Ljutic T.C. LM-6 O/U, 228
Llama Comanche III, 143
Llama Compact Frame Pistol, 125
Llama Large Frame Pistol, 124
Llama M-82 Pistol, 125
Llama M-87 Comp Pistol, 136
Llama Small Frame Pistol, 124
Llama Super Comanche Revolver, 143
London Armory Enfield Musketoon, 259
London Armory 2-Band 1858 Enfield, 259
London Armory 3-Band 1853 Enfield, 259
Lorcin Auto Pistol, 125
Lyman Great Plains Rifle, 255
Lyman Plains Pistol, 246
Lyman Trade Rifle, 256

M

MAS 223 Auto Rifle, 164
Mandall/Cabanas Pistol, 158
Mapiz Zanardini Oxford 89, 197
Mark X American Field Series Rifles, 181
Mark X LTW Sporter Rifle, 181
Mark X Sporter Rifle, 181
Mark X Viscount Rifle, 181
Marksman Model 17 Air Pistol, 268
Marksman Model 28 International, 278
Marksman Model 29 Air Rifle, 278
Marksman Model 40 International, 278
Marksman Model 55, 59 Air Rifles, 278
Marksman Model 56-FTS Field Target, 278
Marksman Model 58-S, 58-K Silhouette, 278
Marksman Model 70 Air Rifle, 278
Marksman Model 1010, 1010X, 1015, 268
Marksman Model 1740 Air Rifle, 279
Marksman Model 1790 Biathlon Trainer, 279
Marksman Plainsman 1049 CO$_2$ Pistol, 268
Marlin Golden 39AS Rifle, 204
Marlin Model 9 Camp Carbine, 169
Marlin Model 15YN, 208
Marlin Model 25MN, 208
Marlin Model 25N, 208

Marlin Model 39TDS Carbine, 204
Marlin Model 45 Carbine, 169
Marlin Model 55 Goose Gun, 241
Marlin Model 60 Rifle, 201
Marlin Model 70HC Rifle, 201
Marlin Model 70P Papoose, 201
Marlin Model 75C Rifle, 201
Marlin Model 880, 208
Marlin Model 881, 208
Marlin Model 882, 208
Marlin Model 883, 208
Marlin Model 995 Rifle, 201
Marlin 30AS Lever Action, 171
Marlin 336CS Lever Action, 171
Marlin 336LTS Carbine, 171
Marlin 444SS Lever Action, 172
Marlin 1894CL Classic, 172
Marlin 1894CL Lever Action, 172
Marlin 1894CS Lever Action, 172
Marlin 1894S Lever Action, 171
Marlin 1895SS Lever Action, 172
Mauser Model 225 Rifle, 181
Mauser Model 300 SL Air Rifle, 279
Maverick Model 88 Shotgun, 221
Maximum Single Shot Pistol, 158
McMillan Long Range Rifle, 212
McMillan M-86 Sniper, 212
McMillan M-87 50-Cal., 212
McMillan M-88 50-Cal., 212
McMillan Nat'l. Match, 212
McMillan Signature Alaskan, 182
McMillan Signature Classic Sporter, 181
McMillan Signature Safari, 182
McMillan Signature Super Varminter, 182
McMillan Signature Titanium Mountain, 182
Mercury G1032 Double, 236
Merkel 47E, 47S, 147E, 147S, 247S, 347S, 447S, 236
Merkel 200E, 201E, 203E, 303E, 229
Mini-Mark X Rifle, 181
Mississippi Model 1841 Rifle, 261
Mitchell AK-22 Auto Rifle, 201
Mitchell AK-47 H.B. Rifle, 164
Mitchell AK-47 Rifle, 164
Mitchell MAS/22 Rifle, 202
Mitchell M-16/22 Rifle, 202
Mitchell M-59 Rifle, 164
Mitchell M-76 Counter-Sniper, 164
Mitchell PPS/50 Rifle, 202
Mitchell Arms SA Revolvers, 153
Mitchell Galil/22 Rifle, 202
Moore & Patrick Flint Dueler, 248
Mossberg Model 500 Bullpup, 245
Mossberg Model 500 Camo Pump, 221
Mossberg Model 500 Mariner, 244
Mossberg Model 500 Security, 244
Mossberg Model 500 Sporting Pump, Combo, 221
Mossberg Model 500 Trophy Slugster, 221
Mossberg Model 590 Mariner, 245
Mossberg Model 590 Military, 244
Mossberg Model 835 Ulti-Mag, 221
Mossberg Model 5500 Mk. II, 217
J.P. Murray 1862-64 Cavalry Carbine, 260

N

Navy Arms Charleville, 254
Navy Arms Country Boy Rifle, 256
Navy Arms Duckfoot, 249
Navy Arms Fowler Shotgun, 264
Navy Arms Henry Carbine, 172
Navy Arms Henry Iron Frame, 172
Navy Arms Henry Military Rifle, 172
Navy Arms Henry Trapper, 172
Navy Arms Hunter Shotgun, 264

Navy Arms LePage Dueller, 249
Navy Arms Model 83/93 Bird Hunter, 228
Navy Arms Model 95/96 Sportsman, 228
Navy Arms Model 100 Shotgun, 229
Navy Arms Model 105 Shotgun, 241
Navy Arms Rolling Block, 193
Navy Arms T&T Shotgun, 264
Navy Arms 1858 Remington-Style Revolver, 252
Navy Arms 1863 Springfield, 260
Navy Model 1851 Revolver, 251
Navy Model 1861 Revolver, 251
Navy-Sheriff 1851 Revolver, 251
New Advantage Arms Derringer, 158
New England Firearms DA Revolvers, 143
New England Firearms Handi-Gun, 242
New England Firearms Handi-Rifle, 193
New England Firearms Mini-Pardner, 241
New England Firearms Pardner, 241
New England Firearms Ultra Revolver, 143
New England Firearms 10-Ga. Single, 242
New Model 1858 Army Revolver, 251
New Orleans Ace, 249
Norinco Dragunov NDM-86 Rifle, 165
Norinco SKS Rifle, 165
Norinco Type 54-1 Tokarev, 125
Norinco Type 84S AK Rifle, 165
North American Mini-Master, 153
North American Mini-Revolvers, 153

O

Omega Auto Pistol, 125

P

Pachmayr Dominator Pistol, 158
Pachmayr/Perazzi MX-20 O/U, 229
Pardini Fiocchi Free Pistol, 137
Pardini Fiocchi PIO Match Air Pistol, 269
Pardini Fiocchi Rapid Fire Match Pistol, 137
Pardini Fiocchi Standard Pistol, 136
Pardini Fiocchi 32 Match Pistol, 136
Parker DHE Double, 237
Parker-Hale Enfield Pattern 1858 Naval Rifle, 260
Parker-Hale Enfield 1853 Musket, 259
Parker-Hale Enfield 1861 Musketoon, 260
Parker-Hale Model 81 African Rifle, 183
Parker-Hale Model 81 Classic, 183
Parker-Hale Model 87 Target Rifle, 213
Parker-Hale Model 1100 Lightweight, 183
Parker-Hale Model 1100M African Magnum, 182
Parker-Hale Model 1200 Super Bolt, Clip, 182
Parker-Hale Model 2100 Midland, 182
Parker-Hale Volunteer Rifle, 260
Parker-Hale Whitworth Military Target Rifle, 260
Parker-Hale 600 Series Doubles, 237
Partisan Avenger Pistol, 125
Pennsylvania Full Stock Rifle, 255
Perazzi Grand American 88 Special, DB81 Special, 229
Perazzi Mirage Skeet Set, 230
Perazzi Mirage Special Skeet, 229
Perazzi Mirage Special Sporting, 230
Perazzi MX1, MX1B Sporting, 229
Perazzi MX3 Special Single, O/U, 229
Perazzi MX8/MX8 Special Trap, Skeet, 229
Perazzi MX12, MX20 Hunting, 229
Perazzi TM1, TMX, 242

Perugini-Visini Classic Double, 237
Perugini-Visini Liberty Double, 237
Perugini-Visini Selous Double Rifle, 197
Perugini-Visini Victoria-M, -D Doubles, 197
Phelps Heritage 1, Eagle 1, 153
Piotti Model King Extra, 237
Piotti Model King No. 1, 238
Piotti Model Lunik, 238
Piotti Model Monte Carlo, 237
Piotti Model Piuma, 237
Pocket Police 1862 Revolver, 252
Poly Tech AK-47/S Auto Rifle, 165
Poly Tech AKS-762 Folding Stock, 165
Poly Tech AKS-762 Rifle, 166
Poly Tech M-14/S Auto Rifle, 165

R

RPM XL Single Shot Pistol, 159
RSR/Anschutz Woodchucker Rifle, 208
RWS/Diana Model 5G Air Pistol, 269
RWS/Diana Model 5GS Air Pistol, 269
RWS/Diana Model 6M Match Pistol, 269
RWS/Diana Model 10 Match Pistol, 269
RWS/Diana Model 24, 34 Rifles, 279
RWS/Diana Model 36, 38 Rifles, 279
RWS/Diana Model 45 Air Rifle, 279
RWS/Diana Model 52 Rifle, 279
RWS/Diana Model 75KT 01 Running Boar, 279
RWS/Diana Model 75T 01, 75UT 01, 75 U 01, 279
Rahn Deer Series, 183
Rahn Elk Series Rifle, 183
Rahn Himalayan Series Rifle, 183
Rahn Safari Series Rifle, 183
Ranger Model 1911A1 Pistol, 126
Raven MP-25 Pistol, 125
Record Champion Air Pistol, 269
Record Jumbo Air Pistol, 269
Remington Model Seven, 184
Remington Model Seven Custom KS, 185
Remington Model Seven FS, 185
Remington Model 11-87 Premier, 218
Remington Model 11-87 Premier Trap, 218
Remington Model 11-87 Premier Skeet, 218
Remington Model 11-87 Special Purpose Deer Gun, 218
Remington Model 11-87 Special Purpose Magnum, 218
Remington Model 541-T Rifle, 209
Remington Model 552BDL Rifle, 202
Remington Model 572BDL Fieldmaster, · 204
Remington Model 581-S "Sportsman," 209
Remington Model 700ADL, 183
Remington Model 700 AS, 184
Remington Model 700BDL, 184
Remington Model 700BDL Left Hand, 183
Remington Model 700BDL Varmint Special, 184
Remington Model 700 Classic, 184
Remington Model 700 Custom KS Mountain Rifle, 184
Remington Model 700 Mountain Rifle, 184
Remington Model 700 Safari, 184
Remington Model 870 Express, 222
Remington Model 870 High Grade, 222
Remington Model 870 Small Gauges, 222
Remington Model 870 Special Field, 222
Remington Model 870 Special Purpose, Deer, 221
Remington Model 870 Special Purpose Magnum, 222

Remington Model 870 TC Trap, 221
Remington Model 870 Wingmaster, Deer, Youth, 221
Remington Model 870P Police, 245
Remington Model 1100 Auto, 218
Remington Model 1100 LT-20, Small Gauge, 218
Remington Model 1100 Special Field, 219
Remington Model 1100 Tournament Skeet, 219
Remington Model 1100 20 Ga., Deer Gun, 219
Remington Model 1100D Tournament, 218
Remington Model 1100F Premier, 218
Remington Model 7400 Auto, 169
Remington Model 7600 Pump, 172
Remington Parker AHE Double, 238
Remington SP10 Magnum Auto Shotgun, 217
Remington Sportsman 78, 184
Remington XP-100 Custom Long Range Pistol, 159
Remington XP-100 Silhouette Pistol, 137
Remington XP-100 Varmint Special, 159
Remington 40-XB-BR, 213
Remington 40-XB KS Varmint Special, 213
Remington 40-XB Rangemaster CF, 213
Remington 40-XC, 40-XC KS National Match, 213
Remington 40-XR Position Rifle, 213
Remington 40-XR Rimfire Custom Sporter, 208
Rigby-Style Target Rifle, 262
Rizzini Boxlock Double, 238
Rizzini Sidelock Double, 238
Rogers & Spencer Revolver, 253
Rossi Model 59, 62 SA Pump, 204
Rossi Model 62 SAC Carbine, 204
Rossi Model 68, 68/2 Revolvers, 143
Rossi Model 88, 88/2, 89 Revolvers, 143
Rossi Model 92 Puma SRS Short Carbine, 172
Rossi Model 92 Saddle Ring Carbine, 172
Rossi Model 511 Sportsman's 22 Revolver, 143
Rossi Model 851, 951 Revolvers, 144
Rossi Model 971 Revolver, 144
Rossi Squire Double, 238
Ruger GP-100 Revolver, 144
Ruger Mini-14/5F Folding Stock, 166
Ruger Mini-14/5R Ranch Rifle, 166
Ruger Mini Thirty Rifle, 166
Ruger Mk II Bull Barrel, 137
Ruger Mk II Gov't. Target, 137
Ruger Mk II Standard Auto, 126
Ruger Mk II Target Model, 137
Ruger Model 77 Mark II Magnum, 185
Ruger Model 77 Mark II Rifle, 185
Ruger Model 77R, 185
Ruger Model 77RL Ultra Light, 185
Ruger Model 77RLS Ultra Light Carbine, 185
Ruger Model 77RS Magnum, 185
Ruger Model 77RS Tropical, 185
Ruger Model 77RSI International, 185
Ruger Model 77V Varmint, 186
Ruger Model 77/22 Rifle, 209
Ruger New Model Bisley, 154
Ruger New Model Blackhawk, 153
Ruger New Model Single-Six, 154
Ruger New Model Super Blackhawk, 153
Ruger New Model Super Single-Six, 154
Ruger No.1A Light Sporter, 193
Ruger No.1B Single Shot, 193
Ruger No.1H Tropical Rifle, 193

Ruger No.1RSI International, 193
Ruger No.1S Medium Sporter, 193
Ruger No.1V Special Varminter, 193
Ruger P-85 Pistol, 126
Ruger Redhawk Revolver, 144
Ruger Red Label O/U, 230
Ruger Small Frame New Model Bisley, 154
Ruger SP-101 Revolvers, 144
Ruger Super Redhawk, 144
Ruger 10/22 Carbine, 202
Ruger 10/22 Sporter, 202
Ruger 44 Old Army Revolver, 253

S

SIG P-210-2 Auto Pistol, 127
SIG P-210-6 Auto Pistol, 127
SIG SG550SP Auto Rifle, 166
SIG-Sauer P220 DA Pistol, 127
SIG-Sauer P225 DA Pistol, 127
SIG-Sauer P226 DA Pistol, 127
SIG-Sauer P230 DA Pistol, 127
SKB Model 200, 200E, 400 Doubles, 238
SKB Model 505, 505 Trap, Skeet, Skeet Set, 230
SKB Model 605, 605 Trap, Skeet, Skeet Set, 230
SKB Model 885 Trap, Skeet, 230
SKB Model 1300 Auto Shotgun, 219
SKB Model 1900 Auto Shotgun, 219
SKB Model 1900 Trap Shotgun, 219
SKB Model 3000 Auto Shotgun, 219
Safari Arms Enforcer Pistol, 126
Safari Arms Matchmaster Pistol, 126
Sako Carbine, Fiberclass Carbine, 186
Sako Deluxe Sporter, 187
Sako Fiberclass Sporter, 186
Sako Heavy Barrel, 186
Sako Hunter, Left Hand, 186
Sako Hunter LS Rifle, 186
Sako Mannlicher-Style Carbine, 186
Sako Safari Grade, 186
Sako Super Deluxe Sporter, 186
Sam Inc Model 88 Crossfire, 245
Santfl Schuetzen Target Rifle, 261
Sauer Model 90 Rifle, 187
Savage Model 24-F Combo, 197
Savage Model 24F-12T Turkey, 197
Savage Model 24-V, 197
Savage Model 99C Lever Action, 173
Savage Model 110B, 187
Savage Model 110F, 110FX, 187
Savage Model 110G, 110G-X, 187
Savage Model 110-GV, 187
Savage Model 389 Combo, 198
Scarab Skorpion Pistol, 126
Second Model Brown Bess, 254
Sedco SP-22 Pistol, 127
Seecamp LWS 32 Pistol, 127
C. Sharps New Model 1875 Rifle, 193
C. Sharps 1875 Classic Sharps, 193
Sheridan Blue, Silver Streak Rifles, 280
Sheridan CO$_2$ Rifles, 280
Sheridan HB Pneumatic Pistol, 270
Sheriff 1851 Revolver, 251
Shiloh Sharps Sporting Rifles 1, 3, 194
Shiloh Sharps The Jaeger Rifle, 194
Shiloh Sharps 1862 Confederate Carbine, 261
Shiloh Sharps 1863 Military Rifle, Carbine, 261
Shiloh Sharps 1863 Sporting Rifle, 261
Shiloh Sharps 1874 Business, Carbine, Saddle Rifles, 194
Shiloh Sharps 1874 Long Range Express, 194

Shiloh Sharps 1874 Military Carbine, 194
Shiloh Sharps 1874 Military Rifle, 194
Shiloh Sharps 1874 Montana Roughrider, 194
Sile Deluxe Percussion Shotgun, 264
Sile Field King Super Light, Hunter, Slug Master, 231
Sile Field Master II, Hunter I, II, 230
Sile Folding Hunter, 242
Sile Protector Single, 242
Sile Sky Stalker O/U, 231
Sile Trap, Field, Skeet Kings, 231
Sile Valley Combo Gun, 198
Simson/Suhl Model 70E, 74E, 76E, 239
Simson/Suhl Model 85 EJ, EU, 231
Smith & Wesson Model 10, 145
Smith & Wesson Model 10 H.B., 145
Smith & Wesson Model 13 H.B., 65, 145
Smith & Wesson Model 15, 145
Smith & Wesson Model 17 K-22, 145
Smith & Wesson Model 19, 145
Smith & Wesson Model 25, 145
Smith & Wesson Model 27, 146
Smith & Wesson Model 29 Silhouette, 137
Smith & Wesson Model 29, 629, 146
Smith & Wesson Model 31, 146
Smith & Wesson Model 34, 63, 146
Smith & Wesson Model 36, 37, 146
Smith & Wesson Model 36, 60 Lady Smith, 146
Smith & Wesson Model 38, 146
Smith & Wesson Model 41 Target, 138
Smith & Wesson Model 49, 649, 146
Smith & Wesson Model 52, 138
Smith & Wesson Model 57, 657, 147
Smith & Wesson Model 60, 146
Smith & Wesson Model 64, 147
Smith & Wesson Model 66, 147
Smith & Wesson Model 422 Pistol, 128
Smith & Wesson Model 586, 686, 147
Smith & Wesson Model 625-2, 145
Smith & Wesson Model 686 Classic Hunter, 147
Smith & Wesson Model 686 Midnight Black, 147
Smith & Wesson Model 745, 137
Smith & Wesson Model 3904/3906, 128
Smith & Wesson Model 4506/4516, 128
Smith & Wesson Model 5904/5906, 128
Smith & Wesson Model 6904/6906, 128
Snake Charmer Shotgun, 242
Sokolovsky 45 Automaster, 138
Spiller & Burr Revolver, 253
Sportarms Model HS21S SA, 154
Sportarms Model HS38S Revolver, 147
Sportarms Tokarev Model 213 Pistol, 128
Springfield Armory BM-59, 167
Springfield Armory M-1 Garand, M-1 T26, 167
Springfield Armory M1-A, 167
Springfield Armory M1-A Super Match, 214
Springfield Armory M-21 Sniper, 213
Springfield Armory P9 Compact Pistol, 129
Springfield Armory P9 Pistol, 129
Springfield Armory SAR-3 Retractable Stock, 166
Springfield Armory SAR-3 Rifle, 166
Springfield Armory SAR-48, 167
Springfield Armory 1911A1 Commander, 129
Springfield Armory 1911A1 Compact, 129
Springfield Armory 1911A1 Defender Pistol, 129
Springfield Armory 1911A1 Pistol, 129
Springfield Armory 1911A2 S.A.S.S., 159

Star Model BM, BKM Pistols, 130
Star Model PD Pistol, 129
Star Model 30M, 30PK Pistols, 130
Steel City Double Deuce Pistol, 130
Steel City War Eagle Pistol, 130
Sterling HR-81/HR-83 Air Rifles, 280
Steyr A.U.G. Rifle, 167
Steyr-Mannlicher Luxus, 188
Steyr-Mannlicher Match UIT, 214
Steyr-Mannlicher Model M, Professional, 187
Steyr-Mannlicher Model S, S/T, 188
Steyr-Mannlicher Model SL, L, 188
Steyr-Mannlicher SSG Marksman, SSG PII, 214
Steyr-Mannlicher SSG Match, 214
Steyr-Mannlicher Varmint SL, L, 188
Stoeger/IGA Double, Coach Gun, 239
Stoeger/IGA O/U, 231
Stoeger/IGA Single, 242
Sundance Model A-25 Pistol, 130
Super Six Golden Bison Revolver, 154

T

Tanarmi Baby Tayida Pistol, 130
Tanarmi Tayida Pistol, 130
Tanarmi TA76/TA22 SA, 154
Targa GT22, GT32, GT380 Pistols, 131
Targa GT22 Target Pistol, 131
Targa GT26 Pistol, 131
Targa GT27 Pistol, 131
Targa GT380XE Pistol, 131
Taurus Model 65, 66, 148
Taurus Model 73, 148
Taurus Model 80, 148
Taurus Model 82 H.B., 148
Taurus Model 83, 148
Taurus Model 85, 148
Taurus Model 86 Master, 96 Scout Master, 138
Taurus Model 94 H.B., 149
Taurus Model 669, 149
Taurus PT58 Pistol, 131
Taurus PT-92AF Pistol, 131
Taurus PT-99AF Pistol, 131
Techni-Mec SPL 640, 642 Folding O/Us, 231
Techni-Mec SR 692 EM, Slug O/Us, 231
Texas Longhorn Border Special, 155
Texas Longhorn Cased Set, 155
Texas Longhorn Grover's Improved No. 5, 155
Texas Longhorn R.H. SA, 155
Texas Longhorn Sesquicentennial Model, 155
Texas Longhorn The Jezebel, 159
Texas Longhorn West Texas Flat Top Target, 155
Texas Paterson 1836, 250
Theoben-Prometheus Super Sirocco, Grand Prix, Eliminator, 280
Theoben Sirocco Classic, Grand Prix, 280
Theoben Sirocco Eliminator, 280
Thompson/Center Cherokee Rifle, 257
Thompson/Center Contender, 160
Thompson/Center Contender Carbine, 194
Thompson/Center Hawken Rifle, 257
Thompson/Center New Englander Rifle, 257
Thompson/Center New Englander Shotgun, 264
Thompson/Center Pennsylvania Hunter, 254
Thompson/Center Renegade Hunter, 257
Thompson/Center Renegade Rifle, 257

Thompson/Center Super 14 Contender, 138
Thompson/Center Super 16 Contender, 138
Thompson/Center TCR '87, 194
Thompson/Center TCR '87 Hunter Shotgun, 242
Thompson/Center White Mountain Carbine, 257
Thompson/Center Youth Contender Carbine, 194
Tikka Bolt-Action Rifle, 188
Tradewinds H-170 Auto, 219
Tradewinds Model 260-A Rifle, 202
Traditions Hawken, 259
Traditions Hunter, Frontier Rifle, Carbine, 113
Traditions Pennsylvania, Rifle, 255
Traditions Pioneer Rifle, 262
Traditions Trapper, Frontier Scout Rifles, 256
Traditions Trapper Pistol, 249
Traditions Trophy Rifle, 262
Trail Guns Kodiak 10 Ga. Shotgun, 264
Tryon Rifle, 257
Tryon Trailblazer Rifle, 255

U

USAS-12 Auto Shotgun, 245
Uberti Confederate Tucker & Sherrard, 250
Uberti Henry Rifle, 173
Uberti Inspector Revolver, 149
Uberti Phantom Silhouette Pistol, 139
Uberti Rolling Block Carbine, 194
Uberti Rolling Block Pistol, 160
Uberti Santa Fe Hawken, 256
Uberti 1st Model Dragoon, 250
Uberti 2nd Model Dragoon, 250
Uberti 3rd Model Dragoon, 250
Uberti 1858 New Army Revolving Carbine, 259
Uberti 1861 Navy, 251
Uberti 1862 Pocket Navy, 252
Uberti 1866 Red Cloud Commemorative, 173
Uberti 1866 Sporting Rifle, 173
Uberti 1866 Trapper's Model Carbine, 173
Uberti 1866 Yellowboy Carbine, 173
Uberti 1866 Yellowboy Indian Carbine, 173
Uberti 1873 Buckhorn Revolving Carbine, 173
Uberti 1873 Buckhorn SA, 155
Uberti 1873 Buntline SA, 156
Uberti 1873 Cattleman Revolving Carbine, 173
Uberti 1873 Cattleman SAs, 155
Uberti 1873 Sporting Rifle, 173
Uberti 1873 Stallion SA, 156
Uberti 1875 Army Outlaw SA, 156
Uberti 1875 Revolving Carbine, 173
Uberti 1890 Outlaw SA, 156
Ultra Light Model 20, 24, 188
Ultra Light Model 20 REB Pistol, 160
Ultra Light Model 20S, 188
Ultra Light Model 28, 188
UZI Carbine, 168
UZI Mini Carbine, 168
UZI Pistol, 132

V

Valmet Hunter Auto, 169
Valmet M-76 Auto Rifle, 168
Valmet M-78 Auto Rifle, 168

Valmet 412S Combo, 198
Valmet 412S Double Rifle, 198
Valmet 412S Field O/U, 231
Valmet 412ST Trap, Skeet, 231
Varner Favorite Schuetzen, 209
Varner Favorite Single Shot, 209
Victory Model MC5 Pistol, 132
Voere Model 1007/1013 Rifles, 209
Voere Model 2115 Rifle, 203
Voere 2155, 2165 Rifles, 188

W

Walker 1847 Percussion, 250
Walther American PPK Pistol, 132
Walther American PPK/S Pistol, 132
Walther CG 90 Air Rifle, 280
Walther CP CO$_2$ Air Pistol, 270
Walther Free Pistol, 139
Walther GSP, GSP-C, 139
Walther GX-1 Match, 214
Walther KK/MS Silhouette, 214
Walther LGR Running Boar Air Rifle, 280
Walther LGR Universal Match Air Rifle, 280
Walther Model TPH Pistol, 133
Walther OSP Rapid Fire, 139
Walther P-5 Pistol, 133
Walther P-38 Pistol, 133
Walther P-88 Auto Pistol, 132
Walther PP Pistol, 132
Walther Running Boar Match, 215
Walther U.I.T. BV Universal, 214
Walther U.I.T. Match, 215
Weatherby Athena O/U, 232
Weatherby Athena Trap, 242
Weatherby Euromark Rifle, 190
Weatherby Fibermark Rifle, 189
Weatherby Lazermark Mark V Rifle, 189
Weatherby Mark V Crown Custom, 189
Weatherby Mark V Rifle, Left Hand, 189
Weatherby Mark V Safari Grade, 189
Weatherby Mark V Ultramark, 189
Weatherby Mark XXII Clip Model, 203
Weatherby Mark XXII Tube Model, 203
Weatherby Orion O/U, 232
Weatherby Vanguard Classic I, II, 190
Weatherby Vanguard VGX Deluxe, 190
Weatherby Vanguard Weatherguard, 190
Dan Wesson Action Cup, PPC Revolvers, 139
Dan Wesson Model 8-2, 14-2, 149
Dan Wesson Model 9-2, 15-2, 32M, 149
Dan Wesson Model 15 Gold Series, 149
Dan Wesson Model 22, 149
Dan Wesson Model 40 Silhouette, 139
Dan Wesson Model 44V, 45V, 149
Whitworth Safari Express, 190
Wichita Classic Pistol, 140
Wichita Classic Rifle, 190
Wichita Hunter Pistol, 139
Wichita International Pistol, 139
Wichita Mk-40 Silhouette, 139
Wichita Silhouette Pistol, 140
Wichita Silhouette Rifle, 215
Wichita Varmint Rifle, 191
Wildey Auto Pistol, 133
Wilkinson Linda Pistol, 133
Wilkinson Sherry Pistol, 133
Winchester Defender Pump, 245
Winchester Model 70 Featherweight, 192
Winchester Model 70 H.B. Varmint, 191
Winchester Model 70 Lightweight, 191
Winchester Model 70 Sporter, 191
Winchester Model 70 Super Express, 191
Winchester Model 70 Winlite, 191
Winchester Model 94 Big Bore Side Eject, 173

Winchester Model 94 Side Eject, 174
Winchester Model 94 7x30 Waters, 174
Winchester Model 1300 Feather-
    weight, 222
Winchester Model 1300 Rifled Deer
    Gun, 222
Winchester Model 1300 Turkey, 222
Winchester Model 1300 Waterfowl, 222
Winchester Model 1400 Ranger,
    Deer, 219
Winchester Model 9422, 9422M, 204
Winchester Pistol Grip Pump Secu-

rity, 245
Winchester Ranger Bolt Rifle, 191
Winchester Ranger Pump, Combo, 222
Winchester Ranger Pump, Youth, 222
Winchester Ranger Side Eject Car-
    bine, 174
Winchester Stainless Marine Pump, 245

Z
Pietro Zanoletti 2000 Field, 232
A. Zoli Angel Field Grade, Condor, 232

A. Zoli Delfino S.P. O/U, 232
A. Zoli O/U Combo, 198
Zoli Model AZ-1900 Rifle, 192
Zoli Silver Falcon O/U, 232
Zoli Silver Fox Double, 239
Zoli Z90 Mono-Trap, 243
Zoli Z90 Skeet, 233
Zoli Z90 Sporting Clays, 233
Zoli Z90 Trap, 233
Zoli Uplander Double, 239
Zoli Woodsman O/U, 233
Zouave Percussion Rifle, 261

GUNDEX® Departments

Auto Handguns—Service & Sport . . .112-133
Competition Handguns 134-140
Revolvers—Service & Sport 140-149
Single-Action Revolvers 150-156
Miscellaneous Handguns 156-160
Centerfire Military Auto Rifles 160-168
Centerfire Sporting Auto Rifles 168-169
Centerfire Lever, Slide & Misc 170-174
Centerfire Bolt Actions 174-192
Centerfire Single Shots 192-194
Drillings, Combos, Double Rifles 195-198
Rimfire Auto Rifles 198-203
Rimfire Lever & Slide Actions 203-204
Rimfire Bolt Actions & Single Shots . .205-209

Competition Rifles 210-215
Auto Shotguns 215-219
Pump Shotguns 219-222
Over/Under Shotguns 223-233
Side-By-Side Shotguns 233-239
Bolt-Action & Single Shot Shotguns .239-243
Military & Police Shotguns 243-245
Blackpowder Pistols 246-249
Blackpowder Revolvers 250-253
Blackpowder Muskets, Rifles 254-263
Blackpowder Shotguns 263-264
Air Pistols .265-270
Air Rifles 270-280

Includes models suitable for several forms of competition and other sporting purposes.

AA ARMS AP9 AUTO PISTOL
Caliber: 9mm Para., 20-shot magazine.
Barrel: 5″.
Weight: 3.5 lbs. **Length:** 11.8″ overall.
Stocks: Checkered plastic.
Sights: Adjustable post front in ring, fixed open rear.
Features: Matte blue/black finish. Lever safety blocks trigger and sear. Fires from closed bolt. Introduced 1988. made in U.S. by AA Arms, Inc.
Price: $275.00

Action Arms AT-88S

ACTION ARMS AT-88S DA PISTOLS
Caliber: 9mm Para., 15 shots; 41 Action Express, 10 shots.
Barrel: 4.72″.
Weight: 35.3 oz. **Length:** 8.1″ overall.
Stocks: Checkered walnut.
Sights: Blade front, rear drift-adjustable for windage.
Features: Double action; polished blue finish. Introduced 1987. Imported from England by Action Arms Ltd.
Price: $598.00
Price: Model 88P (3.66″ bbl., 7.24″ o.a.l., weighs 32.1 oz., and has 13/8-shot magazine $598.00
Price: Model 88H (3.5″ bbl., 6.9″ o.a.l., weighs 30.5 oz. and has 10/7-shot magazine) $598.00

AMT AUTOMAG II AUTO PISTOL
Caliber: 22 WMR, 10-shot magazine.
Barrel: 3⅜″, 4½″, 6″.
Weight: About 23 oz. **Length:** 9⅜″ overall.
Stocks: Smooth black composition.
Sights: Blade front, Millett adjustable rear.
Features: Made of stainless steel. Gas-assisted action. Exposed hammer. Slide flats have brushed finish, rest is sandblast. Squared trigger guard. Introduced 1986. From AMT.
Price: $329.00

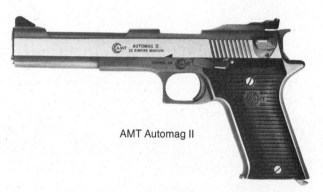

AMT Automag II

AMT 45 ACP HARDBALLER LONG SLIDE
Caliber: 45 ACP.
Barrel: 7″. **Length:** 10½″ overall.
Stocks: Wrap-around rubber.
Sights: Fully adjustable rear sight.
Features: Slide and barrel are 2″ longer than the standard 45, giving less recoil, added velocity, longer sight radius. Has extended combat safety, serrated matte rib, loaded chamber indicator, wide adjustable trigger. From AMT.
Price: $524.00

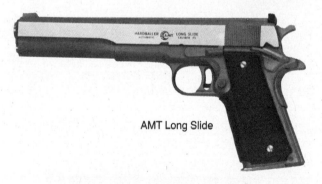

AMT Long Slide

AMT 45 ACP HARDBALLER
Caliber: 45 ACP.
Barrel: 5″.
Weight: 39 oz. **Length:** 8½″ overall.
Stocks: Wrap-around rubber.
Sights: Adjustable.
Features: Extended combat safety, serrated matte slide rib, loaded chamber indicator, long grip safety, beveled magazine well, adjustable target trigger. All stainless steel. From AMT.
Price: $490.00
Price: Government model (as above except no rib, fixed sights) $446.00

American Arms PK22

AMERICAN ARMS PK22 DA AUTO PISTOL
Caliber: 22 LR, 8-shot magazine.
Barrel: 3.3″.
Weight: 22 oz. **Length:** 6.3″ overall.
Stocks: Checkered plastic.
Sights: Fixed
Features: Double action. Polished blue finish. Slide-mounted safety. Made in the U.S. by American Arms, Inc.
Price: $199.00

CAUTION: PRICES CHANGE. CHECK AT GUNSHOP.

AMERICAN ARMS PX-22 AUTO PISTOL
Caliber: 22 LR, 7-shot magazine.
Barrel: 2.85".
Weight: 15 oz. **Length:** 5.39" overall.
Stocks: Black checkered plastic.
Sights: Fixed.
Features: Double action; 7-shot magazine. Polished blue finish. Introduced 1989. Made in U.S. From American Arms, Inc.
Price: **$189.00**

American Arms PX-22

AMERICAN ARMS TT9MM AUTO PISTOL
Caliber: 9mm Para., 9-shot magazine.
Barrel: 4.5".
Weight: 32 oz. **Length:** 8" overall.
Stocks: Grooved plastic
Sights: Fixed.
Features: Single-action mechanism. Blue finish. Imported from Yugoslavia by American Arms, Inc. Introduced 1988.
Price: **$289.00**

AMERICAN ARMS EP380 AUTO PISTOL
Caliber: 380 ACP, 7-shot magazine.
Barrel: 3¹/₂".
Weight: 25 oz. **Length:** 6¹/₂" overall.
Stocks: Checkered wood.
Sights: Fixed.
Features: Double action. Made of stainless steel. Slide-mounted safety. Imported from West Germany by American Arms, Inc. Introduced in 1988.
Price: **$449.00**

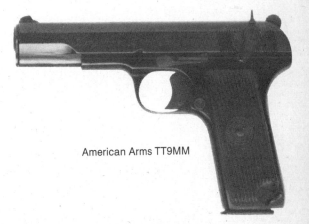
American Arms TT9MM

AMERICAN ARMS ZC380 AUTO PISTOL
Caliber: 380 ACP, 8-shot magazine.
Barrel: 3.75"
Weight: 26 oz. **Length:** 6.5" overall.
Stocks: Checkered plastic.
Sights: Fixed.
Features: Single-action mechanism. Polished blue finish. Imported from Yugoslavia by American Arms, Inc. Introduced 1988.
Price: **$289.00**

Astra Constable

American Arms ZC380

Astra A-60

ASTRA CONSTABLE AUTO PISTOL
Caliber: 22 LR, 10-shot; 380 ACP, 7-shot.
Barrel: 3¹/₂".
Weight: 26 oz.
Stocks: Moulded plastic.
Sights: Adjustable rear.
Features: Double action, quick no-tool takedown, non-glare rib on slide. 380 available in blue, stainless steel, or chrome finish. Engraved guns also available—contact the importer. Imported from Spain by Interarms.
Price: Blue, 22. . . . . **$365.00**
Price: Chrome, 22 . . . . **$375.00**
Price: Blue, 380 . . . . **$350.00**

Astra A-60 Double-Action Pistol
Similar to the Constable except in 380 only, with 13-shot magazine, slide-mounted ambidextrous safety. Available in blued steel only. Introduced 1980.
Price: **$435.00**

CAUTION: PRICES CHANGE. CHECK AT GUNSHOP.

ASTRA A-90 DOUBLE-ACTION AUTO PISTOL
Caliber: 9mm Para. (15-shot), 45 ACP (9-shot).
Barrel: 3.75″.
Weight: 40 oz. **Length:** 7″ overall.
Stocks: Checkered black plastic.
Sights: Square blade front, square notch rear drift-adjustable for windage.
Features: Double or single action; loaded chamber indicator; combat-style trigger guard; optional right-side slide release (for left-handed shooters); automatic internal safety; decocking lever. Introduced 1985. Imported from Spain by Interarms.
Price: Blue **$500.00**

Astra A-90 Pistol

AUTO-ORDNANCE 1911A1 AUTOMATIC PISTOL
Caliber: 9mm Para., 38 Super, 9-shot; 45 ACP, 7-shot magazine.
Barrel: 5″.
Weight: 39 oz. **Length:** 8¹/₂″ overall.
Stocks: Checkered plastic with medallion.
Sights: Blade front, rear adjustable for windage.
Features: Same specs as 1911A1 military guns—parts interchangeable. Frame and slide blued; each radius has non-glare finish. Made in U.S. by Auto-Ordnance Corp.
Price: 45 cal. **$348.95**
Price: 9mm, 38 Super **$385.95**

Auto-Ordnance ZG-51 Pit Bull Auto
Same as the 1911A1 except has 3¹/₂″ barrel, weighs 36 oz. and has a overall length of 7¹/₄″. Available in 45 ACP only; 7-shot magazine. Introduced 1989.
Price: **$385.95**

Auto-Ordnance 1911A1

BEEMAN MODEL P-08 AUTO PISTOL
Caliber: 22 LR, 8-shot magazine.
Barrel: 4″.
Weight: 25 oz. **Length:** 7³/₄″ overall.
Stocks: Checkered hardwood.
Sights: Fixed.
Features: Has toggle action similar to original "Luger" pistol. Action stays open after last shot. Imported from West Germany by Beeman.
Price: **$389.50**

BEEMAN MINI P-08 AUTO PISTOL
Caliber: 380 ACP (5-shot).
Barrel: 3.5″.
Weight: 22¹/₂″ **Length:** 7³/₈″ overall.
Stocks: Checkered hardwood.
Sights: Fixed.
Features: Toggle action similar to original "Luger" pistol. Action stays open after last shot. Has magazine and sear disconnect safety systems. Imported from West Germany by Beeman.
Price: **$389.50**

Auto-Ordnance Pit Bull

> Consult our Directory pages for the location of firms mentioned.

BERNARDELLI MODEL USA AUTO PISTOL
Caliber: 22 LR, 10-shot; 380 ACP, 7-shot.
Barrel: 3¹/₂″.
Weight: 26¹/₂ oz. **Length:** 6¹/₂″ overall.
Stocks: Checkered plastic with thumbrest.
Sights: Ramp front, white outline rear adjustable for w. & e.
Features: Hammer-block slide safety; loaded chamber indicator; dual recoil buffer springs; serrated trigger; inertia-type firing pin. Imported from Italy by Magnum Research, Inc.
Price: **$289.00**
Price: Model AMR (as above except has 6″ bbl., target sights) **$309.00**

Beeman Mini P-O8

BERNARDELLI PO18 DA PISTOL
Caliber: 9mm Para., 16-shot magazine.
Barrel: 4.8".
Weight: 36.3 oz. **Length:** 6.2" overall.
Stocks: Checkered, contoured plastic standard; walnut optional.
Sights: Low profile combat sights.
Features: Manual thumb safety, half-cock, magazine safeties, auto-locking firing pin block safety; ambidextrous magazine release. Introduced 1987. Imported from Italy by Magnum Research, Inc.
Price: With plastic grips **$499.00**
Price: With walnut grips **$539.00**
Price: Compact model (4" bbl., 14-shot) **$519.00**

Bernardelli PO 18

BERETTA MODEL 92F PISTOL
Caliber: 9mm Para., 15-shot magazine.
Barrel: 4.9".
Weight: 34 oz. **Length:** 8.5" overall.
Stocks: Checkered black plastic; wood optional at extra cost.
Sights: Blade front, rear adjustable for w.
Features: Double action. Extractor acts as chamber loaded indicator, squared trigger guard, grooved front- and backstraps, inertia firing pin. Matte finish. Introduced 1977. Imported from Italy by Beretta U.S.A.
Price: With plastic grips **$600.00**
Price: With wood grips **$627.00**

Beretta Model 92FC Pistol
Similar to the Beretta Model 92F except has cut down frame, 4.3" barrel, 7.8" overall length, 13-shot magazine, weighs 31.5 oz. Introduced 1989.
Price: With plastic grips **$620.00**
Price: With wood grips **$647.00**

Beretta Model 92F

BERETTA 80 SERIES DA PISTOLS
Caliber: 380 ACP, 13-shot magazine; 22 LR, 7-shot (M87).
Barrel: 3.82"
Weight: About 23 oz. (M84/85), 20.8 oz. (M87). **Length:** 6.8" overall.
Stocks: Glossy black plastic (wood optional at extra cost).
Sights: Fixed front, drift-adjustable rear.
Features: Double action, quick takedown, convenient magazine release. Introduced 1977. Imported from Italy by Beretta U.S.A.
Price: Model 84 (380 ACP) **$467.00**
Price: Model 84 wood grips **$493.00**
Price: Model 84 nickel finish **$533.00**
Price: Model 85 nickel finish **$480.00**
Price: Model 85 plastic grips **$413.00**
Price: Model 85 wood grips **$440.00**
Price: Model 87, 22 LR, 7-shot magazine, wood grips **$447.00**
Price: Model 87 Long Barrel, 22 LR, single action **$460.00**
Price: Model 89 Sport Wood, single action, 22 LR **$620.00**

Beretta Model 86
Similar to the 380-caliber Model 85 except has tip-up barrel for first-round loading. Barrel length is 4.33", overall length of 7.33". Has 8-shot magazine, walnut or plastic grips. Introduced 1989.
Price: **$480.00**

Beretta Model 86

Beretta Models 84F/85F
Similar to the Beretta 84/85 except both have combat-style frame with grooved trigger guard, manual safety with decocking device, plastic grips, matte black Bruniton finish. Introduced 1989.
Price: Model 84F **$474.00**
Price: Model 85F **$447.00**

BERETTA MODEL 950 BS AUTO PISTOL
Caliber: 22 Short, 6-shot; 25 ACP, 8-shot.
Barrel: 2.5".
Weight: 9.9 oz. (22 Short, 10.2 oz.) **Length:** 4.5" overall.
Stocks: Checkered black plastic.
Sights: Fixed.
Features: Single action, thumb safety; tip-up barrel for direct loading/unloading, cleaning. From Beretta U.S.A.
Price: Blue, 25 . . . . **$153.00**
Price: Blue, 22 . . . . **$153.00**
Price: Engraved **$220.00**

Beretta Model 84F

Beretta Model 21 Pistol

Similar to the Model 950 BS. Chambered for 22 LR and 25 ACP. Both double action. 2.5″ barrel, 4.9″ overall length. 7-round magazine on 22 cal.; 8-round magazine on 25 cal.; 22 cal. available in nickel finish. Both have walnut grips. Introduced in 1985.

Price: 22 cal. **$205.00**
Price: 22 cal, nickel finish **$227.00**
Price: 25 cal. **$205.00**
Price: EL model, 22 or 25 . . . . **$237.00**

Beretta Model 21

BERSA MODEL 85 AUTO PISTOL

Caliber: 380 ACP, 13-shot magazine.
Barrel: 3.5″.
Weight: 25.75 oz. **Length:** 6.6″ overall.
Stocks: Walnut with stippled panels.
Sights: Blade front, notch rear adjustable for windage.
Features: Double action; firing pin and magazine safeties. Available in blue or nickel. Introduced 1989. Imported from Argentina by Eagle Imports, Inc.
Price: Blue **$349.95**
Price: Nickel **$366.95**
Price: Model 83 (as above, except 7-shot magazine), blue **$263.95**
Price: Model 83, nickel **$288.95**

Bersa Model 85

BERSA MODEL 23 AUTO PISTOL

Caliber: 22 LR, 10-shot magazine.
Barrel: 3.5″.
Weight: 24.5 oz. **Length:** 6.6″ overall.
Stocks: Walnut with stippled panels.
Sights: Blade front, notch rear adjustable for windage.
Features: Double action; firing pin and magazine safeties. Available in blue or nickel. Introduced 1989. Imported from Argentina by Eagle Imports, Inc.
Price: Blue **$263.95**
Price: Nickel **$288.95**

BRNO CZ 83 DOUBLE-ACTION PISTOL

Caliber: 32, 15-shot; 380, 13-shot.
Barrel: 3.7″.
Weight: 26.5 oz. **Length:** 6.7″ overall.
Stocks: Checkered black plastic.
Sights: Blade front, rear adjustable for w.
Features: Double action; ambidextrous magazine release and safety. Polished or matte blue. Imported from Czechoslovakia by TD Arms.
Price: **$425.00**

BRNO CZ 75 AUTO PISTOL

Caliber: 9mm Para., 15-shot magazine.
Barrel: 4.7″.
Weight: 35 oz. **Length:** 8″ overall.
Stocks: Checkered wood.
Sights: Blade front, rear adjustable for w.
Features: Double action; blued finish. Imported from Czechoslovakia by TD Arms.
Price: **$599.00**

BRNO CZ 85 Auto Pistol

Same gun as the CZ 75 except has ambidextrous slide release and safety-levers, is available in 9mm Para. and 7.65, contoured composition grips, matte finish on top of slide. Introduced 1986.
Price: **$655.00**

BROWNING BUCK MARK 22 PISTOL

Caliber: 22 LR, 10-shot magazine.
Barrel: 5¹/₂″.
Weight: 32 oz. **Length:** 9¹/₂″ overall.
Stocks: Black moulded composite with skip-line checkering.
Sights: Ramp front, rear adjustable for w. and e.
Features: All steel, matte blue finish, gold-colored trigger. Buck Mark Plus has laminated wood grips. Made in U.S. Introduced 1985. From Browning.
Price: Buck Mark **$207.95**
Price: Buck Mark Plus **$252.95**

Browning Buck Mark Plus

Browning Buck Mark Silhouette

Browning Buck Mark Silhouette

Same as the Buck Mark except has 9⁷/₈″ heavy barrel with .900″ diameter; hooded front sight with interchangeable posts, Millett Gold Cup 360 SIL rear on a special top sighting plane. Grips and forend are black multi-laminated wood. Introduced 1987.
Price: **$352.95**

CAUTION: PRICES CHANGE. CHECK AT GUNSHOP.

Browning Buck Mark Varmint

Browning Buck Mark Varmint
Same as the Buck Mark except has 9⁷/₈″ heavy barrel with .900″ diameter and full-length scope base (no open sights); black multi-laminated wood grips, with optional forend. Over-all length is 14″, weight is 48 oz. Introduced 1987.
Price: **$318.95**

BROWNING HI-POWER 9mm AUTOMATIC PISTOL
Caliber: 9mm Para., 13-shot magazine.
Barrel: 4²¹/₃₂″.
Weight: 32 oz. **Length:** 7³/₄″ overall.
Stocks: Walnut, hand checkered, or black Polyamide.
Sights: ¹/₈″ blade front; rear screw-adjustable for w. and e. Also available with fixed rear (drift-adjustable for w).
Features: External hammer with half-cock and thumb safeties. A blow on the hammer cannot discharge a cartridge; cannot be fired with magazine removed. Fixed rear sight model available. Ambidextrous safety available only with matte finish, moulded grips. Imported from Belgium by Browning.
Price: Fixed sight model, walnut grips **$473.95**
Price: 9mm with rear sight adj. for w. and e., walnut grips **$517.95**
Price: Standard matte black finish, fixed sight, moulded grips, ambidextrous safety. **$436.95**

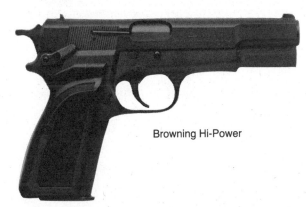

Browning Hi-Power

BROWNING BDA-380 DA AUTO PISTOL
Caliber: 380 ACP, 13-shot magazine.
Barrel: 3¹³/₁₆″.
Weight: 23 oz. **Length:** 6³/₄″ overall.
Stocks: Smooth walnut with inset Browning medallion.
Sights: Blade front, rear drift-adjustable for w.
Features: Combination safety and de-cocking lever will automatically lower a cocked hammer to half-cock and can be operated by right- or left-hand shooters. Inertia firing pin. Introduced 1978. Imported from Italy by Browning.
Price: Blue. **$452.95**
Price: Nickel **$477.95**

Browning BDA-380

Bryco Model 38

BRYCO MODEL 38 AUTO PISTOLS
Caliber: 22 LR, 32 ACP, 380 ACP, 6-shot magazine.
Barrel: 2.8″
Weight: 15 oz. **Length:** 5.3″ overall.
Stocks: Polished resin-impregnated wood.
Sights: Fixed
Features: Safety locks sear and slide. Choice of satin nickel, bright chrome or black Teflon finishes. Introduced 1988. From Jennings Firearms.
Price: 22LR, 32ACP **$109.95**
Price: 380 ACP **$129.95**

BRYCO MODEL 48 AUTO PISTOLS
Caliber: 22 LR, 32 ACP, 380 ACP, 6-shot magazine.
Barrel: 4″.
Weight: 19 oz. **Length:** 6.7″ overall.
Stocks: Polished resin-impregnated wood.
Sights: Fixed.
Features: Safety locks sear and slide. Choice of satin nickel, bright chrome or black Teflon finishes. Announced 1988. From Jennings Firearms.
Price: 22 LR, 32 ACP **$139.00**
Price: 380 ACP **$139.00**

Bryco Model 48

CAUTION: PRICES CHANGE. CHECK AT GUNSHOP.

Calico Model 100-P

CALICO MODEL 950 AUTO PISTOL
Caliber: 9mm Para., 50- or 100-shot magazine.
Barrel: 6″.
Weight: 2.25 lbs. (empty). **Length:** 14″ overall (50-shot magazine).
Stocks: Glass-filled polymer.
Sights: Post front adjustable for w. and e., fixed notch rear.
Features: Helical feed 50- or 100-shot magazine. Ambidextrous safety, static cocking handle. Retarded blowback action. Glass-filled polymer grip. Introduced 1989. From Calico.
Price: $442.95

BUSHMASTER AUTO PISTOL
Caliber: 223, 30-shot magazine.
Barrel: 11½″ (1-10″ twist).
Weight: 5¼ lbs. **Length:** 20½″ overall.
Stocks: Synthetic rotating grip swivel assembly.
Sights: Post front, adjustable open ''Y'' rear
Features: Steel alloy upper receiver with welded barrel assembly, AK-47-type gas system, aluminum lower receiver, one-piece welded steel alloy bolt carrier assembly. From Bushmaster Firearms.
Price: $339.95
Price: With matte electroless nickel finish $379.95

COLT GOV'T MODEL MK IV/SERIES 80
Caliber: 9mm, 38 Super, 45 ACP, 7-shot.
Barrel: 5″.
Weight: 38 oz. **Length:** 8½″ overall.
Stocks: Checkered walnut.
Sights: Ramp front, fixed square notch rear.
Features: Grip and thumb safeties and internal firing pin safety, grooved trigger. Accurizor barrel and bushing.
Price: Blue, 45 ACP. $593.50
Price: Bright stainless, 45 ACP. $691.95
Price: 9mm, blue only $597.50
Price: 38 Super, blue. $597.50
Price: Stainless steel, 45 ACP $628.95

Colt 10mm Delta Elite
Similar to the Government Model except chambered for 10mm auto cartridge. Has three-dot high profile front and rear combat sights, rubber combat stocks with Delta medallion, internal firing pin safety, and new recoil spring/buffer system. Introduced 1987.
Price: Blue. $657.50
Price: STS. $699.95
Price: BSTS. $762.95

COLT COMBAT COMMANDER AUTO PISTOL
Caliber: 9mm Para., 38 Super, 9-shot; 45 ACP, 7-shot.
Barrel: 4¼″.
Weight: 36 oz. **Length:** 7¾″ overall.
Stocks: Checkered walnut.
Sights: Fixed, glare-proofed blade front, square notch rear.
Features: Grooved trigger and hammer spur; arched housing; grip and thumb safeties.
Price: Blue, 9mm. $597.50
Price: Blue, 45. . . . . $593.50
Price: Blue, 38 Super $597.50

Colt Lightweight Commander Mark IV/Series 80
Same as Commander except high strength aluminum alloy frame, wood panel grips, weight 27½ oz. 45 ACP only.
Price: Blue $593.50

CALICO MODEL 110-P AUTO PISTOL
Caliber: 22 LR, 100-shot magazine.
Barrel: 6″.
Weight: 3.7 lbs. (loaded). **Length:** 17.9″ overall.
Stocks: Moulded composition.
Sights: Adjustable post front, notch rear.
Features: Aluminum alloy frame; flash suppressor; pistol grip compartment; ambidextrous safety. Uses same helical-feed magazine as M-100 Carbine. Introduced 1986. Made in U.S. From Calico.
Price: $249.95

Calico Model 950

COLT SERIES 90 DOUBLE EAGLE DA PISTOL
Caliber: 45 ACP, 8-shot magazine.
Barrel: 5″.
Weight: 39 ozs. **Length:** 8½″ overall.
Stocks: Black checkered Xenoy thermoplastic.
Sights: Blade front, rear adjustable for windage. High profile three-dot system.
Features: Made of stainless steel with matte finish. Checkered and curved extended trigger guard, wide steel trigger; decocking lever on left side; traditional magazine release; grooved front strap; bevelled magazine well; extended grip guard; rounded, serrated combat-style hammer. Announced 1989.
Price: About. $675.00

Colt Government Model

Colt Delta Elite

CAUTION: PRICES CHANGE. CHECK AT GUNSHOP.

Colt Combat Elite MK IV/Series 80

Similar to the Government Model except in 45 ACP only, has stainless frame with ordnance steel slide and internal parts. High profile front, rear sights with three-dot system, extended grip safety, beveled magazine well, rubber combat stocks. Introduced 1986.

Price: **$723.50**

Colt Combat Elite

COLT 380 GOVERNMENT MODEL

Caliber: 380 ACP, 7-shot magazine.
Barrel: 3 1/4".
Weight: 21 3/4 oz. **Length:** 6" overall.
Stocks: Checkered composition.
Sights: Ramp front, square notch rear, fixed.
Features: Scaled-down version of the 1911A1 Colt G.M. Has thumb and internal firing pin safeties. Introduced 1983.

Price: Blue.. **$383.95**
Price: Nickel **$426.50**
Price: Coltguard **$405.95**
Price: Stainless **$408.50**

Colt Mustang 380, Mustang Pocket Lite

Similar to the standard 380 Government Model. Mustang has steel frame (18.5 oz.), Pocket Lite has aluminum alloy (12.5 oz.). Both are 1/2" shorter than 380 GM, have 2 3/4" barrel. Introduced 1987.

Price: Mustang 380, blue **$383.95**
Price: As above, nickel **$426.50**
Price: As above, Coltguard **$405.95**
Price: Mustang Pocket Lite, blue **$383.95**

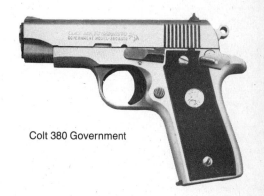

Colt 380 Government

Colt Mustang Plus II

Similar to the 380 Government Model except has the shorter barrel and slide of the Mustang. Blue finish only. Introduced 1988.

Price: **$383.95**

COLT OFFICERS ACP MK IV/SERIES 80

Caliber: 45 ACP, 6-shot magazine.
Barrel: 3 1/2".
Weight: 34 oz. **Length:** 7 1/4" overall.
Stocks: Checkered walnut.
Sights: Ramp blade front with white dot, square notch rear with two white dots.
Features: Trigger safety lock (thumb safety), grip safety, firing pin safety; grooved trigger; flat mainspring housing. Also available with lightweight alloy frame and in stainless steel. Introduced 1985.

Price: Matte finish **$576.50**
Price: Blue... **$593.50**
Price: L.W., matte finish **$593.50**
Price: Stainless **$628.95**
Price: Bright stainless **$691.95**

Coonan 357 Magnum

COONAN 357 MAGNUM PISTOL

Caliber: 357 Mag., 7-shot magazine.
Barrel: 5".
Weight: 42 oz. **Length:** 8.3" overall.
Stocks: Smooth walnut.
Sights: Open, adjustable.
Features: Unique barrel hood improves accuracy and reliability. Many parts interchange with Colt autos. Has grip, hammer, half-cock safeties. From Coonan Arms.
Price: Model B (linkless barrel, interchangeable ramp front sight, new rear sight) **$680.00**

DAVIS P-32 AUTO PISTOL

Caliber: 32 ACP, 6-shot magazine.
Barrel: 2.8".
Weight: 22 oz. **Length:** 5.4" overall.
Stocks: Laminated wood.
Sights: Fixed.
Features: Choice of black Teflon or chrome finish. Announced 1986. Made in U.S. by Davis Industries.
Price: **$87.50**

Davis P-32

CAUTION: PRICES CHANGE. CHECK AT GUNSHOP.

DETONICS "SERVICEMASTER" AUTO PISTOL
Caliber: 45 ACP, 7-shot magazine.
Barrel: 4¼".
Weight: 32 oz. **Length:** 7⅞" overall.
Stocks: Pachmayr rubber.
Sights: Fixed combat.
Features: Stainless steel construction; thumb and grip safeties; extended grip safety. Polished slide flats, rest matte.
Price: **$975.00**

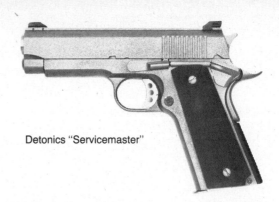

Detonics "Servicemaster"

DETONICS "COMBAT MASTER" MK VI, MC I
Caliber: 45 ACP, 6-shot magazine.
Barrel: 3½".
Weight: 29 oz. **Length:** 6¾" overall, 4½" high.
Stocks: Checkered walnut.
Sights: Combat-type, fixed and adjustable sights avail.
Features: Has a self-adjusting cone barrel centering system, beveled magazine inlet, "full clip" indicator in base of magazine; standard 7-shot (or more) clip can be used in the 45. Throated barrel and polished feed ramp. Introduced 1977. From Detonics.
Price: MC I, matte finish, fixed sights **$725.00**
Price: MK VI, polished stainless, adj. sights **$795.00**

Desert Eagle 357

DESERT EAGLE MAGNUM PISTOL
Caliber: 357 Mag., 9-shot; 41 Mag., 44 Mag., 8-shot.
Barrel: 6", 10", 14", interchangeable.
Weight: 357 Mag.—52 oz. (alloy), 62 oz. (steel); 41 Mag., 44 Mag.—56 oz. (alloy), 66.9 oz. (stainless). **Length:** 10¼" overall (6" bbl.).
Stock: Wrap-around soft rubber.
Sights: Blade on ramp front, combat-style rear. Adjustable available.
Features: Rotating three-lug bolt; ambidextrous safety; combat-style trigger guard; adjustable trigger optional. Military epoxy finish. Satin, bright nickel, hard chrome, polished and blued finishes available. Imported from Israel by Magnum Research Inc.
Price: 357, 6" bbl., standard pistol **$629.00**
Price: As above, alloy frame **$629.00**
Price: As above, stainless steel frame **$669.00**
Price: 41 Mag., 6", standard pistol **$739.00**
Price: 41 Mag., alloy frame **$739.00**
Price: 41 Mag., stainless steel frame **$779.00**
Price: 44 Mag., 6", standard pistol **$749.00**
Price: As above, alloy frame **$749.00**
Price: As above, stainless steel frame **$789.00**

ENCOM MK IV ASSAULT PISTOL
Caliber: 45 ACP, 30-shot magazine.
Barrel: 4.5", 6", 8", 10" optional.
Weight: 6 lbs. **Length:** 12.6" overall (4.5" barrel).
Stocks: Black composition.
Sights: Fixed.
Features: Semi-auto fire only. Side-loading magazine. Interchangeable barrels. Optional retractable stock available with 18½" barrel. Made in the U.S. by Encom America, Inc. Introduced 1988.
Price: **$279.95**

Encom Mk. IV

ENCOM MP-9, MP-45 ASSAULT PISTOLS
Caliber: 9mm, 45 ACP, 10-, 30-, 40- or 50-shot magazine.
Barrel: Interchangeable 4½", 6", 8", 10", 18", 18½".
Weight: 6 lbs. (4½" bbl.). **Length:** 11.8" overall (4½" bbl.).
Stocks: Retractable wire stock.
Sights: Post front, fixed Patridge rear.
Features: Blowback operation, fires from closed breech with floating firing pin; right- or left-hand models available. Made in U.S. From Encom America, Inc.
Price: 9mm or 45 ACP, standard pistol **$275.00**
Price: As above, Mini Pistol (3½" bbl.) **$250.00**
Price: Carbine (18½" bbl., retractable wire stock) **$390.00**

Erma ESP 85A

ERMA SPORTING PISTOL MODEL ESP 85A
Caliber: 22 LR, 8-shot, 32 S&W Long, 5-shot.
Barrel: 6".
Weight: 41 oz. **Length:** 10" overall.
Stocks: Checkered walnut with thumbrest and adjustable left- or right-hand shelf.
Sights: Interchangeable blade front, micro. rear adjustable for windage and elevation.
Features: Interchangeable caliber conversion kit; adjustable trigger, trigger stop. Comes with lockable carrying case. Imported from West Germany by Precision Sales Int'l. Introduced 1988.
Price: 22 LR **$1,119.00**
Price: 32 S&W Long **$1,169.00**

F.I.E. "SUPER TITAN II" PISTOLS
Caliber: 32 ACP, 12-shot; 380 ACP, 11-shot.
Barrel: 3⅞".
Weight: 28 oz. **Length:** 6¾" overall.
Stocks: Smooth, polished walnut.
Sights: Adjustable.
Features: Blue finish only. Introduced 1981. Imported from Italy by F.I.E. Corp.
Price: 32 or 380 . . . . **$279.95**

F.I.E. "TZ-75" SERIES '88 DA AUTO PISTOL
Caliber: 9mm Para., 16-shot magazine; 41 Action Express, 11-shot magazine.
Barrel: 4.72".
Weight: 35.33 oz. **Length:** 8.25" overall.
Stocks: Smooth European walnut. Checkered rubber optional.
Sights: Undercut blade front, open rear adjustable for windage.
Features: Double-action trigger system; squared-off trigger guard; rotating slide-mounted safety. Introduced 1983. Imported from Italy by F.I.E. Corp.
Price: 9mm **$479.95**
Price: 9mm, satin chrome with red outline sights............. **$499.95**
Price: 41 A.E. **$599.95**

F.I.E. Series '88 TZ-75

F.I.E. "TITAN II" PISTOLS
Caliber: 32 ACP, 380 ACP, 6-shot magazine; 22 LR, 10-shot magazine.
Barrel: 3⁷/₈".
Weight: 25³/₄ oz. **Length:** 6³/₄" overall.
Stocks: Checkered nylon, thumbrest-type; walnut optional.
Sights: Adjustable.
Features: Magazine disconnector, firing pin block. Standard slide safety. Available in blue or chrome. Introduced 1978. Imported from Italy by F.I.E. Corp.
Price: 32 or 380, blue **$249.95**
Price: 32 or 380, chrome............................. **$279.95**
Price: 22 LR, blue **$159.95**

F.I.E. Titan II

F.I.E. "TITAN 25" PISTOL
Caliber: 25 ACP, 6-shot magazine.
Barrel: 2⁷/₁₆".
Weight: 12 oz. **Length:** 4⁵/₈" overall.
Stocks: Smooth walnut.
Sights: Fixed.
Features: External hammer; fast simple takedown. Made in U.S.A. by F.I.E. Corp.
Price: Blue.. **$74.95**
Price: Dyna-Chrome **$84.95**
Price: 24K gold with bright blue frame, smooth walnut grips....... **$99.95**
Price: Titan Tigress Lady 25 .... **$159.95**

F.I.E. "Titan 25"

F.I.E. Spectre

Glock 19

Glock 19 Auto Pistol
Similar to the Glock 17 except has a 4" barrel, giving an overall length of 6.9" and weight of 21.2 oz. Magazine capacity is 15 rounds. Introduced 1988.
Price: **$511.60**

F.I.E. SPECTRE DOUBLE-ACTION AUTO PISTOL
Caliber: 9mm Para., 30-shot magazine.
Barrel: 8".
Weight: 2.2 lbs. **Length:** 13.7" overall.
Stocks: Black composition grip.
Sights: Post front, flip rear.
Features: Double-action mechanism fires from closed bolt. Introduced 1987. Imported by F.I.E. Firearms Corp.
Price: **$699.95**

GLOCK 17 AUTO PISTOL
Caliber: 9mm Para., 17-shot magazine.
Barrel: 4.48".
Weight: 21.8 oz. (without magazine). **Length:** 7.40" overall.
Stocks: Black polymer.
Sights: Dot on front blade, white outline rear adjustable for w. and e.
Features: Polymer frame, steel slide; double-action trigger with "Safe Action" system; mechanical firing pin safety, drop safety; simple takedown without tools; locked breech, recoil operated action. Adopted by Austrian armed forces 1983. NATO approved 1984. Imported from Austria by Glock, Inc.
Price: With extra magazine, magazine loader, cleaning kit **$511.60**
Price: Model 17L (6" barrel) **$773.53**

CAUTION: PRICES CHANGE. CHECK AT GUNSHOP.

Grendel P-10

GRENDEL P-10 AUTO PISTOL
Caliber: 380 ACP, 10-shot magazine.
Barrel: 3″.
Weight: 15 oz. **Length:** 5.3″ overall.
Stocks: Checkered polycarbonate metal composite.
Sights: Fixed.
Features: Double action only with a low inertia safety hammer system. Magazine loads from the top. Matte black, electroless nickel or green finish. Introduced 1987. From Grendel, Inc.
Price: Black finish **$150.00**
Price: Green finish. **$155.00**
Price: Electroless nickel **$165.00**
Price: Nickel-green **$167.00**

Heckler & Koch P7-M8

HECKLER & KOCH P7M8 AUTO PISTOL
Caliber: 9mm Para., 8-shot magazine.
Barrel: 4.13″.
Weight: 29 oz. **Length:** 6.73″ overall.
Stocks: Stippled black plastic.
Sights: Fixed, combat-type.
Features: Unique ''squeeze cocker'' in frontstrap cocks the action. Gas-retarded action. Squared combat-type trigger guard. Blue finish. Compact size. Imported from West Germany by Heckler & Koch, Inc.
Price: P7M8. . . . . **$895.00**
Price: P7M13 (13-shot capacity, matte black finish, ambidextrous magazine release, forged steel frame) **$1,104.00**

Heckler & Koch P7K3 Auto Pistol
Similar for the P7M8 and P7M13 except chambered for 380 ACP, 8-shot magazine. Uses an oil-filled buffer to decrease recoil. Introduced 1988.
Price: **$895.00**
Price: 22 LR conversion unit **$467.00**

HECKLER & KOCH HK-94 AUTO PISTOL
Caliber: 9mm Para., 15- or 30-shot magazine.
Barrel: 4.5″.
Weight: 4.4 lbs. **Length:** 12.8″ overall.
Stocks: Black high-impact plastic.
Sights: Post front, diopter rear adjustable for windage and elevation.
Features: Semi-auto pistol inspired by the MP5K submachine gun. Has special flash-hider forend. Introduced 1989. Imported from West Germany by Heckler & Koch, Inc.
Price: **$1,104.00**

Helwan ''Brigadier''

HELWAN ''BRIGADIER'' AUTO PISTOL
Caliber: 9mm Para., 8-shot magazine.
Barrel: 4.5″
Weight: 32 oz. **Length:** 8″ overall.
Stocks: Grooved plastic.
Sights: Blade front, rear adjustable for windage.
Features: Polished blue finish. Single-action design. Cross-bolt safety. Imported by Interarms.
Price: **$260.00**

HOLMES MP-83 AUTO PISTOL
Caliber: 9mm, 16- or 32-shot; 10mm, 12- or 25-shot, 45, 10- or 20-shot.
Barrel: 6″.
Weight: 3½ lbs. **Length:** 14½″ overall.
Stocks: Walnut grip and forend.
Sights: Post front, open adjustable rear.
Features: All steel construction, blue finish. Deluxe package includes gun, foam-lined travel case, Zytel stock, black metal vent. barrel shroud, extra magazine and sling. From Holmes Firearms.
Price: **$500.00**
Price: Deluxe **$525.00**
Price: Caliber conversion kit **$220.00**

Holmes MP-83

Holmes MP-22 Auto Pistol
Similar to the MP-83 except chambered for 22LR, 32-shot capacity. Weighs 2½ lbs., has bolt-notch safety.
Price: **$450.00**
Price: Deluxe. **$525.00**

CAUTION: PRICES CHANGE. CHECK AT GUNSHOP.

IAI Backup

IAI AUTOMAG III PISTOL
Caliber: 30 Carbine, 8-shot magazine.
Barrel: 6³/₈″.
Weight: 43 oz. **Length:** 10¹/₂″ overall.
Stocks: Wraparound rubber.
Sights: Blade front, Millett adjustable rear.
Features: Stainless steel construction. Hammer-drop safety. Slide flats have brushed finish, rest is sandblasted. Introduced 1989. From Irwindale Arms, Inc.
Price: $674.00

INTRATEC TEC-9 AUTO PISTOL
Caliber: 9mm Para., 36-shot magazine.
Barrel: 5″.
Weight: 50 oz. **Length:** 12¹/₂″ overall.
Stock: Moulded composition.
Sights: Fixed.
Features: Semi-auto, fires from closed bolt; firing pin block safety; matte blue finish. Comes wih 1″ black nylon sling. From Intratec.
Price: $313.95
Price: TEC-9S (as above, except stainless) $386.95

Intratec TEC-9M Pistol
Similar to the TEC-9 except smaller. Has 3″ barrel, weighs 44 oz.; 20-shot magazine.
Price: $286.95
Price: TEC-9MS (as above, stainless) $361.95

INTRATEC TEC-22T AUTO PISTOL
Caliber: 22 LR, 30-shot magazine.
Barrel: 4″.
Weight: 30 oz. **Length:** 11³/₁₆″ overall.
Stocks: Moulded composition.
Sights: Protected post front, rear adjustable for windage and elevation.
Features: Ambidextrous cocking knobs and safety. Matte black finish. Accepts any 10/22-type magazine. Introduced 1988. Made in U.S. by Intratec.
Price: $184.95
Price: TEC-22TN (as above, nickel finish) $203.95
Price: TEC-22 (as above, non-threaded bbl.) $172.95

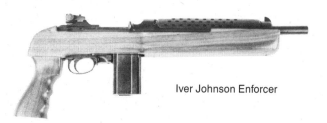

Iver Johnson Enforcer

IAI "BACKUP" AUTO PISTOL
Caliber: 380 ACP, 5-shot magazine
Barrel: 2¹/₂″.
Weight: 18 oz. **Length:** 4.25″ overall. .
Stocks: Checkered Lexon.
Sights: Fixed, open, recessed.
Features: Concealed hammer, blowback operation; manual and grip safeties. All stainless steel construction. Smallest domestically-produced pistol in 380. From Irwindale Arms, Inc.
Price: $237.00

IAI Automag III

IAI JAVELINA 10MM PISTOL
Caliber: 10mm Auto, 8-shot magazine.
Barrel: 7″.
Weight: 40 oz. **Length:** 10¹/₂″ overall.
Stock: Wraparound rubber.
Sights: Blade front, Millett adjustable rear.
Features: All stainless construction. Brushed finish. Introduced 1989. From Irwindale Arms, Inc.
Price: About.. $600.00

Intratec TEC-9

Intratec TEC-22T

IVER JOHNSON ENFORCER MODEL 3000 AUTO
Caliber: 30 M1 Carbine, 15- or 30-shot magazine.
Barrel: 10¹/₂″.
Weight: 4 lbs. **Length:** 18¹/₂″ overall.
Stocks: American walnut with metal handguard.
Sights: Gold bead ramp front. Peep rear.
Features: Accepts 15- or 30-shot magazines. From Iver Johnson.
Price: Blue finish $333.20

Iver Johnson TP22

IVER JOHNSON TP22, TP25 AUTO PISTOLS
Caliber: 22 LR, 25 ACP, 7-shot magazine.
Barrel: 2.85".
Weight: 14½ oz. **Length:** 5.39" overall.
Stocks: Black checkered plastic.
Sights: Fixed.
Features: Double action; 7-shot magazine. Introduced 1981. Made in U.S. From Iver Johnson's.
Price: Either caliber, blue **$191.65**

Jennings J-25

JENNINGS J-22, J-25 AUTO PISTOLS
Caliber: 22 LR, 25 ACP, 6-shot magazine.
Barrel: 2½".
Weight: 13 oz. (J-22). **Length:** 4¹⁵/₁₆" overall (J-22).
Stocks: Walnut on chrome or nickel models; grooved black Cycolac or resin-impregnated wood on Teflon model.
Sights: Fixed.
Features: Choice of bright chrome, satin nickel or black Teflon finish. Introduced 1981. From Jennings Firearms.
Price: J-22, about **$75.00**
Price: J-25, about **$89.95**

L.A.R. Grizzly Win Mag

L.A.R. GRIZZLY WIN MAG MK I PISTOL
Caliber: 357 Mag., 357/45, 10mm, 45 Win. Mag., 45 ACP, 7-shot magazine.
Barrel: 5.4", 6.5".
Weight: 51 oz. **Length:** 10½" overall.
Stocks: Checkered rubber, non-slip combat-type.
Sights: Ramped blade front, fully adjustable rear.
Features: Uses basic Browning/Colt 1911A1 design; interchangeable calibers; beveled magazine well; combat-type flat, checkered rubber mainspring housing; lowered and back-chamfered ejection port; polished feed ramp; throated barrel; solid barrel bushings. Available in satin hard chrome, matte blue, Parkerized finishes. Introduced 1983. From L.A.R. Mfg. Inc.
Price: 45 Win. Mag.. **$725.00**
Price: 357 Mag.. **$750.00**
Price: Conversion units (357 Mag.)..................... **$178.50**
Price: As above, 45 ACP, 10mm, 45 Win. Mag., 357/45 Win. Mag... **$164.00**

Llama Large Frame Auto

L.A.R. Grizzly Win Mag 8" & 10"
Similar to the standard Grizzly Win Mag except has lengthened slide and either 8" or 10" barrel. Available in 45 Win. Mag., 45 ACP, 357/45 Grizzly Win. Mag., 10mm or 357 Magnum. Introduced 1987.
Price: 8", 45 ACP, 45 Win. Mag., 357/45 Grizzly Win. Mag...... **$1,250.00**
Price: As above, 10" **$1,313.00**
Price: 8", 357 Magnum **$1,275.00**
Price: As above, 10" **$1,337.00**

LLAMA LARGE FRAME AUTO PISTOL
Caliber: 38 Super, 45 ACP.
Barrel: 5".
Weight: 40 oz. **Length:** 8½" overall.
Stocks: Checkered walnut.
Sights: Fixed.
Features: Grip and manual safeties, ventilated rib. Imported from Spain by Stoeger Industries.
Price: Blue... **$365.00**
Price: Satin chrome, 45 ACP only..................... **$485.00**

Llama Small Frame Auto

LLAMA SMALL FRAME AUTO PISTOLS
Caliber: 22 LR, 32, 380.
Barrel: 3¹¹/₁₆".
Weight: 23 oz. **Length:** 6½" overall.
Stocks: Checkered plastic, thumb rest.
Sights: Fixed front, adjustable notch rear.
Features: Ventilated rib, manual and grip safeties. Imported from Spain by Stoeger Industries.
Price: Blue, 22 LR, ... **$315.00**
Price: Blue, 32, 380.................................. **$315.00**
Price: Satin chrome, 22 LR or 380 .... **$390.00**

CAUTION: PRICES CHANGE. CHECK AT GUNSHOP.

LLAMA M-82 DA AUTO PISTOL
Caliber: 9mm Para., 15-shot magazine.
Barrel: 4¼".
Weight: 39 oz. **Length:** 8" overall.
Stocks: Matte black ploymer.
Sights: Blade front, rear drift adjustable for windage. High visibility three-dot system.
Features: Double-action mechanism; ambidextrous safety. Introduced 1987. Imported from Spain by Stoeger Industries.
Price: $975.00

LLAMA COMPACT FRAME AUTO PISTOL
Caliber: 9mm Para., 9-shot, 45 ACP, 7-shot.
Barrel: 4⁵/₁₆".
Weight: 37 oz.
Stocks: Smooth walnut.
Sights: Blade front, rear adjustable for windage.
Features: Scaled-down version of the Large Frame gun. Locked breech mechanism; manual and grip safeties. Introduced 1985. Imported from Spain by Stoeger Industries.
Price: Blue only $365.00

LORCIN AUTO PISTOL
Caliber: 25 ACP, 6-shot magazine.
Barrel: 2¼".
Weight: 13.5 oz. **Length:** 4.75" overall.
Stocks: Smooth composition.
Sights: Fixed.
Features: Available in choice of finishes: black and gold, chrome and satin chrome or black. Introduced 1989. From Lorcin Engineering.
Price: $79.95

Lorcin 25 ACP

Norinco Type 54-1

NORINCO TYPE 54-1 TOKAREV PISTOL
Caliber: 7.62 x 25mm, 8-shot magazine.
Barrel: 4.6".
Weight: 29 oz. **Length:** 7.7" overall.
Stocks: Grooved black plastic.
Sights: Fixed.
Features: Matte blue finish. Imported from China by China Sports, Inc.
Price: . . . . NA

OMEGA AUTO PISTOL
Caliber: 38 Super (9-shot), 10mm (8-shot), 45 ACP (7-shot).
Barrel: 5", 6".
Weight: 42.8 oz. (5" barrel).
Stocks: Wraparound checkered rubber.
Sights: Blade front, fully adjustable rear.
Features: Convertible between calibers; ported barrels. Based on 1911A1 but with improved barrel lock-up. Introduced 1987. From Springfield Armory.
Price: Single caliber, 38 Super, 10mm or 45 ACP $849.00

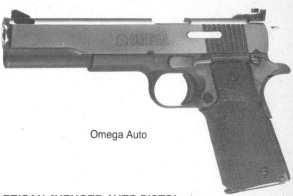

Omega Auto

Partisan Avenger

PARTISAN AVENGER AUTO PISTOL
Caliber: 45 ACP, 30-shot magazine.
Barrel: 6¼".
Weight: 5 lbs., 7 oz. **Length:** 11" overall.
Stocks: Smooth composition.
Sights: Protected blade front, fixed rear.
Features: All steel construction; cam-activated striker; chamber loaded indicator. Easy takedown. Semi-auto only. Fires from a closed bolt. Uses standard M-3 "Grease Gun" magazine. Introduced 1988. Made in U.S. From Patriot Dist. Co.
Price: $445.00

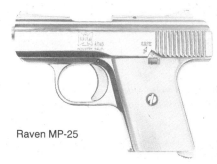

Raven MP-25

RAVEN MP-25 AUTO PISTOL
Caliber: 25 ACP, 6-shot magazine.
Barrel: 2⁷/₁₆".
Weight: 15 oz. **Length:** 4¾" overall.
Stocks: Smooth walnut or ivory-colored plastic.
Sights: Ramped front, fixed rear.
Features: Available in blue, nickel or chrome finish. Made in U.S. Available from Raven Arms.
Price: $69.95

RANGER 1911A1 45 AUTO PISTOL
Caliber: 45 ACP, 7-shot magazine.
Barrel: 5″.
Weight: 38 oz. **Length:** 8¹/₂″ overall.
Stocks: Checkered walnut.
Sights: Millett MK.I front and rear.
Features: Made in U.S. from 4140 steel and other high-strength alloys. Barrel machined from a forged billet. Introduced 1988. From Federal Ordnance, Inc.
Price: Standard model **$439.95**
Price: With extended slide release and safety **$449.95**
Price: With ambidextrous slide release and safety.............. **$459.95**

Ranger 1911A1

RUGER P-85 AUTOMATIC PISTOL
Caliber: 9mm Para., 15-shot magazine.
Barrel: 4.50″.
Weight: 32 oz. **Length:** 7.84″ overall.
Stocks: Grooved "Xenoy" composition.
Sights: Square post front, square notch rear adjustable for windage, both with white dot inserts.
Features: Double action with ambidextrous slide-mounted safety which blocks firing pin and disengages firing mechnaism. Slide is 4140 chrome-moly steel, frame is a lightweight aluminum alloy, both finished matte black. Ambidextrous magazine release. Introduced 1986.
Price: **$325.00**
Price: P-85 C (comes with plastic case, extra magazine).......... **$355.00**

Ruger P-85

Ruger Mark II Stainless

RUGER MARK II STANDARD AUTO PISTOL
Caliber: 22 LR, 10-shot magazine.
Barrel: 4³/₄″ or 6″.
Weight: 36 oz. (4³/₄″ bbl.). **Length:** 8⁵/₁₆″ (4³/₄″ bbl.).
Stocks: Checkered hard rubber.
Sights: Fixed, wide blade front, square notch rear adjustable for w.
Features: Updated design of the original Standard Auto. Has new bolt hold-open device, 10-shot magazine, magazine catch, safety, trigger and new receiver contours. Introduced 1982.
Price: Blued (MK 4, MK 6)................................. **$208.00**
Price: In stainless steel (KMK 4, KMK 6)..................... **$277.00**

SAFARI ARMS MATCHMASTER PISTOL
Caliber: 45 ACP, 6-shot magazine.
Barrel: 5″, 6″, 7″.
Weight: 40 oz. **Length:** 8.7″ overall.
Stocks: Checkered plastic or walnut.
Sights: Combat adjustable.
Features: Beavertail grip safety, ambidextrous extended safety, extended slide release, combat hammer, threaded barrel bushing; throated, ported, tuned. Finishes: blue, Parkerize, matte. Also available in a lightweight version (30 oz.) and stainless steel. Available from SGW/Safari Arms, Inc.
Price: **$649.00**

Safari Arms Enforcer Pistol
Shortened version of the Matchmaster. Has 3.8″ barrel, overall length of 7.7″, and weighs 40 oz. (standard weight), 27 oz. in lightweight version. Other features are the same. From SGW/Safari Arms, Inc.
Price: **$629.00**

Consult our Directory pages for the location of firms mentioned.

SCARAB SKORPION AUTO PISTOL
Caliber: 9mm Para., 32-shot magazine.
Barrel: 4.63″.
Weight: 3.5 lbs. **Length:** 12.25″ overall.
Stocks: Stained polymer.
Sights: Fixed, open.
Features: Semi-auto fire only. Ambidextrous cocking knobs. Comes with one magazine, front hangar and leather hand strap, imitation sound suppressor, padded carrying case, flash hider, leather shoulder strap, 22 LR sub-caliber conversion. Made in U.S. Announced 1988. From Armitage International, Ltd.
Price: **$299.50**

Scarab Skorpion

SEDCO SP-22 AUTO PISTOL
Caliber: 22 LR.
Barrel: 2¹/₂″.
Weight: 11 oz. **Length:** 5″ overall.
Stocks: Simulated pearl.
Sights: Fixed.
Features: Available in polished chrome or black Teflon finish. Rotary safety blocks sear and slide. Made in U.S. by Sedco Industries.
Price: $68.50

SEECAMP LWS 32 STAINLESS DA AUTO
Caliber: 32 ACP Win. Silvertip, 6-shot.
Barrel: 2″, integral with frame.
Weight: 10.5 oz. **Length:** 4¹/₈″ overall.
Stocks: Black plastic.
Sights: Smooth, no-snag, contoured slide and barrel top.
Features: Aircraft quality 17-4 PH stainless steel. Inertia-operated firing pin. Hammer fired double action only. Hammer automatically follows slide down to safety rest position after each shot—no manual safety needed. Magazine safety disconnector. Polished stainless. Introduced 1980. From L.W. Seecamp.
Price: $350.00

SIG P-210-6 AUTO PISTOL
Caliber: 9mm Para., 8-shot magazine.
Barrel: 4³/₄″.
Weight: 36.2 oz. **Length:** 8¹/₂″ overall.
Stocks: Checkered black plastic; walnut optional.
Sights: Blade front, micro. adjustable rear for w. & e.
Features: Adjustable trigger stop; target trigger; ribbed frontstap; sandblasted finish. Conversion unit for 22 LR consists of barrel, recoil spring, slide and magazine. Imported from Switzerland by Mandall Shooting Supplies.
Price: P-210-6 .... $1,900.00
Price: P-210-5 Target $1,900.00

SIG-SAUER P220 ''AMERICAN'' AUTO PISTOL
Caliber: 9mm, 38 Super, 45 ACP. (9-shot in 9mm and 38 Super, 7 in 45).
Barrel: 4³/₈″.
Weight: 28¹/₄ oz. (9mm). **Length:** 7³/₄″ overall.
Stocks: Checkered black plastic.
Sights: Blade front, drift adjustable rear for w.
Features: Double action. De-cocking lever permits lowering hammer onto locked firing pin. Squared combat-type trigger guard. Slide stays open after last shot. Imported from West Germany by SIGARMS, Inc.
Price: ''American'' (side-button magazine release, 45 ACP only) ... $720.00
Price: ''European'' $695.00

SIG-SAUER P225 DA AUTO PISTOL
Caliber: 9mm Para., 8-shot magazine.
Barrel: 3.8″.
Weight: 26 oz. **Length:** 7³/₃₂″ overall.
Stocks: Checkered black plastic.
Sights: Blade front, rear adjustable for windage. Optional ''Siglite'' night sights.
Features: Double action. De-cocking lever permits lowering hammer onto locked firing pin. Squared combat-type trigger guard. Shortened, lightened version of P-220. Imported from West Germany by SIGARMS, Inc.
Price: $750.00
Price: With Siglite night sights $850.00
Price: As above, nickel finish $920.00

SIG-SAUER P226 DA Auto Pistol
Similar to the P-220 pistol except has 15-shot magazine, 4.4″ barrel, and weighs 26¹/₂ oz. 9mm only. Imported from West Germany by SIGARMS, Inc.
Price: Blue $780.00
Price: With Siglite night sights $880.00

SIG P-210-2 AUTO PISTOL
Caliber: 7.65mm or 9mm Para., 8-shot magazine.
Barrel: 4³/₄″.
Weight: 31³/₄ oz. (9mm) **Length:** 8¹/₂″ overall.
Stocks: Checkered black composition.
Sights: Blade front, rear adjustable for windage.
Features: Lanyard loop; matte finish. Conversion unit for 22 LR available. Imported from Switzerland by Mandall Shooting Supplies.
Price: P-210-2 Service Pistol $1,895.00

SIG P-210-6

SIG-Sauer P220 American

SIG-Sauer P230

SIG-SAUER P230 DA AUTO PISTOL
Caliber: 32 ACP, 8-shot; 380 ACP, 7-shot.
Barrel: 3³/₄″.
Weight: 16 oz. **Length:** 6¹/₂″ overall.
Stocks: Checkered black plastic.
Sights: Blade front, rear adjustable for w.
Features: Double action. Same basic action design as P-220. Blowback operation, stationary barrel. Introduced 1977. Imported from West Germany by SIGARMS, Inc.
Price: Blue $495.00
Price: In stainless steel (P-230 SL) $575.00

SMITH & WESSON MODEL 422 AUTO
Caliber: 22 LR, 10-shot magazine.
Barrel: 4¹/₂″, 6″.
Weight: 22 oz. (4¹/₂″ bbl.) **Length:** 7¹/₂″ overall (4¹/₂″ bbl.).
Stocks: Checkered plastic (Field), checkered walnut (Target).
Sights: Field — serrated ramp front, fixed rear; Target — Patridge front, adjustable rear.
Features: Aluminum frame, steel slide, brushed blue finish; internal hammer. Introduced 1987.
Price: 4¹/₂″, 6″, fixed sight.................................. $199.80
Price: Model 622 (stainless) $266.00
Price: As above, adjustable sight $249.75
Price: As above, stainless (Model 622) $316.00

Smith & Wesson 422

SMITH & WESSON MODEL 3904/3906 DOUBLE ACTIONS
Caliber: 9mm Para., 8-shot magazine.
Barrel: 4″.
Weight: About 30 oz. **Length:** 7⁵/₈″ overall.
Stocks: Delrin one-piece wraparound, arched backstrap, textured surface.
Sights: Post front with white dot, fixed or fully adjustable rear with two white dots.
Features: Smooth .365″ trigger, .260″ serrated hammer. Introduced 1989.
Price: Model 3904, blue, fixed sight $495.50
Price: As above, adjustable sight $520.50
Price: Model 3906, stainless, fixed sight $545.00
Price: As above, adjustable sight $572.00

Smith & Wesson 3904

Smith & Wesson 5904/5906 Double-Action Autos
Same as the Models 3904 and 5904 except with 14-shot magazine (20-shot available), and available with straight backstrap. Introduced 1989.
Price: Model 5904, blue, fixed sight $526.50
Price: As above, adjustable sight $553.00
Price: Model 5906, stainless, fixed sight $579.00
Price: As above, adjustable sight $608.00

Smith & Wesson 6904/6906 Double-Action Autos
Similar to the Models 5904/5906 except with 3¹/₂″ barrel, 12-shot magazine (20-shot available), fixed rear sight, .260″ bobbed hammer. Introduced 1989.
Price: Model 6904, blue $502.50
Price: Model 6906, stainless.......................... $553.00

Smith & Wesson 6906

SMITH & WESSON MODEL 4506/4516 AUTOS
Caliber: 45 ACP, 7-shot magazine (M4516), 8-shot magazine (M4506).
Barrel: 3³/₄″ (M4516), 5″ (M4506).
Weight: NA. **Length:** NA.
Stocks: Delrin one-piece wraparound, arched or straight backstrap on M4506, straight only on M4516.
Sights: Post front with white dot, adjustable or fixed on M4506, fixed only on M4516.
Features: M4506 has serrated hammer spur, M4516 has bobbed hammer. Both guns in stainless only. Introduced 1989.
Price: Model 4506, fixed sight $653.00
Price: Model 4506, adjustable sight $686.00
Price: Model 4516 .... $653.00

Smith & Wesson 4506

SPORTARMS TOKAREV MODEL 213
Caliber: 9mm Para., 8-shot magazine.
Barrel: 4.5″.
Weight: 31 oz. **Length:** 7.6″ overall.
Stocks: Grooved plastic.
Sights: Fixed.
Features: Blue finish, hard chrome optional. 9mm version of the famous Russian Tokarev pistol. Made in China by Norinco; imported by Sportarms of Florida. Introduced 1988.
Price: Blue, about $196.95
Price: Hard chrome, about $226.95

CAUTION: PRICES CHANGE. CHECK AT GUNSHOP.

Springfield Armory 1911 A1

Springfield Commander

SPRINGFIELD ARMORY P9 DA PISTOL
Caliber: 9mm Para., 16-shot magazine.
Barrel: 4.72″.
Weight: 35.3 oz. **Length:** 8.1″ overall.
Stocks: Checkered walnut.
Sights: Blade front, open rear drift-adjustable for windage. Three-dot system.
Features: Patterned after the CZ-75. Firing pin safety block, frame-mounted thumb safety. Magazine catch can be switched to opposite side. Commander hammer. Introduced 1989.
Price: Blued. **$454.00**
Price: IPSC Model blued. **$774.00**

Springfield Armory P9 Compact Pistol
Same as the standard P9 except has 3.66″ barrel, 7.24″ overall length and weighs 32.1 oz. Has 10-shot magazine capacity. Introduced 1989.
Price: Blued. **$467.00**

Star PD

SPRINGFIELD ARMORY 1911A1 AUTO PISTOL
Caliber: 9mm or 45 ACP, 8-shot magazine.
Barrel: 5″.
Weight: 2¼ lbs. **Length:** 8½″ overall.
Stocks: NA.
Sights: Blade front, rear drift-adjustable for windage.
Features: All forged parts, including frame, barrel, slide. All new production. Custom slide and parts available. Introduced 1985. From Springfield Armory.
Price: Complete pistol, Parkerized **$420.00**
Price: Complete pistol, blued **$441.00**
Price: 45 to 9mm conversion kit, Parkerized **$169.00**
Price: As above, blued **$177.00**

Springfield Armory 1911A1 Defender
Similar to the standard 1911A1 except has fixed combat-style sights, bevelled magazine well, extended thumb safety, bobbed hammer, walnut stocks, serrated frontstrap, and comes with two stainless steel magazines. Available in 45 ACP only, choice of blue or Parkerized finish. Introduced 1988.
Price: Blue. **$555.00**
Price: Parkerized. **$535.00**

Springfield Armory 1911A1 Commander
Similar to the standard 1911A1 except slide and barrel are ½″ shorter. Has low-profile three-dot sight system. Comes with Commander hammer and walnut stocks. Available in 45 ACP only; choice of blue or Parkerized finish. Introduced 1989.
Price: Blue. **$499.00**
Price: Parkerized. **$479.00**

Springfield Armory 1911A1 Compact
Similar to the Commander model except has a shortened slide with 4.25″ barrel, 7.25″ overall length. Magazine capacity is 6 shots. Has low-profile three-dot sight system, checkered walnut grips. Available in 45 ACP only. Introduced 1989.
Price: Blued. **$499.00**
Price: Parkerized. **$479.00**

Springfield P9

STAR MODEL PD AUTO PISTOL
Caliber: 45 ACP, 6-shot magazine.
Barrel: 3.94″.
Weight: 28 oz. **Length:** 7⁷/₁₆″ overall.
Stocks: Checkered walnut.
Sights: Ramp front, fully adjustable rear.
Features: Rear sight milled into slide; thumb safety; grooved non-slip frontstrap; nylon recoil buffer; inertia firing pin; no grip or magazine safeties. Imported from Spain by Interarms.
Price: Blue. **$415.00**

Star Model BM

STAR MODEL 30M & 30PK DOUBLE-ACTION PISTOLS
Caliber: 9mm Para., 15-shot magazine.
Barrel: 4.33″ (Model M); 3.86″ (Model PK).
Weight: 40 oz. (M); 30 oz. (PK). **Length:** 8″ overall (M); 7.6″ (PK).
Stocks: Checkered black plastic.
Sights: Square blade front, square notch rear click-adjustable for windage and elevation.
Features: Double or single action; grooved front- and backstraps and trigger guard face; ambidextrous safety cams firing pin forward; removable backstrap houses the firing mechanism. Model M has steel frame; Model PK is alloy. Introduced 1984. Imported from Spain by Interarms.
Price: Model M or PK **$535.00**

STEEL CITY "DOUBLE DEUCE" PISTOL
Caliber: 22 LR, 7-shot; 25 ACP, 6-shot.
Barrel: 2¹/₂″.
Weight: 18 oz. **Length:** 5¹/₂″ overall.
Stocks: Rosewood.
Sights: Fixed.
Features: Double action; stainless steel construction with matte finish; ambidextrous slide-mounted safety. From Steel City Arms, Inc.
Price: 22 or 25 cal **$299.95**

Steel City War Eagle

TANARMI TAYIDA DA AUTO PISTOL
Caliber: 9mm Para., 15-shot magazine, 41 A.E., 11-shot magazine.
Barrel: 4.75″.
Weight: 35 oz. **Length:** 8.25″ overall.
Stocks: Checkered neoprene rubber.
Sights: Blade front, white outline rear.
Features: Improved version of the Czech CZ75. Chrome-plated barrel and trigger, extended slide release lever. Available in matte blue or matte chrome. Imported from Italy by Excam.
Price: Matte blue, 9mm **$415.00**
Price: Matte chrome, 9mm **$430.00**
Price: Matte blue, 41 A.E. **$490.00**
Price: Matte chrome, 41 A.E. **$550.00**

STAR BM, BKM AUTO PISTOLS
Caliber: 9mm Para., 8-shot magazine.
Barrel: 3.9″.
Weight: 25 oz.
Stocks: Checkered walnut.
Sights: Fixed.
Features: Blue or chrome finish. Magazine and manual safeties, external hammer. Imported from Spain by Interarms.
Price: Blue, BM **$332.00**
Price: Blue, BKM only **$375.00**
Price: Chrome, BM only **$395.00**

Star Model 30 PK

Steel City Double Deuce

STEEL CITY "WAR EAGLE" PISTOL
Caliber: 9mm Para., 15-shot magazine.
Barrel: 4″.
Weight: NA. **Length:** NA.
Stocks: Rosewood.
Sights: Fixed and adjustable.
Features: Double action; matte-finished stainless steel; ambidextrous safety. Announced 1986.
Price: **$650.00**

SUNDANCE MODEL A-25 AUTO PISTOL
Caliber: 25 ACP, 7-shot magazine.
Barrel: 2″.
Weight: 14 oz. **Length:** 4⁷/₈″ overall.
Stocks: Grooved black ABS or simulated smooth pearl.
Sights: Fixed.
Features: Rotary safety blocks sear. Bright chrome, satin nickel or black Teflon finish. Introduced 1989. From Sundance Ind.
Price: **$65.00**

Tanarmi Baby Tayida Auto Pistol
Similar to the standard TA90 except has ³/₄″ shorter barrel/slide, ¹/₂″ shorter grip. Barrel length 4″, weight is 30 oz., 12-shot magazine.
Price: Matte blue **$430.00**
Price: Matte chrome **$450.00**

CAUTION: PRICES CHANGE. CHECK AT GUNSHOP.

TARGA MODELS GT22, GT32, GT380 AUTO PISTOLS

Caliber: 22 LR, 10-shot; 32 ACP or 380 ACP, 6-shot magazine
Barrel: 4⁷/₈″.
Weight: 26 oz. **Length:** 7³/₈″ overall.
Stocks: Walnut.
Sights: Fixed blade front; rear drift-adjustable for w.
Features: Chrome or blue finish; magazine, thumb, and firing pin safeties; external hammer; safety-lever takedown. Imported from Italy by Excam, Inc.
Price: 22 cal., blue.. $200.00
Price: 22 cal., nickel ....,............. $215.00
Price: 32 cal., blue.. $200.00
Price: 32 cal., chrome $215.00
Price: 380 cal., blue... $212.00
Price: 380 cal., chrome $220.00
Price: 380 cal., chrome, engraved $245.00
Price: 380 cal., blue, engraved $235.00

Targa GT380XE

TARGA GT380XE PISTOL

Caliber: 380 ACP, 11-shot magazine.
Barrel: 3.88″.
Weight: 28 oz. **Length:** 7.38″ overall.
Stocks: Smooth hardwood.
Sights: Adjustable for windage.
Features: Blue finish. Ordnance steel. Magazine disconnector, firing pin and thumb safeties. Introduced 1980. Imported by Excam.
Price: 380 cal., blue................................... $235.00

TARGA MODEL GT27 AUTO PISTOL

Caliber: 25 ACP, 6-shot magazine.
Barrel: 2⁷/₁₆″.
Weight: 12 oz. **Length:** 4⁵/₈″ overall.
Stocks: Smooth walnut.
Sights: Fixed.
Features: Safety-lever takedown; external hammer with half-cock. Assembled in U.S. by Excam, Inc.
Price: Blue... $75.00
Price: Chrome $80.00

Targa GT26

Targa GT26 Auto Pistol

Similar to the GT27 except has steel frame, push-button magazine release and magazine disconnect safety. Contoured smooth walnut grips. Satin blue finish. Imported from Italy by Excam, assembled in U.S.A.
Price: $115.00

TARGA GT22T TARGET AUTO

Caliber: 22LR, 12-shot.
Barrel: 6″.
Weight: 30 oz. **Length:** 9″ overall.
Stocks: Checkered walnut, with thumbrest.
Sights: Blade on ramp front, rear adjustable for windage.
Features: Blue finish. Finger-rest magazine. Imported by Excam.
Price: $200.00

TAURUS MODEL PT-92AF AUTO PISTOL

Caliber: 9mm Para., 15-shot magazine.
Barrel: 4.92″.
Weight: 34 oz. **Length:** 8.54″ overall.
Stocks: Brazilian walnut.
Sights: Fixed notch rear. Three-dot sight system.
Features: Double action, exposed hammer, chamber loaded indicator. Inertia firing pin. Imported by Taurus International.
Price: Blue... $424.75
Price: Satin nickel finish $437.30

Taurus PT-99AF Auto Pistol

Similar to the PT-92 except has fully adjustable rear sight, smooth Brazilian walnut stocks and is available in polished blue or satin nickel. Introduced 1983.
Price: Polished blue $459.65
Price: Satin nickel $474.50

TAURUS MODEL PT58 AUTO PISTOL

Caliber: 380 ACP, 13-shot magazine.
Barrel: 4.01″.
Weight: 30 oz.
Stocks: Brazilian walnut.
Sights: Integral blade on slide front, notch rear. Three-dot system.
Features: Double action with exposed hammer; inertia firing pin. Introduced 1988. Imported by Taurus International.
Price: Blue... $387.80
Price: Satin nickel $394.50

Taurus PT99AF

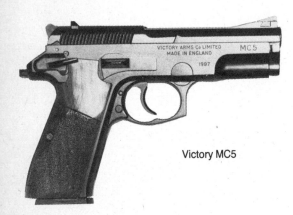

UZI® PISTOL
Caliber: 9mm Para., 45 ACP.
Barrel: 4.5″.
Weight: 3.8 lbs. **Length:** 9.45″ overall.
Stocks: Black plastic.
Sights: Post front with white dot, open rear click adjustable for windage and elevation, two white dots..
Features: Semi-auto blowback action; fires from closed bolt; floating firing pin. Comes in a moulded plastic case with 20-round magazine; 25- and 32-round magazines available. Imported from Israel by Action Arms. Introduced 1984.
Price: **$660.00**

UZI Pistol

Victory MC5

VICTORY MC5 AUTO PISTOL
Caliber: 9mm Para., 38 Super (17-shot magazine), 41 Action Express (12-shot), 45 ACP (10-shot).
Barrel: 4³/8″, 5⁷/8″, 7¹/2″, interchangeable.
Weight: 45 oz. **Length:** 8¹/2″ overall (4³/8″ barrel).
Stocks: High-impact plastic.
Sights: Patridge three-dot system; ramped non-snag front, rear adjustable for windage with different heights available.
Features: Double-action auto; chamber loaded indicator; exposed hammer; ambidextrous safety, magazine catch, slide release; open-top slide. Introduced 1988. Imported from England by Magnum Research, Inc.
Price: MC5. . . . . **$499.00**
Price: Extra barrels **$100.00**
Price: Extra magazines **$25.00**

WALTHER PP AUTO PISTOL
Caliber: 22 LR, 8-shot; 32 ACP, 380 ACP, 7-shot.
Barrel: 3.86″.
Weight: 23¹/2 oz. **Length:** 6.7″ overall.
Stocks: Checkered plastic.
Sights: Fixed, white markings.
Features: Double action; manual safety blocks firing pin and drops hammer; chamber loaded indicator on 32 and 380; extra finger rest magazine provided. Imported from Germany by Interarms.
Price: 22 LR. **$875.00**
Price: 32 . . . . **$850.00**
Price: 380 . . . . **$875.00**
Price: Engraved models . . . . **On Request**

Walther PPK/S American

Walther American PPK/S Auto Pistol
Similar to Walther PP except made entirely in the United States. Has 3.27″ barrel with 6.1″ length overall. Introduced 1980.
Price: 380 ACP only **$529.00**
Price: As above, stainless **$529.00**

Walther American PPK Auto Pistol
Similar to Walther PPK/S except weighs 21 oz., has 6-shot capacity. Made in the U.S. Introduced 1986.
Price: Stainless, 380 ACP only **$529.00**
Price: Blue, 380 ACP only **$529.00**

WALTHER P-88 AUTO PISTOL
Caliber: 9mm Para., 15-shot magazine.
Barrel: 4″.
Weight: 31¹/2 oz. **Length:** 7³/8″ overall.
Stocks: Checkered black composition.
Sights: Blade front, rear adjustable for w. and e.
Features: Double action with ambidextrous decocking lever and magazine release; alloy frame; loaded chamber indicator; matte finish. Imported from Germany by Interarms.
Price: **$1,150.00**

Walther P-88

WALTHER P-38 AUTO PISTOL

Caliber: 22 LR, 9mm Para., 8-shot.
Barrel: 4^{15}/$_{16}$″ (9mm), 5^1/$_{16}$″ (22 LR).
Weight: 28 oz. **Length:** 8^1/$_2$″ overall.
Stocks: Checkered plastic.
Sights: Fixed.
Features: Double action; safety blocks firing pin and drops hammer. Matte finish standard, polished blue, engraving and/or plating available. Imported from Germany by Interarms.
Price: 22 LR **$1,050.00**
Price: 9mm **$995.00**
Price: Steel frame **$1,400.00**
Price: Engraved models .... **On Request**

Walther P-38 Auto Pistol

Walther P-5 Auto Pistol

Latest Walther design that uses the basic P-38 double-action mechanism. Caliber 9mm Para., barrel length 3^1/$_2$″; weight 28 oz., overall length 7″.
Price: **$825.00**
Price: P-5 Compact **$1,100.00**

WALTHER MODEL TPH AUTO PISTOL

Caliber: 22 LR, 6-shot magazine.
Barrel: 2^1/$_4$″.
Weight: 14 oz. **Length:** 5^3/$_8$″ overall
Stocks: Checkered black composition.
Sights: Blade front, rear drift-adjustable for windage.
Features: Made of stainless steel. Scaled-down version of the Walther PP/PPK series. Made in U.S. Introduced 1987. From Interarms.
Price: **$399.00**

Walther P-5

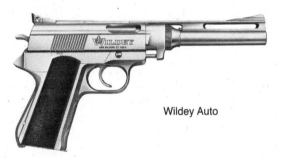

Wildey Auto

Walther TPH

WILDEY AUTOMATIC PISTOL

Caliber: 9mm Win. Mag., 45 Win. Mag., 475 Wildey Mag., 357 Peterbuilt.
Barrel: 5″, 6″, 7″, 8″ (45 Win. Mag.); 8″, 10″ (475 Wildey Mag.). Interchangeable.
Weight: 64 oz. (5″ barrel). **Length:** 11″ overall (7″ barrel).
Stocks: Checkered hardwood.
Sights: Ramp front, fully adjustable rear.
Features: Gas-operated action. Made of stainless steel. Has three-lug rotary bolt. Double action. Made in U.S. by Wildey, Inc.
Price: **$1,099.00**

Wilkinson "Sherry"

WILKINSON "SHERRY" AUTO PISTOL

Caliber: 22 LR, 8-shot magazine.
Barrel: 2^1/$_8$″.
Weight: 9^1/$_4$ oz. **Length:** 4^3/$_8$″ overall.
Stocks: Checkered black plastic.
Sights: Fixed, groove.
Features: Cross-bolt safety locks the sear into the hammer. Available in all blue finish or blue slide and trigger with gold frame. Introduced 1985.
Price: **$149.95**

WILKINSON "LINDA" PISTOL

Caliber: 9mm Para., 31-shot magazine.
Barrel: 8^5/$_{16}$″.
Weight: 4 lbs., 13 oz. **Length:** 12^1/$_4$″ overall.
Stocks: Checkered black plastic pistol grip, maple forend.
Sights: Protected blade front, aperture rear.
Features: Fires from closed bolt. Semi-auto only. Straight blowback action. Cross-bolt safety. Removable barrel. From Wilkinson Arms.
Price: **$324.93**

Models specifically designed for classic competitive shooting sports.

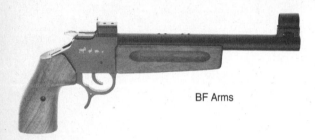

BF Arms

B F ARMS SINGLE SHOT PISTOL
Caliber: 7mm Super Mag., 7mm/375 Super Mag., 32-20, 30 Herrett, 357 Mag., 357 Max.
Barrel: 10″.
Weight: 46 oz.
Stocks: Ambidextrous, oil-finished walnut with forend.
Sights: Hooded front, fully adjustable match rear.
Features: Falling block short-stroke action. Wilson air-gauged match-grade barrel. Flat black oxide finish. Drilled and tapped for standard scope mounts. Made in U.S. by B F Arms. Introduced 1988.
Price: Silhouette, with sights $285.00
Price: Hunter, no sights $259.50

Beeman/Unique 69

BEEMAN/UNIQUE D.E.S. 69 TARGET PISTOL
Caliber: 22 LR, 5-shot magazine.
Barrel: 5.91″.
Weight: 35.3 oz. **Length:** 10.5″ overall.
Stocks: French walnut target-style with thumbrest and adjustable shelf; hand-checkered panels.
Sights: Ramp front, micro. adj. rear mounted on frame; 8.66″ sight radius.
Features: Meets U.I.T. standards. Comes with 260-gram barrel weight; 100, 150, 350 gram weights available. Fully adjustable match trigger; dry-firing safety device. Imported from France by Beeman.
Price: Right-hand $1,065.00
Price: Left-hand $1,130.00

Beeman/Unique 2000-U

BEEMAN/UNIQUE MODEL 2000-U MATCH PISTOL
Caliber: 22 Short, 5-shot magazine.
Barrel: 5.9″.
Weight: 43 oz. **Length:** 11.3″ overall.
Stocks: Anatomically shaped, adjustable, stippled French walnut.
Sights: Blade front, fully adjustable rear; 9.7″ sight radius.
Features: Light alloy frame, steel slide and shock absorber; five barrel vents reduce recoil, three of which can be blocked; trigger adjustable for position and pull weight. Comes with 340-gram weight housing, 160-gram available. Imported from France by Beeman. Introduced 1984.
Price: Right-hand $1,198.00
Price: Left-hand $1,260.00

Bernardelli Model 69

BERNARDELLI MODEL 69 TARGET PISTOL
Caliber: 22 LR, 10-shot magazine.
Barrel: 5.9″.
Weight: 38 oz. **Length:** 9″ overall.
Stocks: Wrap-around, hand-checkered walnut with thumbrest.
Sights: Fully adjustable and interchangeable target-type.
Features: Conforms to U.I.T. regulations. Has 7.1″ sight radius, .27″ wide grooved trigger with 40-45 oz. pull. Manual thumb safety and magazine safety. Introduced 1987. Imported from Italy by Magnum Research, Inc.
Price: $459.00

BERNARDELLI PO10 TARGET PISTOL
Caliber: 22 LR, 5- or 10-shot magazine.
Barrel: 5″.
Weight: About 40.5 oz.
Stocks: Anatomically shaped walnut with thumbrest.
Sights: Fully adjustable and interchangeable target-type.
Features: External hammer with safety notch; pivoted, adjustable trigger; matte black finish, Meets U.I.T. specs. Introduced 1989. Imported from Italy by Magnum Research, Inc.
Price: $519.00
Price: With case $579.00

Chipmunk Silhouette

CHIPMUNK SILHOUETTE PISTOL
Caliber: 22 LR.
Barrel: 14⅞″.
Weight: About 2 lbs. **Length:** 20″ overall.
Stock: American walnut rear grip.
Sights: Post on ramp front, peep rear.
Features: Meets IHMSA 22-cal. unlimited category for competition. Introduced 1985.
Price: $149.95

COLT GOLD CUP NAT'L MATCH MK IV/Series 80
Caliber: 45 ACP, 7-shot magazine.
Barrel: 5″, with new design bushing.
Weight: 39 oz. **Length:** 8 1/2″.
Stocks: Blue—checkered walnut, gold-plated medallion; stainless has black walnut.
Sights: Ramp-style front, Colt-Elliason rear adjustable for w. and e., sight radius 6 3/4″.
Features: Arched or flat housing; wide, grooved trigger with adjustable stop; ribbed-top slide, hand fitted, with improved ejection port.
Price: Blue **$765.50**
Price: Stainless **$821.95**
Price: Bright stainless **$876.50**
Price: Delta Gold Cup (10mm, stainless) . . . . **NA**

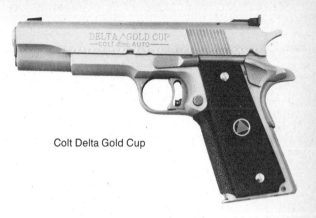

Colt Delta Gold Cup

COMPETITOR SINGLE SHOT PISTOL
Caliber: 22 LR, 223, 7mm TCU, 7mm Int., 30 Herrett, 357 Maximum, 41 Mag., 44 Mag., 454 Casull, 375 Super Mag. Others on special order.
Barrel: 10.5″, 14″.
Weight: NA **Length:** NA
Stocks: Smooth walnut with thumb rest.
Sights: Ramp front, open adjustable rear.
Features: Interchangeable barrels of blue ordnance or bright stainless steel; ventilated barrel shroud; receiver has integral scope mount. Introduced 1987. From TMI Products.
Price: With 10.5″ bbl. **$562.50**
Price: With 14″ bbl. **$578.50**
Price: Extra barrels, 10.5″, standard calibers **$93.75**
Price: Special calibers, add **$62.50**

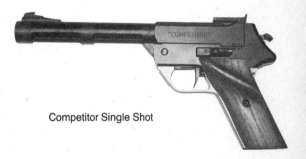

Competitor Single Shot

DETONICS SCOREMASTER TARGET PISTOL
Caliber: 45 ACP, 7-shot magazine.
Barrel: 5″ heavy match barrel with recessed muzzle; 6″ optional.
Weight: 42 oz. **Length:** 8 3/8″ overall.
Stocks: Pachmayr checkered with matching mainspring housing.
Sights: Blade front, Low-Base Bomar rear.
Features: Stainless steel; self-centering barrel system; patented Detonics recoil system; combat tuned; extended grip safety; National Match tolerances; extended magazine release. Comes with two spare magazines, three interchangeable front sights, and carrying case. Introduced 1983. From Detonics.
Price: 45 ACP, 6″ barrel **$1,150.00**
Price: As above, 5″ barrel **$1,110.00**

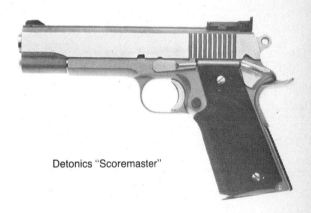

Detonics "Scoremaster"

Detonics Janus Scoremaster Pistol
Similar to the standard Scoremaster except in 45 ACP only and comes with extra 5.6″ compensated barrel and is easily convertible. With longer barrel, the front sight is mounted on the special compensator. Overall length with 5.6″ barrel is 10″, weight is 46 oz. Adjustable Millett rear sight, hand-serrated custom front. Has 8-shot magazine. Made of stainless steel with polished slide flats. Introduced 1988.
Price: **$1,650.00**

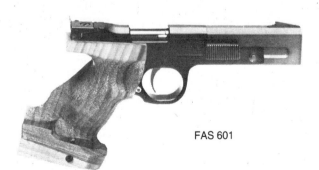

FAS 601

FAS 601 Match Pistol
Similar to SP 602 except has different match stocks with adjustable palm shelf, 22 Short only for rapid fire shooting; weighs 40 oz., 5.6″ bbl.; has gas ports through top of barrel and slide to reduce recoil; slightly different trigger and sear mechanisms.
Price: **$1,295.00**

ERMA ER MATCH REVOLVERS
Caliber: 22 LR, 32 S&W Long, 6-shot.
Barrel: 6″.
Weight: 46 oz. **Length:** 11.2″ overall.
Stocks: Stippled walnut, adjustable match-type.
Sights: Blade front, micrometer rear adjustable for windage and elevation.
Features: Polished blue finish. Introduced 1989. Imported from West Germany by Precision Sales International.
Price: 22 LR or 32 S&W Long **$1,225.00**

FAS 602 MATCH PISTOL
Caliber: 22 LR, 5-shot.
Barrel: 5.6″.
Weight: 37 oz. **Length:** 11″ overall.
Stocks: Walnut wrap-around; sizes small, medium or large, or adjustable.
Sights: Match. Blade front, open notch rear fully adjustable for w. and e. Sight radius is 8.66″.
Features: Line of sight is only 11/32″ above centerline of bore; magazine is inserted from top; adjustable and removable trigger mechanism; single lever takedown. Full 5-year warranty. Imported from Italy by Mandall Shooting Supplies.
Price: **$1,295.00**

HAMMERLI MODEL 150 FREE PISTOL
Caliber: 22 LR, single shot.
Barrel: 11.3".
Weight: 43 oz. **Length:** 15.35" overall.
Stocks: Walnut with adjustable palm shelf.
Sights: Sight radius of 14.6". Micro rear sight adjustable for w. and e.
Features: Single shot Martini action. Cocking lever on left side of action with vertical operation. Set trigger adjustable for length and angle. Trigger pull weight adjustable between 5 and 100 grams. Guaranteed accuracy of .78", 10 shots from machine rest. Imported from Switzerland by Mandall Shooting Supplies.
Price: About $1,980.00
Price: With electric trigger (Model 152), about $2,015.00

Hammerli 152

HAMMERLI MODEL 208s PISTOL
Caliber: 22 LR, 8-shot magazine.
Barrel: 5.9".
Weight: 37.5 oz. **Length:** 10" overall.
Stocks: Walnut, target-type with thumbrest.
Sights: Blade front, open fully adjustable rear.
Features: Adjustable trigger, including length; interchangeable rear sight elements. Imported from Switzerland by Mandall.
Price: $1,755.00

HAMMERLI STANDARD, MODELS 208, 211, 215
Caliber: 22 LR.
Barrel: 5.9", 6-groove.
Weight: 37.6 oz. (45 oz. with extra heavy barrel weight). **Length:** 10".
Stocks: Walnut. Adjustable palm rest (208), 211 has thumbrest grip.
Sights: Match sights, fully adjustable for w. and e. (click adjustable). Interchangeable front and rear blades.
Features: Semi-automatic, recoil operated. 8-shot clip. Slide stop. Fully adjustable trigger (2¼ lbs. and 3 lbs.). Extra barrel weight available. Imported from Switzerland by Mandall Shooting Supplies, Beeman.
Price: Model 208, approx. (Mandall) $1,399.00
Price: Model 211, approx. (Mandall) $1,295.00
Price: Model 215, approx. (Mandall) $1,295.00
Price: Model 208 (Beeman) $1,960.00
Price: Model 211 (Beeman) $1,570.00
Price: Model 215 (Beeman) $1,560.00

Hammerli 208

HAMMERLI MODEL 232 RAPID FIRE PISTOL
Caliber: 22 Short, 6-shot.
Barrel: 5", with six exhaust ports.
Weight: 44 oz. **Length:** 10.4" overall.
Stocks: Stippled walnut; wrap-around on Model 232-2, adjustable on 232-1.
Sights: Interchangeable front and rear blades, fully adjustable micrometer rear.
Features: Recoil operated semi-automatic; nearly recoilless design; trigger adjustable from 8.4 to 10.6 oz. with three lengths offered. Wrap-around grips available in small, medium and large sizes. Imported from Switzerland by Beeman, Mandall. Introduced 1984.
Price: Model 232-1, about $1,500.00
Price: Model 232-1 (Beeman) $1,445.00
Price: Model 232-2 (Beeman) $1.655.00

LLAMA M-87 9MM COMP
Caliber: 9mm Para., 14-shot magazine.
Barrel: 6".
Weight: 47 oz. **Length:** 9.5" overall.
Stocks: Polymer composition.
Sights: Patridge front, fully adjustable rear.
Features: A match-ready Comp pistol. Built-in ported compensator, over-size magazine and safety releases, fixed barrel bushing, bevelled magazine well, extended trigger guard. Introduced 1989. Imported by Stoeger Industries.
Price: $1,450.00

Llama M-87 Comp

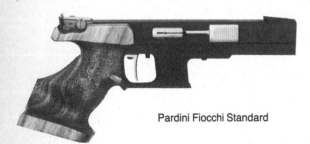

Pardini Fiocchi Standard

PARDINI FIOCCHI 32 MATCH PISTOL
Caliber: 32 S&W Long, 5-shot magazine.
Barrel: 4.9".
Weight: 38.7 oz. **Length:** 11.7" overall.
Stocks: Stippled walnut match-type with adjustable plam shelf.
Sights: Match. Undercut blade front, fully adjustable open rear.
Features: Match trigger. Recoil compensation system. Imported from Italy by Fiocchi of America.
Price: $906.25

PARDINI FIOCCHI STANDARD PISTOL
Caliber: 22 LR, 5-shot magazine.
Barrel: 4.9".
Weight: 37 oz. **Length:** 11.7" overall.
Stocks: Match-type stippled walnut.
Sights: Match-type undercut blade front, fully adjustable open rear.
Features: Match trigger. Matte blue finish. Comes with locking case. Imported from Italy by Fiocchi of America.
Price: $868.75

CAUTION: PRICES CHANGE. CHECK AT GUNSHOP.

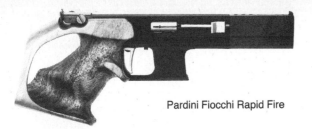

Pardini Fiocchi Rapid Fire

PARDINI FIOCCHI RAPID FIRE MATCH
Caliber: 22 Short, 5-shot magazine.
Barrel: 5.1".
Weight: 34.5 oz. **Length:** 11.7" overall.
Stocks: Stippled walnut, match-type.
Sights: Post front, fully adjustable rear.
Features: Alloy bolt. Has 14.9" sight radius. Imported from Italy by Fiocchi of America.
Price: **$893.75**

Pardini Fiocchi Free Pistol

PARDINI FIOCCHI FREE PISTOL
Caliber: 22 LR, single shot.
Barrel: 4.9".
Weight: 37 oz. **Length:** 11.7" overall.
Stocks: Walnut, special hand-fitting free-pistol design.
Sights: Post front, fully adjustable open rear.
Features: Rotating bolt-action design. Has 8.6" sight radius. Imported from Italy by Fiocchi of America.
Price: . . . . **$962.50.**

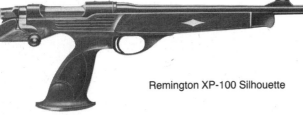

Remington XP-100 Silhouette

REMINGTON XP-100 SILHOUETTE PISTOL
Caliber: 7mm BR Remington, 35 Remington, single shot.
Barrel: 14³/₄".
Weight: 4¹/₈ lbs. **Length:** 21¹/₄" overall.
Stock: Brown nylon, one piece, checkered grip.
Sights: None furnished. Drilled and tapped for scope mounts.
Features: Universal grip fits right or left hand; match-type grooved trigger, two-position thumb safety.
Price: 7mm BR Rem **$380.00**
Price: 35 Rem **$393.00**

RUGER MARK II TARGET MODEL AUTO PISTOL
Caliber: 22 LR, 10-shot magazine.
Barrel: 6⁷/₈".
Weight: 42 oz. **Length:** 11¹/₈" overall.
Stocks: Checkered hard rubber.
Sights: .125" blade front, micro click rear, adjustable for w. and e. Sight radius 9³/₈". Introduced 1982.
Price: Blued (MK-678) **$259.75**
Price: Stainless (KMK-678) **$329.00**

Ruger Mark II Government Target Model
Same gun as the Mark II Target Model except has higher sights and is roll marked "Government Target Model" on the right side of the receiver below the rear sight. Identical in all respects to the military model used for training U.S. armed forces except for markings. Comes with factory test target. Introduced 1987.
Price: Blued (MK678G) **$300.25**

Ruger Mark II Bull Barrel
Same gun as the Target Model except has 5¹/₂" or 10" heavy barrel (10" meets all IHMSA regulations). Weight with 5¹/₂" barrel is 42 oz., with 10" barrel, 52 oz.
Price: Blued (MK-512, MK-10) **$259.75**
Price: Stainless (KMK-512, KMK-10) **$329.00**

Ruger Government Target

Smith & Wesson 29 Silhouette

SMITH & WESSON MODEL 29 SILHOUETTE
Caliber: 44 Magnum, 6-shot.
Barrel: 10⁵/₈".
Weight: 58 oz. **Length:** 16³/₁₆" overall.
Stocks: Over-size target-type, checkered Goncalo Alves.
Sights: Four-position front to match the four distances of silhouette targets; micro-click rear adjustable for windage and elevation.
Features: Designed specifically for silhouette shooting. Front sight has click stops for the four pre-set ranges. Introduced 1983.
Price: **$535.50**

SMITH & WESSON MODEL 745 AUTO
Caliber: 45 ACP, 8-shot magazine.
Barrel: 5".
Weight: 38.75 oz. **Length:** 8⁵/₈" overall.
Stocks: Checkered walnut.
Sights: Serrated ramp front, square notch high visibility rear adjustable for w.
Features: Stainless steel frame, blued slide, hammer, trigger, sights. Comes with two magazines. Introduced 1987.
Price: **$699.00**

COMPETITION HANDGUNS

SMITH & WESSON MODEL 41 TARGET
Caliber: 22 LR, 10-shot clip.
Barrel: 5½", 7".
Weight: 44½ oz. **Length:** 9" overall.
Stocks: Checkered walnut with modified thumbrest, usable with either hand.
Sights: ⅛" Patridge on ramp base. S&W micro click rear adjustable for w. and e.
Features: ⅜" wide, grooved trigger; adjustable trigger stop.
Price: S&W Bright Blue, satin matted top area. **$549.50**

SMITH & WESSON 38 MASTER Model 52 AUTO
Caliber: 38 Special (for mid-range W.C. with flush-seated bullet only), 5-shot magazine.
Barrel: 5".
Weight: 40.5 oz. with empty magazine. **Length:** 8⅝" overall.
Stocks: Checkered walnut.
Sights: ⅛" Patridge front, S&W micro-click rear adjustable for w. and e.
Features: Top sighting surfaces matte finished. Locked breech, moving barrel system; checked for 10-ring groups at 50 yards. Coin-adjustable sight screws. Dry-firing permissible if manual safety on.
Price: S&W Bright Blue. **$711.50**

Smith & Wesson Model 41

Smith & Wesson Model 52

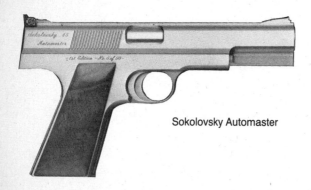

Sokolovsky Automaster

TAURUS MODEL 86 MASTER REVOLVER
Caliber: 38 Spec., 6-shot.
Barrel: 6" only.
Weight: 34 oz. **Length:** 11¼" overall.
Stocks: Oversize target-type, checkered Brazilian walnut.
Sights: Patridge front, micro-click rear adjustable for w. and e.
Features: Blue finish with non-reflective finish on barrel. Imported from Brazil by Taurus International.
Price: **$276.50**
Price: Model 96 Scout Master, same except in 22 cal. **$276.50**

SOKOLOVSKY 45 AUTOMASTER
Caliber: 45 ACP, 6-shot magazine.
Barrel: 6".
Weight: 3.6 lbs. **Length:** 9½" overall.
Stocks: Smooth walnut.
Sights: Ramp front, Millett fully adjustable rear.
Features: Intended for target shooting, not combat. Semi-custom built with precise tolerances. Has special "safety trigger" next to regular trigger. Most parts made of stainless steel. Introduced 1985. From Sokolovsky Corp.
Price: **$4,500.00**

Taurus Model 96

Thompson/Center Super 14 Contender

THOMPSON/CENTER SUPER 14 CONTENDER
Caliber: 22 LR, 222 Rem., 223 Rem., 7mm TCU, 7 x 30 Waters, 30-30 Win., 35 Rem., 357 Rem. Maximum, 44 Mag., 10mm Auto, 445 Super Mag., single shot.
Barrel: 14".
Weight: 45 oz. **Length:** 17¼" overall.
Stocks: T/C "Competitor Grip" (walnut and rubber).
Sights: Fully adjustable target-type.
Features: Break-open action with auto safety. Interchangeable barrels for both rimfire and centerfire calibers. Introduced 1978.
Price: **$345.00**
Price: With Armour Alloy II finish **$425.00**
Price: Extra barrels, blued **$155.00**
Price: As above, Armour Alloy **$205.00**

Thompson/Center Super 16 Contender
Same as the T/C Super 14 Contender except has 16¼" barrel. Rear sight can be mounted at mid-barrel position (10¾" radius) or moved to the rear (using scope mount position) for 14¾" radius. Overall length is 20¼". Comes with T/C Competitor Grip of walnut and rubber. Available in 22 LR, 22 WMR, 223 Rem., 7x30 Waters, 30-30 Win., 35 Rem., 44 Mag., 45-70 Gov't. Also available with 16" vent rib barrel with internal choke, caliber 45 Colt/410 shotshell.
Price: **$350.00**
Price: 45-70 Gov't **$365.00**
Price: Extra 16" barrels (blued) **$160.00**
Price: As above, 45-70 . . . . **$175.00**
Price: Super 16 Vent Rib (45-410). **$375.00**
Price: Extra vent rib barrel **$185.00**

Walther Free Pistol

UBERTI "PHANTOM" SA SILHOUETTE
Caliber: 357 Mag., 44 Mag.
Barrel: 10 1/2".
Weight: NA. **Length:** NA.
Stocks: Walnut target-style.
Sights: Blade on ramp front, fully adjustable rear.
Features: Hooked trigger guard. Introduced 1986. Imported by Uberti USA.
Price: **$518.00**

WALTHER GSP MATCH PISTOL
Caliber: 22 LR, 32 S&W wadcutter (GSP-C), 5-shot.
Barrel: 5 3/4".
Weight: 44.8 oz. (22 LR), 49.4 oz. (32). **Length:** 11.8" overall.
Stocks: Walnut, special hand-fitting design.
Sights: Fixed front, rear adjustable for w. and e.
Features: Available with either 2.2 lb. (1000 gm) or 3 lb. (1360 gm) trigger. Spare mag., bbl. weight, tools supplied in Match Pistol Kit. Imported from Germany by Interarms.
Price: GSP **$1,400.00**
Price: GSP-C **$1,650.00**
Price: 22 LR conversion unit for GSP-C **$875.00**
Price: 22 Short conversion unit for GSP-C **$875.00**
Price: 32 S&W conversion unit for GSP-C **$1,050.00**

DAN WESSON MODEL 40 SILHOUETTE
Caliber: 357 Maximum, 6-shot.
Barrel: 6", 8", 10".
Weight: 64 oz. (8" bbl.) **Length:** 14.3" overall (8" bbl.).
Stocks: Smooth walnut, target-style.
Sights: 1/8" serrated front, fully adjustable rear.
Features: Meets criteria for IHMSA competition with 8" slotted barrel. Blue or stainless steel.
Price: Blue, 6" **$508.32**
Price: Blue, 8" **$525.19**
Price: Blue, 10" **$543.41**
Price: Stainless, 6" **$568.97**
Price: Stainless, 8" slotted **$595.13**
Price: Stainless, 10" **$609.03**

DAN WESSON ACTION CUP/PPC COMPETITION REVOLVERS
Caliber: 38 Spec., 357 Mag., 6-shot.
Barrel: Extra heavy 6" bull shroud with removable underweight.
Weight: 4 lbs., 7 oz. (PPC, with weight).
Stocks: Pachmayr Gripper.
Sights: Tasco Pro Point II on Action Cup; Aristocrat with three-position rear on PPC model.
Features: Competition tuned with narrow trigger, chamfered cylinder chambers. Action Cup available in stainless only, PPC in bright blue or stainless. Introduced 1989.
Price: Action Cup **$913.30**
Price: PPC, blue **$779.83**
Price: PPC, stainless **$857.48**

WICHITA HUNTER, INTERNATIONAL PISTOL
Caliber: 22 LR, 22 WMR, 7mm INT-R, 7x30 Waters, 30-30 Win., 32 H&R Mag., 357 Mag., 357 Super Mag., single shot.
Barrel: 10 1/2".
Weight: International — 3 lbs., 13 oz.; Hunter — 3 lbs., 14 oz.
Stocks: Walnut grip and forend.
Sights: International — target front, adjustable rear; Hunter has scope mount only.
Features: Made of 17-4PH stainless steel. Break-open action. Grip dimensions same as Colt 45 auto. Safety supplied only on Hunter model. Extra barrels are factory fitted. Introduced 1983. Available from Wichita Arms.
Price: International **$484.95**
Price: Hunter **$484.95**
Price: Extra barrels **$295.00**

WALTHER FREE PISTOL
Caliber: 22 LR, single shot.
Barrel: 11.7".
Weight: 48 oz. **Length:** 17.2" overall.
Stocks: Walnut, special hand-fitting design.
Sights: Fully adjustable match sights.
Features: Special electronic trigger. Matte finish blue. Introduced 1980. Imported from Germany by Interarms.
Price: **$1,850.00**

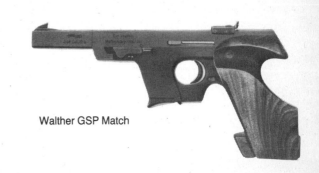

Walther GSP Match

Walther OSP Rapid-Fire Pistol
Similar to Model GSP except 22 Short only, stock has adjustable free-style hand rest.
Price: **$1,550.00**

Dan Wesson Model 40

WICHITA MK-40 SILHOUETTE PISTOL
Caliber: 22-250, 7mm IHMSA, 308 Win. F.L. Other calibers available on special order. Single shot.
Barrel: 13", non-glare blue; .700" dia. muzzle.
Weight: 4 1/2 lbs. **Length:** 19 3/8" overall.
Stock: American walnut with oil finish.
Sights: Wichita Multi-Range sighting system.
Features: Aluminum receiver with steel insert locking lugs, measures 1.360" O.D.; three locking lug bolts, three gas ports; flat bolt handle; completely adjustable Wichita trigger. Introduced 1981. From Wichita Arms.
Price: **$1,100.00**

Wichita Silhouette/Hunter

WICHITA SILHOUETTE PISTOL

Caliber: 22-250, 7mm IHMSA, 308. Other calibers available on special order. Single shot.
Barrel: 14¹⁵/₁₆″.
Weight: 4¹/₂ lbs. **Length:** 21³/₈″ overall.
Stock: American walnut with oil finish. Glass bedded.
Sights: Wichita Multi-Range sight system.
Features: Comes with left-hand action with right-hand grip. Fluted bolt, flat bolt handle. Action drilled and tapped for Burris scope mounts. Non-glare satin blue finish. Wichita adjustable trigger. Introduced 1979. From Wichita Arms.
Price: Center grip stock $1,100.00
Price: As above except with Rear Position Stock and target-type Lightpull trigger $1,100.00

Wichita Silhouette

WICHITA CLASSIC PISTOL

Caliber: Any, up to and including 308 Win.
Barrel: 11¹/₄″, octagon.
Weight: About 5 lbs.
Stock: Exhibition grade American black walnut. Checkered 20 lpi. Other woods available on special order.
Sights: Micro open sights standard. Receiver drilled and tapped for scope mount.

Features: Receiver and barrel octagonally shaped, finished in non-glare blue. Bolt has three locking lugs and three gas escape ports. Completely adjustable Wichita trigger. Introduced 1980. From Wichita Arms.
Price: 2,950.00
Price: Engraved, in walnut presentation case $4,850.00

HANDGUNS—DOUBLE ACTION REVOLVERS, SERVICE & SPORT

Includes models suitable for hunting and competitive courses for fire, both police and international.

Armscor 38

ARMSCOR MODEL 200SE REVOLVER

Caliber: 22 LR, 22 WMR, 38 Spec., 6-shot.
Barrel: 2″, 3″, 4″, 6″.
Weight: 36 oz. (4″ barrel). **Length:** 9.25″ overall (4″ barrel).
Stocks: Checkered mahogany.
Sights: Ramp front, fully adjustable rear.
Features: Blue finish, ventilated barrel rib. Introduced 1989. Imported from the Philippines by Armscor.
Price: $199.95

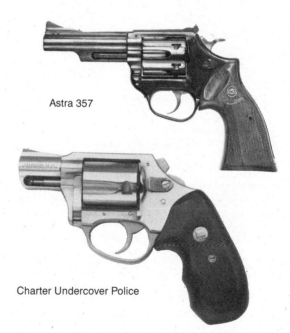

Astra 357

Charter Undercover Police

ASTRA 357/9mm CONVERTIBLE REVOLVER

Caliber: 357 Magnum, 6-shot.
Barrel: 3″, 4″, 6″, 8¹/₂″.
Weight: 40 oz. (6″ bbl.) **Length:** 11¹/₄″ (6″ bbl.).
Stocks: Checkered walnut.
Sights: Fixed front, rear adjustable for w. and e.
Features: Swing-out cylinder with countersunk chambers, floating firing pin. Target-type hammer and trigger. Imported from Spain by Interarms.
Price: $395.00

Astra Model 44, 45 Double-Action Revolver

Similar to the 357 Mag. except chambered for 44 Mag. or 45 Colt. Barrel length of 6″ only, giving overall length of 11³/₈″. Weight is 2³/₄ lbs. Introduced 1980.
Price: 44 Mag., 6″, stainless $450.00

CHARTER ARMS UNDERCOVER POLICE SPECIAL

Caliber: 38 Special, 5-shot.
Barrel: 2.1″.
Weight: 21 oz. **Length:** 6.5″ overall.
Stocks: Smooth combat-style of laminated wood.
Sights: Blade front, fixed rear.
Features: Stainless steel or Service Blue. Double-action mode only. Spurless hammer. Full ejector rod shroud. Made in U.S. by Charter Arms.
Price: Service Blue, about $184.00
Price: Stainless, about $264.00

Charter Arms "Bonnie" and "Clyde" Revolvers

Similar to the Undercover Police Special except in blue only with 2¹/₂″ full-shroud barrel; one gun barrel is marked "Bonnie," the other "Clyde." Grips of laminated wood in choice of nine colors: Rosewood, Camo, Oak, Burnt Orange, Golden Brown, Aqua, Scarlet, Ebony, Blonde. Both have fixed sights. Introduced 1989.
Price: $259.00

CHARTER ARMS POLICE BULLDOG
Caliber: 32 H&R Mag., 38 Special (6-shot), 357 Mag., 44 Special (5-shot).
Barrel: 32 H&R Mag., 44 Spec. — 3½"; 38 Special, 357 Mag. — 4".
Weight: 23.5 oz. (44 Spec.) to 28 oz. (357 Mag.)
Length: 8½" overall (357 Mag., 4" bbl.).
Stocks: Checkered neoprene; walnut or neoprene or 44 Special.
Sights: Blade front, fixed rear on 4", adjustable on 3½" barrel.
Features: Stainless steel or Service Blue. All have full barrel shrouds. Made in U.S. by Charter Arms.
Price: Stainless, 32 H&R Mag., about $285.00
Price: Stainless, 38 Special, about $275.00
Price: Stainless, 357 Mag., about........................... $299.00
Price: Stainless, 44 Spec., about $307.00
Price: Service Blue, 32, 38, 3½" barrel, about $260.00
Price: Service Blue, 32, 38, 4" barrel, about $235.00
Price: Service Blue, 44 Spec., about $260.00

Charter Police Bulldog

Charter Arms Bulldog Tracker
Similar to the standard Bulldog except chambered for 357 Mag., has adjustable rear sight, 2½" bull barrel, ramp front sight, square butt checkered walnut grips. Available in blue finish only.
Price: $250.00

CHARTER ARMS BULLDOG
Caliber: 44 Special, 5-shot.
Barrel: 2½".
Weight: 19 oz. **Length:** 7¾" overall.
Stocks: Checkered walnut, Bulldog.
Sights: Patridge-type front, square-notch rear.
Features: Wide trigger and hammer; beryllium copper firing pin.
Price: Service Blue, 2½" $242.00
Price: Stainless steel, 2½" $290.00

CHARTER ARMS TARGET BULLDOG
Caliber: 357 Mag., 9mm Federal, 44 Spec., 5-shot.
Barrel: 5½", vent. rib, full shroud.
Weight: 29 oz. **Length:** 10" overall.
Stocks: Walnut, smooth target-type.
Sights: Blade front, adjustable rear.
Features: Made of stainless steel. Shrouded ejector rod. Made in U.S. by Charter Arms.
Price: $375.00

Charter Target Bulldog

CHARTER ARMS PATHFINDER REVOLVER
Caliber: 22 LR, 6-shot.
Barrel: 3½".
Weight: 26 oz. **Length:** 8¼" overall.
Stocks: Checkered Neoprene.
Sights: Blade front, adjustable rear.
Features: Stainless steel or Service Blue. Full-length ejector rod shroud. Made in U.S. by Charter Arms.
Price: Service Blue (does not have shroud), about $230.00
Price: Stainless, about $282.00

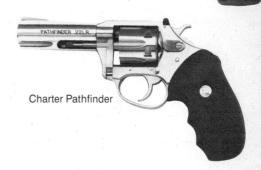

Charter Pathfinder

CHARTER ARMS PIT BULL REVOLVER
Caliber: 9mm Federal, 5-shot.
Barrel: 2½", 3½".
Weight: 24.5 oz. (2½" bbl.). **Length:** 7¼" overall (2½" bbl.).
Stocks: Checkered neoprene.
Sights: Blade front, fixed rear on 2½", adjustable on 3½".
Features: Stainless steel or Service Blue. Both barrels have full-length ejector rod shroud. Made in U.S. by Charter Arms.
Price: Service Blue, 2½", about $286.00
Price: Service Blue, 3½", about $293.00
Price: Stainless, 2½", about $300.00
Price: Stainless, 3½", about $307.00

CHARTER ARMS UNDERCOVER REVOLVER
Caliber: 38 Special, 5-shot.
Barrel: 2".
Weight: 16 oz. **Length:** 6¼" overall (2").
Stocks: Checkered walnut.
Sights: Patridge-type ramp front, notched rear.
Features: Wide trigger and hammer spur. Steel frame. Police Undercover, 2" bbl. (for 38 Spec. +P loads) carry same prices as regular 38 Spec. guns.
Price: Polished blue, about................................ $216.00
Price: Stainless, about $272.00

Charter Pit Bull

Charter Arms Off-Duty Revolver
Similar to the Undercover except 38 Special or 22 LR, 2" barrel, Mat-Black non glare finish. This all-steel gun comes with Red-Dot front sight. Also available in stainless steel. Introduced 1984.
Price: Mat-Black finish, about............................. $184.00
Price: Stainless steel, about $241.00

CHARTER ARMS BULLDOG PUG
Caliber: 44 Special, 5-shot.
Barrel: 2½".
Weight: 19 oz. **Length:** 7¼" overall.
Stocks: Bulldog walnut or neoprene.
Sights: Ramp front, notch rear.
Features: Shrouded ejector rod; wide trigger and hammer spur. Introduced 1986.
Price: About... $250.00

COLT KING COBRA REVOLVER
Caliber: 357 Magnum, 6-shot.
Barrel: 2¹/₂″, 4″, 6″ (STS); 4″, 6″ (BSTS); 4″, 6″ (blue).
Weight: 42 oz. (4″ bbl.). **Length:** 9″ overall (4″ bbl.).
Stocks: Checkered rubber.
Sights: Red insert ramp front, adjustable white outline rear.
Features: Stainless steel; full-length contoured ejector rod housing, barrel rib; matte finish. Introduced 1986.
Price: STS, 2¹/₂″, 4″, 6″ **$434.95**
Price: BSTS, 4″, 6″ **$471.95**
Price: Blue, 4″, 6″ **$408.95**

Colt King Cobra

COLT PYTHON REVOLVER
Caliber: 357 Magnum (handles all 38 Spec.), 6-shot.
Barrel: 2¹/₂″, 4″, 6″ or 8″, with ventilated rib.
Weight: 38 oz. (4″ bbl.). **Length:** 9¹/₄″ (4″ bbl.).
Stocks: Checkered walnut, target-type.
Sights: ¹/₈″ ramp front, adjustable notch rear.
Features: Ventilated rib; grooved, crisp trigger; swing-out cylinder; target hammer.
Price: Blue, 2¹/₂″, 4″, 6″, 8″ **$729.95**
Price: Stainless, 2¹/₂″, 4″, 6″, 8″ **$835.95**
Price: Bright stainless, 2¹/₂″, 4″, 6″, 8″ **$859.95**

Colt Python

ERMA ER-777 SPORTING REVOLVER
Caliber: 357 Mag., 6-shot.
Barrel: 4″, 5¹/₂″, 6″.
Weight: 44 to 48 oz. **Length:** 9¹/₂″ overall (4″ barrel).
Stocks: Stippled walnut service-type.
Sights: Interchangeable blade front, micro-adjustable rear for windage and elevation.
Features: Polished blue finish. Adjustable trigger. Imported from West Germany by Precision Sales Int'l. Introduced 1988.
Price: **$1,093.00**

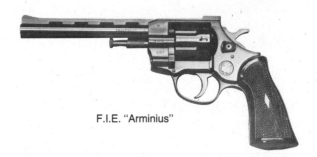

Erma ER-777

Consult our Directory pages for
the location of firms mentioned.

F.I.E. ARMINIUS REVOLVERS
Caliber: 38 Special, 357 WMR, 32 S&W, 22 WMR, 22 LR.
Barrel: 2″, 3″, 4″, 6″.
Weight: 35 oz. (6″ bbl.). **Length:** 11″ overall (6″ bbl.).
Stocks: Checkered plastic; walnut optional.
Sights: Ramp front, fixed rear on standard models, w. and e. adjustments on target models.
Features: Thumb-release, swing-out cylinder. Ventilated rib, solid frame. Interchangeable 22 WMR cylinder available with 22 cal. versions. Imported from West Germany by F.I.E. Corp.
Price: .... **$199.95 to $279.95**

F.I.E. "Arminius"

F.I.E. "TITAN TIGER" REVOLVER
Caliber: 38 Special.
Barrel: 2″ or 4″.
Weight: 27 oz. **Length:** 6¹/₄″ overall (2″ bbl.).
Stocks: Checkered plastic, Bulldog style. Walnut optional.
Sights: Fixed.
Features: Thumb-release swing-out cylinder, one stroke ejection. Made in U.S.A. by F.I.E. Corp.
Price: Blue **$189.95**

F.I.E. "STANDARD" REVOLVER
Caliber: 32 S&W, 32 S&W Long, 32 H&R Mag., 38 Spec., 6-shot.
Barrel: 2″ or 4″.
Weight: 23 oz. (2″ barrel). **Length:** 6¹/₄″ overall (2″ barrel).
Stocks: Magnum-style round butt; checkered plastic.
Sights: Ramp front, fixed square notch rear.
Features: One-piece solid frame; checkered hammer spur, serrated trigger; blue finish. Introduced 1989. Imported by F.I.E. Firearms Corp.
Price: **$129.95**

F.I.E. "Standard"

CAUTION: PRICES CHANGE. CHECK AT GUNSHOP.

LLAMA COMANCHE III REVOLVERS
Caliber: 357 Mag.
Barrel: 4″, 6″.
Weight: 28 oz. **Length:** 9¼″ (4″ bbl.).
Stocks: Checkered walnut.
Sights: Fixed blade front, rear adjustable for w. and e.
Features: Ventilated rib, wide spur hammer. Satin chrome finish available. Imported from Spain by Stoeger Industries.
Price: Blue finish **$325.00**
Price: Satin chrome **$380.00**

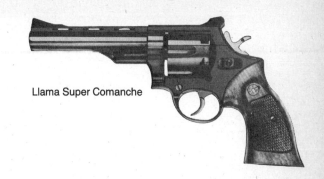

Llama Super Comanche

Llama Super Comanche IV Revolver
Similar to the Comanche except: large frame, 44 Mag. with 6″, 8½″ barrel, 6-shot cylinder; smooth, extra wide trigger; wide spur hammer; over-size walnut, target-style grips. Weight is 3 lbs., 2 oz. Blue finish only.
Price: 44 Mag. **$420.00**

NEW ENGLAND FIREARMS DA REVOLVERS
Caliber: 22 LR (9-shot), 22 WMR (6-shot), 32 H&R Mag. (5-shot).
Barrel: 2½″, 4″, 6″.
Weight: 25 oz. (22 LR, 2½″). **l ength:** 7″ overall (2½ bbl.).
Stocks: American hardwood.
Sights: Fixed.
Features: Choice of blue or nickel finish. Introduced 1988. From New England Firearms Co.
Price: . . . . **NA**

New England Revolver

New England Ultra

NEW ENGLAND FIREARMS ULTRA REVOLVER
Caliber: 22 LR (9-shot), 22 WMR (6-shot), 32 H&R Mag. (5-shot).
Barrel: 4″, 6″.
Weight: 32 oz. (4″ bbl.). **Length:** 8⅝″ overall (4″ bbl.).
Stocks: Walnut-finished hardwood.
Sights: Blade front, fully adjustable rear.
Features: Blue finish. Bull-style barrel with recessed muzzle, high "Lustre" blue/black finish on 22 LR with 6″ barrel. Introduced 1989. From New England Firearms.
Price: . . . . **NA**

ROSSI MODEL 68 REVOLVER
Caliber: 38 Spec.
Barrel: 2″, 3″.
Weight: 22 oz.
Stocks: Checkered wood.
Sights: Ramp front, low profile adjustable rear.
Features: All-steel frame, Thumb latch operated swing-out cylinder. Introduced 1978. Imported from Brazil by Interarms.
Price: 38, blue, 3″ **$180.00**
Price: M68/2 (2″ barrel) **$185.00**
Price: 3″, nickel **$195.00**

Rossi Model 68

ROSSI MODEL 88 STAINLESS REVOLVER
Caliber: 32 S&W, 38 Spec., 5-shot.
Barrel: 2″, 3″.
Weight: 22 oz. **Length:** 7.5″ overall.
Stocks: Checkered wood, service-style.
Sights: Ramp front, square notch rear drift adjustable for windage.
Features: All metal parts except springs are of 440 stainless steel; matte finish; small frame for concealability. Introduced 1983. Imported from Brazil by Interarms.
Price: 3″ barrel **$215.00**
Price: M88/2 (2″ barrel) **$215.00**
Price: M89 stainless (3″, 32 S&W) **$210.00**

Rossi Model 88 Stainless

ROSSI MODEL 511 SPORTSMAN'S 22 REVOLVER
Caliber: 22 LR, 6-shot.
Barrel: 4″.
Weight: 30 oz. **Length:** 9″ overall.
Stocks: Checkered wood.
Sights: Orange-insert ramp front, fully adjustable square notch rear.
Features: All stainless steel. Shrouded ejector rod; heavy barrel; integral sight rib. Introduced 1986. Imported from Brazil by Interarms.
Price: **$235.00**

Rossi Model 511

ROSSI MODEL 951 REVOLVER
Caliber: 38 Special, 6-shot.
Barrel: 3″, 4″, vent. rib.
Weight: 30 oz. **Length:** 9″ overall.
Stocks: Checkered hardwood, combat-style.
Sights: Colored insert front, fully adjustable rear.
Features: Polished blue finish, shrouded ejector rod. Medium-size frame. Introduced 1985. Imported from Brazil by Interarms.
Price: M951, blue **$225.00**
Price: M851 (as above, stainless, 3″, 4″) **$245.00**

ROSSI MODEL 971 REVOLVER
Caliber: 357 Mag., 6-shot.
Barrel: 4″, heavy.
Weight: 36 oz. **Length:** 9″ overall.
Stocks: Checkered Brazilian hardwood.
Sights: Blade front, fully adjustable rear.
Features: Full-length ejector rod shroud; matted sight rib; target-type trigger, wide checkered hammer spur. Introduced 1988. Imported from Brazil by Interarms.
Price: **$245.00**
Price: M971 stainless, 4″, 6″ .... **NA**

RUGER GP-100 REVOLVERS
Caliber: 38 Special, 357 Magnum, 6-shot.
Barrel: 3″, 3″ heavy, 4″, 4″ heavy.
Weight: 3″ barrel — 35 oz., 3″ heavy barrel — 36 oz., 4″ barrel — 37 oz., 4″ heavy barrel — 38 oz.
Sights: Fixed.
Stocks: Ruger Cushioned Grip (live rubber with Goncalo Alves inserts).
Features: Uses all new action and frame incorporating improvements and features of both the Security-Six and Redhawk revolvers. Full length and short ejector shroud. Satin blue and stainless steel. Introduced 1988.
Price: GPF-330 (357, 3″), GPF-830 (38 Spec.) **$360.00**
Price: GPF-331 (357, 3″ heavy), GPF-831 (38 Spec.) **$360.00**
Price: GPF-340 (357, 4″), GPF-840 (38 Spec.) **$360.00**
Price: GPF-341 (357, 4″ heavy), GPF-841 (38 Spec.) **$360.00**
Price: KGPF-330 (357, 3″, stainless), KGPF-830 (38 Spec.) **$390.00**
Price: KGPF-331 (357, 3″ heavy, stainless), KGPF-831 (38 Spec.).. **$390.00**
Price: KGPF-340 (357, 4″, stainless), KGPF-840 (38 Spec.) **$390.00**
Price: KGPF-341 (357, 4″ heavy, stainless), KGPF-841 (38 Spec.).. **$390.00**

Rossi Model 951

Rossi Model 971

Ruger GP-100

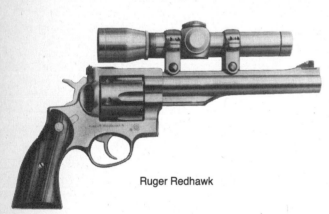

Ruger Redhawk

Ruger Super Redhawk

RUGER SP101 REVOLVERS
Caliber: 38 Special + P, 5-shot.
Barrel: 2¼″, 3″.
Weight: 2¼″ — 25 oz.; 3″ — 27 oz.
Sights: Fixed.
Stocks: Ruger Cushioned Grip (live rubber with plastic inserts). Goncalo Alves wood inserts are available as an accessory.
Features: Incorporates improvements and features found in the GP-100 revolvers into a compact, small frame, double-action revolver. Full-length ejector shroud. Stainless steel only. Introduced 1988.
Price: KSP-182 (2¼″ barrel) **$370.00**
Price: KSP-183 (3″ barrel) **$370.00**

RUGER REDHAWK
Caliber: 41 Mag., 44 Rem. Mag., 6-shot.
Barrel: 5½″, 7½″.
Weight: About 54 oz. (7½″ bbl.). **Length:** 13″ overall (7½″ barrel).
Stocks: Square butt Goncalo Alves.
Sights: Interchangeable Patridge-type front, rear adjustable for w. and e.
Features: Stainless steel, brushed satin finish, or blued ordnance steel. Has a 9½″ sight radius. Introduced 1979.
Price: Blued, 41 Mag., 44 Mag., 5½″, 7½″ **$397.00**
Price: Blued, 41 Mag., 44 Mag., 7½″, with scope mount, rings **$430.00**
Price: Stainless, 41 Mag., 44 Mag., 5½″, 7½″ **$447.50**
Price: Stainless, 41 Mag., 44 Mag., 7½″, with scope mount, rings . **$482.50**

Ruger Super Redhawk Revolver
Similar to the standard Redhawk except has a heavy extended frame with the Ruger Integral Scope Mounting System on the wide topstrap. The wide hammer spur has been lowered for better scope clearance. Incorporates the mechanical design features and improvements of the GP-100. Choice of 7½″ or 9½″ barrrel, both with ramp front sight base with Redhawk-style interchangeable insert sight blades, adjustable rear sight. Comes with Ruger "Cushioned Grip" panels of live rubber and Goncalo Alves wood. Satin polished stainless steel, 44 Magnum only. Introduced 1987.
Price: KSRH-7 (7½″), KSRH-9 (9½″) **$510.00**

CAUTION: PRICES CHANGE. CHECK AT GUNSHOP.

SMITH & WESSON M&P Model 10 REVOLVER
Caliber: 38 Special, 6-shot.
Barrel: 2″, 4″.
Weight: 30½ oz. **Length:** 9¼″ overall.
Stocks: Checkered walnut, Service. Round or square butt.
Sights: Fixed, ramp front, square notch rear.
Price: Blued $323.00

S&W Model 10

Smith & Wesson 38 M&P Heavy Barrel Model 10
Same as regular M&P except: 4″ heavy ribbed bbl. with ramp front sight, square rear, square butt, wgt. 33½ oz.
Price: Blued $323.00
Price: Nickeled $334.50

SMITH & WESSON Model 13 H.B. M&P
Caliber: 357 and 38 Special, 6-shot.
Barrel: 3″ or 4″.
Weight: 34 oz. **Length:** 9⁵/₁₆″ overall (4″ bbl.).
Stocks: Checkered walnut, Service.
Sights: ⅛″ serrated ramp front, fixed square notch rear.
Features: Heavy barrel, K-frame, square butt (4″), round butt (3″).
Price: Blue $329.00
Price: Model 65, as above in stainless steel $357.00

S&W Model 15

SMITH & WESSON MODEL 15 COMBAT MASTERPIECE
Caliber: 38 Special, 6-shot.
Barrel: 4″, 6″.
Weight: 32 oz. **Length:** 9⁵/₁₆″ (4″ bbl.).
Stocks: Checkered walnut. Grooved tangs.
Sights: Front, Baughman Quick Draw on ramp, micro-click rear, adjustable for w. and e.
Price: Blued, 4″, 6″ $350.00

S&W Model 17

SMITH & WESSON MODEL 17 K-22 MASTERPIECE
Caliber: 22 LR, 6-shot.
Barrel: 4″, 6″, 8³/₈″.
Weight: 39 oz. (6″ bbl.). **Length:** 11⅛″ overall.
Stocks: Checkered walnut, Service.
Sights: Patridge front with 6″, 8³/₈″, serrated on 4″, S&W micro-click rear adjustable for windage and elevation.
Features: Grooved tang, polished blue finish.
Price: 4″, 6″ bbl. $368.00
Price: 8³/₈″ bbl. $414.50

SMITH & WESSON 357 COMBAT MAGNUM Model 19
Caliber: 357 Magnum and 38 Special, 6-shot.
Barrel: 2½″, 4″, 6″.
Weight: 36 oz. **Length:** 9⁹/₁₆″ (4″ bbl.).
Stocks: Checkered Goncalo Alves, target. Grooved tangs.
Sights: Front, ⅛″ Baughman Quick Draw on 2½″ or 4″ bbl., Patridge on 6″ bbl., micro-click rear adjustable for w. and e.
Features: Also available in nickel finish.
Price: S&W Bright Blue, adj. sights, from $338.50
Price: Nickel, 4″, 6″ only $357.00

S&W Model 19

SMITH & WESSON MODEL 25 REVOLVER
Caliber: 45 Colt, 6-shot.
Barrel: 4″, 6″, 8³/₈″.
Weight: About 46 oz. **Length:** 11³/₈″ overall (6″ bbl.).
Stocks: Checkered Goncalo Alves, target-type.
Sights: S&W red ramp front, S&W micrometer click rear with white outline.
Features: Available in Bright Blue or nickel finish; target trigger, target hammer. Contact S&W for complete price list.
Price: 4″, 6″, blue $429.00
Price: 8³/₈″, blue or nickel $436.50

S&W Model 25

Smith & Wesson Model 625-2
Similar to the Model 25 except chambered for 45 ACP, is made of stainless steel. Has pinned black front sight ramp, micrometer rear with plain blade, semi-target hammer, combat trigger, round butt Pachmayr stocks, full lug barrel. Introduced 1989.
Price: $535.00

CAUTION: PRICES CHANGE. CHECK AT GUNSHOP.

SMITH & WESSON 44 MAGNUM Model 29 REVOLVER
Caliber: 44 Magnum, 44 Special or 44 Russian, 6-shot.
Barrel: 4″, 6″, 8³/₈″, 10⁵/₈″.
Weight: 47 oz. (6″ bbl.), 44 oz. (4″ bbl.). **Length:** 11³/₈″ overall (6″ bbl.).
Stocks: Oversize target-type, checkered Goncalo Alves. Tangs and target trigger grooved, checkered target hammer.
Sights: ¹/₈″ red ramp front, micro-click rear, adjustable for w. and e.
Price: S&W Bright Blue or nickel, 4″, 6″ $481.50
Price: 8³/₈″ bbl., blue $492.00
Price: As above with scope mount $527.00
Price: 10⁵/₈″, blue only (AF) $535.50
Price: Model 629 (stainless steel), 4″, 6″ $509.50
Price: Model 629, 8³/₈″ barrel $526.50
Price: As above with scope mount $561.50

SMITH & WESSON 357 MAGNUM M-27 REVOLVER
Caliber: 357 Magnum and 38 Special, 6-shot.
Barrel: 4″, 6″, 8³/₈″.
Weight: 45¹/₂ oz. (6″ bbl.). **Length:** 11⁵/₁₆″ (6″ bbl.).
Stocks: Checkered walnut, Magna. Grooved tangs and trigger.
Sights: Serrated ramp front, micro-click rear, adjustable for w. and e.
Price: S&W Bright Blue, 4″ $451.00
Price: As above, 6″ $423.00
Price: 8³/₈″ bbl., sq. butt, target hammer, trigger, stocks $430.50

SMITH & WESSON 32 REGULATION POLICE Model 31
Caliber: 32 S&W Long, 6-shot.
Barrel: 2″, 3″.
Weight: 18³/₄ oz. (3″ bbl.). **Length:** 7¹/₂″ (3″ bbl.).
Stocks: Checkered walnut, Magna.
Sights: Fixed, ¹/₁₀″ serrated ramp front, square notch rear.
Features: Blued.
Price: $354.00

SMITH & WESSON 1953 Model 34, 22/32 KIT GUN
Caliber: 22 LR, 6-shot.
Barrel: 2″, 4″.
Weight: 24 oz. (4″ bbl.). **Length:** 8³/₈″ (4″ bbl. and round butt).
Stocks: Checkered walnut, round or square butt.
Sights: Front, serrated ramp, micro-click rear, adjustable for w. and e.
Price: Blued $355.50
Price: Model 63, as above in stainless, 4″ $390.00

SMITH & WESSON BODYGUARD MODEL 38
Caliber: 38 Special, 5-shot.
Barrel: 2″.
Weight: 14¹/₂ oz. **Length:** 6⁵/₁₆″ overall.
Stocks: Checkered walnut.
Sights: Fixed serrated ramp front, square notch rear.
Features: Alloy frame; internal hammer.
Price: Blued $368.00
Price: Nickeled $381.00

SMITH & WESSON 38 CHIEFS SPECIAL & AIRWEIGHT
Caliber: 38 Special, 5-shot.
Barrel: 2″, 3″.
Weight: 19¹/₂ oz. (2″ bbl.); 13¹/₂ oz. (Airweight). **Length:** 6¹/₂″ (2″ bbl. and round butt).
Stocks: Checkered walnut, round or square butt.
Sights: Fixed, serrated ramp front, square notch rear.
Price: Blued, standard Model 36, 2″ $328.00
Price: As above, nickel 2″ $339.00
Price: Blued, Airweight Model 37 .... $347.50
Price: As above, nickel $361.00

Smith & Wesson Model 36-LS LadySmith
Similar to the standard Model 36. Available with 2″ or 3″ barrel. The 2″ comes with smooth, contoured rosewood grips with the S&W monogram; 3″ has smooth, finger-grooved Goncalo Alves grips. Each has a speedloader cutout. Comes in a fitted carry/storage case. Introduced 1989.
Price: Model 36-LS $368.00
Price: Model 60-LS (as above except in stainless) $415.00

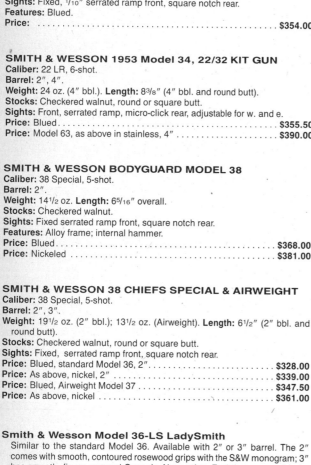

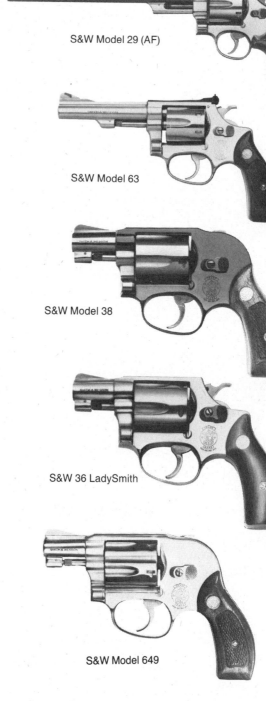

S&W Model 29 (AF)

S&W Model 63

S&W Model 38

S&W 36 LadySmith

S&W Model 649

Smith & Wesson Bodyguard Model 49, 649 Revolvers
Same as Model 38 except steel construction, weight 20¹/₂ oz.
Price: Blued, Model 49 .... $348.00
Price: Stainless, Model 649 .... $396.50

Smith & Wesson Model 60 Chiefs Special Stainless
Same as Model 36 except: 2″ bbl. and round butt only.
Price: Stainless steel $375.00

SMITH & WESSON 41 MAGNUM MODEL 57 REVOLVER
Caliber: 41 Magnum, 6-shot.
Barrel: 4″, 6″ or 8³/₈″.
Weight: 48 oz. (6″ bbl.). **Length:** 11⁹/₈″ (6″ bbl.).
Stocks: Oversize target-type checkered Goncalo Alves.
Sights: ¹/₈″ red ramp front, micro-click rear adjustable for w. and e.
Price: S&W Bright Blue or nickel 4″, 6″ $427.00
Price: 8³/₈″ bbl. $442.00
Price: Stainless, Model 657, 4″, 6″ $455.00
Price: As above, 8³/₈″ $470.50

S&W Model 57

SMITH & WESSON MODEL 64 STAINLESS M&P
Caliber: 38 Special, 6-shot.
Barrel: 2″, 3″, 4″.
Weight: 34 oz. **Length:** 9⁵/₁₆″ overall.
Stocks: Checkered walnut, Service style.
Sights: Fixed, ¹/₈″ serrated ramp front, square notch rear.
Features: Satin finished stainless steel, square butt.
Price: $351.00

S&W Model 66

SMITH & WESSON MODEL 66 STAINLESS COMBAT MAGNUM
Caliber: 357 Magnum and 38 Special, 6-shot.
Barrel: 2¹/₂″, 4″, 6″.
Weight: 36 oz. **Length:** 9⁹/₁₆″ overall.
Stocks: Checkered Goncalo Alves target.
Sights: Front, Baughman Quick Draw on ramp, micro-click rear adjustable for windage and elevation.
Features: Satin finish stainless steel.
Price: From $385.00

SMITH & WESSON MODELS 586, 686 DISTINGUISHED COMBAT MAGNUM
Caliber: 357 Magnum.
Barrel: 4″, 6″, 8³/₈″, full shroud.
Weight: 46 oz. (6″), 41 oz. (4″).
Stocks: Goncalo Alves target-type with speed loader cutaway.
Sights: Baughman red ramp front, four-position click-adjustable front, S&W micro-meter click rear (or fixed).
Features: Uses new L-frame, but takes all K-frame grips. Full-length ejector rod shroud. Smooth combat-type trigger, semi-target type hammer. Trigger stop on 6″ models. Also available in stainless as Model 686. Introduced 1981.
Price: Model 586, blue, 4″ $381.50
Price: Model 586, nickel, from $393.00
Price: Model 686, stainless, from $410.00
Price: Model 586, 6″, adjustable front sight, blue $423.50
Price: As above, 8³/₈″ $410.50
Price: Model 686, 6″, adjustable front sight $447.50
Price: As above, 8³/₈″ $465.00

S&W Model 586

Smith & Wesson 686 Midnight Black
Similar ot the standard Model 686 except has Midnight Black finish, combat trigger, semi-target hammer. Comes with red ramp front sight, plain or white outline micrometer rear, Goncalo Alves target stocks with speedloader cut, full lug barrel. Introduced 1989.
Price: $445.00

Smith & Wesson 686 Classic Hunter
Similar to the stainless Model 686 except available in 6″ barrel only, has a pinned black ramp front sight with S&W micrometer click rear, .375″ semi-target hammer, .312″ smooth combat trigger, Hogue soft neoprene grips, full lug barrel and unfluted cylinder. Introduced 1989.
Price: $470.00

> Consult our Directory pages for
> the location of firms mentioned

Sportarms HS38S

SPORTARMS MODEL HS38S REVOLVER
Caliber: 38 Special, 6-shot.
Barrel: 3″, 4″.
Weight: 31.3 oz. **Length:** 8″ overall (3″ barrel).
Stocks: Checkered hardwood; round butt on 3″ model, target-style on 4″.
Sights: Blade front, adjustable rear.
Features: Polished blue finish; ventilated rib on 4″ barrel. Made in West Germany by Herbert Schmidt; imported by Sportarms of Florida.
Price: About $150.00

TAURUS MODEL 66 REVOLVER
Caliber: 357 Magnum, 6-shot.
Barrel: 3″, 4″, 6″.
Weight: 35 oz.
Stocks: Checkered walnut, target-type. Standard stocks on 3″.
Sights: Serrated ramp front, micro-click rear adjustable for w. and e. Red ramp front with white outline rear on stainless models only.
Features: Wide target-type hammer spur, floating firing pin, heavy barrel with shrouded ejector rod. Introduced 1978. From Taurus International.
Price: Blue $248.35
Price: Nickel $259.45
Price: Stainless steel $315.35
Price: Model 65 (similar to M66 except has a fixed rear sight and ramp front), blue, 3″ or 4″ only $228.00
Price: Model 65, satin nickel, 3″ or 4″ only $239.70

Taurus Model 66

TAURUS MODEL 73 SPORT REVOLVER
Caliber: 32 S&W Long, 6-shot.
Barrel: 3″, heavy.
Weight: 22 oz. **Length:** 8¼″ overall.
Stocks: Oversize target-type, checkered Brazilian walnut.
Sights: Ramp front, notch rear.
Features: Imported from Brazil by Taurus International.
Price: Blue $204.25
Price: Satin nickel $222.35

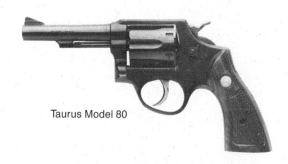

Taurus Model 73

TAURUS MODEL 80 STANDARD REVOLVER
Caliber: 38 Spec., 6-shot.
Barrel: 3″ or 4″.
Weight: 31 oz. (4″ bbl.). **Length:** 9¼″ overall (4″ bbl.).
Stocks: Checkered Brazilian walnut.
Sights: Serrated ramp front, square notch rear.
Features: Imported from Brazil by Taurus International.
Price: Blue $197.90
Price: Satin nickel $210.00

TAURUS MODEL 82 HEAVY BARREL REVOLVER
Caliber: 38 Spec., 6-shot.
Barrel: 3″ or 4″, heavy.
Weight: 33 oz. (4″ bbl.). **Length:** 9¼″ overall (4″ bbl.).
Stocks: Checkered Brazilian walnut.
Sights: Serrated ramp front, square notch rear.
Features: Imported from Brazil by Taurus International.
Price: Blue, about $197.90
Price: Satin nickel, about $210.00

Taurus Model 80

TAURUS MODEL 83 REVOLVER
Caliber: 38 Spec., 6-shot.
Barrel: 4″ only, heavy.
Weight: 34½ oz.
Stocks: Oversize checkered walnut.
Sights: Ramp front, micro-click rear adjustable for w. and e.
Features: Blue or nickel finish. Introduced 1977. Imported from Brazil by Taurus International.
Price: Blue $208.35
Price: Satin nickel $219.25

Taurus Model 82

TAURUS MODEL 85 REVOLVER
Caliber: 38 Spec., 5-shot.
Barrel: 2″, 3″.
Weight: 21 oz.
Stocks: Checkered walnut.
Sights: Ramp front, square notch rear.
Features: Blue, satin nickel finish or stainless steel. Introduced 1980. Imported from Brazil by Taurus International.
Price: Blue $216.90
Price: Satin nickel, 3″ only $232.70
Price: Stainless steel $274.60

Taurus Model 83

CAUTION: PRICES CHANGE. CHECK AT GUNSHOP.

TAURUS MODEL 94 H.B. REVOLVER
Caliber: 22 LR, 9-shot cylinder.
Barrel: 3″, 4″.
Weight: 25 oz.
Stocks: Checkered Brazilian hardwood.
Sights: Serrated ramp front, click-adjustable rear for w. and e.
Features: Floating firing pin, color case-hardened hammer and trigger. Introduced 1989. Imported from Brazil by Taurus International.
Price: **$230.95**

TAURUS MODEL 669 REVOLVER
Caliber: 357 Mag., 6-shot.
Barrel: 4″, 6″.
Weight: 37 oz. (4″ bbl.).
Stocks: Checkered walnut, target-type.
Sights: Serrated ramp front, micro-click rear adjustable for windage and elevation.
Features: Wide target-type hammer, floating firing pin, full-length barrel shroud. Introduced 1988. Imported by Taurus International.
Price: Blue **$257.35**
Price: Stainless **$324.30**

UBERTI "INSPECTOR" REVOLVER
Caliber: 32 S&W Long, 38 Spec., 6-shot.
Barrel: 3″, 4″, 6″.
Weight: 24 oz. (3″ bbl.). **Length:** 8″ overall (3″ bbl.).
Stocks: Checkered walnut.
Sights: Blade on ramp front, fixed or adjustable rear.
Features: Blue or chrome finish. Introduced 1986. Imported from Italy by Uberti USA.
Price: Blue, fixed sights **$413.00**
Price: Blue, adjustable sights, 4″, 6″ only **$450.00**
Price: Chrome, fixed sights **$441.00**
Price: Chrome, adjustable sights, 4″, 6″ only **$481.00**

DAN WESSON MODEL 44V, 45V REVOLVERS
Caliber: 41 Mag., 44 Mag., 45 Colt, 6-shot.
Barrel: 4″, 6″, 8″, 10″; interchangeable.
Weight: 48 oz. (4″). **Length:** 12″ overall (6″ bbl.).
Stocks: Smooth.
Sights: 1/8″ serrated front, white outline rear adjustable for windage and elevation.
Features: Available in blue or stainless steel. Smooth, wide trigger with adjustable over-travel; wide hammer spur. Available in Pistol Pac set also. Contact Dan Wesson Arms for complete price list.
Price: 41 Mag., 4″, vent. **$412.80**
Price: As above except in stainless. **$461.98**
Price: 44 Mag., 4″, blue **$431.45**
Price: As above except in stainless. **$507.30**
Price: 45 Colt, 4″, vent. **$431.45**
Price: As above except in stainless. **$507.30**

Dan Wesson 9-2, 15-2 & 32M Revolvers
Same as Models 8-2 and 14-2 except they have adjustable sight. Model 9-2 chambered for 38 Special, Model 15-2 for 357 Magnum. Model 32M is chambered for 32 H&R Mag. Same specs and prices as for 15-2 guns. Available in blue or stainless. Contact Dan Wesson for complete price list.
Price: Model 9-2 or 15-2, 2¹/₂″, blue. **$337.64**
Price: As above except in stainless. **$366.07**

DAN WESSON MODEL 22 REVOLVER
Caliber: 22 LR, 22 WMR, 6-shot.
Barrel: 2¹/₂″, 4″, 6″, 8″, 10″; interchangeable.
Weight: 36 oz. (2¹/₂″), 44 oz. (6″). **Length:** 9¹/₄″ overall (4″ barrel).
Stocks: Checkered; undercover, service or over-size target.
Sights: 1/8″ serrated, interchangeable front, white outline rear adjustable for windage and elevation.
Features: Built on the same frame as the Dan Wesson 357; smooth, wide trigger with over-travel adjustment, wide spur hammer, with short double-action travel. Available in Brite blue or stainless steel. Contact Dan Wesson for complete price list.
Price: 2¹/₂″ bbl., blue **$337.64**
Price: As above, stainless **$366.07**
Price: With 4″, vent. rib, blue **$369.97**
Price: As above, stainless **$398.41**
Price: Stainless Pistol Pac, 22 LR. **$689.01**

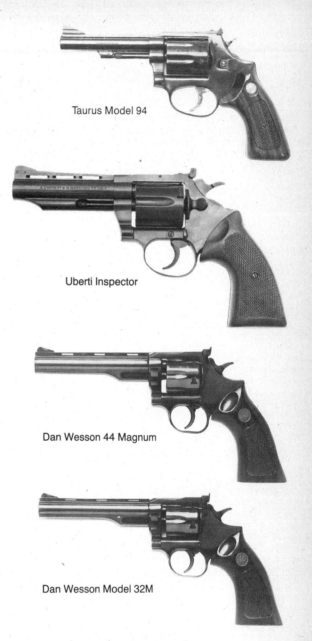

Taurus Model 94

Uberti Inspector

Dan Wesson 44 Magnum

Dan Wesson Model 32M

DAN WESSON MODEL 8-2 & MODEL 14-2
Caliber: 38 Special (Model 8-2); 357 (14-2), both 6-shot.
Barrel: 2¹/₂″, 4″, 6″, 8″; interchangeable.
Weight: 30 oz. (2¹/₂″). **Length:** 9¹/₄″ overall (4″ bbl.).
Stocks: Checkered, interchangeable.
Sights: 1/8″ serrated front, fixed rear.
Features: Interchangeable barrels and grips; smooth, wide trigger; wide hammer spur with short double-action travel. Available in stainless or Brite blue. Contact Dan Wesson for complete price list.
Price: Model 8-2, 2¹/₂″, blue. **$267.15**
Price: As above except in stainless. **$311.38**
Price: Model 714-2 Pistol Pac, stainless. **$516.68**

Dan Wesson Model 15 Gold Series
Similar to the Model 15 except has smoother action to reduce DA pull to 8-10 lbs.; comes with either 6″ or 8″ vent heavy slotted barrel shroud with bright blue barrel. Shroud is stamped "Gold Series" with the Dan Wesson signature engraved and gold filled. Hammer and trigger are polished bright; rosewood grips. New sights with orange dot Patridge front, white triangle on rear blade. Introduced 1989.
Price: 6″ **$543.59**
Price: 8″ **$554.26**

Both classic six-shooters and modern adaptations for hunting and sport.

CENTURY MODEL 100-SINGLE ACTION
Caliber: 30-30, 375 Win., 444 Marlin, 45-70, 50-70.
Barrel: 6¹/₂″, 8″ (standard), 10″, 12″. Other lengths to order.
Weight: 6 lbs. (loaded). **Length:** 15″ overall (8″ bbl.).
Stocks: Smooth walnut.
Sights: Ramp front, Millett adjustable square notch rear.
Features: Highly polished high tensile strength manganese bronze frame, blue cylinder and barrel; coil spring trigger mechanism. Calibers other than 45-70 start at $1,500.00. Introduced 1975. Made in U.S. From Century Gun Dist., Inc.
Price: 8″ barrel, 45-70.............................$780.00
Price: 10″ barrel, 45-70...........................$810.00
Price: 12″ barrel, 45-70...........................$840.00

Century Model 100

CIMARRON 1873 PEACEMAKER REPRO
Caliber: 22 LR, 22 WMR, 38 WCF, 357 Mag., 44 WCF, 45 Colt.
Barrel: 3″, 4″, 4³/₄″, 5¹/₂″, 7¹/₂″.
Weight: 39 oz. **Length:** 10″ overall (4″ barrel).
Stocks: Walnut.
Sights: Blade front, fixed or adjustable rear.
Features: Uses "old model" blackpowder frame with "Bullseye" ejector or New Model frame. Imported by Cimarron Arms.
Price: Standard model (Old Model or New Model)..............$389.00
Price: "A" engraving (30 percent coverage)...................$589.00
Price: "B" engraving (50 percent coverage)...................$699.00
Price: "C" engraving (100 percent coverage)...............$1,099.00

Cimarron 1873 Peacemaker

CIMARRON U.S. CAVALRY MODEL SINGLE ACTION
Caliber: 45 Colt.
Barrel: 7¹/₂″.
Weight: 42 oz. **Length:** 13¹/₂″ overall.
Stocks: Walnut.
Sights: Fixed.
Features: Has "A.P. Casey" markings; "U.S." plus patent dates on frame, serial number on backstrap, trigger guard, frame and cylinder, "APC" cartouche on left grip; color case-hardened frame and hammer, rest charcoal blue. Exact copy of the original. Imported by Cimarron Arms.
Price: $459.00

Cimarron U.S. Cavalry

Cimarron Artillery Model Single Action
Similar to the U.S. Cavalry model except has 5¹/₂″ barrel, weighs 39 oz., and is 11¹/₂″ overall. U.S. markings and cartouche, case-hardened frame and hammer; 45 Colt only.
Price: $459.00

CIMARRON SHERIFF MODEL SINGLE ACTION
Caliber: 22 LR, 22 WMR, 38 Spec., 357 Mag., 44 WCF, 45 Colt.
Barrel: 3″ or 4″.
Weight: 38 oz. **Length:** 10″ overall.
Stocks: Walnut.
Sights: Fixed.
Features: Patent dates on frame; serial number on backstrap, trigger guard, frame and cylinder. Modern or old-style blue. Uses blackpowder frame. Imported by Cimarron Arms.
Price: $389.00

Cimarron 1875 Remington

Cimarron 1890 Remington

CIMARRON 1875 REMINGTON
Caliber: 357 Mag., 44-40, 45 Colt, 6-shot.
Barrel: 7¹/₂″.
Weight: 44 oz. **Length:** 13³/₄″ overall.
Stocks: Smooth walnut.
Sights: Blade front, notch rear.
Features: Replica of the 1875 Remington S.A. Army revolver. Brass trigger guard, color case-hardened frame, rest blued, or nickel finish. Imported by Cimarron Arms Co.
Price: $349.00

CIMARRON 1890 REMINGTON REVOLVER
Caliber: 357 Mag., 44-40, 45 Colt, 6-shot.
Barrel: 5¹/₂″.
Weight: 37 oz. **Length:** 12¹/₂″ overall.
Stocks: American walnut.
Sights: Blade front, groove rear.
Features: Replica of the 1890 Remington single-action. Brass trigger guard, rest is blued, or nickel finish. Lanyard ring in butt. Imported by Cimarron Arms Co.
Price: $349.00

CAUTION: PRICES CHANGE. CHECK AT GUNSHOP.

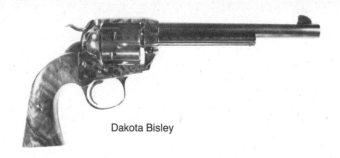

Dakota Bisley

DAKOTA 1875 OUTLAW REVOLVER
Caliber: 357, 44-40, 45 Colt.
Barrel: 7¹/2".
Weight: 46 oz. **Length:** 13¹/2" overall.
Stocks: Smooth walnut.
Sights: Blade front, fixed groove rear.
Features: Authentic copy of 1875 Remington with firing pin in hammer; color case-hardened frame, blue cylinder, barrel, steel backstrap and brass trigger guard. Also available in nickel, factory engraved. Imported by E.M.F.
Price: All calibers. **$485.00**
Price: Nickel **$520.00**
Price: Engraved. **$600.00**

DAKOTA SINGLE-ACTION REVOLVERS
Caliber: 22 LR, 22 WMR, 357 Mag., 30 Carbine, 32-20, 32 H&R Mag., 38-40, 44-40, 44 Spec., 45 Colt, 45 ACP.
Barrel: 3¹/2", 4⁵/8", 5¹/2", 7¹/2", 12", 16¹/4".
Weight: 45 oz. **Length:** 13" overall (7¹/2" bbl.).
Stocks: Smooth walnut.
Sights: Blade front, fixed rear.
Features: Colt-type hammer with firing pin, color case-hardened frame, blue barrel and cylinder, brass grip frame and trigger guard. Available in blue or nickel-plated, plain or engraved. Imported by E.M.F.
Price: 22 LR, 30 Car., 357, 44-40, 45 Colt, 4⁵/8", 5¹/2", 7¹/2" **$480.00**
Price: 22 LR/22 WMR, 45 Colt/ 45 ACP, 32-20/32 H&R, 357/9mm, 44-40/44 Spec., 5¹/2", 7¹/2" **$580.00**
Price: 357, 44-40, 45, 12" **$520.00**
Price: 357, 44-40, 45, 3¹/2" **$520.00**

Dakota 1890 Police Revolver
Similar to the 1875 Outlaw except has 5¹/2" barrel, weighs 40 oz., with 12¹/2" overall length. Has lanyard ring in butt. Calibers 357, 44-40, 45 Colt. Imported by E.M.F.
Price: All calibers. **$500.00**
Price: Nickel **$540.00**
Price: Engraved **$600.00**

F.I.E. "COWBOY" SINGLE-ACTION REVOLVER
Caliber: 22 LR, 22 LR/22 WMR, 6-shot.
Barrel: 3¹/4" or 6¹/2".
Weight: 28 oz. (3¹/4" barrel).
Stocks: Smooth nylon.
Sights: Blade front, fixed rear.
Features: Floating firing pin, hammer block safety. Available as combo with extra cylinder. Made in U.S. by F.I.E. Firearms Corp.
Price: 22 LR. **$99.95**
Price: 22 LR/22 WMR combo **$114.95**

F.I.E. "BUFFALO SCOUT" REVOLVER
Caliber: 22 LR/22 WMR.
Barrel: 4³/4".
Weight: 32 oz. **Length:** 10" overall.
Stocks: Black checkered nylon, walnut optional.
Sights: Blade front, fixed rear.
Features: Slide spring ejector. Blue, chrome, gold or blue with gold backstrap and trigger guard models available. Imported from Italy by F.I.E.
Price: Blue, 22 LR **$99.95**
Price: Blue, 22 convertible **$124.95**
Price: Chrome, 22 LR **$114.95**
Price: Chrome, convertible **$139.95**
Price: "Yellow Rose," gold, 22 convertible **$179.95**

COLT SINGLE ACTION ARMY REVOLVER
Caliber: 44-40, 45 Colt, 6-shot.
Barrel: 3", 4³/4", 5¹/2", 7¹/2".
Weight: 37 oz. (5¹/2" bbl.). **Length:** 10⁷/8" overall (5¹/2" bbl.).
Stocks: Black composite rubber with eagle and shield crest.
Sights: Fixed. Grooved topstrap, blade front.
Features: Blue or all nickel with walnut stocks. Available in limited quantities through the Colt Custom Shop only.
Price: From. **$1,095.00**

DAKOTA BISLEY MODEL SINGLE ACTION
Caliber: 22 LR, 22 WMR, 32-20, 32 H&R Mag., 357, 30 Carbine, 38-40, 44 Spec., 44-40, 45 Colt, 45 ACP.
Barrel: 4⁵/8", 5¹/2", 7¹/2".
Weight: 37 oz. **Length:** 10¹/2" overall with 5¹/2" barrel.
Stocks: Smooth walnut.
Sights: Blade front, fixed groove rear.
Features: Colt-type firing pin in hammer; color case-hardened frame, blue barrel, cylinder, steel backstrap and trigger guard. Also available in nickel, factory engraved. Imported by E.M.F.
Price: All calibers, bbl. lengths **$540.00**
Price: Combo models—22 LR/22 WMR, 32-20/32 H&R, 357/9mm, 44-40/44 Spec., 45 Colt/45 ACP **$600.00**
Price: Nickel, all cals. **$640.00**
Price: Engraved, all cals., lengths **$700.00**

Dakota Single Action

Dakota 1890 Police

F.I.E. "Cowboy"

F.I.E. "Buffalo Scout"

F.I.E. "TEXAS RANGER" REVOLVER
Caliber: 22 LR, 22 WMR.
Barrel: 4¾", 6½", 9".
Weight: 31 oz. (4¾" bbl.). **Length:** 10" overall.
Stocks: American walnut.
Sights: Blade front, notch rear.
Features: Single action, blue/black finish. Introduced 1983. Made in the U.S. by F.I.E.
Price: 22 LR, 4¾" $104.95
Price: As above, convertible (22 LR/22 WMR) $124.95
Price: 22 LR, 6½" $104.95
Price: As above, convertible (22 LR/22 WMR) $124.95
Price: 22 LR, 9" $104.95
Price: As above, convertible (22 LR/22 WMR) $124.95

F.I.E. "Texas Ranger"

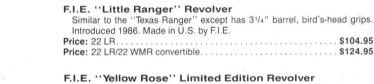

F.I.E. "Little Ranger"

F.I.E. "LITTLE RANGER" Revolver
Similar to the "Texas Ranger" except has 3¼" barrel, bird's-head grips. Introduced 1986. Made in U.S. by F.I.E.
Price: 22 LR... $104.95
Price: 22 LR/22 WMR convertible.......................... $124.95

F.I.E. "Yellow Rose" Limited Edition Revolver
Same gun as the "Buffalo Scout" revolver except is completely 24 karat gold-plated and has ivory polymer grips scrimshawed with a map of Texas, the Texas state flag and a single yellow rose highlighted with green leaves. Comes in a French fitted presentation case of American walnut, lined and fitted with contrasting velvet. Polished brass-plated hinge and lock. From F.I.E. Introduced 1987.
Price: $349.95

F.I.E. "HOMBRE" SINGLE-ACTION REVOLVER
Caliber: 357 Mag., 44 Mag., 45 Colt.
Barrel: 6" or 7½".
Weight: 45 oz. (6" bbl.).
Stocks: Smooth walnut with medallion.
Sights: Blade front, grooved topstrap (fixed) rear.
Features: Color case-hardened frame. Bright blue finish. Super-smooth action. Introduced 1979. Imported from West Germany by F.I.E. Corp.
Price: $259.95
Price: 24K gold-plated.................................. $339.95

FREEDOM ARMS 454 CASULL
Caliber: 44 Mag., 45 Colt, 454 Casull, 5-shot.
Barrel: 4¾", 6", 7½", 10".
Weight: 50 oz. **Length:** 14" overall (7½" bbl.).
Stocks: Impregnated hardwood.
Sights: Blade front, notch or adjustable rear.
Features: All stainless steel construction; sliding bar safety system. Lifetime warranty. Made in U.S.A.
Price: Fixed sight $1,044.75
Price: Adjustable sight................................ $1,149.75
Price: Field Grade, adjustable sight, (matte stainless finish, Pachmayr Presentation grips, 4¾", 7½", 10")......................... $795.00
Price: Field Grade, fixed sights, 4¾" only.................... $725.00

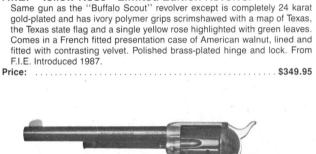

F.I.E. "Hombre"

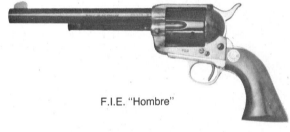

Freedom 454 Field Grade

Freedom Arms Mini Revolver

Freedom Boot Gun

FREEDOM ARMS MINI REVOLVER
Caliber: 22 Short, Long, Long Rifle, 5-shot; 22 WMR, 4-shot.
Barrel: 1".
Weight: 4 oz. **Length:** 4" overall.
Stocks: Impregnated hardwood.
Sights: Blade front, notch rear.
Features: Made of stainless steel, simple takedown; half-cock safety; floating firing pin; cartridge rims recessed in cylinder. Comes in gun rug. Lifetime warranty. Also available in percussion — see blackpowder section. From Freedom Arms.
Price: 22 LR, 1" barrel $153.12
Price: 22 WMR, 1" barrel $176.50

Freedom Arms Boot Gun
Similar to the Mini Revolver except 22 WMR only, has 3" barrel, weighs 5 oz. and is 5⅞" overall. Has oversize grips, floating firing pin. Made of stainless steel. Lifetime warranty. Comes in rectangular gun rug. Introduced 1982. From Freedom Arms.
Price: 22 WMR $219.95

MITCHELL SINGLE-ACTION ARMY REVOLVERS

Caliber: 22 LR, 357 Mag., 44 Mag., 45 Colt, 6-shot.
Barrel: 4³/₄", 5¹/₂", 6", 6¹/₂", 7¹/₂", 10", 12", 18".
Weight: NA. **Length:** NA
Stocks: One-piece walnut.
Sights: Serrated ramp front, fixed or adjustable rear.
Features: Color case-hardened frame, brass backstrap, balance blued; hammer block safety. Stainless steel and dual cylinder models available. Imported by Mitchell Arms.
Price: Fixed sight, 22 LR, 4³/₄", 5¹/₂", 7¹/₂" **$279.69**
Price: As above, 357,45 . . . . **$295.95**
Price: As above, 44 Mag. **$295.95**
Price: Adjustable sight, 22 LR, 4³/₄", 5¹/₂", 7¹/₂" **$310.00**
Price: As above, 357, 45 . . . . **$328.00**
Price: As above, 44 Mag. **$328.00**
Price: Stainless steel, 22 LR, 4³/₄", 5¹/₂", 7¹/₂" **$328.00**
Price: As above, 357 Mag. **$359.00**
Price: 44 Mag./44-40, dual cylinder, 4³/₄", 6", 7¹/₂" **$328.00**
Price: 22 LR/22 WMR, dual cylinder, 4³/₄", 5¹/₂", 7¹/₂" **$345.00**
Price: Silhouette Model, 44 Mag., 10", 12", 18" **$395.95**

Mitchell Single Action

North American Mini

North American Mini-Master

NORTH AMERICAN MINI-REVOLVERS

Caliber: 22 S, 22 LR, 22 WMR, 5-shot.
Barrel: 1¹/₈", 1⁵/₈", 2¹/₂".
Weight: 4 to 6.6 oz. **Length:** 3⁵/₈" to 6¹/₈" overall.
Stocks: Laminated wood.
Sights: Blade front, notch fixed rear.
Features: All stainless steel construction. Polished satin and matte finish. Engraved models available. From North American Arms.
Price: 22 Short, 1¹/₈" bbl. **$138.00**
Price: 22 LR, 1¹/₈" bbl. **$139.00**
Price: 22 LR, 1⁵/₈" bbl. **$139.00**
Price: 22 WMR, 1⁵/₈" bbl. **$158.00**
Price: 22 WMR, 2¹/₂" bbl. **$174.00**
Price: 22 WMR, 1¹/₈" or 1⁵/₈" bbl. with extra 22 LR cylinder **$190.00**
Price: As above, 2¹/₂" bbl. **$206.00**

NORTH AMERICAN MINI-MASTER

Caliber: 22 LR, 22 WMR, 5-shot cylinder.
Barrel: 4".
Weight: 10.7 oz. **Length:** 7.75" overall.
Stocks: Checkered hard black rubber.
Sights: Blade front, white outline rear adjustable for elevation.
Features: Heavy vent barrel; full-size grips. Non-fluted cylinder. Introduced 1989.
Price: **$250.00**

Phelps Heritage I

Ruger N.M. Blackhawk

PHELPS HERITAGE I, EAGLE I REVOLVERS

Caliber: 444 Marlin, 45-70, 6-shot.
Barrel: 8" or 12", 16" (45-70).
Weight: 5¹/₂ lbs. **Length:** 19¹/₂" overall (12" bbl.).
Stocks: Smooth walnut.
Sights: Ramp front, adjustable rear.
Features: Single action; polished blue finish; safety bar. From E. Phelps Mfg. Co.
Price: 8", 45-70 . . . . **$765.00**
Price: 12", 45-70 . . . . **$790.00**
Price: 8", 444 Marlin **$865.00**
Price: 12", 444 Marlin **$890.00**

RUGER NEW MODEL BLACKHAWK REVOLVER

Caliber: 30 Carbine, 357 Mag./38Spec., 41 Mag., 44 Mag., 45 Colt, 6-shot.
Barrel: 4⁵/₈" or 6¹/₂", either caliber, 5¹/₂" (44 Mag. only), 7¹/₂" (30 Carbine, 45 Colt only).
Weight: 42 oz. (6¹/₂" bbl.). **Length:** 12¹/₄" overall (6¹/₂" bbl.).
Stocks: American walnut.
Sights: ¹/₈" ramp front, micro-click rear adjustable for w. and e.
Features: New Ruger interlocked mechanism, independent firing pin, hardened chrome-moly steel frame, music wire springs throughout.
Price: Blue, 30 Carbine (7¹/₂" bbl.), BN31 . . . . **$286.00**
Price: Blue, 357 Mag. (4⁵/₈", 6¹/₂"), BN34, BN36 . . . . **$297.50**
Price: Blue, 357/9mm (4⁵/₈", 6¹/₂"), BN34X, BN36X **$311.75**
Price: Blue, 44 Mag. (5¹/₂"), S45N **$343.50**
Price: Stainless, 44 Mag. (5¹/₂"), KS45N **$375.25**
Price: Blue, 41 Mag., 44 Mag., 45 Colt (4⁵/₈", 6¹/₂"), BN41, BN42, BN44, BN45 . . . . **$297.50**
Price: Stainless, 357 Mag. (4⁵/₈", 6¹/₂"), KBN34, KBN36 . . . . **$366.50**

RUGER NEW MODEL SUPER BLACKHAWK

Caliber: 44 Magnum, 6-shot. Also fires 44 Spec.
Barrel: 7¹/₂" (6-groove, 20" twist), 10¹/₂".
Weight: 48 oz. (7¹/₂" bbl.), 51 oz. (10¹/₂" bbl.). **Length:** 13³/₈" overall (7¹/₂" bbl.).
Stocks: Genuine American walnut.
Sights: ¹/₈" ramp front, micro-click rear adjustable for w. and e.
Features: Ruger interlocked mechanism, non-fluted cylinder, steel grip and cylinder frame, square back trigger guard, wide serrated trigger and wide spur hammer.
Price: Blue (S-47N, S-411N) **$343.50**
Price: Stainless (KS-47N, KS-411N) **$375.25**

Ruger N.M. Bisley Blackhawk

RUGER NEW MODEL SUPER SINGLE-SIX CONVERTIBLE REVOLVER

Caliber: 22 LR, 6-shot; 22 WMR in extra cylinder.
Barrel: 4⁵/₈″, 5¹/₂″, 6¹/₂″, or 9¹/₂″ (6-groove).
Weight: 34¹/₂ oz. (6¹/₂″ bbl.). **Length:** 11¹³/₁₆″ overall (6¹/₂″ bbl.).
Stocks: Smooth American walnut.
Sights: Improved Patridge front on ramp, fully adjustable rear protected by integral frame ribs.
Features: Ruger interlocked mechanism, transfer bar ignition, gate-controlled loading, hardened chrome-moly steel frame, wide trigger, music wire springs throughout, independent firing pin.
Price: 4⁵/₈″, 5¹/₂″, 6¹/₂″, 9¹/₂″ barrel **$255.00**
Price: 5¹/₂″, 6¹/₂″ bbl. only, stainless steel. **$321.00**

Ruger Small Frame New Model Bisley

Similar to the New Model Single-Six except frame is styled after the classic Bisley "flat-top." Most mechanical parts are unchanged. Hammer is lower and smoothly curved with a deeply checkered spur. Trigger is strongly curved with a wide smooth surface. Longer grip frame designed with a hand-filling shape, and the trigger guard is a large oval. Dovetail rear sight drift-adjustable for windage; front sight base accepts interchangeable square blades of various heights and styles. Available with an unfluted cylinder and roll engraving, or with a fluted cylinder and no engraving. Weight about 41 oz. Chambered for 22 LR and 32 H&R Mag., 6¹/₂″ barrel only. Introduced 1985.
Price: **$298.00**

SPORTARMS MODEL HS21S SINGLE ACTION

Caliber: 22 LR or 22 LR/22 WMR combo, 6-shot.
Barrel: 5¹/₂″.
Weight: 33.5 oz. **Length:** 11″ overall.
Stocks: Smooth hardwood.
Sights: Blade front, rear drift adjustable for windage.
Features: Available in blue with imitation stag or wood stocks. Made in West Germany by Herbert Schmidt; imported by Sportarms of Florida.
Price: 22 LR, blue, "stag" grips, about **$80.00**
Price: 22 LR/22 WMR Combo, blue, wood stocks, about **$110.00**

Super Six Golden Bison

Tanarmi TA76

Ruger New Model Bisley

Similar to standard New Model Blackhawk except the hammer is lower with a smoothly curved, deeply checkered wide spur. The trigger is strongly curved with a wide smooth surface. Longer grip frame has a hand-filling shape. Adjustable rear sight, ramp-style front. Available with an unfluted cylinder and roll engraving, or with a fluted cylinder and no engraving. Fixed or adjustable sights. Chambered for 357, 41, 44 Mags. and 45 Colt; 7¹/₂″ barrel; overall length of 13″. Introduced 1985.
Price: **$354.50**

Ruger New Model Single-Six Revolver

Similar to the Super Single-Six revolver except chambered for 32 H&R Magnum (also handles 32 S&W and 32 S&W Long). Weight is about 34 oz. with 6¹/₂″ barrel. Barrel lengths: 4⁵/₈″, 5¹/₂″, 6¹/₂″, 9¹/₂″. Introduced 1985.
Price: **$244.75**

Ruger Bisley Single-Six

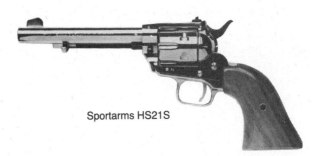

Sportarms HS21S

SUPER SIX GOLDEN BISON 45-70 REVOLVER

Caliber: 45-70, 6-shot.
Barrel: 8″, 10¹/₂″, octagonal.
Weight: 5 lbs., 12 oz. (8″ bbl.) **Length:** 15″ overall (8″ bbl.).
Stocks: Smooth walnut.
Sights: Blaze orange blade front on ramp, Millett fully adjustable rear.
Features: Cylinder frame and grip frame of high tensile Manganese bronze; hammer of Manganese bronze with a hardened steel pad for firing pin contact; all coil springs; full-cock, cross-bolt interlocking safety and traveling safeties. Choice of antique brown or blue/black finish. Lifetime warranty. Comes in a fitted walnut presentation case. Made in the U.S. by Super Six Limited.
Price: Golden Bison (8″ bbl.)............................. **$1,895.00**
Price: Golden Bison Bull (10¹/₂″ bbl.) **$1,995.00**

TANARMI S.A. REVOLVER MODEL TA76/TA22

Caliber: 22 LR, 22 WMR, 6-shot.
Barrel: 4³/₄, 6″ or 9″.
Weight: 32 oz. **Length:** 10″ overall.
Stocks: Walnut.
Sights: Blade front, rear adjustable for w. and e.
Features: Manual hammer block safety. Imported from Italy by Excam.
Price: 22 LR, blue, 4³/₄″ **$95.00**
Price: Combo, blue, 4³/₄″ **$105.00**
Price: 22 LR, chrome, 4³/₄″ **$99.00**
Price: Combo, chrome, 4³/₄″ **$121.00**
Price: Combo, blue, 6″ **$115.00**
Price: Combo, blue, 9″ **$115.00**

     CAUTION: PRICES CHANGE. CHECK AT GUNSHOP.

TEXAS LONGHORN GROVER'S IMPROVED NO. FIVE
Caliber: 44 Magnum, 6-shot.
Barrel: 5½″.
Weight: 44 oz. **Length:** NA.
Stocks: Fancy AAA walnut.
Sights: Square blade front on ramp, fully adjustable rear.
Features: Music wire coil spring action with double locking bolt; polished blue finish. Hand-made in limited 1,200-gun production. Grip contour, straps, oversized base pin, lever latch and lockwork identical copies of Elmer Keith design. Lifetime warranty to original owner. Introduced 1988.
Price: **$985.00**

Texas Longhorn Grover's No. 5

TEXAS LONGHORN RIGHT-HAND SINGLE ACTION
Caliber: All centerfire pistol calibers.
Barrel: 4¾″.
Weight: NA. **Length:** NA.
Stocks: One-piece fancy walnut, or any fancy AAA wood.
Sights: Blade front, grooved topstrap rear.
Features: Loading gate and ejector housing on left side of gun. Cylinder rotates to the left. All steel construction; color case-hardened frame; high polish blue; music wire coil springs. Lifetime guarantee to original owner. Introduced 1984. From Texas Longhorn Arms.
Price: South Texas Army Limited Edition — hand-made, only 1,000 to be produced; "One of One Thousand" engraved on barrel. **$1,500.00**

Texas Longhorn Sesquicentennial Model Revolver
Similar to the South Texas Army Model except has ¾-coverage Nimschke-style engraving, antique golden nickel plate finish, one-piece elephant ivory grips. Comes with hand-made solid walnut presentation case, factory letter to owner. Limited edition of 150 units. Introduced 1986.
Price: **$2,500.00**

Texas Longhorn Arms Texas Border Special
Similar to the South Texas Army Limited Edition except has 3½″ barrel, bird's-head style grip. Same special features. Introduced 1984.
Price: **$1,500.00**

Texas Longhorn Arms West Texas Flat Top Target
Similar to the South Texas Army Limited Edition except choice of barrel length from 7½″ through 15″; flat-top style frame; ⅛″ contoured ramp front sight, old model steel micro-click rear adjustable for w. and e. Same special features. Introduced 1984.
Price: **$1,500.00**

Texas Longhorn Border Special

Texas Longhorn Arms Cased Set
Set contains one each of the Texas Longhorn Right-Hand Single Actions, all in the same caliber, same serial numbers (100, 200, 300, 400, 500, 600, 700, 800, 900). Ten sets to be made (#1000 donated to NRA museum). Comes in hand-tooled leather case. All other specs same as Limited Edition guns. Introduced 1984.
Price: **$5,750.00**
Price: With ¾-coverage "C-style" engraving. **$7,650.00**

Texas Longhorn Flat Top

UBERTI 1873 CATTLEMAN SINGLE ACTIONS
Caliber: 22 LR, 22 WMR, 32-20, 38 Spec., 38-40, 357 Mag., 44 Spec., 44-40, 45 Colt, 6-shot.
Barrel: 4¾″, 5½″, 7½″; 44-40, 45 Colt also with 3″.
Weight: 38 oz. (5½″ bbl.). **Length:** 10¾″ overall (5½″ bbl.).
Stocks: One-piece smooth walnut.
Sights: Blade front, groove rear; fully adjustable rear available.
Features: Steel or brass backstrap, trigger guard; color case-hardened frame, blued barrel, cylinder. Imported from Italy by Uberti USA.
Price: Steel backstrap, trigger guard, fixed sights **$361.00**
Price: As above, adjustable sight **$385.00**
Price: Brass backstrap, trigger guard, fixed sights **$333.00**
Price: As above, adjustable sight **$358.00**

Uberti Cattleman

Uberti 1873 Buckhorn Single Action
A slightly larger version of the Cattleman revolver. Available in 44 Magnum or 44 Magnum/44-40 convertible, otherwise has same specs.
Price: Steel backstrap, trigger guard, fixed sights **$371.00**
Price: As above, brass. **$343.00**
Price: Convertible (two cylinders) add **$40.00**

UBERTI 1873 STALLION SINGLE ACTION

Caliber: 22 LR/22 WMR convertible.
Barrel: 4³/₄″, 5¹/₂″, 6¹/₂″, round.
Weight: 36 oz. **Length:** 10³/₄″ overall.
Stocks: One-piece walnut.
Sights: Blade front, groove rear or ramp front, adjustable rear.
Features: Smaller version of the Cattleman with same frame options. Imported from Italy by Uberti USA.
Price: Steel backstrap, trigger guard, fixed sights **$361.00**
Price: As above, adjustable sight **$385.00**
Price: Brass, fixed sights. **$333.00**
Price: As above, adjustable sight **$357.00**
Price: Stainless, fixed sight **$406.00**
Price: As above, adjustable sight **$429.00**

Uberti 1873 Stallion

Uberti 1873 Buntline Single Action

Available in 357 Mag., 44-40 or 45 Colt (Cattleman frame), 44 Mag./44-40 convertible (Buckhorn frame) with 18″ barrel. Weight is 3.6 lbs. with an overall length of 23″. Same sight and frame options as Cattleman and Buckhorn.
Price: Steel backstrap, trigger guard, fixed sight **$390.00**
Price: As above, adj sight **$417.00**
Price: Brass backstrap, trigger guard, fixed sight **$366.00**
Price: As above, adjustable sight **$390.00**
Price: Convertible, add **$65.00**
Price: Shoulder stock **$125.00**

UBERTI 1875 SA ARMY "OUTLAW" REVOLVER

Caliber: 357 Mag., 44-40, 45 Colt, 6-shot.
Barrel: 7¹/₂″.
Weight: 44 oz. **Length:** 13³/₄″ overall.
Stocks: Smooth walnut.
Sights: Blade front, notch rear.
Features: Replica of the 1875 Remington S.A. Army revolver. Brass trigger guard, color case-hardened frame, rest blued. Imported by Uberti USA.
Price: **$343.00**
Price: Nickel-plated **$378.00**

UBERTI 1890 ARMY "OUTLAW" REVOLVER

Caliber: 357 Mag., 44-40, 45 Colt, 6-shot.
Barrel: 5¹/₂″.
Weight: 37 oz. **Length:** 12¹/₂″ overall.
Stocks: American Walnut.
Sights: Blade front, groove rear.
Features: Replica of the 1890 Remington single action. Brass trigger guard, rest is blued. Imported by Uberti, USA.
Price: **$357.00**
Price: Nickle-plated **$399.00**

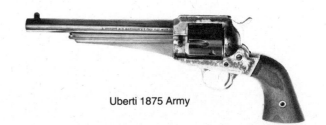

Uberti 1875 Army

HANDGUNS—MISCELLANEOUS

Specially adapted single-shot and multi-barrel arms.

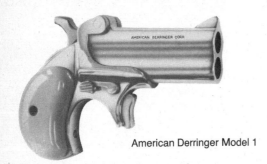

American Derringer Model 1

American Derringer Model 10 Lightweight

Similar to the Model 1 except frame is of aluminum, giving weight of 10 oz. Available in 45 Colt or 45 ACP only. Matte gray finish. Introduced 1989.
Price: 45 Colt. **$237.50**
Price: 45 ACP **$218.00**
Price: Model 11 (38 Spec., aluminum bbls., wgt. 11 oz.) **$159.95**

American Derringer Texas Commemorative

A Model 1 Derringer with solid brass frame, stainless steel barrel and stag grips. Available in 32 H&R Mag., 38 Special, 44-40 Win., or 45 Colt. Introduced 1987.
Price: **$218.00**

AMERICAN DERRINGER MODEL 1

Caliber: 22 LR, 22 WMR, 22 Hornet, 223 Rem., 30 Luger, 30-30 Win., 32 ACP, 38 Super, 380 ACP, 38 Spec., 9x18, 9mm Para., 357 Mag., 357 Maximum, 10mm, 41 Mag., 38-40, 44-40 Win., 44 Spec., 44 American, 44 Mag., 45 Colt, 45 ACP, 410-ga. (2¹/₂″).
Barrel: 3″.
Weight: 15¹/₂ oz. (38 Spec.). **Length:** 4.82″ overall.
Stocks: Rosewood, Zebra wood.
Sights: Blade front.
Features: Made of stainless steel with high-polish or satin finish. Two-shot capacity. Manual hammer block safety. Introduced 1980. Available in almost any pistol caliber. Contact the factory for complete list of available calibers and prices. From American Derringer Corp.
Price: 22 LR or WMR **$218.00**
Price: 22 Hornet, 223 Rem.. . . . . **$369.00**
Price: 38 Spec. **$187.50**
Price: 357 Maximum **$250.00**
Price: 357 Mag. **$225.00**
Price: 9x18, 9mm, 380, 38 Super **$179.95**
Price: 10mm **$218.00**
Price: 44 Spec., 44 American **$275.00**
Price: 38-40, 44-40 Win., 45 Colt, 45 Auto Rim **$275.00**
Price: 30-30, 41, 44 Mags., 45 Win. Mag. **$369.00**
Price: 45-70, single shot **$312.00**
Price: 45 Colt, 410, 2¹/₂″. **$312.00**
Price: 45 ACP, 10mm Auto **$218.00**

CAUTION: PRICES CHANGE. CHECK AT GUNSHOP.

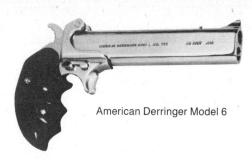
American Derringer Model 6

American Derringer Model 7
Similar to Model 1 except made of high strength aircraft aluminum. Weighs 7½ oz., 4.82″ o.a.l., rosewood stocks. Available in 22 LR, 32 S&W Long, 32 H&R Mag., 380 ACP, 38 S&W, 38 Spec., 44 Spec. Introduced 1986.
Price: 22 LR or 38 Spec. **$187.50**
Price: 38 S&W, 380 ACP, 32 S&W Long **$157.50**
Price: 32 H&R Mag. **$172.50**
Price: 44 Spec. **$500.00**

AMERICAN DERRINGER DA 38
Caliber: 38 Spec.
Barrel: 2½″.
Weight: 14 oz. **Length:** 4.8″ overall.
Stocks: Checkered plastic.
Sights: Fixed.
Features: Double-action only; two-shots. Manual safety. Made of satin-finished stainless steel and aluminum. Introduced 1989. From American Derringer Corp.
Price: **$225.00**

American Derringer Semmerling

ANSCHUTZ EXEMPLAR BOLT-ACTION PISTOL
Caliber: 22 LR, 5-shot; 22 WMR, 22 Hornet, 5-shot.
Barrel: 10″, 14″.
Weight: 3½ lbs. **Length:** 17″ overall.
Stock: European walnut with stippled grip and forend.
Sights: Hooded front on ramp, open notch rear adjustable for w. and e.
Features: Uses Match 64 action with left-hand bolt; Anshultz #5091 two-stage trigger set at 9.85 oz. Receiver grooved for scope mounting; open sights easily removed. Introduced 1987. Imported from West Germany by PSI.
Price: 22 LR. **$395.00**
Price: 22 LR, left-hand **$405.00**
Price: 22 LR, 14″ barrel **$419.50**
Price: 22 Hornet **$744.50**
Price: 22 Hornet with laminated stock **$774.50**

Davis Derringer

AMERICAN DERRINGER MODEL 3
Caliber: 38 Special.
Barrel: 2.5″.
Weight: 8.5 oz. **Length:** 4.9″ overall.
Stocks: Rosewood.
Sights: Blade front.
Features: Made of stainless steel. Single shot with manual hammer block safety. Introduced 1985. From American Derringer Corp.
Price: **$115.00**

American Derringer Model 4
Similar to the Model 1 except has 4.1″ barrel, overall length of 6″, and weighs 16½ oz.; chambered for 3″ 410-ga. shotshells or 45 Colt. Can be had with 45-70 upper barrel and 3″ 410-ga. or 45 Colt bottom barrel. Made of stainless steel. Manual hammer block safety. Introduced 1985.
Price: 3″ 410/45 Colt (either barrel) **$350.00**
Price: 3″ 410/45 Colt or 45-70 (Alaskan Survival model) **$369.00**

American Derringer Model 6
Similar to the Model 1 except has 6″ barrels chambered for 3″ 410 shotshells or 45 Colt, rosewood stocks, 8.2″ o.a.l. and weighs 21 oz. Shoots either round for each barrel. Manual hammer block safety. Introduced 1986.
Price: High polish or satin finish **$369.00**
Price: Gray matte finish. **$350.00**

AMERICAN DERRINGER SEMMERLING LM-4
Caliber: 9mm Para., 7-shot magazine; 45 ACP, 5-shot magazine.
Barrel: 3.625″.
Weight: 24 oz. **Length:** 5.2″ overall.
Stocks: Checkered plastic on blued guns, rosewood on stainless guns.
Sights: Open, fixed.
Features: Manually-operated repeater. Height is 3.7″, width is 1″. Comes with manual, leather carrying case, spare stock screws, wrench. From American Derringer Corp.
Price: Blued **$1,250.00**
Price: Stainless steel **$1,500.00**

Anschutz Exemplar Hornet

Consult our Directory pages for
the location of firms mentioned.

DAVIS DERRINGERS
Caliber: 22 LR, 22 WMR, 25 ACP, 32 ACP.
Barrel: 2.4″.
Weight: 9.5 oz. **Length:** 4″ overall.
Stocks: Laminated wood.
Sights: Blade front, fixed notch rear.
Features: Choice of black Teflon or chrome finish; spur trigger. Introduced 1986. Made in U.S. by Davis Industries.
Price: **$64.90**

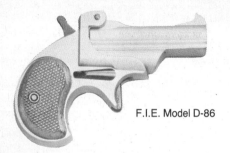

F.I.E. Model D-86

FEATHER GUARDIAN ANGEL PISTOL
Caliber: 9mm Para., 38 Special.
Barrel: 3″.
Weight: 17 oz. **Length:** 5¹/₂″ overall.
Stocks: Black composition.
Sights: Fixed.
Features: Uses a pre-loaded two-shot drop-in "magazine." Stainless steel construction; matte finish. From Feather Industries. Introduced 1988.
Price: **$139.95**

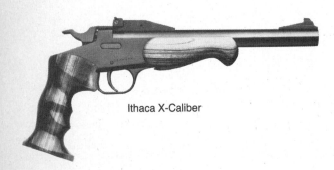

Ithaca X-Caliber

MANDALL/CABANAS PISTOL
Caliber: 177, pellet or round ball; single shot.
Barrel: 9″.
Weight: 51 oz. **Length:** 19″ overall.
Stock: Smooth wood with thumb rest.
Sights: Blade front on ramp, open adjustable rear.
Features: Fires round ball or pellets with 22 blank cartridge. Automatic safety; muzzlebrake. Imported from Mexico by Mandall Shooting Supplies.
Price: **$125.00**

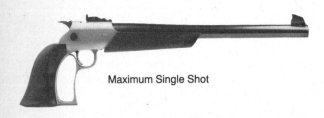

Maximum Single Shot

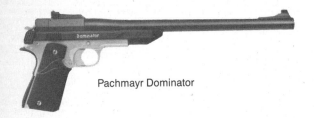

Pachmayr Dominator

F.I.E. D-86 DERRINGER
Caliber: 38 Special.
Barrel: 3″.
Weight: 14 oz.
Stocks: Checkered black nylon, walnut optional.
Sights: Fixed.
Features: Dyna-Chrome or blue finish. Spur trigger. Tip-up barrel; extractors. Made in U.S. by F.I.E. Corp.
Price: With nylon grips **$94.95**
Price: With walnut grips **$114.95**

Feather Guardian Angel

ITHACA X-CALIBER SINGLE SHOT
Caliber: 22 LR, 44 Mag.
Barrel: 10″, 15″.
Weight: 3¹/₄ lbs. **Length:** 15″ overall (10″ barrel).
Stocks: Goncalo Alves grip and forend on Model 20; American walnut on Model 30.
Sights: Blade on ramp front; Model 20 has adjustable, removeable target-type rear. Drilled and tapped for scope mounting.
Features: Dual firing pin for RF/CF use. Polished blue finish.
Price: 22 LR, 10″, 44 Mag., 10″ or 15″ **$270.00**
Price: 22 LR/44 Mag. combo, 10″ and 15″ **$365.00**
Price: As above, both 10″ barrels **$365.00**

MAXIMUM SINGLE SHOT PISTOL
Caliber: 22 Hornet, 22 BR, 223 Rem., 22-250, 6mm BR, 6mm-223, 243, 250 Savage, 6.5mm-35, 7mm TCU, 7mm BR, 7mm-35, 7mm INT-R, 7mm-08, 7mm Rocket, 7mm Super Mag., 30 Herrett, 308 Win., 7.62 x 39, 32-20, 357 Mag., 357 Maximum, 358 Win., 44 Mag.
Barrel: 8³/₄″, 10¹/₂″, 14″.
Weight: 61 oz. (10¹/₂″ bbl.), 78 oz. (14″ bbl.). **Length:** 15″, 18¹/₂″ overall (with 10¹/₂″ and 14″ bbl., respectively).
Stocks: Smooth walnut stocks and forend.
Sights: Ramp front, fully adjustable open rear.
Features: Falling block action; drilled and tapped for M.O.A. scope mounts; integral grip frame/receiver; adjustable trigger; Douglas barrel (interchangeable); Armoloy finish. Introduced 1983. Made in U.S. by M.O.A. Corp.
Price: 8³/₄″, 10″, 14″ **$499.00**
Price: Extra barrels **$139.00**
Price: Scope mount **$49.00**

NEW ADVANTAGE ARMS DERRINGER
Caliber: 22 LR, 22 WMR, 4-shot.
Barrel: 2¹/₂″.
Weight: 15 oz. **Length:** 4¹/₂ overall.
Stocks: Smooth walnut.
Sights: Fixed.
Features: Double-action mechanism, four barrels, revolving firing pin. Rebounding hammer, automatic safety. Polished blue finish. Reintroduced 1989. From TMI Products.
Price: 22 LR **$149.95**
Price: 22 WMR **$159.95**

PACHMAYR DOMINATOR PISTOL
Caliber: 22 Hornet 223, 7mm-06, 308, 35 Rem., 44 Mag., single shot.
Barrel: 10¹/₂″ (44 Mag.), 14″ all other calibers.
Weight: 4 lbs. (14″ barrel). **Length:** 16″ overall (14″ barrel).
Stocks: Pachmayr Signature system.
Sights: Optional sights or drilled and tapped for scope mounting.
Features: Bolt-action pistol on 1911A1 frame. Comes as complete gun. Introduced 1988. From Pachmayr.
Price: Either barrel **$524.50**

RPM XL SINGLE SHOT PISTOL

Caliber: 22 LR, 22 WMR, 225 Win., 25 Rocket, 6.5 Rocket, 32 H&R Mag., 357 Max., 357 Mag., 30-30 Win., 30 Herrett, 357 Herrett, 41 Mag., 44 Mag., 454 Casull, 375 Win., 7mm UR, 7mm Merrill, 30 Merrill, 7mm Rocket, 270 Ren, 270 Rocket, 270 Max., 45-70.

Barrel: 8" slab, 10¾", 12", 14" bull; .450" wide vent. rib, matted to prevent glare.

Weight: About 60 oz. **Length:** 12¼" overall (10¾" bbl.).

Stocks: Smooth Goncalo with thumb and heel rest.

Sights: Front .100" blade, Millett rear adjustable for w. and e. Hooded front with interchangeable post optional

Features: Polished blue finish, hard chrome optional. Barrel is drilled and tapped for scope mounting. Cocking indicator visible from rear of gun. Has spring-loaded barrel lock, positive hammer block thumb safety. Trigger adjustable for weight of pull and over-travel. For complete price list contact RPM.

Price: Regular ¾" frame, right-hand action **$750.00**
Price: As above, left-hand action **$775.00**
Price: Wide ⅞" frame, right-hand action only **$800.00**
Price: Extra barrel, 8"-10¾" **$230.00**
Price: Extra barrel, 12"-14" **$300.00**

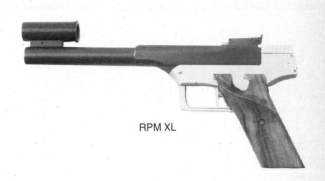

RPM XL

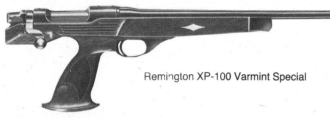

Remington XP-100 Varmint Special

Remington XP-100 Custom

REMINGTON XP-100 "VARMINT SPECIAL"

Caliber: 223 Rem., single shot.

Barrel: 10½", ventilated rib.

Weight: 60 oz. **Length:** 16¾".

Stock: Brown nylon one-piece, checkered grip with white spacers.

Sights: Tapped for scope mount.

Features: Fits left or right hand, is shaped to fit fingers and heel of hand. Grooved trigger. Rotating thumb safety, cavity in forend permits insertion of up to five 38 cal., 130-gr. metal jacketed bullets to adjust weight and balance. Included is a black vinyl, zippered case.

Price: Including case, about **$373.00**

Remington XP-100 Custom Long Range Pistol

Similar to the XP-100 "Varmint Special" except chambered for 223 Rem. (heavy barrel), 7mm-08 Rem., 35 Rem., 250 Savage, 6mm BR, 7mm BR. Offered with standard 14½" barrel with adjustable rear leaf and front bead sights, or with heavy 15½" barrel without sights (except 35 Rem.). Custom Shop 14½" barrel, Custom Shop English walnut stock in right- or left-hand configuration. Action tuned in Custom Shop. Weight is under 4½ lbs. (heavy barrel, 5½ lbs.). Introduced 1986.

Price: **$907.00**

SPRINGFIELD ARMORY 1911A2 S.A.S.S. PISTOL

Caliber: 22 LR, 223, 7mm BR, 7mm-08, 308, 357 Mag., 358 Win., 44 Mag., single shot.

Barrel: 10¾" or 14.9".

Weight: 4 lbs. 2 oz. (14.9" bbl.). **Length:** 17.2" overall (14.9" bbl.).

Stocks: Rubberized wraparound.

Sights: Blade on ramp front, fully adjustable open rear. Drilled and tapped for scope mounting.

Features: Uses standard 1911A1 frame with a break-open top half interchangeable barrel system. Available as complete gun or as conversion unit only (requires fitting). Introduced 1989.

Price: Complete pistol, 15" bbl. **$519.00**
Price: As above 10¾" bbl. **$506.00**
Price: Conversion unit, 15" bbl. **$259.00**
Price: As above, 10¾" **$246.00**
Price: Interchangeable barrel, 15" **$128.70**
Price: As above, 10¾" **$115.70**

Springfield S.A.S.S.

Texas Longhorn "Jezebel"

TEXAS LONGHORN "THE JEZEBEL" PISTOL

Caliber: 22 Short, Long, Long Rifle, single shot.

Barrel: 6".

Weight: 15 oz. **Length:** 8" overall.

Stocks: One-piece fancy walnut grip (right or left hand), walnut forend.

Sights: Bead front, fixed rear.

Features: Hand-made gun. Top-break action; all stainless steel; automatic hammer block safety; music wire coil springs. Barrel is half-round, half-octagon. Announced 1986. From Texas Longhorn Arms.

Price: About. **$250.00**

Thompson/Center Contender

THOMPSON/CENTER ARMS CONTENDER
Caliber: 7mm TCU, 30-30 Win., 22 S, L, LR, 22 WMR, 22 Hornet, 223 Rem., 7x30 Waters, 32 H&R Mag., 32-20 Win., 357 Mag., 357 Rem. Max., 44 Mag., 10mm Auto, 445 Super Mag., 45/410, single shot.
Barrel: 10″, tapered octagon, bull barrel and vent. rib.
Weight: 43 oz. (10″ bbl). **Length:** 13¼″ (10″ bbl).
Stocks: T/C "Competitor Grip." Right or left hand.

Sights: Under-cut blade ramp front, rear adjustable for w. & e.
Features: Break-open action with automatic safety. Single-action only. Interchangeable bbls., both caliber (rim & centerfire), and length. Drilled and tapped for scope. Engraved frame. See T/C catalog for exact barrel/caliber availability.
Price: Blued (rimfire cals.) **$335.00**
Price: Blued (centerfire cals.) **$335.00**
Price: With Armour Alloy II finish **$415.00**
Price: With internal choke **$420.00**
Price: As above, vent. rib **$435.00**
Price: Extra bbls. (standard octagon) **$145.00**
Price: Bushnell Phantom scope base **$15.00**
Price: 45/410, vent. rib, internal choke bbl. **$165.00**

UBERTI ROLLING BLOCK TARGET PISTOL
Caliber: 22 LR, 22 WMR, 22 Hornet, 357 Mag., single shot.
Barrel: 9⅞″, half-round, half-octagon.
Weight: 44 oz. **Length:** 14″ overall.
Stocks: Walnut grip and forend.
Sights: Blade front, fully adjustable rear.
Features: Replica of the 1871 rolling block target pistol. Brass trigger guard, color case-hardened frame, blue barrel. Imported by Uberti USA.
Price: **$294.00**

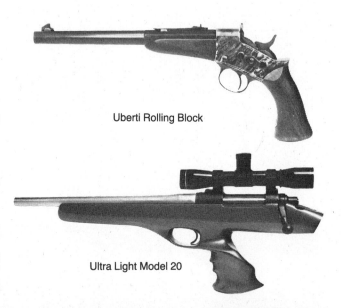

Uberti Rolling Block

Ultra Light Model 20

ULTRA LIGHT ARMS MODEL 20 REB HUNTER'S PISTOL
Caliber: 22-250 thru 308 Win. standard. Most silhouette calibers and others on request. 5-shot magazine.
Barrel: 14″, Douglas No. 3.
Weight: 4 lbs.
Stock: Composite Kevlar, graphite reinforced. Du Pont Imron paint in green, brown, black and camo.
Sights: None furnished. Scope mount included.
Features: Timney adjustable trigger; two position, three-function safety; benchrest quality action; matte or bright stock and metal finish; right- or left-hand action. Shipped in hard case. Introduced 1987. From Ultra Light Arms.
Price: **$1,300.00**

CENTERFIRE RIFLES—MILITARY STYLE AUTOLOADERS

Suitable for, and adaptable to, certain kinds of competitions as well as sporting purposes, such as hunting.

Prices shown were correct at presstime, but may not reflect current market trends.

American Arms AKY39

AMAC LONG-RANGE RIFLE
Caliber: 50 BMG.
Barrel: 33″, fully fluted, free-floating.
Weight: 30 lbs. **Length:** 55.5″ overall.
Stocks: Composition. Adjustable drop and comb.
Sights: Comes with Leupold Ultra M1 20 x scope.
Features: Bolt-action long-range rife. Comes with Automatic Ranging Scope Base. Ajustable trigger. Rifle breaks down for transport, storage. From Iver Johnson.
Price: **$8,500.00**

AMERICAN ARMS AKY39, AKF39 RIFLES
Caliber: 7.62x39, 30-shot magazine.
Barrel: 19.6″.
Weight: 9.1 lbs. **Length:** 40.6″ overall.
Stocks: Teakwood (AKY39), folding metal (AKF39).
Sights: Hooded post front, open adjustable rear. Flip-up Tritium night sights front and rear.
Features: Matte blue finish on metal, oil-finished wood. Imported from Yugoslavia by American Arms, Inc.
Price: Wood stock (AKY39) **$559.00**
Price: Folding metal stock (AKF39) **$589.00**

American Arms AKC 47 Rifle
Same as the AKY39 except does not have Tritium night sights, comes with blade bayonet, three magazines and cleaning kit. Imported from China by American Arms, Inc. Introduced 1989.
Price: **$365.00**
Price: AKF 47 (as above except has underfolding metal stock) **$365.00**

CAUTION: PRICES CHANGE. CHECK AT GUNSHOP.

Thompson M1

Auto-Ordnance Thompson M1

Similar to the Model 27 A-1 except is in the M-1 configuration with side cocking knob, horizontal forend, smooth unfinned barrel, sling swivels on butt and forend. Matte black finish. Introduced 1985.

Price: $625.00

AUTO-ORDNANCE MODEL 27 A-1 THOMPSON

Caliber: 45 ACP, 30-shot magazine.
Barrel: 16″.
Weight: 11½ lbs. **Length:** About 42″ overall (Deluxe).
Stock: Walnut stock and vertical forend.
Sights: Blade front, open rear adjustable for w.
Features: Recreation of Thompson Model 1927. Semi-auto only. Deluxe model has finned barrel, adjustable rear sight and compensator; Standard model has plain barrel and military sight. From Auto-Ordnance Corp.
Price: Deluxe $716.00
Price: 1927A5 Pistol (M27A1 without stock; wgt. 7 lbs.) $622.50
Price: Lightweight model. $631.50

Barrett Model 82 A-1

BARRETT LIGHT-FIFTY MODEL 82 A-1

Caliber: 50 BMG, 11-shot detachable box magazine.
Barrel: 33″.
Weight: 32.5 lbs. **Length:** 61″ overall.
Stock: Composition.
Sights: Open, iron. Scope optional.
Features: Semi-automatic, recoil operated with recoiling barrel. Three-lug locking bolt; muzzlebrake. Self-leveling bipod. Fires same 50-cal. ammunition as the M2HB machinegun. Introduced 1985. From Barrett Firearms.
Price: With one magazine, case $4,995.00
Price: With two magazines, Leupold M3 Ultra scope, Barrett Ranging reticle, rings, case $5,795.00

Bushmaster Auto Rifle

BUSHMASTER AUTO RIFLE

Caliber: 223, 30-shot magazine
Barrel: 18½″.
Weight: 6¼ lbs. **Length:** 37.5″ overall.
Stock: Rock maple.
Sights: Protected post front adjustable for elevation, protected quick-flip rear peep adjustable for windage; short and long range.
Features: Steel alloy upper receiver with welded barrel assembly; AK-47-type gas system, aluminum lower receiver; silent sling and swivels; bayonet lug; one-piece welded steel alloy bolt carrier assembly. From Bushmaster Firearms.
Price: With maple stock $384.95
Price: With nylon-coated folding stock $394.95
Price: Matte electroless finish, maple stock $394.95
Price: As above, folding stock $394.95

BERETTA AR70 SPORTER RIFLE

Caliber: 223, 8- and 30-shot magazines.
Barrel: 17.2″.
Weight: 8.3 lbs. **Length:** 38″ overall.
Stock: Black high-impact plastic.
Sights: Blade front, diopter rear adjustable for windage and elevation.
Features: Matte black epoxy finish; easy takedown. Comes with both magazines, cleaning kit, carrying strap. Imported from Italy by Beretta U.S.A. Corp. Introduced 1984.
Price: $1,065.00

Colt AR-15A2 Rifle

COLT AR-15A2 GOVERNMENT MODEL RIFLE

Caliber: 223 Rem., 5-shot magazine.
Barrel: 20″.
Weight: 7.5 lbs. **Length:** 39″ overall.
Stock: Composition stock, grip, forend.
Sights: Post front, aperture rear adjustable for windage and elevation.
Features: Five-round detachable box magazine, standard-weight barrel, flash suppressor, sling swivels. Has forward bolt assist. Military matte black finish. Model introduced 1989.
Price: $815.95

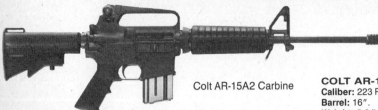

Colt AR-15A2 Carbine

Colt AR-15A2 Sporter II Rifle
Same as the AR-15A2 Government Model rifle except rear sight adjustable for windage only.
Price: $739.95

Colt AR-15A2 Delta H-BAR
Similar to the AR-15A2 Government Model except has standard stock, heavy barrel, is refined and inspected by the Colt Custom Shop. Comes with a 3-9x rubber armored scope and removeable cheekpiece, adjustable scope mount, black leather military-style sling, cleaning kit, and hard carrying case. Pistol grip has Delta medallion. Introduced 1987.
Price: $1,359.95

COLT AR-15A2 GOVERNMENT MODEL CARBINE
Caliber: 223 Rem.
Barrel: 16".
Weight: 5.8 lbs. **Length:** 35" overall (extended).
Stock: Telescoping aluminum.
Sights: Post front, adjustable for elevation, flip-type rear for short, long range, windage.
Features: 5-round detachable box magazine, flash suppressor, sling swivels. Forward bolt assist included. Introduced 1985.
Price: $835.95

Colt AR-15A2 H-BAR
Similar to the AR-15A2 Delta H-BAR except has heavy barrel, 800-meter M-16A2 rear sight adjustable for windage and elevation, case deflector for left-hand shooters, target-style nylon sling. Introduced 1986.
Price: $869.95

Daewoo AR100

Daewoo AR110C Auto Carbine
Similar to the MAX-1 except has a folding buttstock giving overall length of 38.9" (extended). 28.7" (folded). Weight is 7.5 lbs.; barrel length is 18.3". Has hooded post front sight, adjustable peep rear. Uses AR-15/M-16 magazines. Introduced 1985. Imported from Korea by Pacific International.
Price: $399.95

DAEWOO AR100 AUTO RIFLE
Caliber: 5.56mm (223), 30-round magazine.
Barrel: 17".
Weight: 6.5 lbs. **Length:** 38.4" overall (butt extended).
Stock: Retractable.
Sights: Post front, adjustable peep rear.
Features: Machine-forged receiver; gas-operated action; uses AR-15/M-16 magazines. Introduced 1985. Imported from Korea by Pacific International.
Price: $429.95

FEATHER AT-9 SEMI-AUTO CARBINE
Caliber: 9mm Para., 25-shot magazine.
Barrel: 16".
Weight: 5 lbs. **Length:** 33 1/2 overall (stock extended).
Stock: Telescoping wire, composition pistol grip.
Sights: Hooded post front, adjustable aperture rear.
Features: Semi-auto only. Matte black finish. From Feather Industries. Announced 1988.
Price: $499.95

Feather AT-9

FEDERAL XC-900/XC-450 AUTO CARBINES
Caliber: 9mm Para., 32-shot magazine; 45 ACP.
Barrel: 16.5" (with flash hider).
Weight: 8 lbs. **Length:** 34 1/2" overall.
Stock: Detachable tube steel; adjustable stock optional.
Sights: Hooded post front, peep rear adjustable for w. and e.
Features: Quick takedown for transport, storage. All heli-arc welded steel construction. Made in U.S. by Federal Engineering Corp.
Price: Phosphate finish, either cal. $513.50
Price: As above, with adj. stock $561.54
Price: With Teflon finish, nylon covered forend, hard-chrome bolt. . . $610.94
Price: As above, with adj. stock $656.44

Federal XC-900/XC-450

Spectre Carbine

F.I.E. SPECTRE AUTO CARBINE
Caliber: 9mm Para., 30-shot magazine.
Barrel: 16.5″.
Weight: 5.3 lbs. **Length:** 35.5″ overall (stock extended).
Stock: Folding metal.
Sights: Post front, two-position flip rear.
Features: Double- or single-action fire; 50-shot magazine available. Introduced 1987. Imported by F.I.E. Firearms Corp.
Price: $699.95

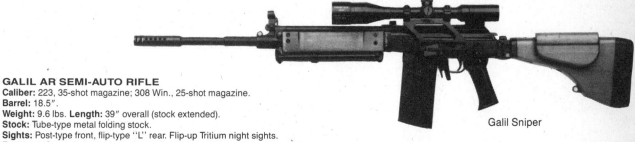

Galil Sniper

GALIL AR SEMI-AUTO RIFLE
Caliber: 223, 35-shot magazine; 308 Win., 25-shot magazine.
Barrel: 18.5″.
Weight: 9.6 lbs. **Length:** 39″ overall (stock extended).
Stock: Tube-type metal folding stock.
Sights: Post-type front, flip-type ''L'' rear. Flip-up Tritium night sights.
Features: Gas-operated, rotating bolt. Cocking handle, safety and magazine catch can be operated from either side. Introduced 1982. Imported from Israel by Action Arms Ltd.
Price: 308 .... $1,060.00
Price: As above in 223 (16.1″ bbl., 36.5″ o.a.l., 35-shot magazine) $1,000.00

Galil Model ARM Semi-Auto Rifle
Similar to the standard AR models except comes with folding bipod with integral wire cutter, vented hardwood handguard and carrying handle. Other specs are the same. Introduced 1987.
Price: 223 .... $1,100.00
Price: 308 .... $1,200.00

Galil Sniper Rifle
Similar to the Galil AR except has 20″ barrel; folding, adjustable hardwood buttstock, hardwood forend; comes with detachable 6x40 Nimrod scope. Available in 308 only. Length with stock folded 33″, weight is 14.1 lbs. Black finish. Introduced 1989.
Price: $4,100.00

Galil Hadar II

Galil Hadar II Auto Rifle
Similar to the Galil AR except in 308 only with 18.5″ barrel, fixed walnut stock and forend. Overall length of 38.4″. Does not have the Tritium night sights. Introduced 1989.
Price: $1,060.00

Heckler & Koch HK-91

HECKLER & KOCH HK-91 AUTO RIFLE
Caliber: 308 Win., 5- or 20-shot magazine.
Barrel: 17.71″.
Weight: 9½ lbs. **Length:** 40¼″ overall.
Stock: Black high-impact plastic.
Sights: Post front, aperture rear adjustable for w. and e.
Features: Delayed roller-lock action. Sporting version of West German service rifle. Takes special H&K clamp scope mount. Imported from West Germany by Heckler & Koch, Inc.
Price: HK-91 A-2 with plastic stock $946.00
Price: HK-91 A-3 with retractable metal stock $1,114.00
Price: HK-91/94 scope mount with 1″ rings $351.00

Heckler & Koch HK-93 Auto Rifle
Similar to HK-91 except in 223 cal., 16.13″ barrel, overall length of 35½″, weighs 7¾ lbs. Same stock, forend.
Price: HK-93 A-2 with plastic stock $946.00
Price: HK-93 A-3 with retractable metal stock $1,114.00

Consult our Directory pages for the location of firms mentioned.

CENTERFIRE RIFLES—MILITARY STYLE AUTOLOADERS

Heckler & Koch HK-94

HECKLER & KOCH HK-94 AUTO CARBINE
Caliber: 9mm Para., 15-shot magazine.
Barrel: 16″.
Weight: 6½ lbs. (fixed stock). **Length:** 34¾″ overall.
Stock: High-impact plastic butt and forend or retractable metal stock.
Sights: Hooded post front, aperture rear adjustable for windage and elevation.
Features: Delayed roller-locked action; accepts H&K quick-detachable scope mount. Introduced 1983. Imported from West Germany by Heckler & Koch, Inc.
Price: HK-94-A2 (fixed stock) **$946.00**
Price: HK-94-A3 (retractable metal stock) **$1,114.00**
Price: 30-shot magazine **$34.00**
Price: Clamp to hold two magazines **$26.00**

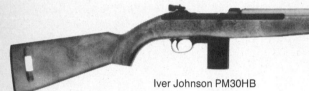

Iver Johnson PM30HB

IVER JOHNSON PM30HB CARBINE
Caliber: 30 U.S. Carbine
Barrel: 18″ four-groove.
Weight: 6½ lbs. **Length:** 35½″ overall.
Stock: Glossy-finished hardwood or walnut.
Sights: Click-adjustable peep rear.
Features: Gas-operated semi-auto carbine. 15-shot detachable magazine. Made in U.S.A.
Price: Blue finish, hardwood stock **$265.00**
Price: Blue finish, walnut stock **$291.50**
Price: Paratrooper **$291.50**

MAS 223 Auto

MAS 223 SEMI-AUTO RIFLE
Caliber: 223, 25-shot magazine.
Barrel: 19.2″.
Weight: About 8 lbs. **Length:** 29.8″ overall.
Stock: Rubber-covered adjustable cheekpiece converts to left- or right-hand shooters.
Sights: Adjustable blade front with luminescent spot for night use, aperture adjustable rear.
Features: Converts to left- or right-hand ejection. Armored plastic guards vital parts, including sights. Civilian version of the French FAMAS assault rifle. Introduced 1986. Imported from France by Century Arms.
Price: With spare parts kit, bipod, sling, spare magazine, about . . **$1,325.00**

Mitchell AK-47

MITCHELL AK-47 SEMI-AUTO RIFLE
Caliber: 308, 7.62x39, 30-shot magazine.
Barrel: 19.6″.
Weight: 9.1 lbs. **Length:** 40.6″ overall with wood stock.
Stock: Teak.
Sights: Hooded post front, open adjustable rear.
Features: Gas operated semi-automatic. Last-round bolt hold-open. Imported from Yugoslavia by Mitchell Arms.
Price: Wood stock **$675.00**
Price: With folding metal stock **$698.00**

Mitchell Heavy Barrel AK-47
Same gun as the standard AK-47 except has heavy finned barrel, heavy forend, fully adjustable day or night sights. Available with or without folding, detachable bipod.
Price: **$995.00**

MITCHELL M-59 SEMI-AUTO RIFLE
Caliber: 7.62x39, 10-shot magazine.
Barrel: 18″.
Weight: 9 lbs. **Length:** 44″ overall.
Stock: Walnut.
Sights: Hooded post front, open adjustable rear with night sights front and rear.
Features: Gas-operated likeness of the SKS rifle. Imported from Yugoslavia by Mitchell Arms.
Price: **$699.00**

MITCHELL M-76 COUNTER-SNIPER RIFLE
Caliber: 7.9mm (8mm Mauser).
Barrel: 21.8″. Muzzlebrake, flash hider.
Weight: 10.9 lbs. **Length:** 44.6″ overall.
Stock: Teak.
Features: Uses AK-47 action. Optional scope, night sight, mounts available. Imported from Yugoslavia by Mitchell Arms.
Price: **$1,995.00**

CAUTION: PRICES CHANGE. CHECK AT GUNSHOP.

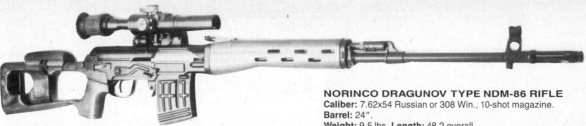

Norinco Dragunov

NORINCO DRAGUNOV TYPE NDM-86 RIFLE
Caliber: 7.62x54 Russian or 308 Win., 10-shot magazine.
Barrel: 24″.
Weight: 9.5 lbs. **Length:** 48.2 overall.
Stock: Skeleton-type wood butt with cheekpiece, ventilated wood forend.
Sights: Protected post front, open adjustable rear and 4x scope with lighted reticle.
Features: Matte blue finish. Comes with scope and mount. Imported from China by China Sports, Inc.
Price: .... NA

Norinco SKS

NORINCO SKS SEMI-AUTO RIFLE
Caliber: 223 or 7.62x39, 30-shot magazine.
Barrel: 20.47″.
Weight: 8.8 lbs. **Length:** 40.16″ overall.
Stock: Oil-finished wood.
Sights: Protected post front, open adjustable rear.
Features: Uses detachable AK-type magazine; folding bayonet; blue finish. Imported from China by China Sports, Inc.
Price: .... NA

Norinco Type 84S

NORINCO TYPE 84S AK RIFLE
Caliber: 223 (5.56mm NATO), 30-shot magazine.
Barrel: 16.34″.
Weight: 8.87 lbs. **Length:** 34.25″ overall.
Stock: Wood butt, grip, forend.
Sights: Protected post front, open adjustable rear.
Features: Available with under-folding metal butt or composition butt, grip, forend. Imported from China by China Sports, Inc.
Price: .... NA

Poly Tech AK47/S

POLY TECH AKS-47/S AUTO RIFLE
Caliber: 7.62x39, 30-shot magazine; optional 5-, 20- and 40-shot box magazines, 75-round drum magazine available.
Barrel: 16³/₈″.
Weight: 8.2 lbs. **Length:** 34³/₈″ overall.
Stock: Oil-finished Chiu wood. Also available with down-folding stock.
Sights: Protected post front, leaf rear graduated to 800 meters.
Features: Semi-auto version of the original AK-47. Receiver is machined from bar stock. Chrome-lined barrel, chromed gas piston; phosphated bolt and bolt carrier. Spring-loaded firing pin. Comes with three 30-shot magazines, cleaning kit, web sling, oil bottle and an original AK-47-pattern bayonet. Imported from China by Poly Technologies, Inc.
Price: $899.95

POLY TECH M-14/S AUTO RIFLE
Caliber: 7.62mm NATO, 20-shot box magazine.
Barrel: 22″ (without flash hider).
Weight: 9.2 lbs. **Length:** 43³/₁₀″ overall.
Stock: Oil-finished Chinese walnut, fiberglass handguard (walnut optional).
Sights: Square blade front, click-adjustable aperture rear.
Features: Semi-auto only. Receiver is machined from chrome-moly steel. Chrome-lined barrel, chromed gas piston. Parkerized finish. Announced 1988. Imported from China by Poly Technologies, Inc.
Price: .... NA

Poly Tech AKS-762 Folding Stock Rifle
Similar to the AKS-762 Wood Stock rifle except has side-folding skeleton stock. Semi-auto version of the Chinese Type 56-2 assault rifle. No bayonet mount.
Price: $799.95

POLY TECH AKS-762 AUTO RIFLE
Caliber: 7.62x39, 30-shot magazine; optional 5-, 20- and 40-shot, 75-round drum magazines available.
Barrel: 16³/₈".
Weight: About 8.4 lbs. **Length:** 34³/₈" overall.
Stock: Oil-finished Chiu wood.
Sights: Hooded post front, leaf rear graduated to 800 meters.
Features: Semi-auto version of the Chinese Type 56 (AKM) rifle. Chrome-lined barrel, chromed gas piston, phospaded bolt and bolt carrier, rest blued. Spring-loaded firing pin. Comes with detachable Type 56 spike bayonet, sling, cleaning kit, oil bottle. Imported from China by Poly Technologies, Inc.
Price: Wood or folding metal stock $799.95

RUGER MINI-14/5R RANCH RIFLE
Caliber: 223 Rem., 5-shot detachable box magazine.
Barrel: 18¹/₂".
Weight: 6.4 lbs. **Length:** 37¹/₄" overall.
Stock: American hardwood, steel reinforced.
Sights: Ramp front, fully adjustable rear.
Features: Fixed piston gas-operated, positive primary extraction. New buffer system, redesigned ejector system. Ruger S100RH scope rings included. 20-shot magazines available from Ruger dealers, 30-shot magazine available only to police departments and government agencies.
Price: Mini-14/5R, blued $454.50
Price: Mini-14/5RF, blued, folding stock $515.00
Price: K-Mini-14/5R, stainless $497.75
Price: K-Mini-14/5RF, stainless, folding stock $562.75

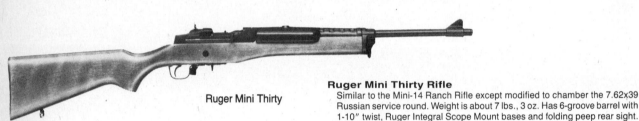

Ruger Mini Thirty

Ruger Mini Thirty Rifle
Similar to the Mini-14 Ranch Rifle except modified to chamber the 7.62x39 Russian service round. Weight is about 7 lbs., 3 oz. Has 6-groove barrel with 1-10" twist, Ruger Integral Scope Mount bases and folding peep rear sight. Detachable 5-shot staggered box magazine. Blued finish. Introduced 1987.
Price: $454.50

Ruger Mini-14/5F

Ruger Mini-14/5F Folding Stock
Same as the Ranch Rifle except available with folding stock, checkered high impact plastic vertical pistol grip. Over-all length with stock open is 37³/₄", length closed is 27¹/₂". Weight is about 7³/₄ lbs.
Price: Blued ordnance steel, standard stock, Mini-14/5 . . . . $421.75
Price: Stainless, K-Mini 14/5 . . . . $465.00
Price: Blued, folding stock, Mini-14/5 F $503.00
Price: Stainless, folding stock, K-Mini-14/5 F $535.00

SIG SG550SP

SIG SG550SP AUTO RIFLE
Caliber: 223, 20-shot magazine.
Barrel: 20.8".
Weight: 9 lbs. **Length:** 39.3" overall.
Stock: Synthetic.
Sights: Protected post front, adjustable diopter rear.
Features: Semi-auto only. Ambidextrous controls. Introduced 1989. Imported by Sigarms.
Price: $2,400.00
Price: SG551SP (16" bbl., 7.7 lbs.) $2,400.00

Springfield Armory SAR-3

SPRINGFIELD ARMORY SAR-3 RIFLE
Caliber: 308 Win., 20-shot magazine.
Barrel: 18".
Weight: 8.7 lbs. **Length:** 40.3" overall.
Stock: Black composition butt and forend.
Sights: Protected post front, rotary-style adjustable rear.
Features: Delayed roller-lock action, fluted chamber; matte black finish. Introduced 1988. From Springfield Armory.
Price: $844.00

Springfield Armory SAR-3 Retractable Stock Model
Same as standard SAR-3 except has retractable metal buttstock giving 33.1" overall length (retracted). Introduced 1988.
Price: $1,038.70

CAUTION: PRICES CHANGE. CHECK AT GUNSHOP.

SPRINGFIELD ARMORY SAR-48 RIFLE
Caliber: 7.62mm NATO (308 Win.), 20-shot magazine.
Barrel: 21".
Weight: 9.5 lbs. **Length:** 43.3" overall.
Stock: Fiberglass.
Sights: Protected post, adjustable peep rear.
Features: New production. Introduced 1985. From Springfield Armory.
Price: Standard model **$899.00**
Price: "Bush" rifle, 18" barrel **$899.00**
Price: Para model, folding stock **$1,020.00**

Springfield Armory SAR-48 Bush

Springfield Armory M1A

SPRINGFIELD ARMORY M-1A RIFLE
Caliber: 7.62mm NATO (308), 243 Win., 5-, 10- or 20-shot box magazine.
Barrel: 25 1/16" with flash suppressor, 22" without suppressor.
Weight: 8 3/4 lbs. **Length:** 44 1/4" overall.
Stock: American walnut with walnut colored heat-resistant fiberglass hand-guard. Matching walnut handguard available. Also available with fiberglass stock.
Sights: Military, square blade front, full click-adjustable aperture rear.
Features: Commercial equivalent of the U.S. M-14 service rifle with no provision for automatic firing. From Springfield Armory. Military accessories available including 3x-9x56 ART scope and mount.
Price: Standard M1A rifle, about $844.00
Price: Match Grade, about $1,104.00
Price: Super Match (heavy premium barrel), about $1,329.00
Price: M1A-A1 Assault Rifle, walnut stock, about $870.00
Price: As above, folding stock, about $1,007.00

SPRINGFIELD ARMORY BM-59
Caliber: 7.62mm NATO (308 Win.), 20-shot box magazine.
Barrel: 19.3".
Weight: 9 1/4 lbs. **Length:** 43.7" overall.
Stock: Walnut, with trapped rubber butt pad.
Sights: Military square blade front, click adjustable peep rear.
Features: Full military-dress Italian service rifle. Available in selective fire or semi-auto only. Refined version of the M-1 Garand. Accessories available include: folding Alpine stock, muzzlebrake/flash suppressor/grenade launcher combo, bipod, winter trigger, grenade launcher sights, bayonet, oiler. Extremely limited quantities. Introduced 1981.
Price: Standard Italian model, about **$1,373.00**
Price: Alpine model, about **$1,580.00**
Price: Alpine Paratrooper model, about **$1,787.00**
Price: Nigerian Mark IV model, about **$1,502.00**

Springfield Armory M1

Consult our Directory pages for
the location of firms mentioned

SPRINGFIELD ARMORY M-1 GARAND RIFLE
Caliber: 308, 30-06, 8-shot clip.
Barrel: 24".
Weight: 9 1/2 lbs. **Length:** 43 1/2" overall.
Stock: Walnut, military.
Sights: Military square blade front, click adjustable peep rear.
Features: Commercially-made M-1 Garand duplicates the original service rifle. Introduced 1979. From Springfield Armory.
Price: Standard, about $761.00
Price: National Match, about. $897.00
Price: Ultra Match, about $1033.00
Price: M-1-T26 "Tanker," walnut stock, about $797.00
Price: Standard M-1 Garand with Beretta-made receiver, about . . **$1,665.00**

STEYR A.U.G. AUTOLOADING RIFLE
Caliber: 223 Rem.
Barrel: 20".
Weight: 8 1/2 lbs. **Length:** 31" overall.
Stock: Synthetic, green. One-piece moulding houses receiver group, hammer mechanism and magazine.
Sights: 1.5x scope only; scope and mount form the carrying handle.
Features: Semi-automatic, gas-operated action; can be converted to suit right- or left-handed shooters, including ejection port. Transparent 30- or 42-shot magazines. Folding vertical front grip. Introduced 1983. Imported from Austria by Gun South, Inc.
Price: Right- or left-hand model **$1,362.00**

Steyr A.U.G. Rifle

CENTERFIRE RIFLES—MILITARY STYLE AUTOLOADERS

UZI Carbine

UZI® CARBINE
Caliber: 9mm Para., 41 Action Express, 45 ACP.
Barrel: 16.1″.
Weight: 8.4 lbs. **Length:** 24.4″ (stock folded).
Stock: Folding metal stock. Wood stock available as an accessory.
Sights: Post-type front, ''L'' flip-type rear adjustable for 100 meters and 200 meters. Both click-adjustable for w. and e.
Features: Adapted to meet BATF regulations, this semi-auto has the same qualities as the famous submachine gun. Made by Israel Military Industries. Comes in moulded carrying case with sling, magazine, sight adjustment key. Exclusively imported from Israel by Action Arms Ltd. 9mm introduced 1980; 45 ACP introduced 1985; 41 A.E. introduced 1987.
Price: $775.00

UZI® Mini Carbine
Similar to the UZI Carbine except shorter receiver dimensions and has a forward-folding metal stock. Available in 9mm Para. or 41 Action Express; 19.75″ barrel; overall length of 35.75″ (26.1″ folded); weight is 7.2 lbs. Introduced 1987.
Price: $775.00

Valmet M-76

VALMET M-76 STANDARD RIFLE
Caliber: 223, 15- or 30-shot magazine, or 308, 20-shot magazine.
Barrel: 16³/₄″.
Weight: About 8¹/₂ lbs. **Length:** 37³/₄″ overall.
Stock: Wood, synthetic or folding metal type; composition forend.
Sights: Hooded adjustable post front, peep rear with luminous night sight.
Features: Semi-automatic only. Has sling swivels, flash suppressor. Bayonet, cleaning kit, 30-shot magazine, scope adaptor cover optional. Imported from Finland by Stoeger.
Price: Wood stock $740.00
Price: Folding stock $825.00
Price: Synthetic stock $840.00

Valmet M78 Semi-Auto
Similar to M76 except chambered only for 308 Win., has 24¹/₄″ heavy barrel, weighs 11 lbs., 43¹/₄″ overall; 20-shot magazine; bipod; machined receiver. Length of pull on wood stock dimensioned for American shooters. Rear sight adjustable for w. and e., open-aperture front sight; folding carrying handle. Imported from Finland by Stoeger.
Price: $1,060.00

CENTERFIRE RIFLES—SPORTING AUTOLOADERS

Includes models for hunting, adaptable to and suitable for certain competition.

Browning High Power Rifle

BROWNING HIGH-POWER SEMI-AUTO RIFLE
Caliber: 243, 270, 280, 30-06, 308.
Barrel: 22″ round tapered.
Weight: 7³/₈ lbs. **Length:** 43″ overall.
Stock: French walnut p.g. stock and forend, hand checkered.
Sights: Adj. folding-leaf rear, gold bead on hooded ramp front, or no sights.
Features: Detachable 4-round magazine. Receiver tapped for scope mounts. Trigger pull 3¹/₂ lbs. Imported from Belgium by Browning.
Price: Grade I, with sights $594.95
Price: Grade 1, no sights. $579.95

Browning Big Game BAR
Similar to the standard BAR except has silver-gray receiver with engraved and gold inlaid whitetail deer on the right side, a mule deer on the left; a gold edged scroll banner frames ''One of Six Hundred'' on the left side, the numerical edition number replaces ''One'' on the right. Chambered only in 30-06. Fancy, highly figured walnut stock and forend. Introduced 1983.
Price: $3,550.00

Browning Magnum Semi-Auto Rifle
Same as the standard caliber model, except weighs 8³/₈ lbs., 45″ overall, 24″ bbl., 3-round mag. Cals. 7mm Mag., 300 Win. Mag., 338 Win. Mag.
Price: Grade 1, with sights $644.95
Price: Grade 1, no sights. $629.95

CALICO MODEL 900 CARBINE
Caliber: 9mm Para., 50- or 100-shot magazine.
Barrel: 16″.
Weight: 3.7 lbs. (empty). **Length:** 28¹/₂″ overall (stock collapsed).
Stock: Sliding steel buttstock.
Sights: Post front adjustable for w. and e., fixed notch rear.
Features: Helical feed 50- or 100-shot magazine. Ambidextrous safety, static cocking handle. Retarded blowback action. Glass-filled polymer grip. Introduced 1989. From Calico.
Price: $458.95

Calico Model 900

CAUTION: PRICES CHANGE. CHECK AT GUNSHOP.

Heckler & Koch HK770

HECKLER & KOCH HK770 AUTO RIFLE
Caliber: 308 Win., 3-shot magazine.
Barrel: 19.6".
Weight: 7½ lbs. **Length:** 42.8" overall.
Stock: European walnut. Checkered p.g. and forend.
Sights: Vertically adjustable blade front, open fold-down, rear adj. for w.
Features: Has the delayed roller-locked system and polygonal rifling. Magazine catch located at front of trigger guard. Receiver top is dovetailed to accept clamp-type scope mount. Imported from West Germany by Heckler & Koch, Inc. Limited availability.
Price: $813.00

Heckler & Koch SL6

HECKLER & KOCH SL6 AUTO RIFLE
Caliber: 223, 4-shot magazine.
Barrel: 17".
Weight: 8 lbs. **Length:** 39¾" overall.
Stock: European walnut, oil finished.
Sights: Hooded post front, adjustable aperture rear.
Features: Delayed roller-locked action; polygon rifling; receiver is dovetailed for H&K quick-detachable scope mount. Introduced 1983. Imported from West Germany by Heckler & Koch, Inc. Limited availability.
Price: $813.00

Marlin Model 45

MARLIN MODEL 9 CAMP CARBINE
Caliber: 9mm Para., 12-shot magazine (20-shot available).
Barrel: 16½", Micro-Groove® rifling.
Weight: 6¼ lbs. **Length:** 35½" overall.
Stock: Walnut-finished hardwood; rubber butt pad; Mar-Shield® finish.
Sights: Ramp front with red post cutaway Wide-Scan™ hood, adjustable open rear.
Features: Manual bolt hold-open; Garand-type safety, magazine safety; loaded chamber indicator; receiver drilled, tapped for scope mounting. Introduced 1985.
Price: $311.95

Marlin Model 45 Carbine
Similar to the Model 9 except chambered for 45 ACP, 7-shot magazine. Introduced 1986.
Price: $311.95

Remington 7400

Sights: Gold bead front sight on ramp; step rear sight with windage adj.
Features: Redesigned and improved version of the Model 742. Positive cross-bolt safety. Receiver tapped for scope mount. 4-shot clip mag. Introduced 1981.
Price: About.. $459.00
Price: Carbine (18½" bbl., 30-06 only) $459.00
Price: D Grade, about $2,291.00
Price: F Grade, about.................................... $4,720.00
Price: F Grade with gold inlays, about..................... $7,079.00

REMINGTON MODEL 7400 AUTO RIFLE
Caliber: 243 Win., 270 Win., 280 Rem., 308 Win. and 30-06, 4-shot magazine.
Barrel: 22" round tapered.
Weight: 7½ lbs. **Length:** 42" overall.
Stock: Walnut, deluxe cut checkered p.g. and forend.

Valmet Hunter

Weight: 8 lbs. **Length:** 42" overall.
Stock: American walnut butt and forend. Checkered palm-swell p.g. and forend.
Sights: Blade front, open flip-type rear.
Features: Uses semi-auto Kalashnikov-type gas-operated action with rotating bolt. Stock is adjustable for length via spacers. Optional cleaning kit, sling, ejection buffer, scope mount. Introduced 1986. Imported from Finland by Valmet.
Price: $795.00

VALMET HUNTER AUTO RIFLE
Caliber: 223, 15-, 30-shot magazines; 243, 9-shot magazine; 308, 5-, 9- and 20-shot magazines.
Barrel: 20½".

Both classic arms and recent designs in American-style repeaters for sport and field shooting.

Action Arms Timber Wolf

ACTION ARMS TIMBER WOLF PUMP RIFLE
Caliber: 38 Spec./357 Mag., 10-shot magazine.
Barrel: 18.5″.
Weight: 5.5 lbs. **Length:** 36.5″ overall.
Stock: Walnut.
Sights: Blade front, adjustable rear.
Features: Push-button safety on trigger guard; integral scope mount on receiver. Blue finish. Introduced 1989. Imported from Israel by Action Arms Ltd.
Price: $475.00

Browning Model 65

BROWNING MODEL 65 LEVER-ACTION RIFLE
Caliber: 218 Bee, 7-shot magazine.
Barrel: 24″ round tapered.
Weight: 6 lbs., 12 oz. **Length:** 41.75″ overall.
Stock: Select walnut. Full pistol grip, semi-beavertail forend.

Sights: Hooded ramp front, adjustable buckhorn-style rear.
Features: Reproduction of the Winchester Model 65 with half-length magazine, uncheckered wood, blue finish. High Grade model has better wood with cut checkering and high gloss finish; receiver has grayed finish with scroll engraving and game scenes — a coyote on the left side, bobcat on the right, both gold-plated, as is the trigger. Production limited to 3500 Grade I guns, 1500 High Grades. Introduced 1989. Imported from Japan by Browning.
Price: Grade I $550.00
Price: High Grade $850.00

Browning Model 71

BROWNING MODEL 71 LEVER-ACTION RIFLE
Caliber: 348 Win., 4-shot magazine.
Barrel: 20″ (Carbine), 24″ (Rifle).
Weight: 8 lbs., 2 oz. (Rifle). **Length:** 45″ overall (Rifle).

Stock: Select walnut, pistol grip type, classic-style forend. Flat metal buttplate. Satin finish.
Sights: Hooded front, open buckhorn rear.
Features: Reproduction of the Winchester Model 71 with half-length magazine tube, uncheckered wood; blue finish. High Grade model has extra quality wood with high gloss finish and fine checkering. Barrel and magazine are blued, receiver and lever are grayed and have scroll engraving with gold-plated big game. Production limited to 3,000 Rifles, 3,000 Carbines. Introduced 1987. Imported from Japan by Browning.
Price: Grade I, Rifle or Carbine $599.95
Price: High Grade, Rifle or Carbine $979.95

Browning BLR

BROWNING BLR MODEL 81 LEVER-ACTION RIFLE
Caliber: 222, 223, 22-250, 243, 257 Roberts, 7mm-08, 308 Win. or 358 Win., 4-shot detachable magazine.
Barrel: 20″ round tapered.

Weight: 6 lbs. 15 oz. **Length:** 39¾″ overall.
Stock: Checkered straight grip and forend, oil-finished walnut.
Sights: Gold bead on hooded ramp front; low profile square notch adj. rear.
Features: Wide, grooved trigger; half-cock hammer safety. Receiver tapped for scope mount. Recoil pad installed. Imported from Japan by Browning.
Price: With sights $472.50
Price: No sights $457.50

Cimarron 1873 ''Short''

CIMARRON 1873 ''SHORT'' RIFLE
Caliber: 22 LR, 22 WMR, 357 Magnum, 44-40, 45 Colt.
Barrel: 20″ tapered octagon.
Weight: 7.5 lbs. **Length:** 39″ overall.
Stock: Walnut.
Sights: Bead front, adjustable semi-buckhorn rear.
Features: Has half, ''button'' magazine. Original-type markings, including caliber, on barrel and elevator and ''Kings'' patent. From Cimarron Arms Co.
Price: $695.00

CAUTION: PRICES CHANGE. CHECK AT GUNSHOP.

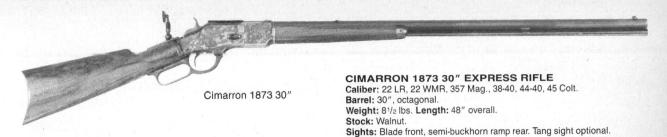

Cimarron 1873 30″

Cimarron 1873 ''Button'' Half-Magazine
Similar to the 1873 Express except has 24″ barrel with half-magazine.
Price: **$695.00**

CIMARRON 1873 30″ EXPRESS RIFLE
Caliber: 22 LR, 22 WMR, 357 Mag., 38-40, 44-40, 45 Colt.
Barrel: 30″, octagonal.
Weight: 8¹/₂ lbs. **Length:** 48″ overall.
Stock: Walnut.
Sights: Blade front, semi-buckhorn ramp rear. Tang sight optional.
Features: Color case-hardened frame; choice of modern blue-black or charcoal blue for other parts. Barrel marked ''Kings Improvement.'' From Cimarron Arms.
Price: **$695.00**

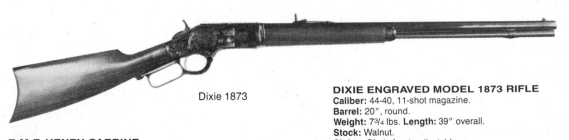

Dixie 1873

E.M.F. HENRY CARBINE
Caliber: 44-40 or 44 rimfire.
Barrel: 21″.
Weight: About 9 lbs. **Length:** About 39″ overall.
Stock: Oil-stained American walnut.
Sights: Blade front, rear adjustable for e.
Features: Reproduction of the original Henry carbine with brass frame and buttplate, rest blued. From E.M.F.
Price: Standard **$1,380.00**
Price: Engraved **$1,598.00**

DIXIE ENGRAVED MODEL 1873 RIFLE
Caliber: 44-40, 11-shot magazine.
Barrel: 20″, round.
Weight: 7³/₄ lbs. **Length:** 39″ overall.
Stock: Walnut.
Sights: Blade front, adjustable rear.
Features: Engraved and case-hardened frame. Duplicate of Winchester 1873. Made in Italy. From Dixie Gun Works.
Price: **$595.00**
Price: Plain, blued carbine **$495.00**

Marlin 336CS

Marlin 336LTS Lever-Action Carbine
Similar to the 336CS except has 16¹/₄″ barrel, weighs 6¹/₂ lbs., and overall length of 34³/₈″. Rubber rifle buttpad. Introduced 1988.
Price: **$345.95**

Marlin 30AS Lever-Action Carbine
Same as the Marlin 336CS except has walnut-finished hardwood p.g. stock, 30-30 only, 6-shot. Hammer-block safety.
Price: **$286.95**

MARLIN 336CS LEVER-ACTION CARBINE
Caliber: 30-30 or 35 Rem., 6-shot tubular magazine.
Barrel: 20″ Micro-Groove®.
Weight: 7 lbs. **Length:** 38¹/₂″ overall.
Stock: Select American black walnut, capped p.g. with white line spacers. Mar-Shield® finish.
Sights: Ramp front with Wide-Scan™ hood, semi-buckhorn folding rear adjustable for w. and e.
Features: Hammer-block safety. Receiver tapped for scope mount, offset hammer spur; top of receiver sand blasted to prevent glare.
Price: Less scope **$337.95**

Marlin 1894S

MARLIN 1894S LEVER-ACTION CARBINE
Caliber: 41 Magnum, 44 Special/44 Magnum, 45 Colt, 10-shot tubular magazine
Barrel: 20″ Micro-Groove®.
Weight: 6 lbs. **Length:** 37¹/₂″ overall.
Stock: American black walnut, straight grip and forend. Mar-Shield® finish. Rubber rifle buttpad.
Sights: Wide-Scan™ hooded ramp front, semi-buckhorn folding rear adjustable for w. and e.
Features: Hammer-block safety. Receiver tapped for scope mount, offset hammer spur, solid top receiver sand blasted to prevent glare.
Price: **$379.95**

Marlin 1894CL

Marlin Model 1894CL Rifle
Similar to the 1894S except chambered for 25-20 Win. and 32-20 Win. Has 6-shot magazine. 22″ barrel with standard rifling, overall length of 38³/₄″, weight of 6¹/₄ lbs. Introduced 1988.
Price: **$406.95**

Marlin Model 1894CS Carbine
Similar to the standard Model 1894S except chambered for 38 Special/357 Magnum with 9-shot magazine, 18¹/₂″ barrel, hammer-block safety, brass bead front sight. Introduced 1983.
Price: **$379.95**

Marlin Model 1894 CL Classic
Similar to the 1894CS except chambered for 25-20 and 32-20 Win. Has 6-shot magazine. 22″ barrel with 6-groove rifling, brass bead front sight, adjustable semi-buckhorn folding rear. Hammer-block safety. Weighs 6¹/₄ lbs., overall length of 38³/₄″. Introduced 1988.
Price: **$406.95**

MARLIN 1895SS LEVER-ACTION RIFLE
Caliber: 45-70, 4-shot tubular magazine.
Barrel: 22″ round.
Weight: 7¹/₂ lbs. **Length:** 40¹/₂″ overall.
Stock: American black walnut, full pistol grip. Mar-Shield® finish; rubber butt-pad; q.d. swivels studs.
Sights: Bead front with Wide-Scan™ hood, semi-buckhorn folding rear adjustable for w. and e.
Features: Hammer-block safety. Solid receiver tapped for scope mounts or receiver sights; offset hammer spur.
Price: **$408.95**

MARLIN 444SS LEVER-ACTION SPORTER
Caliber: 444 Marlin, 5-shot tubular magazine.
Barrel: 22″ Micro-Groove®.
Weight: 7¹/₂ lbs. **Length:** 40¹/₂″ overall.
Stock: American black walnut, capped p.g. with white line spacers, rubber rifle buttpad. Mar-Shield® finish; swivels studs.
Sights: Hooded ramp front, folding semi-buckhorn rear adjustable for w. & e.
Features: Hammer-block safety. Receiver tapped for scope mount; offset hammer spur.
Price: **$408.95**

NAVY ARMS HENRY CARBINE
Caliber: 44-40 or 44 rimfire.
Barrel: 24″.
Weight: About 8¹/₄ lbs. **Length:** 39″ overall.
Stock: Oil-stained American walnut.
Sights: Blade front, rear adjustable for e.
Features: Reproduction of the original Henry carbine with brass frame and buttplate, rest blued. Will be produced in limited edition of 1,000 standard models, plus 50 engraved guns. Made in U.S. by Navy Arms.
Price: Standard **$769.00**
Price: Engraved **$1,849.00**

Navy Arms Henry

Price: Iron Frame rifle (similar to Carbine except has blued frame). . **$769.00**
Price: Military Rifle (similar to Carbine except has sling swivels, different rear sight) **$769.00**
Price: Trapper model (16¹/₂″ bbl., 7¹/₄ lbs., 34¹/₂″ o.a.l.) **$769.00**

Remington Model 7600

REMINGTON MODEL 7600 SLIDE ACTION
Caliber: 243, 270, 280, 30-06, 308, 35 Whelen.
Barrel: 22″ round tapered.
Weight: 7¹/₂ lbs. **Length:** 42″ overall.

Stock: Cut-checkered walnut p.g. and forend, Monte Carlo with full cheek-piece.
Sights: Gold bead front sight on matted ramp, open step adjustable sporting rear.
Features: Redesigned and improved version of the Model 760. Detachable 4-shot clip. Cross-bolt safety. Receiver tapped for scope mount. Also available in high grade versions. Introduced 1981.
Price: About **$439.00**
Price: Carbine (18¹/₂″ bbl., 30-06 only) **$439.00**

ROSSI SADDLE-RING CARBINE M92 SRC
Caliber: 38 Spec./357 Mag., 44 Spec./44-40, 44 Mag., 10-shot magazine.
Barrel: 20″.
Weight: 5³/₄ lbs. **Length:** 37″ overall.
Stock: Walnut.
Sights: Blade front, buckhorn rear.
Features: Recreation of the famous lever-action carbine. Handles 38 and 357 interchangeably. Has high-relief puma medallion inlaid in the receiver. Introduced 1978. Imported by Interarms.
Price: **$282.00**
Price: Blue, engraved **$327.00**
Price: 44 Spec./44 Mag. (Model 65) **$297.00**

Rossi Carbine

Rossi Puma M92 SRS Short Carbine
Similar to the standard M92 except has 16″ barrel, overall length of 33″, in 38/357 only. Puma medallion on side of receiver. Introduced 1986.
Price: **$282.00**

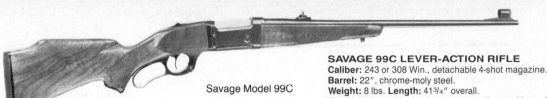

Savage Model 99C

SAVAGE 99C LEVER-ACTION RIFLE
Caliber: 243 or 308 Win., detachable 4-shot magazine.
Barrel: 22", chrome-moly steel.
Weight: 8 lbs. **Length:** 41³/₄" overall.
Stock: Walnut with checkered p.g. and forend, Monte Carlo comb.
Sights: Hooded ramp front, adjustable ramp rear sight. Tapped for scope mounts.
Features: Grooved trigger, top tang slide safety locks trigger and lever. Brown rubber buttpad, q.d. swivel studs, push-button magazine release.
Price: **$588.00**

UBERTI MODEL 1866 SPORTING RIFLE
Caliber: 22 LR, 22 WMR, 38 Spec., 44-40.
Barrel: 24¹/₄", octagonal.
Weight: 8.1 lbs. **Length:** 43¹/₄" overall.
Stock: Walnut.
Sights: Blade front adjustable for w., rear adjustable for e.
Features: Frame buttplate, forend cap of polished brass, balance charcoal blued. Imported by Uberti USA.
Price: **$635.00**
Price: Yellowboy Carbine (19" round bbl.) **$597.00**
Price: Yellowboy "Indian" Carbine (engraved receiver, "nails" in wood). **$686.00**
Price: 1866 "Red Cloud Commemorative" Carbine **$672.00**
Price: 1866 "Trapper's Model" Carbine (16" bbl.). **$688.00**

Uberti 1866 Rifle

UBERTI HENRY RIFLE
Caliber: 44-40.
Barrel: 24¹/₄", half-octagon.
Weight: 9.2 lbs. **Length:** 43³/₄" overall.
Stock: American walnut.
Sights: Blade front, rear adjustable for e.
Features: Frame, elevator, magazine follower, buttplate are brass, balance blue (also available in polished steel). Imported by Uberti USA.
Price: **$770.00**
Price: Henry Carbine (22¹/₄" bbl.) **$770.00**

UBERTI 1873 SPORTING RIFLE
Caliber: 22 LR, 22 WMR, 38 Spec., 357 Mag., 44-40, 45 Colt.
Barrel: 24¹/₄", octagonal.
Weight: 8.1 lbs. **Length:** 43¹/₄" overall.
Stock: Walnut.
Sights: Blade front adjustable for w., open rear adjustable for e.
Features: Color case-hardened frame, blued barrel, hammer, lever, buttplate, brass elevator. Imported by Uberti USA.
Price: **$756.00**
Price: 1873 Carbine (19" round bbl.) **$721.00**
Price: 1873 Carbine, nickel-plated **$818.00**
Price: 1873 "Trapper's Model" Carbine (16" bbl.). **$721.00**

Uberti 1873 Rifle

Consult our Directory pages for the location of firms mentioned.

UBERTI 1873 CATTLEMAN REVOLVING CARBINE
Caliber: 22 LR/22 WMR, 38 Spec., 357 Mag., 44-40, 45 Colt, 6-shot.
Barrel: 18".
Weight: 4.4 lbs. **Length:** 34" overall.
Stock: Walnut.
Sights: Blade front, groove rear, or adjustable target.
Features: Carbine version of the single-action revolver. Brass buttplate, color case-hardened frame, blued cylinder and barrel. Imported by Uberti USA.
Price: Fixed Sight **$448.00**
Price: Target sight **$483.00**
Price: 22 convertible (two cyls.) fixed sight. **$483.00**
Price: As above, target sights **$516.00**

UBERTI 1875 ARMY TARGET REVOLVING CARBINE
Caliber: 357 Mag., 44-40, 45 Colt, 6-shot.
Barrel: 18".
Weight: 4.9 lbs. **Length:** 37" overall.
Stock: Walnut.
Sights: Ramp front, rear adjustable for elevation.
Features: Polished brass trigger guard and buttplate, color case-hardened frame. Carbine version of the 1875 revolver. Imported by Uberti USA.
Price: Blue barrel, cylinder **$513.00**
Price: Nickeled barrel, cylinder. **$627.00**

WINCHESTER MODEL 94 BIG BORE SIDE EJECT
Caliber: 307 Win., 356 Win., 6-shot magazine.
Barrel: 20".
Weight: 7 lbs. **Length:** 38⁵/₈" overall.
Stock: Monte Carlo-style American walnut. Satin finish.
Sights: Hooded ramp front, semi-buckhorn rear adjustable for w. & e.
Features: All external metal parts have Winchester's deep blue high polish finish. Rifling twist 1-in-12". Rubber recoil pad fitted to buttstock. Introduced 1983. Made under license by U.S. Repeating Arms Co.
Price: About. **$299.00**

Uberti 1873 Buckhorn 44-Cal. Revolving Carbine
Similar to 1873 Cattleman Carbine except slightly larger proportions. Available in 44 Mag. or 44 Mag./44-40 convertible.
Price: Fixed sights **$460.00**
Price: Target sights **$495.00**
Price: Convertible (two cylinders), fixed sights. **$490.00**
Price: Convertible, target sights **$534.00**

Winchester Model 94

Winchester Model 94 Side Eject, 7x30 Waters

Same as Model 94 Side Eject except has 24″ barrel, chambered for 7x30 Waters, 7-shot magazine, overall length of 37³/₄″ and weight is 7 lbs. Barrel twist is 1-in-12″. Rubber buttpad instead of plastic. Introduced 1984.
Price: About **$283.00**

Winchester Ranger Side Eject Carbine

Same as Model 94 Side Eject except has 5-shot magazine, American hardwood stock and forend, no front sight hood. Introduced 1985.
Price: About **$251.00**
Price: With 4x32 Bushnell scope, mounts, about **$287.00**

WINCHESTER MODEL 94 SIDE EJECT RIFLE

Caliber: 30-30 (12″ twist), 6-shot tubular magazine.
Barrel: 16″, 20″.
Weight: 6¹/₂ lbs. **Length:** 37³/₄″ overall.
Stock: Straight grip walnut stock and forend.
Sights: Hooded blade front, semi-buckhorn rear. Drilled and tapped for scope mount.
Features: Solid frame, forged steel receiver; side ejection, exposed rebounding hammer with automatic trigger-activated safety transfer bar. Introduced 1984.
Price: 30-30, about **$299.00**
Price: With 1.5-4.5 x Bushnell scope, mounts **$342.00**
Price: Trapper model (16″ bbl.), about **$283.00**
Price: As above, 45 Colt, 44 Mag./44 Spec., about **$299.00**
Price: With Win-Tuff laminated hardwood stock **$299.00**

CENTERFIRE RIFLES—BOLT ACTIONS

Includes models for a wide variety of sporting and competitive purposes and uses.

Alpine Rifle

ALPINE BOLT-ACTION RIFLE

Caliber: 22-250, 243 Win., 270, 30-06, 308, 7mm Rem. Mag., 8mm, 5-shot magazine (3 for magnum).
Barrel: 23″ (std. cals.), 24″ (mag.).
Weight: 7¹/₂ lbs.
Stock: European walnut. Full p.g. and Monte Carlo; checkered p.g. and forend; rubber recoil pad; white line spacers; sling swivels.
Sights: Ramp front, open rear adjustable for w. and e.
Features: Made by Firearms Co. Ltd. in England. Imported by Mandall Shooting Supplies.
Price: Standard Grade **375.00**
Price: Supreme Grade **$395.00**
Price: Custom Grade **$425.00**

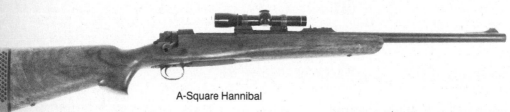

A-Square Hannibal

A-SQUARE CAESAR BOLT-ACTION RIFLE

Caliber: Group I — 270, 30-06, 9.3x62; Group II — 7mm Rem. Mag., 300 Win. Mag., 338 Win. Mag., 416 Taylor, 458 Win. Mag.; Group III — 300 H&H, 300 Wea., 8mm Rem. Mag., 340 Wea., 9.3x64, 375 H&H, 375 Wea., 416 Hoffman, 450 Ackley.
Barrel: 20″ to 26″ (no-cost customer option).
Weight: 8¹/₂ to 11 lbs.
Stock: Claro walnut with hand-rubbed oil finish; classic style with A-Square Coil-Chek® features for reduced recoil; flush detachable swivels. Customer choice of length of pull.
Sights: Choice of three-leaf express, forward or normal-mount scope, or combination (at extra cost).
Features: Matte non-reflective blue, double cross-bolts, steel and fiberglass reinforcement of wood from tang to forend tip; Mauser-style claw extractor; expanded magazine capacity. Right or left hand. Introduced 1984. Made in U.S. by A-Square Co., Inc.
Price: Group I calibers **$1,575.00**
Price: Group II calibers **$1,650.00**
Price: Group III calibers **$1,650.00**

A-SQUARE HANNIBAL BOLT-ACTION RIFLE

Caliber: Group I — 270, 30-06, 9.3x62; Group II — 7mm Rem. Mag., 300 Win. Mag., 338 Win. Mag., 416 Taylor, 458 Win. Mag.; Group III — 300 H&H, 300 Wea., 8mm Rem. Mag., 340 Wea., 9.3x64, 375 H&H, 375 Wea., 416 Hoffman, 450 Ackley; Group IV — 338 A-Square, 378 Wea., 416 Rigby, 404 Jeffery, 460 Short A-Square, 460 Wea., 500 A-Square.
Barrel: 20″ to 26″ (no-cost customer option).
Weight: 8¹/₂ to 11 lbs.
Stock: Claro walnut with hand-rubbed oil finish; classic style with A-Square Coil-Chek® features for reduced recoil; flush detachable swivels. Customer choice of length of pull.
Sights: Choice of three-leaf express, forward or normal-mount scope, or combination (at extra cost).
Features: Matte non-reflective blue, double cross-bolts, steel and fiberglass reinforcement of wood from tang to forend tip; Mauser-style claw extractor; expanded magazine capacity. Right-hand only. Introduced 1983. Made in U.S. by A-Square Co., Inc.
Price: Group I calibers **$1,480.00**
Price: Group II calibers **$1,550.00**
Price: Group III calibers **$1,580.00**
Price: Group IV calibers **$1,600.00**

CAUTION: PRICES CHANGE. CHECK AT GUNSHOP.

Anschutz Classic 1700

Anschutz Custom 1700 Rifles
Similar to the Classic models except have roll-over Monte Carlo cheekpiece, slim forend with Schnabel tip, Wundhammer palm swell on pistol grip, rosewood grip cap with white diamond insert. Skip-line checkering on grip and forend. Introduced 1988. Imported from Germany by PSI.
Price: $1,130.00

ARMSPORT 2801 BOLT-ACTION RIFLE
Caliber: 243, 308, 30-06, 7mm Rem. Mag., 300 Win. Mag.
Barrel: 24″.
Weight: 8 lbs.
Stock: European walnut with Monte Carlo comb.
Sights: Ramp front, open adjustable rear.
Features: Blue metal finish, glossy wood. Introduced 1986. Imported from Italy by Armsport.
Price: $575.00

ANSCHUTZ CLASSIC 1700 RIFLES
Caliber: 22 Hornet, 5-shot clip; 222 Rem., 2-shot clip.
Barrel: 23¹/₂″, ¹³/₁₆″ dia. heavy.
Weight: 7³/₄ lbs. Length: 42¹/₂″ overall.
Stock: Select European walnut with checkered pistol grip and forend.
Sights: None furnished, drilled and tapped for scope mounting.
Features: Adjustable single stage trigger. Receiver drilled and tapped for scope mounting. Introduced 1988. Imported from Germany by PSI.
Price: $1,100.00

ANSCHUTZ BAVARIAN BOLT-ACTION RIFLE
Caliber: 22 Hornet, 222 Rem., detachable clip.
Barrel: 24″.
Weight: 7¹/₄ lbs. Length: 43″ overall.
Stock: European walnut with Bavarian cheek rest. Checkered p.g. and forend.
Sights: Hooded ramp front, folding leaf rear.
Features: Uses the improved 1700 Match 54 action with adjustable trigger. Drilled and tapped for scope mounting. Introduced 1988. Imported from Germany by Precision Sales International.
Price: $1,130.00

Beeman/HW 60J

BEEMAN/HW 60J BOLT-ACTION RIFLE
Caliber: 222 Rem.
Barrel: 22.8″.
Weight: 6.5 lbs. Length: 41.7″ overall.
Stock: Walnut with cheekpiece; cut checkered p.g. and forend.
Sights: Hooded blade on ramp front, open rear.
Features: Polished blue finish; oil-finished wood. Imported from West Germany by Beeman. Introduced 1988.
Price: $688.00

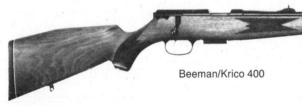

Beeman/Krico 400

BEEMAN/KRICO MODEL 600/700 BIG GAME RIFLE
Caliber: 243 (M600), 30-06 M700).
Barrel: 23¹/₂″.
Weight: 7 lbs. Length: 43¹/₂″ overall.
Stock: European classic-style walnut. Wundhammer palm swell. Rosewood schnabel tip; checkered grip and forend; rubber buttpad.
Sights: Hooded ramp front, open rear adjustable for windage.
Features: Silent safety, hammer swaged barrel. Detachable three-shot magazine. Imported from West Germany by Beeman.
Price: Model 600 . . . . $1,098.00
Price: Model 700 . . . . $999.00

BEEMAN/KRICO MODEL 400 BOLT-ACTION RIFLE
Caliber: 22 Hornet, 5-shot magazine.
Barrel: 23.5″.
Weight: 6.8 lbs. Length: 43″ overall.
Stock: Select European walnut, curved European comb with cheekpiece; solid rubber buttpad; cut checkered grip and forend.
Sights: Blade front on ramp, open rear adjustable for windage.
Features: Detachable box magazine; action has rear locking lugs, twin extractors. Available with single or optional match and double set trigger. Receiver grooved for scope mounts. Made in West Germany. Imported by Beeman.
Price: $695.00

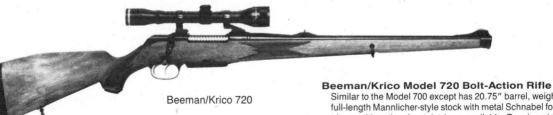

Beeman/Krico 720

Beeman/Krico Model 720 Bolt-Action Rifle
Similar to the Model 700 except has 20.75″ barrel, weighs 6.8 lbs., and has full-length Mannlicher-style stock with metal Schnabel forend tip; double set trigger with optional match trigger available. Receiver drilled and tapped for scope mounting. Imported from West Germany by Beeman.
Price: Model 720 (270 Win.) $899.00
Price: Model 720 (30-06) $799.00

Blaser R84

BLASER R84 BOLT-ACTION RIFLE
Caliber: 22-250, 243, 6mm Rem., 25-06, 270, 280, 30-06, 257 Wea., 264 Win. Mag., 7mm Rem. Mag., 300 Win. Mag., 300 Wea., 338 Win. Mag., 375 H&H.
Barrel: 23″ (24″ in magnum cals.).

Weight: 7-7¼ lbs. **Length:** 41″ overall (23″ barrel).
Stock: Two-piece Turkish walnut. Solid black buttpad.
Sights: None furnished. Comes with low-profile Blaser scope mounts.
Features: Interchangeable barrels (scope mounts on barrel), and magnum/standard caliber bolt assemblies. Left-hand models available in all calibers. Imported from West Germany by Autumn Sales, Inc.
Price: Right-hand, standard or magnum calibers **$1,595.00**
Price: Left-hand, standard or magnum calibers **$1,645.00**
Price: Interchangeable barrels, standard or magnum calibers **$545.00**

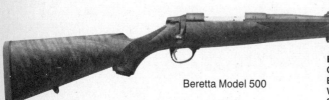

Beretta Model 500

BRNO ZKK 600, 601, 602 BOLT-ACTION RIFLES
Caliber: 30-06, 270, 7x57, 7x64 (M600); 223, 243, 308 (M601); 8x68S, 375 H&H, 458 Win. Mag. (M602), 5-shot magazine.
Barrel: 23½″ (M600, 601), 25″ (M602).
Weight: 6 lbs., 3 oz. to 9 lbs., 4 oz. **Length:** 43″ overall (M601).
Stock: Walnut.
Sights: Hooded ramp front, open folding leaf adjustable rear.
Features: Adjustable set trigger (standard trigger included); easy-release floorplate; sling swivels. Imported from Czechoslovakia by TD Arms.
Price: ZKK 600 Standard **$599.00**
Price: As above, Monte Carlo stock **$649.00**
Price: ZKK 601 Standard **$549.00**
Price: As above, Monte Carlo stock **$599.00**
Price: ZKK 602, Monte Carlo stock **$749.00**
Price: As above, standard stock **$689.00**

BERETTA 500 SERIES CUSTOM BOLT-ACTION RIFLES
Caliber: 222, 243, 308 (M501); 30-06.
Barrel: 23″ to 24″.
Weight: 6.8 to 8.4 lbs. **Length:** NA.
Stock: Close-grained walnut, with oil finish, hand checkering.
Sights: None furnished; drilled and tapped for scope mounting.
Features: Model 500 — short action; 501 — medium action. All models have rubber buttpad. Imported from Italy by Beretta U.S.A. Corp. Introduced 1984.
Price: Model 500 and 501 .... **$725.00**

BRNO ZKB 680 FOX BOLT-ACTION RIFLE
Caliber: 22 Hornet, 222 Rem., 5-shot magazine.
Barrel: 23½″.
Weight: 5 lbs., 12 oz. **Length:** 42½″ overall.
Stock: Turkish walnut, with Monte Carlo.
Sights: Hooded front, open adjustable rear.
Features: Detachable box magazine; adjustable double set triggers. Imported from Czechoslovakia by TD Arms.
Price: **$499.00**

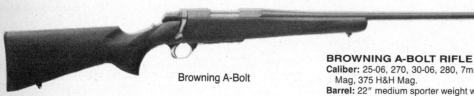

Browning A-Bolt

Browning A-Bolt ''Stainless Stalker''
Similar to the Hunter model A-Bolt except receiver is made of stainless steel; the rest of the exposed metal surfaces are finished with a durable matte silver-gray. Graphite-Fiberglass composite textured stock. No sights are furnished. Available in 270, 30-06, 7mm Rem. Mag. Introduced 1987.
Price: **$579.95**
Price: Composite Stalker (as above with checkered stock) **$454.95**

Browning A-Bolt Left Hand
Same as the Medallion model A-Bolt except has left-hand action and is available only in 270, 30-06, 7mm Rem. Mag. Introduced 1987.
Price: **$550.95**

BROWNING A-BOLT RIFLE
Caliber: 25-06, 270, 30-06, 280, 7mm Rem. Mag., 300 Win. Mag., 338 Win. Mag, 375 H&H Mag.
Barrel: 22″ medium sporter weight with recessed muzzle; 26″ on mag. cals.
Weight: 6½ to 7½ lbs. **Length:** 44¾″ overall (Magnum and standard), 41¾″ (short action).
Stock: Classic style American walnut; recoil pad standard on magnum calibers.
Features: Short-throw (60°) fluted bolt, 3 locking lugs, plunger-type ejector; adjustable trigger is grooved and gold-plated. Hinged floorplate, detachable box magazine (4 rounds std. cals., 3 for magnums). Slide tang safety. Medallion has glossy stock finish, rosewood grip and forend caps, high polish blue. Introduced 1985. Imported from Japan by Browning.
Price: Medallion, no sights **$527.95**
Price: Hunter, no sights **$454.95**
Price: Hunter, with sights **$512.95**
Price: Medallion, 375 H&H Mag., with sights **$617.95**

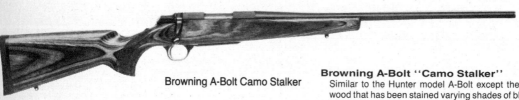

Browning A-Bolt Camo Stalker

Browning A-Bolt ''Camo Stalker''
Similar to the Hunter model A-Bolt except the stock is of multi-laminated wood that has been stained varying shades of black and green; cut checkering; metal parts have a matte, non-glare finish. No sights are furnished. Available in 270, 30-06, 7mm Rem. Mag. Introduced 1987.
Price: **$482.95**

CAUTION: PRICES CHANGE. CHECK AT GUNSHOP.

Browning Micro Medallion

Browning A-Bolt Pronghorn Antelope Issue

Same specifications as standard A-Bolt except available only in 243 Win. and has detailed engraving on the receiver flats, floorplate, trigger guard and at the rear of the barrel. Each side of the receiver has a different pronghorn study in 24 karat gold plating. Stock is a high grade of walnut with skip-line checkering and a pearl border and high gloss finish. Brass spacers separate the rosewood caps and recoil pad. Limited edition of 500 rifles. Introduced 1987.

Price: **$1,302.00**

Browning Short Action A-Bolt

Similar to the standard A-Bolt except has short action for 22-250, 243, 257 Roberts, 7mm-08, 308 chamberings. Available in Hunter or Medallion grades. Weighs 6½ lbs. Other specs essentially the same. Introduced 1985.

Price: Medallion, no sights **$527.95**
Price: Hunter, no sights **$454.95**
Price: Hunter, with sights **$512.95**

Browning A-Bolt Micro Medallion

Similar to the standard A-Bolt except is a scaled-down version. Comes with 20″ barrel, shortened length of pull (13⁵⁄₁₆″); three-shot magazine capacity; weighs 6 lbs., l oz. Available in 243, 308, 7mm-08, 257 Roberts, 223, 22-250. Introduced 1988.

Price: No sights **$527.95**

Consult our Directory pages for the location of firms mentioned.

Browning A-Bolt Gold Medallion

Similar to the standard A-Bolt except has select walnut stock with brass spacers between rubber recoil pad and between the rosewood grip cap and forend tip; gold-filled barrel inscription; palm-swell pistol grip, Monte Carlo comb. 22 lpi checkering with double borders; engraved receiver flats. In 270, 30-06, 7mm Rem. Mag only. Introduced 1988.

Price: **$689.95**

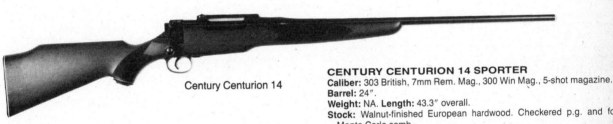

Century Centurion 14

CENTURY CENTURION 14 SPORTER

Caliber: 303 British, 7mm Rem. Mag., 300 Win Mag., 5-shot magazine.
Barrel: 24″.
Weight: NA. **Length:** 43.3″ overall.
Stock: Walnut-finished European hardwood. Checkered p.g. and forend. Monte Carlo comb.
Sights: None furnished.
Features: Uses modified Pattern 14 Enfield action. Drilled and tapped for scope mounting. Blue finish. From Century International Arms.
Price: 303, about **$225.95**
Price: Magnum calibers, about **$251.95**

Century Enfield

CENTURY ENFIELD SPORTER #4

Caliber: 303 British, 10-shot magazine.
Barrel: 25.2″.
Weight: NA. **Length:** 44.5″ overall.
Stock: Beechwood with checkered p.g. and forend, Monte Carlo comb.
Sights: Blade front, adjustable aperture rear.
Features: Uses Lee-Enfield action; blue finish. Introduced 1987. From Century International Arms.
Price: **$185.95**
Price: Jungle Sporter (20½″ bbl.) **$212.95**

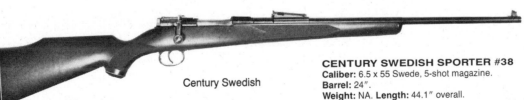

Century Swedish

CENTURY SWEDISH SPORTER #38

Caliber: 6.5 x 55 Swede, 5-shot magazine.
Barrel: 24″.
Weight: NA. **Length:** 44.1″ overall.
Stock: Walnut-finished European hardwood with checkered p.g. and forend; Monte Carlo comb.
Sights: Blade front, adjustable rear.
Features: Uses M38 Swedish Mauser action; comes with Holden Ironsighter see-through scope mount. Introduced 1987. From Century International Arms.
Price: About **$212.95**

Churchill Regent

Churchill Highlander Bolt-Action Rifle

Similar to the Regent except has a classic-style stock of standard-grade European walnut. Highlander Combo includes rifle without iron sights, q.d. swivels, cobra-style sling, rings, bases, and 3-9x32 scope.
Price: Highlander with sights **$379.00**
Price: Highlander Combo **$409.00**
Price: Highlander without sights **$349.00**

CHURCHILL BOLT-ACTION RIFLE

Caliber: 243, 25-06, 270, 308, 30-06 (4-shot magazine), 7mm Rem. Mag., 300 Win. Mag. (3-shot).
Barrel: 22″ (7mm Rem. Mag. has 24″).
Weight: 7½ lbs. **Length:** 42½″ overall with 22″ barrel.
Stock: European walnut, checkered p.g. and forend. Regent grade has Monte Carlo, Highlander has classic design.
Sights: Gold bead on ramp front, fully adjustable rear.
Features: Positive safety locks trigger; oil-finished wood; swivel posts; recoil pad. Imported by Ellett Bros. Introduced 1986.
Price: Highlander, without sights, either cal. **$350.00**
Price: As above, with sights **$380.00**
Price: Regent, without sights **$549.00**
Price: As above, with sights **$579.00**

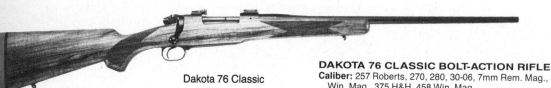

Dakota 76 Classic

Dakota 76 Short Action Rifles

A scaled-down version of the standard Model 76. Standard chamberings are 22-250, 243, 6mm Rem., 250-3000, 7mm-08, 308 and 358; others on special order. Short Classic Grade has 21″ barrel; Alpine Grade is lighter (6½ lbs.), has a blind magaizne and slimmer stock. Introduced 1989.
Price: Short Classic **$1,950.00**
Price: Alpine **$1,850.00**

DAKOTA 76 CLASSIC BOLT-ACTION RIFLE

Caliber: 257 Roberts, 270, 280, 30-06, 7mm Rem. Mag., 338 Win. Mag., 300 Win. Mag., 375 H&H, 458 Win. Mag.
Barrel: 23″.
Weight: 7½ lbs. **Length:** NA.
Stock: Medium fancy grade walnut in classic style. Checkered p.g. and forend; solid buttpad. Composite stock also available.
Sights: None furnished; drilled and tapped for scope mounts.
Features: Has many features of the original Model 70 Winchester. One-piece rail trigger guard assembly; steel grip cap. Adjustable trigger. Many options available. Left-hand rifle available at same price. Introduced 1988. From Dakota Arms, Inc.
Price: Wood or composite stock **$1,950.00**

Dakota 76 Safari

Dakota 416 Rigby African

Similar to the 76 Safari except chambered for 416 Rigby, four-round magazine, select wood, two stock cross-bolts. Has 24″ barrel, weight of 9.4 lbs. Ramp front sight, standing leaf rear. Introduced 1989.
Price: **$3,500.00**

DAKOTA 76 SAFARI BOLT-ACTION RIFLE

Caliber: 338 Win. Mag., 300 Win. Mag., 375 H&H, 458 Win. Mag.
Barrel: 23″.
Weight: 8½ lbs. **Length:** NA.
Stock: Fancy walnut with ebony forend tip; point-pattern with wrap-around forend checkering. Composite stock also available.
Sights: Ramp front, standing leaf rear.
Features: Has many features of the original Model 70 Winchester. Barrel band front swivel, inletted rear. Cheekpiece with shadow line. Steel grip cap. Introduced 1988. From Dakota Arms, Inc.
Price: Wood stock **$2,850.00**
Price: Composite stock **$2,450.00**

Du Biel Modern Classic

AUGUSTE FRANCOTTE BOLT-ACTION RIFLES

Caliber: 243, 270, 7×64, 30-06, 308, 300 Win. Mag., 338, 7mm Rem. Mag., 375 H&H, 416 Rigby, 458 Win. Mag.
Barrel: 23½″ standard; other lengths on request.
Weight: 7.61 lbs. (medium cals.), 11.1 lbs. (magnum cals.).
Stock: Fancy European walnut. To customer specs.
Sights: To customer specs.
Features: Basically a custom gun, Francotte offers many options. Imported from Belgium by Armes de Chasse.
Price: . . . . **NA**

Du BIEL ARMS BOLT-ACTION RIFLES

Caliber: Standard calibers 22-250 thru 458 Win. Mag. Selected wildcat calibers available.
Barrel: Selected weights and lengths. Douglas Premium.
Weight: About 7½ lbs.
Stock: Five styles. Walnut, maple, laminates. Hand checkered.
Sights: None furnished. Receiver has integral milled bases.
Features: Basically a custom-made rifle. Left or right-hand models available. Five-lug locking mechanism; 36-degree bolt rotation; adjustable Canjar trigger; oil or epoxy stock finish; Presentation recoil pad; jeweled and chromed bolt body; sling swivel studs; lever latch or button floorplate release. All steel action and parts. Introduced 1978. From Du Biel Arms.
Price: Rollover Model, left- or right-hand. **$2,500.00**
Price: Thumbhole, left- or right-hand. **$2,500.00**
Price: Classic, left- or right-hand **$2,500.00**
Price: Modern Classic, left- or right-hand **$2,500.00**
Price: Thumbhole Mannlicher, left- or right-hand **$2,500.00**

Grendel SRT

GRENDEL SRT COMPACT RIFLE
Caliber: 308 Win., 9-shot magazine.
Barrel: 20″ (Models 20F [fluted], 20L [not fluted]), 24″ (Model 24, not fluted).
Weight: 6.7 lbs. (Model 20F). **Length:** 40.8″ overall (Model 20F). open; folds to 30″ length.
Stock: Folding Du Pont Zytel reinforced with glass fiber.
Sights: None furnished. Integral scope bases.
Features: Uses Sako A-2 action. Muzzlebrake. Forend has a rod for sling swivel and will accept M-16 clip-on bipod. Uses Sako scope mount. Introduced 1987. From Grendel, Inc.
Price: SRT-20F (fluted barrel) $525.00

Heym SR 20 Fiberglass

HEYM SR 20 TROPHY SERIES RIFLE
Caliber: 243, 7x57, 270, 308, 30-06, 7mm Rem. Mag., 338 Win. Mag., 375 H&H.
Barrel: 22″ (standard cals.), 24″ (magnum cals.).
Weight: About 7 lbs.
Stock: AAA-grade European walnut with cheekpiece, solid rubber buttpad, checkered grip and forend, oil finish, rosewood grip cap.
Sights: Silver bead ramp front, open rear on quater-rib. Drilled and tapped for scope mounting.
Features: Octagonal barrel, single set trigger, barrel-mounted q.d. swivel, standard q.d. rear swivel. Imported from West Germany by Heym America, Inc.
Price: $2,300.00
Price: For left-hand rifle, add.............................. $400.00
Price: For fiberglass stock, add............................ $450.00

Heym SR 20 Classic Safari Rifle
Similar to the Trophy Series except in 404 Jeffery, 425 Express, 458 Win. Mag. 24″ barrel; has large post front sight, express rear; barrel-mounted ring-type front q.d. swivel, q.d. rear; double-lug recoil bolt in stock. Introduced 1989. Imported from West Germany by Heym America, Inc.
Price: $2,200.00
Price: For left-hand rifle, add.............................. $500.00

Heym SR 20 Alpine

HEYM SR 20 Alpine Series Rifle
Similar to the Trophy Series except available in 243, 270, 7x57, 308, 30-06, 6.5x55, 7x64, 8x57JS with 20″ barrel, open sights; full-length "Mountain rifle" stock with schnabel forend cap, steel grip cap. Introduced 1989. Imported from West Germany by Heym America, Inc.
Price: $1,750.00

Heym SR 20 Classic Sportsman Series Rifle
Similar to the Trophy Series except has round barrel without sights. Imported from West Germany by Heym America, Inc. Introduced 1989.
Price: $1,700.00

Heym Express

HEYM MAGNUM EXPRESS SERIES RIFLE
Caliber: 404 Jeffery, 416 Rigby, 500 Nitro Express 3″, 460 Wea. Mag., 500 A-Square, 450 Ackley.
Barrel: 24″.
Weight: About 9.9 lbs. **Length:** 45¼″ overall.
Stock: Classic English design of AAA-grade European walnut with cheekpiece, solid rubber buttpad, steel grip cap.
Sights: Post front on ramp, three-leaf express rear.
Features: Modified magnum Mauser action, Timney single trigger; special hinged floorplate; barrel-mounted q.d. swivel, q.d. rear; double recoil lug in stock. Introduced 1989. Imported from West Germany by Heym America, Inc.
Price: $3,500.00
Price: For left-hand rifle, add.............................. $500.00

HOWA M1500 TROPHY BOLT-ACTION RIFLE
Caliber: 223, 22-250, 243, 270, 30-06, 308, 7mm Rem. Mag., 300 Win. Mag., 338 Win. Mag.
Barrel: 22″ (24″ in magnum calibers).
Weight: 7½-7¾ lbs. **Length:** 42″ over-all (42½″ for 270, 30-06, 7mm).
Stock: American walnut with Monte Carlo comb and cheekpiece; 18 lpi checkering on p.g. and forend.
Sights: Hooded ramp gold bead front, open round-notch rear adjustable for w. and e. Drilled and tapped for scope mounts.
Features: Trigger guard and magazine box are a single unit with a hinged floorplate. Comes with q.d. swivel studs. Composition non-slip buttplate with white spacer. Magnum models have rubber recoil pad. Introduced 1979. Imported from Japan by Interarms.
Price: $495.00
Price: 7mm Rem. Mag., 300 Win. Mag. $510.00

Howa Heavy Barrel Varmint Rifle
Similar to the Trophy model except has heavy 24″ barrel, available in 223 and 22-250 only, Parkerized finish. No sights furnished; drilled and tapped for scope mounts. Introduced 1989. Imported from Japan by Interarms.
Price: $535.00

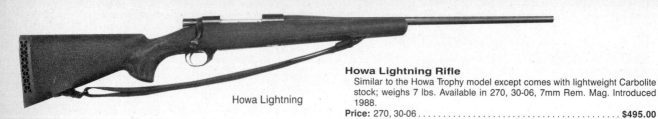

Howa Lightning

Howa Model 1500
Similar to the standard 1500 except has a 22″ heavy barrel and fully adjustable trigger. Chambered for 22-250 and 223. Weighs 9 lbs. 5 oz. Skipline checkering, q.d. swivels. Introduced 1982.
Price: Parkerized, oil-finished stock **$535.00**

Howa Lightning Rifle
Similar to the Howa Trophy model except comes with lightweight Carbolite stock; weighs 7 lbs. Available in 270, 30-06, 7mm Rem. Mag. Introduced 1988.
Price: 270, 30-06 . . . . **$495.00**
Price: 7mm Rem. Mag. **$510.00**

Jaeger Hunter

Jaeger "Alaskan" Rifle
Similar to the "Hunter" except chambered for 7mm Rem. Mag., 300 Win. Mag. and 338 Win. Mag. Has Jaeger ramp front sight with silver bead, Williams open rear. Weight is 8 lbs. Bead-blasted blue/black finish. Douglas Premium barrel. Custom options available. Introduced 1989.
Price: From **$749.00**

Jaeger "African" Rifle
Similar to the "Hunter" except has Deluxe stock with graphite reinforcing, swivel studs. Weight is 9 lbs., magazine holds three rounds. Chambered for 375 H&H, 416 Taylor, 458 Win. Mag. Has Jaeger custom banded front ramp with flip-up night-sight and hood; rear sight is Jaeger single leaf with deep V-notch regulated at 50 yards. Bead-blasted blue/black finish. Introduced 1989.
Price: From **$995.00**

JAEGER "HUNTER" RIFLE
Caliber: 243, 257 Roberts, 25-06, 7x57, 7mm-08, 308, 280 Rem., 30-06, 4-shot magazine.
Barrel: 22″ or 24″; Douglas Premium.
Weight: About 7 lbs.
Stock: Bell & Carlson Kevlar/fiberglass with intergral sling, 1″ rubber recoil pad, black wrinkle finish. Checkered grip and forend.
Sights: None furnished. Drilled and tapped for scope mounting.
Features: Uses Mauser-type action with claw extractor, hinged floorplate, single stage adjustable trigger. Custom options available. Introduced 1989. From Paul Jaeger, Inc.
Price: From **$595.00**
Price: With laminated stock from **$870.00**

Kimber Big Game

KIMBER BIG GAME RIFLE
Caliber: 270, 280, 7mm Rem. Mag., 30-06, 300 Win. Mag., 338 Win. Mag., 375 H&H.
Barrel: 22″ (24″ for magnum).

Weight: 7¹/₂-8¹/₂ lbs. **Length:** 42″ overall (22″ bbl.).
Stock: Deluxe has AA Claro walnut, Super Grade has AAA fancy Claro or straight grain English walnut.
Sights: None furnished.
Features: Two styles available—Deluxe and Super Grade. Mauser-style extractor; Model 70-type override trigger design, ejector, three-position safety; Mauser-style bolt stop; Featherweight M70 barrel profile (except 7mm, 338, 375). Introduced 1988.
Price: Deluxe (all cals. except 375 H&H). **$1,395.00**
Price: As above, 375 H&H **$1,495.00**
Price: Super Grade, square bridge receiver, all except 375 H&H . **$1,495.00**
Price: As above, 375 H&H **$1,595.00**

Kimber Ultra Varmint

KIMBER MODEL 84 SPORTER
Caliber: 17 Rem., 221 Rem., 223 Rem., 5-shot magazine.
Barrel: 22″ (Sporter), 24″ (Varmint), 24″ stainless (Ultra Varmint).
Weight: About 6¹/₄ lbs. **Length:** 40¹/₂″ overall (Sporter).
Stock: Two styles available—Deluxe has AA Claro walnut ebony forend tip, no cheekpiece; Super Grade has AAA Claro walnut, ebony forend tip, beaded cheekpiece. Both hand checkered 20 lpi, Niedner-style buttplate, steel grip cap, fully inletted swivel studs. Ultra Varmint stock is of laminated birch, no

cheekpiece, hand checkered, curved rubber buttpad, conventional swivel studs. Super Varmint stock is AAA Claro walnut with ebony forend tip, has beaded cheekpiece, wrap-around checkering, curved buttpad, inletted swivel studs.
Sights: Hooded ramp front with bead, folding leaf rear (optional).
Features: All new Mauser-type head locking bolt action; steel trigger guard and hinged floorplate; Mauser-type extractor; fully adjustable trigger; chrome-moly barrel. Rotating disc-safety. Round-top receiver with bases for scope mounting. Varmint gun prices same as others. Introduced 1984. Contact Kimber for full details.
Price: Deluxe Grade. **$1,150.00**
Price: Super Grade **$1,250.00**
Price: Ultra Varmint (laminated stock, stainless bbl.) **$1,165.00**
Price: Super Varmint (24″ medium heavy bbl.). **$1,265.00**
Price: Continental (Mannlicher stock) . . . . **P.O.R.**

CAUTION: PRICES CHANGE. CHECK AT GUNSHOP.

Kimber 89 African

Kimber Model 82, 84 Super Grade

Super-grade version of the Models 82 and 84. Has a Classic stock only of specially selected, high-grade, California Claro walnut, with Continental beaded cheekpiece and ebony forend tip; borderless, full coverage 20 lpi checkering; Niedner-type checkered steel buttplate. Options include barrel quarter-rib with express rear sight. Available in 22 Long Rifle, 17 Rem., 221 Rem., 223 Rem.

Price: Model 82, 22 Long Rifle **$1,095.00**
Price: Model 84, 17 Rem., 221 Rem., 223 Rem................ **$1,250.00**

KIMBER MODEL 89 AFRICAN

Caliber: 375 H&H (5-shot); 404 Jeffery, 416 Rigby (4-shot); 460 Wea. Mag., 505 Gibbs (3-shot).
Barrel: 24″, six-groove.
Weight: 10-10½ lbs. **Length:** 47″ overall.
Stock: AA grade English walnut with ebony forend tip. Beaded English-style cheekpiece, borderless wrap-around hand checkering.
Sights: Blade front on ramp, express rear on contoured quarter-rib.
Features: Controlled feed head locking Kimber magnum action with Mauser-style extractor and bolt-stop. Winchester pre-'64-type three-position safety and ejection system. Twin recoil cross pins in stock. Barrel mounted recoil lug in addition to integral receiver lug. Drop box magazine, trapdoor grip cap. Rubber buttpad, barrel-mounted front swivel stud. Announced 1989.
Price: **$3,200.00**

Mark X LTW

Mark X LTW Sporter Bolt-Action Rifle

Similar to the standard Mark X except comes with lightweight Carbolite composition stock, 20″ barrel; weights 7 lbs. Available in 270, 30-06, 7mm Rem. Mag. Introduced 1988.

Price: 270, 30-06 .... **$480.00**
Price: 7mm Rem. Mag. **$495.00**

MARK X AMERICAN FIELD SERIES

Caliber: 22-250, 243, 25-06, 270, 7x57, 7mm Rem. Mag., 308 Win., 30-06, 300 Win. Mag.
Barrel: 24″.
Weight: 7 lbs. **Length:** 45″ overall.
Stock: Genuine walnut stock, hand checkered with 1″ sling swivels.
Sights: Ramp front with removable hood, open rear sight adjustable for windage and elevation.
Features: Mauser-system action. One-piece trigger guard with hinged floorplate, drilled and tapped for scope mounts and receiver sight, hammer-forged chrome vanadium steel barrel. Imported from Yugoslavia by Interarms.
Price: With adj. trigger, sights **$570.00**
Price: 7mm Rem. Mag., 300 Win. Mag. **$585.00**

Mini-Mark X

Mark X Viscount Rifle

Same gun and features as the Mark X American Field except has stock of European hardwood. Imported from Yugoslavia by Interarms. Reintroduced 1987.

Price: **$460.00**
Price: 7mm Rem. Mag., 300 Win. Mag. **$475.00**

MAUSER 225 BOLT-ACTION RIFLE

Caliber: 243, 25-06, 270, 7x57, 308, 30-06, 4-shot magazine (standard); 257 Wea., 270 Wea., 7mm Rem. Mag., 300 Win. Mag., 300 Wea., 308 Norma Mag., 375 H&H, 3-shot magazine (magnum).
Barrel: 24″ (standard), 26″ (magnum).
Weight: About 8 lbs. **Length:** 44½″ overall (24″ bbl.).

Mini-Mark X Rifle

Scaled-down version of the Mark X American Field. Uses miniature M98 Mauser-system action, chambered for 223 Rem.; 20″ barrel with open adjustable sights. Overall length of 39¾″, weight 6.35 lbs. Drilled and tapped for scope mounting. Checkered hardwood stock. Adjustable trigger. Introduced 1987. Imported from Yugoslavia by Interarms.
Price: **$385.00**

Stock: Oil-finished hand-checkered European walnut with Monte Carlo. Recoil pad and swivel studs standard.
Sights: None furnished. Drilled and tapped for scope mounts. Open sights, rings, bases available from KDF.
Features: Three-lug, front-locking action with ultra-fast lock time. Imported from West Germany by KDF, Inc.
Price: Standard Calibers **$1,075.00**
Price: Magnum calibers................................. **$1,125.00**

McMillan Signature Sporter

McMILLAN SIGNATURE CLASSIC SPORTER

Caliber: 22-250, 243, 6mm Rem., 7mm-08, 284, 308 (short action); 25-06, 270, 280 Rem., 30-06, 7mm Rem. Mag., 300 Win. Mag., 300 Wea. (long action); 338 Win. Mag., 340 Wea., 375 H&H (magnum action).
Barrel: 22″, 24″, 26″.

Weight: 7 lbs. (short action).
Stock: McMillan fiberglass in green, beige, brown or black. Recoil pad and 1″ swivels installed. Length of pull up to 14¼″.
Sights: None furnished. Comes with 1″ rings and bases.
Features: Uses McMillan right- or left-hand action with matte black finish. Trigger pull set at 3 lbs. Four-round magazine for standard calibers, three for magnums. Aluminum floorplate. Fibergrain and wood stocks optional. Introduced 1987. From G. McMillan & Co.
Price: **$1,750.00**

McMillian Super Varminter

McMillan Signature Super Varminter

Similar to the Classic Sporter except has heavy contoured barrel, adjustable trigger, field bipod and special hand-bedded fiberglass stock (Fibergrain optional). Chambered for 223, 22-250, 220 Swift, 243, 6mm Rem., 25-06, 7mm-08 and 308. Comes with 1″ rings and bases. Introduced 1989.
Price: $1,850.00

McMillan Signature Titanium Mountain Rifle

Similar to the Classic Sporter except action made of titanium alloy, barrel of chrome-moly steel (titanium match-grade barrel optional). Stock is of graphite reinforced fiberglass. Weight is 5½ lbs. Chambered for 270, 280 Rem., 30-06, 7mm Rem. Mag., 300 Win. Mag. Fibergrain stock optional. Introduced 1989.
Price: $2,450.00
Price: With titanium barrel $2,950.00

McMillan Safari

McMillan Signature Alaskan

Similar to the Classic Sporter except has match-grade barrel with single leaf rear sight, barrel band front, 1″ detachable rings and mounts, steel floorplate, electroless nickel finish. Has wood Monte Carlo stock with cheekpiece, palm-swell grip, solid buttpad. Chambered for 270, 280 Rem., 30-06, 7mm Rem. Mag., 300 Win. Mag., 300 Wea., 358 Win., 340 Wea., 375 H&H. Introduced 1989.
Price: $2,450.00

McMILLAN SIGNATURE SAFARI RIFLE

Caliber: 300 Win. Mag., 300 Wea., 338 Win. Mag., 340 Wea., 375 H&H, 378 Wea., 416 Taylor, 416 Rem., 416 Rigby, 458 Win. Mag.
Barrel: 24″.
Weight: About 9-10 lbs. **Length:** 43″ overall.
Stock: McMillan fiberglass Safari.
Sights: Barrel band front ramp, multi-leaf express rear.
Features: Uses McMillan Safari action. Has q.d. 1″ scope mounts, positive locking steel floorplate, barrel band sling swivel. Match-grade barrel. Matte black finish standard. Introduced 1989. From G. McMillan & Co.
Price: $3,150.00

Parker-Hale 1200 Super

Parker-Hale Model 1200 Super Clip Rifle

Same as the Model 1200 Super except has a detachable steel box magazine and steel trigger guard. Imported from England by Precision Sports, Inc. Introduced 1984.
Price: $759.95
Price: Optional set trigger $89.95

PARKER-HALE MODEL 1200 SUPER BOLT ACTION

Caliber: 22-250, 243, 6mm, 25-06, 270, 6.5x55, 7x57, 7x64, 308, 30-06, 8mm, 7mm Rem. Mag., 300 Win. Mag.
Barrel: 24″.
Weight: About 7½ lbs. **Length:** 44½″ overall.
Stock: European walnut, rosewood grip and forend tips, hand-cut checkering; roll-over cheekpiece; palm-swell pistol grip; ventilated recoil pad; wrap-around checkering.
Sights: Hooded post front, open rear.
Features: Uses Mauser-style action with claw extractor; gold-plated adjustable; silent side safety locks trigger, sear and bolt; aluminum trigger guard. Imported from England by Precision Sports, Inc. Introduced 1984.
Price: $699.95
Price: Optional set trigger $89.95

Parker-Hale 2100

Parker-Hale Model 1100 Lightweight Rifle

Similar to the Model 1200 Super except has slim barrel profile, hollow bolt handle, alloy trigger guard/floorplate. The Monte Carlo stock has a schnabel forend, hand-cut checkering, swivel studs, palm-swell pistol grip. Comes with hooded ramp front sight, open Williams rear adjustable for windage and elevation. Same calibers as Model 81. Overall length is 43″, weight 6½ lbs., with 22″ barrel. Imported from England by Precision Sports, Inc. Introduced 1984.
Price: $599.95
Price: Optional set trigger $89.95

PARKER-HALE MODEL 2100 MIDLAND RIFLE

Caliber: 22-250, 243, 6mm, 270, 6.5x55, 7x57, 7x64, 308, 30-06, 300 Win. Mag., 7mm Rem. Mag.
Barrel: 22″.
Weight: About 7 lbs. **Length:** 43″ overall.
Stock: European walnut, cut-checkered pistol grip and forend; sling swivels.
Sights: Hooded post front, flip-up open rear.
Features: Mauser-type action has twin front locking lugs, rear safety lug, and claw extractor; hinged floorplate; adjustable single stage trigger; silent side safety. Imported from England by Precision Sports, Inc. Introduced 1984.
Price: $399.95
Price: 300 Win. Mag., 7mm Rem. Mag. $429.95

CAUTION: PRICES CHANGE. CHECK AT GUNSHOP.

Parker-Hale 81 Classic

Parker-Hale Model 1100 Lightweight Rifle

Similar to the Model 81 Classic except has slim barrel profile, hollow bolt handle, alloy trigger guard/floorplate. The Monte Carlo stock has a schnabel forend, hand-cut checkering, swivel studs, palm-swell pistol grip. Comes with hooded ramp front sight, open Williams rear adjustable for windage and elevation. Same calibers as Model 81. Overall length is 43″, weight 6¹/₂ lbs., with 22″ barrel. Imported from England by Precision Sports, Inc. Introduced 1984.
Price: **$599.95**
Price: Optional set trigger **$89.95**

PARKER-HALE MODEL 81 CLASSIC RIFLE

Caliber: 22-250, 243, 6mm Rem., 270, 6.5x55, 7x57, 7x64, 308, 30-06, 300 Win. Mag., 7mm Rem. Mag., 4-shot magazine.
Barrel: 24″.
Weight: About 7³/₄ lbs. **Length:** 44¹/₂″ overall.
Stock: European walnut in classic style with oil finish, hand-cut checkering; palm-swell pistol grip, rosewood grip cap.
Sights: Drilled and tapped for open sights and scope mounting. Scope bases included.
Features: Uses Mauser-style action; one-piece steel, Oberndorf-style trigger guard with hinged floorplate; rubber buttpad; quick-detachable sling swivels. Imported from England by Precision Sports, Inc. Introduced 1984.
Price: **$879.95**
Price: Optional set trigger **$89.95**

Parker-Hale Model 81 African

Parker-Hale Model 81 African Rifle

Similar to the Model 81 Classic except chambered only for 375 H&H and 9.3x62. Has adjustable trigger, barrel band front swivel, African express rear sight, engraved receiver. Classic-style stock has a solid buttpad, checkered p.g. and forend. Introduced 1986.
Price: **$1,149.00**

Rahn Elk

Rahn "Elk Series" Rifle

Similar to the "Deer Series" except chambered for 6mmx56, 30-06, 7mm Rem. Mag. and has elk head engraving on floorplate. Introduced 1986.
Price: **$940.00**
Price: With stock made to customer specs. **$990.00**

RAHN "DEER SERIES" BOLT-ACTION RIFLE

Caliber: 25-06, 308, 270.
Barrel: 24″.
Weight: NA. **Length:** NA.
Stock: Circassian walnut with rosewood forend and grip caps, Monte Carlo cheekpiece, semi-Schnabel forend; hand checkered.
Sights: Bead front, open adjustable rear. Drilled and tapped for scope mount.
Features: Free-floating barrel; rubber recoil pad; one-piece trigger guard with hinged, engraved floorplate; 22 rimfire conversion insert available. Introduced 1986. From Rahn Gun Works, Inc.
Price: **$875.00**
Price: With custom stock made to customer specs **$925.00**

Rahn "Himalayan Series" Rifle

Similar to the "Deer Series" except chambered for 5.6x57 or 6.5x68S, short stock of walnut or fiberglass, and floorplate engravings of a yak with scroll border. Introduced 1986.
Price: **$910.00**
Price: With walnut stock made to customer specs. **$960.00**

Rahn "Safari Series" Rifle

Similar to the "Deer Series" except chambered for 308 Norma Mag., 300 Win. Mag., 8x68S, 9x64. Choice of Cape buffalo, rhino or elephant engraving. Gold oval nameplate with three initials. Introduced 1986.
Price: **$950.00**
Price: With stock made to customer specs **$1,000.00**

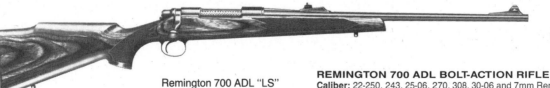

Remington 700 ADL "LS"

Remington 700 BDL Left Hand

Same as 700 BDL except mirror-image left-hand action, stock. Available in 243, 308, 270, 30-06 only.
Price: About. **$516.00**
Price: 7mm Rem. Mag., about **$537.00**

REMINGTON 700 ADL BOLT-ACTION RIFLE

Caliber: 22-250, 243, 25-06, 270, 308, 30-06 and 7mm Rem. Mag.
Barrel: 22″ or 24″ round tapered.
Weight: 7 lbs. **Length:** 41¹/₂″ to 43¹/₂″ overall.
Stock: Walnut. RKW finished p.g. stock with impressed checkering, Monte Carlo.
Sights: Gold bead ramp front; removable, step-adj. rear with windage screw.
Features: Side safety, receiver tapped for scope mounts.
Price: About. **$392.00**
Price: 7mm Rem. Mag., about **$415.00**
Price: Model 700 ADL/LS (laminated stock, 243, 270, 30-06 only) .. **$440.00**
Price: As above, 7mm Rem. Mag. **$459.00**

CAUTION: PRICES CHANGE. CHECK AT GUNSHOP.

Remington 700 BDL

Remington Model 700 "Mountain Rifle"

Similar to the 700 BDL except weighs 6³/₄ lbs., has a 22″ tapered barrel. Redesigned pistol grip, straight comb, contoured cheekpiece, satin stock finish, fine checkering, hinged floorplate and magazine follower, two-position thumb safety. Chambered for 243 270 Win., 7mm-08, 280 Rem., 30-06, 308, 4-shot magazine. Over-all length is 42¹/₂″. Introduced 1986.
Price: About $469.00

Remington 700 BDL Bolt-Action Rifle

Same as 700 ADL, except also available in 222, 223, 6mm, 7mm-08 Rem.; skip-line checkering; black forend tip and p.g. cap, white line spacers. Matted receiver top, quick release floorplate. Hooded ramp front sight. Q.D. swivels and 1″ sling.
Price: About $462.00
Available also in 17 Rem., 7mm Rem. Mag, 300 Win. Mag., 338 Win. Mag., 35 Whelen calibers. 44¹/₂″ overall, weight 7¹/₂ lbs.
Price: About $485.00
Price: Custom Grade I, about $1,263.00
Price: Custom Grade II, about $2,245.00
Price: Custom Grade III, about $3,508.00
Price: Custom Grade IV, about $5,473.00

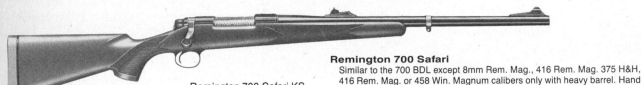

Remington 700 Safari KS

Remington 700 BDL Varmint Special

Same as 700 BDL, except 24″ heavy bbl., 43¹/₂″ overall, wgt. 9 lbs. Cals. 222, 223, 22-250, 243, 6mm Rem., 7mm-08 Rem. and 308. No sights.
Price: About $493.00

Remington Model 700 Custom "KS" Mountain Rifle

Similar to the 700 "Mountain Rifle" except has Kevlar reinforced resin synthetic stock. Available in both left- and right-hand versions. Chambered for 270 Win., 30-06, 7mm Rem. Mag., 300 Win. Mag., 300 Wea. Mag., 35 Whelen, 338 Win. Mag., 8mm Rem. Mag., 375 H&H, all with 24″ barrel only. Weight is 6 lbs., 6 oz. Introduced 1986.
Price: About $867.00

Remington 700 Safari

Similar to the 700 BDL except 8mm Rem. Mag., 416 Rem. Mag. 375 H&H, 416 Rem. Mag. or 458 Win. Magnum calibers only with heavy barrel. Hand checkered, oil-finished stock in classic or Monte Carlo style with recoil pad installed. Delivery time is about 5 months.
Price: About $871.00
Price: Safari Custom KS (Kevlar stock). $1,004.00

Remington Model 700 "AS" Rifle

Similar to the 700 "Mountain Rifle" except stock is of "Arylon" thermoplastic resin. Same style as the "Mountain Rifle," available in black with lightly textured finish (cheekpiece left smooth). Solid buttpad, grip cap with Remington logo. Right-hand action only with hinged floorplate in 22-250, 243, 270, 280 Rem., 308, 30-06, 7mm Rem. Mag., 22″ barrel, weight 6³/₄ lbs. Introduced 1989.
Price: $479.00
Price: 7mm Rem. Mag. $499.00

Remington 700 Classic

REMINGTON 700 "CLASSIC" RIFLE

Caliber: 300 Weatherby Magnum only, 4-shot magazine.
Barrel: 24″.
Weight: About 7³/₄ lbs. Length: 44¹/₂″ overall.
Stock: American walnut, 20 lpi checkering on p.g. and forend. Classic styling. Satin finish.
Sights: None furnished. Receiver drilled and tapped for scope mounting.
Features: A "classic" version of the M700ADL with straight comb stock. Fitted with rubber recoil pad. Sling swivel studs installed. Hinged floorplate. Limited production in 1989 only.
Price: About $485.00

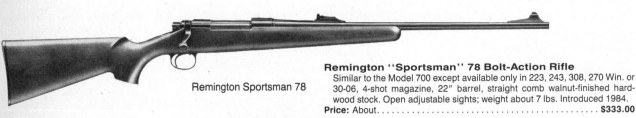

Remington Sportsman 78

Remington "Sportsman" 78 Bolt-Action Rifle

Similar to the Model 700 except available only in 223, 243, 308, 270 Win. or 30-06, 4-shot magazine, 22″ barrel, straight comb walnut-finished hardwood stock. Open adjustable sights; weight about 7 lbs. Introduced 1984.
Price: About $333.00

Remington Model Seven

REMINGTON MODEL SEVEN BOLT-ACTION RIFLE

Caliber: 223 Rem. (5-shot), 243, 7mm-08, 6mm, 308 (4-shot).
Barrel: 18¹/₂″.
Weight: 6¹/₄ lbs. Length: 37¹/₂″ overall.
Stock: Walnut, with modified Schnabel forend. Cut checkering.
Sights: Ramp front, adjustable open rear.
Features: New short-action design; silent side safety; free-floated barrel except for single pressure point at forend tip. Introduced 1983.
Price: About $440.00

CAUTION: PRICES CHANGE. CHECK AT GUNSHOP.

Remington Model Seven "FS" Rifle

Similar to the standard Model Seven except has a fiberglass stock reinforced with Du Pont Kevlar aramid fiber. Classic style in gray or camo, rubber buttpad. Weight is 5¼ lbs. Calibers 243, 7mm-08, 308. Introduced 1907.
Price: **$600.00**

Remington Model Seven Custom "KS"

Similar to the standard Model Seven except has a stock of lightweight Kevlar aramid fiber and chambered for 223 Rem., 7mm BR, 7mm-08, 35 Rem. and 350 Rem. Mag. Barrel length is 20″, weight 5¾ lbs. Same stock features, design as the "FS" rifle. Comes with iron sights and is drilled and tapped for scope mounting. Special order through Remington Custom Shop. Introduced 1987.
Price: **$867.00**

Ruger Magnum Rifle

RUGER M-77 MARK II MAGNUM RIFLE

Caliber: 375 H&H (4-shot magazine), 416 Rigby (3-shot magazine).
Barrel: NA.
Weight: 9.25 lbs. (375), 10.25 lbs. (416). **Length:** NA.
Stock: Circassian walnut.
Sights: Ramp front, three leaf express on serrated rib. Rib also serves as base for front scope ring.
Features: Uses an enlarged Mark II action, safety, trigger mechanism, trigger guard, floorplate. Introduced 1989.
Price: About **$1,500.00**

RUGER M-77 MARK II RIFLE

Caliber: 223, 4-shot magazine.
Barrel: 20″.
Weight: 6 lbs., 7 oz. **Length:** 39¾″ overall.
Stock: American walnut.
Sights: None furnished. Receiver has Ruger integral scope mount base, comes with Ruger 1″ rings.
Features: Short action with new trigger and three-position safety. New trigger guard with redesigned floorplate latch. Introduced 1989.
Price: **$483.00**

Ruger Model 77R

Ruger Model M-77RS Magnum Rifle

Similar to Ruger 77 except magnum-size action. Calibers 270, 7x57, 30-06, 243, 308, 25-06, 7mm Rem. Mag., 300 Win. Mag., 338 Win. Mag., 35 Whelen, with 24″ barrel. Weight about 7 lbs. Integral-base receiver, Ruger 1″ rings and open sights.
Price: **$533.50**

RUGER M-77R BOLT-ACTION RIFLE

Caliber: 22-250, 6mm, 243, 308, 220 Swift (Short Stroke action); 270, 7x57, 257 Roberts, 280 Rem., 30-06, 25-06, 7mm Rem. Mag., 300 Win. Mag., 338 Win. Mag. (Magnum action).
Barrel: 22″ round tapered (24″ in 220 Swift and magnum action calibers).
Weight: 6¾ lbs. **Length:** 42″ overall (22″ barrel).
Stock: Hand checkered American walnut, p.g. cap, sling swivel studs and recoil pad.
Sights: None supplied; comes with scope rings.
Features: Integral scope mount bases, diagonal bedding system, hinged floorplate, adjustable trigger, tang safety.
Price: With Ruger steel scope rings, no sights (M-77R) **$483.00**

Ruger Model M-77RL Ultra Light

Similar to the standard Model 77 except weighs only 6 lbs., chambered for 243, 270, 30-06, 257, 22-250, 250-3000 and 308; barrel tapped for target scope blocks; has 20″ Ultra Light barrel. Over-all length 40″. Ruger's steel 1″ scope rings supplied. Introduced 1983.
Price: **$513.00**

Ruger Model M-77RS Tropical Rifle

Similar to the Model 77RS Magnum except chambered only for 458 Win. Mag., 24″ barrel, steel trigger guard and floorplate. Weight about 8¾ lbs. Comes with open sights and Ruger 1″ scope rings.
Price: **$618.00**

Ruger International 77

Ruger International Model M-77RSI Rifle

Same as the Model 77 except has 18½″ barrel, full-length Mannlicher-style stock, with steel forend cap, loop-type sling swivel. Integral-base receiver, open sights, Ruger 1″ steel rings. Improved front sight. Available in 22-250, 250-3000, 243, 308, 270, 30-06. Weighs 7 lbs. Length overall is 38⅜″.
Price: **$539.75**

Ruger Ultra Light

Ruger Model M-77RLS Ultra Light Carbine

Similar to the Model 77RL Ultra Light except has 18½″ barrel, Ruger Integral Scope Mounting System, iron sights, and hinged floorplate. Available in 270, 30-06 (Magnum action); 243, 308 (Short Stroke action). Weight is 6 lbs., overall length 38⅞″. Introduced 1987.
Price: **$513.00**

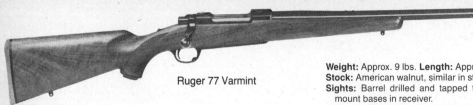

Ruger 77 Varmint

RUGER MODEL 77V VARMINT
Caliber: 22-250, 220 Swift, 243, 6mm, 25-06, 308.
Barrel: 24″ heavy straight tapered, 24″ in 220 Swift.

Weight: Approx. 9 lbs. **Length:** Approx. 44″ overall (24″ barrel).
Stock: American walnut, similar in style to Magnum Rifle.
Sights: Barrel drilled and tapped for target scope blocks. Integral scope mount bases in receiver.
Features: Ruger diagonal bedding system. Ruger steel 1″ scope rings supplied. Fully adjustable trigger. Barreled actions available in any of the standard calibers and barrel lengths.
Price: **$496.50**

Sako Hunter

SAKO HUNTER RIFLE
Caliber: 17 Rem., 222 PPC, 222, 223, 6mm PPC (short action); 22-250, 243, 7mm-08, 308 (medium action); 25-06, 6.5 × 55, 270, 30-06, 7mm Rem. Mag., 7 × 64, 300 Win. Mag., 338 Win. Mag., 9.3 × 62, 375 H&H Mag., 300 Wea. Mag. (long action).
Barrel: 22″ to 24″ depending on caliber.
Weight: 5³/₄ lbs. (short); 6¹/₄ lbs. (med.); 7¹/₄ lbs. (long).
Stock: Hand-checkered European walnut.
Sights: None furnished. Scope mounts included.
Features: Adj. trigger, hinged floorplate. Imported from Finland by Stoeger.
Price: 17 Rem. **$900.00**
Price: 222, 223, 22-250, 243, 308, 7mm-08 .... **$860.00**
Price: Long action cals. (except magnums) **$890.00**
Price: Magnum cals. **$900.00**
Price: 375 H&H **$920.00**
Price: 300 Wea. **$935.00**
Price: 22 PPC, 6mm PPC, Hunter. **$1,085.00**
Price: As above, Deluxe **$1,360.00**

Sako Hunter Left-Hand Rifle
Same gun as the Sako Hunter except has left-hand action, stock with dull finish. Available in long action and magnum calibers only. Introduced 1987.
Price: Standard calibers **$1,010.00**
Price: Magnum calibers **$1,025.00**
Price: 375 H&H **$1,040.00**

Sako Hunter LS

Sako Hunter LS Rifle
Same gun as the Sako Hunter except has laminated stock with dull finish. Chambered for same calibers. Introduced 1987.
Price: Short and medium action **$1,075.00**
Price: Long action **$1,100.00**
Price: Magnum cals. **$1,115.00**

Sako Mannlicher-Style Carbine
Same as the Hunter except has full "Mannlicher" style stock, 18¹/₂″ barrel, weighs 7¹/₂ lbs., chambered for 222 Rem., 243, 25-06 270, 308 and 30-06, 7mm Rem. Mag., 300 Win. Mag., 338 Win. Mag., 375 H&H. Introduced 1977. From Stoeger.
Price: **$945.00**
Price: Magnum cals **$980.00**
Price: 375 H&H **$1,020.00**

Sako Fiberclass Sporter
Similar to the Hunter except has a black fiberglass stock in the classic style, with wrinkle finish, rubber buttpad. Barrel length is 23″, weight 7 lbs., 2 oz. Comes with scope mounts. Introduced 1985.
Price: 17 Rem. **$1,175.00**
Price: Short, medium, long action, std. cals. **$1,175.00**
Price: Magnum cals. **$1,220.00**

Sako Carbine

Sako Carbine
Similar to the Hunter except with 18¹/₂″ barrel, same calibers and with conventional oil-finished stock of the Hunter model. Introduced 1986.
Price: 22-250, 243, 7mm-08, 308 Win. **$860.00**
Price: 25-06, 6.5x55, 270, 7x64, 30-06 .... **$890.00**
Price: 7mm Rem. Mag., 300 Win., 338 Win., 375 H&H ... **$910.00**
Price: As Fiberclass with black fiberglass stock, 25-06, 270, 30-06 **$1,190.00**
Price: As above, 7mm Rem. Mag., 308 Mag., 338 Win., 375 H&H **$1,220.00**

Sako Safari Grade Bolt Action
Similar to the Hunter except available in long action, calibers 300 Win. Mag., 338 Win. Mag. or 375 H&H Mag. only. Stocked in French walnut, checkered 20 lpi, solid rubber buttpad; grip cap and forend tip; quarter-rib "express" rear sight, hooded ramp front. Front sling swivel band-mounted on barrel.
Price: **$2,225.00**

Sako Heavy Barrel
Same as std. Super Sporter except has beavertail forend; available in 222, 223 (short action), 22 PPC, 6mm PPC (single shot), 22-250, 243, 308 (medium action). Weight from 8¹/₄ to 8¹/₂ lbs. 5-shot magazine capacity.
Price: 222, 223 (short action) **$965.00**
Price: 22-250, 243, 308 (medium action) **$965.00**
Price: 22 PPC, 6mm PPC (single shot) **$1,085.00**

Sako Super Deluxe Sporter
Similar to Deluxe Sporter except has select European walnut with high gloss finish and deep cut oak leaf carving. Metal has super high polish, deep blue finish.
Price: **$2,225.00**

CAUTION: PRICES CHANGE. CHECK AT GUNSHOP.

Sako Deluxe Sporter

Sako Deluxe Sporter

Same action as Hunter except has select wood, rosewood p.g. cap and forend tip. Fine checkering on top surfaces of integral dovetail bases, bolt sleeve, bolt handle root and bolt knob. Vent. recoil pad, skip-line checkering, mirror finish bluing.
Price: **$1,065.00**
Price: 7mm Rem. Mag., 300 Win. Mag., 338 Mag., 375 H&H **$1,090.00**

SAUER 90 RIFLE

Caliber: 243, 308, 25-06, 270, 30-06, 7mm Rem. Mag., 300 Win., 300 Wea., 375 H&H.
Barrel: 20″ (Stutzen), 24″, 26″.
Weight: 7 lbs., 6 oz. (Junior). **Length:** 42½″ overall.
Stock: Supreme grade has California Claro walnut with Monte Carlo, high gloss; Lux has European walnut, Monte Carlo comb, oil finish; Stutzen Lux has European walnut, European Monte Carlo comb, oil finish.
Sights: Post front on ramp, open rear adjustable for w.

Features: Detachable 3-4 round box magazine; rear bolt locking lugs; 65° bolt throw; front sling swivel on barrel band. Introduced 1986. Imported from West Germany by Sigarms.
Price: Supreme (std. cals.).............................. **$1,475.00**
Price: As above, magnum cals............................ **$1,575.00**
Price: Lux (std. cals.) **$1,325.00**
Price: As above, magnum cals............................ **$1,375.00**
Price: Stutzen Lux (270, 30-06 only) **$1,325.00**

Savage Model 110G

SAVAGE 110G BOLT-ACTION RIFLE

Caliber: 223, 270, 308, 30-06, 243, 5-shot; 7mm Rem. Mag., 300 Win. Mag., 4-shot.
Barrel: 22″ round tapered, 24″ for magnum.

Weight: 6¾ lbs. **Length:** 42⅜″ (22″ barrel).
Stock: Walnut-finished checkered hardwood with Monte Carlo; hard rubber buttplate.
Sights: Ramp front, step adjustable rear.
Features: Top tang safety, receiver tapped for scope mount. Full floating barrel; adjustable trigger. Introduced 1989.
Price: **$366.98**
Price: 110-G-X, no sights, Weaver-type integral bases **$351.30**

Savage Model 110-GV

Savage 110-GV Varmint Rifle

Similar to the Model 110-G except has medium-weight varmint barrel, no sights, receiver driled and tapped for scope mounting. Introduced 1989.
Price: **$400.00**

Savage Model 110F Bolt-Action Rifle

Similar to the Model 110G except has a black Du Pont Rynite® stock with black buttpad, swivel studs, removable open sights. Introduced 1988.
Price: **$465.00**
Price: Model 110-FX (no sights, integral Weaver-type bases)...... **$450.00**

Savage Model 110B Bolt-Action Rifle

Similar to the Model 110G except has brown laminated Monte Carlo stock with brown buttpad. Cals. 223, 22-250, 243, 308, 270, 30-06, 7mm Rem. Mag., 300 Win. Mag. Weighs 6¾ lbs. Introduced 1989.
Price: **$442.25**

Savage Model 110B

Steyr-Mannlicher Professional

Weight: 6.8 lbs. to 7.5 lbs. **Length:** 39″ (full-stock); 43″ (half-stock).
Stock: Hand checkered walnut. Full Mannlicher or std. half-stock with M.C. and rubber recoil pad.
Sights: Ramp front, open U-notch rear.
Features: Choice of interchangeable single or double set triggers. Detachable 5-shot rotary magazine. Drilled and tapped for scope mounting. Available as "Professional" model with Parkerized finish and synthetic stock (right-hand action only). Imported by Gun South, Inc.
Price: Full-stock (carbine) **$1,939.00**
Price: Half-stock (rifle) **$1,812.00**
Price: For left-hand action (full-stock) add about **$173.00**
Price: Professional model with iron sights.................. **$1,532.00**

STEYR-MANNLICHER MODEL M

Caliber: 7x64, 7x57, 25-06, 270, 30-06. Left-hand action cals.—7x64, 25-06, 270, 30-06. Optional cals.—6.5x57, 8x57JS, 9.3x62, 6.5x55, 7.5x55.
Barrel: 20″ (full-stock); 23.6″ (half-stock).

Steyr-Mannlicher L

STEYR-MANNLICHER MODELS SL & L
Caliber: SL—222, 222 Rem. Mag., 223; SL Varmint—222; L—22-250, 6mm, 243, 308 Win.; L Varmint—22-250, 243, 308 Win.
Barrel: 20″ (full-stock); 23.6″ (half-stock).
Weight: 6 lbs. (full-stock). **Length:** 38¼″ (full-stock).
Stock: Hand checkered walnut. Full Mannlicher or standard half-stock with Monte Carlo.
Sights: Ramp front, open U-notch rear.
Features: Choice of interchangeable single or double set triggers. Five-shot detachable ''Makrolon'' rotary magazine, 6 rear locking lugs. Drilled and tapped for scope mounts. Imported by Gun South, Inc.
Price: Full-Stock **$1,939.00**
Price: Half-stock **$1,812.00**

Steyr-Mannlicher ''Luxus''
Similar to Steyr-Mannlicher Models L and M except has single set trigger and detachable 3-shot steel magazine. Same calibers as L and M. Oil finish or high gloss lacquer on stock.
Price: Full-stock **$2,495.00**
Price: Half-stock **$2,364.00**

STEYR-MANNLICHER MODELS S & S/T
Caliber: Model S—300 Win. Mag., 7mm Rem. Mag., 300 H&H Mag., 375 H&H Mag. (6.5x68, 8x68S, 9.3x64 optional); S/T—375 H&H Mag., 458 Win. Mag. (9.3x64 optional).
Barrel: 25.6″.
Weight: 8.4 lbs. (Model S). **Length:** 45″ overall.
Stock: Half-stock with M.C. and rubber recoil pad. Hand checkered walnut. Available with optional spare magazine inletted in butt.
Sights: Ramp front, U-notch rear.
Features: Choice of interchangeable single or double set triggers, detachable 4-shot magazine. Drilled and tapped for scope mounts. Imported by Gun South, Inc.
Price: Model S **$1,952.00**
Price: Model S/T 375 H&H, 458 Win. Mag. **$2,176.00**

Steyr-Mannlicher Varmint, Models SL and L
Similar to standard SL and L except chambered only for 222 Rem., 22-250, 243, 308. Has 26″ heavy barrel, no sights (drilled and tapped for scope mounts). Choice of single or double set triggers. Five-shot detachable magazine.
Price: **$1,939.00**

Tikka Rifle

TIKKA BOLT-ACTION RIFLE
Caliber: 223, 243, 270, 30-06, 7mm Rem. Mag., 338 Win. Mag.
Barrel: 22″ (std. cals.), 24″ (magnum cals.).

Weight: 7⅛ lbs. **Length:** 43″ overall (std. cals.).
Stock: European walnut with Monte Carlo comb, rubber buttpad, checkered grip and forend.
Sights: None furnished.
Features: Detachable four-shot magazine (standard calibers), three-shot in magnums. Receiver dovetailed for scope mounting. Introduced 1988. Imported from Finland by Stoeger Industries.
Price: Standard calibers **$720.00**
Price: Magnum calibers **$740.00**

Ultra Light Model 20

Ultra Light Arms Model 20S Rifle
Similar to the Model 20 except uses short action chambered for 17 Rem., 222 Rem., 223 Rem., 22 Hornet. Has 22″ Douglas Premium No. 1 contour barrel, weighs 4¾ lbs., 41″ overall length.
Price: **$2,000.00**
Price: Model 20S Left Hand (left-hand action and stock) **$2,100.00**

Ultra Light Arms Model 28 Rifle
Similar to the Model 20 except in 264, 7mm Rem. Mag., 300 Win. Mag., 338 Win. Mag. Uses 24″ Douglas Premium No. 2 contour barrel. Weighs 5½ lbs., 45″ overall length. KDF or U.L.A. recoil arrestor built in. Any custom feature available on any U.L.A. product can be incorporated.
Price: Right hand **$2,500.00**
Price: Left hand **$2,600.00**

ULTRA LIGHT ARMS MODEL 20 RIFLE
Caliber: 17 Rem., 22 Hornet, 222 Rem., 222 Rem. Mag., 223 Rem., 22-250, 6mm Rem., 243, 250-3000, 257 Roberts, 257 Ackley, 7 x 57, 7 x 57 Ackley, 7mm-08, 284 Win., 300 Savage, 358 Win.
Barrel: 22″ or 24″ Douglas Premium No. 1 contour.
Weight: 4½ lbs. **Length:** 41½″ overall.
Stock: Composite Kevlar, graphite reinforced. Dupont Imron paint colors — green, black, brown and camo options. Choice of length of pull.
Sights: None furnished. Scope mount included.
Features: Timney adjustable trigger; two-position three-function safety. Benchrest quality action. Matte or bright stock and metal finish. 3″ magazine length. Shipped in a hard case. From Ultra Light Arms, Inc.
Price: Right hand **$2,000.00**
Price: Model 20 Left Hand (left-hand action and stock) **$2,100.00**
Price: Model 24 (25-06, 270, 7mm Express Rem., 30-06, 3⅜″ magazine length) **$2,100.00**
Price: Model 24 Left Hand (left-hand action and stock) **$2,200.00**

VOERE 2155, 2165 BOLT-ACTION RIFLE
Caliber: 22-250, 270, 308, 243, 30-06, 7x64, 5.6x57, 6.5x55, 8x57 JRS, 7mm Rem. Mag., 300 Win. Mag., 8x68S, 9.3x62, 9.3x64, 6.5x68.
Stock: European walnut, hog-back style; checkered pistol grip and forend.
Sights: Ramp front, open adjustable rear.
Features: Mauser-type action with 5-shot detachable box magazine; double set or single trigger; drilled and tapped for scope mounting. Imported from Austria by L. Joseph Rahn. Introduced 1984.

Price: M2165, standard calibers, single trigger **$885.00**
Price: As above, double set triggers **$925.00**
Price: M2165, magnum calibers, single trigger **$915.00**
Price: As above, double set triggers **$955.00**
Price: M2165, full-stock, single trigger **$925.00**
Price: As above, double set triggers **$985.00**
Price: M2155 (as above, no jeweling, military safety, single trigger) . **$700.00**
Price: As above, double triggers **$750.00**

CAUTION: PRICES CHANGE. CHECK AT GUNSHOP.

Weatherby Mark V

Weatherby Mark V ''Safari Grade'' Custom Rifles

Uses the Mark V barreled action. Stock is of European walnut with satin oil finish, rounded ebony tip and cap, black presentation recoil pad, no white spacers, and pattern #16 fine-line checkering. Matte finish bluing, floorplate is engraved ''Weatherby Safari Grade''; 24" barrel. Standard rear stock swivel, barrel band front swivel. Has quarter-rib rear sight with a stationary leaf and one folding shallow V leaf. Front sight is a hooded ramp with brass bead. Right- or left-hand. Allow 8-10 months delivery. Introduced 1989.
Price: 300 W.M. **$2,866.00**
Price: 340 W.M. **$2,882.00**
Price: 378 W.M. **$3,018.00**
Price: 416 W.M. **$3,098.00**
Price: 460 W.M. **$3,063.00**

WEATHERBY MARK V BOLT-ACTION RIFLE

Caliber: All Weatherby cals., plus 22-250 and 30-06
Barrel: 24" or 26" round tapered.
Weight: 6¹/₂-10¹/₂ lbs. **Length:** 43¹/₄"-46¹/₂" overall.
Stock: Walnut, Monte Carlo with cheekpiece, high luster finish, checkered p.g. and forend, recoil pad.
Sights: Optional (extra).
Features: Cocking indicator, adjustable trigger, hinged floorplate, thumb safety, quick detachable sling swivels.
Price: Cals. 224 and 22-250, std. bbl., right-hand only **$971.00**
Price: With 26" semi-target bbl., right-hand only **$987.00**
Price: Cals. 240, 257, 270, 7mm, 30-06 and 300 (24" bbl.) right- or left-hand **$991.00**
Price: With 26" No. 2 contour bbl., right-hand or 300 W.M. left only **$1,011.00**
Price: Cal. 340 (26" bbl.), right- or left-hand **$1,011.00**
Price: Cal. 378 (26" bbl.), right- or left-hand **$1,165.00**
Price: 416 W.M., 24", right- or left-hand **$1,270.00**
Price: As above, 26" **$1,290.00**
Price: 460 W.M., 24", right- or left-hand **$1,330.00**
Price: As above, 26" **$1,350.00**

Weatherby Ultramark

Weatherby Mark V ''Crown'' Custom Rifles

Uses hand-honed, engraved Mark V barreled action with fully-checkered bolt knob, damascened bolt and follower. Floorplate is engraved ''Weatherby Custom.'' Super fancy walnut stock with inlays and stock carving. Gold monogram with name or initials. Right-hand only. Available in 240, 257, 270, 7mm, 300 Wea. Mag. or 30-06. Introduced 1989.
Price: From . . . . **$3,117.00** to **$4,320.00**
Price: For 340 W.M., add. **$16.00**

Weatherby Mark V Ultramark Rifle

Similar to the Mark V except stock is of select Claro walnut with basket-weave checkering; hand-honed, jeweled action with a floorplate engraved ''Weatherby Ultramark.'' Available in all Weatherby calibers and 30-06 except 224 Wea. Mag., 460 Wea. Mag. and 22-250. Introduced 1989.
Price: 240, 257, 270, 7mm, 300 Wea. Mag., 30-06, 24", right- or left-hand action **$1,250.00**
Price: As above, 26" **$1,275.00**
Price: 340 Wea. Mag., 26" right- or left-hand **$1,275.00**
Price: As above, 378 Wea. Mag. **$1,470.00**
Price: 416 Wea. Mag., 24", right- or left-hand **$1,575.00**
Price: As above, 26" **$1,595.00**

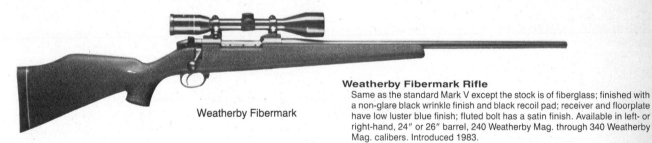

Weatherby Fibermark

Weatherby Fibermark Rifle

Same as the standard Mark V except the stock is of fiberglass; finished with a non-glare black wrinkle finish and black recoil pad; receiver and floorplate have low luster blue finish; fluted bolt has a satin finish. Available in left- or right-hand, 24" or 26" barrel, 240 Weatherby Mag. through 340 Weatherby Mag. calibers. Introduced 1983.
Price: 240 W.M. through 300 W.M., 24" bbl. **$1,123.00**
Price: 240 W.M. through 340 W.M., 26" bbl., right-hand or 300, 340 W.M. left-hand only **$1,143.00**

Consult our Directory pages for the location of firms mentioned.

Weatherby Lazermark V Rifle

Same as standard Mark V except stock has extensive laser carving under cheekpiece on butt, p.g. and forend. Introduced 1981.
Price: 22-250, 224 Wea., 24" bbl., right-hand only **$1,085.00**
Price: As above, 26" bbl., right-hand only. **$1,100.00**
Price: 240 Wea. thru 300 Wea., 24" bbl., right- or left-hand **$1,105.00**
Price: As above, 26" bbl., right-hand or 300 W.M. left-hand **$1,125.00**
Price: 340 Wea., right- or left-hand **$1,127.00**
Price: 378 Wea., right- or left-hand **$1,281.00**
Price: 416 W.M., 24", right- or left-hand **$1,390.00**
Price: As above, 26" **$1,410.00**
Price: 460 W.M., 24" right- or left-hand. **$1,450.00**
Price: As above, 26" **$1,470.00**

Weatherby Mark V Rifle Left Hand

Available in all Weatherby calibers, plus 30-06 with 24" barrel. Left-hand 26" barrel available in 300 and 340 calibers. Not available in 224 WM and 22-250 Varmintmaster.

Weatherby Weatherguard

Weatherby Vanguard Weatherguard Rifle
Has a forest green or black wrinkle-finished synthetic stock. All metal is matte blue. Has a 24″ barrel, weighs 7½ lbs., measures 44½″. In 223, 243, and 308; 40½″ in 270, 7mm-08, 7mm Rem. Mag., 30-06. Accepts same scope mount bases as Mark V action. Introduced 1989.
Price: Right-hand only.......................................$399.00

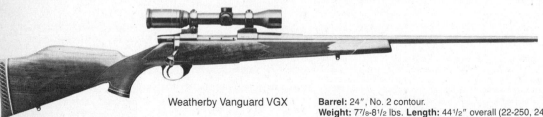

Weatherby Vanguard VGX

Barrel: 24″, No. 2 contour.
Weight: 7⅞-8½ lbs. **Length:** 44½″ overall (22-250, 243 are 44″).
Stock: Walnut with high luster finish; rosewood grip cap and forend tip.
Sights: Optional, available at extra cost.
Features: Fully adjustable trigger; side safety; rubber recoil pad. Introduced 1989. Imported from Japan by Weatherby.
Price: $600.00

WEATHERBY VANGUARD VGX DELUXE RIFLE
Caliber: 22-250, 243, 270, 270 Wea. Mag., 7mm Rem. Mag., 30-06, 300 Win. Mag., 300 Wea. Mag., 338 Win. Mag.; 5-shot magazine (3-shot for magnums).

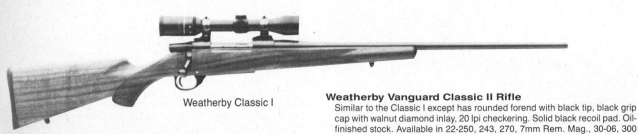

Weatherby Classic I

Weatherby Vanguard Classic II Rifle
Similar to the Classic I except has rounded forend with black tip, black grip cap with walnut diamond inlay, 20 lpi checkering. Solid black recoil pad. Oil-finished stock. Available in 22-250, 243, 270, 7mm Rem. Mag., 30-06, 300 Win. Mag., 338 Win. Mag., 270 Wea. Mag., 300 Wea. Mag. Introduced 1989.
Price: $600.00

Weatherby Vanguard Classic I Rifle
Similar to the Vanguard VGX Deluxe except has a ''classic'' style stock without Monte Carlo comb, no forend tip. Has distinctive Weatherby grip cap. Satin finish on stock. Available in 223, 243, 270, 7mm-08, 7mm Rem. Mag. 30-06, 308; 24″ barrel. Introduced 1989.
Price: $465.00

WEATHERBY EUROMARK BOLT-ACTION RIFLE
Caliber: All Weatherby calibers except 224, 22-250.
Barrel: 24″ or 26″ round tapered.
Weight: 6½ to 10½ lbs. **Length:** 44¼″ overall (24″ bbl.).
Stock: Walnut, Monte Carlo with extended tail, fine-line hand checkering, satin oil finish, ebony forend tip and grip cap with maple diamond, solid buttpad.
Sights: Optional (extra).

Features: Cocking indicator; adjustable trigger; hinged floorplate; thumb safety; q.d. sling swivels. Introduced 1986.
Price: With 24″ barrel (240, 257, 270, 7mm, 30-06, 300), right- or left-hand...$1,040.00
Price: 26″ No. 2 contour barrel, right- or left-hand (300 only).....$1,060.00
Price: 340 W.M., 26″, right- or left-hand.....................$1,060.00
Price: 416 W.M., 24″, right- or left-hand.....................$1,320.00
Price: As above, 26″.......................................$1,340.00
Price: 460 W.M., 24″, right- or left-hand.....................$1,385.00
Price: As above, 26″.......................................$1,405.00

Whitworth Express Rifle

WHITWORTH SAFARI EXPRESS RIFLE
Caliber: 375 H&H, 458 Win. Mag.
Barrel: 24″.
Weight: 7½-8 lbs. **Length:** 44″.
Stock: Classic English Express rifle design of hand checkered, select European walnut.
Sights: Three-leaf open sight calibrated for 100, 200, 300 yards on ¼-rib, ramp front with removable hood.
Features: Solid rubber recoil pad, barrel-mounted sling swivel, adjustable trigger, hinged floorplate, solid steel recoil cross bolt.
Price: 375, 458, with express sights.........................$710.00

WICHITA CLASSIC RIFLE
Caliber: 17 Rem. thru 308 Win., including 22 and 6mm PPC.
Barrel: 21⅛″.
Weight: 8 lbs. **Length:** 41″ overall.
Stock: AAA Fancy American walnut. Hand-rubbed and checkered (20 lpi). Hand-inletted, glass bedded, steel grip cap. Pachmayr rubber recoil pad.
Sights: None. Drilled and tapped for scope mounting.
Features: Available as single shot or repeater. Octagonal barrel and Wichita action, right- or left-hand. Checkered bolt handle. Bolt is hand-fitted, lapped and jeweled. Adjustable Canjar trigger is set at 2 lbs. Side thumb safety. Firing pin fall is ³⁄₁₆″. Non-glare blue finish. From Wichita Arms.
Price: Single shot.......................................$2,950.00

CAUTION: PRICES CHANGE. CHECK AT GUNSHOP.

Wichita Varmint Rifle

WICHITA VARMINT RIFLE
Caliber: 17 Rem. thru 308 Win., including 22 and 6mm PPC.
Barrel: 20 1/8″.

Weight: 0 lbs. **Length:** 40 1/8″ overall.
Stock: AAA Fancy American walnut. Hand-rubbed finish, hand checkered, 20 lpi pattern. Hand-inletted, glass bedded, steel grip cap, Pachmayr rubber recoil pad.
Sights: None. Drilled and tapped for scope mounts.
Features: Right- or left-hand Wichita action with three locking lugs. Available as a single shot or repeater with 3-shot magazine. Checkered bolt handle. Bolt is hand fitted, lapped and jeweled. Side thumb safety. Firing pin fall is 3/16″. Non-glare blue finish. From Wichita Arms.
Price: Single shot **$1,975.00**

Winchester 70 Super Express

WINCHESTER 70 SPORTER
Caliber: 22-250, 223, 243, 270, 270 Wea., 30-06, 264 Win. Mag., 7mm Rem. Mag., 300 H&H, 300 Win. Mag., 300 Wea. Mag., 338 Win. Mag., 3-shot magazine.
Barrel: 24″.
Weight: 7 3/4 lbs. **Length:** 44 1/2″ overall.
Stock: American walnut with Monte Carlo cheekpiece. XTR checkering and satin finish.
Sights: None furnished; optional hooded ramp front, adjustable folding leaf rear.
Features: Three-position safety, detachable sling swivels, stainless steel magazine follower, rubber buttpad, epoxy bedded receiver recoil lug. From U.S. Repeating Arms Co.
Price: With sights, about **$472.00**
Price: Without sights, about **$472.00**
Price: 300 Wea. Mag., about **$472.00**

Winchester Model 70 Winlite Rifle
Similar to the Model 70 Sporter except has McMillan black fiberglass stock. No sights are furnished but receiver is drilled and tapped for scope mounting. Available in 270, 280, 30-06 (22″ barrel, 4-shot magazine), 7mm Rem. Mag., 300 Wea., 300 Win. Mag., 338 Win. Mag. (24″ barrel, 3-shot magazine). Weight is 6 1/4-6 1/2 lbs. for 270, 30-06; 6 3/4-7 lbs. for 7mm Mag., 338. Introduced 1986.
Price: About **$637.00**
Price: 300 Weatherby, about **$637.00**

WINCHESTER 70 SUPER EXPRESS MAGNUM
Caliber: 375 H&H Mag., 458 Win. Mag., 3-shot magazine.
Barrel: 24″ (375), 22″ (458).
Weight: 8 1/2 lbs.
Stock: American walnut with Monte Carlo cheekpiece. Wrap-around checkering and finish.
Sights: Hooded ramp front, open rear.
Features: Two steel cross bolts in stock for added strength. Front sling swivel mounted on barrel. Contoured rubber buttpad. From U.S. Repeating Arms Co.
Price: About **$792.00**

WINCHESTER MODEL 70 LIGHTWEIGHT RIFLE
Caliber: 270, 280, 30-06 (standard action); 22-250, 223, 243, 308 (short action), both from 5-shot magazine, except 6-shot in 223.
Barrel: 22″.
Weight: 6 1/4 lbs. **Length:** 40 1/2″ overall (std.), 40″ (short).
Stock: American walnut with satin finish, deep-cut checkering.
Sights: None furnished. Drilled and tapped for scope mounting.
Features: Three position safety; stainless steel magazine follower; hinged floorplate; sling swivel studs. Introduced 1984.
Price: With sights, about **$430.00**
Price: With Win-Tuff laminated stock, 270, 30-06 only **$442.00**
Price: With Win-Cam green laminated stock, 270, 30-06 only **$442.00**

Winchester Model 70 Heavy Barrel Varmint
Similr to the Model 70 Sporter except has heavy 26″ barrel with counterbored muzzle. Available in 22-250, 223 and 243. Receiver bedded in sporter-style stock. Has rubber buttpad. Receiver drilled and tapped for scope mounting. Weight about 9 lbs., overall length 46″. Introduced 1989.
Price: **$482.00**

Winchester 70 Lightweight

Winchester Model 70 Lightweight Rifle
Similar to the Model 70 Sporter except has 22″ barrel, walnut, classic-style stock with diamond-point pattern checkering, and available in 22-250, 223, 243, 270, 280, 30-06 and 308. Model 70 Win-Tuff has brown laminate stock (cals. 223, 243, 270, 30-06, 308); Win-Cam has camo green laminate stock (cals. 270, 30-06 only).
Price: Walnut **$430.00**
Price: Win-Tuff **$442.00**
Price: Win-Cam **$442.00**

Winchester Ranger

Winchester Ranger Rifle
Similar to Model 70 Sporter except chambered only for 243, 270, 30-06, with 22″ barrel. American hardwood stock, no checkering, composition butt plate. Metal has matte blue finish. Introduced 1985.
Price: About **$387.00**
Price: Ranger Youth, 243 only, scaled-down stock **$396.00**

CENTERFIRE RIFLES — BOLT ACTIONS

Winchester 70 Featherweight

Winchester Model 70 Featherweight
Available with standard action in 270 Win., 280 Rem., 30-06, short action in 22-250, 223, 243, 308; 22″ tapered Featherweight barrel; classic-style American walnut stock with Schnabel forend, wrap-around checkering fashioned after early Model 70 custom rifle patterns. Red rubber buttpad, sling swivel studs. Weighs 6¾ lbs. (standard action), 6½ lbs. (short action). Introduced 1984.
Price: About **$472.00**

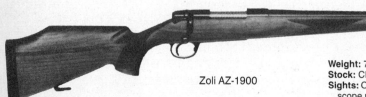

Zoli AZ-1900

Weight: 7¼ lbs. **Length:** 41¾″ overall (21″ bbl.).
Stock: Checkered Turkish circassian walnut.
Sights: Open sights supplied with gun but not mounted. Drilled and tapped for scope mounts.
Features: Polished blue finish, oil-finished stock. Engine-turned bolt. Introduced 1989. Imported from Italy by Antonio Zoli, USA.

ZOLI MODEL AZ-1900 BOLT-ACTION RIFLE
Caliber: 243, 6.5x55, 270, 308, 30-06, 7mm Rem. Mag., 300 Win. Mag.
Barrel: 21″ (24″ on 7mm Rem. Mag., 300 Win. Mag.).

Price: Model AZ-1900, standard cals. **$750.00**
Price: As above, magnum, cals. **$800.00**
Price: Model AZ-1900 DL (engraved receiver, no sights) **$850.00**
Price: As above, magnum cals. **$900.00**

CENTERFIRE RIFLES—SINGLE SHOTS

Classic and modern designs for sporting and competitive use.

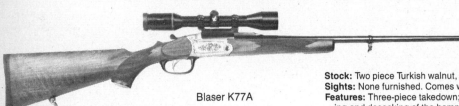

Blaser K77A

BLASER K77A SINGLE SHOT RIFLE
Caliber: 22-250, 243, 6.5x55, 270, 280, 7x57R, 7x65R, 30-06, 7mm Rem. Mag., 300 Win. Mag., 300 Wea. Mag.
Barrel: 23″ (24″ magnum).
Weight: 5½-5¾ lbs. **Length:** 39½″ overall (23″ barrel).

Stock: Two piece Turkish walnut, checkered 18 lpi. Solid black buttpad.
Sights: None furnished. Comes with low-profile Blaser scope mount.
Features: Three-piece takedown; tang-mounted sliding safety provides cocking and decocking of the hammer spring. Optional interchangeable barrels must be factory fitted. Introduced 1989. Imported from West Germany by Autumn Sales, Inc.
Price: Standard calibers **$2,280.00**
Price: Magnum calibers **$2,380.00**
Price: Interchangeable barrel, standard calibers **$730.00**
Price: As above, magnum calibers **$778.00**

Browning Model 1885

BROWNING MODEL 1885 SINGLE SHOT RIFLE
Caliber: 223, 22-250, 30-06, 270, 7mm Rem. Mag., 45-70.
Barrel: 28″.
Weight: About 8½ lbs. **Length:** 43½″ overall.

Stock: Walnut with straight grip, Schnabel forend.
Sights: None furnished; drilled and tapped for scope mounting.
Features: Replica of J.M. Browning's high-wall falling block rifle. Octagon barrel with recessed muzzle. Imported from Japan by Browning. Introduced 1985.
Price: **$699.95**

HEYM-RUGER Model HR 30/38 RIFLE
Caliber: 243 Win., 6.5x55, 6.5x57R, 7x57R, 7x64R, 8x57JRS, 9.3x62, 270 Win., 308 Win., 30-06 (standard); 6.5x68, 8x68S, 9.3x64, 7mm Rem. Mag., 300 Win. Mag., 375 H&H, 470 N.E. (magnum).
Barrel: 24″ (standard cals.), 25″ (magnum cals.).
Weight: 6½ to 7 lbs.
Stock: Dark European walnut, hand-checkered p.g. and forend. Oil finish, recoil pad. Full Mannlicher-type or sporter-style with schnabel forend, Bavarian cheekpiece.
Sights: Bead on ramp front, leaf rear.
Features: Ruger No. 1 action and safety, Canjar single set trigger, hand-engraved animal motif. Options available include deluxe engraving and stock carving. Imported from West Germany by Paul Jaeger, Inc.

> Consult our directory pages for the location of firms mentioned.

Price: HR-30N, round bbl., sporter stock, std. cals. **$3,100.00**
Price: HR-30G, as above except in mag. cals. **$3,300.00**
Price: HR-30L, round bbl., full stock, std. cals. **$3,500.00**
Price: For octagon barrel, (HR 38) add **$490.00**
Price: For sideplates with large hunting scenes, add **$1,700.00**

CAUTION: PRICES CHANGE. CHECK AT GUNSHOP.

NEW ENGLAND FIREARMS "HANDI-RIFLE"
Caliber: 22 Hornet, 223, 30-30, 45-70.
Barrel: 22".
Weight: 7 lbs.
Stock: Walnut-finished hardwood.
Sights: Ramp front, folding rear. Drilled and tapped for scope mount; 223 Rem. has no open sights, comes with scope mounts.
Features: Break-open action with side-lever release. Blue finish. Introduced 1989. From New England Firearms.
Price: . . . . **NA**

New England "Handi-Rifle"

Ruger No. 1B Rifle

Ruger No. 1A Light Sporter
Similar to the No. 1B Standard Rifle except has lightweight 22" barrel, Alexander Henry-style forend, adjustable folding leaf rear sight on quarter-rib, dovetailed ramp front with gold bead. Calibers 243, 30-06, 270 and 7x57. Weight about 7¼ lbs.
Price: No. 1A **$575.00**
Price: Barreled action **$389.50**

RUGER NO. 1B SINGLE SHOT
Caliber: 220 Swift, 22-250, 223, 243, 6mm Rem., 25-06, 257 Roberts, 270, 280, 30-06, 7mm Rem. Mag., 300 Win. Mag., 338 Win. Mag., 270 Wea., 300 Wea.
Barrel: 26" round tapered with quarter-rib; with Ruger 1" rings.
Weight: 8 lbs. **Length:** 43⅜" overall.
Stock: Walnut, two-piece, checkered p.g. and semi-beavertail forend.
Sights: None, 1" scope rings supplied for integral mounts.
Features: Under-lever, hammerless falling block design has auto ejector, top tang safety.
Price: **$575.00**
Price: Barreled action **$389.50**

Ruger No. 1 International

Ruger No. 1S Medium Sporter
Similar to the No. 1B Standard Rifle except has Alexander Henry-style forend, adjustable folding leaf rear sight on quarter-rib, ramp front sight base and dovetail-type gold bead front sight. Calibers 7mm Rem. Mag., 338 Win. Mag., 300 Win. Mag. with 26" barrel, 45-70 with 22" barrel. Weight about 7½ lbs. in 45-70.
Price: No. 1S **$575.00**
Price: Barreled action **$389.50**

Ruger No. 1H Tropical Rifle
Similar to the No. 1B Standard Rifle except has Alexander Henry forend, adjustable folding leaf rear sight on quarter-rib, ramp front with dovetail gold bead front, 24" heavy barrel. Calibers 375 H&H (weight about 8¼ lbs.) and 458 Win. Mag. (weight about 9 lbs.).
Price: No. 1H **$575.00**
Price: Barreled action **$389.50**

C. Sharps Arms 1875 Classic Sharps
Similar to the New Model 1875 Sporting Rifle except has 30" full octagon barrel, crescent buttplate with toe plate, Hartford-style forend with cast German silver nose cap. Blade front sight, Rocky Mountain buckhorn rear. Weight is 10 lbs. Introduced 1987. From C. Sharps Arms Co.
Price: **$995.00**

Ruger No. 1 RSI International
Similar to the No. 1B Standard Rifle except has lightweight 20" barrel, full-length Mannlicher-style forend with loop sling swivel, adjustable folding leaf rear sight on quarter-rib, ramp front with gold bead. Calibers 243, 30-06, 270 and 7x57. Weight is about 7¼ lbs.
Price: No. 1RSI **$595.00**
Price: Barreled action **$389.50**

Ruger No. 1V Special Varminter
Similar to the No. 1B Standard Rifle except has 24" heavy barrel. Semi-beavertail forend, barrel tapped for target scope block, with 1" Ruger scope rings. Calibers 22-250, 220 Swift, 223, 25-06, 6mm. Weight about 9 lbs.
Price: No. 1V **$575.00**
Price: Barreled action **$389.50**

NAVY ARMS ROLLING BLOCK RIFLE
Caliber: 45-70.
Barrel: 30".
Stocks: Walnut finished.
Sights: Fixed front, adjustable rear.
Features: Reproduction of classic rolling block action. Available in Buffalo Rifle (octagonal bbl.) and Creedmoor (half-round, half-octagonal bbl.) models. From Navy Arms.
Price: 26", 30" full octagon barrel **$489.00**
Price: Creedmoor Model, 30" full octagon **$521.00**
Price: 30", half-round **$489.00**
Price: 26", half-round **$489.00**
Price: Half-round Creedmoor **$521.00**

C. Sharps 1875

C. SHARPS ARMS NEW MODEL 1875 RIFLE
Caliber: 22 LR Stevens, 32-40 & 38-55 Ballard, 38-56 WCF, 40-65 WCF, 40-90 3¼", 40-90 2⅝", 40-70 2¹/₁₀", 40-70 2¼", 40-70 2½", 40-50 1¹¹/₁₆", 40-50 1⁷/₈", 45-90 2⁴/₁₀", 45-70 2¹/₁₀".

Barrel: 24", 26", 30", (standard); 32", 34" optional.
Weight: 8-12 lbs.
Stocks: Walnut, straight grip, shotgun butt with checkered steel buttplate.
Sights: Silver blade front, Rocky Mountain buckhorn rear.
Features: Recreation of the 1875 Sharps rifle. Production guns will have case colored receiver. Available in Custom Sporting and Target versions upon request. Announced 1986. From C. Sharps Arms Co.
Price: 1875 Carbine (24" tapered round bbl.) **$575.00**
Price: 1875 Saddle Rifle (26" tapered oct. bbl.) **$685.00**
Price: 1875 Sporting Rifle (30" tapered oct. bbl.) **$695.00**
Price: 1875 Business Rifle (28" tapered round bbl.) **$565.00**

Sharps Long Range Express

Shiloh Sharps 1874 Montana Roughrider

Similar to the No. 1 Sporting Rifle except available with half-octagon or full-octagon barrel in 24″, 26″, 28″, 30″, 34″ lengths; standard supreme or semi-fancy wood, shotgun, pistol grip or military-style butt. Weight about 8½ lbs. Calibers 30-40, 30-30, 40-50x1¹¹/₁₆″ BN, 40-70x2¹/₁₀″ BN, 45-70x2¹/₁₀″ ST. Globe front and tang sight optional.

Price: Standard supreme **$725.00**
Price: Semi-fancy **$810.00**

Shiloh Sharps 1874 Business Rifle

Similar to No. 3 Rifle except has 28″ heavy round barrel, military-style buttstock and steel buttplate. Weight about 9½ lbs. Calibers 40-50 BN, 40-70 BN, 40-90 BN, 45-70 ST, 45-90 ST, 50-70 ST, 50-100 ST, 32-40, 38-55, 40-70 ST, 40-90 ST.

Price: **$725.00**
Price: 1874 Carbine (similar to above except 24″ round bbl., single trigger—double set avail.). **$725.00**
Price: 1874 Saddle Rifle (similar to Carbine except has 26″ octagon barrel, semi-fancy shotgun butt) **$790.00**

Shiloh Sharps ''The Jaeger''

Similar to the Montana Roughrider except has half-octagon 26″ lightweight barrel, calibers 30-40, 30-30, 45-70. Standard supreme black walnut.

Price: **$795.00**

SHILOH SHARPS 1874 LONG RANGE EXPRESS

Caliber: 40-50 BN, 40-70 BN, 40-90 BN, 45-70 ST, 45-90 ST, 45-110 ST, 50-70 ST, 50-90 ST, 50-110 ST, 32-40, 38-55, 40-70 ST, 40-90 ST.
Barrel: 34″ tapered octagon.
Weight: 10½ lbs. **51″ overall.**
Stock: Oil-finished semi-fancy walnut with pistol grip, shotgun-style butt, traditional cheek rest and accent line. Schnabel forend.
Sights: Globe front, sporting tang rear.
Features: Recreation of the Model 1874 Sharps rifle. Double set triggers. Made in U.S. by Shiloh Rifle Mfg. Co.
Price: **$850.00**
Price: Sporting Rifle No. 1 (similar to above except with 30″ bbl., blade front, buckhorn rear sight) **$820.00**
Price: Sporting Rifle No. 3 (similar to No. 1 except straight-grip stock, standard wood) **$725.00**

Shiloh Sharps 1874 Military Rifle

Has 30″ round barrel. Iron block front sight and Lawrence-style rear ladder sight. Military butt, buttplate with patchbox assembly, three barrel bands; single trigger (double set available). Calibers 40-50x1¹¹/₁₆″ BN, 40-70x2¹/₁₀″ BN, 40-90 BN, 45-70x2¹/₁₀″ ST, 50-70 ST.
Price: **$845.00**

Shiloh Sharps 1874 Military Carbine

Has 22″ round barrel with blade front sight and full buckhorn ladder-type rear. Military-style buttstock with barrel band on military-style forend. Steel buttplate, saddle bar and ring. Standard supreme grade only. Weight is about 8½ lbs. Calibers 40-70 BN, 45-70, 50-70. Introduced 1989.
Price: **$765.00**

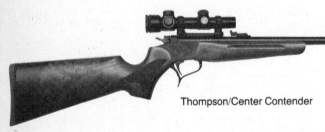

Thompson/Center Contender

Thompson/Center Youth Model Contender Carbine

Same as the standard Contender Carbine except has 16¼″ barrel, shorter buttstock with 12″ length of pull. Comes with fully adjustable open sights. Overall length is 29″, weight about 4 lbs., 9 oz. Available in 22 LR, 22 WMR, 223 Rem., 7x30 Waters, 30-30, 35 Rem., 44 Mag. Also available with 16¼″, rifled vent. rib barrel chambered for 45/410.

Price: **$345.00**
Price: With 45/410 barrel **$370.00**
Price: Extra barrels **$160.00**
Price: Extra 45/410 barrel **$185.00**

THOMPSON/CENTER CONTENDER CARBINE

Caliber: 22 LR, 22 Hornet, 223 Rem., 7mm T.C.U., 7x30 Waters, 30-30 Win., 357 Rem. Maximum, 35 Rem., 44 Mag., 410, single shot.
Barrel: 21″.
Weight: 5 lbs., 2 oz. **Length:** 35″ overall.
Stock: Checkered American walnut with rubber buttpad.
Sights: Blade front, open adjustable rear.
Features: Uses the T/C Contender action. Eleven interchangeable barrels available, all with sights, drilled and tapped for scope mounting. Introduced 1985. Offered as a complete Carbine only.
Price: Rifle calibers **$375.00**
Price: Extra barrels, rifle calibers, each **$165.00**
Price: 410 shotgun **$395.00**
Price: Extra 410 barrel **$185.00**

Thompson/Center TCR Hunter

UBERTI ROLLING BLOCK BABY CARBINE

Caliber: 22 LR, 22 WMR, 22 Hornet, 357 Mag., single shot.
Barrel: 22″.
Weight: 4.8 lbs. **Length:** 35½″ overall.
Stock: Walnut stock and forend.
Sights: Blade front, fully adjustable open rear.
Features: Resembles Remington New Model No. 4 carbine. Brass trigger guard and buttplate; color case-hardened frame, blued barrel. Imported by Uberti USA.
Price: **$350.00**

THOMPSON/CENTER TCR '87 SINGLE SHOT RIFLE

Caliber: 22 Hornet, 222 Rem., 223 Rem., 22-250, 243 Win., 270, 308, 7mm-08, 30-06, 32-40 Win., 12-ga. slug. Also 10-ga. and 12-ga. field barrels.
Barrel: 23″ (standard), 25⁷/₈″ (heavy).
Weight: About 6¾ lbs. **Length:** 39½″ overall.
Stock: American black walnut, checkered p.g. and forend.
Sights: None furnished.
Features: Break-open design with interchangeable barrels. Single-stage trigger. Cross-bolt safety. Made in U.S. by T/C. Introduced 1983.
Price: With Medium Sporter barrel (223, 22-250, 7mm-08, 308, 32-40 Win.) **$425.00**
Price: With Light Sporter barrel (22 Hornet, 222, 223, 22-250, 243, 270, 308, 30-06) **$425.00**
Price: 12-ga. slug barrel **$185.00**
Price: Extra Medium or Light Sporter barrel **$185.00**
Price: 10-, 12-ga. field barrels **$185.00**

CAUTION: PRICES CHANGE. CHECK AT GUNSHOP.

Designs for sporting and utility purposes worldwide.

American Arms RS

AMERICAN ARMS RS COMBO
Caliber/Gauge: 222 or 308 and 12 ga., 3″.
Barrel: 24″ with vent. rib over rifle. Full choke tube.

Weight: 7 lbs., 14 oz.
Stock: Walnut with Monte Carlo, pistol grip, cut checkering; schnabel forend tip.
Sights: Vent. rib with blade front, folding rear; grooved for scope mounting.
Features: Boxlock action with antique silver finish and engraving; double triggers; extractors. Barrel connectors allow for windage and elevation adjustments on rifle barrel. Introduced 1989. Imported from Italy by American Arms, Inc.
Price: $749.00

Armsport 2783 Combo

ARMSPORT 2783 O/U COMBINATION GUN
Caliber/Gauge: 12 ga. (3″) over 222 Rem., 270 Win.; 20 ga. over 222, 243, 270.
Barrel: 28″ (Full).

Weight: 8 lbs.
Stock: European walnut.
Sights: Blade front, leaf rear.
Features: Ventilated top and middle ribs; flip-up rear sight; silvered receiver. Introduced 1986. Imported from Italy by Armsport.
Price: Turkey Gun, 12/222................................. $750.00
Price: Combination Gun, all other listed calibers $1,495.00

BERETTA EXPRESS S689, SSO DOUBLE RIFLES
Caliber: 30-06, 9.3x74R, 375 H&H, 458 Win. Mag.
Barrel: 23″, 25.5″.
Weight: 7.7 lbs.
Stock: European walnut, hand-checkered grip and forend.
Sights: Blade front on ramp, open V-notch rear.
Features: Boxlock action (689), sidelock action (SSO) with silvered, engraved receiver; ejectors; double triggers; recoil pad. Imported from Italy by Beretta U.S.A. Corp. Introduced 1984.
Price: S689, 30-06, 9.3x74R $4,907.00
Price: SSO, 375 H&H, 458 Win. Mag.................... $17,533.00
Price: SSO5, 375 H&H, 458 Win. Mag.................... $19,600.00

BRNO SUPER EXPRESS O/U DOUBLE RIFLE
Caliber: 7x65R, 9.3x74R, 375 H&H, 458 Win. Mag.
Barrel: 23½.″
Weight: 8½ to 9 lbs. **Length:** 40″ overall.
Stock: European walnut with raised cheekpiece, skip-line checkering.
Sights: Bead on ramp front, quarter-rib with open rear.
Features: Sidelock action with engraved sideplates; double set triggers; selective automatic ejectors; rubber recoil pad. Barrels regulated for 100 meters. Imported from Czechoslovakia by TD Arms.
Price: $3,900.00

BRNO ZH SERIES 300 COMBINATION GUN
Caliber/Gauge: 5.6x52R/12 ga., 5.6x50R Mag./12, 7x57R/12, 7x57R/16.
Barrel: 23½″ (Full).
Weight: 7.9 lbs. **Length:** 40½″ overall.
Stock: Walnut.
Sights: Bead on blade front, folding leaf rear.
Features: Boxlock action; 8-barrel set for combination calibers and o/u shotgun barrels in 12 ga. (Field, Trap, Skeet) and 16 ga. (Field). Imported from Czechoslovakia by TD Arms.
Price: $3,500.00

CHAPUIS RGEXPRESS MODEL 89 DOUBLE RIFLE
Caliber: 7x65R, 8x57 JRS, 9.3x74R, 375 H&H.
Barrel: 23.6″.
Weight: About 7½ lbs. **Length:** 40.3″ overall.
Stock: European walnut with cheekpiece, oil finish.
Sights: Bead on ramp front, adjustable express rear on quarter-rib.
Features: Boxlock action; engraved, coin-finish receiver. Automatic ejectors, double triggers, double hook barrels. Imported from France by Armes de Chasse.
Price: $6,500.00

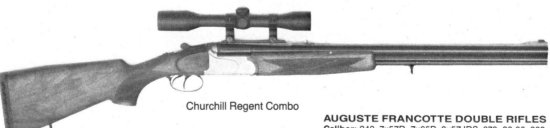

Churchill Regent Combo

CHURCHILL REGENT COMBINATION GUN
Caliber/Gauge: 12 (3″) over 222, 223, 243, 270, 308, 30-06.
Barrel: 25″ (Imp. Mod.)
Weight: 8 lbs. **Length:** 42″ overall.
Stock: Hand checkered European walnut, oil finish, Monte Carlo comb.
Sights: Blade on ramp front, open rear.
Features: Silvered, engraved receiver; double triggers; dovetail scope mount. Imported by Ellett Bros. Introduced 1985.
Price: $739.00

AUGUSTE FRANCOTTE DOUBLE RIFLES
Caliber: 243, 7x57R, 7x65R, 8x57JRS, 270, 30-06, 308, 338, 300 Win. Mag., 9.3x74R, 375 H&H, 416 Rigby, 458 Win. Mag.; others on request.
Barrel: 23½″ standard; other lengths on request.
Weight: 7.61 lbs. (medium calibers), 11.1 lbs. (mag. calibers).
Stock: Fancy European walnut; dimensions to customer specs. Straight or pistol grip style.
Sights: Bead on ramp front, leaf rear on quarter-rib; to customer specs.
Features: Chopper lump barrels; special extractor for rimmed cartridges; back-action sidelocks; double trigger with hinged front trigger. Automatic or free safety. Wide range of options available. Imported from Belgium by Armes de Chasse.
Price: .... NA

Heym 88B Safari

HEYM MODEL 22S SAFETY COMBO GUN

Caliber/Gauge: 16 or 20 ga. (2³/₄″, 3″), 12 ga. (2³/₄″) over 22 Hornet, 22 WMR, 222 Rem., 223, 243 Win., 5.6x50R, 5.6x52R, 6.5x55, 6.5x57R, 7x57R, 8x57 JRS.
Barrel: 24″, solid rib.
Weight: About 5¹/₂ lbs.
Stock: Dark European walnut, hand-checkered p.g. and forend. Oil finish.
Sights: Silver bead ramp front, folding leaf rear.
Features: Tang-mounted cocking slide, separate barrel selector, single set trigger. Base supplied for quick-detachable scope mounts. Patented rocker-weight system automatically uncocks gun if accidentally dropped or bumped hard. Imported from West Germany by Heym America, Inc.
Price: Model 22S **$2,400.00**
Price: Model 22SZ takedown **$2,770.00**
Price: Model 22SM (rail scope mount, 12 ga.) **$2,500.00**
Price: 22SMZ (as above except takedown) **$2,870.00**

HEYM MODEL 88B SAFARI DOUBLE RIFLE

Caliber: 375 H&H, 458 Win. Mag., 470 Nitro Express, 500 Nitro Express.
Action: Boxlock with interceptor sear. Automatic ejectors with disengagement sear.
Barrel: 25″.
Weight: About 10 lbs.
Stock: Best quality Circassian walnut; classic design with cheekpiece; oil finish, hand checkering; Presentation buttpad; steel grip cap.
Sights: Large silver bead on ramp front, quarter-rib with three-leaf express rear.
Features: Double triggers; engraved, silvered frame. Introduced 1985. Imported from West Germany by Paul Jaeger, Inc.
Price: 375 and 458 . . . . **$13,600.00**
Price: 470 Nitro Express, 500 Nitro Express **$13,600.00**

Heym Model 88B

HEYM MODEL 33 BOXLOCK DRILLING

Caliber/Gauge: 5.6x50R Mag., 5.6x52R, 6.5x55, 6.5x57R, 7x57R, 7x65R, 8x57JRS, 9.3x74R, 243, 308, 30-06; 16x16 (2³/₄″), 20x20 (3″).
Barrel: 25″ (Full & Mod.).
Weight: About 6¹/₂ lbs. **Length:** 42″ overall.
Stock: Dark European walnut, checkered p.g. and forend; oil finish.
Sights: Silver bead front, folding leaf rear. Automatic sight positioner. Availalbe with scope and Suhler claw mounts.
Features: Boxlock action with Greener-type cross bolt and safety, double under-lugs. Double set triggers. Plastic or steel trigger guard. Engraving coverage varies with model. Imported from West Germany by Heym America, Inc.
Price: Model 33 Standard **$6,000.00**
Price: Model 33 Deluxe (hunting scene engraving) **$6,400.00**

HEYM MODEL 88B SIDE-BY-SIDE DOUBLE RIFLE

Caliber: 30-06, 8x57JRS, 9.3x74R, 375 H&H.
Barrel: 25″.
Weight: 7¹/₂ lbs. (std. cals.), 8¹/₂ lbs. (mag.). **Length:** 42″ overall.
Stock: Fancy French walnut, classic North American design.
Sights: Silver bead post on ramp front, fixed or three-leaf express rear.
Features: Action has complete coverage hunting scene engraving. Available as boxlock or with q.d. sidelocks. Imported from West Germany by Heym America, Inc.
Price: Boxlock, from **$9,600.00**
Price: Sidelock, Model 88B-SS, from **$13,800.00**
Price: Disengageable ejectors, add **$380.00**

HEYM MODEL 55B/55SS O/U DOUBLE RIFLE

Caliber: 7x65R, 308, 30-06, 8x57JRS, 9.3x74R.
Barrel: 25″.
Weight: About 8 lbs., depending upon caliber. **Length:** 42″ overall.
Stock: Dark European walnut, hand-checkered p.g. and forend. Oil finish.
Sights: Silver bead ramp front, open V-type rear.
Features: Boxlock or full sidelock; Kersten double cross bolt, cocking indicators; hand-engraved hunting scenes. Options available include interchangeable barrels, Zeiss scopes in claw mounts, deluxe engravings and stock carving, etc. Imported from West Germany by Heym America, Inc.
Price: Model 55B boxlock **$7,230.00**
Price: Model 55SS sidelock **$11,230.00**
Price: Interchangeable shotgun barrels, add **$3,200.00**
Price: Interchangeable rifle barrels, add **$4,700.00**

HEYM MODEL 37B DOUBLE RIFLE DRILLING

Caliber/Gauge: 7x65R, 30-06, 8x57JRS, 9.3x74R; 20 ga. (3″).
Barrel: 25″ (shotgun barrel choked Full or Mod.).
Weight: About 8¹/₂ lbs. **Length:** 42″ overall.
Stock: Dark European walnut, hand-checkered p.g. and forend. Oil finish.
Sights: Silver bead front, folding leaf rear. Available with scope and Suhler claw mounts.
Features: Full sidelock construction. Greener-type cross bolt, double under-lugs, cocking indicators. Imported from West Germany by Heym America, Inc.
Price: Model 37B double rifle drilling **$12,000.00**
Price: Model 37B Deluxe (hunting scene engraving) **$13,900.00**

Heym Model 55BF O/U Combo Gun

Similar to Model 55B o/u rifle except chambered for 12, 16, or 20 ga. (2³/₄″ or 3″) over 5.6x50R, 222 Rem., 223 Rem., 5.6x52R, 243, 6.5x57R, 270, 7x57R, 7x65R, 308, 30-06, 8x57JRS, 9.3x74R. Has solid rib barrel. Available with interchangeable shotgun and rifle barrels.
Price: Model 55BF boxlock **$5,200.00**

Heym Model 37 Sidelock Drilling

Similar to Model 37 Double Rifle Drilling except has 12 x 12, 16 x 16 or 20x20 over 5.6x50R Mag., 5.6x52R, 6.5x55, 6.5x57R, 7x57R, 7x65R, 8x57JRS, 9.3x74R, 243, 308 or 30-06. Rifle barrel is manually cocked and uncocked.
Price: Model 37 with border engraving **$9,400.00**
Price: As above with engraved hunting scenes **$11,000.00**

Kodiak Mk. IV

KODIAK MK. IV DOUBLE RIFLE

Caliber: 45-70.
Barrel: 24″.
Weight: 10 lbs. **Length:** 42¹/₂″ overall.
Stock: European walnut with semi-pistol grip.
Sights: Ramp front with bead, adjustable two-leaf rear.
Features: Exposed hammers, color case-hardened locks. Rubber recoil pad. Comes cased. Introduced 1988. Imported from Italy by Trail Guns Armory.
Price: **$1,495.00**

Krieghoff Trumpf

KRIEGHOFF TRUMPF DRILLING
Caliber/Gauge: 12, 16, 20/22 Hornet, 222 Rem., 243, 270, 30-06, 308. Standard European calibers also available.
Barrel: 25″. Shot barrels choked Imp. Mod. & Full. Optional free-floating rifle barrel available.
Weight: About 7½ lbs.
Stock: Hand-checkered European walnut with German-style grip and cheekpiece. Oil finish.
Sights: Bead front, automatic pop-up open rear.
Features: Boxlock action with double or optional single trigger, top tang shotgun safety. Fine, light scroll engraving. Imported from West Germany by Krieghoff International, Inc.
Price: **$6,990.00**
Price: Neptune (full sidelock drilling), from **$11,850.00**

MAPIZ ZANARDINI OXFORD 89 DOUBLE RIFLE
Caliber: 444 Marlin, 7x65R, 6.5x57R, 9.3x74R, 375 H&H, 458 Win. Mag., 465 N.E., 470 N.E., 577 N.E., 600 N.E., 375 Flanged N.E.
Barrel: 24″, 25″, 25½″.
Weight: NA. **Length:** NA.
Stock: European walnut with Bavarian-style cheekpiece, oil finish, rubber or hard buttplate.
Sights: Blade on ramp front, express-type rear.
Features: Boxlock action with extensive engraving; automatic ejectors, double triggers. Introduced 1989. Imported from Italy by Armes de Chasse.
Price: **$6,850.00**

KRIEGHOFF TECK O/U COMBINATION GUN
Caliber/Gauge: 12, 16, 20/22 Hornet, 222, 243, 270, 30-06, 308 and standard European calibers. O/U rifle also available in 458 Win. on special order.
Barrel: 25″ on double rifle or combo. 28″ or o/u shotgun. Optional free-floating rifle barrel available.
Weight: 7-7½ lbs.
Stock: Hand-checkered European walnut with German-style grip and cheekpiece.
Sights: White bead front on shotgun, open or folding on rifle or combo.
Features: Boxlock action with non-selective single trigger or optional single/double trigger. Greener cross bolt. Ejectors standard on all but o/u rifle. Top tang safety. Light scroll engraving. Imported from West Germany by Krieghoff International, Inc.
Price: From .... **$5,450.00 to $8,750.00**
Price: Ulm (full sidelock model) from **$10,500.00**

Perugini-Visini "Selous"

PERUGINI-VISINI MODEL "SELOUS" SIDELOCK DOUBLE RIFLE
Caliber: 30-06, 7mm Rem. Mag., 7x65R, 9.3x74R, 270 Win., 300 H&H, 338 Win., 375 H&H, 458 Win. Mag., 470 Nitro.

Barrel: 22″-26″.
Weight: 7¼ to 10½ lbs., depending upon caliber. **Length:** 41″ overall (24″ bbl.).
Stocks: Oil-finished walnut, checkered grip and forend; cheekpiece.
Sights: Bead on ramp front, express rear on quarter-rib.
Features: True sidelock action with ejectors; sideplates are hand detachable; comes with leather trunk case. Introduced 1983. Imported from Italy by Wm. Larkin Moore.
Price: **$21,800.00**

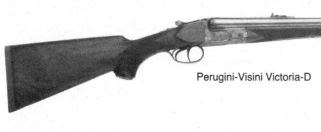

Perugini-Visini Victoria-D

Perugini-Visini Victoria Double Rifles
A boxlock double rifle which shares many of the same features of the Selous model. Calibers 7x65R, 30-06, 9.3x74R, 375 H&H Mag., 458 Win. Mag., 470; double triggers; automatic ejectors. Many options available, including an extra 20-ga. barrel set.
Price: Victoria-M (7x65R, 30-06, 9.3x74R), from about **$6,800.00**
Price: Victoria-D (375, 458, 470), from about **$12,500.00**

Savage 24F

Savage Model 24-V Combination Gun
Similar to the Model 24-F except has walnut-finished hardwood stock, 222, 223 or 30-30 over 20 gauge with 3″ chamber. Introduced 1989.
Price: **$343.50**

Savage Model 24F-12T Turkey Gun
Similar to the Model 24F except has camouflage Rynite stock and extra Full choke tube. Available only in 222 or 223 over 12 gauge with 3″ chamber. Introduced 1989.
Price: **$421.85**

SAVAGE MODEL 24-F O/U
Caliber/Gauge: 222, 223, 30-30 over 12 or 20 ga.
Action: Takedown, low rebounding visible hammer. Single trigger, barrel selector spur on hammer.
Barrel: 24″ separated barrels; 12 ga. has Mod. choke tube, 20 ga. has fixed Mod. choke.
Weight: 7 lbs. **Length:** 40½″ overall.
Stock: Black Rynite composition.
Sights: Ramp front, open rear adjustable for e. Grooved for tip-off scope mount.
Features: Removable butt cap for storage and accessories. Removable grip cap with integral screwdriver, compass. Introduced 1989.
Price: 20 ga. **$390.50**
Price: 12 ga. **$406.15**

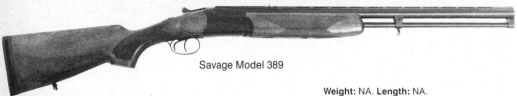

Savage Model 389

SAVAGE MODEL 389 O/U COMBINATION
Caliber/Gauge: 12 ga. over 222 or 308.
Barrel: 25³/₄" separated barrels with floating front mount for windage, elevation adjustment. Has choke tubes.

Weight: NA. **Length:** NA.
Stock: Oil-finished walnut with recoil pad, cut-checkered grip and forend.
Sights: Blade front, folding leaf rear. Vent. rib milled for scope mount.
Features: Matte finish, extractors, double triggers, q.d. swivel studs. Introduced 1988.
Price: **$599.00**

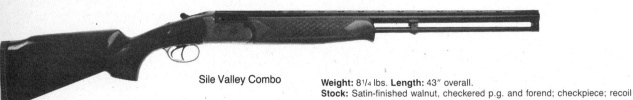

Sile Valley Combo

SILE VALLEY COMBO GUN
Caliber/Gauge: 12 ga. over 222 Rem. or 308 Win., 3" chamber.
Barrel: 23¹/₂" (Cyl.).

Weight: 8¹/₄ lbs. **Length:** 43" overall.
Stock: Satin-finished walnut, checkered p.g. and forend; checkpiece; recoil pad.
Sights: Ramp front, folding rear. Accepts claw-type scope mount.
Features: Automatic safety; double triggers; engraved and silvered receiver. Imported by Sile.
Price: **$679.95**

Valmet 412S Double

VALMET 412S DOUBLE RIFLE
Caliber: 30-06, 9.3x74R.
Barrel: 24".

Weight: 8⁵/₈ lbs.
Stock: American walnut with Monte Carlo style.
Sights: Ramp front, adjustable open rear.
Features: Barrel selector mounted in trigger. Cocking indicators in tang. Recoil pad. Valmet scope mounts available. Interchangeable barrels. Introduced 1980. Imported from Finland by Valmet.
Price: Extractors, 30-06 .... **$1,275.00**
Price: With ejectors, 9.3x74R **$1,315.00**

VALMET 412S COMBINATION GUN
Caliber/Gauge: 12 over 222, 308, 30-06, 9.3x74R.
Barrel: 24" (Imp. Mod.).
Weight: 7⁵/₈ lbs.
Stock: American walnut, with recoil pad. Monte Carlo style. Standard measurements 14"x1³/₅"x2"x2³/₅".
Sights: Blade front, flip-up-type open rear.
Features: Barrel selector on trigger. Hand-checkered stock and forend. Barrels are screw-adjustable to change bullet point of impact. Barrels are interchangeable. Introduced 1980. Imported from Finland by Valmet.
Price: **$1,165.00**
Price: Extra barrels, from **$540.00**

A. ZOLI RIFLE-SHOTGUN O/U COMBO
Caliber/Gauge: 12 ga. over 222, 308 or 30-06.
Barrel: Combo—24", shotgun—28" (Mod. & Full).
Weight: About 8 lbs. **Length:** 41" overall (24" bbl.)
Stock: European walnut.
Sights: Blade front, flip-up rear.
Features: Available with German claw scope mounts on rifle/shotgun barrels. Comes with set of 12/12 (Mod. & Full) barrels. Imported from Italy by Mandall Shooting Supplies.
Price: With two barrel sets **$1,695.00**
Price: As above with claw mounts, scope **$2,495.00**

RIMFIRE RIFLES—AUTOLOADERS

Designs for hunting, utility and sporting purposes, including training for competition.

AMT Lightning 25/22

AMT Lightning Small-Game Hunter Rifle
Same as the Lightning 25/22 except has conventional stock of black fiberglass-filled nylon, checkered at the grip and forend, and fitted with Uncle Mike's swivel studs. Removable recoil pad provides storage for ammo, cleaning rod and survival knife. No iron sights—comes with 4x, 1" scope and mounts. Has a 22" target weight barrel, weighs 6³/₄ lbs., overall length of 40¹/₂". Introduced 1987. From AMT.
Price: With scope **$278.00**

AMT LIGHTNING 25/22 RIFLE
Caliber: 22 LR, 25-shot magazine.
Barrel: 18", tapered or bull.
Weight: 6 lbs. **Length:** 26¹/₂" (folded), 37" (open).
Stock: Folding stainless steel.
Sights: Ramp front, rear adjustable for windage.
Features: Made of stainless steel with matte finish. Receiver dovetailed for scope mounting. Extended magazine release. Standard or "bull" barrel. Youth stock available. Introduced 1984. From AMT.
Price: **$278.00**

Anschutz Model 525

AMERICAN ARMS EXP-64 AUTO RIFLE
Caliber: 22 LR, 10-shot magazine.
Barrel: 21".
Weight: 7 lbs. **Length:** 40" (22" taken down).
Stock: Synthetic. Rifle takes down for storage in buttstock.
Sights: Blade front, adjustable rear.
Features: Quick takedown for storage, carry. Receiver grooved for scope mounting. Cross-boilt safety. Introduced 1989. Imported from Italy by American Arms, Inc.
Price: **$165.00**
Price: With hardwood stock, forend (Model SM-64) **$149.00**

ARMSCOR MODEL 20P AUTO RIFLE
Caliber: 22 LR, 15-shot magazine.
Barrel: 20¾".
Weight: 5.5 lbs. **Length:** 39¾" overall.
Stock: Walnut-finished mahogany.
Sights: Bead front, rear adjustable for e.
Features: Receiver grooved for scope mounting. Blued finish. Introduced 1987. Imported from the Philippines by Armscor.
Price: About.. **$99.95**
Price: Model 2000 (as above except has checkered stock, fully adjustable sight), about **$102.95**

Auto-Ordnance 1927A-3

Browning Auto-22

Browning Auto-22 Grade VI
Same as the Grade I Auto-22 except available with either grayed or blued receiver with extensive engraving with gold-plated animals: right side pictures a fox and squirrel in a woodland scene; left side shows a beagle chasing a rabbit. On top is a portrait of the beagle. Stock and forend are of high-grade walnut with a double-bordered cut checkering design. Introduced 1987.
Price: Grade VI, blue or gray receiver. **$674.95**

CALICO MODEL 100 CARBINE
Caliber: 22 LR, 100-shot magazine.
Barrel: 16".
Weight: 5.7 lbs. (loaded). **Length:** 35.8" overall (stock extended).
Stock: Folding steel.
Sights: Post front adjustable for e., notch rear adjustable for w.
Features: Uses alloy frame and helical-feed magazine; ambidextrous safety; removable barrel assembly; pistol grip compartment; flash suppressor; bolt stop. Made in U.S. From Calico.
Price: **$299.95**

ANSCHUTZ DELUXE MODEL 525 AUTO
Caliber: 22 LR, 10-shot clip.
Barrel: 24".
Weight: 6½ lbs. **Length:** 43" overall.
Stock: European hardwood; checkered pistol grip, Monte Carlo comb, beavertail forend.
Sights: Hooded ramp front, folding leaf rear.
Features: Rotary safety, empty shell deflector, single stage trigger. Receiver grooved for scope mounting. Introduced 1982. Imported from Germany by PSI.
Price: **$435.00**

ARMSCOR AK22 AUTO RIFLE
Caliber: 22 LR, 15-shot magazine.
Barrel: 18½".
Weight: 7 lbs. **Length:** 36" overall.
Stock: Plain mahogany.
Sights: Post front, open rear adjustable for w. and e.
Features: Resembles the AK-47. Matte black finish. Introduced 1987. Imported from the Philippines by Armscor.
Price: About.. **$179.35**
Price: With folding steel stock, about **$199.95**

ARMSCOR MODEL 1600 AUTO RIFLE
Caliber: 22 LR, 15-shot magazine.
Barrel: 18".
Weight: 5¼ lbs. **Length:** 38½" overall.
Stock: Black ebony wood.
Sights: Post front, aperture rear.
Features: Resembles Colt AR-15. Matte black finish. Introduced 1987. Imported from the Philippines by Armscor.
Price: About.. **$126.45**
Price: M1600R (as above except has retractable buttstock, ventilated forend), about...................................... **$139.95**

AUTO-ORDNANCE MODEL 1927A-3
Caliber: 22 LR, 10-, 30- or 50-shot magazine.
Barrel: 16", finned.
Weight: About 7 lbs.
Stock: Walnut stock and forend.
Sights: Blade front, open rear adjustable for windage and elevation.
Features: Recreation of the Thompson Model 1927, only in 22 Long Rifle. Alloy receiver, finned barrel.
Price: **$487.50**

BROWNING AUTO-22 RIFLE
Caliber: 22 LR, 11-shot.
Barrel: 19¼".
Weight: 4¾ lbs. **Length:** 37" overall.
Stock: Checkered select walnut with p.g. and semi-beavertail forend.
Sights: Gold bead front, folding leaf rear.
Features: Engraved receiver with polished blue finish; cross-bolt safety; tubular magazine in buttstock; easy take down for carrying or storage. Imported from Japan by Browning.
Price: Grade I **$328.50**

Calico Model 100

Calico Model 105 Sporter
Similar to the Model 100 except has hand-rubbed wood buttstock and forend. Weight is 4¾ lbs. Introduced 1987.
Price: **$318.95**

Charter AR-7 Explorer

CHARTER AR-7 EXPLORER CARBINE
Caliber: 22 LR, 8-shot clip.
Barrel: 16″ alloy (steel-lined).
Weight: 2¹/₂ lbs. **Length:** 34¹/₂″/16¹/₂″ stowed.
Stock: Moulded black Cycloac, snap-on rubber buttpad.
Sights: Square blade front, aperture rear adjustable for e.
Features: Takedown design stores barrel and action in hollow stock. Light enough to float.
Price: Black, Silvertone or camoflage finish, about $146.25

Daisy Model 2213

DAISY MODEL 2213 AUTO RIFLE
Caliber: 22 LR, 7-shot clip.
Barrel: 19″.
Weight: 6.5 lbs. **Length:** 34.75″ overall.
Stock: Walnut.
Sights: Blade on ramp front, fully adjustable, removable notch rear.
Features: Removable trigger assembly; receiver dovetailed for scope mounting. Introduced 1988.
Price: About. $139.00

Daisy Model 2203 Auto Rifle
Similar to the Model 2213 except has a moulded copolymer stock that is adjustable for length of pull. Introduced 1988.
Price: About. $99.00

Feather SAR-180

Weight: 6.25 lbs. **Length:** 37″ overall.
Stock: Walnut butt, grip, forend.
Sights: Protected post front, adjustable rear; receiver grooved for scope mounting or laser sight.
Features: Top-mounted 165-round magazine, matte blue-black finish. Parts interchange with the American 180. Made in U.S. Introduced 1988. From Feather Industries.
Price: $499.95

FEATHER SAR-180 CARBINE
Caliber: 22 LR, 165-round magazine.
Barrel: 18″.

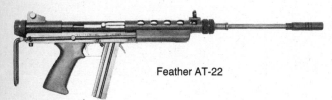

Feather AT-22

FEATHER AT-22 SEMI-AUTO CARBINE
Caliber: 22 LR, 20-shot magazine.
Barrel: 17″.
Weight: 3.25 lbs. **Length:** 34.75″ overall (stock extended).
Stock: Telescoping wire; composition pistol grip.
Sights: Protected post front, adjustable aperture rear.
Features: Removable barrel. Length when folded is 26″. Matte black finish. From Feather Industries. Introduced 1986.
Price: $239.95

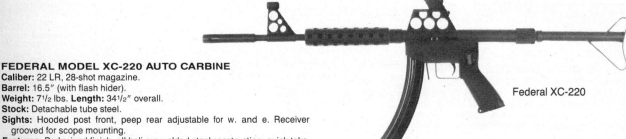

Federal XC-220

FEDERAL MODEL XC-220 AUTO CARBINE
Caliber: 22 LR, 28-shot magazine.
Barrel: 16.5″ (with flash hider).
Weight: 7¹/₂ lbs. **Length:** 34¹/₂″ overall.
Stock: Detachable tube steel.
Sights: Hooded post front, peep rear adjustable for w. and e. Receiver grooved for scope mounting.
Features: Parkerized finish; all heli-arc welded steel construction; quick takedown. From Federal Engineering Corp.
Price: $341.25

HECKLER & KOCH MODEL 300 AUTO RIFLE
Caliber: 22 WMR, 5-shot box mag.
Barrel: 19³/₄″.
Weight: 5³/₄ lbs. **Length:** 39¹/₂″ overall.
Stock: European walnut, Monte Carlo with cheek rest; checkered p.g. and Schnabel forend.

Sights: Post front adjustable for elevation, V-notch rear adjustable for windage.
Features: Polygonal rifling, comes with sling swivels; straight blowback inertia bolt action; single-stage trigger (3¹/₂-lb. pull). Clamp scope mount with 1″ rings available at extra cost. Limited quantity available. Imported from West Germany by Heckler & Koch, Inc.
Price: HK300 . . . . $608.00

CAUTION: PRICES CHANGE. CHECK AT GUNSHOP.

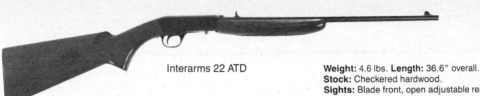

Interarms 22 ATD

INTERARMS MODEL 22 ATD RIFLE
Caliber: 22 LR, 11-shot magazine.
Barrel: 19.4″.

Weight: 4.6 lbs. **Length:** 36.6″ overall.
Stock: Checkered hardwood.
Sights: Blade front, open adjustable rear.
Features: Browning-design takedown action for storage, transport. Cross-bolt safety. Tube magazine loads through buttplate. Blue finish with engraved receiver. Introduced 1987. Imported from China by Interarms.
Price: $179.00
Price: With camoflage case. $195.00

Marlin Model 60

MARLIN 60 SEMI-AUTO RIFLE
Caliber: 22 LR, 17-shot tubular magazine.
Barrel: 22″ round tapered.

Weight: About 5½ lbs. **Length:** 40½″ overall.
Stock: Walnut-finished Monte Carlo, full pistol grip; Mar-Shield® finish.
Sights: Ramp front, open adjustable rear.
Features: Matted receiver is grooved for tip-off mounts. Manual bolt hold-open; automatic last-shot bolt hold-open.
Price: $123.95

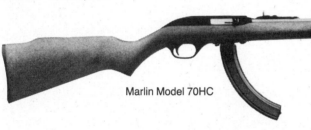

Marlin Model 70HC

MARLIN MODEL 70 HC AUTO
Caliber: 22 LR, 25-shot clip magazine.
Barrel: 18″ (16-groove rifling).
Weight: 5 lbs. **Length:** 36½″ overall.
Stock: Walnut-finished hardwood with Monte Carlo, full p.g. Mar-Shield® finish.
Sights: Ramp front, adjustable open rear. Receiver grooved for scope mount.
Features: Receiver top has serrated, non-glare finish; cross-bolt safety; manual bolt hold-open.
Price: $138.95

Marlin 70P Papoose

Marlin Model 70P Papoose
Similar to the Model 70 except is a takedown model with easily removable barrel—no tools needed. Has 16¼″ Micro-Groove® barrel, walnut-finished hardwood stock, ramp front, adjustable open rear sights, cross-bolt safety. Takedown feature allows removal of barrel without tools. Overall length is 35¼″, weight is 3¾ lbs. Receiver grooved for scope mounting. Comes with 4x scope, mounts and zippered case. Introduced 1986.
Price: With scope $155.95

MARLIN MODEL 995 SEMI-AUTO RIFLE
Caliber: 22 LR, 7-shot clip magazine
Barrel: 18″ Micro-Groove®.
Weight: 5 lbs. **Length:** 36¼″ overall.
Stock: American black walnut, Monte Carlo-style, with full pistol grip. Checkered p.g. and forend; white buttplate spacer; Mar-Shield® finish.
Sights: Ramp bead front with Wide-Scan™ hood; adjustable folding semi-buckhorn rear.
Features: Receiver grooved for tip-off scope mount; bolt hold-open device; cross-bolt safety. Introduced 1979.
Price: $165.95

MARLIN MODEL 75C SEMI-AUTO RIFLE
Caliber: 22 LR, 13-shot tubular magazine.
Barrel: 18″.
Weight: 5 lbs. **Length:** 36½″ overall.
Stock: Walnut-finished hardwood; Monte Carlo with full p.g.
Sights: Ramp front, adjustable open rear.
Features: Manual bolt hold-open; automatic last-shot bolt hold-open; cross-bolt safety; receiver grooved for scope mounting.
Price: $123.95

Mitchell AK-22

MITCHELL AK-22 SEMI-AUTO RIFLE
Caliber: 22 LR, 20-shot magazine; 22 WMR, 10-shot magazine.
Barrel: 16½″.
Weight: 3.1 lbs. **Length:** 38″ overall.
Stock: European walnut.
Sights: Post front, open adjustable rear.
Features: Replica of the AK-47 assault rifle. Wide magazine to maintain appearance. Imported from Italy by Mitchell Arms.
Price: 22 LR. $279.68
Price: 22 WMR $296.87

Mitchell M-16/22

MITCHELL M-16/22 RIFLE
Caliber: 22 LR.
Barrel: 18.5".
Weight: 6.1 lbs. **Length:** 39" overall.
Stock: Black composition.
Sights: Adjustable post front, adjustable aperture rear.
Features: Replica of the AR-15 rifle. Full width magazine. Comes with military-type sling. Introduced 1987. Imported by Mitchell Arms, Inc.
Price: 22 LR $279.68

MITCHELL PPS/50 RIFLE
Caliber: 22 LR, 20-shot magazine (50-shot drum optional).
Barrel: 16½".
Weight: 5¾ lbs. **Length:** 31" overall.
Stock: Walnut.
Sights: Blade front, adjustable rear.
Features: Full-length perforated barrel shroud. Matte finish. Introduced 1989. Imported by Mitchell Arms.
Price: With 20-shot "banana" magazine $279.68
Price: With 50-shot drum magazine $329.63

MITCHELL GALIL/22 AUTO RIFLE
Caliber: 22 LR, 20-shot magazine; 22 WMR, 10-shot magazine.
Barrel: 16.5".
Weight: 5.7 lbs. **Length:** 36" overall.
Stock: European walnut butt, grip, forend.
Sights: Post front adjustable for elevation, rear adjustable for windage.
Features: Replica of the Israeli Galil rifle. Introduced 1987. Imported by Mitchell Arms, Inc.
Price: 22 LR $279.68
Price: 22 WMR $296.87

Mitchell MAS/22

MITCHELL MAS/22 AUTO RIFLE
Caliber: 22 LR, 20-shot magazine.
Barrel: 16.5".
Weight: 4.7 lbs. **Length:** 28.5" overall.
Stock: Walnut butt, grip and forend.
Sights: Adjustable post front, flip-type aperture rear.
Features: Bullpup design resembles French armed forces rifle. Top cocking lever, flash hider. Introduced 1987. Imported by Mitchell Arms, Inc.
Price: 22 LR $279.68

Remington 552 BDL

REMINGTON 552BDL SPEEDMASTER RIFLE
Caliber: 22 S (20), L (17) or LR (15) tubular mag.
Barrel: 21" round tapered.
Weight: About 5¾ lbs. **Length:** 40" overall.
Stock: Walnut. Checkered grip and forend.
Sights: Bead front, step open rear adjustable for w. and e.
Features: Positive cross-bolt safety, receiver grooved for tip-off mount.
Price: About $198.00

Ruger 10/22 RB

RUGER 10/22 AUTOLOADING CARBINE
Caliber: 22 LR, 10-shot rotary magazine.
Barrel: 18½" round tapered.
Weight: 5 lbs. **Length:** 37¼" overall.
Stock: American hardwood with p.g. and bbl. band.
Sights: Gold bead front, folding leaf rear adjustable for e.
Features: Detachable rotary magazine fits flush into stock, cross-bolt safety, receiver tapped and grooved for scope blocks or tip-off mount. Scope base adapter furnished with each rifle.
Price: Model 10/22 RB (birch stock) $183.00
Price: Model 10/22 R (American walnut stock) $203.85

TRADEWINDS MODEL 260-A AUTO RIFLE
Caliber: 22 LR, 5-shot (10-shot mag. avail.).
Barrel: 22½".
Weight: 5¾ lbs. **Length:** 41½".
Stock: Walnut. with hand checkered p.g. and forend.
Sights: Ramp front with hood, three-leaf folding rear, receiver grooved for scope mount.
Features: Double extractors, sliding safety. Imported by Tradewinds.
Price: $250.00

Ruger 10/22 Auto Sporter
Same as 10/22 Carbine except walnut stock with hand checkered p.g. and forend; straight buttplate, no barrel band, has sling swivels.
Price: Model 10/22 DSP $231.00

CAUTION: PRICES CHANGE. CHECK AT GUNSHOP.

Weatherby Mark XXII

VOERE MODEL 2115 AUTO RIFLE
Caliber: 22 LR, 8- or 15-shot magazine.
Barrel: 18.1".
Weight: 5.75 lbs. **Length:** 37.7" overall.
Stock: Walnut-finished beechwood with cheekpiece; checkered pistol grip and forend.
Sights: Post front with hooded ramp, leaf rear.
Features: Clip-fed autoloader with single stage trigger, wing-type safety. Imported from Austria by L. Joseph Rahn. Introduced 1984.
Price: Model 2115 . . . . $325.00
Price: Model 2114S (as above except no cheekpiece, checkering or white line spacers at grip, buttplate). $330.00

WEATHERBY MARK XXII AUTO RIFLE, CLIP MODEL
Caliber: 22 LR only, 5- or 10-shot clip.
Barrel: 24" round contoured.
Weight: 6 lbs. **Length:** 42¼" overall.
Stocks: Walnut, Monte Carlo comb and cheekpiece, rosewood p.g. cap and forend tip. Skip-line checkering.
Sights: Gold bead ramp front, three-leaf folding rear.
Features: Thumb operated tang safety. Single shot or semi-automatic side lever selector. Receiver grooved for tip-off scope mount. Single pin release for quick takedown.
Price: $454.00

Weatherby Mark XXII Tubular Model
Same as Mark XXII Clip Model except 15-shot tubular magazine.
Price: $454.00

RIMFIRE RIFLES—LEVER & SLIDE ACTIONS

Classic and modern models for sport and utility, including training.

AMAC Targetmaster

AMAC TARGETMASTER RIFLE
Caliber: 22 Long Rifle (19 Short, 15 Long, 12 Long Rifle).
Barrel: 18".
Weight: 5¾ lbs. **Length:** 36½" overall.
Stock: Walnut-finished hardwood.
Sights: Hooded ramp front, open adjustable rear.
Features: Polished blue finish. Receiver grooved for scope mounting. Introduced 1985. From Iver Johnson.
Price: Standard or Youth Model $166.50

AMAC Wagonmaster

AMAC WAGONMASTER RIFLE
Caliber: 22 Long Rifle (21 Short, 17 Long, 15 Long Rifle), 22 WMR (12-shot magazine).
Barrel: 19".
Weight: 5¾ lbs. **Length:** 36½" overall.
Stock: Walnut-finished hardwood.
Sights: Hooded ramp front, open adjustable rear.
Features: Polished blue finish. Receiver grooved for scope mounting. Introduced 1985. From Iver Johnson.
Price: 22 Long Rifle. $166.50
Price: 22 WMR $187.50

Browning BL-22

BROWNING BL-22 LEVER-ACTION RIFLE
Caliber: 22 S (22), L (17) or LR (15). Tubular magazine.
Barrel: 20" round tapered.
Weight: 5 lbs. **Length:** 36¾" overall.
Stock: Walnut, two-piece straight grip Western style.
Sights: Bead post front, folding-leaf rear.
Features: Short throw lever, half-cock safety, receiver grooved for tip-off scope mounts. Imported from Japan by Browning.
Price: Grade I $286.95
Price: Grade II (engraved receiver, checkered grip and forend). $326.95

Marlin Golden 39AS

MARLIN GOLDEN 39AS LEVER-ACTION RIFLE
Caliber: 22 S (26), L (21), LR (19), tubular magazine.
Barrel: 24" Micro-Groove®.
Weight: 6¹/₂ lbs. **Length:** 40" overall.

Stock: American black walnut with white line spacers at p.g. cap and butt-plate; Mar-Shield® finish. Swivel studs.
Sights: Bead ramp front with detachable Wide-Scan™ hood, folding rear semi-buckhorn adjustable for w. and e.
Features: Hammer-block safety; rebounding hammer. Takedown action, receiver tapped for scope mount (supplied), offset hammer spur; gold-plated steel trigger.
Price: $338.95

Marlin 39TDS

MARLIN MODEL 39TDS CARBINE
Caliber: 22 S (16), 22 L (12), 22 LR (10).
Barrel: 16¹/₂" Micro-Groove®.
Weight: 5¹/₄ lbs. **Length:** 32⁵/₈" overall.

Stock: American black walnut with straight grip; short forend with blued tip. Mar-Shield® finish.
Sights: Ramp front with Wide-Scan™ hood, adjustable semi-buckhorn rear.
Features: Takedown style, comes with carrying case. Hammer-block safety, rebounding hammer; blued metal, gold-plated steel trigger. Introduced 1988.
Price: With case $376.95

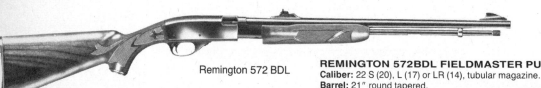

Remington 572 BDL

REMINGTON 572BDL FIELDMASTER PUMP RIFLE
Caliber: 22 S (20), L (17) or LR (14), tubular magazine.
Barrel: 21" round tapered.
Weight: 5¹/₂ lbs. **Length:** 42" overall.
Stock: Walnut with checkered p.g. and slide handle.
Sights: Blade ramp front; sliding ramp rear adjustable for w. and e.
Features: Cross-bolt safety; removing inner magazine tube converts rifle to single shot; receiver grooved for tip-off scope mount.
Price: About....................................... $208.00

Rossi 62 SA

Rossi 62 SAC Carbine
Same as standard model except 22 LR only, has 16¹/₄" barrel. Magazine holds slightly fewer cartridges.
Price: Blue.. $195.00
Price: Nickel $210.00

ROSSI 62 SA PUMP RIFLE
Caliber: 22 LR, 22 WMR.
Barrel: 23", round or octagon.
Weight: 5³/₄ lbs. **Length:** 39¹/₄" overall.
Stock: Walnut, straight grip, grooved forend.
Sights: Fixed front, adjustable rear.
Features: Capacity 20 Short, 16 Long or 14 Long Rifle. Quick takedown. Imported from Brazil by Interarms.
Price: Blue.. $195.00
Price: Nickel $210.00
Price: Blue, with octagon barrel $220.00
Price: 22 WMR, as Model 59 .... $240.00

Winchester 9422

Winchester 9422M Lever-Action Rifle
Same as the 9422 except chambered for 22 WMR cartridge, has 11-round mag. capacity.
Price: About... $331.00
Price: With Win-Cam green stock, about $335.00
Price: With Win-Tuff brown laminated stock, about $335.00

WINCHESTER 9422 LEVER-ACTION RIFLE
Caliber: 22 S (21), L (17), LR (15), tubular mag.
Barrel: 20¹/₂".
Weight: 6¹/₄ lbs. **Length:** 37¹/₈" overall.
Stock: American walnut, two-piece, straight grip (no p.g.).
Sights: Hooded ramp front, adjustable semi-buckhorn rear.
Features: Side ejection; receiver grooved for scope mounting, takedown action. Has XTR wood and metal finish. Made under license by U.S. Repeating Arms Co.
Price: About.. $323.00
Price: With Win-Tuff laminated stock, about............ $331.00

CAUTION: PRICES CHANGE. CHECK AT GUNSHOP.

Includes models for a variety of sports, utility and competitive shooting.

Anschutz 1416/1516

Anschutz 1418D/1518D Deluxe Rifles

Similar to the 1416D/1516D rifles except has full-length Mannlicher-style stock, shorter 19³/₄″ barrel. Weighs 5¹/₂ lbs. Stock has buffalo horn Schnabel tip. Double set trigger available on special order. Model 1418D chambered for 22 LR, 1518D for 22 WMR Imported from Germany by PSI.

Price: 1418D $830.00
Price: 1518D $847.00

ANSCHUTZ DELUXE 1416/1516 RIFLES

Caliber: 22 LR (1416D), 5-shot clip; 22 WMR (1516D), 4-shot clip.
Barrel: 22¹/₂″.
Weight: 6 lbs. **Length:** 41″ overall.
Stock: European walnut; Monte Carlo with cheekpiece, Schnabel forend, checkered pistol grip and forend.
Sights: Hooded ramp front, folding leaf rear.
Features: Uses Model 1403 target rifle action. Adjustable single stage trigger. Receiver grooved for scope mounting. Imported from Germany by PSI.
Price: 1416D, 22 LR $552.00
Price: 1516D, 22 WMR $589.00
Price: 1416D Classic left-hand $630.00

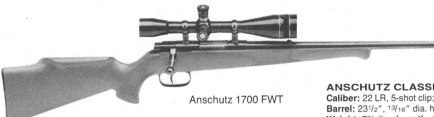

Anschutz 1700 FWT

Anschutz 1700 FWT Bolt-Action Rifle

Similar to the Anschutz Custom except has McMillan fiberglass stock with Monte Carlo, roll-over cheekpiece, Wundhammar swell, and checkering. Comes without sights but the receiver is drilled and tapped for scope mounting. Has 24″ barrel, single stage #5095 trigger. Introduced 1989.
Price: $995.00

ANSCHUTZ CLASSIC 1700 RIFLES

Caliber: 22 LR, 5-shot clip; 22 WMR, 4-shot clip.
Barrel: 23¹/₂″, ¹³/₁₆″ dia. heavy.
Weight: 7³/₄ lbs. **Length:** 42¹/₂″ overall.
Stock: Select European walnut with checkered pistol grip and forend.
Sights: None furnished, drilled and tapped for scope mounting.
Features: Adjustable single stage trigger. Receiver drilled and tapped for scope mounting. Introduced 1988. Imported from Germany by PSI.
Price: 22 LR $958.50
Price: 22 WMR $1,015.00

Anschutz Bavarian

Anschutz Custom 1700 Rifles

Similar to the Classic models except have roll-over Monte Carlo cheekpiece, slim forend with schnabel tip, Wundhammar palm swell on pistol grip, rosewood grip cap with white diamond insert. Skip-line checkering on grip and forend. Introduced 1988. Imported from Germany by PSI.

Price: 22 LR $999.50
Price: 22 WRM $1,029.00

ANSCHUTZ BAVARIAN BOLT-ACTION RIFLE

Caliber: 22 LR, 22 WMR, 5-shot clip.
Barrel: 24″.
Weight: 7¹/₄ lbs. **Length:** 43″ overall.
Stock: European walnut with Bavarian cheek rest. Checkered p.g. and forend.
Sights: Hooded ramp front, folding leaf rear.
Features: Uses the improved 1700 Match 54 action with adjustable 5096 trigger. Drilled and tapped for scope mounting. Introduced in 1988. Imported from Germany by Precision Sales International.
Price: 22 LR $999.50
Price: 22 WMR $1,029.00

Anschutz Achiever

ANSHUTZ ACHIEVER BOLT-ACTION RIFLE

Caliber: 22 LR, 5-shot clip.
Barrel: 19¹/₂″.
Weight: 5 lbs. **Length:** 35¹/₂″ to 36²/₃″ overall.
Stock: Walnut-finished hardwood with adjustable buttplate, vented forend, stippled pistol grip. Length of pull adjustable from 11⁷/₈″ to 13″.
Sights: Hooded front, open rear adjustable for w. and e.
Features: Uses Mark 2000-type action with adjustable two-stage trigger. Receiver grooved for scope mounting. Designed for training in junior rifle clubs and for starting young shooters. Introduced 1987. Imported from West Germany by PSI.
Price: $319.50
Price: Sight Set #1 .... $54.00

Beeman/HW 60J-ST

BEEMAN/HW 60J-ST BOLT ACTION RIFLE
Caliber: 22 LR.
Barrel: 22.8".
Weight: 6.5 lbs. **Length:** 41.7" overall.
Stock: Walnut with cheekpiece, cut checkered p.g. and forend.
Sights: Hooded blade on ramp front, open rear.
Features: Polished blue finish; oil-finished walnut. Imported from West Germany by Beeman. Introduced 1988.
Price: **$488.00**

Armscor Model 1500 Rifle
Similar to the Model 14P except chambered for 22 WMR. Has 21.5" barrel, double lug bolt, checkered stock, weighs 6.5 lbs. Introduced 1987.
Price: About **$149.95**

BRNO ZKM 452 BOLT-ACTION RIFLE
Caliber: 22 LR, 5- or 10-shot magazine.
Barrel: 25".
Weight: 6 lbs., 10 oz. **Length:** 43½" overall.
Stock: Beechwood.
Sights: Hooded bead front, open rear adjustable for e.
Features: Blue finish; oiled stock with checkered p.g. Imported from Czechoslovakia by TD Arms.
Price: **$399.00**

ARMSCOR MODEL 14P BOLT-ACTION RIFLE
Caliber: 22 LR, 5-shot magazine.
Barrel: 23".
Weight: 6 lbs. **Length:** 41.5" overall.
Stock: Walnut-finished mahogany.
Sights: Bead front, rear adjustable for e.
Features: Receiver grooved for scope mounting. Blued finish. Introduced 1987. Imported from the Philippines by Armscor.
Price: About **$101.35**

> Consult our Directory pages for
> the location of firms mentioned.

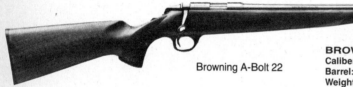

Browning A-Bolt 22

Browning A-Bolt Gold Medallion
Similar to the standard A-Bolt except stock is of high-grade walnut with brass spacers between stock and rubber recoil pad and between the rosewood grip cap and forend. Medallion-style engraving covers the receiver flats, and the words "Gold Medallion" are engraved and gold filled on the right side of the barrel. High gloss stock finish. Introduced 1988.
Price: **$449.95**

BROWNING A-BOLT 22 BOLT-ACTION RIFLE
Caliber: 22 LR, 22 WMR, 5-shot magazines standard.
Barrel: 22".
Weight: 5 lbs., 9 oz. **Length:** 40¼" overall.
Stock: Walnut with cut checkering, rosewood grip cap and forend tip.
Sights: Offered with or without open sights. Open sight model has ramp front and adjustable folding leaf rear.
Features: Short 60-degree bolt throw. Top tang safety. Grooved for 22 scope mount. Drilled and tapped for full-size scope mounts. Detachable magazines. Gold-colored trigger preset at about 4 lbs. Imported from Japan by Browning. Introduced 1986.
Price: A-Bolt 22, no sights **$339.95**
Price: A-Bolt 22, with open sights **$349.95**
Price: A-Bolt 22 WMR, no sights **$389.95**
Price: As above, with sights **$399.95**

Cabanas Master

Cabanas Espronceda IV Bolt-Action Rifle
Similar to the Leyre model except has full sporter stock, 18¾" barrel, 40" overall length, weighs 5½ lbs.
Price: **$119.95**

CABANAS LASER RIFLE
Caliber: 177.
Barrel: 19".
Weight: 6 lbs., 12 oz. **Length:** 42" overall.
Stock: Target-type thumbhole.
Sights: Blade front, open fully adjustable rear.
Features: Fires round ball or pellets with 22 blank cartridge. Imported from Mexico by Mandall Shooting Supplies.
Price: **$159.95**

CABANAS MASTER BOLT-ACTION RIFLE
Caliber: 177, round ball or pellet; single shot.
Barrel: 19½".
Weight: 8 lbs. **Length:** 45½" overall.
Stocks: Walnut target-type with Monte Carlo.
Sights: Blade front, fully adjustable rear.
Features: Fires round ball or pellet with 22-cal. blank cartridge. Bolt action. Imported from Mexico by Mandall Shooting Supplies. Introduced 1984.
Price: **$150.00**
Price: Varmint model (has 21½" barrel, 4½ lbs., 41" o.a.l., varmint-type stock) **$109.95**

Cabanas Leyre Bolt-Action Rifle
Similar to Master model except 44" overall, has sport/target stock.
Price: **$134.95**
Price: Model R83 (17" barrel, hardwood stock, 40" o.a.l.) **$79.95**
Price: Mini 82 Youth (16½" barrel, 33" o.a.l., 3½ lbs.) **$69.95**
Price: Pony Youth (16" barrel, 34" o.a.l., 3.2 lbs.) **$79.95**
Price: Safari **$99.95**

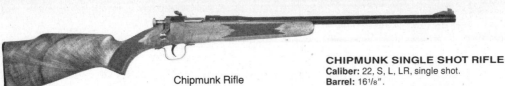

Chipmunk Rifle

CHIPMUNK SINGLE SHOT RIFLE
Caliber: 22, S, L, LR, single shot.
Barrel: 16¹/₈″.
Weight: About 2¹/₂ lbs. **Length:** 30″ overall.
Stocks: American walnut, or camouflage.
Sights: Post on ramp front, peep rear adjustable for windage and elevation.
Features: Drilled and tapped for scope mounting using special Chipmunk base ($9.95). Made in U.S.A. Introduced 1982. From Oregon Arms.
Price: **$129.95**
Price: Deluxe Model with hand checkered fancy stock **$179.95**

Daisy Legacy 2202

DAISY LEGACY 2202 BOLT-ACTION REPEATER
Caliber: 22 LR, 10-shot rotary magazine.
Barrel: 19″. Octagonal barrel shroud.
Weight: 6.5 lbs. **Length:** 34.75″ to 36.75″ (variable).
Stock: Moulded lightweight copolymer.
Sights: Blade on ramp front, fully adjustable removeable rear.
Features: Adjustable buttstock length; removeable bolt and trigger assembly; barrel interchanges with smoothbore unit. Receiver dovetailed for scope mounting. Introduced 1988. Made in U.S. by Daisy.
Price: About **$89.00**

Daisy Legacy 2212 Bolt-Action Repeater
Same as the Model 2202 except has walnut stock, fixed length of pull.
Price: About **$129.00**

DAISY LEGACY 2201 BOLT-ACTION SINGLE SHOT
Caliber: 22 LR.
Barrel: 19″. Octagonal barrel shroud.
Weight: 6.5 lbs. **Length:** 34.75″ to 36.75″ (variable).
Stock: Moulded copolymer.
Sights: Blade on ramp front, fully adjustable removeable notch rear.
Features: Adjustable buttstock length; removeable bolt and trigger assembly; adjustable trigger pull; barrel interchanges with smoothbore unit. Receiver dovetailed for scope mounting. Introduced 1988. Made in U.S. by Daisy.
Price: About **$79.00**

Daisy Legacy 2211 Bolt-Action Single Shot
Same gun as the Model 2201 except comes with walnut stock, fixed length of pull.
Price: About **$119.00**

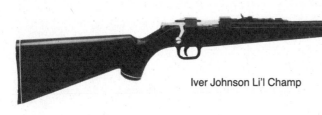

Iver Johnson Li'l Champ

IVER JOHNSON LI'L CHAMP RIFLE
Caliber: 22 S, L, LR, single shot.
Barrel: 16¹/₄″.
Weight: 3 lbs., 2 oz. **Length:** 32¹/₂″ overall.
Stock: Moulded composition.
Sights: Blade on ramp front, adjustable rear.
Features: Sized for junior shooters. Nickel-plated bolt. Made in U.S.A. Introduced 1986. From Iver Johnson.
Price: **$91.50**

Kimber 82B

KIMBER MODEL 82B BOLT-ACTION RIFLE
Caliber: 22 LR, 5-shot detachable magazine.
Barrel: 22″; 6-grooves; 1-in-16″ twist.
Weight: About 6¹/₄ lbs. **Length:** 40¹/₂″ overall (Sporter).
Stock: Super Grade is of AAA Claro walnut with ebony forend tip, beaded cheekpiece, hand checkered 20 lpi borderless, full coverage, wrap-around; Niedner-style buttplate, fully inletted swivel studs.
Sights: Hooded ramp front with bead, folding leaf rear (optional).
Features: High quality, adult-sized, bolt-action rifle. Barrel screwed into receiver; rocker-type silent safety; twin rear locking lugs. All steel construction. Fully adjustable trigger; round-top receiver with bases for Kimber scope mounts. High polish blue. Barreled actions available. Also available in true left-hand version in selected models. Made in U.S.A. Introduced 1979. Contact Kimber for full details.
Price: Deluxe Grade **$995.00**
Price: Super Grade **$1,095.00**
Price: Deluxe Grade, left-hand. .... **P.O.R.**
Price: Continental (Mannlicher stock, 18″ bbl.). .... **P.O.R.**

Kimber Model 82, 84 Super Grade
Super-grade version of the Models 82 and 84. Has the Classic stock only of specially selected, high-grade, California Claro walnut, with Continental beaded cheekpiece and ebony forend tip; borderless, full-coverage 20 lpi checkering; Niedner-type checkered steel buttplate. Options include barrel quarter-rib with express rear sight. Available in 22 Long Rifle, 17 Rem., Rem., 221 Rem., 223 Rem.
Price: Model 82 22 Long Rifle **$1,095.00**
Price: Model 84, 17, 221, 223 .... **$1,250.00**

Marlin 880

MARLIN 880 BOLT-ACTION RIFLE
Caliber: 22 LR; 7-shot clip magazine.
Barrel: 22″ Micro-Groove®.
Weight: 5½ lbs. **Length:** 41″.
Stock: Monte Carlo American black walnut with checkered p.g. and forend. Rubber buttpad, swivel studs. Mar-Shield® finish.
Sights: Wide-Scan® ramp front, folding semi-buckhorn rear adjustable for w. and e.
Features: Receiver grooved for tip-off scope mount. Introduced 1989.
Price: **$181.95**

Marlin 881 Bolt-Action Rifle
Same as the Marlin 880 except tubular magazine, holds 17 Long Rifle cartridges. Weight 6 lbs.
Price: **$188.95**

Marlin 883

Marlin 883 Bolt-Action Rifle
Same as Marlin 882 except tubular magazine holds 12 rounds of 22 WMR ammunition.
Price: **$207.95**

Marlin 882 Bolt-Action Rifle
Same as the Marlin 880 except 22 WMR cal. only with 7-shot clip magazine, weight about 6 lbs. Comes with swivel studs.
Price: **$199.95**

Marlin 25N Bolt-Action Repeater
Similar to Marlin 880, except walnut-finished p.g. stock, adjustable open rear sight, ramp front.
Price: **$131.95**

Marlin 25 MN

Marlin Model 25MN Bolt-Action Rifle
Similar to the Model 25N except chambered for 22 WMR. Has 7-shot clip magazine, 22″ Micro-Groove® barrel, walnut-finished hardwood stock. Introduced 1989.
Price: **$150.95**

Marlin 15YN

MARLIN 15YN "LITTLE BUCKAROO"
Caliber: 22 LR, single shot.
Barrel: 16¼″ Micro-Groove®.
Weight: 4¼ lbs. **Length:** 33¼″ overall.
Stock: One-piece walnut-finished hardwood with Monte Carlo; Mar-Shield® finish.
Sights: Ramp front, adjustable open rear.
Features: Beginner's rifle with thumb safety, easy-load feed throat, red cocking indicator. Receiver grooved for scope mounting. Introduced 1989.
Price: **$126.95**

RSR/Anschutz Woodchucker

RSR/ANSCHUTZ WOODCHUCKER RIFLE
Caliber: 22 LR, 5-shot clip.
Barrel: 16¼″.
Weight: 3 lbs., 10 oz. **Length:** 32¼″ overall.
Stock: Hardwood; 12″ length of pull.
Sights: Bead front, U-notch rear with step elevator.
Features: Dual opposing extractors; receiver grooved for scope mounting. Made in Germany by Anschutz; imported by RSR Wholesale Guns, Inc.
Price: **$175.95**

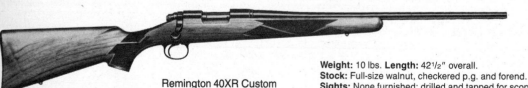

Remington 40XR Custom

Weight: 10 lbs. **Length:** 42½″ overall.
Stock: Full-size walnut, checkered p.g. and forend.
Sights: None furnished; drilled and tapped for scope mounting.
Features: Customer Shop gun. Duplicates Model 700 centerfire rifle.
Price: Grade 1 . . . . **$1,263.00**
Price: Grade II **$2,245.00**
Price: Grade III **$3,508.00**
Price: Grade IV **$5,473.00**

REMINGTON 40XR RIMFIRE CUSTOM SPORTER
Caliber: 22 LR.
Barrel: 24″.

Remington Model 541-T

REMINGTON MODEL 541-T
Caliber: 22 S, L, LR, 5-shot clip.
Barrel: 24".
Weight: 5⅞ lbs. **Length:** 42½" overall.
Stock: Walnut, cut-checkered p.g. and forend. Satin finish.
Sights: None. Drilled and tapped for scope mounts.
Features: Clip repeater. Thumb safety. Re-introduced 1986.
Price: About **$333.00**

Remington 581-S

REMINGTON MODEL 581-S "SPORTSMAN" RIFLE
Caliber: 22 S, L or LR. 5-shot clip magazine.
Barrel: 24" round.
Weight: 4¾ lbs. **Length:** 42⅜" overall.
Stock: Walnut finished hardwood, Monte Carlo with p.g.
Sights: Bead post front, screw adjustable open rear.
Features: Sliding side safety, wide trigger, receiver grooved for tip-off scope
mounts. Comes with single-shot adapter. Reintroduced 1986.
Price: About **$184.00**

Ruger 77/22

Features: Mauser-type action uses Ruger's 10-shot rotary magazine. Three-
position safety, simplified bolt stop, patented bolt locking system. Uses the
dual screw barrel attachemnt system of the 10/22 rifle. Integral scope
mounting system with 1" Ruger rings. Blued model introduced in 1983.
Stainless steel model and blued model with the synthetic stock introduced
in 1989.
Price: 77/22R (no sights, rings, walnut stock) **$364.50**
Price: 77/22S (open sights, walnut stock). **$364.50**
Price: 77/22RS (open sights, rings, walnut stock) **$364.50**
Price: 77/22RP (no sights, rings, synthetic stock) **$300.00**
Price: 77/22SP (open sights, synthetic stock) **$300.00**
Price: 77/22RSP (open sights, rings, synthetic stock) **$320.00**
Price: K77/22RP (stainless, no sights, rings, synthetic stock) **$360.00**
Price: K77/22SP (stainless, open sights, synthetic stock) **$360.00**
Price: K77/22RSP (stainless, open sights, rings, synthetic stock). . . **$380.00**

RUGER 77/22 RIMFIRE BOLT-ACTION RIFLE
Caliber: 22 Long Rifle, 10-shot rotary magazine.
Barrel: 20".
Weight: About 5¾ lbs. **Length:** 39¾" overall.
Stock: Checkered American walnut or injection-moulded Du Pont Zytel rein-
forced with nylon.
Sights: Gold bead front, adjustable folding leaf rear or plain barrel with 1"
Ruger rings.

Varner Favorite

VARNER FAVORITE SINGLE SHOT RIFLE
Caliber: 22 LR.
Barrel: 21½"; half-round, half-octagon.
Weight: 5 lbs.
Stock: American walnut.
Sights: Blade front, open step-adjustable rear and peep.
Features: Recreation of the Stevens Favorite rifle with takedown barrel. Target
grade barrel. Made in U.S. Introduced 1988. From Varner Sporting Arms,
Inc.
Price: Hunter Grade (checkered walnut) **$369.00**
Price: Hunter Deluxe (AAA Fancy walnut) **$499.00**
Price: Presentation Grade (AAA Fancy walnut, checkered grip and forend, in-
cludes hard custom takedown case) **$569.00**

Varner Favorite Schuetzen
Similar to the Favorite except is a recreation of the Stevens Ladies Favorite
Schuetzen (1910-1916). Color case-hardened frame and lever hand engraved wtih Ulrich-style scrolls. Pistol grip perch belly stock, extended
forend of AAA Fancy walnut with extensive checkering. Ladder-style, tang-
mounted peep sight adjustable for windage and elevation, globe-type front
with six inserts. Has 24" target-grade barrel, half-round, half-octagon. Introduced 1989.
Price: **$1,000.00**

Voere Model 1007/1013

Weight: About 5½ lbs. (M1007).
Stock: Oil-finished beechwood.
Sights: Hooded front, open adjustable rear.
Features: Single-stage trigger (M1013 available with double set). Military-look
stock; sling swivels. Convertible to single shot. Imported from Austria by L.
Joseph Rahn. Introduced 1984.
Price: 1007 Biathlon **$310.00**
Price: 1013, 22 WMR **$350.00**

VOERE MODEL 1007/1013 BOLT-ACTION RIFLE
Caliber: 22 LR (M1007 Biathlon), 22 WMR (M1013).
Barrel: 18".

Includes models for classic American and ISU target competition and other sporting and competitive shooting.

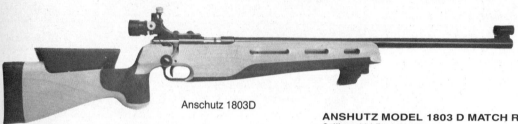

Anschutz 1803D

ANSCHUTZ MODEL 64-MS, 64-MS LEFT
Caliber: 22 LR, single shot.
Barrel: 21³/₄″, medium heavy; ⁷/₈″ diameter.
Weight: 8 lbs., 1 oz. **Length:** 39¹/₂″ overall.
Stock: Walnut-finished hardwood, silhouette-type.
Sights: None furnished. Receiver drilled and tapped for scope mounting.
Features: Designed for metallic silhouette competition. Stock has stippled checkering, contoured thumb groove with Wundhammer swell. Two-stage #5091 trigger. Slide safety locks sear and bolt. Introduced 1980. Imported from West Germany by PSI.
Price: Model 64-MS **$717.00**
Price: Model 64-MS Left **$793.00**

Anschutz Model 54.18 MS Silhouette Rifle
Same basic features as Anschutz 1913 Super Match but with special metallic silhoutte European hardwood stock and two-stage trigger. Has 22″ barrel; receiver drilled and tapped.
Price: **$1,212.00**
Price: Model 54.18 MSL (true left-hand version of above) **$1,273.00**

ANSHUTZ MODEL 1803 D MATCH RIFLE
Caliber: 22 LR, single shot.
Barrel: 25¹/₂″, ³/₄″ diameter.
Weight: 8.6 lbs. **Length:** 43³/₄″ overall.
Stock: Walnut-finished hardwood with adjustable cheekpiece; stippled grip and forend.
Sights: None furnished.
Features: Uses Anshultz Match 64 action and #5091 two-stage trigger. A medium weight rifle for intermediate and advanced Junior Match competition. Introduced 1987. Imported from West Germany by PSI.
Price: Right-hand **$806.00**
Price: Left-hand **$859.00**

ANSCHUTZ 1911 MATCH RIFLE
Caliber: 22 LR, single shot.
Barrel: 27¹/₄″ round (1″ dia.).
Weight: 11 lbs. **Length:** 46″ overall.
Stock: Walnut-finished European hardwood; American prone style with Monte Carlo, cast-off cheekpiece, checkered p.g., beavertail forend with swivel rail and adjustable swivel, adjustable rubber buttplate.
Sights: None. Receiver grooved for Anschutz sights (extra). Scope blocks.
Features: Two-stage #5018 trigger adjustable from 2.1 to 8.6 oz. Extremely fast lock time. Imported from West Germany by PSI.
Price: Right-hand, no sights **$1,576.00**
Price: M1911-L (true left-hand action and stock) **$1,714.00**

Anschutz Model 1913

Anschutz 1913 Super Match Rifle
Same as the Model 1911 except European walnut International-type stock with adjustable cheekpiece, adjustable aluminum hook buttplate, adjustable hand stop, weight 15¹/₂ lbs., 46″ overall. Imported from West Germany by PSI.
Price: Right-hand, no sights **$2,255.00**
Price: M1913-L (left-hand action and stock) **$2,440.00**

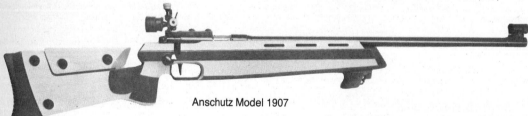

Anschutz Model 1907

Anschutz 1907 Match Rifle
Same action as Model 1913 but with ⁷/₈″ diameter 26″ barrel. Length is 44¹/₂″ overall, weight 10 lbs. Blonde wood finish with vented forend. Designed for ISU requirements, suitable for NRA matches.
Price: Right-hand, no sights **$1,344.00**
Price: M1907-L (true left-hand action and stock) **$1,462.00**

Anschutz Model 1910 Super Match II
Similar to the Super Match 1913 rifle except has a stock of European hardwood with tapered forend and deep receiver area. Hand and palm rests not included. Uses Match 54 action. Adjustable hook buttplate and cheekpiece. Sights not included. Introduced 1982. Imported from Germany by PSI.
Price: Right-hand **$2,013.00**
Price: Left-hand **$2,183.00**

CAUTION: PRICES CHANGE. CHECK AT GUNSHOP.

ANSCHUTZ 1808ED SUPER RUNNING TARGET
Caliber: 22 LR, single shot.
Barrel: 20½"; ⅞" diameter.
Weight: 9¼ lbs. **Length:** 42" overall.
Stock: European hardwood. Heavy beavertail forend, adjustable cheekpiece, buttplate, stippled pistol grip and forend.
Sights: None furnished. Receiver grooved for scope mounting.
Features: Uses Super Match 54 action. Adjustable trigger from 14 oz. to 3.5 lbs. Removable sectioned barrel weights. **Special Order Only.** Introduced 1982. Imported from Germany by PSI.
Price: Right-hand $1,290.00
Price: Left-hand, 1808EDL $1,400.00

ANSCHUTZ MODEL 1403D MATCH RIFLE
Caliber: 22 LR only, single shot.
Barrel: 26"; ¹¹⁄₁₆" dia.
Weight: 7¾ lbs. **Length:** 44" overall.
Stock: Walnut-finished hardwood, cheekpiece, checkered p.g., beavertail forend, adjustable buttplate.
Sights: None furnished.
Features: Sliding side safety, adjustable #5053 single stage trigger, receiver grooved for Anschutz sights. Imported from West Germany by PSI.
Price: Without sights $699.50

BEEMAN/HW 660 MATCH RIFLE
Caliber: 22 LR.
Barrel: 26".
Weight: 10.7 lbs. **Length:** 45.3" overall.
Stock: Match-type walnut with adjustable cheekpiece and buttplate.
Sights: Globe front, match aperture rear.
Features: Adjustable match trigger; stippled p.g. and forend; forend accessory rail. Imported from West Germany by Beeman. Introduced 1988.
Price: $725.00

Beeman/HW 660

BEEMAN/WEIHRAUCH HW60 TARGET RIFLE
Caliber: 22 LR, single shot.
Barrel: 26.8".
Weight: 10.8 lbs. **Length:** 45.7" overall.
Stock: Walnut with adjustable buttplate. Stippled p.g. and forend. Rail with adjustable swivel.
Sights: Hooded ramp front, match-type aperture rear.
Features: Adjustable match trigger with push-button safety. Left-hand version also available. Introduced 1981. Imported from West Germany by Beeman.
Price: Right-hand $698.00
Price: Left-hand. $739.95

Heckler & Koch PSG-1

HECKLER & KOCH PSG-1 MARKSMAN RIFLE
Caliber: 308, 5- and 20-shot magazines.
Barrel: 25.6", heavy.
Weight: 17.8 lbs. **Length:** 47.5" overall.
Stock: Matte black high impact plastic, adjustable for length, pivoting butt cap, vertically-adjustable cheekpiece; target-type pistol grip with adjustable palm shelf.
Sights: Hendsoldt 6x42 scope.
Features: Uses HK-91 action with low-noise bolt closing device; special forend with T-way rail for sling swivel or tripod. Gun comes in special foam-fitted metal transport case with tripod, two 20-shot and two-5-shot magazines, cleaning rod. Imported from West Germany by Heckler & Koch, Inc. Introduced 1986.
Price: $8,728.00

ANSCHUTZ 1827B BIATHLON RIFLE
Caliber: 22 LR, 5-shot magazine.
Barrel: 21½".
Weight: 9 lbs. with sights. **Length:** 42½" overall.
Stock: Walnut-finished hardwood; cheekpiece, stippled pistol grip and forend.
Sights: Globe front specially designed for Biathlon shooting, micrometer rear with hinged snow cap.
Features: Uses Match 54 action and adjustable trigger; adjustable wooden buttplate, Biathlon butthook, adjustable hand-stop rail. **Special Order Only.** Introduced 1982. Imported from Germany by PSI.
Price: Right-hand $1,744.00
Price: Left-hand $1,863.00

BEEMAN/FEINWERKBAU 2600 TARGET RIFLE
Caliber: 22 LR, single shot.
Barrel: 26.3".
Weight: 10.6 lbs. **Length:** 43.7" overall.
Stock: Laminated hardwood and hard rubber.
Sights: Globe front with interchangeable inserts; micrometer match aperture rear.
Features: Identical smallbore companion to the Beeman/FWB 600 air rifle. Free floating barrel. Match trigger has fingertip weight adjustment dial. Introduced 1986. Imported from West Germany by Beeman.
Price: Right-hand $1,375.00
Price: Left-hand $1,550.00

FEDERAL ORDNANCE M14SA TARGET RIFLE
Caliber: 7.62mm NATO (308 Win.).
Barrel: 22".
Weight: 8 lbs., 9 oz. **Length:** 44" overall.
Stock: Fiberglass or wood.
Sights: G.I., fully adjustable for windage and elevation.
Features: Civilian version of the M-14 service rifle. All metal has military blue finish. Comes with G.I.-type manual. Introduced 1988. Made in the U.S. by Federal Ordnance.
Price: With fiberglass stock $624.95
Price: With wood stock $674.95

FINNISH LION STANDARD TARGET RIFLE
Caliber: 22 LR, single shot.
Barrel: 27⅝".
Weight: 10½ lbs. **Length:** 44⁹⁄₁₆" overall.
Stock: French walnut, target style.
Sights: Globe front, International micrometer rear.
Features: Optional accessories: palm rest, hook buttplate, forend stop and swivel assembly, buttplate extension, five front sight aperture inserts, three rear sight apertures, Allen wrench. Adjustable trigger. Imported from Finland by Mandall Shooting Supplies.
Price: $695.00

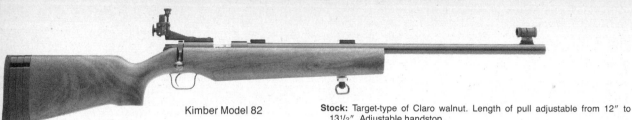

Kimber Model 82

KIMBER MODEL 82 GOVERNMENT
Caliber: 22 LR, single shot.
Barrel: 25″, six groove. Match grade.
Weight: 10-10³/₄ lbs. **Length:** 43¹/₂″ overall.

Stock: Target-type of Claro walnut. Length of pull adjustable from 12″ to 13¹/₂″. Adjustable handstop.
Sights: Receiver grooved for Kimber scope mounts or optional aperture sight package. Barrel has two rear bases for scope mounting.
Features: Single-stage trigger adjustable for over travel, sear engagement and weight. Super-fast lock time. Meets U.S. Army requirements. Introduced 1988.
Price: Without sights $575.00
Price: Front and rear sight package $160.00

McMillan National Match

McMILLAN NATIONAL MATCH RIFLE
Caliber: 308, 5-shot magazine.
Barrel: 24″, stainless steel.

Weight: About 11 lbs. (std. bbl.). **Length:** 43″ overall.
Stock: Modified ISU fiberglass with adjustable buttplate.
Sights: Barrel band and Tompkins front; no rear sight furnished.
Features: McMillan repeating action with clip slot, Canjar trigger. Match-grade barrel. Available in right-hand only. Fibergrain stock, sight installation, special machining and triggers optional. Introduced 1989. From G. McMillan & Co.
Price: $2,000.00

McMillan Long Range

McMILLAN LONG RANGE RIFLE
Caliber: 300 Win. Mag., single shot.
Barrel: 26″, stainless steel, match grade.

Weight: 14 lbs. **Length:** 46¹/₂″ overall.
Stock: Fiberglass with adjustable buttplate and cheekpiece. Adjustable for length of pull, drop, cant and cast-off.
Sights: Barrel band and Tompkins front; no rear sight furnished.
Features: Uses McMillan solid bottom single shot action and Canjar trigger. Barrel twist 1-in-12″. Introduced 1989. From G. McMillan & Co.
Price: $2,000.00

McMILLAN M-87 50-CALIBER RIFLE
Caliber: 50 BMG, single shot.
Barrel: 29″, with muzzlebrake.
Weight: About 21¹/₂ lbs. **Length:** 53″ overall.
Stock: McMillan fiberglass.
Sights: None furnished.
Features: Right-hand McMillan stainless steel receiver, chrome-moly barrel with 1-in-15″ twist. Introduced 1987. From G. McMillan & Co.
Price: $2,950.00

McMILLAN M-86 SNIPER RIFLE
Caliber: 308, 30-06 (4-shot magazine), 300 Win. Mag. (3-shot magazine).
Barrel: 24″, McMillan match-grade in heavy contour.
Weight: 11¹/₄ lbs. (308), 11¹/₂ lbs. (30-06, 300). **Length:** 43¹/₂″ overall.
Stock: Specially designed McHale fiberglass stock with textured grip and forend, recoil pad.
Sights: None furnished.
Features: Uses McMillan repeating action. Comes with bipod. Matte black finish. Sling swivels. Introduced 1989. From G. McMillan & Co.
Price: $1,650.00

McMillan M-88

Consult our Directory pages for the location of firms mentioned.

McMillan M-88 50-Caliber Rifle
Similar to the M-87 except has a fully adjustable fiberglass stock, single shot shellholder bolt receiver. Uses McMillan Quick Takedown system. Weight is about 21 lbs. Introduced 1988.
Price: $3,250.00

CAUTION: PRICES CHANGE. CHECK AT GUNSHOP.

Parker-Hale M87

PARKER-HALE M87 TARGET RIFLE
Caliber: 308 Win., 243, 6.5x55, 30-06, 300 Win. Mag. (other calibers on request), 5-shot detachable box magazine.

Barrel: 26″ heavy.
Weight: About 10 lbs. **Length:** 45″ overall.
Stock: Walnut target-style, adjustable for length of pull; solid buttpad; accessory rail with hand-stop. Deeply stippled grip and forend.
Sights: None furnished. Receiver dovetailed for Parker-Hale "Roll-Off" scope mounts.
Features: Mauser-style action with large bolt knob. Parkerized finish. Introduced 1987. Imported from England by Precision Sports.
Price: $1,299.00

Remington Model 40-XB

Remington 40-XB KS Varmint Special
Similar to the standard Model 40-XB except has Du Pont Kevlar aramid fiber stock with straight comb, cheekpiece, palm-swell grip, black recoil pad. Swivel studs easily removable. Stock color is satin black with light texture. Single shot or repeater. Chamberings include 220 Swift. Introduced 1987. Custom Shop order.
Price: Single shot $1,123.00
Price: Repeater $1,277.00
Price: Extra for 2-oz. trigger $140.00

REMINGTON 40-XB RANGEMASTER TARGET Centerfire
Caliber: 222 Rem., 222 Rem. Mag., 223, 220 Swift, 22-250, 6mm Rem., 243, 25-06, 7mm BR Rem., 7mm Rem. Mag., 30-338 (30-7mm Rem. Mag.), 300 Win. Mag., 7.62 NATO (308 Win.), 30-06, single shot.
Barrel: 27¼″.
Weight: 11¼ lbs. **Length:** 47″ overall.
Stock: American walnut with high comb and beavertail forend stop. Rubber non-slip buttplate.
Sights: None. Scope blocks installed.
Features: Adjustable trigger pull. Receiver drilled and tapped for sights.
Price: Standard s.s., stainless steel barrel, about $983.00
Price: Repeating model, about $1,067.00
Price: Extra for 2-oz. trigger, about $140.00

Remington Model 40XB-BR

REMINGTON 40-XR RIMFIRE POSITION RIFLE
Caliber: 22 LR, single-shot.
Barrel: 24″, heavy target.
Weight: 10 lbs. **Length:** 43″ overall.
Stock: Birch or Kevlar. Position-style with front swivel block on forend guide rail.
Sights: Drilled and tapped. Furnished with scope blocks.
Features: Meets all I.S.U. specifications. Deep forend, buttplate vertically adjustable, wide adjustable trigger.
Price: About $983.00
Price: Model 40-XR KS (Kevlar stock) $1,123.00

REMINGTON MODEL 40XB-BR
Caliber: 22 BR Rem., 222 Rem., 222 Rem. Mag., 223, 6mmx47, 6mm BR Rem., 7.62 NATO (308 Win.).
Barrel: 20″ (light varmint class), 24″ (heavy varmint class).
Weight: Light varmint class, 7¼ lbs.; heavy varmint class, 12 lbs.
Length: 38″ (20″ bbl.), 42″ (24″ bbl.).
Stock: Select walnut or Kevlar.
Sights: None. Supplied with scope blocks.
Features: Unblued stainless steel barrel, trigger adjustable from 1½ lbs. to 3½ lbs. Special 2-oz. trigger at extra cost. Scope and mounts extra.
Price: With walnut stock $1,052.00
Price: With Kevlar stock $1,193.00
Price: Extra for 2-oz. trigger, about $140.00

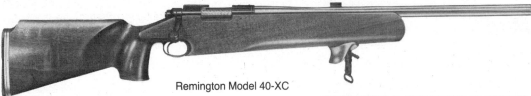

Remington Model 40-XC

REMINGTON 40-XC NAT'L MATCH COURSE RIFLE
Caliber: 7.62 NATO, 5-shot.
Barrel: 24″, stainless steel.
Weight: 11 lbs. without sights. **Length:** 43½″ overall.
Stock: Birch or Kevlar, position-style, with palm swell, handstop.
Sights: None furnished.
Features: Designed to meet the needs of competitive shooters firing the national match courses. Position-style stock, top loading clip slot magazine, anti-bind bolt and receiver, bright stainless steel barrel. Meets all I.S.U. Army Rifle specifications. Adjustable buttplate, adjustable trigger.
Price: About $1,052.00
Price: Model 40-XC KS (Kevlar stock) $1,193.00

SPRINGFIELD ARMORY M-21 SNIPER RIFLE
Caliber: 308 Win.
Barrel: 22″, Douglas heavy, air-gauged.
Weight: 15.25 lbs. (with bipod, scope mount). **Length:** 44¼″ overall.
Stock: Heavy walnut with adjustable comb, ventilated recoil pad. Glass bedded.
Sights: National Match front and rear.
Features: Refinement of the standard M-1A rifle. Has specially knurled shoulder for new figure-eight operating rod guide. New style folding and removable bipod. Guaranteed to deliver MOA accuracy. Comes with six 20-round magazines, leather military sling, cleaning kit. Introduced 1987. From Springfield Armory.
Price: $1,881.00

Springfield M1A Match

SPRINGFIELD ARMORY M1A SUPER MATCH
Caliber: 308 Win.
Barrel: 22″, heavy Douglas Premium, or Hart stainless steel.

Weight: About 10 lbs. **Length:** 44½″ overall.
Stock: Heavy walnut competition stock with longer pistol grip, contoured area behind the rear sight, thicker butt and forend, glass bedded.
Sights: National Match front and rear.
Features: Has new figure-eight style operating rod guide, new stock design. Introduced 1987. From Springfield Armory, Inc.
Price: About **$1,329.00**

Steyr SSG Marksman

Steyr-Mannlicher SSG Match
Same as Model SSG Marksman except has heavy barrel, match bolt, Walther target peep sights and adjustable rail in forend to adjustable sling travel. Weight is 11 lbs.
Price: Synthetic half-stock **$1,875.00**
Price: Walnut half-stock **$2,125.00**

STEYR-MANNLICHER SSG MARKSMAN
Caliber: 308 Win.
Barrel: 25.6″.
Weight: 8.6 lbs. **Length:** 44.5″ overall.
Stock: Choice of ABS "Cycolac" synthetic half-stock or walnut. Removable spacers in butt adjusts length of pull from 12¾″ to 14″.
Sights: Hooded blade front, folding leaf rear.
Features: Parkerized finish. Choice of interchangeable single or double set triggers. Detachable 5-shot rotary magazine (10-shot optional). Drilled and tapped for scope mounts. Imported from Austria by Gun South, Inc.
Price: Synthetic half-stock **$1,592.00**
Price: Walnut half-stock **$1,995.00**
Price: SSG PII (large bolt knob, heavy bbl., no sights, forend rail). **$1,995.00**

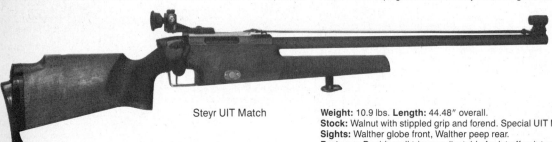

Steyr UIT Match

STEYR-MANNLICHER MATCH UIT RIFLE
Caliber: 243 Win. or 308 Win., 10-shot magazine.
Barrel: 25.5″.

Weight: 10.9 lbs. **Length:** 44.48″ overall.
Stock: Walnut with stippled grip and forend. Special UIT Match design.
Sights: Walther globe front, Walther peep rear.
Features: Double-pull trigger adjustable for let-off point, slack, weight of first-stage pull, release force and length; buttplate adjustable for height and length. Meets UIT specifications. Introduced 1984. Imported from Austria by Gun South, Inc.
Price: **$2,350.00**

Walther U.I.T. BV

WALTHER U.I.T BV UNIVERSAL
Caliber: 22 LR, single shot.
Barrel: 25½″.
Weight: 10 lbs., 3 oz. **Length:** 44¾″ overall.
Stock: Walnut, adjustable for length and drop; forend guide rail for sling or palm rest.
Sights: Globe-type front, fully adjustable aperture rear.
Features: Conforms to both NRA and U.I.T. requirements. Fully adjustable trigger. Left-hand stock available on special order. Imported from Germany by Interarms.
Price: **$1,700.00**

WALTHER KK/MS SILHOUETTE RIFLE
Caliber: 22 LR, single shot.
Barrel: 25.5″.
Weight: 8.75 lbs. **Length:** 44.75″ overall.
Stock: Walnut with thumbhole, stippled grip and forend.
Sights: None furnished. Receiver grooved for scope mounting.
Features: Over-size bolt knob. Adjustable trigger. Rubber buttpad. Introduced 1989. Imported from Germany by Interarms.
Price: **$1,100.00**

Walther GX-1 Match Rifle
Same general specs as U.I.T. except has 25½″ barrel, overall length of 44½″, weight of 15½ lbs. Stock is designed to provide every conceivable adjustment for individual preference and anatomical compatibility. Left-hand stock available on special order. Imported from Germany by Interarms.
Price: **$2,200.00**

CAUTION: PRICES CHANGE. CHECK AT GUNSHOP.

Walther U.I.T. Match

WALTHER RUNNING BOAR MATCH RIFLE
Caliber: 22 LR, single shot.
Barrel: 23.6″.
Weight: 8 lbs., 5 oz. **Length:** 42″ overall.
Stock: Walnut thumbhole type. Forend and p.g. stippled.
Features: Especially designed for running boar competition. Receiver grooved to accept dovetail scope mounts. Adjustable cheekpiece and buttplate. 1.1 lb. trigger pull. Left-hand stock available on special order. Imported from Germany by Interarms.
Price: $1,300.00

Walther U.I.T. Match
Same specifications and features as standard U.I.T. Super rifle but has scope mount bases. Forend has new tapered profile, fully stippled. Imported from Germany by Interarms.
Price: $1,300.00

Wichita Silhouette

WICHITA SILHOUETTE RIFLE
Caliber: All standard calibers with maximum overall cartridge length of 2.800″.
Barrel: 24″ free-floated Matchgrade.
Weight: About 9 lbs.
Stock: Metallic gray fiberthane with ventilated rubber recoil pad.
Sights: None furnished. Drilled and tapped for scope mounts.
Features: Legal for all NRA competitions. Single shot action. Fluted bolt, 2-oz. Canjar trigger; glass-bedded stock. Introduced 1983. From Wichita Arms.
Price: $2,150.00
Price: Left-hand $2,325.00

SHOTGUNS—AUTOLOADERS

Includes a wide variety of sporting guns and guns suitable for various competitions.

Benelli Black Eagle

BENELLI BLACK EAGLE AUTO SHOTGUN
Gauge: 12, 3″ chamber.
Barrel: 21″, 24″, 26″ (Full, Mod., Imp. Cyl. choke tubes).
Weight: 7.1 to 7.6 lbs. **Length:** 42½″ overall (21″ barrel).
Stock: European walnut with high gloss finish. Comes with drop adjustment kit.
Features: Uses the Montefeltro rotating bolt inertia recoil operating system with a two-piece steel/aluminum receiver. Drop adjustment kit allows the stock to be custom fitted without modifying the stock. Black lower receiver finish, blued upper. Introduced 1989. Imported from Italy by Heckler & Koch, Inc.
Price: $795.00

ARMSPORT 2751 GAS AUTO SHOTGUN
Gauge: 12, 3″ chamber.
Barrel: 28″ (Mod.), 30″ (Full).
Weight: 7 lbs.
Stock: European walnut.
Features: Gas-operated action; blued receiver with light engraving. Introduced 1986. Imported from Italy by Armsport.
Price: With fixed chokes $575.00
Price: Blue, choke tubes, 28″ bbl. $650.00
Price: With silvered receiver $675.00

Benelli M1 Super 90

BENELLI M1 SUPER 90 FIELD AUTO SHOTGUN
Gauge: 12, 3″ chamber.
Barrel: 26″, 28″ (choke tubes).
Weight: 7 lbs., 4 oz.
Stock: High impact polymer.
Sights: Metal bead front.
Features: Sporting version of the military & police gun. Uses the rotating Montefeltro bolt system. Ventilated rib; blue finish. Imported from Italy by Heckler & Koch
Price: $648.00
Price: M1 Super Field with short magazine $648.00

Benelli Montefeltro Super 90 Shotgun
Similar to the M1 Super 90 except has checkered walnut stock with high-gloss finish. Uses the Montefeltro rotating bolt system with a simple inertia recoil design. Imp., Mod., Full choke tubes. Weight is 7-7½ lbs. Finish is matte black. Introduced 1987.
Price: Standard Hunter, 26″, 28″ $675.00
Price: Left-hand. $734.00
Price: Turkey Gun, 24″ bbl. $675.00
Price: Uplander, 21″ bbl. $675.00

CAUTION: PRICES CHANGE. CHECK AT GUNSHOP.

BERETTA A-303 AUTO SHOTGUN

Gauge: 12 or 20, 2³/₄" or 3" chamber.
Barrel: 12 ga., 3"—24", 26", 28", 30", 32"; 12 ga., 2³/₄"—26", 28", 30"; 20 ga., 2³/₄" or 3"—26", 28". All equipped with Mobilchoke choke tubes. Slug model has 22" (Cyl.) barrel.
Weight: About 6¹/₂ lbs., 20 gauge; about 7¹/₂ lbs., 12 gauge.
Stock: American walnut; hand-checkered grip and forend.
Features: Gas-operated action, alloy receiver, magazine cut-off, push-button safety. Mobilchoke models come with three interchangeable flush-mounted screw-in choke tubes. Imported from Italy by Beretta U.S.A. Introduced 1983.
Price: Mobilchoke, 12 ga. or 20 ga. $653.00
Price: 12 ga. trap with Monte Carlo stock $727.00
Price: 12 ga. trap with standard trap stock $673.00
Price: 12 or 20 ga., Skeet $673.00
Price: Slug, 12 or 20 ga. $680.00
Price: A-303 Youth Gun, 20 ga., 2³/₄" chamber, 24" barrel. $733.00
Price: A-303 Sporting clays with Mobilchoke $733.00

BERETTA 1200F AUTO SHOTGUN

Gauge: 12 ga., 2³/₄" and 3" chamber.
Barrel: 28" vent. rib with Mobilchoke choke tubes.
Weight: 7.3 lbs.
Stock: Special strengthened technopolymer, matte black finish.
Features: Resists abrasion and adverse effects of water, salt and other damaging materials associated with tough field conditions. Imported from Italy by Beretta U.S.A. Introduced 1988.
Price: $580.00

Beretta A-303 Upland Model

Similar to the 12-gauge field A-303 except has 24" vent. rib barrel with Mobilchoke choke tubes, 2³/₄" chamber, straight English-style stock. Introduced 1989.
Price: $680.00

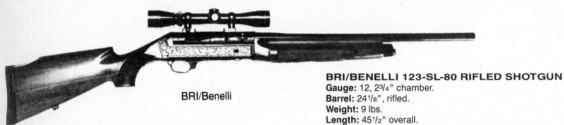

BRI/Benelli

BRI/BENELLI 123-SL-80 RIFLED SHOTGUN

Gauge: 12, 2³/₄" chamber.
Barrel: 24¹/₈", rifled.
Weight: 9 lbs.
Length: 45¹/₂" overall.
Stock: European walnut with checkered p.g. and forend.
Sights: None furnished. Drilled and tapped for scope mounting.
Features: Rifled bore. Quick interchangeable barrels; cross-bolt safety; engraved receiver; recoil pad. From Ballistic Research Industries.
Price: $995.00

Browning Sweet Sixteen

Browning Auto-5 Gold Classic

Same as the standard Auto-5 Light 12 with 28" (Mod.) barrel. Has engraved hunting and wildlife scenes with gold animals and portrait. Only 500 will be made, each numbered "1 of Five Hundred," etc. with "Browning Gold Classic." Select, figured walnut, special checkering with carved border, and the semi-pistol grip stock. Introduced 1984.
Price: Auto-5 Gold Classic $6,500.00

Browning Auto-5 Magnum 12

Same as standard Auto-5 except chambered for 3" magnum shells (also handles 2³/₄" magnum and 2³/₄" HV loads). 28" Mod., Full; 30" and 32" (Full) bbls. Comes with Invector choke tubes. 14" x 1⁵/₈" x 2¹/₂" stock. Recoil pad. Wgt. 8³/₄ lbs.
Price: With Invector choke tubes $685.95
Price: Extra Invector barrel $230.95

BROWNING AUTO-5 LIGHT 12 and 20, SWEET 16

Gauge: 12, 16, 20, 5-shot; 3-shot plug furnished; 2³/₄" or 3" chamber.
Action: Recoil operated autoloader; takedown.
Barrel: 26", 28", 30" Invector (choke tube) barrel; also available with Light 20 ga. 28" (Mod.) or 26" (Imp. Cyl.) barrel.
Weight: 12, 16 ga. 7¹/₄ lbs., 20 ga. 6³/₈ lbs.
Stock: French walnut, hand checkered half-p.g. and forend. 14¹/₄" x 1⁵/₈" x 2¹/₂".
Features: Receiver hand engraved with scroll designs and border. Double extractors, extra bbls. interchangeable without factory fitting; mag. cut-off; cross-bolt safety. Buck Special no longer inventoried, but can be ordered as a Buck Special extra barrel, plus an action only. Imported from Japan by Browning.
Price: Light 12, 20, Sweet 16, vent. rib., Invector $684.95
Price: Extra Invector barrel $237.95
Price: Extra fixed-choke barrel (Light 20 only) $194.95
Price: 12, 16, 20 Buck Special barrel $240.95

Browning Auto-5 Magnum 20

Same as Magnum 12 except 26" or 28" barrel with Invector choke tubes. With ventilated rib, 7¹/₂ lbs.
Price: Invector only $685.95
Price: Extra Invector barrel $230.95

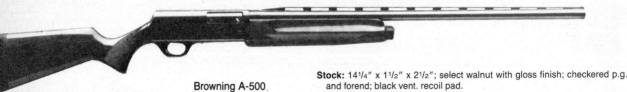

Browning A-500

BROWNING A-500 AUTO SHOTGUN

Gauge: 12 only, 3" chamber.
Barrel: 24" Buck Special, 26", 28", 30" with Invector choke tubes.
Weight: 7 lbs., 7 oz. (30" barrel).
Length: 49¹/₂" overall (30" bbl.).

Stock: 14¹/₄" x 1¹/₂" x 2¹/₂"; select walnut with gloss finish; checkered p.g. and forend; black vent. recoil pad.
Sights: Metal bead front.
Features: Uses a short-recoil action with four-lug rotary bolt and composite and coil spring buffering system. Shoots all loads without adjustment. Has a magazine cut-off, Invector chokes. Introduced 1987. Imported from Belgium by Browning.
Price: $559.95
Price: Extra Invector and Buck Special barrels $199.95

SHOTGUNS—AUTOLOADERS

COSMI AUTOMATIC SHOTGUN

Gauge: 12 or 20, 2³/₄″ or 3″ chamber.
Barrel: 22″ to 34″. Choke (including choke tubes) and length to customer specs. Boehler steel.
Weight: About 6¹/₄ lbs. (20 ga.).
Stock: Length and style to customer specs. Hand-checkered exhibition grade circassian walnut standard.
Features: Hand-made, essentially a custom gun. Recoil-operated auto with tip-up barrel. Made completely of stainless steel (lower receiver polished); magazine tube in buttstock holds 7 rounds. Double ejectors, double safety system. Comes with fitted leather case. Imported from Italy by Incor Inc.
Price: From. **$7,400.00**

Cosmi Auto

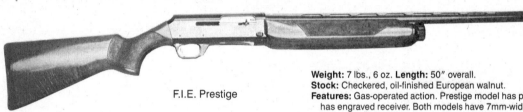

F.I.E. Prestige

F.I.E./FRANCHI PRESTIGE, ELITE SHOTGUNS

Gauge: 12, 2³/₄″ or 3″ chamber.
Barrel: 26″, 28″, 30″, 32″ with Full, Mod., Imp. Cyl. Franchoke choke tubes.

Weight: 7 lbs., 6 oz. **Length:** 50″ overall.
Stock: Checkered, oil-finished European walnut.
Features: Gas-operated action. Prestige model has plain blued receiver, Elite has engraved receiver. Both models have 7mm-wide vent. rib. Gas piston is stainless steel. Introduced 1985. Choke tubes introduced 1989. Imported from Italy by F.I.E. Corp.
Price: Prestige. **$759.95**
Price: Elite. **$799.95**
Price: Extra barrels **$179.95**

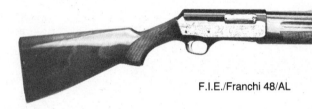

F.I.E./Franchi 48/AL

F.I.E./Franchi Slug Gun

Same as Standard 48/AL automatic except 24″ Cylinder bored plain barrel, adjustable rifle-type sights.
Price: 12 or 20 ga., standard. **$524.95**
Price: As above, Hunter grade **$559.95**
Price: Extra barrel **$179.95**

F.I.E./FRANCHI 48/AL AUTO SHOTGUN

Gauge: 12 or 20, 5-shot, 2³/₄″ or 3″ chamber.
Action: Recoil-operated automatic.
Barrel: 26″, 28″, 30″, 32″ with Full, Mod., Imp. Cyl. Franchoke choke tubes.
Weight: 12 ga. 6¹/₄ lbs., 20 ga. 5 lbs. 2 oz.
Stock: Epoxy-finished walnut, with cut-checkered pistol grip and forend.
Features: Chrome-lined barrel, easy takedown, three-round plug provided. Ventilated rib barrel. Imported from Italy by F.I.E.
Price: Vent. rib 12, 20 . . . . **$599.95**
Price: Hunter model (engraved) **$649.95**
Price: 12 ga. Magnum, 32″ **$559.95**
Price: Extra barrel **$174.95**

Mossberg 5500 MKII

MOSSBERG MODEL 5500 MKII AUTO SHOTGUN

Gauge: 12, 2³/₄″ and 3″ chamber.
Barrel: 28″ (2³/₄″ chamber, ACCU-II tubes — Imp. Cyl., Mod., Full); 28″ (3″ chamber, ACCU-STEEL tubes — Mod., Full). Both vent. rib.
Weight: 7¹/₂ lbs. **Length:** 48″ overall with 28″ barrel.
Stock: 14″x1¹/₂″x2¹/₂″. Walnut-stained hardwood.
Features: Comes with both barrels listed above. Gas-operated action. Blue finish. Introduced 1988.
Price: **$433.00**

Remington SP 10

REMINGTON SP 10 MAGNUM AUTO SHOTGUN

Gauge: 10, 3¹/₂″ chamber, 3-shot magazine.
Barrel: 26″, 30″ (Full and Mod. Rem Chokes).
Weight: 11 to 11¹/₄ lbs. **Length:** 47¹/₂″ overall (26″ barrel).
Stock: Walnut with satin finish. Checkered grip and forend.
Sights: Metal bead front.
Features: Stainless steel gas system with moving cylinder; ³/₈″ ventilated rib. Receiver and barrel have matte finish. Brown recoil pad. Comes with padded Cordura nylon sling. Introduced 1989.
Price: **$1,265.00**

CAUTION: PRICES CHANGE. CHECK AT GUNSHOP.

Remington 11-87

REMINGTON MODEL 11-87 PREMIER SHOTGUN
Gauge: 12 ga., 3″ chamber.
Barrel: 26″, 28″, 30″ Rem Choke tubes.
Weight: About 8¼ lbs.
Length: 46″ overall (26″ bbl.).
Stock: Walnut with satin finish; cut checkering; solid brown buttpad; no white spacers.
Sights: Bradley-type white-faced front, metal bead middle.
Features: Pressure compensating gas system allows shooting 2¾″ or 3″ loads interchangeably with no adjustments. Stainless magazine tube; redesigned feed latch, barrel support ring on operating bars; pinned forend. Introduced 1987.
Price: $559.00
Price: Left-hand $612.00

Remington Model 11-87 Premier Skeet
Similar to 11-87 Premier except Skeet dimension stock with cut checkering, satin finish, two-piece buttplate; 26″ barrel with Skeet or Rem Chokes (Skeet, Imp. Skeet). Gas system set for 2¾ shells only. Introduced 1987.
Price: $612.00
Price: With Skeet choke $597.00

Remington 11-87 Deer

Remington Model 11-87 Special Purpose Deer Gun
Similar to the 11-87 Special Purpose Magnum except has 21″ barrel with rifle sights, rifled and Imp. Cyl. choke tubes. Gas system set to handle all 2¾″ and 3″ slug, buckshot, high velocity field and magnum loads. Not designed to function with light 2¾″ field loads. Introduced 1987.
Price: $543.00
Price: With cantilever scope mount, rings $596.00

Remington Model 11-87 Special Purpose Magnum
Similar to the 11-87 Premier except has dull stock finish, Parkerized exposed metal surfaces. Bolt and carrier have dull blackened coloring. Comes with 26″ or 30″ barrel with Rem Chokes, padded Cordura nylon sling and q.d. swivels. Introduced 1987.
Price: $559.00

Remington 11-87 Trap

Remington Model 11-87 Premier Trap
Similar to 11-87 Premier except trap dimension stock with straight or Monte Carlo comb; select walnut with satin finish and Tournament-grade cut checkering; 30″ barrel with Trap Full or Rem Chokes (Trap Full, Trap Extra Full, Trap Super Full). Gas system set for 2¾″ shells only. Introduced 1987.
Price: With straight stock, Rem Choke $618.00
Price: As above, Trap Full choke $605.00
Price: With Monte Carlo stock $633.00
Price: As above, Trap Full choke $618.00

Remington Model 1100

REMINGTON MODEL 1100 AUTO
Gauge: 20, 28, 410.
Barrel: 25″ (Full, Mod.), 26″, 28″, with Rem Chokes.
Weight: 7½ lbs.
Stock: 14″x1½″x2½″. American walnut, checkered p.g. and forend.
Features: Quickly interchangeable barrels. Matted receiver top with scroll work on both sides of receiver. Cross-bolt safety.
Price: With Rem Chokes, 20 ga. about $545.00
Price: 28 and 410 .... $587.00

Remington 1100D Tournament Auto
Same as 1100 Standard except vent. rib, better wood, more extensive engraving.
Price: About $2,291.00

Remington 1100 LT-20

Remington 1100 LT-20 and Small Gauge
Same as 1100 except 20, 28 ga., 2¾″, 410 bore, 3″ (5-shot). 45½″ overall. Available in 25″ barrel (Full, Mod., or Imp. Cyl.) only.
Price: With vent rib, about $532.00
Price: 20 ga., 3″ Magnum $545.00

Remington 1100F Premier Auto
Same as 1100D except select wood, better engraving.
Price: About $4,720.00
Price: With gold inlay, about $7,079.00

CAUTION: PRICES CHANGE. CHECK AT GUNSHOP.

Remington 1100 Special Field

Remington 1100 Tournament Skeet

Same as the 1100 except 26″ barrel, special Skeet boring, vent. rib (high rib on LT-20), ivory bead front and metal bead middle sights. 14″ × 1¹/₂″ × 2¹/₂″ stock. 20, 28, 410 ga. Wgt. 7¹/₂ lbs., cut checkering, walnut, new receiver scroll.
Price: Tournament Skeet (28, 410), about **$618.00**
Price: Tournament Skeet (20), about **$618.00**

SKB MODEL 1300 UPLAND MAG SHOTGUN

Gauge: 12, 2³/₄″ or 3″, 20, 3″.
Barrel: 22″ (Slug), 26″, 28″ (Inter Choke tubes).
Weight: 6¹/₂ to 7¹/₄ lbs.
Length: 48¹/₄″ overall (28″ barrel).
Stock: 14¹/₂″ × 1¹/₂″ × 2¹/₂″. Walnut, with hand checkered grip and forend.
Sights: Metal bead front.
Features: Gas operated with Universal Automatic System. Blued receiver. Magazine cut-off system. Introduced 1988. Imported from Japan by Ernie Simmons Ent.
Price: Field **$495.00**
Price: 1300 Slug **$499.00**

SKB Model 3000 Auto Shotgun

Similar to the Model 1900 except has more elaborate engraving, initial plate in buttstock.
Price: Field **$585.00**
Price: Trap **$595.00**

Remington 1100 ''Special Field''

Similar to standard Model 1100 except 12 and 20 ga. only, comes with 21″ Rem Choke barrel. LT-20 version 6¹/₂ lbs.; has straight-grip stock, shorter forend, both with cut checkering. Comes with vent rib only; matte finish receiver without engraving. Introduced 1983.
Price: 12 and 20 ga., 21″ Rem Choke, about **$545.00**

Remington 1100 20 Ga. Deer Gun

Same as 1100 except 20 ga. only, 21″ barrel (Imp. Cyl.), rifle sights adjustable for w. and e.; recoil pad with white spacer. Weight 7¹/₄ lbs.
Price: About **$492.00**

SKB Model 1900 Auto Shotgun

Similar to the Model 1300 except has engraved bright-finish receiver, grip cap, gold-plated trigger. Introduced 1988.
Price: Field **$550.00**
Price: Slug gun (22″ barrel, rifle sights) **$550.00**
Price: Deluxe Trap (2³/₄″ chamber, 30″ barrel with Inter Choke tubes, Monte Carlo stock) **$575.00**

SKB Model 1900 Trap

Similar to the Model 1900 Field except in 12 gauge only (2³/₄″ chamber), 30″ barrel with Inter Choke tubes and 9.5mm wide rib. Introduced 1988.
Price: **$575.00**

TRADEWINDS H-170 AUTO SHOTGUN

Gauge: 12 only, 2³/₄″ chamber.
Action: Recoil-operated automatic.
Barrel: 26″, 28″ (Mod.) and 28″ (Full), chrome-lined.
Weight: 7 lbs.
Stock: Select European walnut stock, p.g. and forend hand checkered.
Features: Light alloy receiver, five-shot tubular magazine, ventilated rib. Imported from Italy by Tradewinds.
Price: **$395.00**

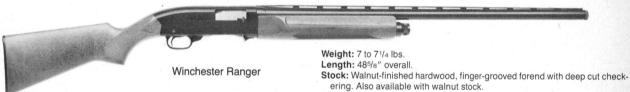

Winchester Ranger

WINCHESTER MODEL 1400 RANGER AUTO SHOTGUN

Gauge: 12 and 20, 2³/₄″ chamber.
Barrel: 28″ vent. rib with Winchoke tubes (Imp. Cyl., Mod., Full), or 22″ plain barrel (Mod.).

Weight: 7 to 7¹/₄ lbs.
Length: 48⁵/₈″ overall.
Stock: Walnut-finished hardwood, finger-grooved forend with deep cut checkering. Also available with walnut stock.
Sights: Metal bead front.
Features: Cross-bolt safety, front-locking rotating bolt, black serrated buttplate, gas-operated action. From U.S. Repeating Arms Co.
Price: Vent. rib with Winchoke, about **$341.00**
Price: As above with walnut stock **$399.00**
Price: Deer barrel combo, about **$406.00**
Price: Deer gun, about **$326.00**

SHOTGUNS—SLIDE ACTIONS

Includes a wide variety of sporting guns and guns suitable for competitive shooting.

ARMSCOR MODEL 30 PUMP SHOTGUN

Gauge: 12, 5-shot magazine.
Barrel: 28″ (Mod.), 30″ (Full).
Weight: 7.3 lbs.
Length: 47″ overall. (28″).
Stock: Plain mahogany.
Sights: Metal bead front.
Features: Double action bars; blue finish; grooved forend. Introduced 1987. Imported from the Philippines by Armscor.
Price: **$209.25**

ARMSPORT 2755 PUMP SHOTGUN

Gauge: 12, 3″ chamber.
Barrel: 28″ (Mod.), 30″ (Full).
Weight: 7 lbs.
Stock: European walnut.
Features: Ventilated rib; rubber recoil pad; polished blue finish. Introduced 1986. Imported from Italy by Armsport.
Price: Fixed chokes **$395.00**
Price: 28″, 30″, choke tubes **$465.00**
Price: Police model with 20″ (Imp. Cyl.), black receiver **$375.00**

CAUTION: PRICES CHANGE. CHECK AT GUNSHOP.

Browning Model 12

BRI "SPECIAL" RIFLED PUMP SHOTGUN
Gauge: 12, 3" chamber.
Barrel: 24" (Cyl.) rifled.
Weight: 7¹/₂ lbs.
Length: 44" overall.
Stock: Walnut with high straight comb. Rubber recoil pad.
Sights: None. Comes with scope mount on barrel.
Features: Uses Mossberg Model 500 Trophy Slugster action; double slide bars, twin extractors, dual shell latches; top receiver safety. From Ballistic Research Industries. Introduced 1988.
Price: About **$695.00**

BROWNING MODEL 12 PUMP SHOTGUN
Gauge: 20, 2³/₄" chamber.
Barrel: 26" (Mod.).
Weight: 7 lbs., 1 oz. **Length:** 45" overall.
Stock: 14" × 2¹/₂" × 1 1¹/₂". Select walnut with cut checkering, semi-gloss finish; Grade V has high-grade walnut.
Features: Reproduction of the Winchester Model 12. Has high post floating rib with grooved sighting plane; cross-bolt safety in trigger guard; polished blue finish. Limited to 8,500 Grade I and 4,000 Grade V guns. Introduced 1988. Imported from Japan by Browning.
Price: Grade I **$734.95**
Price: Grade V **$1,187.00**

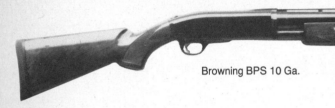

Browning BPS 10 Ga.

Browning BPS Pump Shotgun (Ladies and Youth Model)
Same as BPS Upland Special except 20 ga. only, 22" Invector barrel, stock has pistol grip with recoil pad. Length of pull is 13¹/₄". Introduced 1986.
Price: **$433.50**

Browning BPS "Stalker" Pump Shotgun
Same gun as the standard BPS except all exposed metal parts have a matte blued finish and the stock has a durable black finish with a black recoil pad. Available in 10 ga. (3¹/₂") and 12 ga. with 3" or 3¹/₂" chamber, 22", 28", 30" barrel with Invector choke system. Introduced 1987.
Price: 12 ga., 3" chamber **$433.50**
Price: 10, 12 ga., 3¹/₂" chamber **$508.50**

BROWNING BPS PUMP SHOTGUN
Gauge: 10, 12, 3¹/₂" chamber; 12 or 20 gauge, 3" chamber (2³/₄" in target guns), 5-shot magazine.
Barrel: 10 ga.—24" Buck Special, 28", 30", 32" Invector; 12, 20 ga. — 22", 24", 26", 28", 30", 32" (Imp. Cyl., Mod. or Full). Also available with Invector choke tubes, 12 or 20 ga.; Upland Special has 22" barrel with Invector tubes. BPS 3¹/₂" has back-bored barrel.
Weight: 7 lbs., 8 oz. (28" barrel). **Length:** 48³/₄" overall (28" barrel).
Stock: 14¹/₄"×1 1¹/₂"×2¹/₂". Select walnut, semi-beavertail forend, full p.g. stock.
Features: Bottom feeding and ejection, receiver top safety, high post vent. rib. Double action bars eliminate binding. Vent. rib barrels only. Introduced 1977. Imported from Japan by Browning.
Price: Grade I Hunting, Upland Special, Invector **$433.50**
Price: Extra Invector barrel **$185.95**
Price: Buck Special barrel with rifle sights **$191.95**
Price: Grade I Hunting, 10 ga. **$508.50**
Price: Extra 10 ga. Invector barrel **$218.95**
Price: Extra Buck Special barrel **$224.95**
Price: 12 ga., 3¹/₂", 28", 30" only, Invector PLUS **$508.50**

Ithaca 87 Supreme

Ithaca Model 87 Ultra Field Pump Shotgun
Similar to the Model 87 Supreme except the receiver is made of aircraft-quality aluminum. Available in 12 ga., 2³/₄" chamber or 20 ga., 2³/₄" chamber, 25" (Mod.) with choke tube. Weight is 5 lbs. (20 ga.), 6 lbs. (12 ga.). Reintroduced 1988.
Price: **$514.00**

Ithaca Model 87 Deluxe Pump Shotgun
Similar to the Model 87 Supreme Vent. Rib except comes with choke tubes in 25", 26", 28" (Mod.), 30" (Full). Standard-grade walnut.
Price: **$495.00**

Ithaca Deerslayer II Rifled Shotgun
Similar to the Deerslayer except has rifled 25" barrel and uncheckered American walnut stock and forend. Monte Carlo comb. Solid frame construction. Introduced 1988.
Price: **$525.00**

ITHACA MODEL 87 SUPREME PUMP SHOTGUN
Gauge: 12, 20, 3" chamber, 5-shot magazine.
Barrel: 26" (Imp. Cyl., Mod., Full), 28" (Mod.), 30" (Full). Vent. rib.
Weight: 6³/₄ to 7 lbs.
Stock: 14" × 1 1¹/₂" × 2¹/₄". Full fancy-grade walnut, checkered p.g. and slide handle.
Sights: Raybar front.
Features: Bottom ejection, cross-bolt-safety. Polished and blued engraved receiver. Reintroduced 1988. From Ithaca Acquisition Corp.
Price: **$819.00**
Price: M87 Camo Vent (28", Mod. choke tube, camouflage finish) . . **$524.00**

ITHACA MODEL 87 DEERSLAYER SHOTGUN
Gauge: 12, 20, 3" chamber.
Barrel: 20", 25" (Special Bore), or rifled bore.
Weight: 6 to 6³/₄ lbs.
Stock: 14" × 1 1¹/₂" × 2¹/₄". American walnut. Checkered p.g. and slide handle.
Sights: Raybar blade front on ramp, rear adjustable for windage and elevation, and grooved for scope mounting.
Features: Bored for slug shooting. Bottom ejection, cross-bolt safety. Reintroduced 1988. From Ithaca Acquisition Corp.
Price: **$391.00**
Price: Ultralight Deerslayer (20 ga. only, 2³/₄", 5 lbs.) **$444.00**
Price: Deluxe Combo (12 and 20 ga. barrels) **$525.00**

MAVERICK MODEL 88 PUMP SHOTGUN

Gauge: 12, 3″ chamber.
Barrel: 28″ (Mod.), plain or vent. rib; 30″ (Full), plain or vent. rib.
Weight: 7¼ lbs. **Length:** 48″ overall with 28″ bbl.
Stock: Black synthetic with ribbed synthetic forend.
Sights: Bead front.
Features: Alloy receiver with blue finish; cross-bolt safety in trigger guard; interchangeable barrels. Rubber recoil pad. Introduced 1989. From Maverick Arms, Inc.
Price: 28″ or 30″, plain barrel **$175.00**
Price: As above, vent. rib **$195.00**

MOSSBERG MODEL 500 TROPHY SLUGSTER

Gauge: 12, 3″ chamber.
Barrel: 24″, smooth or rifled bore. Plain (no rib).
Weight: 7¼ lbs. **Length:** 44″ overall.
Stock: 14″ pull, 1⅜″ drop at heel. Walnut-stained hardwood; high comb design with recoil pad and q.d. swivel studs.
Features: Ambidextrous thumb safety, twin extractors, dual slide bars. Comes with scope mount. Introduced 1988.
Price: Smoothbore, about **$304.00**
Price: Rifled bore, about **$324.00**

Mossberg 500 Sporting

MOSSBERG MODEL 500 SPORTING PUMP

Gauge: 12, 20, 410, 3″ chamber.
Barrel: 18½″ to 30″ with ACCU-CHOKE tubes, plain or vent. rib; ACCU-STEEL tubes for steel shot.
Weight: 6¼ lbs. (410), 7¼ lbs. (12).
Length: 48″ overall (28″ barrel).
Stock: 14″ × 1½″ × 2½″. Walnut-stained hardwood. Checkered grip and forend.
Sights: White bead front, brass mid-bead.
Features: Ambidextrous thumb safety, twin extractors, disconnecting safety, dual action bars. From Mossberg.
Price: From about **$258.00**
Price: Sporting Combos (field barrel and Slugster barrel), from **$294.00**

Mossberg Model 500 Camo Pump

Same as the Model 500 Sporting Pump except entire gun is covered with special camouflage finish. Available with synthetic field or Speedfeed stock. Receiver drilled and tapped for scope mounting. Comes with q.d. swivel studs, swivels, camouflage sling. In 12 ga. only.
Price: From about **$304.00**
Price: Camo Combo (as above with extra Slugster barrel), from about **$358.00**

Mossberg Model 835

Weight: 7¾ lbs.
Length: 48½″ overall.
Stock: 14″ × 1½″ × 2½″. Walnut-stained hardwood or camo synthetic; both have recoil pad.
Sights: White bead front, brass mid-bead.
Features: Backbored barrel to reduce recoil, improve patterns. Ambidextrous thumb safety, twin extractors, dual slide bars. Announced 1988.
Price: Blued, wood stock **$416.00**
Price: Camo finish, synthetic stock **$443.00**

MOSSBERG MODEL 835 ULTI-MAG PUMP

Gauge: 12, 3½″ chamber.
Barrel: 28″, ACCU-MAG choke tubes.

Remington 870 "Wingmaster"

REMINGTON MODEL 870 WINGMASTER

Gauge: 12, 3″ chamber.
Barrel: 26″, 28″, 30″ (Rem Chokes).
Weight: 7¼ lbs.
Length: 46½″ overall (26″ bbl.).
Stock: 14″ × 2½″ × 1″. American walnut with satin finish, cut-checkered p.g. and forend. Rubber buttpad.
Sights: Ivory bead front, metal mid-bead.
Features: Double action bars; cross-bolt safety; blue finish. Available in right- or left-hand style. Introduced 1986.
Price: **$439.00**
Price: Left-hand **$495.00**
Price: Brushmaster Deer Gun (rifle sights, 20″ bbl., fixed choke) . . . **$386.00**
Price: Deer Gun, left-hand **$454.00**
Price: 20 ga., vent. rib, 26″, 28″ (Rem Choke) **$439.00**
Price: As above, Youth Gun (21″ Rem Choke, 13″ stock) **$423.00**

Remington 870 TC Trap

Same as the M870 except 12 ga. only, 30″ fixed Full or Rem Choke, vent. rib barrel, ivory front and white metal middle beads. Special sear, hammer and trigger assy. 14⅜″ × 1½″ × 1⅞″ stock with recoil pad. Hand fitted action and parts. Wgt. 8 lbs.
Price: Model 870TC Trap, Rem Choke, about **$572.00**
Price: As above, fixed choke **$559.00**
Price: TC Trap with Monte Carlo stock, about **$585.00**
Price: As above, fixed choke **$572.00**

Remington 870 Deer

Remington Model 870 Special Purpose Deer Gun

Similar to the 870 Wingmaster except available with 20″ barrel with rifled and Imp. Cyl. choke tubes; rifle sights or cantilever scope mount with rings. Metal has black, non-glare finish, satin finish on wood. Recoil pad, detachable sling of camo Cordura nylon. Introduced 1989.
Price: With rifle sights **$414.00**
Price: With scope mount and rings **$476.00**

Remington 870 Express

Remington 870 "Special Purpose" Magnum

Similar to the Model 870 except chambered only for 12-ga., 3″ shells, vent. rib. 26″ or 30″ Rem Choke barrel. All exposed metal surfaces are finished in dull, non-reflective black. Wood has an oil finish. Comes with padded Cordura 2″ wide sling, quick-detachable swivels. Chrome-lined bores. Dark recoil pad. Introduced 1985.
Price: About **$439.00**

Remington 870 Small Gauges

Exact copies of the large gauge Model 870, except that guns are offered in 28 ga. and 410 bore, 25″ barrel (Full, Mod., Imp. Cyl.). D and F grade prices same as large-gauge M870 prices.
Price: With vent. rib barrel, about **$465.00**

Remington Model 870 Express

Similar to the 870 Wingmaster except has a walnut-toned hardwood stock with solid, black recoil pad and pressed checkering on grip and forend. Outside metal surfaces have a black oxide finish. Comes only with 28″ vent. rib barrel with a Mod. Rem Choke tube. Introduced 1987.
Price: **$238.00**
Price: Express Combo (with extra 20″ Deer barrel) **$335.00**

Remington 870 High Grades

Same as 870 except better walnut, hand checkering. Engraved receiver and barrel. Vent. rib. Stock dimensions to order.
Price: 870D, about **$2,291.00**
Price: 870F, about **$4,720.00**
Price: 870F with gold inlay, about **$7,079.00**

Remington 870 Special Field

Remington Model 870 "Special Field"

Similar to the standard Model 870 except comes with 21″ barrel only, 3″ chamber, choked Imp. Cyl., Mod., Full and Rem Choke; 12 ga. weighs 6³/₄ lbs., Ltwt. 20 weighs 6 lbs.; has straight-grip stock, shorter forend, both with cut checkering. Vent. rib barrel only. Introduced 1984.
Price: 12 or 20 ga., Rem Choke, about **$439.00**

Winchester 1300

Winchester Model 1300 Rifled Deer Gun

Same as the Model 1300 except has rifled 22″ barrel, Win-Tuff laminated stock or walnut, rifle-type sights. Introduced 1988.
Price: Walnut stock **$367.00**
Price: Laminated stock **$378.00**

Winchester Model 1300 Turkey

Similar to the standard Model 1300 Featherweight except 12 ga. only, 30″ barrel with Mod., Full and Extra Full Winchoke tubes, matte finish wood and metal, and comes with recoil pad, Cordura sling and swivels.
Price: With Win-Cam green-shaded laminated stock, about **$368.00**
Price: National Wild Turkey Federation edition **$387.00**

WINCHESTER MODEL 1300 FEATHERWEIGHT PUMP

Gauge: 12 and 20, 3″ chamber, 5-shot capacity.
Barrel: 22″, vent. rib, with Full, Mod., Imp. Cyl. Winchoke tubes.
Weight: 6³/₈ lbs.
Length: 42⁵/₈″ overall.
Stock: American walnut, with deep cut checkering on pistol grip, traditional ribbed forend; high luster finish.
Sights: Metal bead front.
Features: Twin action slide bars; front-locking rotating bolt; roll-engraved receiver; blued, highly polished metal; cross-bolt safety with red indicator. Introduced 1984.
Price: About **$338.00**

Winchester 1300 Waterfowl Pump

Similar to the 1300 Featherweight except in 3″ 12 ga. only, 30″ vent. rib barrel with Winchoke system; stock and forend of walnut with low-luster finish. All metal surfaces have special non-glare matte finish. Introduced 1985.
Price: About **$338.00**
Price: With laminated stock. **$349.00**

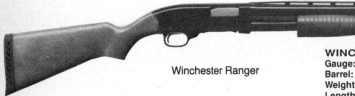

Winchester Ranger

Winchester Ranger Youth Pump Gun

Similar to the standard Ranger except chambered only for 3″ 20 ga., 22″ vent. rib barrel with Winchoke tubes (Full, Mod., Imp. Cyl.) or 22″ plain barrel with fixed Mod. choke. Weighs 6¹/₂ lbs., measures 41⁵/₈″ o.a.l. Stock has 13″ pull length and gun comes with discount certificate for full-size stock. Introduced 1983. Made under license by U.S. Repeating Arms Co.
Price: Vent. rib barrel, Winchoke, about **$286.00**
Price: Plain barrel, Mod. choke, about **$257.00**
Price: With walnut stock **$344.00**

WINCHESTER RANGER PUMP GUN

Gauge: 12 or 20, 3″ chamber, 4-shot magazine.
Barrel: 28″ vent. rib with Full, Mod., Imp. Cyl. Winchoke tubes.
Weight: 7 to 7¹/₄ lbs.
Length: 48⁵/₈″ to 50⁵/₈″ overall.
Stock: Walnut-finished hardwood with ribbed forend.
Sights: Metal bead front.
Features: Cross-bolt safety, black rubber buttpad, twin action slide bars, front-locking rotating bolt. From U.S. Repeating Arms Co.
Price: Vent. rib barrel, Winchoke, about **$268.00**

Winchester Ranger Pump Gun Combination

Similar to the standard Ranger except comes with two barrels: 22″ (Cyl.) deer barrel with rifle-type sights and an interchangeable 28″ vent. rib Winchoke barrel with Full, Mod. and Imp. Cyl. choke tubes. Available in 12 and 20 gauge 3″ only, with recoil pad. Introduced 1983.
Price: With two barrels, about **$333.00**

    CAUTION: PRICES CHANGE. CHECK AT GUNSHOP.

Includes a variety of game guns and guns for competitive shooting.

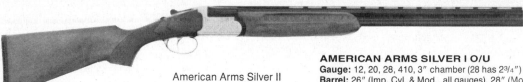

American Arms Silver II

American Arms Silver II Shotgun

Similar to the Silver I except 26" barrel (Imp. Cyl., Mod., Full choke tubes, 12 and 20 ga.), 28" (Imp. Cyl., Mod., Full choke tubes, 12 ga. only), 26" (Imp. Cyl. & Mod. fixed chokes, 28 and 410), 26" two-barrel set (Imp. Cyl. & Mod., fixed, 28 and 410); automatic selective ejectors. Weight is about 6 lbs., 15 oz. (12 ga., 26").
Price: **$579.00**
Price: Two-barrel set (28, 410) **$789.00**

AMERICAN ARMS SILVER I O/U

Gauge: 12, 20, 28, 410, 3" chamber (28 has 2³/₄")
Barrel: 26" (Imp. Cyl. & Mod., all gauges), 28" (Mod. & Full, 12, 20).
Weight: About 6³/₄ lbs.
Stock: 14¹/₈" × 1³/₈" × 2³/₈". Checkered walnut.
Sights: Metal bead front.
Features: Boxlock action with scroll engraving, silver finish. Single selective trigger, extractors. Chrome-lined barrels. Manual safety. Rubber recoil pad. Introduced 1987. Imported from Italy and Spain by American Arms, Inc.
Price: 12 or 20 gauge **$439.00**
Price: 28 or 410 . . . . **$499.00**

American Arms Sterling

American Arms 12-Ga. Waterfowl Special

Similar to the 10-ga. Waterfowl Special except chambered for 3¹/₂" 12-ga. shell. Single selective trigger with top tang selector; automatic selctive ejectors; recoil pad; swivels and camo sling included; matte metal finish. Boxlock action.
Price: **$609.00**

AMERICAN ARMS STERLING O/U SHOTGUN

Gauge: 12 or 20, 3" chamber.
Barrel: 26" (12 and 20), 28" (12 only). Imp. Cyl., Mod., Full choke tubes.
Weight: 7 lbs., 1 oz. (12 ga.), 6 lbs., 12 oz. (20 ga.).
Stock: 14¹/₈" × 1³/₈" × 2³/₈". Hand-checkered walnut with oil finish.
Sights: Metal bead front.
Features: Boxlock action with false sideplates and silver finish, scroll engraving; single selective, gold-colored trigger; chrome-lined bores; manual safety; automatic selective ejectors. Imported from Spain by American Arms, Inc. Introduced 1987.
Price: **$825.00**

American Arms Waterfowl

American Arms Turkey Special

Similar to the Waterfowl Special 10-gauge gun except has 26" barrels with Full & Full choke tubes. Double triggers, extractors. Weighs 9 lbs., 15 oz.
Price: **$875.00**

AMERICAN ARMS WATERFOWL SPECIAL O/Us

Gauge: 10, 3¹/₂" chambers.
Barrel: 32" vent. rib (steel Full & Full).
Weight: 10 lbs., 13 oz.
Stock: 14¹/₂" × 1³/₈" × 2³/₈". Checkered walnut with dull finish.
Sights: Metal bead front.
Features: Boxlock action with non-reflective sideplates and barrels; chrome-lined barrels; double triggers; extractors; sling swivels. Comes with camouflage sling. Introduced 1988. Imported from Spain by American Arms, Inc.
Price: **$829.00**

AMERICAN ARMS/FRANCHI BLACK MAGIC GAME GUN

Gauge: 12 or 20, 3" chamber.
Barrel: 24", 26", 28" (Imp. Cyl., Mod., Full choke tubes).
Weight: 7 lbs.
Stock: 14¹/₄"x1¹/₂"x2³/₈". Walnut, checkered grip and forend; recoil pad.
Features: Vent. rib with bead front sight; cross-bolt safety; magazine cut-off. Introduced 1989. Imported from Italy by American Arms, Inc.
Price: **$599.00**

American Arms/Franchi Black Magic Skeet Gun

Similar to the Black Magic Game Gun except has 2³/₄" chamber, 26" (Skeet), ported barrel; weight 7¹/₄ lbs. Stock dimensions of 14¹/₂"x1¹/₂"x2¹/₄". Introduced 1989.
Price: **$669.00**

> Consult our Directory pages for the location of firms mentioned.

AMERICAN ARMS/FRANCHI BLACK MAGIC TRAP

Gauge: 12, 2³/₄" chamber.
Barrel: 30", choke tubes.
Weight: 7.5 lbs.
Stock: 14¹/₂"x1¹/₄"x1³/₈". Walnut, cut checkering.
Features: Cross-bolt safety; magazine cut-off; recoil pad. Introduced 1989. Imported from Italy by American Arms, Inc.
Price: **$689.00**

Armsport 2730

ARMSPORT MODEL 2700 O/U

Gauge: 12 or 20 ga.
Barrel: 26" (Imp. Cyl. & Mod.); 28" (Mod. & Full); vent. rib.

Weight: 8 lbs.
Stock: European walnut, hand-checkered p.g. and forend.
Features: Single selective trigger, automatic ejectors, engraved receiver. Imported by Armsport.
Price: M2733/2735 (Boss-type action, 12, 20, extractors) **$575.00**
Price: M2741/2743 (as above with ejectors) **$620.00**
Price: M2730/2731 (as above with single trigger, screw-in chokes) . **$730.00**
Price: M2705 (410 ga., 26" Imp. & Mod., double triggers) **$595.00**
Price: M2720 (as above with single trigger) **$650.00**

Armsport Goose Gun

ARMSPORT MODEL 2700 O/U GOOSE GUN
Gauge: 10 ga., 3¹/₂″ chambers.
Barrel: 27″ (Imp. & Mod.), 32″ (Full & Full). Available with choke tubes.

Weight: About 9.8 lbs.
Stock: European walnut.
Features: Boss-type action; double triggers; extractors. Introduced 1986. Imported from Italy by Armsport.
Price: Fixed chokes **$915.00**
Price: Choke tubes **$995.00**

Armsport Tri-Barrel

ARMSPORT 2900 TRI-BARREL SHOTGUN
Gauge: 12, 3″ chambers.
Barrel: 28″ (Imp. Cyl. & Mod. & Full).
Weight: 7³/₄ lbs.
Stock: European walnut.
Features: Top-tang barrel selector; double triggers; silvered, engraved frame. Introduced 1986. Imported from Italy by Armsport.
Price: **$1,500.00**

Beretta 682 Sporting

BERETTA MODEL S05, S06 SO9 SHOTGUNS
Gauge: 12, 2³/₄″ chambers.
Barrel: To customer's specs.
Stock: To customer's specs.
Features: SO5—Trap, Skeet and Sporting Clays models available in standard SO5 and SO5 EELL; SO6—SO6 and SO6 EELL are field models made to customer specifications. SO6 has a case-hardened receiver with contour hand engraving. SO6 EELL has hand-engraved receiver in a fine floral or "fine English" pattern, with bas-relief chisel work and gold inlays. SO6 and SO6 EELL are available, at no extra charge, with sidelocks removable by hand. Imported from Italy by Beretta U.S.A.
Price: SO5 Trap, Skeet, Sporting **$13,693.00**
Price: SO5 Combo, two-bbl. set **$17,020.00**
Price: SO6 Trap, Skeet, Sporting **$15,480.00**
Price: SO6 EELL Field, custom specs **$23,973.00**
Price: SO9 (12, 20, 28, 410, 26″, 28″, 30″, any choke) . . . . **NA**

BERETTA SERIES 682 OVER/UNDERS
Gauge: 12, 2³/₄″ chambers.
Barrel: Skeet—26″ and 28″; trap—30″ and 32″, Imp. Mod. & Full and Mobilchoke; trap mono shotguns—32″ and 34″ Mobilchoke; trap top single guns—32″ and 34″ Full and Mobilchoke; trap combo sets—from 30″ o/u, 32″ unsingle to 32″ o/u, 34″ top single.
Stock: Close-grained walnut, hand checkered.
Sights: Luminous front sight and center bead.
Features: Trap Monte Carlo stock has deluxe trap recoil pad. Various grades available; contact Beretta U.S.A. for details. Imported from Italy by Beretta U.S.A. Corp.
Price: 682 Skeet **$2,073.00**
Price: 682 Trap **$2,053.00**
Price: 682 Trap Mono shotguns **$2,827.00**
Price: 682 Trap Top Single shotguns **$2,187.00**
Price: 682 Trap Combo sets . . . . **$2,773.00** to 2,827.00
Price: 687 EELL Trap . . . . **$3,800.00** to 4,887.00
Price: 687 EELL Skeet (4-bbl. set) **$6,767.00**

Beretta Onyx

BERETTA OVER/UNDER FIELD SHOTGUNS
Gauge: 12, 20, 28, 2³/₄″ and 3″ chambers.
Barrel: 26″ and 28″ (fixed chokes or Mobilchoke tubes.)
Stock: Close-grained walnut.
Features: Highly-figured, American walnut stocks and forends, and a unique, weather-resistant finish on barrels. Available in two grades: Golden Onyx has individual game scenes of flushing pheasant and rising ducks on the receiver; the 686 Onyx bears a gold P. Beretta signature on each side of the receiver. Imported from Italy by Beretta U.S.A.
Price: 686 Onyx **$1,167.00**
Price: 686 two bbl. set **$1,713.00**
Price: 686 Field **$1,147.00**
Price: 687L Field **$1,573.00**
Price: 687 Golden Onyx **$1,800.00**
Price: 687 EL **$2,607.00**
Price: 687 EELL . . . . **$3,767.00** to $3,820.00

BERETTA SPORTING CLAYS SHOTGUNS
Gauge: 12 and 20, 2³/₄″ chambers
Barrel: 28″, Mobilchoke.
Stock: Close-grained walnut.
Sights: Luminous front sight and center bead.
Features: Equipped with Beretta Mobilchoke flush-mounted screw-in choke tube system. Models vary according to grade, from field-grade Beretta 686 Sporting with its floral engraving pattern, to competition-grade Beretta 682 Sporting with its brushed satin finish and adjustable length of pull to the 687 Sporting with intricately hand-engraved game scenes, fine line, deep-cut checkering. Imported from Italy by Beretta U.S.A. Corp.
Price: 686 Sporting **$1,653.00**
Price: 682 Sporting, 30″ **$2,153.00**
Price: 682 Super Sport, 28″, 30″, tapered rib **$2,287.00**
Price: 687 Sporting **$2,173.00**
Price: 687 Sporting (20-gauge) **$2,173.00**
Price: 687 EELL Sporter (hand engraved sideplates, deluxe wood) **$3,600.00**

BRNO SUPER OVER/UNDER SHOTGUN
Gauge: 12, 2³/₄" or 3" chambers.
Barrel: 27¹/₂" (Full & Mod.).
Weight: 7 lbs., 4 oz. (Field). **Length:** 44" overall.
Stock: Walnut, with raised cheekpiece.
Features: Sidelock action with double safety interceptor sears; double triggers on Field model; automatic selective ejectors; engraved sideplates. Trap and Skeet models available. Imported from Czechoslovakia by TD Arms.
Price: $899.00

BRNO 500 OVER/UNDER SHOTGUN
Gauge: 12, 2³/₄" chambers.
Barrel: 27¹/₂" (Full & Mod.).
Weight: 7 lbs. **Length:** 44¹/₂" overall.
Stock: Walnut, with raised cheekpiece.
Features: Boxlock action with ejectors; double triggers; acid-etched engraving. Imported from Czechoslovakia by TD Arms.
Price: $899.00

BRNO ZH 301 OVER/UNDER SHOTGUN
Gauge: 12, 2³/₄" or 3" chambers.
Barrel: 27¹/₂" (Full & Mod.).
Weight: 7 lbs. **Length:** 44¹/₂" overall.
Stock: Walnut.
Features: Boxlock action with acid-etch engraving; double triggers. Imported from Czechoslovakia by TD Arms.
Price: $599.00

BRNO Super

BABY BRETTON OVER/UNDER SHOTGUN
Gauge: 12 or 20, 2³/₄" chambers.
Barrel: 27¹/₂" (Cyl., Imp. Cyl., Mod., Full choke tubes).
Weight: About 5 lbs.
Stock: Walnut, checkered pistol grip and forend, oil finish.
Features: Receiver slides open on two guide rods, is locked by a large thumb lever on the right side. Extractors only. Light alloy barrels. Imported from France by Mandall Shooting Supplies.
Price: $895.00

BRNO CZ 581 OVER/UNDER SHOTGUN
Gauge: 12, 2³/₄" or 3" chambers.
Barrel: 28" (Full & Mod.).
Weight: 7 lbs., 6 oz. **Length:** 45¹/₂" overall.
Stock: Turkish walnut with raised cheekpiece.
Features: Boxlock action; automatic selective ejectors; automatic safety; sling swivels; vent. rib; double triggers. Imported from Czechoslovakia by TD Arms.
Price: $649.00

Browning Citori 16

Browning Citori O/U Skeet Models
Similar to standard Citori except 26", 28" (Skeet & Skeet) only; stock dimensions of 14³/₈"x1¹/₂"x2", fitted with Skeet-style recoil pad; conventional target rib and high post target rib.
Price: Grade I Invector (high post rib) $1,090.00
Price: Grade I, 12 & 20 (high post rib) $1,055.00
Price: Grade I, 28 & 410 (high post rib) $1,100.00
Price: Grade III, 12 and 20 (high post rib) $1,525.00
Price: Grade VI, 12 and 20 (high post rib) $2,125.00
Price: Four barrel Skeet set—12, 20, 28, 410 barrels, with case, Grade I only $3,530.00
Price: Grade III, four-barrel set (high post rib) $4,025.00
Price: Grade VI, four-barrel set (high post rib) $4,515.00
Price: Grade I, three-barrel set $2,460.00
Price: Grade III, three-barrel set $2,835.00
Price: Grade VI, three-barrel set $3,465.00

BROWNING CITORI O/U SHOTGUN
Gauge: 12, 16, 20, 28 and 410.
Barrel: 26", 28" (Mod. & Full, Imp. Cyl. & Mod.), in 28 and 410. Also offered with Invector choke tubes. Lightning 3¹/₂" has Invector PLUS back-bored barrels.
Weight: 6 lbs., 8 oz. (26" 410) to 7 lbs., 13 oz. (30" 12-ga.).
Length: 43" overall (26" bbl.).
Stock: Dense walnut, hand checkered, full p.g., beavertail forend. Field-type recoil pad on 12 ga. field guns and trap and Skeet models.
Sights: Medium raised beads, German nickel silver.
Features: Barrel selector integral with safety, automatic ejectors, three-piece takedown. Imported from Japan by Browning.
Price: Grade I Hunting, Invector $985.00
Price: Grade III, Invector, 12 and 20 .... $1,385.00
Price: Grade VI, Invector, 12 and 20 .... $1,995.00
Price: Grade I, 28 and 410, fixed chokes $975.00
Price: Grade III, 28 and 410, fixed chokes $1,525.00
Price: Grade VI, 28 and 410, high post rib, fixed chokes $2,125.00
Price: Grade I Lightning, Invector, 12, 16, 20 .... $995.00
Price: Grade I Lightning, 28", 30" only, 3¹/₂", Invector PLUS .. $1,050.00
Price: Grade III Lightning, Invector, 12, 16, 20 .... $1,400.00
Price: Grade VI Lightning, Invector, 12, 16, 20 .... $2,035.00

Browning Lightning Clays

Browning Citori PLUS Trap Gun
Similar to the Grade I Citori Trap except comes only with 30" barrels with .745" over-bore, Invector PLUS choke system with Full, Imp. Mod. and Mod. choke tubes; high post, ventilated, tapered, target rib for adjustable impact from 3" to 12" above point of aim. Available with or without ported barrels. Select walnut stock has high-gloss finish, Monte Carlo comb, modified beavertail forend and is fully adjustable for length of pull, drop at comb and drop at Monte Carlo. Has Browning Recoil Reduction System. Introduced 1989.
Price: Grade I, with ported barrel $1,550.00
Price: Grade I, non-ported barrel $1,500.00

Browning Lightning Sporting Clays
Similar to the Citori Lightning with rounded pistol grip and classic forend. Has high post tapered rib or lower hunting-style rib with 30" Imp. Cyl. & Mod. chokes. Gloss stock finish, radiused recoil pad. Has "Lightning Sporting Clays Edition" engraved and gold filled on receiver. Introduced 1989.
Price: Low-rib version $1,050.00
Price: High-rib version $1,100.00

Browning Special Sporting Clays
Similar to the GTI except has full pistol grip stock with palm swell, gloss finish, 28", 30" or 32" barrels with fixed Imp. Cyl. & Mod. chokes; high post tapered rib. Also available as 28" and 30" two-barrel set. Introduced 1989.
Price: $1,100.00
Price: Two-barrel set $1,700.00

Browning GTI

Browning Citori O/U Trap Models

Similar to standard Citori except 12 gauge only; 30″, 32″ (Full & Full, Imp. Mod. & Full, Mod. & Full), 34″ single barrel in Combo Set (Full, Imp. Mod., Mod.), or Invector model; Monte Carlo cheekpiece (14³/₈″x1³/₈″x1³/₈″x2″); fitted with trap-style recoil pad; conventional target rib and high post target rib.

Price: Grade I, Invector, high post target rib $1,105.00
Price: Grade III, Invector, high post target rib $1,525.00
Price: Grade VI, Invector, high post target rib $2,125.00

Browning Limited Edition Waterfowl Superposed

Same specs as the Superposed Gold Classic. Available in 12 ga. only, 28″ (Mod. & Full). Limited to 500 guns, the edition number of each gun is inscribed in gold on the bottom of the receiver with ''Black Duck'' and its scientific name. Sides of receiver have two gold inlayed black ducks, bottom has two, and one on the trigger guard. Receiver is completely engraved and grayed. Stock and forend are highly figured dark French walnut with 24 lpi checkering, hand-oiled finish, checkered butt. Comes with form-fitted, velvet-lined, black walnut case. Introduced 1983.

Price: $8,800.00
Price: Similar treatment as above except for the Pintail Duck Issue $8,800.00

Browning Citori GTI Sporting Clays

Similar to the Citori Hunting except has semi-pistol grip with slightly grooved, semi-beavertail forend, satin-finish stock, radiused rubber butt-pad. Has three interchangeable trigger shoes, trigger has three lengths of pull adjustments. Wide 13mm vent. rib, 28″ or 30″ barrels with Imp. Cyl. Invector choke tubes. Ventilated side ribs. Introduced 1989.

Price: $1,125.00

Browning Superlight Citori Over/Under

Similar to the standard Citori except available in 12, 20 with 24″, 26″ or 28″ Invector barrels, 28 or 410 with 26″ barrels choked Imp. Cyl. & Mod. or 28″ choked Mod. & Full. Has straight grip stock, Schnabel forend tip. Superlight 12 weighs 6 lbs., 9 oz. (26″ barrels); Superlight 20, 5 lbs., 12 oz. (26″ barrels). Introduced 1982.

Price: Grade I only, 28 or 410 . . . . $975.00
Price: Grade III, Invector, 12 or 20 . . . . $1,410.00
Price: Grade III, 28 or 410 . . . . $1,525.00
Price: Grade VI, Invector, 12 or 20 . . . . $2,035.00
Price: Grade VI, 28 or 410 . . . . $2,125.00
Price: Grade I Invector, 12 or 20 . . . . $1,005.00
Price: Grade I Invector, Upland Special (24″ bbls.), 12 or 20 . . . . . $1,005.00

BROWNING OVER/UNDER GOLD CLASSIC

Gauge: 20, 2³/₄″ chambers.
Barrel: 26″ (Imp. Cyl. & Mod.).
Weight: 6³/₈ lbs.
Stock: 14¹/₄″x1⁵/₈″x2¹/₂″. Select walnut with straight grip, schnabel forend.
Features: Receiver has upland setting of bird dogs, pheasant and quail in inlaid gold on satin gray finish. Stock has fine checkering and decorative carving with oil finish. Introduced 1984. Made in Belgium.

Price: $6,000.00

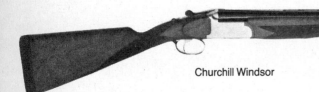

Churchill Windsor

Churchill Regent Over/Under Shotguns

Similar to the Windsor Grade except better wood with oil finish, better engraving; available only in 12 or 20 gauge (3″ chambers), 27″ barrels, with ICT interchangeable choke tubes (Imp. Cyl., Mod., Full). Regent VII has dummy sideplates. Introduced 1984.

Price: Regent VII, 12 or 20 ga. $889.00

CHURCHILL WINDSOR OVER/UNDER SHOTGUNS

Gauge: 12, 20, 28, 410, 3″ chambers.
Barrel: 26″ (Skeet & Skeet, Imp. Cyl. & Mod.), 28″ (Mod. & Full), 30″ (Mod. & Full, Full & Full), 12 ga.; 26″ (Skeet & Skeet, Imp. Cyl. & Mod.), 28″ (Mod. & Full), 20 ga.; 25″, 26″ (Imp. Cyl. & Mod), 28″ (Mod & Full), 28 ga.; 24″, 26″ (Full & Full), 410 ga.; or 27″, 30″ ICT choke tubes.
Stock: European walnut, checkered pistol grip, oil finish.
Features: Boxlock action with silvered, engraved finish; single selective trigger; automatic ejectors on Windsor IV, extractors only on Windsor III. Also available in Flyweight version with 23″, 25″ barrels, fixed or ICT chokes, straight-grip stock. Imported from Italy by Ellett Bros. Introduced 1984.
Price: Windsor III . . . . $549.00 to $649.00
Price: Windsor IV . . . . $619.00 to $719.00

Churchill Monarch

Churchill Regent Trap & Skeet

Trap has ventilated side rib, Monte Carlo stock, Churchill recoil pad. Oil-finished wood, fine checkering, chrome bores. Weight is 8 lbs. Regent Skeet available in 12 or 20 ga., 26″ (Skeet & Skeet); oil-finished stock measures 14¹/₂″x1¹/₂″x2³/₈″. Both guns have silvered and engraved receivers. Introduced 1984.

Price: Regent Trap (30″ Imp. Mod. & Full) $869.00
Price: Regent Skeet, 12 or 20 ga. $809.00

Charles Daly Lux Over/Under

Similar to the Field Grade except has automatic selective ejectors, antique silver finish on frame, and has choke tubes for Imp. Cyl., Mod. and Full. Introduced 1989.

Price: $585.00

CHURCHILL MONARCH OVER/UNDER SHOTGUNS

Gauge: 12 or 20, 3″ chambers.
Barrel: 26″ (Imp. Cyl. & Mod.), 28″ (Mod. & Full). Chrome-lined.
Weight: 12 ga.—7¹/₂ lbs., 20 ga.—6¹/₂ lbs.
Stock: European walnut with checkered p.g. and forend.
Features: Single selective trigger; blued, engraved receiver; vent. rib. Introduced 1986. Imported by Ellett Bros.
Price: . . . . $419.00 to $449.00

CHARLES DALY FIELD GRADE O/U

Gauge: 12 or 20, 3″ chambers.
Barrel: 12 and 20 ga. — 26″ (Imp. Cyl. & Mod.), 12 ga. — 28″ (Mod. & Full).
Weight: 6 lbs., 15 oz. (12 ga.), 6 lbs., 10 oz. (20 ga.). **Length:** 43¹/₂″ overall (26″ bbl.).
Stock: 14¹/₈″x1³/₈″x2³/₈″. Walnut with cut-checkered grip and forend. Black, vent. rubber recoil pad. Semi-gloss finish.
Features: Boxlock action with manual safety; extractors; single selective trigger. Color case-hardened receiver with engraving. Introduced 1989. Imported from Europe by Outdoor Sports Headquarters.
Price: $425.00

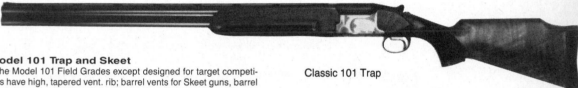

CLASSIC MODEL 101 FIELD GRADE I
Gauge: 12 or 20, 3″ chambers.
Action: Top lever, break open. Manual safety combined with bbl. selector at top of receiver tang.
Barrel: 25½″, 28″, interchangeable choke tubes.
Weight: 12 ga. 7 lbs. **Length:** 44⅞″ overall.
Stock: 14½″x1½″2½″. Checkered walnut p.g. and forend; fluted comb. Straight English or standard.
Features: Single selective adjustable trigger, auto ejectors. Hand engraved blued receiver. Suitable for steel shot. Chrome-lined bores and chambers. Comes with hard gun case. Manufactured in and imported from Japan by Classic Doubles.
Price: $1,905.00

Classic 101 Field I

Classic Model 101 Field Grade II
Similar to the Field Grade I except has engraved satin gray receiver. Available in 12, 20, 28, 410, plus a 12/20 gauge set (12 ga. 28″, 20 ga. 26″).
Price: $2,190.00
Price: 12/20 set $3,420.00

Classic Model 101 Waterfowler
Same as Model 101 Field Grade except in 12 ga. only, 3″ chambers, 30″ barrels. Comes with four choke tubes: Mod., Imp. Mod., Full, Extra-Full. Non-glare wood finish, matte blued receiver with hand etching and engraving. Introduced 1981. Manufactured in and imported from Japan by Classic Doubles.
Price: $1,520.00

Classic Model 101 Trap and Skeet
Similar to the Model 101 Field Grades except designed for target competition. Barrels have high, tapered vent. rib; barrel vents for Skeet guns, barrel ports for trap guns; Skeet models have mechanical trigger, trap have inertia trigger. Stocks pre-drilled for recoil reducer, and are quick detachable. Standard or Monte Carlo stock. Trap available as o/u, single barrel or Combo.
Price: Trap, from $1,905.00
Price: Skeet, 12 and 20 . . . . $1,905.00
Price: Skeet, 410 . . . . $4,765.00

Classic 101 Trap

Classic Model 101 Sporter O/U
Similar to the Field Grade II except designed for Sporting Clays and has different balance than a field gun. Available in 12 ga. only with 28″ or 30″ barrels with six choke tubes. Top of frame and top lever have matte finish. Frame has silvered finish, light engraving.
Price: $1,980.00
Price: Combo includes both barrel sets $2,945.00

Krieghoff K-80 Trap

F.I.E./FRANCHI "ALCIONE S" OVER/UNDER
Gauge: 12 ga. only, 3″ chambers.
Barrel: 26″, 28″, 30″, 32″ with Full, Mod., Imp. Cyl. Franchoke choke tubes.
Weight: 6 lbs. 13 oz.
Stock: French walnut with cut checkered pistol grip and forend. Recoil pad; epoxy finish.
Features: Top tang safety, automatic ejectors, single selective trigger. Chrome-plated bores. Decorative scroll on silvered receiver. Introduced 1982. Choke tubes introduced 1989. Imported from Italy by F.I.E. Firearms Corp.
Price: Diamond Grade $1,599.95

KRIEGHOFF K-80 O/U TRAP SHOTGUN
Gauge: 12, 2¾″ chambers.
Barrel: 30″, 32″, (Imp. Mod. & Full or choke tubes).
Weight: About 8½ lbs.
Stock: Four stock dimensions or adjustable stock available; all have palm-swell grips. Checkered European walnut.
Features: Satin nickel receiver. Selective mechanical trigger, adjustable for position. Ventilated step rib. Introduced 1980. Imported from West Germany by Krieghoff International, Inc.
Price: K-80 O/U, (30″, 32″, Imp. Mod. & Full) $4,850.00
Price: K-80 Unsingle (32″, 34″, Full), Standard $5,675.00
Price: K-80 Topsingle (34″, Full), Standard $4,995.00
Price: K-80 Combo (two-barrel set), Standard $7,295.00

KRIEGHOFF K-80 SKEET SHOTGUN
Gauge: 12, 2¾″ chambers.
Barrel: 28″ (Skeet & Skeet, optional Tula or choke tubes).
Weight: About 7¾ lbs.
Stock: American Skeet or straight Skeet stocks, with palm-swell grips. Walnut.
Features: Satin gray receiver finish. Selective mechanical trigger adjustable for position. Choice of ventilated 8mm parallel flat rib or ventilated 8-12mm tapered flat rib. Introduced 1980. Imported from West Germany by Krieghoff International, Inc.
Price: Standard, Skeet chokes $4,750.00
Price: As above, Tula chokes $4,950.00
Price: Lightweight model (weighs 7 lbs.), Standard $4,750.00
Price: Two-Barrel Set (tube concept), 12 ga., Standard $8,745.00

KRIEGHOFF K-80 PIGEON SHOTGUN
Gauge: 12, 2¾″ chambers.
Barrel: 28″, 30″ (Imp. Mod. & Super Full or choke tubes), 29″ optional (Imp. Mod. & Special Full).
Weight: About 8 lbs.
Stock: Four stock dimensions available. Checkered walnut.
Features: Steel receiver with satin gray finish, engraving. Selective mechanical trigger adjustable for position. Ventilated step rib. Free-floating barrels. Comes with aluminum case. Introduced 1980. Imported from West Germany by Krieghoff International.
Price: Standard grade $4,850.00

Krieghoff K-80 Four-Barrel Skeet Set
Similar to the Standard Skeet except comes with barrels for 12, 20, 28, 410. Comes with fitted aluminum case.
Price: Standard grade $9,650.00

Krieghoff K-80 International Skeet
Similar to the Standard Skeet except has ½″ ventilated Broadway-style rib, special Tula chokes with gas release holes at muzzle. International Skeet stock. Comes in fitted aluminum case.
Price: Standard grade $5,100.00

Krieghoff K-80 Clays

KRIEGHOFF K-80 SPORTING CLAYS O/U
Gauge: 12, 2¾″ chambers.
Barrel: 28″ or 30″ with choke tubes.

Weight: About 8 lbs.
Stock: #3 Sporting stock designed for gun-down shooting.
Features: Choice of standard or lightweight receiver with satin nickel finish and classic scroll engraving. Selective mechanical trigger adjustable for position. Choice of tapered flat, 8mm parallel flat, or step-tapered barrel rib. Free-floating barrels. Aluminum case. Imported from West Germany by Krieghoff International.
Price: Standard grade with five choke tubes **$5,350.00**

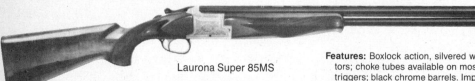

Laurona Super 85MS

LAURONA SUPER MODEL OVER/UNDERS
Gauge: 12, 20, 2¾″ or 3″ chambers.
Barrel: 26″ (Multichokes), 28″ (Mod. & Full, Imp. Cyl. & Imp. Mod.), 29″ (Multichokes or Full).
Weight: About 7 lbs.
Stock: European walnut. Dimensions vary according to model. Full pistol grip.

Features: Boxlock action, silvered with engraving. Automatic selective ejectors; choke tubes available on most models; single selective or twin single triggers; black chrome barrels. Imported from Spain by Galaxy Imports.
Price: Model 82G, 82S, 12 or 20 ga. **$984.00**
Price: Model 83 MG, 12 or 20 ga. **$995.00**
Price: Model 84S Super Trap (fixed chokes) **$1,095.00**
Price: Model 85 Super Game, 12 or 20 ga. **$995.00**
Price: Model 85 MS Super Trap (Full/Multichoke) **$1,135.00**
Price: Model 85 MS Super Pigeon **$1,117.00**
Price: Model 85 S Super Skeet, 12 ga. **$1,061.00**
Price: Model 85 MS Spec. Sporting, 12 ga. **$1,085.00**

Laurona Sporting Clays

LAURONA SILHOUETTE 300 SPORTING CLAYS
Gauge: 12, 2¾″ chambers.
Barrel: 28″ (Multichoke tubes, flush-type or knurled).
Weight: 7 lbs., 4 oz.
Stock: 14³⁄₈″x1³⁄₈″x2½″. European walnut with full pistol grip, beavertail forend. Rubber buttpad.
Features: Selective single trigger, automatic selective ejectors, automatic safety. Introduced 1988. Imported from Spain by Galaxy Imports.
Price: **$1,019.00**

Laurona Silhouette 300 Trap
Same gun as the Silhouette 300 Sporting Clays except has 29″ barrels, trap stock dimensions of 14³⁄₈″x1⁷⁄₁₆″x1⁵⁄₈″, weighs 7 lbs., 15 oz. Available with flush or knurled Multichokes.
Price: **$1,159.00**

Ljutic LM-6

LJUTIC T.C. LM-6 DELUXE O/U SHOTGUN
Gauge: 12 ga.
Barrel: 28″ to 34″, choked to customer specs for live birds, trap, International Trap.
Weight: To customer specs.
Stock: To customer specs. Oil finish, hand checkered.
Features: Custom-made gun. Hollow-milled rib, pull or release trigger, push-button opener in front of trigger guard. From Ljutic Industries.
Price: Super Deluxe LM-6 o/u **$9,984.00**
Price: Over/under Combo (interchangeable single barrel, two trigger guards, one for single trigger, one for doubles) **$14,995.00**
Price: Extra over/under barrel sets, 29″-32″ **$4,995.00**

Ljutic Four-Barrel Skeet Set
LM-6 over/under 12-ga. frame with matched set of four 28″ barrels in 12, 20, 28 and 410. Ljutic Paternator chokes and barrel are integral. Stock is to customer specs, of fine American or French walnut with EX (or Extra) Fancy checkering.
Price: Four-barrel set **$26,995.00**

Navy Bird Hunter

NAVY ARMS MODEL 83/93 BIRD HUNTER O/U
Gauge: 12, 20, 3″ chambers.
Barrel: 28″ (Imp. Cyl. & Mod., Mod. & Full).
Weight: About 7½ lbs.
Stock: European walnut, checkered grip and forend.
Sights: Metal bead front.
Features: Boxlock action with double triggers; extractors only; silvered, engraved receiver; vented top and middle ribs. Imported from Italy by Navy Arms. Introduced 1984.
Price: Model 83 (extractors) **$389.00**
Price: Model 93 (ejectors) **$450.00**

Navy Arms Model 95/96
Same as the 83/93 Bird Hunter except comes with five interchangeable choke tubes. Model 96 has gold-plated single trigger and ejectors.
Price: Model 95 (extractors) **$475.00**
Price: Model 96 (ejectors) **$575.00**

CAUTION: PRICES CHANGE. CHECK AT GUNSHOP.

MERKEL OVER/UNDER SHOTGUNS

Gauge: 12, 16, 20, 28, 410, 2³/₄″, 3″ chambers.
Barrel: 26″, 26³/₄″, 28″ (standard chokes).
Weight: 6 to 7 lbs.
Stock: European walnut. Straight English or pistol grip.
Features: Models 200E and 201E are boxlocks, 203E and 303E are sidelocks. All have auto. ejectors, articulated front triggers. Auto. safety, selective and non-selective triggers optional. Imported from East Germany by Armes de Chasse.
Price: 200E, about **$2,835.00**
Price: 201E, about **$3,675.00**
Price: 203E (sidelock), about **$8,020.00**
Price: 303E (sidelock), about **$9,060.00**

NAVY ARMS MODEL 100 O/U SHOTGUN

Gauge: 12, 20, 28, 2³/₄″ chambers, 410, 3″ chambers.
Barrel: 12 ga. — 28″ (Imp. Cyl. & Mod., Mod. & Full); 20 ga. — 28″ (Imp. Cyl. & Mod., Skeet & Skeet); 28 ga. — 28″ (Full & Mod., Skeet & Skeet); 410 bore — 26″ (Full & Full, Skeet & Skeet).
Weight: 6¹/₄ lbs.
Stock: European walnut; checkered p.g. and forend.
Features: Chrome-lined barrels, hard chrome finished receiver with engraving, vent. rib. Single trigger. Imported from Italy by Navy Arms. Introduced 1986.
Price: **$299.00**

Pachmayr/Perazzi

PACHMAYR/PERAZZI MX-20 OVER/UNDER

Gauge: 20, 3″ chambers.
Barrel: 26″ (Cyl., Imp. Cyl., Mod., Imp. Mod., Full choke tubes). Fixed chokes available.
Weight: 6 lbs., 8 oz.
Stock: 14¹/₂″x1³/₈″x2¹/₄″x1¹/₂″; select European walnut with 26 lpi checkering, checkered butt.
Sights: Nickel silver front bead.

Features: Boxlock action, uses special 20-gauge frame. Carved schnabel-type forend. Single selective trigger, automatic selective ejectors, manual safety. Comes with lockable fitted case. Introduced 1986. From Pachmayr, Ltd.
Price: **$4,995.00**

Perazzi MX8 Skeet

PERAZZI MX8/MX8 SPECIAL TRAP, SKEET

Gauge: 12, 2³/₄″ chambers.
Barrel: Trap — 29¹/₂″ (Imp. Mod. & Extra Full), 31¹/₂″ (Full & Extra Full). Choke tubes optional. Skeet — 27⁵/₈″ (Skeet & Skeet).
Weight: About 8¹/₂ lbs. (Trap); 7 lbs., 15 oz. (Skeet).
Stock: Interchangeable and custom made to customer specs.
Features: Has detachable and interchangeable trigger group with flat V springs. Flat ⁷/₁₆″ ventilated rib. Many options available. Imported from Italy by Perazzi U.S.A., Inc.
Price: From. **$5,350.00**
Price: MX8 Special (adj. four-position trigger), from **$5,600.00**
Price: MX8 Special Single (32″ or 34″ single barrel, step rib), from **$5,350.00**
Price: MX8 special Combo (o/u and single barrel sets), from **$7,650.00**

Perazzi Grand American 88 Special
Similar to the MX8 except has tapered ⁷/₁₆″x⁵/₁₆″ high ramped rib. Choked Imp. Mod. & Full, 29¹/₂″ barrels.
Price: From. **$7,650.00**
Price: Special Single (32″ or 34″ single barrel), from **$5,350.00**
Price: DB81 Special, from **$5,550.00**

Perazzi MX3 Special

Perazzi MX3 Special Single, Over/Under
Similar to the MX8 Special except has an adjustable four-position trigger, high ⁷/₁₆″x⁵/₁₆″ rib, weighs 8¹/₂ lbs. Choked Mod. & Full.
Price: From. **$5,030.00**
Price: MX3 Special Single (32″ or 34″ single barrel), from **$4,750.00**
Price: MX3 Special Combo (o/u and single barrel sets), from **$6,650.00**

Perazzi MX1, MX1B Sporting Over/Under
Similar to the MX8 except has ramped, tapered rib, interchangeable trigger assembly with leaf hammer springs, 27⁵/₈″ barrels choked Imp. Mod. & Extra Full. Weight is 7 lbs., 12 oz.
Price: From. **$5,350.00**
Price: MX1B (as above except has flat conventional rib), from **$5,350.00**

Perazzi Mirage Special Skeet Over/Under
Similar to the MX8 Skeet except has adjustable four-position trigger, Skeet stock dimensions.
Price: From. **$5,600.00**

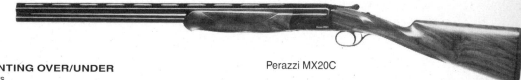

Perazzi MX20C

PERAZZI MX12 HUNTING OVER/UNDER

Gauge: 12, 2³/₄″ chambers.
Barrel: 26″, 27⁵/₈″ (Mod. & Full) choke tubes available (MX12C).
Weight: 7 lbs., 4 oz.
Stock: To customer specs; interchangeable.
Features: Single selective trigger; coil springs used in action; schnabel forend tip. Imported from Italy by Perazzi U.S.A., Inc.
Price: From. **$5,200.00**
Price: MX12C (with choke tubes), from **$5,500.00**

Perazzi MX20 Hunting Over/Under
Similar to the MX12 except 20-ga. frame size. Available in 20, 28, 410 with 2³/₄″ or 3″ chambers. 26″ only, and choked Mod. & Full. Weight is 6 lbs., 6 oz.
Price: From. **$5,700.00**
Price: MX20C (as above, 20 ga. only, choke tubes), from **$6,000.00**

CAUTION: PRICES CHANGE. CHECK AT GUNSHOP.

GUNS ILLUSTRATED 1990 **229**

Sile Field King Super Light, Field Hunter, Slug Master O/U
Similar to the Field Master II except in 12 ga. only with 28″ barrels (Mod. & Full). Weight 6¼ lbs. Imported by Sile.
Price: $489.95
Price: Field Hunter (similar to above, with 23½″ Cyl. & Cyl. barrels, ramp front sight, folding rear) $391.95
Price: Slug Master.. $461.95

SILE SKY STALKER OVER/UNDER
Gauge: 20, 28, 410, 3″ chambers.
Barrel: 26″, 28″ (Imp. Cyl. & Mod., Mod. & Full, Full & Full, Skeet & Skeet).
Weight: About 6¾ lbs.
Stock: Walnut-finished hardwood, checkered p.g. and forend.
Features: Folds in half for storage or carry. Mechanical extractors; single non-selective trigger. Imported by Sile.
Price: $239.95

STOEGER/IGA OVER/UNDER SHOTGUN
Gauge: 12, 20, 3″ chambers.
Barrel: 26″ (Full & Full, Imp. Cyl. & Mod.), 28″ (Mod. & Full).
Weight: 6¾ to 7 lbs.
Stock: 14½″x1½″x2½″. Oil-finished hardwood with checkered pistol grip and forend.
Features: Manual safety, single trigger, extractors only, ventilated top rib. Introduced 1983. Imported from Brazil by Stoeger Industries.
Price: $380.00

Sile Field King, Skeet King O/U Shotgun
Similar to the Field Master II except 26″, 28″ (Imp. Cyl. & Mod.), 28″ (Mod. & Full) for Field; Skeet has 26″ (Skeet & Skeet); both fixed chokes. Single non-selective trigger.
Price: $391.95

Sile Trap King O/U Shotgun
Similar to the Field Master II except has 2¾″ chambers, 30″ barrels choked Mod. & Full or Full & Full. Walnut Monte Carlo stock with palm swell and recoil pad. Weight is 8½ lbs. Automatic ejectors.
Price: $559.95

SIMSON/SUHL MODEL 85 EJ OVER/UNDER
Gauge: 12, 2¾″ chambers.
Barrel: 28″ (Imp. Cyl. & Mod.).
Weight: 6¾ lbs.
Stock: European walnut; pistol grip style.
Features: Anson & Deeley modified boxlock action with double triggers, manual safety. Cold hammer forged barrels, double locking lugs. Choking and patterning for steel shot (by importer). Auto safety, vent. rib optional. Imported from East Germany by Armes de Chasse.
Price: $1,600.00
Price: Model EU (single non-selective trigger, vent. rib) $1,900.00

Techi-Mec SPL 640

TECHNI-MEC MODEL SPL 640 FOLDING O/U
Gauge: 12, 16, 20, 28, 2¾″ chambers; 410, 3″ chambers.
Barrel: 26″ (Mod. & Full).
Weight: 5½ lbs.
Stock: European walnut.
Features: Gun folds in half for storage, transportation. Chrome-lined barrels; ventilated rib; photo-engraved silvered receiver. Imported from Italy by L. Joseph Rahn, Mandall. Introduced 1984.
Price: Double triggers......................... $280.00 to $299.95
Price: Single trigger .... $300.00 to $350.95
Price: Model SPL 642, double triggers (Rahn) $300.00
Price: As above, single trigger (Rahn) $315.00

TECHNI-MEC MODEL SR 692 EM OVER/UNDER
Gauge: 12, 16, 20, 2¾″ or 3″ chambers.
Barrel: 26″, 28″, 30″ (Mod., Full, Imp. Cyl., Cyl.).
Weight: 6½ lbs.
Stock: 14½″x ½″x2½″. European walnut with checkered grip and forend.
Features: Boxlock action with dummy sideplates, fine game scene engraving; single selective trigger; automatic ejectors available. Imported from Italy by L. Joseph Rahn. Introduced 1984.
Price: $750.00
Price: Slug gun $700.00

> Consult our Directory pages for the location of firms mentioned.

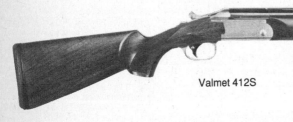

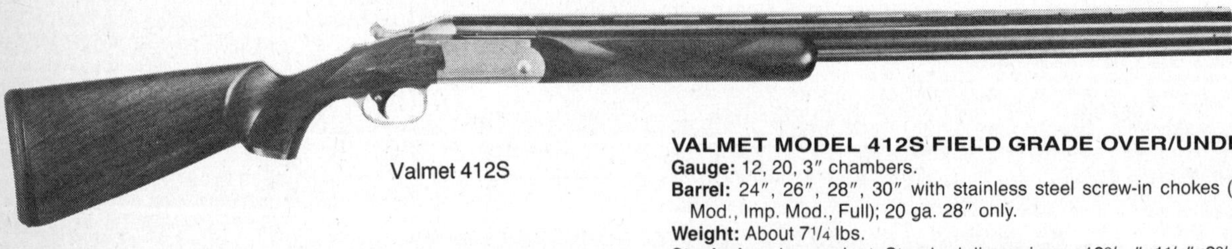

Valmet 412S

Valmet 412 ST Trap and Skeet
Target versions of the 412S gun with hand-honed actions, mechanical single triggers, elongated forcing cones and stainless steel choke tubes. Target safety is locked in "Fire" position (removal of a screw converts it to automatic safety); automatic ejectors; cocking indicators. Walnut stocks with double palm swells are quickly interchangeable. Trap guns have high stepped rib, 30″, 32″ O/U and 32″, 34″ single barrels; Skeet guns in 12, 20 ga. with 28″ barrels.
Grade II guns have semi-fancy wood, matte nickel finished receiver with matte blue locking bolt and lever, gold trigger, pre-drilled stock for insertion of a recoil reducer, more checkering at stock wrist. Introduced 1987.
Price: Grade I.................................... $1,215.00
Price: Grade II $1,550.00

VALMET MODEL 412S FIELD GRADE OVER/UNDER
Gauge: 12, 20, 3″ chambers.
Barrel: 24″, 26″, 28″, 30″ with stainless steel screw-in chokes (Imp. Cyl., Mod., Imp. Mod., Full); 20 ga. 28″ only.
Weight: About 7¼ lbs.
Stock: American walnut. Standard dimensions—13⁹⁄₁₀″x1½″x2²⁄₅″. Checkered p.g. and forend.
Features: Free interchangeability of barrels, stocks and forends into double rifle model, combination gun, etc. Barrel selector in trigger; auto. top tang safety; barrel cocking indicators. Introduced 1980. Imported from Finland by Valmet.
Price: Model 412S (ejectors)............................... $999.00

Perazzi Mirage Sporting

PERAZZI MIRAGE SPECIAL SPORTING O/U
Gauge: 12, 2³/₄″ chambers.
Barrel: 27⁵/₈″, 28³/₈″ (Imp. Mod. & Extra Full).
Weight: 7 lbs., 12 oz.
Stock: To customer specs; interchangeable.
Features: Has adjustable four-position trigger; flat ⁷/₁₆″ x ⁵/₁₆″ vent. rib. Many options available. Imported from Italy by Perazzi U.S.A., Inc.
Price: **$5,350.00**

Perazzi Mirage Special Four-Gauge Skeet
Similar to the Mirage Sporting model except has Skeet dimensions, interchangeable, adjustable four-position trigger assembly. Comes with four barrel sets in 12, 20, 28, 410, flat ⁵/₁₆″x⁵/₁₆″ rib.
Price: From **$13,050.00**
Price: MX3 Special Set, from **$11,650.00**

Ruger 12 Ga. Red Label

Weight: About 7 lbs. (20 ga.), 7¹/₂ lbs. (12 ga.). **Length:** 43″ overall (26″ barrels).
Stock: 14″ x 1¹/₂″ x 2¹/₂″. Straight grain American walnut. Checkered p.g. and forend, rubber recoil pad.
Features: Automatic safety/barrel selector, stainless steel trigger. Patented barrel side spacers may be removed if desired. Available only with stainless receiver. 20 ga. introduced 1977; 12 ga. introduced 1982.
Price: 20 ga. **$920.00**
Price: 12 ga., stainless receiver **$920.00**
Price: As above, screw-in choke tubes **$1,050.00**

RUGER "RED LABEL" O/U SHOTGUN
Gauge: 20 and 12, 3″ chambers.
Barrel: 20 ga.—26″, 28″ (Skeet & Skeet, Imp. Cyl. & Mod. choke tubes), 28″ (Full & Mod.); 12 ga.—26″, 28″ (Skeet & Skeet, Imp. Cyl. & Mod., Full & Mod.); 12 ga.—26″, 28″ (Skeet, Imp. Cyl., Full, Mod. Screw-In choke tubes).

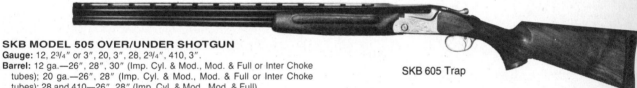

SKB 605 Trap

SKB MODEL 505 OVER/UNDER SHOTGUN
Gauge: 12, 2³/₄″ or 3″, 20, 3″, 28, 2³/₄″, 410, 3″.
Barrel: 12 ga.—26″, 28″, 30″ (Imp. Cyl. & Mod., Mod. & Full or Inter Choke tubes); 20 ga.—26″, 28″ (Imp. Cyl. & Mod., Mod. & Full or Inter Choke tubes); 28 and 410—26″, 28″ (Imp. Cyl. & Mod., Mod. & Full).
Weight: 6.6 to 7.4 lbs.
Length: 45³/₁₆″ overall.
Stock: 14¹/₈″ x 1¹/₂″ x 2³/₁₆″. Hand checkered walnut.
Sights: Metal bead front.
Features: Blued boxlock action; ejectors; single selective trigger. Introduced 1988. Imported from Japan by Ernie Simmons Enterprises.
Price: **$795.00**
Price: Two-barrel Field Set, 12 and 20, choke tubes **$1,250.00**
Price: As above, 28 and 410, fixed chokes **$1,250.00**
Price: Model 505 Trap, Skeet **$825.00**
Price: Model 505 Single Barrel Trap **$825.00**
Price: Skeet set, 20, 28, 410 . . . . **$1,850.00**

SKB Model 605 Over/Under Shotgun
Similar to the Model 505 except has silvered, engraved receiver.
Price: **$975.00**
Price: Two-barrel Field Set, 12 and 20 ga., choke tubes **$1,450.00**
Price: As above, 28 and 410, fixed chokes **$1,450.00**
Price: Model 605 Trap, Skeet **$995.00**
Price: Model 605 Single Barrel Trap **$995.00**
Price: Skeet Set, 20, 28, 410 . . . . **$1,995.00**

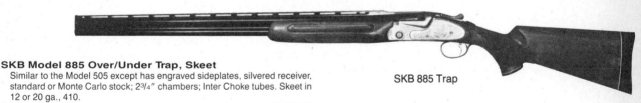

SKB 885 Trap

SKB Model 885 Over/Under Trap, Skeet
Similar to the Model 505 except has engraved sideplates, silvered receiver, standard or Monte Carlo stock; 2³/₄″ chambers; Inter Choke tubes. Skeet in 12 or 20 ga., 410.
Price: **$1,495.00**
Price: Skeet Set, 20, 28, 410 . . . . **$2,650.00**

Sile Field Master II

Weight: 7¹/₂ lbs. **Length:** 45¹/₄″ overall.
Stock: Satin-finished walnut, cut-checkered p.g. and forend.
Features: Single selective trigger; extractors; automatic safety; engraved silvered receiver. Imported by Sile.
Price: **$475.95**
Price: Field Hunter I (similar to above except 26″ [Imp. Cyl. & Mod.] or 28″ [Mod. & Full]) **$335.95**
Price: Field Hunter II (as above except with choke tubes) **$391.95**

SILE FIELD MASTER II O/U SHOTGUN
Gauge: 12, 3″ chambers.
Barrel: 28″ (Imp. Cyl., Mod., Imp. Mod., Full choke tubes).

Weatherby Orion III

WEATHERBY ORION O/U SHOTGUNS
Gauge: 12, 20, 410, 3″ chambers, 28, 2³/₄″ chambers.
Barrel: Fixed choke, 12, 20, 28, 410—26″, 28″, 30″ (Imp. Cyl. & Mod., Full & Mod., Skeet & Skeet); IMC Multi-Choke, 12, 20, Field models — 26″ (Imp. Cyl., Mod., Full, Skeet), 28″ (Imp. Cyl., Mod., Full), 30″ (Mod., Full); O/U Trap models — 30″, 32″ (Imp. Mod., Mod., Full); Single bbl. Trap — 32″, 34″ (Imp. Mod., Mod., Full).

Weight: 6¹/₂″ to 9 lbs.
Stock: American walnut, checkered grip and forend. Rubber recoil pad. Dimensions for Field and Skeet models, 14¹/₄″x1¹/₂″x2¹/₂″.
Features: Selective automatic ejectors, single selective mechanical trigger. Top tang safety, Greener crossbolt. Orion I has plain blued receiver, no engraving; Orion II has engraved, blued receiver; Orion III has silver-gray receiver with engraving. Imported from Japan by Weatherby.
Price: Orion I, Field, 12 or 20, IMC $850.00
Price: Orion II, Field, 12 or 20, IMC $1,000.00
Price: Orion II, Field, 28 or 410, fixed chokes $1,000.00
Price: Orion II, Skeet, 12 or 20, fixed chokes $1,011.00
Price: Orion II, Trap, 12, IMC $1,051.00
Price: Orion III, Field, 12 or 20, IMC $1,100.00

Weatherby Athena V

WEATHERBY ATHENA O/U SHOTGUNS
Gauge: 12, 20, 28, 410 ga, 3″ chambers; 2³/₄″ on Trap gun.
Action: Boxlock (simulated sidelock) top lever break-open. Selective auto ejectors, single selective trigger (selector inside trigger guard).
Barrel: Fixed choke, 12, 20 ga.—26″, 28″ (Skeet & Skeet); IMC Multi-Choke tubes 12, 20, 410, Field models—26″ (Skeet, Imp. Cyl., Mod.), 28″ (Imp. Cyl., Mod., Full), 30″ (12 ga. only. Full, Mod., Full); o/u Trap models—30″, 32″ (Mod., Imp. Mod., Full).

Weight: 12 ga. 7³/₈ lbs., 20 ga. 6⁷/₈ lbs.
Stock: American walnut, checkered p.g. and forend (14¹/₄″ × 1¹/₂″ × 2¹/₂″).
Features: Mechanically operated trigger. Top tang safety, Greener cross-bolt, fully engraved receiver, recoil pad installed. IMC models furnished with three interchangeable flush-fitting choke tubes. Imported from Japan by Weatherby. Introduced 1982.
Price: Skeet, fixed choke $1,601.00
Price: 12 or 20 ga., IMC Multi-Choke, Field $1,590.00
Price: IMC Multi-Choke Trap $1,611.00
Price: Athena Grade V (more elaborate engraving) $2,000.00
Price: Extra IMC Choke tubes $16.00
Price: Master Skeet Tube Set (12-ga. gun with six Briley tubes in 20, 28, 410) $3,200.00

Zanoletti 2000 Field

A. ZOLI DELFINO S.P. O/U
Gauge: 12 or 20, 3″ chambers.
Barrel: 28″ (Mod. & Full); vent. rib.
Weight: 5¹/₂ lbs.
Stock: Walnut. Hand checkered p.g. and forend; cheekpiece.
Features: Color case-hardened receiver with light engraving; chrome-lined barrels; automatic sliding safety; double triggers; ejectors. From Mandall Shooting Supplies.
Price: $895.00

PIETRO ZANOLETTI MODEL 2000 FIELD O/U
Gauge: 12 only.
Barrel: 28″ (Mod. & Full).
Weight: 7 lbs.
Stock: European walnut, checkered grip and forend.
Sights: Gold bead front.
Features: Boxlock action with auto ejectors, double triggers; engraved receiver. Imported from Italy by Mandall Shooting Supplies. Introduced 1984.
Price: $895.00

Zoli Angel

A. ZOLI MODEL ANGEL FIELD GRADE O/U
Gauge: 12, 20.
Barrel: 26″, 28″, 30″ (Mod. & Full).

Weight: About 7¹/₂ lbs.
Stock: Straight-grained walnut with checkered grip and forend.
Sights: Gold bead front.
Features: Boxlock action with single selective trigger, auto ejectors; extra-wide vent. top rib. Imported from Italy by Mandall Shooting Supplies.
Price: $895.00
Price: Condor model $895.00

Zoli Silver Falcon

ZOLI SILVER FALCON OVER/UNDER
Gauge: 12 or 20, 3″ chambers.

Barrel: 12 ga. — 26″, 28″; 20 ga. — 26″; Imp. Cyl., Mod., Imp. Mod., Full choke tubes.
Weight: 6¹/₄ to 7¹/₄ lbs.
Stock: 14¹/₄″x2¹/₈″x1⁵/₁₆″. Oil-finished Turkish circassian walnut.
Features: Boxlock action with silver finish, floral engraving; single selective trigger, automatic ejectors. Introduced 1989. Imported from Italy by Antonio Zoli, USA.
Price: $1,200.00

CAUTION: PRICES CHANGE. CHECK AT GUNSHOP.

ZOLI Z90 TRAP GUN

Gauge: 12, 2³/₄″ chambers.
Barrel: 29¹/₂″ or 32″. Comes with Mod., Imp. Mod. and Full choke tubes.
Weight: 8¹/₂ lbs.
Stock: 14¹/₂″x2¹/₈″x1¹/₂″x1¹/₂″. Checkered Turkish circassian walnut with Monte Carlo, recoil pad, oil finish.
Features: Boxlock action with automatic selective ejectors, single selective trigger adjustable for pull length; step-type vent. rib and vent. center rib. Introduced 1989. Imported from Italy by Antonio Zoli, USA.
Price: **$1,800.00**

Zoli Z90 Trap

Zoli Z90 Skeet Gun

Similar to the Z90 Trap except has 28″ barrels with fixed Skeet & Skeet chokes, 14¹/₄″x2¹/₄″x1¹/₂″ stock dimensions (drop at heel also available at 2¹/₈″, 2³/₈″ or 2¹/₂″). Weighs 7³/₄ lbs. Available in 12 gauge only. Introduced 1989.
Price: **$1,800.00**

Zoli Woodsman

ZOLI Z90 SPORTING CLAYS SHOTGUN

Gauge: 12, 2³/₄″ chambers.
Barrel: 28″. Comes with four choke tubes — two Skeet, one each Imp. Cyl. and Mod.
Weight: 7¹/₄ lbs.
Stock: 14¹/₄″x2¹/₈″x1¹/₂″. Turkish circassian walnut with checkered grip and forend; oil finish.
Features: Sidelock action with silvered and engraved frame, single selective trigger, selective automatic ejectors. Schnabel forend tip; solid rubber buttpad. Introduced 1989. Imported from Italy by Antonio Zoli, USA.
Price: **$1,500.00**

ZOLI WOODSMAN OVER/UNDER SHOTGUN

Gauge: 12, 3″ chambers.
Barrel: 23″ (five choke tubes furnished — two each Cyl., plus Imp. Cyl., Mod., Full).
Weight: 6³/₄ lbs.
Stock: 14¹/₂″x2⁵/₁₆″x1³/₈″. Turkish circassian walnut with skip-line checkering, rubber buttpad; oil finish.
Sights: Rifle-type sights on raised rib. Folding leaf rear, bead front.
Features: Boxlock action with silvered and engraved frame, single selective trigger, automatic selective ejectors. Available with or without sling swivels. Introduced 1989. Imported from Italy by Antonio Zoli, USA.
Price: **$1,350.00**

SHOTGUNS—SIDE-BY-SIDES

Variety of models for utility and sporting use, including some competitive shooting.

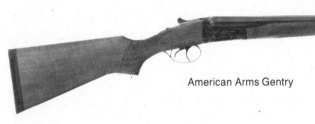

American Arms Gentry

American Arms Derby Side-by-Side

Has sidelock action with English-style engraving on the sideplates. Straight-grip, hand-checkered walnut stock with splinter forend, hand rubbed oil finish. Double or single non-selective trigger, automatic selective ejectors. Same chokes, rib, barrel lengths as the York. Has 5-year warranty. From American Arms, Inc.

Price: 12 and 20, double trigger **$789.00**
Price: As above, single trigger **$825.00**
Price: 28 and 410, double trigger **$825.00**
Price: As above, single trigger **$859.00**
Price: Two-barrel set, 20/28 ga., double triggers **$1,029.00**
Price: As above, single trigger........................... **$1,069.00**

AMERICAN ARMS GENTRY DOUBLE SHOTGUN

Gauge: 12, 16, 20, 28, 410, 3″ chambers except 16, 28, 2³/₄″.
Barrel: 26″ (Imp. Cyl. & Mod., all gauges), 28″ (Mod. & Full, 12 and 20 gauges).
Weight: 6¹/₄ to 6³/₄ lbs.
Stock: 14¹/₈″ × 1³/₈″ × 2³/₈″. Hand-checkered walnut with semi-gloss finish.
Sights: Metal bead front.
Features: Boxlock action with English-style scroll engraving, color case-hardened finish. Double triggers, extractors. Independent floating firing pins. Manual safety. Five-year warranty. Introduced 1987. Imported from Spain by American Arms, Inc.
Price: 12, 16 or 20 gauge **$469.00**
Price: 28 or 410 .... **$499.00**

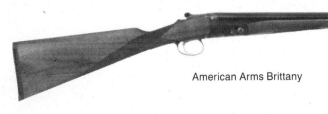

American Arms Brittany

AMERICAN ARMS BRITTANY SHOTGUN

Gauge: 12, 20, 3″ chambers.
Barrel: 12 ga. —27″; 20 ga. — 25″ (Imp. Cyl., Mod., Full choke tubes).
Weight: 6 lbs., 7 oz. (20 ga.).
Stock: 14¹/₈″x1³/₈″x2³/₈″. Hand-checkered walnut with oil finish, straight English-style with semi-beavertail forend.
Features: Boxlock action with case-color finish, engraving; single selective trigger, automatic selective ejectors; rubber recoil pad. Introduced 1989. Imported from Spain by American Arms, Inc.
Price: **$649.00**

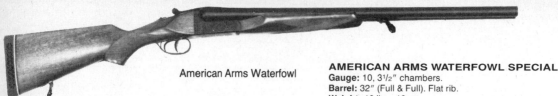

American Arms Waterfowl

American Arms Turkey Special Side-by-Side

Similar to the Waterfowl Special except in 12 ga. with 3¹/₂″ chambers, 26″ barrels with Full & Full choke tubes, single selective trigger, extractors. Comes with camouflage sling, swivels, 5-year warranty. From American Arms, Inc.

Price: $559.00
Price: As above, 10 ga. $655.00

AMERICAN ARMS WATERFOWL SPECIAL

Gauge: 10, 3¹/₂″ chambers.
Barrel: 32″ (Full & Full). Flat rib.
Weight: 10 lbs., 13 oz.
Stock: 14⁵/₁₆″ × 1³/₈″ × 2³/₈″. Hand-checkered walnut with beavertail forend, full pistol grip, dull finish, rubber recoil pad.
Features: Boxlock action with double triggers and extractors. All metal has Parkerized finish. Comes with camouflaged sling, sling swivels, 5-year warranty. Introduced 1987. Imported from Spain by American Arms, Inc.
Price: $609.00

American Arms Grulla

AMERICAN ARMS GRULLA #2 DOUBLE SHOTGUN

Gauge: 12, 20, 28, 410.
Barrel: 12 ga. — 28″ (Mod. & Full); 26″ (Imp. Cyl. & Mod.) all gauges.

Weight: 5 lbs., 13 oz. to 6 lbs. 4 oz.
Stock: Select walnut with straight English grip, splinter forend; hand-rubbed oil finish; checkered grip, forend, butt.
Features: True sidelock action with double triggers, detachable locks, automatic selective ejectors, cocking indicators, gas escape valves. Color case-hardened receiver with scroll engraving. English-style concave rib. Introduced 1989. Imported from Spain by American Arms, Inc.
Price: 12, 20, 28, 410 .... $2,099.00
Price: Two-barrel sets $3,030.00

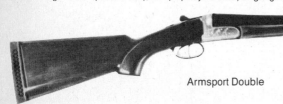

Armsport Double

BGJ 10 GAUGE MAGNUM SHOTGUN

Gauge: 10 ga. (3¹/₂″ chambers).
Action: Boxlock.
Barrel: 32″ (Full).
Weight: 11 lbs.
Stock: 14¹/₂″x1¹/₂″x2⁵/₈″. European walnut, checkered at p.g. and forend.
Features: Double triggers; color hardened action, rest blued. Front and center metal beads on matted rib; ventilated rubber recoil pad. Forend release has positive Purdey-type mechanism. Imported from Spain by Mandall Shooting Supplies.
Price: $599.95

ARMSPORT DOUBLE SHOTGUN

Gauge: 12, 20, 410; 3″ chambers.
Barrel: 12 ga. — 28″ (Mod. & Full); 20 ga. — 26″ (Imp. & Mod.); 410 — 26″ (Imp. & Mod.)
Weight: About 6³/₄ lbs.
Stock: European walnut.
Features: Chrome-lined barrels. Boxlock action with engraving. Imported from Italy by Armsport.
Price: $595.00

ARIZAGA MODEL 31 DOUBLE SHOTGUN

Gauge: 12, 16, 20, 28, 410.
Barrel: 26″, 28″ (standard chokes).
Weight: 6 lbs., 9 oz. **Length:** 45″ overall.
Stock: Straight English style or pistol grip.
Features: Boxlock action with double triggers; blued, engraved receiver. Imported by Mandall Shooting Supplies.
Price: $425.00

Consult our Directory pages for the location of firms mentioned.

Bernardelli Series Roma Shotguns

Similar to the Series S. Uberto Models except with dummy sideplates to simulate sidelock action. In 12, 20, 28 gauge, 25¹/₂″, 26³/₄″, 28″, 29″ barrels. Straight English or pistol grip stock. Chrome-lined barrels, boxlock action, double triggers, ejectors, automatic safety. Checkered butt. Special choke combinations, barrel lengths optional.

Price: Roma 3, about $1,400.00
Price: Roma 4, about $1,600.00
Price: Roma 6, about $2,000.00
Price: Roma 3 .... $1,283.00
Price: As above with ejectors $1,391.00
Price: Roma 4 .... $1,459.00
Price: As above with ejectors $1,566.00
Price: Roma 6 .... $1,726.00
Price: As above with ejectors $1,833.00

BERNARDELLI SERIES S. UBERTO DOUBLES

Gauge: 12, 16, 20, 28, 2³/₄″ or 3″ chambers.
Barrel: 25⁵/₈″, 26³/₄″, 28″, 29¹/₈″ (Mod. & Full).
Weight: 6 to 6¹/₂ lbs.
Stock: 14³/₁₆″x2³/₈″x1⁹/₁₆″ standard dimensions. Select walnut with hand checkering.
Features: Anson & Deeley boxlock action with Purdey locks, choice of extractors or ejectors. Uberto 1 has color case-hardened receiver, Uberto 2 and F.S. silvered and differ in amount and quality of engraving. Custom options available. Prices vary with importer and are shown respectively. Imported from Italy by Armes De Chasse and Mandall Shooting Supplies.

Price: S. Uberto 1 .... $1,297.20 to $1,217.96
Price: As above with ejectors .... $1,428.00 to $1,373.52
Price: S. Uberto 2 .... $1,356.00 to $1,275.58
Price: As above with ejectors .... $1,486.80 to $1,430.16
Price: S. Uberto F.S. .... $1,560.00 to $1,492.46
Price: As above with ejectors .... $1,690.80 to $1,647.00
Price: S. Uberto 1 .... $1,173.00
Price: As above with ejectors $1,279.00
Price: S. Uberto 2E $1,343.00
Price: S. Uberto 2EM $1,409.00

Bernardelli System Holland H. Side-by-Side

True sidelock action. Available in 12 gauge only, reinforced breech, three round Purdey locks, automatic ejectors, folding right trigger. Model VB Liscio has color case-hardened receiver and sideplates with light engraving. VB and VB Tipo Lusso are silvered and engraved.

Price: VB Liscio .... $6,840.00 to $6,716.00
Price: VB .... $7,680.00 to $7,782.00
Price: VB Tipo Lusso .... $9,240.00 to $9,107.00

CAUTION: PRICES CHANGE. CHECK AT GUNSHOP.

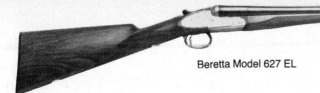

Beretta Model 627 EL

BERETTA SIDE-BY-SIDE FIELD SHOTGUNS
Gauge: 12 and 20, 2³/₄" and 3" chambers.
Barrel: 26" and 28" (fixed and Mobilchoke tubes).
Stock: Close-grained American walnut.
Features: Front and center beads on a raised ventilated rib. Has P. Beretta signature on each side of the receiver, while a gold gauge marking is inscribed atop the rib. Imported from Italy by Beretta U.S.A.
Price: 626 Onyx $1,533.00
Price: 627 EL $2,655.00
Price: 627 EELL (pistol grip or straight English stock) $4,453.00

BRNO ZP149, ZP349 SIDE-BY-SIDE
Gauge: 12, 2³/₄" or 3" chambers.
Barrel: 28¹/₂" (Full & Mod.).
Weight: 7 lbs., 3 oz. **Length:** 45" overall.
Stock: Turkish or Yugoslavian walnut with raised cheekpiece.
Features: Sidelock action with double triggers, automatic ejectors, barrel indicators, auto safety. Imported from Czechoslovakia by TD Arms.
Price: ZP 149, standard $589.00
Price: As above, engraved $609.00
Price: ZP 349, extractors, standard $629.00
Price: As above, engraved $649.00

CHAPUIS RG PROGRESS SIDE-BY-SIDE
Gauge: 12, 16 (2³/₄"), 20 ga. (3").
Barrel: 26¹/₂" or 27¹/₂" depending on choke (any choke available). Chrome-moly steel with chrome-plated bores.
Weight: 5¹/₂ to 6¹/₄ lbs.
Stock: Select French walnut, oil or varnish finish. Fine checkering on p.g. and forend. Straight English or pistol grip.
Features: Single barrel joining rib. Auto ejectors are standard. Double triggers. Scroll engraving on frame and sideplates. Extra barrel set available. Imported from France by Armes de Chasse.
Price: $2,800.00

Churchill Windsor I

CHURCHILL ROYAL SIDE-BY-SIDE SHOTGUN
Gauge: 12 (3"), 16 (2³/₄"), 20, 28, 410 (3").
Barrel: 12 ga. — 26" (Imp. Cyl. & Mod.), 28" (Mod. & Full); 16 ga. — 28" (Mod. & Full); 20 ga. — 28" (Imp. Cyl. & Mod., Mod. & Full); 410 — 26" (Full & Full).
Weight: 5³/₄ to 6¹/₂ lbs.
Stock: Straight-grip style of checkered European walnut.
Features: Color case-hardened boxlock action with double triggers, extractors; chromed barrels with concave rib. Introduced 1988. Imported by Ellett Bros.
Price: . . . . $559.00 to $589.00

CHURCHILL WINDSOR SIDE-BY-SIDE SHOTGUNS
Gauge: 10 (3¹/₂"), 12, 16, 20, 28, 410 (2³/₄" 16 ga., 3" others).
Barrel: 24" (Mod. & Full), 410 and 20 ga.; 26" (Imp. Cyl. & Mod., Mod. & Full); 28" (Mod. & Full, Skeet & Skeet—28 ga.); 30" (Full & Full, Mod. & Full); 32" (Full & Full—10 ga.).
Weight: About 7¹/₂ lbs. (12 ga.).
Stock: Hand-checkered European walnut with rubber buttpad.
Features: Anson & Deeley boxlock action with silvered and engraved finish; automatic top tang safety; double triggers; beavertail forend. Windsor I with extractors only. Also available in Flyweight versions, 23", 25", fixed or ICT chokes, straight stock. Imported from Spain by Ellett Bros. Introduced 1984.
Price: Windsor I, 10 ga. . . . . $679.00 to $969.00
Price: Windsor I, 12 through 410 ga. . . . . $559.00 to $629.00

CLASSIC MODEL 201 DOUBLE
Gauge: 12, 20, 28/410.
Barrel: 26" (Imp. Cyl. & Mod.); choke tubes available on 12 ga. model only; 28" (Imp. Cyl. & Mod., Mod. & Full) for 28/410 set.
Weight: About 7 lbs. **Length:** 43¹/₄" overall (26" barrel).
Stock: 14¹/₂"x1¹/₂"x2¹/₄". Fancy grade American walnut. Straight English on 20 ga. only.
Features: Automatic selective ejectors; elongated forcing cones; top automatic tang safety. Suitable for steel shot. Blued frame. Imported from Japan by Classic Doubles.
Price: 12 ga. $2,190.00
Price: 20 ga. $2,310.00
Price: 28/410 set $3,675.00

Classic Model 201

CRUCELEGUI HERMANOS MODEL 150 DOUBLE
Gauge: 12, 16 or 20, 2³/₄" chambers.
Action: Greener triple cross-bolt.
Barrel: 20", 26", 28", 30", 32" (Cyl. & Cyl., Full & Full, Mod. & Full, Mod. & Imp. Cyl., Imp. Cyl. & Full, Mod. & Mod.).
Weight: 5 to 7¹/₄ lbs.
Stock: Hand-checkered walnut, beavertail forend.
Features: Exposed hammers; double triggers; color case-hardened receiver; sling swivels; chrome-lined bores. Imported from Spain by Mandall Shooting Supplies.
Price: $399.95

Ferlib Model F VII

FERLIB MODEL F VII DOUBLE SHOTGUN
Gauge: 12, 20, 28, 410.
Barrel: 25" to 28".
Weight: 5¹/₂ lbs. (20 ga.).
Stock: Oil-finished walnut, checkered straight grip and forend.
Features: Boxlock action with fine scroll engraved, silvered receiver. Double triggers standard. Introduced 1983. Imported from Italy by Wm. Larkin Moore.
Price: 12 or 20 ga. $4,750.00
Price: 28 or 410 ga. $5,488.00
Price: Extra for single trigger $375.00

Francotte Double

AUGUSTE FRANCOTTE SIDE-BY-SIDE SHOTGUNS
Gauge: 12, 16, 20, 28, 410.
Barrel: 26″ thru 30″. To customer specs.
Weight: 6.61 lbs. (12 ga.).
Stock: To customer specs. English, pistol grip, half-pistol grip; European walnut.
Features: Chopper lump barrels; bar action sidelocks or boxlock. Full selection of options available from the maker. Imported from Belgium by Armes de Chasse.
Price: .... **NA**

Garbi Model 100

GARBI MODEL 100 DOUBLE
Gauge: 12, 16, 20, 28.
Barrel: 26″, 28″, choked to customer specs.
Weight: 5¹/₂ to 7¹/₂ lbs.
Stock: 14¹/₂″x2¹/₄″x1¹/₂″. European walnut. Straight grip, checkered butt, classic forend.
Features: Sidelock action, automatic ejectors, double triggers standard. Color case-hardened action, coin finish optional. Single trigger; beavertail forend, etc. optional. Five other models are available. Imported from Spain by Wm. Larkin Moore and L. Joseph Rahn.
Price: From .... **$2,450.00 to $2,800.00**

Garbi Model 103A, B Side-by-Side
Similar to the Garbi Model 100 except has Purdey-type fine scroll and rosette engraving. Better overall quality than the Model 101. Model 103B has nickel-chrome steel barrels, H&H-type easy opening mechanism; other mechanical details remain the same. Imported from Spain by Wm. Larkin Moore and L. Joseph Rahn, Inc.
Price: Model 103A, from .... **$4,300.00 to $4,500.00**
Price: Model 103B, from .... **$5,700.00 to $6,000.00**

Garbi Model 101 Side-by-Side
Similar to the Garbi Model 100 except is available with optional level, file-cut, Churchill or ventilated top rib, and in a 12-ga. pigeon or wildfowl gun. Has Continental-style floral and scroll engraving, select walnut stock. Better overall quality than the Model 100. Imported from Spain by Wm. Larkin Moore and L. Joseph Rahn.
Price: .... **$4,300.00 to $4,500.00**

Garbi Model 200 Side-by-Side
Similar to the Garbi Model 100 except has barrels of nickel-chrome steel, heavy-duty locks, magnum proofed. Very fine continental-style floral and scroll engraving, well figured walnut stock. Other mechanical features remain the same. Imported from Spain by L. Joseph Rahn and Wm. Larkin Moore.
Price: .... **$5,800.00 to $6,250.00**

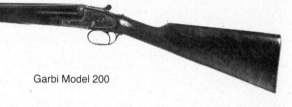

Garbi Model 200

HATFIELD UPLANDER SHOTGUN
Gauge: 20, 3″ chambers.
Barrel: 26″ (Imp. Cyl. & Mod.).
Weight: 5³/₄ lbs.
Stock: Straight English style, special select XXX fancy walnut. Hand-rubbed oil finish. Splinter forend.
Features: Double locking under-lug boxlock action; color case-hardened frame; single non-selective trigger. Introduced 1988. From Hatfield.
Price: Grade 1 .... **$1,120.00**
Price: Grade 2 .... **$1,995.00**
Price: Grade 3 .... **$2,495.00**
Price: Grade 4 .... **$3,995.00**
Price: Grade 5 .... **$5,595.00**

Hatfield Uplander

MERCURY MODEL G1032 DOUBLE BARREL SHOTGUN
Gauge: 10, 3¹/₂″ chambers.
Action: Triple-lock Anson & Deeley type.
Barrel: 32″ (Full & Full).
Weight: 10¹/₈ lbs.
Stock: 14″x1⁵/₈″x2¹/₄″ walnut, checkered p.g. stock and beavertail forend, recoil pad.
Features: Double triggers, front hinged, automatic safety, extractors; safety gas ports, engraved frame. Imported from Spain by Tradewinds.
Price: **$480.00**

MERKEL SIDE-BY-SIDE SHOTGUNS
Gauge: 12, 16, 20, 2³/₄″ or 3″ chambers.
Barrel: 26″, 26³/₄″, 28″ (standard chokes).
Weight: 6 to 7 lbs.
Stock: European walnut. Straight English or pistol grip.
Features: Models 47E, 147E, 122 are boxlocks; others are sidelocks. All have double triggers, double lugs and Greener cross-bolt locking and automatic ejectors. Choking and patterning for steel shot (by importer). Upgraded wood, engraving, etc. optional. Imported from East Germany by Armes de Chasse.

Price: Model 47E, about	**$1,335.00**
Price: Model 147E, about	**$1,610.00**
Price: Model 47S, about	**$3,275.00**
Price: Model 147S, about	**$4,030.00**
Price: Model 247S, about	**$4,030.00**
Price: Model 347S, about	**$4,715.00**
Price: Model 447S, about	**$5,360.00**

CAUTION: PRICES CHANGE. CHECK AT GUNSHOP.

Parker DHE

Weight: About 6³/₄ lbs. (12 ga.), 6¹/₂ lbs. (20 ga.), 5¹/₂ lbs. (28 ga.), 5 lbs. (410).
Stock: Fancy American walnut, checkered grip and forend. Straight stock or pistol grip, splinter or beavertail forend; 28 lpi checkering.
Features: Reproduction of the original Parker—most parts interchangeable with original. Double or single selective trigger; checkered skeleton buttplate; selective ejectors; bores hard chromed, excluding choke area. Two-barrel sets available. Hand engraved scroll and scenes on case-hardened frame. Fitted leather trunk included. Limited production. Introduced 1984. Made by Winchester in Japan. Imported by Parker Div. of Reagent Chemical.

PARKER DHE SIDE-BY-SIDE SHOTGUN
Gauge: 12, 20, 28, 2³/₄″ or 3″ chambers.
Barrel: 26″ (Imp. Cyl. & Mod., 2³/₄″ chambers), Skeet & Skeet available, 28″ (Mod. & Full, 3″ chambers only).

Price: D Grade, one barrel set $2,970.00
Price: B Grade $3,970.00
Price: A-1 Special $8,740.00

Parker-Hale 645E

PARKER-HALE MODEL "600" SERIES DOUBLES
Gauge: 12, 16, 20, 2³/₄″ chambers; 28, 410, 3″ chambers.
Barrel: 25″, 26″, 27″, 28″ (Imp. Cyl. & Mod., Mod. & Full).
Weight: 12 ga., 6³/₄-7 lbs.; 20 ga., 5³/₄-6 lbs.
Stock: 14¹/₂″x1¹/₂″x2¹/₂″. Hand-checkered walnut with oil finish. "E" (English) models have straight grip, splinter forend, checkered butt. "A" (American) models have p.g. stock, beavertail forend, buttplate.
Features: Boxlock action; silvered, engraved action; automatic safety; ejectors or extractors. E-models have double triggers, concave rib (XXV models have Churchill-type rib); A-models have single, non-selective trigger, raised matted rib. Made in Spain by Ugartechea. Imported by Precision Sports. Introduced 1986.

PERUGINI-VISINI CLASSIC DOUBLE SHOTGUN
Gauge: 12, 20, 2³/₄″ or 3″.
Barrel: NA.
Weight: NA. **Length:** NA.
Stock: Straight English type of high grade European briar walnut; oil finish.
Features: H&H-type hand-detachable sidelocks internally gold-plated; single or double triggers; automatic ejectors. Many options available. Imported from Italy by Wm. Larkin Moore.
Price: From about $12,000.00

Price: 640E (12, 16, 20; 26″, 28″), extractors. $564.95
Price: 640E (28, 410; 27″ only), extractors. $634.95
Price: 640A (12, 16, 20; 26″, 28″), extractors. $664.95
Price: 640A (28, 410, 27″ only), ejectors $734.95
Price: 640M "Big Ten" 10-ga. $674.95
Price: 645E (12, 16, 20; 26″, 28″), with ejectors $714.95
Price: 645E (28, 410; 27″), with ejectors $784.95
Price: 645A (12, 16, 20; 26″, 28″), with ejectors $814.95
Price: 645A (28, 410; 27″ only), ejectors $884.95
Price: 645E-XXV (12, 16, 20; 25″), with ejectors $744.95
Price: 645E-XXV (28, 410; 27″), with ejectors $814.95
Price: 645E Bi-Gauge (20/28 or 28/410), ejectors. $1,299.95
Price: 645A Bi-Gauge (20/28 or 28/410), ejectors. $1,399.95
Price: 670E (12, 16, 20; 26″, 28″) sidelock, with ejectors $3,100.00
Price: 670E (28, 410; 27″) sidelock, with ejectors. $3,300.00
Price: 680E-XXV (12, 16, 20; 25″) sidelock, ejectors, case-color action $2,900.00
Price: 680E-XXV (28, 410; 25″) sidelock, ejectors, case-color action $3,100.00

Perugini-Visini Liberty Double Shotgun
A boxlock gun that shares many of the same features of the Classic model. Available in 12, 20, 28, 410, 2³/₄″ or 3″ chambers. Many options available and can be had as a matched pair.
Price: From about $5,900.00

Piotti Model Piuma

PIOTTI MODEL PIUMA SIDE-BY-SIDE
Gauge: 12, 16, 20, 28, 410.
Barrel: 25″ to 30″ (12 ga.), 25″ to 28″ (16, 20, 28, 410).
Weight: 5¹/₂ to 6¹/₄ lbs. (20 ga.).
Stock: Dimensions to customer specs. Straight grip stock with checkered butt, classic splinter forend, hand-rubbed oil finish are standard; pistol grip, beavertail forend, satin luster finish optional.
Features: Anson & Deeley boxlock ejector double with chopper lump barrels. Level, file-cut rib, light scroll and rosette engraving, scalloped frame. Double triggers with hinged front standard, single non-selective optional. Coin finish standard, color case-hardened optional. Imported from Italy by Wm. Larkin Moore.
Price: $6,600.00

Piotti Model King Extra Side-by-Side
Similar to the Piotti King No. 1 except highest quality wood and metal work. Choice of either bulino game scene engraving or game scene engraving with gold inlays. Engraved and signed by a master engraver. Exhibition grade wood. Other mechanical specifications remain the same. Imported from Italy by Wm. Larkin Moore.
Price: $20,000.00

Piotti Monte Carlo

Piotti Model Monte Carlo Side-by-Side
Similar to the Piotti King No. 1 except has Purdey-style scroll and rosette engraving, no gold inlays, overall workmanship not as finely detailed. Other mechanical specifications remain the same. Imported from Italy by Wm. Larkin Moore.
Price: $11,400.00

PIOTTI KING NO. 1 SIDE-BY-SIDE

Gauge: 12, 16, 20, 28, 410.
Barrel: 25″ to 30″ (12 ga.), 25″ to 28″ (16, 20, 28, 410). To customer specs. Chokes as specified.
Weight: 6½ lbs. to 8 lbs. (12 ga. to customer specs.)
Stock: Dimensions to customer specs. Finely figured walnut; straight grip with checkered butt with classic splinter forend and hand-rubbed oil finish standard. Pistol grip, beavertail forend, satin luster finish optional.
Features: Holland & Holland pattern sidelock action, automatic ejectors. Double trigger with front trigger hinged standard; non-selective single trigger optional. Coin finish standard; color case-hardened optional. Top rib: level, file cut standard; concave, ventilated optional. Very fine, full coverage scroll engraving with small floral bouquets, gold crown in top lever, name in gold, and gold crest in forend. Imported from Italy by Wm. Larkin Moore.
Price: **$13,500.00**

Piotti Model Lunik Side-by-Side

Similar to the Piotti King No. 1 except better overall quality. Has Renaissance-style large scroll engraving in relief, gold crown in top lever, gold name and gold crest in forend. Best quality Holland & Holland-pattern sidelock ejector double with chopper lump (demi-bloc) barrels. Other mechanical specifications remain the same. Imported from Italy by Wm. Larkin Moore.
Price: **$14,400.00**

Remington Parker

REMINGTON PARKER AHE SIDE-BY-SIDE

Gauge: 20, 2¾″ chambers.
Barrel: 28″ (any combination of Skeet, Imp. Cyl., Mod., Full chokes.)
Weight: About 6½ lbs.
Stock: Circassian or American walnut; straight or pistol grip; beavertail or splinter forend; rubber recoil pad, Parker buttplate or engraved skeleton steel buttplate. Checkered 28 lpi.

Features: Custom-made gun. Single selective trigger, automatic ejectors; scroll-engraved color case-hardened receiver. Automatic ejectors. Limited production. Reintroduced 1988. From Remington.
Price: From. **$12,750.00**

Rizzini Sidelock

RIZZINI SIDELOCK SIDE-BY-SIDE

Gauge: 12, 20, 28, 410.
Barrel: 25″ to 30″ (12 ga.), 25″ to 28″ (20, 28, 410). To customer specs. Chokes as specified.
Weight: 6½ lbs. to 8 lbs. (12 ga., to customer specs.)
Stock: Dimensions to customer specs. Finely figured walnut; straight grip with checkered butt with classic splinter forend and hand-rubbed oil finish standard. Pistol grip, beavertail forend, satin luster finish optional.
Features: Holland & Holland pattern sidelock action, auto ejectors. Double triggers with front trigger hinged standard; non-selective single trigger optional. Coin finish standard; color case-hardened optional. Top rib level, file cut standard; concave, ventilated optional. Very fine, full coverage scroll engraving with small floral bouquets, gold crown in top lever, name in gold, and gold crest in forend. Imported from Italy by Wm. Larkin Moore.
Price: 12, 20 ga., from **$22,500.00**
Price: 28, 410 ga., from **$25,200.00**

RIZZINI BOXLOCK SIDE-BY-SIDE

Gauge: 12, 20, 28, 410.
Barrel: 25″ to 30″ (12 ga.), 25″ to 28″ (20, 28, 410).
Weight: 5½ to 6¼ lbs. (20 ga.).
Stock: Dimensions to customer specs. Straight grip stock with checkered butt, classic splinter forend, hand-rubbed oil finish are standard; pistol grip, beavertail forend, satin luster finish optional.
Features: Anson & Deeley boxlock ejector double with chopper lump barrels. Level, file-cut rib, light scroll and rosette engraving, scalloped frame. Double triggers with hinged front standard, single non-selective optional. Coin finish standard, color case-hardened optional. Imported from Italy by Wm. Larkin Moore.
Price: 12, 20 ga., from **$14,200.00**
Price: 28, 410 ga., from **$15,700.00**

Rossi "Squire"

ROSSI "SQUIRE" DOUBLE BARREL

Gauge: 12, 20, 410, 3″ chambers.
Barrel: 12—28″ (Mod. & Full); 20 ga.—26″ (Imp. Cyl. & Mod.), 28″ (Mod. & Full); 410—26″ (Full & Full).
Weight: About 7½ lbs.
Stock: Walnut-finished hardwood.
Features: Double triggers, raised matted rib, beavertail forend. Massive twin underlugs mesh with synchronized sliding bolts. Introduced 1978. Imported by Interarms.
Price: 12 or 20 ga. **$340.00**
Price: 410 .... **$345.00**

SKB Model 200

SKB MODEL 200 DOUBLE SHOTGUN

Gauge: 12, 20, 3″ chambers.
Barrel: 25″, 26″ (Inter Choke tubes).
Weight: 6 lbs., 10 oz. (12 ga.). **Length:** 42⅛″ overall (26″ barrels).
Stock: 14″x1½″x2⅝″. Walnut with checkered grip and forend, recoil pad.
Sights: Metal bead front.
Features: Engraved boxlock action with silvered finish. Gold-plated trigger. Introduced in 1988. Imported from Japan by Ernie Simmons Enterprises.
Price: **$895.00**
Price: Model 200E with straight English-style stock. **$895.00**

SKB Model 400 Double Shotgun

Similar to the Model 200 except has engraved and silvered sideplates. Standard or straight English-style stock.
Price: **$1,195.00**

IGA Side-by-Side

STOEGER/IGA SIDE-BY-SIDE SHOTGUN
Gauge: 12, 20, 28, 2³/₄″ chambers; 410, 3″ chambers.
Barrel: 26″ (Full & Full, 410 only, Imp. Cyl. & Mod.), 28″ (Mod. & Full).
Weight: 6³/₄ to 7 lbs.
Stock: 14¹/₂″x1¹/₂″x2¹/₂″. Oil-finished hardwood. Checkered pistol grip and forend.
Features: Automatic safety, extractors only, solid matted barrel rib. Double triggers only. Introduced 1983. Imported from Brazil by Stoeger Industries.
Price: $265.00
Price: Coach Gun, 12 or 20 ga., 20″ bbls. $260.00

SIMSON/SUHL MODEL 70E SIDE-BY-SIDE SHOTGUN
Gauge: 12, 16, 20, 2³/₄″ or 3″ chambers.
Barrel: 26³/₄″, 28″ (standard chokes), solid rib.
Weight: 6 to 7 lbs.
Stock: European walnut. Straight English or pistol grip.
Features: Anson & Deeley action with Greener crossbolt, ejectors, double triggers; color case-hardened frame with light engraving. Imported from E. Germany by Armes de Chasse.
Price: Model 70E $1,000.00
Price: Model 74E, 76E (as above except game scene engraving, upgraded wood) .... NA
Price: Model 76E (as above except with dummy sideplates, hunting scene engraving) $1,900.00

> Consult our Directory pages for the location of firms mentioned.

Zoli Silver Fox

ZOLI SILVER FOX SIDE-BY-SIDE SHOTGUN
Gauge: 12 or 20, 3″ chambers.
Barrel: 12 ga. — 26″ (Imp. Cyl. & Mod.), 28″ (Mod. & Full); 20 ga. — 26″ (Imp. Cyl. & Mod.).

Weight: 6¹/₄ to 7¹/₄ lbs.
Stock: 14¹/₂″x2⁵/₁₆″x1¹/₂″. Select Turkish circassian walnut with straight grip, splinter forend, oil finish; solid recoil pad.
Features: Boxlock action with single trigger, selective ejectors, polished, engraved, silver receiver. "Best Grade" gun. Introduced 1989. Imported from Italy by Antonio Zoli, USA.
Price: Either gauge $2,850.00

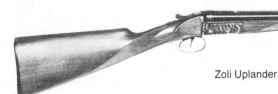

Zoli Uplander

ZOLI UPLANDER SIDE-BY-SIDE SHOTGUN
Gauge: 12 or 20, 3″ chambers.
Barrel: 25″ (Imp. Cyl. & Mod.).
Weight: 6¹/₄ to 7¹/₄ lbs.
Stock: 14¹/₂″x2⁵/₁₆″x1¹/₂″. Oil-finished Turkish circassian walnut.
Features: Color case-hardened boxlock action with double triggers, auto. ejecteors. Straight English-style stock, splinter forend. Introdued 1989. Imported from Italy by Antonio Zoli, USA.
Price: Either gauge $1,050.00

SHOTGUNS—BOLT ACTIONS & SINGLE SHOTS

Variety of designs for utility and sporting purposes, as well as for competitive shooting.

AMERICAN ARMS SINGLE BARREL SHOTGUN
Gauge: 12, 20, 410, 3″ chamber.
Barrel: 26″ (Full, 410 ga.), 28″ (Mod., Full).
Weight: About 6¹/₂ lbs.
Stock: Walnut-finished hardwood with checkered grip, forend.
Sights: Bead front.
Features: Manual thumb safety; chrome-lined barrel. Imported from Italy by American Arms, Inc. Introduced 1988.
Price: $99.00
Price: Youth model, 20 ga., 26″ (Mod.) or 410, 26″ (Full), 12¹/₂″ pull **$115.00**

American Arms Single

American Arms Slugger

American Arms Slugger
Similar to the Single Barrel except in 12 or 20 ga. with 24″ slug barrel; rifle-type sights; recoil pad. Introduced 1989.
Price: $115.00

American Arms Combo

American Arms Waterfowl Special
Similar to the Single Barrel model except chambered for 10 ga. 3¹/₂″, has 30″ (Full) barrel. Matte finish.
Price: $149.00

American Arms Camper Special
Similar to the Single Barrel except has 21″ barrel (Mod.), overall length of 27″, pistol grip instead of buttstock, 12, 20, 410. Gun folds for storage, carry. Matte finish.
Price: $107.00

American Arms Combo
Similar to the Single Barrel except comes with interchangeable rifle and shotgun barrels fitted to one frame: 22 Long Rifle and 20 ga. (28″, Mod.) or 22 Hornet and 12 ga. (28″, Full). Rifle barrel has tunnel front blade, adjustable rear sights. Comes with hard carrying case. Introduced 1989.
Price: $235.00

American Arms Camper

American Arms Turkey Special
Similar to the Single Barrel except chambered for 10 ga. 3¹/₂″, has 26″ barrel with choke tube. Matte finish.
Price: $179.00

Armsport Single

ARMSPORT SINGLE BARREL SHOTGUN
Gauge: 12, 20, 410; 3″ chamber.
Barrel: 12 ga. — 28″ (Mod., Full); 20 ga. — 26″ (Mod.); 410 — 26″ (Full).
Weight: About 6¹/₂ lbs.
Stock: Hardwood with oil finish.
Features: Chrome-lined barrel, manual safety, cocking indicator. Opening lever behind trigger guard. Imported by Armsport.
Price: $110.00

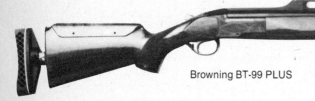

Browning BT-99 PLUS

Browning BT-99 PLUS Trap Gun
Similar to the Grade I BT-99 except comes only with 34″ barrel with .745″ over bore, Invector PLUS choke system with Full, Imp. Mod. and Mod. choke tubes; high post, ventilated, tapered, target rib adjustable from 3″ to 12″ above point of aim. Available with or without ported barrel. Select walnut stock has high-gloss finish, Monte Carlo comb, modified beavertail forend and is fully adjustable for length of pull, drop at comb and drop at Monte Carlo. Has Browning Recoil Reduction System. Introduced 1989.
Price: Grade I, with ported barrel $1,570.00
Price: Grade I, non-ported barrel $1,520.00

BROWNING BT-99 COMPETITION TRAP SPECIAL
Gauge: 12 gauge, 2³/₄″ chamber.
Action: Top lever break-open, hammerless.
Barrel: 32″ or 34″ with 1¹/₃₂″ wide high post floating vent. rib. Comes with Invector choke tubes or fixed Full, Imp. Mod.
Weight: 8 lbs. (32″ bbl.).
Stock: French walnut; hand-checkered, full pistol grip, full beavertail forend; recoil pad. Trap dimensions with M.C. 14³/₈″ x 1³/₈″ x 1³/₈″ x 2″.
Sights: Ivory front and middle beads.
Features: Gold-plated trigger with 3¹/₂-lb. pull, deluxe trap-style recoil pad, automatic ejector, no safety. Available with either Monte Carlo or standard stock. Imported from Japan by Browning.
Price: Grade I Invector $1,005.00
Price: As above, non-Invector $981.00
Price: Grade I Invector PLUS, ported bbl. $1,570.00
Price: As above, non-ported bbl. $1,520.00

Ithaca Custom Trap

ITHACA 5E CUSTOM TRAP SINGLE BARREL
Gauge: 12, 2³/₄″ chamber.
Barrel: 32″, 34″ (Full).
Weight: 8¹/₂ lbs.
Stock: 14³/₈″ x 1³/₈″ x 1³/₈″. AA Fancy American walnut.
Sights: White bead front, brass middle bead.
Features: Frame, top lever, trigger guard extensively engraved and gold inlaid. Reintroduced 1988. From Ithaca Acquisition Corp.
Price: 5E $7,176.00
Price: Dollar Grade Trap $10,000.00

F.I.E. "S.S.S." SINGLE BARREL
Gauge: 12, 20, 410, 3″ chamber.
Action: Button-break on trigger guard.
Barrel: 18¹/₂″ (Cyl.).
Weight: 6¹/₂ lbs.
Stock: Walnut-finished hardwood, full beavertail forend.
Features: Exposed hammer. Automatic ejector. Imported from Brazil by F.I.E. Corp.
Price: $99.95

KRIEGHOFF KS-5 TRAP GUN

Gauge: 12, 2³/₄″ chamber.
Barrel: 32″, 34″; Full choke or choke tubes.
Weight: About 8¹/₂ lbs.
Stock: Choice of high Monte Carlo (1¹/₂″), low Monte Carlo (1³/₈″) or factory adjustable stock. European walnut.
Features: Ventilated tapered step rib. Adjustable trigger or optional release trigger. Choice of blue or nickeled receiver. Comes with fitted aluminum case. Introduced 1988. Imported from West Germany by Krieghoff International, Inc.
Price: Fixed choke, cased $2,670.00

KRIEGHOFF K-80 SINGLE BARREL TRAP GUN

Gauge: 12, 2³/₄″ chamber.
Barrel: 32″ or 34″ Unsingle; 34″ Top Single. Fixed Full or choke tubes.
Weight: About 8³/₄ lbs.
Stock: Four stock dimensions or adjustable stock available. All hand-checkered European walnut.
Features: Satin nickel finish with K-80 logo. Selective mechanical trigger adjustable for finger position. Tapered step vent. rib. Adjustable point of impact on Unsingle.
Price: Standard grade full Unsingle. $5,675.00
Price: Standard grade full Top Single $4,995.00

Ljutic Mono Gun

LJUTIC MONO GUN SINGLE BARREL

Gauge: 12 ga. only.
Barrel: 34″, choked to customer specs; hollow-milled rib, 35¹/₂″ sight plane.
Weight: Approx. 9 lbs.
Stock: To customer specs. Oil finish, hand checkered.
Features: Totally custom made. Pull or release trigger; removable trigger guard contains trigger and hammer mechanism; Ljutic pushbutton opener on front of trigger guard. From Ljutic Industries.
Price: $3,795.00
Price: With standard, medium or Olympic rib, custom 32″-34″ bbls. $3,895.00
Price: As above with screw-in choke barrel $3,995.00

Ljutic LTX Super Deluxe Mono Gun

Super Deluxe version of the standard Mono Gun with high quality wood, extra-fancy checkering pattern in 24 lpi, double recessed choking. Available in two weights: 8¹/₄ lbs. or 8³/₄ lbs. Extra light 33″ barrel; medium-height rib. Introduced 1984. From Ljutic Industries.
Price: $4,995.00
Price: With three screw-in choke tubes $5,595.00

Ljutic Space Shotgun

LJUTIC RECOILLESS SPACE GUN SHOTGUN

Gauge: 12 only, 2³/₄″ chamber.
Barrel: 30″ (Full). Screw-in or fixed-choke barrel.
Weight: 8¹/₂ lbs.
Stock: 14¹/₂″ to 15″ pull length; universal comb; medium or large p.g.
Sights: Vent. rib.
Features: Pull trigger standard, release trigger available; anti-recoil mechanism. Revolutionary new design. Introduced 1981. From Ljutic Industries.
Price: From. $3,695.00

Marlin Model 55

MARLIN MODEL 55 GOOSE GUN BOLT ACTION

Gauge: 12 only, 2³/₄″ or 3″ chamber.
Action: Bolt action, thumb safety, detachable two-shot clip. Red cocking indicator.
Barrel: 36″ (Full).
Weight: 8 lbs. **Length:** 56³/₄″ overall.
Stock: Walnut-finished hardwood, p.g., ventilated recoil pad. Swivel studs, Mar-Shield® finish.
Features: Brass bead front sight, U-groove rear sight.
Price: $228.95

NAVY ARMS MODEL 105 FOLDING SHOTGUN

Gauge: 12, 20, 410, 3″ chamber.
Barrel: 28″ (Full); 26″ (Full) in 410 ga.
Stock: Walnut-stained hardwood. Checkered p.g. and forend. Metal bead front.
Features: Folding, hammerless, top-lever action with cross-bar action. Chrome-lined barrel, blued receiver. Deluxe has vent. rib, engraved hard-chrome receiver. Introduced 1987. From Navy Arms.
Price: Model 105S Standard $100.00
Price: Model 105L Deluxe $115.00

New England "Pardner"

NEW ENGLAND FIREARMS "PARDNER" SHOTGUN

Gauge: 12, 16 (2³/₄″), 20, 410, 3″ chamber.
Barrel: 12 ga.—24″ (Cyl.), rifle sights, 28″ (Mod., Full); 16 ga.—28″ (Full); 20 ga.—24″ (Cyl.), rifle sights, 26″ (Mod., Full); 410 ga.—26″ (Full).
Weight: About 5¹/₂ lbs. **Length:** 43″ overall (28″ barrel).
Stock: Walnut-finished hardwood; 13³/₄″ pull length (12¹/₂″ youth).
Features: Transfer-bar ignition; side-lever action release. Color case-hardened receiver, blued barrel. Youth model available. Introduced 1987. From New England Firearms Co.
Price: . . . . NA

New England Firearms "Mini-Pardner"

Same as the "Pardner" except has 18¹/₂″ barrel, shortened butt, swivel studs; available in 20 or 410, 3″ chamber. Introduced 1989.
Price: . . . . NA

NEW ENGLAND FIREARMS "HANDI-GUN"
Caliber/Gauge: 22 Hornet, 223, 30-30 or 45-70; 20 ga., 3" chamber.
Barrel: 22", interchangeable.
Weight: 6¹/₂ lbs. **Length:** 37" overall.
Stock: American hardwood.
Sights: Rifle—ramp front, open adjustable rear; shotgun barrel has front bead. Drilled and tapped for scope mounts.
Features: Break-open single shot with interchangeable barrels. Matte electroless nickel or blue finish. Introduced 1987. From New England Firearms Co.
Price: . . . . **NA**

New England "Handi-Gun"

NEW ENGLAND FIREARMS 10-GAUGE SHOTGUN
Similar of the 12 ga. "Pardner" except chambered for 3¹/₂" 10 ga. shell, has 32" (Full) barrel, giving 47" o.a.l. Introduced 1987.
Price: . . . . **NA**

PERAZZI TM1 SPECIAL SINGLE TRAP
Gauge: 12, 2³/₄" chambers.
Barrel: 32" or 34" (Extra Full).
Weight: 8 lbs., 6 oz.
Stock: To customer specs; interchangeable.
Features: Tapered and stepped high rib; adjustable four-position trigger. Also available with choke tubes. Imported from Italy by Perazzi U.S.A., Inc.
Price: From **$4,250.00**
Price: TMX Special Single (as above except special high rib), from **$4,250.00**

Perazzi TM1

Sile Protector Single Barrel Shotgun
Similar to the Folding Hunter except has grooved walnut pistol grip (no buttstock), forend; 19³/₄" barrel; weighs 4.1 lbs., 27" overall. In 12, 20, 410 ga. Extractor only. Folds for carry or storage. From Sile.
Price: **$111.95**

SILE FOLDING HUNTER SINGLE BARREL
Gauge: 12, 20, 410, 3" chamber.
Barrel: 12 and 20 ga.—28" (Mod.); 410—26" (Full). Vent. rib or plain barrel.
Weight: 5¹/₄ to 6 lbs. **Length:** 45" overall (28" barrel).
Stock: Walnut, checkered p.g. and forend.
Features: Folds in half for storage or carry. Manual safety. Engraved, chromed receiver. Imported by Sile.
Price: Vent. Rib **$139.95**
Price: Plain barrel **$125.95**

Snake Charmer II

SNAKE CHARMER II SHOTGUN
Gauge: 410, 3" chamber.
Barrel: 18¹/₄".
Weight: About 3¹/₂ lbs. **Length:** 28⁵/₈" overall.
Stock: ABS grade impact resistant plastic.
Features: Thumbhole-type stock holds four extra rounds. Stainless steel barrel and frame. Reintroduced 1989. From Sporting Arms Mfg., Inc
Price: **$149.00**
Price: New Generation Snake Charmer (as above except with black carbon steel bbl.) **$139.00**

STOEGER/IGA SINGLE BARREL SHOTGUN
Gauge: 12, 2³/₄", 20, 410, 3".
Barrel: 12, 20 ga.—26", 28" (Imp. Cyl., Mod., Full); 410—28" (Imp. Cyl., Mod., Full).
Weight: 5¹/₄ lbs.
Stock: 14" × 1¹/₂" × 2¹/₂". Brazilian hardwood.
Sights: Metal bead front.
Features: Exposed hammer with half-cock safety; extractor; blue finish. Introduced 1987. Imported from Brazil by Stoeger Industries.
Price: **$95.00**

THOMPSON/CENTER TCR '87 HUNTER SHOTGUN
Gauge: 10, 3¹/₂", 12, 3¹/₂".
Barrel: 25" (Full).
Weight: 8 lbs.
Stock: Uncheckered walnut.
Sights: Bead front.
Features: Uses same receiver as TCR '87 rifle models, and stock has extra ⁷/₁₆" drop at heel. Choke designed for steel shot. Introduced 1989.
Price: **$425.00**

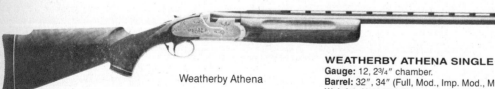

Weatherby Athena

WEATHERBY ATHENA SINGLE BARREL TRAP
Gauge: 12, 2³/₄" chamber.
Barrel: 32", 34" (Full, Mod., Imp. Mod., Multi-Choke tubes).
Weight: About 8¹/₂ lbs.
Length: 49¹/₂" overall with 32" barrel.
Stock: 14³/₈" × 1³/₈" × 2¹/₈" × 1³/₄". American walnut with checkered p.g. and forend.
Sights: White front, brass middle bead.
Features: Engraved, silvered sideplate receiver; ventilated rubber recoil pad. Can be ordered with an extra over-under barrel set. Introduced 1988. Imported from Japan by Weatherby.
Price: **$1,611.00**
Price: Combo **$2,100.00**

Consult our Directory pages for the location of firms mentioned.

CAUTION: PRICES CHANGE. CHECK AT GUNSHOP.

Zoli Z90

ZOLI Z90 MONO-TRAP GUN
Gauge: 12, 2³/₄" chamber.
Barrel: 32" or 34" (choke tubes).
Weight: 8¹/₂ lbs.
Stock: 14¹/₂"x2¹/₈"x1¹/₄"x1¹/₄". Checkered Turkish circassion walnut with Monte Carlo; oil finish.
Features: Boxlock action with automatic ejector; trigger adjustable for length of pull; step-type vent. rib with two sight beads. Matte blue finish on receiver. Introduced 1989. Imported from Italy by Antonio Zoli, USA.
Price: **$1,800.00**

SHOTGUNS—MILITARY & POLICE

Designs for utility, suitable for and adaptable to competitions and other sporting purposes.

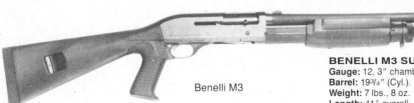

Benelli M3

BENELLI M3 SUPER 90 DEFENSE SHOTGUN
Gauge: 12, 3" chamber, 7-shot magazine.
Barrel: 19³/₄" (Cyl.).
Weight: 7 lbs., 8 oz.
Length: 41" overall.
Stock: High-impact polymer with sling loop in side of butt; rubberized pistol grip on optional SWAT stock.
Sights: Post front, buckhorn rear adjustable for w.
Features: Combination pump/auto action. Alloy receiver with rotating locking lug bolt; matte finish; automatic shell release lever. Comes with carrier for speed loading and magazine reducer plug. Optional vent. rib and interchangeable barrels available. Introduced 1989. Imported by Heckler & Koch, Inc.
Price: **$801.00**

ARMSCOR MODEL 30R RIOT GUN
Gauge: 12, 6- or 8-shot capacity.
Barrel: 20" (Cyl.).
Weight: 6³/₄ lbs.
Length: 39" overall.
Stock: Plain mahogany.
Sights: Metal bead front.
Features: Double action bars; blue finish; grooved forend. Introduced 1987. Imported from the Philippines by Armscor.
Price: About **$209.25**

Benelli M1 Super 90 Defense
Similar to the M3 Super 90 Defense except is semi-automatic only, has overall length of 39³/₄" and weighs 7 lbs., 4 oz. Introduced 1986.
Price: Slug Gun with standard stock. **$606.00**
Price: With pistol grip stock. **$644.00**

Beretta 1200FP

BERETTA MODEL 1200 FP AUTO SHOTGUN
Gauge: 12, 2³/₄" or 3" chamber.
Barrel: 20" (Cyl.).
Weight: 7.3 lbs.
Length: NA
Stock: Special strengthened technopolymer, matte black finish.
Sights: Fixed rifle type.
Features: Has 6-shot magazine. Introduced 1988. Imported from Italy by Beretta U.S.A.
Price: **$560.00**

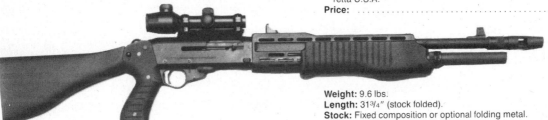

F.I.E./Franchi SPAS 12

Weight: 9.6 lbs.
Length: 31³/₄" (stock folded).
Stock: Fixed composition or optional folding metal.
Sights: Blade front, aperture rear.
Features: Functions as pump and/or gas-operated auto. Has 8-shot magazine. Parkerized alloy receiver, chrome-lined bore, resin pistol grip and pump handle. Made in Italy by Franchi. Introduced 1983. Imported by F.I.E. Corp.
Price: **$699.95**
Price: Mod. or Full choke tube **$44.95**
Price: Optional fixed or folding stock **$79.95**

F.I.E./FRANCHI SPAS 12 PUMP/AUTO SHOTGUN
Gauge: 12, 2³/₄" chamber.
Barrel: 21¹/₂". Barrel threaded for SPAS accessories.

F.I.E./Franchi SAS 12

F.I.E/Franchi LAW 12 Auto Shotgun

A semi-automatic-only lightweight variation of the SPAS 12 pump/auto. Has a 21¹/₂″ barrel, 8-shot magazine, matte black finish. Over-all length is 41¹/₂″, weight about 7¹/₂ lbs. Stock and pistol grip of nylon resin is detachable. Accessories include shot diverter tube, Full or Modified choke tubes, scope mount, olive drab sling, takedown tool, carry handle. Introduced 1987. Imported from Italy by F.I.E.
Price: $599.95

F.I.E./Franchi SAS 12 Pump Shotgun

A slide-action-only, lightweight variation of the SPAS 12 pump/auto shotgun, with the same specifications as the LAW 12. Introduced 1987. Imported from Italy by F.I.E.
Price: $399.95

Holmes Model 88

HOLMES MODEL 88 PUMP SHOTGUN

Gauge: 12, 2³/₄″ chamber, 5- or 10-shot magazine.
Barrel: 18¹/₄″ (Cyl.); 20″ (choke tubes).
Weight: 9 lbs.
Length: 38¹/₄″ overall (18¹/₄″ barrel).
Stock: Synthetic.
Sights: Post front, fixed rear.
Features: Double action bars; matte blue finish. Announced 1988. From Holmes Firearms.
Price: With one magazine $495.00
Price: Extra magazines, each $40.00

ITHACA MODEL 87 M&P DSPS SHOTGUNS

Gauge: 12, 3″ chamber, 5- or 8-shot magazine.
Barrel: 20″ (Cyl.).
Weight: 7 lbs.
Stock: Walnut.
Sights: Bead front on 5-shot, rifle sights on 8-shot.
Features: Parkerized finish; bottom ejection; cross-bolt safety. Reintroduced 1988. From Ithaca Acquisition Corp.
Price: M&P, 5-shot $407.00
Price: DSPS, 8-shot $407.00

Ithaca Model 87 Hand Grip Shotgun

Similar to the Model 87 M&P except has black polymer pistol grip and slide handle with nylon sling. In 12 or 20 gauge, 18¹/₂″ barrel (Cyl.), 5-shot magazine. Reintroduced 1988.
Price: $391.00

Mossberg 500

Mossberg Model 590 Military Shotgun

Similar to the Model 500 Security except has 20″ barrel only, 9-shot magazine. Available with wood stock, synthetic field, Speedfeed stock. Introduced 1987.
Price: Wood stock, blue $328.95
Price: Speedfeed stock, Parkerized $395.00
Price: Synthetic stock, Parkerized $378.00

MOSSBERG MODEL 500 SECURITY SHOTGUNS

Gauge: 12, 2³/₄″ chamber.
Barrel: 18¹/₂″, 20″ (Cyl.).
Weight: 7 lbs.
Stock: Walnut-finished hardwood; synthetic field or Speedfeed.
Sights: Metal bead front.
Features: Available in 6- or 8-shot models. Top-mounted safety, double action slide bars, swivel studs, rubber recoil pad. Blue, Parkerized or electroless nickel finishes. Price list not complete—contact Mossberg for full list.
Price: From about $259.00
Price: Mini Combo (as above except also comes with a handguard and pistol grip kit), from about $268.00
Price: Maxi Combo (as above except also comes with an extra field barrel), from about $294.00

Mossberg 500 Mariner

Mossberg Model 500 Mariner Pump

Similar to the Model 500 Security except all metal parts finished with MARINECOAT, a Teflon and metal coating to resist rust and corrosion. Choice of synthetic field or Speedfeed stocks or pistol grip.
Price: 6-shot $358.00
Price: Mini Combo (as above except includes handguard and pistol grip kit), 6-shot $383.00
Price: Mini Combo, 9-shot $436.00

Mossberg 590

Mossberg Model 590 Mariner Shotgun

Same gun as the 590 Military except all metal parts are finished with MARINECOAT, a Teflon and metal coating to resist rust and corrosion. Has 20″ barrel, 9-shot capacity. Introduced 1989.
Price: With synthetic field or pistol grip stock **$428.00**
Price: With Speedfeed stock **$443.00**

Mossberg Bullpup

MOSSBERG 500 BULLPUP

Gauge: 12, 2³/₄″ chamber; 6- or 9-shot.
Barrel: 18¹/₂″, 20″ (Cyl.).
Weight: 9¹/₂ lbs. (6-shot).
Length: 28¹/₂″ overall (18¹/₂″ bbl.).
Stock: Bullpup design of high-impact plastics.
Sights: Fixed, mounted in carrying handle.
Features: Uses the M500 pump shotgun action. Cross-bolt and grip safeties. Introduced 1986.
Price: 6-shot **$403.00**
Price: 9-shot **$472.00**

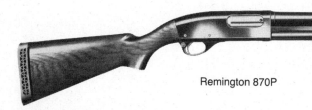

Remington 870P

REMINGTON MODEL 870P POLICE SHOTGUN

Gauge: 12, 3″ chamber.
Barrel: 18″, 20″ (Police Cyl.), 20″ (Imp. Cyl.).
Weight: About 7 lbs.
Stock: Lacquer-finished hardwood or folding stock.
Sights: Metal bead front or rifle sights.
Features: Solid steel receiver, double action slide bars. Blued or Parkerized finish.
Price: Wood stock, 18″ or 20″, bead sight, about **$326.00**
Price: Wood stock, 20″, rifle sights, about **$349.00**

SAM INC MODEL 88 CROSSFIRE SHOTGUN

Caliber/Gauge: 308 Win./12 ga., 2³/₄″ chamber.
Barrel: 20″.
Weight: 9.5 lbs. **Length:** 39.75″ overall.
Stock: Lightweight composite.
Sights: Optional. Adjustable open or optical battle sight.
Features: Combination pump/semi-auto action; each can be independently reloaded while the other is in operation. Has two barrels. Uses 20-shot M-14 magazine for 308, seven-shot box magazine for 12 ga. First round chambered by pump action, fires semi-auto thereafter. **Announced 1989.** From Sam Inc.
Price: Less sights **$1,177.00**

USAS-12 AUTO SHOTGUN

Gauge: 12, 2³/₄″; 7-, 10- or 20-shot drum magazine.
Barrel: 18¹/₄″ (Cyl.).
Weight: 10 lbs. **Length:** 38″ overall.
Stock: Composition butt, pistol grip, forend.
Sights: Fixed.
Features: Gas-operated action; Parkerized finish. Imported from Korea by Gilbert Equipment Co.
Price: **$775.00**

Winchester Defender

WINCHESTER DEFENDER PUMP GUN

Gauge: 12, 3″ chamber, 5- or 8-shot capacity.
Barrel: 18″ (Cyl.).
Weight: 6³/₄ lbs.
Length: 38⁵/₈″ overall.
Stock: Walnut-finished hardwood stock and ribbed forend.
Sights: Metal bead front.
Features: Cross-bolt safety, front-locking rotating bolt, twin action slide bars. Black rubber buttpad. Made under license by U.S. Repeating Arms Co.
Price: 8-shot, about **$244.00**
Price: 5-shot, about **$238.00**
Price: Defender Combo (with p.g. and extra vent. rib 28″ bbl.) **$316.00**

> Consult our Directory pages for the location of firms mentioned.

Winchester "Stainless Marine" Pump Gun

Same as the Defender except has bright chrome finish, stainless steel barrel, rifle-type sights only. Has special forend cap for easy cleaning and inspection. Phosphate coated for corrosion resistance.
Price: About **$423.00**

Winchester Pistol Grip Pump Security Shotguns

Same as regular Security Series but with pistol grip and forend of high-impact resistant ABS plastic with non-glare black finish. Introduced 1984.
Price: Pistol Grip Defender, about **$244.00**

The following pages catalog the blackpowder arms currently available to U.S. shooters. These range from quite precise replicas of historically significant arms to toally new designs created expressly to give the blackpowder shooter the benefits of modern technology.

Most of the replicas are imported, and many are available from more than one source. Thus, examples of a given model such as the 1860 Army revolver or Zouave rifle purchased from different importers may vary in price, finish and fitting. Most of them bear proofmarks, indicating that they have been testfired in the proof house of their country of origin.

A list of the importers and the retail price ranges are included with the description for each model. Many local dealers handle more than one importer's products, giving the prospective buyer an opportunity to make his own judgment in selecting a blackpowder gun. Most importers have catalogs available free or at

nominal cost, and some are well worth having for the useful information on blackpowder shooting they provide in addition to their detailed descriptions and specifications of the guns.

A number of special accessories are also available for the blackpowder shooter. These include replica powder flasks, bullet moulds, cappers and tools, as well as more modern devices to facilitate blackpowder cleaning and maintenance. Ornate presentation cases and even detachable shoulder stocks are also available for some blackpowder pistols from their importers. Again, dealers or the importers will have catalogs.

The blackpowder guns are arranged in four sections: Single Shot Pistols, Revolvers, Muskets & Rifles, and Shotguns. The guns within each section are arranged roughly by date of the original, with the oldest first. Thus the 1836 Paterson replica leads off the revolver section, and flintlocks precede percussion arms in the other sections.

BLACKPOWDER SINGLE SHOT PISTOLS — FLINT & PERCUSSION

Scottish Black Watch

Dixie Charleville

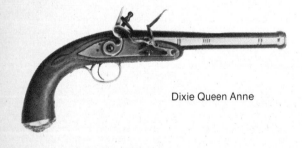

Dixie Queen Anne

Lyman Plains Pistol

BLACK WATCH SCOTCH PISTOL
Caliber: 577 (.550″ round ball).
Barrel: 7″, smoothbore.
Weight: 1 1/2 lbs. **Length:** 12″ overall.
Stock: Brass.
Sights: None.
Features: Faithful reproduction of this military flintlock. From Dixie.
Price: **$145.00**

CHARLEVILLE FLINTLOCK PISTOL
Caliber: 69 (.680″ round ball).
Barrel: 7 1/2″.
Weight: 48 oz. **Length:** 13 1/2″ overall.
Stock: Walnut.
Sights: None.
Features: Brass frame, polished steel barrel, iron belt hook, brass buttcap and backstrap. Replica of original 1777 pistol. Imported by Dixie.
Price: **$145.00**

DIXIE QUEEN ANNE FLINTLOCK PISTOL
Caliber: 50 (.490″ round ball).
Barrel: 7 1/2″, smoothbore.
Stock: Walnut.
Sights: None.
Features: Browned steel barrel, fluted brass trigger guard, brass mask on butt. Lockplate left in the white. Made by Pedersoli in Italy. Introduced 1983. Imported by Dixie Gun Works.
Price: **$131.00**
Price: Kit **$115.00**

LYMAN PLAINS PISTOL
Caliber: 50 or 54.
Barrel: 8″, 1-in-30″ twist, both calibers.
Weight: 50 oz. **Length:** 15″ overall.
Stock: Walnut half-stock.
Sights: Blade front, square notch rear adjustable for windage.
Features: Polished brass trigger guard and ramrod tip, color case-hardened coil spring lock, spring-loaded trigger, stainless steel nipple, blackened iron furniture. Hooked patent breech, detachable belt hook. Introduced 1981. From Lyman Products.
Price: Finished **$174.95**
Price: Kit **$144.95**

DIXIE PENNSYLVANIA PISTOL
Caliber: 44 (.430″ round ball).
Barrel: 10″ (7/8″ octagon).
Weight: 2 1/2 lbs.
Stock: Walnut-stained hardwood.
Sights: Blade front, open rear drift-adjustable for windage; brass.
Features: Available in flint only. Brass trigger guard, thimbles, nosecap, wedgeplates; high-luster blue barrel. Imported from Italy by Dixie Gun Works.
Price: Finished **$119.95**
Price: Kit. **$88.75**

CAUTION: PRICES CHANGE. CHECK AT GUNSHOP.

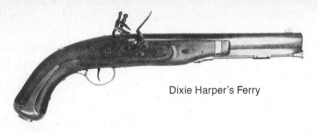

Dixie Harper's Ferry

CVA Kentucky

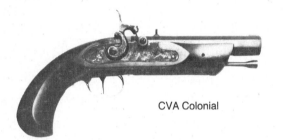

CVA Colonial

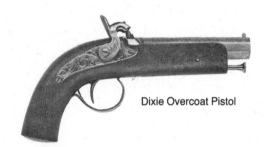

Dixie Overcoat Pistol

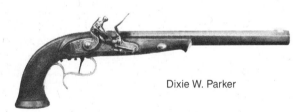

Dixie W. Parker

CVA Hawken

HARPER'S FERRY 1806 PISTOL
Caliber: 58 (.570" round ball).
Barrel: 10".
Weight: 40 oz. **Length:** 16" overall.
Stock: Walnut.
Sights: Fixed.
Features: Case-hardened lock, brass mounted browned barrel. Replica of the first U.S. Gov't.-made flintlock pistol. Imported by Navy Arms, Dixie, EMF.
Price: $165.00
Price: Kit (Dixie) $135.00

KENTUCKY FLINTLOCK PISTOL
Caliber: 44, 45.
Barrel: 10 1/8".
Weight: 32 oz. **Length:** 15 1/2" overall.
Stock: Walnut.
Sights: Fixed.
Features: Specifications, including caliber, weight and length may vary with importer. Case-hardened lock, blued barrel; available also as brass barrel flint Model 1821. Imported by Navy Arms (44 only), The Armoury.
Price: .... $40.95 to $207.00
Price: In kit form, from .... $90.00 to $112.00
Price: Single cased set (Navy Arms) $195.00
Price: Double cased set (Navy Arms) $295.00

Kentucky Percussion Pistol
Similar to flint version but percussion lock. Imported by The Armoury, Navy Arms, CVA (50 cal.).
Price: .... $97.50 to $141.95
Price: In kit form (CVA, Armoury) $93.95
Price: Single cased set (Navy Arms) $175.00
Price: Double cased set (Navy Arms) $270.00

CVA COLONIAL PISTOL
Caliber: 45.
Barrel: 6 3/4", octagonal, rifled. **Length:** 12 3/4" overall.
Stock: Selected hardwood.
Features: Case-hardened lock, brass furniture, fixed sights. Steel ramrod. Available in percussion only. Imported by CVA.
Price: Finished $107.95
Price: Kit $71.95

DIXIE OVERCOAT PISTOL
Caliber: 39.
Barrel: 4" smoothbore.
Weight: 13 oz. **Length:** 8" overall.
Stock: Walnut-finished hardwood. Checkered p.g.
Sights: Bead front.
Features: Shoots .380" balls. Breech plug and engraved lock are burnished steel finish; barrel and trigger guard blued.
Price: Engraved model $34.50

DIXIE W. PARKER FLINTLOCK PISTOL
Caliber: 45.
Barrel: 11", rifled.
Weight: 40 oz. **Length:** 16 1/2" overall.
Stock: Walnut.
Sights: Blade front, notch rear.
Features: Browned barrel, silver-plated trigger guard, finger rest, polished and engraved lock. Double set triggers. Imported by Dixie Gun Works.
Price: $270.00

CVA HAWKEN PISTOL
Caliber: 50.
Barrel: 9 3/4"; 1" flats.
Weight: 50 oz. **Length:** 16 1/2" overall.
Stock: Select hardwood.
Sights: Beaded blade front, fully adjustable open rear.
Features: Color case-hardened lock, polished brass wedge plate, nose cap, ramrod thimbles, trigger guard, grip cap. Hooked breech. Imported by CVA.
Price: $145.95
Price: Kit $105.95

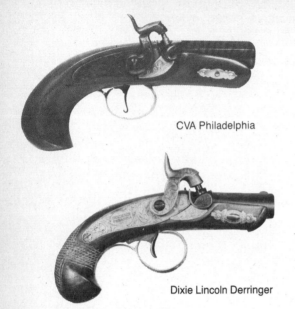

CVA Philadelphia

Dixie Lincoln Derringer

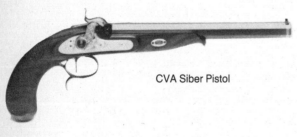

Dixie Brass Frame

CVA PHILADELPHIA DERRINGER PISTOL
Caliber: 45.
Barrel: 3¹/₈″.
Weight: 16 oz. **Length:** 7″ overall.
Stock: Select hardwood.
Sights: Fixed.
Features: Engraved wedge holder and barrel. Imported by CVA.
Price: $93.95
Price: Kit form $51.95

DIXIE LINCOLN DERRINGER
Caliber: 41.
Barrel: 2″, 8 lands, 8 grooves.
Weight: 7 oz. **Length:** 5¹/₂″ overall.
Stock: Walnut finish, checkered.
Sights: Fixed.
Features: Authentic copy of the ''Lincoln Derringer.'' Shoots .400'' patched ball. German silver furniture includes trigger guard with pineapple finial, wedge plates, nose, wrist, side and teardrop inlays. All furniture, lockplate, hammer, and breech plug engraved. Imported from Italy by Dixie Gun Works.
Price: With wooden case. $285.95
Price: Kit (not engraved) $89.95

DIXIE PHILADELPHIA DERRINGER
Caliber: 41.
Barrel: 3¹/₂″, octagon.
Weight: 8 oz. **Length:** 5¹/₂″ overall.
Stock: Walnut, checkered p.g.
Sights: Fixed.
Features: Barrel and lock are blued; brass furniture. From Dixie Gun Works.
Price: $45.00

DIXIE BRASS FRAME DERRINGER
Caliber: 41.
Barrel: 2¹/₂″.
Weight: 7 oz. **Length:** 5¹/₂″ overall.
Stock: Walnut.
Features: Brass frame, color case-hardened hammer and trigger. Shoots .395″ round ball. Engraved model available. From Dixie Gun Works.
Price: Plain model $49.95
Price: Engraved model $85.95
Price: Kit form, plain model. $42.50

FRENCH-STYLE DUELING PISTOL
Caliber: 44.
Barrel: 10″.
Weight: 35 oz. **Length:** 15³/₄″ overall.
Stock: Carved walnut.
Sights: Fixed.
Features: Comes with velvet-lined case and accessories. Imported by Mandall Shooting Supplies.
Price: $295.00

DIXIE ABILENE DERRINGER
Caliber: 41.
Barrel: 2¹/₂″, six-groove rifling.
Weight: 8 oz. **Length:** 6¹/₂″ overall.
Stock: Walnut.
Features: All steel version of Dixie's brass-framed derringers. Blued barrel, color case-hardened frame and hammer. Shoots .395″ patched ball. Comes with wood presentation case.
Price: $81.50
Price: Kit form $51.95

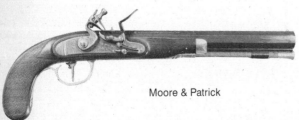

CVA Siber Pistol

CVA SIBER PISTOL
Caliber: 45.
Barrel: 10¹/₂″.
Weight: 34 oz. **Length:** 15¹/₂″ overall.
Stock: High-grade French walnut, checkered grip.
Sights: Barleycorn front, micro-adjustable rear.
Features: Reproduction of pistol made by Swiss watchmaker Jean Siber in the 1800s. Precise lock and set trigger give fast lock time. Has engraving, blackened stainless barrel, trigger guard. Imported by CVA.
Price: $393.95

Moore & Patrick

MOORE & PATRICK FLINT DUELING PISTOL
Caliber: 45.
Barrel: 10″, rifled.
Weight: 32 oz. **Length:** 14¹/₂″ overall.
Stock: European walnut, checkered.
Sights: Fixed.
Features: Engraved, silvered lockplate, blue barrel. German silver furniture. Imported from Italy by Dixie.
Price: $285.00

CAUTION: PRICES CHANGE. CHECK AT GUNSHOP.

BLACKPOWDER SINGLE SHOT PISTOLS — FLINT & PERCUSSION

Dixie LePage

DIXIE SCREW BARREL PISTOL
Caliber: .445".
Barrel: 2¹⁄₂".
Weight: 8 oz. **Length:** 6¹⁄₂" overall.
Stock: Walnut.
Features: Trigger folds down when hammer is cocked. Close copy of the origi-
nals once made in Belgium. Uses No. 11 percussion caps.
Price: **$89.00**
Price: Kit **$53.00**

ELGIN CUTLASS PISTOL
Caliber: 44 (.440").
Barrel: 4¹⁄₄"".
Weight: 21 oz. **Length:** 12" overall.
Stock: Walnut.
Sights: None.
Features: Replica of the pistol used by the U.S. Navy as a boarding weapon.
Smoothbore barrel. Available as a kit or finished. Made in U.S. by Navy
Arms.
Price: Kit **$60.00**
Price: Finished **$80.00**

NAVY ARMS DUCKFOOT
Caliber: 36.
Barrel: 2⁷⁄₈", three barrels.
Weight: 32 oz. **Length:** 10¹⁄₂" overall.
Stock: Walnut.
Sights: None.
Features: Steel barrels and receiver, brass frame. Also comes in kit form, 90%
completed, no drilling or tapping. From Navy Arms.
Price: Complete **$55.00**
Price: Kit **$35.00**

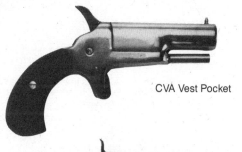

CVA Vest Pocket

Traditions Trapper

Dixie Tornado

NAVY ARMS LE PAGE DUELING PISTOL
Caliber: 45.
Barrel: 9", octagon, rifled.
Weight: 34 oz. **Length:** 15" overall.
Stock: European walnut.
Sights: Adjustable rear.
Features: Single set trigger. Polished metal finish. From Navy Arms.
Price: Percussion **$315.00**
Price: Single cased set, percussion **$420.00**
Price: Double cased set, percussion **$700.00**
Price: Flintlock, rifled **$340.00**
Price: Flintlock, smoothbore **$340.00**
Price: Flintlock, single cased set **$495.00**
Price: Flintlock, double cased set **$850.00**

DIXIE LE PAGE PERCUSSION DUELING PISTOL
Caliber: 45.
Barrel: 10", rifled.
Weight: 40 oz. **Length:** 16" overall.
Stock: Walnut, fluted butt.
Sights: Blade front, notch rear.
Features: Double set triggers. Blued barrel; trigger guard and butt cap are
polished silver. Imported by Dixie Gun Works.
Price: **$225.00**

Elgin Cutlass Pistol

CVA VEST POCKET DERRINGER
Caliber: 44.
Barrel: 2¹⁄₂", brass.
Weight: 7 oz.
Stock: Two-piece walnut.
Features: All brass frame with brass ramrod. A muzzle-loading version of the
Colt No. 3 derringer.
Price: Finished **$57.95**
Price: Kit **$49.95**

TRADITIONS TRAPPER PISTOL
Caliber: 45, 50.
Barrel: 9³⁄₄", ⁷⁄₈" flats.
Weight: 2³⁄₄ lbs. **Length:** 16⁵⁄₈" overall.
Stock: Beech.
Sights: Blade front, adjustable rear.
Features: Double set triggers; brass butt cap, trigger guard, wedge plate,
forend tip, thimble. From Traditions Inc.
Price: **$128.00**
Price: Kit **$98.00**

NEW ORLEANS ACE
Caliber: 44.
Barrel: 3¹⁄₂", rifled or smoothbore.
Weight: 16 oz. **Length:** 9" overall.
Stock: Walnut.
Sights: None.
Features: Solid brass frame (receiver). Available complete or in kit form. Kit is
90% complete, no drilling or tapping, fully inletted. From Navy Arms.
Price: Complete (smoothbore) **$45.00**
Price: Kit (smoothbore) **$30.00**

DIXIE TORNADO TARGET PISTOL
Caliber: 44 (.430" round ball).
Barrel: 10", octagonal, 1-in-22" twist.
Stocks: Walnut, target-style. Left unfinished for custom fitting. Walnut forend.
Sights: Blade on ramp front, micro-type open rear adjustable for windage and
elevation.
Features: Grip frame style of 1860 Colt revolver. Improved model of the Tingle
and B.W. Southgate pistol. Trigger adjustable for pull. Frame, barrel, ham-
mer and sights in the white, brass trigger guard. Comes with solid brass,
walnut-handled cleaning rod with jag and nylon muzzle protector. Introduced 1983. From Dixie Gun Works.
Price: **$151.95**

Texas Patterson

WALKER 1847 PERCUSSION REVOLVER
Caliber: 44, 6-shot.
Barrel: 9".
Weight: 84 oz. **Length:** 15 1/2" overall.
Stocks: Walnut.
Sights: Fixed.
Features: Case-hardened frame, loading lever and hammer; iron backstrap; brass trigger guard; engraved cylinder. Imported by CVA, Navy Arms, Dixie, Armsport.
Price: About . . . . $185.00 to $295.00
Price: Single cased set (Navy Arms). $275.00

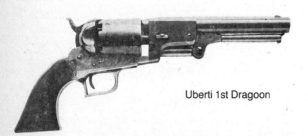

Uberti 1st Dragoon

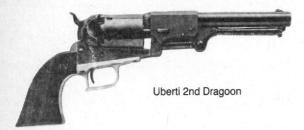

Uberti 2nd Dragoon

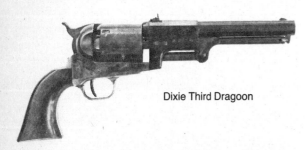

Dixie Third Dragoon

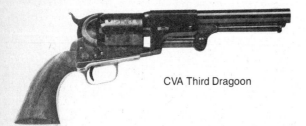

CVA Third Dragoon

TEXAS PATERSON 1836 REVOLVER
Caliber: 36 (.376" round ball).
Barrel: 7 1/2".
Weight: 42 oz.
Stocks: One-piece walnut.
Sights: Fixed.
Features: Copy of Sam Colt's first commercially-made revolving pistol. Has no loading lever but comes with loading tool. From Dixie Gun Works, Navy Arms.
Price: About. $185.00

Walker 1847

UBERTI 1st MODEL DRAGOON
Caliber: 44.
Barrel: 7 1/2", part round, part octagon.
Weight: 64 oz.
Stocks: One-piece walnut.
Sights: German silver blade front, hammer notch rear.
Features: First model has oval bolt cuts in cylinder, square-back flared trigger guard, V-type mainspring, short trigger. Ranger and Indian scene roll-engraved on cylinder. Color case-hardened frame, loading lever, plunger and hammer; blue barrel, cylinder, trigger and wedge. Available with old-time charcoal blue or standard blue-black finish. Polished brass backstrap and trigger guard. From Uberti USA.
Price: $238.00

Uberti 2nd Model Dragoon Revolver
Similar to the 1st Model except this model is distinguished by its rectangular bolt cuts in the cylinder.
Price: $240.00
Price: As Confederate Tucker & Sherrard, with 3rd Model loading lever and special cylinder engraving. $238.00

Uberti 3rd Model Dragoon Revolver
Similar to the 2nd Model except for oval trigger guard, long trigger, modifications to the loading lever and latch. Imported by Benson Firearms, Uberti USA
Price: Military (frame cut for shoulder stock, steel backstrap) $259.00
Price: Civilian (brass backstrap, trigger guard) $240.00
Price: Western (silver-plated backstrap, trigger guard) $269.00
Price: Shoulder stock $125.00

> Consult our Directory pages for the location of firms mentioned

DIXIE THIRD MODEL DRAGOON
Caliber: 44 (.454" round ball).
Barrel: 7 3/8".
Weight: 4 lbs., 2 1/2 oz.
Stocks: One-piece walnut.
Sights: Brass pin front, hammer notch rear, or adjustable folding leaf rear.
Features: Cylinder engraved with Indian fight scene. This is the only Dragoon replica with folding leaf sight. Brass backstrap and trigger guard; color case-hardened steel frame, blue-black barrel. Imported by Dixie Gun Works.
Price: $185.00

CVA Third Model Colt Dragoon
Similar to the Dixie Third Dragoon except has 7 1/2" barrel, weighs 4 lbs., 6 oz., blade front sight. Overall length of 14". 44 caliber, 6-shot.
Price: $225.95

CAUTION: PRICES CHANGE. CHECK AT GUNSHOP.

BLACKPOWDER REVOLVERS

Dixie 1849 Pocket

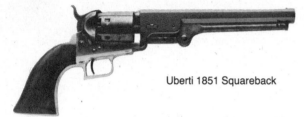

Uberti 1851 Squareback

CVA Sheriff's Model

CVA Colt Sheriff's Model
Similar to the Uberti 1861 Navy except has 5¹/₂" barrel, brass or steel frame, semi-fluted cylinder. In 36 caliber only.
Price: Brass frame, finished $143.95
Price: As above, kit $125.95
Price: Steel frame, finished. $169.95

1851 SHERIFF MODEL PERCUSSION REVOLVER
Caliber: 36, 44, 6-shot.
Barrel: 5".
Weight: 40 oz. Length: 10¹/₂" overall.
Stocks: Walnut.
Sights: Fixed.
Features: Brass backstrap and trigger guard; engraved navy scene; case-hardened frame, hammer, loading lever. Imported by E.M.F., Sile.
Price: Steel frame $170.00
Price: Brass frame .... $90.95 to $125.00
Price: Kit, brass or steel frame .... $114.00 to $160.00

1851 NAVY-SHERIFF
Same as 1851 Sheriff model except has 4" barrel. Imported by E.M.F., Uberti USA.
Price: About. $229.00
Price: Stainless steel (Uberti USA) $295.00

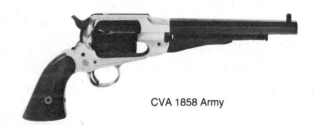

CVA 1858 Army

CVA 1858 Remington Target
Similar to the New Model 1858 Remington except has ramped blade front sight, adjustable rear.
Price: $229.95

1848 BABY DRAGOON, 1849 POCKET, WELLS FARGO REVOLVERS
Caliber: 31.
Barrel: 3", 4", 5"; seven-groove, RH twist.
Weight: About 21 oz.
Stocks: Varnished walnut.
Sights: Brass pin front, hammer notch rear.
Features: No loading lever on Baby Dragoon or Wells Fargo models. Unfluted cylinder with stagecoach holdup scene; cupped cylinder pin; no grease grooves; one safety pin on cylinder and slot in hammer face; straight (flat) mainspring. From Dixie, Uberti USA.
Price: 6" barrel, with loading lever (Dixie) $150.00
Price: Brass backstrap, trigger guard (Uberti USA) $229.00
Price: As above, silver-plated (Uberti USA) $240.00

NAVY MODEL 1851 PERCUSSION REVOLVER
Caliber: 36, 44, 6-shot.
Barrel: 7¹/₂".
Weight: 44 oz. Length: 13" overall.
Stocks: Walnut finish.
Sights: Post front, hammer notch rear.
Features: Brass backstrap and trigger guard; some have 1st Model square-back trigger guard, engraved cylinder with navy battle scene; case-hardened frame, hammer, loading lever. Imported by The Armoury, Navy Arms, E.M.F., Dixie, Euroarms of America, Armsport, CVA, Sile, Uberti USA.
Price: Brass frame .... $150.00 to $229.00
Price: Steel frame .... $125.00 to $229.00
Price: Stainless (Uberti USA) $295.00
Price: Sillver-plated backstrap, trigger guard (Uberti USA) $249.00
Price: Kit form .... $95.00 to $119.95
Price: Engraved model (Dixie) $135.00
Price: Single cased set, steel frame (Navy Arms) $199.00
Price: Double cased set, steel frame (Navy Arms) $325.00
Price: London Model with iron backstrap (Uberti USA) $245.00

Uberti 1861 Navy Percussion Revolver
Similar to 1851 Navy except has round 7¹/₂" barrel, rounded trigger guard, German silver blade front sight, "creeping" loading lever. Available with fluted or round cylinder. Imported by Uberti USA.
Price: Steel backstrap, trigger guard, cut for stock $245.00
Price: Brass backstrap, trigger guard. $229.00
Price: Silver-plated backstrap, trigger guard $249.00
Price: Stainless steel. $305.00

ARMY 1851 PERCUSSION REVOLVER
Caliber: 44, 6-shot.
Barrel: 7¹/₂".
Weight: 45 oz. Length: 13" overall.
Stocks: Walnut finish.
Sights: Fixed.
Features: 44-caliber version of the 1851 Navy. Imported by The Armoury, E.M.F.
Price: .... $95.00 to $140.00

NEW MODEL 1858 ARMY PERCUSSION REVOLVER
Caliber: 36 or 44, 6-shot.
Barrel: 6¹/₂" or 8".
Weight: 40 oz. Length: 13¹/₂" overall.
Stocks: Walnut.
Sights: Blade front, groove-in-frame rear.
Features: Replica of Remington Model 1858. Also available from some importers as Army Model Belt Revolver in 36 cal., shortened and lightened version of the 44. Target Model (Uberti USA, Navy) has fully adjustable target rear sight, target front, 36 or 44. Imported by CVA (as 1858 Remington Army), Dixie, Navy Arms, The Armoury, E.M.F., Euroarms of America (engraved, stainless and plain), Armsport, Sile, Uberti USA.
Price: Steel frame, about $213.95
Price: Steel frame kit (Euroarms) .... $105.00 to $150.00
Price: Single cased set (Navy Arms). $205.00
Price: Double cased set (Navy Arms) $330.00
Price: Nickel finish (E.M.F.) $152.75
Price: Stainless steel Model 1858 (Euroarms, Uberti, Sile, Navy Arms, Armsport) .... $140.00 to $220.00
Price: Target Model (Euroarms, Uberti, Sile, Navy, E.M.F.) $95.95 to $239.00
Price: Brass frame, finished (CVA, Navy Arms, Sile) ..... $97.95 to $159.95
Price: As above, kit (CVA, Dixie, Navy Arms) .... $94.75 to $139.95

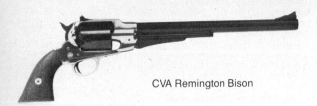

CVA Remington Bison

Navy 1858 Remington-Style

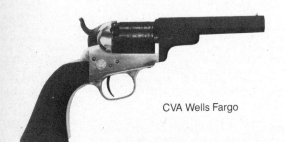

CVA Wells Fargo

CVA Pocket Remington

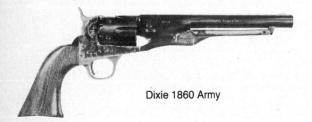

Dixie 1860 Army

CVA Remington Bison

Similar to the CVA 1858 Remington Target except has 10¼″ octagonal barrel, 44 caliber, brass frame.
Price: Finished **$247.95**

NAVY DELUXE 1858 REMINGTON-STYLE REVOLVER

Caliber: 44.
Barrel: 8″.
Weight: 2 lbs., 13 oz.
Stocks: Smooth walnut.
Sights: Dovetailed blade front.
Features: First exact reproduction—correct in size and weight to the original, with progressive rifling; highly polished with blue finish, silver-plated trigger guard. From Navy Arms.
Price: Deluxe model **$300.00**

CVA WELLS FARGO MODEL

Caliber: 31.
Barrel: 4″, octagonal.
Weight: 28 oz. (with extra cylinder). **Length:** 9″ overall.
Stocks: Walnut.
Sights: Post front, hammer notch rear.
Features: Brass frame and backstrap or steel frame; blue finish. Comes with extra cylinder. Imported by CVA.
Price: Brass frame, finished **$117.95**
Price: As above, kit **$105.95**
Price: Steel frame, finished **$175.95**

CVA POCKET REMINGTON

Caliber: 31.
Barrel: 4″, octagonal.
Weight: 15½ oz. **Length:** 7½″ overall.
Stocks: Two-piece walnut.
Sights: Post front, grooved topstrap rear.
Features: Spur trigger, brass frame with blued barrel and cylinder. Available finished or in kit form. Introduced 1984.
Price: Finished **$117.95**
Price: Kit **$93.95**

1860 ARMY PERCUSSION REVOLVER

Caliber: 44, 6-shot.
Barrel: 8″.
Weight: 40 oz. **Length:** 13⅝″ overall.
Stocks: Walnut.
Sights: Fixed.
Features: Engraved navy scene on cylinder; brass trigger guard; case-hardened frame, loading lever and hammer. Some importers supply pistol cut for detachable shoulder stock, have accessory stock available. Imported by E.M.F., CVA, Navy Arms, The Armoury, Dixie (half-fluted cylinder, not roll engraved), Euroarms of America (brass or steel model), Armsport, Sile, Uberti USA.
Price: About . . . . **$150.00** to **235.00**
Price: Single cased set (Navy Arms) **$225.00**
Price: Double cased set (Navy Arms) **$350.00**
Price: 1861 Navy: Same as Army except 36 cal., 7½″ bbl., wgt. 41 oz., cut for shoulder stock; round cylinder (fluted avail.), from Armsport, E.M.F., CVA (brass frame) . . . . **$150.00** to **249.00**
Price: Steel frame kit (E.M.F., Navy, Euroarms) . . . . **$120.00** to **146.00**
Price: Stainless steel (Uberti USA) **$305.00**

1862 POCKET POLICE PERCUSSION REVOLVER

Caliber: 36, 5-shot.
Barrel: 4½″, 5½″, 6½″, 7½″.
Weight: 26 oz. **Length:** 12″ overall (6½″ bbl.).
Stocks: Walnut.
Sights: Fixed.
Features: Round tapered barrel; half-fluted and rebated cylinder; case-hardened frame, loading lever and hammer; silver or brass trigger guard and backstrap. Imported by CVA (5½″ only), Navy Arms (5½″ only), Uberti USA.
Price: About **$179.95**
Price: Single cased set with accessories (Navy Arms) **$275.00**
Price: Stainless steel (Uberti USA) 4½″, 5½″ **$289.00**
Price: Kit (CVA) **$109.95**
Price: With silver-plated backstrap, trigger guard (Uberti USA) **$245.00**

UBERTI 1862 POCKET NAVY PERCUSSION REVOLVER

Caliber: 36, 5-shot.
Barrel: 4½″, 5½″, 6½″, octagonal, 7-groove, LH twist.
Weight: 27 oz. (5½″ barrel). **Length:** 10½″ overall (5½″ bbl.).
Stocks: One-piece varnished walnut.
Sights: Brass pin front, hammer notch rear.
Features: Rebated cylinder, hinged loading lever, brass or silver-plated backstrap and trigger guard, color cased frame, hammer, loading lever, plunger and latch, rest blued. Has original-type markings. From Uberti USA.
Price: With brass backstrap, trigger guard **$229.00**
Price: With silver-plated backstrap, trigger guard **$245.00**
Price: Stainless steel (4½″, 5½″ only) **$289.00**

CAUTION: PRICES CHANGE. CHECK AT GUNSHOP.

BLACKPOWDER REVOLVERS

Dixie Spiller & Burr

SPILLER & BURR REVOLVER
Caliber: 36 (.375″ round ball).
Barrel: 7″, octagon.
Weight: 2¹/₂ lbs. **Length:** 12¹/₂″ overall.
Stocks: Two-piece walnut.
Sights: Fixed.
Features: Reproduction of the C.S.A. revolver. Brass frame and trigger guard. Also available as a kit. From Dixie, Navy Arms.
Price: .... **$125.00** to **$142.00**
Price: Kit form **$65.00**
Price: Single cased set (Navy Arms).................... **$199.00**
Price: Double cased set (Navy Arms).................... **$325.00**

GRISWOLD & GUNNISON PERCUSSION REVOLVER
Caliber: 36 or 44, 6-shot.
Barrel: 7¹/₂″.
Weight: 44 oz. (36 cal.). **Length:** 13″ overall.
Stocks: Walnut.
Sights: Fixed.
Features: Replica of famous Confederate pistol. Brass frame, backstrap and trigger guard; case-hardened loading lever; rebated cylinder (44 cal. only). Rounded Dragoon-type barrel. Imported by Navy Arms (as Reb Model 1860), E.M.F., Uberti USA
Price: About.. **$229.00**
Price: Kit (E.M.F.)...................................... **$95.00**
Price: Single cased set (Navy Arms)..................... **$199.00**
Price: Double cased set (Navy Arms).................... **$325.00**
Price: Reb 1860 (Navy Arms) **$100.00**

LE MAT CAVALRY MODEL REVOLVER
Caliber: 44/65.
Barrel: 6³/₄″ (revolver); 4⁷/₈″ (single shot).
Weight: NA.
Stocks: Hand-checkered walnut.
Sights: Post front, hammer notch rear.
Features: Exact reproduction with all-steel construction; 44-cal. 9-shot cylinder, 65-cal. single barrel; color case-hardened hammer with selector; spur trigger guard; ring at butt; lever-type barrel release. From Navy Arms.
Price: Cavalry model (lanyard ring, spur trigger guard) **$550.00**
Price: Army model (round trigger guard, pin-type barrel release) ... **$550.00**
Price: Naval-style (thumb selector on hammer) **$550.00**

DIXIE "WYATT EARP" REVOLVER
Caliber: 44.
Barrel: 12″ octagon.
Weight: 46 oz. **Length:** 18″ overall.
Stocks: Two-piece walnut.
Sights: Fixed.
Features: Highly polished brass frame, backstrap and trigger guard; blued barrel and cylinder; case-hardened hammer, trigger and loading lever. Navy-size shoulder stock ($45.00) will fit with minor fitting. From Dixie Gun Works.
Price: **$130.00**

Freedom Mini Percussion

Ruger Old Army

Consult our Directory pages for the location of firms mentioned

ROGERS & SPENCER PERCUSSION REVOLVER
Caliber: 44.
Barrel: 7¹/₂″.
Weight: 47 oz. **Length:** 13³/₄″ overall.
Stocks: Walnut.
Sights: Cone front, integral groove in frame for rear.
Features: Accurate reproduction of a Civil War design. Solid frame; extra large nipple cut-out on rear of cylinder; loading lever and cylinder easily removed for cleaning. From Euroarms of America (standard blue, engraved, burnished, target models), Navy Arms.
Price: .... **$160.00** to **$240.00**
Price: Nickel-plated.. **$120.00**
Price: Engraved (Euroarms) **$286.00**
Price: Kit version **$95.00**
Price: Target version (Euroarms).......................... **$234.00**
Price: Brushed satin chrome (Navy Arms) **$180.00**
Price: Burnished London Gray (Euroarms)................. **$234.00**

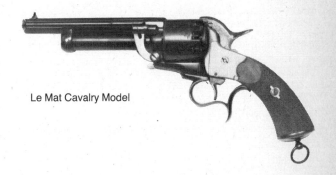

Le Mat Cavalry Model

FREEDOM ARMS PERCUSSION MINI REVOLVER
Caliber: 22, 5-shot.
Barrel: 1″, 1³/₄″, 3″.
Weight: 4³/₄ oz. (1″ bbl.).
Stocks: Simulated ebony.
Sights: Fixed.
Features: Percussion version of the 22 RF gun. All stainless steel; spur trigger. Gun comes with leather carrying pouch, bullet seating tool, powder measure, 20 29-gr. bullets. Introduced 1983. From Freedom Arms.
Price: 1″ barrel **$203.02**

RUGER 44 OLD ARMY PERCUSSION REVOLVER
Caliber: 44, 6-shot. Uses .457″ dia. lead bullets.
Barrel: 7¹/₂″ (6-groove, 16″ twist).
Weight: 46 oz. **Length:** 13³/₄″ overall.
Stocks: Smooth walnut.
Sights: Ramp front, rear adjustable for w. and e.
Features: Stainless steel standard size nipples, chrome-moly steel cylinder and frame, same lockwork as in original Super Blackhawk. Also available in stainless steel in very limited quantities. Made in USA. From Sturm, Ruger & Co.
Price: Stainless steel (Model KBP-7) **$370.50**
Price: Blued steel (Model BP-7) **$290.50**

Navy Brown Bess

SECOND MODEL BROWN BESS MUSKET
Caliber: 75, uses .735″ round ball.
Barrel: 42″, smoothbore.
Weight: 9¹/₂ lbs. **Length:** 59″ overall.
Stock: Walnut (Navy); walnut-stained hardwood (Dixie).
Sights: Fixed.
Features: Polished barrel and lock with brass trigger guard and buttplate. Bayonet and scabbard available. From Navy Arms, Dixie, E.M.F.
Price: Finished . . . . **$399.00 to $750.00**
Price: Kit (Dixie, Navy) . . . . **$375.00 to $430.00**

NAVY ARMS CHARLEVILLE MUSKET
Caliber: 69.
Barrel: 44⁵/₈″.
Weight: 8³/₄ lbs. **Length:** 59³/₈″ overall.
Stock: Walnut.
Sights: Blade front.
Features: Replica of Revolutionary War 1763 musket. Bright metal, walnut stock. From Navy Arms.
Price: Finished **$550.00**
Price: Kit **$450.00**

HARPERS FERRY 1803 FLINTLOCK RIFLE
Caliber: 54 or 58.
Barrel: 35″.
Weight: 9 lbs. **Length:** 59¹/₂″ overall.
Stock: Walnut with cheekpiece.
Sights: Brass blade front, fixed steel rear.
Features: Brass trigger guard, sideplate, buttplate; steel patch box. Imported by Euroarms of America.
Price: **$512.00**

Dixie Indian Gun

DIXIE INDIAN GUN
Caliber: 75.
Barrel: 31″, round tapered.
Weight: About 9 lbs. **Length:** 47″ overall.
Stock: Hardwood.
Sights: Blade front.
Features: Modified Brown Bess musket; brass furniture, browned lock and barrel. Lock is marked "GRICE 1762" with crown over "GR." Serpent-style sideplate. Introduced 1983.
Price: Complete. **$375.00**
Price: As above, in kit form **$360.00**

KENTUCKY FLINTLOCK RIFLE
Caliber: 44, 45, or 50.
Barrel: 35″.
Weight: 7 lbs. **Length:** 50″ overall.
Stock: Walnut stained, brass fittings.
Sights: Fixed.
Features: Available in Carbine model also, 28″ bbl. Some variations in detail, finish. Kits also available from some importers. Imported by Navy Arms, The Armoury, Armsport.
Price: About . . . . $217.95 to $324.00
Price: Deluxe model, flint or percussion, 50-cal. (Navy Arms) **$275.00**

KENTUCKIAN RIFLE & CARBINE
Caliber: 44.
Barrel: 35″ (Rifle), 27¹/₂″ (Carbine).
Weight: 7 lbs. (Rifle), 5¹/₂ lbs. (Carbine). **Length:** 51″ (Rifle) overall, Carbine 43″.
Stock: Walnut stain.
Sights: Brass blade front, steel V-ramp rear.
Features: Octagon bbl., case-hardened and engraved lockplate. Brass furniture. Imported by Dixie, Armsport.
Price: Rifle or carbine, flint, about **$225.00**
Price: As above, percussion, about **$210.00**

Kentucky Percussion Rifle
Similar to flintlock except percussion lock. Finish and features vary with importer. Imported by Navy Arms (45 cal.), The Armoury, CVA, Armsport (rifle-shotgun combo).
Price: About **$259.95**
Price: Armsport combo **$235.00**
Price: 50 cal. (Navy Arms). **$299.00**
Price: Kit, 50 cal. (CVA) **$143.95**

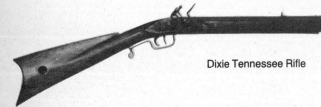

Dixie Tennessee Rifle

DIXIE TENNESSEE MOUNTAIN RIFLE
Caliber: 32 or 50.
Barrel: 41¹/₂″, 6-groove rifling, brown finish. **Length:** 56″ overall.
Sights: Walnut, oil finish; Kentucky-style.
Stock: Silver blade front, open buckhorn rear.
Features: Recreation of the original mountain rifles. Early Schultz lock, interchangeable flint or percussion with vent plug or drum and nipple. Tumbler has fly. Double-set triggers. All metal parts browned. From Dixie.
Price: Flint or percussion, finished rifle, 50 cal. **$335.00**
Price: Kit, 50 cal **$275.00**
Price: Left-hand model, flint or perc. **$335.00**
Price: Left-hand kit, flint or perc., 50 cal. **$275.00**
Price: Squirrel Rifle (as above except in 32 cal. with ¹³/₁₆″ barrel flats), flint or percussion **$335.00**
Price: Kit, 32 cal., flint or percussion **$275.00**

THOMPSON/CENTER PENNSYLVANIA HUNTER RIFLE
Caliber: 50.
Barrel: 31″, half-octagon, half-round.
Weight: About 7¹/₂ lbs. **Length:** 48″ overall.
Stock: Black walnut.
Sights: Open, adjustable.
Features: Rifled 1-in-66″ for round ball shooting. Available in flintlock or percussion.
Price: Percussion **$265.00**
Price: Flintlock. **$280.00**

HATFIELD SQUIRREL RIFLE
Caliber: 36, 45, 50.
Barrel: 39¹/₂″, octagon, 32″ on half-stock.
Weight: 8 lbs. (32 cal.).
Stock: American fancy maple full-stock.
Sights: Silver blade front, buckhorn rear.
Features: Recreation of the traditional squirrel rifle. Available in flint or percussion with brass trigger guard and buttplate. From Hatfield Rifle Works. Introduced 1983.

Hatfield Squirrel Rifle

Price: Full stock, flint or percussion Grade **$465.00**
Price: As above, Grade II **$532.00**
Price: As above, Grade III **$630.00**

CVA Pennsylvania

CVA PENNSYLVANIA LONG RIFLE
Caliber: 50.
Barrel: 40″, octagonal; ⁷/₈″ flats.

Weight: 8 lbs., 3 oz. **Length:** 55³/₄″ overall.
Stock: Select walnut.
Sights: Brass blade front, fixed semi-buckhorn rear.
Features: Color case-hardened lockplate, brass buttplate, toe plate, patch-box, trigger guard, thimbles, nosecap; blued barrel, double-set triggers; authentic V-type mainspring. Introduced 1983. From CVA.
Price: Finished, percussion **$475.95**
Price: Finished, flintlock **$485.95**

PENNSYLVANIA FULL-STOCK RIFLE
Caliber: 45 or 50.
Barrel: 32″ rifled, ¹⁵/₁₆″ dia.
Weight: 8¹/₂ lbs.
Stock: Walnut.
Sights: Fixed.
Features: Available in flint or percussion. Blued lock and barrel, brass furniture. Offered complete or in kit form. From The Armoury.
Price: Flint **$250.00**
Price: Percussion **$225.00**

TRADITIONS PENNSYLVANIA RIFLE
Caliber: 45, 50.
Barrel: 40¹/₄″, ⁷/₈″ flats.
Weight: 9 lbs. **Length:** 57¹/₂″ overall.
Stock: Walnut.
Sights: Blade front, adjustable rear.
Features: Brass patch box and ornamentation. Double set triggers. From Traditions Inc.
Price: Flintlock **$369.00**
Price: Percussion **$354.00**

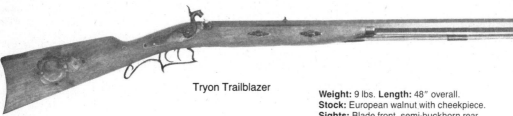

Tryon Trailblazer

TRYON TRAILBLAZER RIFLE
Caliber: 50.
Barrel: 32″, 1″ flats.

Weight: 9 lbs. **Length:** 48″ overall.
Stock: European walnut with cheekpiece.
Sights: Blade front, semi-buckhorn rear.
Features: Reproduction of a rifle made by George Tryon about 1820. Double-set triggers, back action lock, hooked breech with long tang. From Armsport.
Price: **$445.00**

CVA Squirrel Rifle

CVA SQUIRREL RIFLE
Caliber: 36, 36/50 Combo.
Barrel: 25″, octagonal; ⁷/₈″ flats.
Weight: 6 lbs. **Length:** 40³/₄″ overall.
Stock: Hardwood.
Sights: Beaded blade front, fully adjustable hunting-style rear.
Features: Color case-hardened lockplate, brass buttplate, trigger guard, wedge plates, thimbles; double set triggers; hooked breech; authentic V-type mainspring. From CVA.
Price: Finished, percussion, 36 cal. **$227.95**
Price: Kit, percussion, 36 cal. **$169.95**
Price: As above, with 36- and 50-cal. bbls. **$142.95**

LYMAN GREAT PLAINS RIFLE
Caliber: 50 or 54 cal.
Barrel: 32″, 1-in-66″ twist.
Weight: 9 lbs.
Stock: Walnut.
Sights: Steel blade front, buckhorn rear adjustable for w. & e. and fixed notch primitive sight included.
Features: Blued steel furniture. Stainless steel nipple. Coil spring lock, Hawken-style trigger guard and double set triggers. Round thimbles recessed and sweated into rib. Steel wedge plates and toe plate. Introduced 1979. From Lyman.
Price: Percussion **$329.95**
Price: Flintlock **$349.95**
Price: Percussion kit **$259.95**

BLACKPOWDER MUSKETS & RIFLES

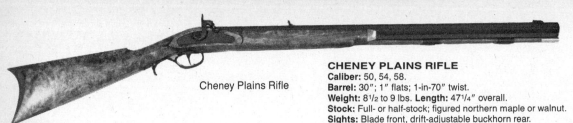

Cheney Plains Rifle

CHENEY PLAINS RIFLE
Caliber: 50, 54, 58.
Barrel: 30″; 1″ flats; 1-in-70″ twist.
Weight: 8¹/₂ to 9 lbs. **Length:** 47¹/₄″ overall.
Stock: Full- or half-stock; figured northern maple or walnut.
Sights: Blade front, drift-adjustable buckhorn rear.
Features: Browned steel, polished brass or browned furniture, hand-rubbed oil on wood; single or double set trigger; sweated rib and recessed thimbles; poured pewter nosecap. Introduced 1983. From Cheney Firearms Co.
Price: Percussion or flintlock.................................$449.00

Traditions Trapper

TRADITIONS TRAPPER RIFLE
Caliber: 36, 45, 50.
Barrel: 24″, ⁷/₈″ flats.
Weight: 5 lbs. **Length:** 40¹/₂″ overall.
Stock: Beech.
Sights: Beaded blade front, adjustable rear.
Features: Metal ramrod, brass furniture. From Traditions Inc.
Price: $188.00
Price: Frontier Scout (similar to above except shorter length of pull, weighs 6 lbs., 26″ bbl., 36, 45 or 50 cal.) $172.00

Lyman Trade Rifle

LYMAN TRADE RIFLE
Caliber: 50 or 54.
Barrel: 28″ octagon, 1-in-48″ twist.
Weight: 8³/₄ lbs. **Length:** 45″ overall.
Stock: European walnut.
Sights: Blade front, open rear adjustable for w. or optional fixed sights.
Features: Fast twist rifling for conical bullets. Polished brass furniture with blue steel parts, stainless steel nipple. Hook breech, single trigger, coil spring percussion lock. Steel barrel rib and ramrod ferrules. Introduced 1980. From Lyman.
Price: Percussion $244.95
Price: Kit, percussion $194.95
Price: Flintlock...$269.95
Price: Kit, flintlock $224.95

CVA KENTUCKY RIFLE
Caliber: 50.
Barrel: 33¹/₂″, rifled, octagon (⁷/₈″ flats).
Weight: 7¹/₂ lbs. **Length:** 48″ overall.
Stock: Select hardwood.
Sights: Brass Kentucky blade-type front, fixed open rear.
Features: Available in either flint or percussion. Stainless steel nipple included. From CVA.
Price: Percussion $259.95
Price: Percussion kit $143.95

Navy Country Boy

NAVY ARMS COUNTRY BOY RIFLE
Caliber: 32, 36, 45, 50.
Barrel: 26″.
Weight: 6 lbs.
Stock: Walnut.
Sights: Blade front, adjustable rear.
Features: Octagonal rifled barrel; blue finish; hooked breech; Mule Ear lock for fast ignition. From Navy Arms.
Price: $250.00
Price: Kit $192.00

Uberti Santa Fe

UBERTI SANTA FE HAWKEN RIFLE
Caliber: 50 or 54.
Barrel: 32″, octagonal.
Weight: 9.8 lbs. **Length:** 50″ overall.
Stock: Walnut, with beavertail cheekpiece.
Sights: German silver blade front, buckhorn rear.
Features: Browned finish, color case-hardened lock, double triggers, German silver ferrule, wedge plates. Imported by Uberti USA.
Price: $385.00
Price: Kit $339.00

CAUTION: PRICES CHANGE. CHECK AT GUNSHOP.

Dixie Tryon

DIXIE DELUX CUB RIFLE
Caliber: 40.
Barrel: 28″.
Weight: 6½ lbs.
Stock: Walnut.
Sights: Fixed.
Features: Short rifle for small game and beginning shooters. Brass patchbox and furniture. Flint or percussion.
Price: Finished $225.00
Price: Kit $210.00

Thompson/Center Renegade Hunter
Similar to standard Renegade except has single trigger in a large-bow shotgun-style trigger guard, no brass trim. Available in 50 or 54 caliber. Color case-hardened lock, rest blued. Introduced 1987. From Thompson/Center.
Price: $255.00

TRYON RIFLE
Caliber: 50, 54.
Barrel: 34″, octagon; 1-in-63″ twist.
Weight: 9 lbs. **Length:** 49″ overall.
Stock: European walnut with steel furniture.
Sights: Blade front, fixed rear.
Features: Reproduction of an American plains rifle with double set triggers and back-action lock. Imported from Italy by Dixie.
Price: $299.00
Price: Kit $249.00

THOMPSON/CENTER RENEGADE RIFLE
Caliber: 50 and 54 plus 56 cal., smoothbore.
Barrel: 26″, 1″ across the flats.
Weight: 8 lbs.
Stock: American walnut.
Sights: Open hunting (Patridge) style, fully adjustable for w. and e.
Features: Coil spring lock, double set triggers, blued steel trim.
Price: Percussion model $275.00
Price: Flintlock model, 50 cal. only.................... $290.00
Price: Percussion kit $200.00
Price: Flintlock kit $215.00
Price: Left-hand percussion, 50 or 54 cal. $285.00

T/C New Englander

THOMPSON/CENTER NEW ENGLANDER RIFLE
Caliber: 50, 54.
Barrel: 28″, round.

Weight: 7 lbs., 15 oz.
Stock: American walnut.
Sights: Open, adjustable.
Features: Color case-hardened percussion lock with engraving, rest blued. Also accepts 12-ga. shotgun barrel. Introduced 1987. From Thompson/Center.
Price: Right-hand model.................................. $220.00
Price: Left-hand model $235.00
Price: Accessory 12 ga. barrel, right-hand $102.50
Price: As above, left-hand................................ $110.00

T/C Hawken

THOMPSON/CENTER HAWKEN RIFLE
Caliber: 45, 50 or 54.
Barrel: 28″ octagon, hooked breech.
Stocks: American walnut.
Sights: Blade front, rear adjustable for w. & e.
Features: Solid brass furniture, double set triggers, button rifled barrel, coil-type mainspring. From Thompson/Center Arms.
Price: Percussion model (45, 50 or 54 cal.) $325.00
Price: Flintlock model (50 cal.) $340.00
Price: Percussion kit $230.00
Price: Flintlock kit $245.00

THOMPSON/CENTER CHEROKEE RIFLE
Caliber: 32, 45.
Barrel: 24″, ¹³⁄₁₆″ across flats.
Weight: About 6 lbs.
Stock: American walnut.
Sights: Open hunting style; round notch rear fully adjustable for w. and e.
Features: Single trigger only. Interchangeable barrels. Brass buttplate, trigger guard, forend escutcheons and lockplate screw bushing. Introduced 1984.
Price: 32, 45 caliber $265.00
Price: Interchangeable 32, 45-cal. barrel $115.00
Price: Kit, percussion, 32, 45 .... $210.00
Price: Kit barrels $90.00

T/C White Mountain

THOMPSON/CENTER WHITE MOUNTAIN CARBINE
Caliber: 50.
Barrel: 21″, half-octagon, half-round.
Weight: 6½ lbs. **Length:** 38″ overall.
Stock: American black walnut.
Sights: Open hunting (Patridge) style, fully adjustable rear.
Features: Percussion only. Single trigger, large trigger guard; rubber buttpad; rear q.d. swivel, front swivel mounted on thimble; comes with sling. Introduced 1989.
Price: $275.00

CAUTION: PRICES CHANGE. CHECK AT GUNSHOP.

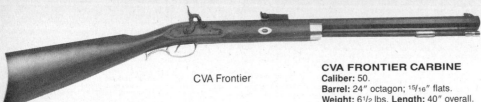

CVA Frontier

CVA MOUNTAIN RIFLE
Caliber: 50, 54.
Barrel: 32″ octagon, 15/16″ flats.
Weight: 9 lbs. **Length:** 48″ overall.
Stock: European walnut with cheekpiece.
Sights: German silver blade front, adjustable open rear.
Features: Color case-hardened and engraved lockplate; bridle, fly, screw-adjustable sear engagement. Double set triggers. Pewter nose cap, trigger guard, buttplate. From CVA.
Price: 50 cal., chrome bore **$397.95**

CVA FRONTIER CARBINE
Caliber: 50.
Barrel: 24″ octagon; 15/16″ flats.
Weight: 6 1/2 lbs. **Length:** 40″ overall.
Stock: Selected hardwood.
Sights: Brass blade front, fixed open rear.
Features: Color case-hardened lockplate, screw-adjustable sear engagement, V-type mainspring. Early style brass trigger with tension spring. Brass buttplate, trigger guard, wedge plate, nose cap, thimble. From CVA.
Price: **$215.95**
Price: Kit **$149.95**

Charles Daly Hawken

ARMOURY R140 HAWKIN RIFLE
Caliber: 45, 50 or 54.
Barrel: 29″
Weight: 8 3/4 to 9 lbs. **Length:** 45 3/4″ overall.
Stock: Walnut, with cheekpiece.
Sights: Dovetail front, fully adjustable rear.
Features: Octagon barrel, removable breech plug; double set triggers; blued barrel, brass stock fittings, color case-hardened percussion lock. From Armsport, The Armoury.
Price: . . . . **$225.00 to $280.00**

ITHACA-NAVY HAWKEN RIFLE
Caliber: 50 and 54.
Barrel: 32″ octagonal, 1″ dia.
Weight: About 9 lbs.
Stocks: Walnut.
Sights: Blade front, rear adjustable for w.
Features: Hooked breech, 1 7/8″ throw percussion lock. Attached twin thimbles and under-rib. German silver barrel key inlays, Hawken-style toe and buttplates, lock bolt inlays, barrel wedges, entry thimble, trigger guard, ramrod and cleaning jag, nipple and nipple wrench. Introduced 1977. From Navy Arms
Price: Complete, percussion. **$480.00**
Price: Kit, percussion **$374.00**

CHARLES DALY HAWKEN RIFLE
Caliber: 45, 50, 54.
Barrel: 28″ octagonal, 7/8″ flats.
Weight: 7 1/2 lbs. **Length:** 45 1/2″ overall.
Stock: European hardwood.
Sights: Blade front, open fully adjustable rear.
Features: Color case-hardened lock uses coil springs; trigger guard, buttplate, forend cap, ferrules and ramrod fittings are polished brass. Left-hand model available in 50-cal. only. Imported by Outdoor Sports Headquarters. Introduced 1984.
Price: Right-hand, percussion **$259.95**
Price: Left-hand, percussion (50-cal. only) **$289.00**
Price: Right-hand, flintlock **$299.00**
Price: Left-hand, flintlock (50-cal. only) **$319.00**
Price: Wilderness Hawken (50-cal. only) **$189.95**

CVA HAWKEN RIFLE
Caliber: 50, 58.
Barrel: 28″, octagon; 1″ across flats; 1-in-66″ twist.
Weight: 8 lbs. **Length:** 44″ overall.
Stock: Select walnut.
Sights: Beaded blade front, fully adjustable open rear.
Features: Fully adjustable double set triggers; brass patch box, wedge plates, nose-cap, thimbles, trigger guard and buttplate; blued barrel; color case-hardened, engraved lockplate. Percussion only. Hooked breech, chrome bore. Introduced 1981.
Price: Finished rifle, percussion **$389.95**
Price: St. Louis Hawken (as above, except does not have chrome bore; hardwood stock), finished **$253.95**
Price: As above, combo kit (50, 54-cal. bbls.). **$241.95**
Price: 50-cal./12-ga. combo, finished **$343.95**
Price: As above, kit **$269.95**

Traditions Hunter

Traditions Hunter Rifle
Similar to the Hawken except has blackened and German silver furniture. Has 28 1/4″ barrel with 1″ flats.
Price: Percussion only, 50 or 54 cal. **$321.00**
Price: Hawken Woodsman (similar to above, brass furniture, 50 cal. only, beech stock) **$206.00**
Price: As above, kit **$160.00**
Price: Frontier (beech stock, flintlock). **$203.00**
Price: As above, percussion **$188.00**
Price: Frontier Carbine (24″ bbl., 45, 50 cal., percussion) **$188.00**

HAWKEN RIFLE
Caliber: 45, 50, 54 or 58.
Barrel: 28″, blued, 6-groove rifling.
Weight: 8 3/4 lbs. **Length:** 44″ overall.
Stock: Walnut with cheekpiece.
Sights: Blade front, fully adjustable rear.
Features: Coil mainspring, double set triggers, polished brass furniture. Features vary slightly with maker. From CVA, Armsport, Sile.
Price: . . . . **$245.00 to $275.00**
Price: Hawken Deluxe rifle or carbine with hard chrome bore (Sile) . **$219.95**
Price: Hawken Hunter, as above except has black-finished furniture (Sile, CVA). **$243.95**
Price: Hawken Deluxe Prefinished Kit (Sile) **$195.00**

Dixie Hawken

TRADITIONS HAWKEN RIFLE
Caliber: 50, 54.
Barrel: 32¼″; 1″ flats.
Weight: 9 lbs. **Length:** 50″ overall.
Stock: Walnut with cheekpiece.
Sights: Hunting style, click adjustable for windage and elevation.
Features: Fiberglass ramrod, double set triggers, polished brass furniture. From Traditions, Inc.
Price: Percussion $316.00
Price: Kit $213.00

DIXIE HAWKEN RIFLE
Caliber: 45, 50, 54.
Barrel: 30″.
Weight: 8 lbs. **Length:** 46½″ overall.
Stock: Walnut.
Sights: Blade front, adjustable rear.
Features: Blued barrel, double set triggers, steel crescent buttplate. Imported by Dixie.
Price: Finished $225.00
Price: Kit $185.00

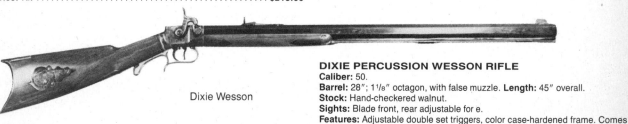

Dixie Wesson

DIXIE PERCUSSION WESSON RIFLE
Caliber: 50.
Barrel: 28″; 1⅛″ octagon, with false muzzle. **Length:** 45″ overall.
Stock: Hand-checkered walnut.
Sights: Blade front, rear adjustable for e.
Features: Adjustable double set triggers, color case-hardened frame. Comes with loading rod and loading accessories. From Dixie Gun Works.
Price: With false muzzle $395.00

Parker-Hale 1853

PARKER-HALE ENFIELD 1853 MUSKET
Caliber: .577″.
Barrel: 39″, 3-groove cold-forged rifling.
Weight: About 9 lbs. **Length:** 55″ overall.
Stock: Seasoned walnut.
Sights: Fixed front, rear step adjustable for elevation.
Features: Three-band musket made to original specs from original gauges. Solid brass stock furniture, color hardened lockplate, hammer; blued barrel, trigger. Imported from England by Navy Arms.
Price: $475.00

LONDON ARMORY 3-BAND 1853 ENFIELD
Caliber: 58 (.577″ Minie, .575″ round ball, .580″ maxi ball).
Barrel: 39″.
Weight: 9½ lbs. **Length:** 54″ overall.
Stock: European walnut.
Sights: Inverted "V" front, traditional Enfield folding ladder rear.
Features: Recreation of the famed London Armory Company Pattern 1862 Enfield Musket. One-piece walnut stock, brass buttplate, trigger guard and nose cap. Lockplate marked "London Armoury Co." and with a British crown. Blued Baddeley barrel bands. From Dixie, Euroarms of America, Navy Arms, Muzzle Loaders, Inc..
Price: About . . . . $395.00 to $427.00
Price: Assembled kit (Euroarms) $380.00

Uberti 1858 New Model

UBERTI 1858 NEW ARMY REVOLVING CARBINE
Caliber: 44.
Barrel: 18″.
Weight: 4.6 lbs. **Length:** 37″ overall.
Stock: Walnut.
Sights: Ramp front, rear adjustable for e.
Features: Carbine version of the 1858 New Army revolver. Brass trigger guard and buttplate; blued, tapered octagonal barrel. Imported from Italy by Uberti USA.
Price: $385.00

LONDON ARMORY 2-BAND ENFIELD 1858
Caliber: .577″ Minie, .575″ round ball.
Barrel: 33″.
Weight: 10 lbs. **Length:** 49″ overall.
Stock: Walnut.
Sights: Folding leaf rear adjustable for elevation.
Features: Blued barrel, color case-hardened lock and hammer, polished brass buttplate, trigger guard, nose cap. From Navy Arms, Euroarms of America, Dixie.
Price: . . . . $325.00 to $450.00
Price: Assembled kit (Euroarms) $365.00

LONDON ARMORY ENFIELD MUSKETOON
Caliber: 58, Minie ball.
Barrel: 24″, round.
Weight: 7-7½ lbs. **Length:** 40½″ overall.
Stock: Walnut, with sling swivels.
Sights: Blade front, graduated military-leaf rear.
Features: Brass trigger guard, nose cap, buttplate; blued barrel, bands, lockplate, swivels. Imported by Euroarms of America.
Price: Kit (fully assembled) $322.00

BLACKPOWDER MUSKETS & RIFLES

Parker-Hale 1861

PARKER-HALE ENFIELD 1861 MUSKETOON
Caliber: 58.
Barrel: 24″.
Weight: 7 lbs. **Length:** 40¹/₂″ overall.
Stock: Walnut.
Sights: Fixed front, adjustable rear.
Features: Percussion muzzleloader, made to original 1861 English patterns. Imported from England by Navy Arms.
Price: **$400.00**

PARKER-HALE VOLUNTEER RIFLE
Caliber: .451″.
Barrel: 32″.
Weight: 9¹/₂ lbs. **Length:** 49″ overall.
Stocks: Walnut, checkered wrist and forend.
Sights: Globe front, adjustable ladder-type rear.
Features: Recreation of the type of gun issued to volunteer regiments during the 1860s. Rigby-pattern rifling, patent breech, detented lock. Stock is glass bedded for accuracy. Comes with comprehensive accessory/shooting kit. From Navy Arms.
Price: **$725.00**

PARKER-HALE ENFIELD PATTERN 1858 NAVAL RIFLE
Caliber: .577″.
Barrel: 33″.
Weight: 8¹/₂ lbs. **Length:** 48¹/₂″ overall.
Stock: European walnut.
Sights: Blade front, step adjustable rear.
Features: Two-band Enfield percussion rifle with heavy barrel. Five-groove progressive depth rifling, solid brass furniture. All parts made exactly to original patterns. Imported from England by Navy Arms.
Price: **$500.00**

Parker-Hale Whitworth

PARKER-HALE WHITWORTH MILITARY TARGET RIFLE
Caliber: 45.
Barrel: 36″.
Weight: 9¹/₄ lbs. **Length:** 52¹/₂″ overall.
Stock: Walnut. Checkered at wrist and forend.
Sights: Hooded post front, open step-adjustable rear.
Features: Faithful reproduction of the Whitworth rifle, only bored for 45-cal. Trigger has a detented lock, capable of being adjusted very finely without risk of the sear nose catching on the half-cock bent and damaging both parts. Introduced 1978. Imported from England by Navy Arms.
Price: **$750.00**

Dixie 1861

DIXIE U.S. MODEL 1861 SPRINGFIELD
Caliber: 58.
Barrel: 40″.
Weight: About 8 lbs. **Length:** 55¹³/₁₆″ overall.
Stock: Oil-finished walnut.
Sights: Blade front, step adjustable rear.
Features: Exact recreation of original rifle. Sling swivels attached to trigger guard bow and middle barrel band. Lockplate marked "1861" with eagle motif and "U.S. Springfield" in front of hammer; "U.S." stamped on top of buttplate. From Dixie.
Price: **$450.00**
Price: Kit **$420.00**

COOK & BROTHER CONFEDERATE CARBINE
Caliber: 58.
Barrel: 24″.
Weight: 7¹/₂ lbs. **Length:** 40¹/₂″ overall.
Stock: Select walnut.
Features: Recreation of the 1861 New Orleans-made artillery carbine. Color case-hardened lock, browned barrel. Buttplate, trigger guard, barrel bands, sling swivels and nose cap of polished brass. From Euroarms of America.
Price: **$366.00**

J.P. Murray Carbine

J.P. MURRAY 1862-1864 CAVALRY CARBINE
Caliber: 58 (.577″ Minie).
Barrel: 23″.
Weight: 7 lbs., 9 oz. **Length:** 39″ overall.
Stock: Walnut.
Sights: Blade front, rear drift adjustable for windage..
Features: Browned barrel, color case-hardened lock, blued swivel and band springs, polished brass buttplate, trigger guard, barrel bands. From Euroarms of America.
Price: **$358.00**

NAVY ARMS 1863 SPRINGFIELD
Caliber: 58, uses .575″ mini-ball.
Barrel: 40″, rifled.
Weight: 9¹/₂ lbs. **Length:** 56″ overall.
Stock: Walnut.
Sights: Open rear adjustable for elevation.
Features: Full-size three-band musket. Polished bright metal, including lock. From Navy Arms.
Price: Finished rifle **$500.00**
Price: Kit **$400.00**

BLACKPOWDER MUSKETS & RIFLES

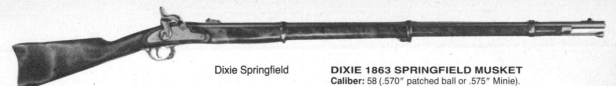

Dixie Springfield

DIXIE 1863 SPRINGFIELD MUSKET
Caliber: 58 (.570″ patched ball or .575″ Minie).
Barrel: 50″, rifled.
Stocks: Walnut stained.
Sights: Blade front, adjustable ladder-type rear.
Features: Bright-finish lock, barrel, furniture. Reproduction of the last of the regulation muzzleloaders. Imported from Japan by Dixie Gun Works.
Price: Finished **$475.00**
Price: Kit **$330.00**

Dixie Zouave

ZOUAVE PERCUSSION RIFLE
Caliber: 58, 59.
Barrel: 32½″.
Weight: 9½ lbs. **Length:** 48½″ overall.
Stock: Walnut finish, brass patch box and buttplate.
Sights: Fixed front, rear adjustable for e.
Features: Color case-hardened lockplate, blued barrel. From Dixie, Euroarms (M1863).
Price: About.. **$275.00**
Price: Kit (Euroarms 58 cal. only) **$263.00**

Mississippi Model 1841 Percussion Rifle
Similar to Zouave rifle but patterned after U.S. Model 1841. Imported by Dixie, Euroarms.
Price: .... **$430.00 to $463.00**

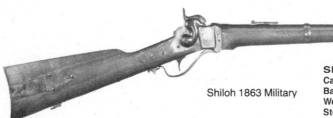

Shiloh 1863 Military

SHILOH SHARPS 1863 MILITARY RIFLE
Caliber: 54.
Barrel: 30″, round.
Weight: 8 lbs., 12 oz.
Stock: Military-style butt, steel buttplate and patch box. Standard-grade walnut.
Sights: Iron block front, Lawrence-style ladder rear.
Features: Recreation of the 1863 percussion rifle. Made in U.S. by Shiloh Rifle Mfg. Co.
Price: **$850.00**
Price: 1863 Military Carbine (as above except has 22″ round bbl. band on military-style forend, saddle bar and ring) **$740.00**

Shiloh Sharps 1862 Confederate Carbine Robinson
Recreation of the 54-cal. 1862 Confederate Robinson carbine with 21½″ round barrel; iron block front, fixed V-notch rear sights; brass buttplate and barrel band; sling swivel on buttstock. Weight is about 7½ lbs.
Price: **$800.00**

Shiloh 1863 Sporting

Shiloh Sharps Model 1863 Sporting Rifle
Similar to the Military Carbine except has 30″ octagon barrel, blade front and sporting rear sights, shotgun butt available, steel buttplate, schnabel forend. Standard-grade wood (semi-fancy available).
Price: **$740.00**

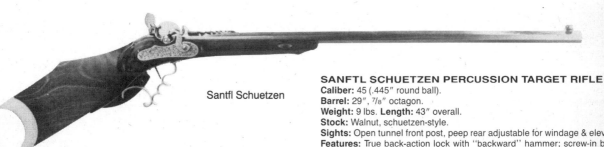

Santfl Schuetzen

SANFTL SCHUETZEN PERCUSSION TARGET RIFLE
Caliber: 45 (.445″ round ball).
Barrel: 29″, ⅞″ octagon.
Weight: 9 lbs. **Length:** 43″ overall.
Stock: Walnut, schuetzen-style.
Sights: Open tunnel front post, peep rear adjustable for windage & elevation.
Features: True back-action lock with "backward" hammer; screw-in breech plug; buttplate, trigger guard and stock inlays are polished brass. Imported from Italy by Dixie Gun Works.
Price: **$595.00**

Rigby-style Target

RIGBY-STYLE TARGET RIFLE
Caliber: .451″.
Barrel: 32¹/₂″.

Weight: 7³/₄ lbs.
Stock: Walnut; hand-checkered pistol grip, forend.
Sights: Target front with micrometer adjustment; adjustable Vernier peep rear.
Features: Comes cased with loading accessories—bullet starter, bullet sizer, special ramrod. Introduced 1985. From Navy Arms.
Price: **$550.00**

CVA Express

CVA EXPRESS RIFLE
Caliber: 50, 54.
Barrel: 28″, round.

Weight: 9 lbs.
Stock: Walnut-stained hardwood.
Sights: Bead and post front, adjustable rear.
Features: Double rifle with twin percussion locks and triggers. Hooked breech. Introduced 1985. From CVA.
Price: Finished **$519.95**
Price: Kit, 50 cal. only **$439.95**

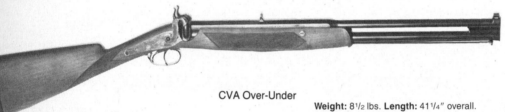

CVA Over-Under

CVA O/U CARBINE-RIFLE
Caliber: 50.
Barrel: 26″.

Weight: 8¹/₂ lbs. **Length:** 41¹/₄″ overall.
Stock: Checkered walnut.
Sights: Blade front with gold bead, folding rear adjustable for w. and e.
Features: Two-shot over/under with two hammers, two triggers. Polished blue finish. From CVA.
Price: **$579.95**

KODIAK MK III DOUBLE RIFLE
Caliber: 54x54, 58x58, 50x50.
Barrel: 28″, 5 grooves, 1-in-48″ twist.
Weight: 9¹/₂ lbs. **Length:** 43¹/₄″ overall.
Stock: Czechoslovakian walnut, hand-checkered.
Sights: Adjustable bead front, adjustable open rear.
Features: Hooked breech allows interchangeability of barrels. Comes with sling and swivels, adjustable powder measure, bullet mould and bullet starter. Engraved lockplates, top tang and trigger guard. Locks and top tang polished, rest blued. Introduced 1976. Imported from Italy by Trail Guns Armory, Inc.

Kodiak MK III

Price: 50, 54, 58 cal. SxS **$550.00**
Price: Spare barrels, all calibers.......................... **$294.25**
Price: Spare barrels, 12 ga. x 12 ga. **$195.00**

Traditions Pioneer

TRADITIONS TROPHY RIFLE
Caliber: 50, 54.
Barrel: 27¹/₄″, part octagon, part round.
Weight: 7 lbs. **Length:** 44³/₄″ overall.
Stock: Walnut with full pistol grip and cheekpiece.
Sights: Patridge-style blade front, hunting-style rear click adjustable for windage and elevation.
Features: Engraved, color case-hardened lock with bridle, claw mainspring; single trigger adjustable for weight. Sling swivels; fiberglass ramrod; recoil pad. From Traditions, Inc.
Price: Percussion only..................................... **$321.00**

TRADITIONS PIONEER RIFLE
Caliber: 50, 54.
Barrel: 27¹/₄″; ¹⁵/₁₆″ flats.
Weight: 7 lbs. **Length:** 44″ overall.
Stock: Beech with pistol grip, recoil pad.
Sights: Beaded blade front, buckhorn rear with elevation ramp.
Features: V-type mainspring, adjustable single trigger; blackened furniture; color case-hardened lock; large trigger guard. From Traditions, Inc.
Price: Percussion only.................................... **$161.00**

CAUTION: PRICES CHANGE. CHECK AT GUNSHOP.

BLACKPOWDER MUSKETS & RIFLES

CVA Blazer

CVA BLAZER RIFLE
Caliber: 50 (.490″ ball).
Barrel: 28″, octagon.

Weight: 6 lbs., 13 oz.
Stock: Hardwood.
Sights: Brass blade front, fixed semi-buckhorn rear.
Features: Straight-line percussion with pistol-grip stock of modern design. From CVA.
Price: Finished $149.95
Price: Kit $121.95

Gonic GA-87

GONIC GA-87 M/L RIFLE
Caliber: 458 Express.
Barrel: 24″ (Carbine), 26″ (Rifle).
Weight: 6 to 6½ lbs. **Length:** 41″ overall (Carbine).
Stock: American walnut with checkered grip and forend.

Sights: Bead front, open rear adjustable for windage and elevation; drilled and tapped for scope bases.
Features: Closed-breech action with straight-line ignition. Modern trigger mechanism with ambidextrous safety. Satin blue finish on metal, satin stock finish. Introduced 1989. From Gonic Arms, Inc.
Price: Standard Rifle or Carbine, no sights $385.00
Price: As above, with sights $427.70
Price: Deluxe Rifle or Carbine, no sights $410.50
Price: As above, with sights $453.20

Knight MK-85

KNIGHT MK-85 HUNTER RIFLE
Caliber: 45, 50, 54.
Barrel: 20″, 22″, 24″.
Weight: 7 lbs.

Stock: Classic, walnut; recoil pad; swivel studs.
Sights: Hooded blade front on ramp, open adjustable rear.
Features: One-piece in-line bolt assembly with straight through Sure-Fire ignition system. Adjustable Timney Featherweight trigger. Drilled and tapped for scope mounting. Made in U.S. From Modern Muzzleloading, Inc.
Price: $479.95
Price: Stalker (laminated, colored stock) $519.95
Price: Predator (stainless steel, composition stock) $559.95

BLACKPOWDER SHOTGUNS

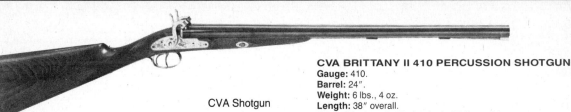

CVA Shotgun

CVA BRITTANY II 410 PERCUSSION SHOTGUN
Gauge: 410.
Barrel: 24″.
Weight: 6 lbs., 4 oz.
Length: 38″ overall.
Stock: Hardwood with pistol grip, M.C. comb.
Sights: Brass bead front.
Features: Color case-hardened lockplates; double triggers (front is hinged); brass wedge plates; stainless nipple. Introduced 1986. From CVA.
Price: Finished $209.95
Price: Kit $151.95

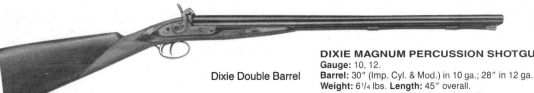

Dixie Double Barrel

DIXIE MAGNUM PERCUSSION SHOTGUN
Gauge: 10, 12.
Barrel: 30″ (Imp. Cyl. & Mod.) in 10 ga.; 28″ in 12 ga.
Weight: 6¼ lbs. **Length:** 45″ overall.
Stock: Hand-checkered walnut, 14″ pull.
Features: Double triggers, light hand engraving. Case-hardened locks in 12 ga.; polished steel in 10 ga. with sling swivels. From Dixie.
Price: Upland $325.00
Price: 12 ga. kit $305.00
Price: 10 ga. $365.00
Price: 10 ga. kit $305.00

CVA Trapper

NAVY ARMS HUNTER SHOTGUN
Gauge: 20.
Barrel: 28¹/₂″, interchangeable choke tubes (Full, Mod.).
Stock: Walnut, Hawken-style, checkered p.g. and forend.
Sights: Bead front.
Features: Chrome-lined barrel; rubber butt pad; color case-hardened lock; double set triggers; blued furniture. Comes with two flush-mounting choke tubes. Introduced 1986. From Navy Arms.
Price: $315.00

CVA TRAPPER PERCUSSION
Gauge: 12.
Barrel: 28″.Choke tubes (Mod., Imp., Full).
Weight: NA.
Length: 46″ overall.
Stock: English-style straight grip of walnut-finished hardwood.
Sights: Brass bead front.
Features: Single blued barrel; color case-hardened lockplate and hammer; screw adjustable sear engagements, V-type mainspring; brass wedge plates; black trigger guard and tang. From CVA.
Price: Finished $283.95
Price: Kit $237.95
Price: 12-ga./50-cal. combo, finished $399.95

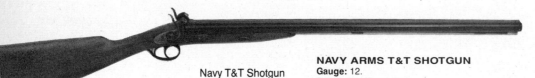

Navy T&T Shotgun

NAVY ARMS T&T SHOTGUN
Gauge: 12.
Barrel: 28″ (Full & Full).
Weight: 7¹/₂ lbs.
Stock: Walnut.
Sights: Bead front.
Features: Color case-hardened locks, blued steel furniture. From Navy Arms.
Price: $432.00

Navy Fowler

NAVY ARMS FOWLER SHOTGUN
Gauge: 12.
Barrel: 28″.
Weight: 7 lbs., 12 oz. **Length:** 45″ overall.
Stock: Walnut.
Features: Color case-hardened lockplates and hammers; checkered stock. Imported by Navy Arms.
Price: Fowler model, 12 ga. only $332.00
Price: Fowler kit, 12 ga. only $249.00

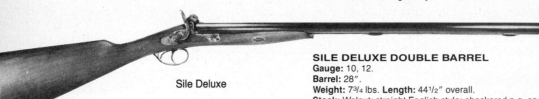

Sile Deluxe

SILE DELUXE DOUBLE BARREL
Gauge: 10, 12.
Barrel: 28″.
Weight: 7³/₄ lbs. **Length:** 44¹/₂″ overall.
Stock: Walnut; straight English style; checkered p.g. and forend.
Features: Percussion locks with double triggers; chrome-lined bores; engraved color case-hardened lockplates and hammers. Imported by Sile.
Price: $325.00
Price: Confederate Cavalry Model (as above except 14″ barrels, weighs 6¹/₂ lbs., overall length of 30¹/₂″) $325.00

T/C New Englander

TRAIL GUNS KODIAK 10-GAUGE DOUBLE
Gauge: 10.
Barrel: 20″, 30³/₄″ (Cyl. bore).
Weight: About 9 lbs. **Length:** 47¹/₈″ overall.
Stock: Walnut, with cheek rest. Checkered wrist and forend.
Features: Chrome-plated bores; engraved lockplates, brass bead front and middle sights; sling swivels. Introduced 1980. Imported from Italy by Trail Guns Armory.
Price: $425.00

THOMPSON/CENTER "NEW ENGLANDER" SHOTGUN
Gauge: 12.
Barrel: 28″ (Imp. Cyl.), round.
Weight: 5 lbs., 2 oz.
Stock: Select American black walnut with straight grip.
Features: Percussion lock is color case-hardened, rest blued. Also accepts 26″ round 50- and 54-cal. rifle barrel. Introduced 1986.
Price: Right-hand $220.00
Price: Left-hand $235.00
Price: Accessory rifle barrel, right-hand, 50 or 54 .... $102.50
Price: As above, left-hand $110.00

AMERICAN ARMS IDEAL #83 AIR PISTOL
Caliber: 177, single shot.
Barrel: 7.5".
Weight: 3 lbs. **Length:** 14³/4" overall.
Power: Spring-air, barrel cocking.
Sights: Adjustable.
Features: Velocity of 400 fps. Automatic safety. Imported from Spain by American Arms, Inc.
Price: **$105.00**

BEEMAN P1 MAGNUM AIR PISTOL
Caliber: 177, 20, 22, single shot.
Barrel: 8.4".
Weight: 2.5 lbs. **Length:** 11" overall.
Power: Top lever cocking; spring piston.
Stocks: Checkered walnut.
Sights: Blade front, square notch rear with click micrometer adjustments for w. and e. Grooved for scope mounting.
Features: Dual power for 177 and 20 cal: low setting gives 350-400 fps; high setting 500-600 fps. Rearward expanding mainspring simulates firearm recoil. All Colt 45 auto grips fit gun. Dry-firing feature for practice. Optional wooden shoulder stock. Introduced 1985. Imported by Beeman.
Price: 177, 22 cal. **$288.00**
Price: 20 cal. **$295.00**

Beeman P1 Magnum

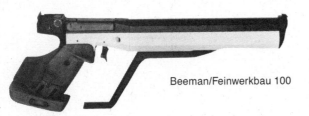

Beeman/Feinwerkbau 100

Beeman/Feinwerkbau C10

BEEMAN/FEINWERKBAU MODEL 100 PISTOL
Caliber: 177, single shot.
Barrel: 10.1", 12 groove rifling.
Weight: 2.5 lbs. **Length:** 16.5" overall
Power: Single-stroke pneumatic, sidelever cocking.
Stocks: Stippled walnut with adjustable palm shelf.
Sights: Blade front, open rear adjustable for w. and e. Notch size adjustable for width. Interchangeable front blades.
Features: Velocity 460 fps. Fully adjustable trigger. Cocking effort 12 lbs. Introduced 1988. Imported by Beeman.
Price: Right-hand **$890.00**
Price: Left-hand... **$920.00**

BEEMAN/FEINWERKBAU MODEL C10 CO₂ PISTOL
Caliber: 177, single-shot.
Barrel: 10.1", 12-groove rifling.
Weight: 2.5 lbs. **Length:** 16" overall.
Power: Special CO_2 cylinder.
Stocks: Stippled walnut with adjustable palm shelf.
Sights: Blade front, open rear adjustable for w. and e. Notch size adjustable for width. Interchangeable front blades.
Features: Fully adjustable trigger; can be set for dry firing. Separate gas chamber for uniform power. Cylinders interchangeable even when full. Short-barrel model also available. Introduced 1988. Imported by Beeman.
Price: Right-hand **$785.00**
Price: Left-hand... **$815.00**
Price: Mini-C10, right-hand............................ **$785.00**
Price: Mini-C10, left-hand............................. **$815.00**

Beeman/Webley Hurricane

BEEMAN/WEBLEY HURRICANE PISTOL
Caliber: 177 or 22, single shot.
Barrel: 8", rifled.
Weight: 2.4 lbs. **Length:** 11¹/2" overall.
Power: Spring piston.
Stocks: Thumbrest, checkered high-impact synthetic.
Sights: Hooded front; micro-click rear adjustable for w. and e.
Features: Velocity of 470 fps (177-cal.). Single stroke cocking, adjustable trigger pull, manual safety. Rearward recoil like a firearm pistol. Steel piston and cylinder. Scope base included; 1.5x scope **$49.95** up extra. Shoulder stock available. Introduced 1977. Imported from England by Beeman.
Price: **$149.95**

Beeman/Webley Tempest

BEEMAN/WEBLEY TEMPEST AIR PISTOL
Caliber: 177 or 22, single shot.
Barrel: 6.75", rifled ordnance steel.
Weight: 32 oz. **Length:** 9" overall.
Power: Spring piston.
Stocks: Checkered black epoxy with thumbrest.
Sights: Post front; rear has sliding leaf adjustable for w. and e.
Features: Adjustable trigger pull, manual safety. Velocity 470 fps (177 cal.). Steel piston in steel liner for maximum performance and durability. Unique rearward spring simulates firearm recoil. Shoulder stock available. Introduced 1979. Imported from England by Beeman.
Price: **$129.95**

BEEMAN/FEINWERKBAU FWB-65 MKII AIR PISTOL
Caliber: 177, single shot.
Barrel: 6.1″ or 7.5″, removeable bbl. wgt. avail.
Weight: 42 oz. **Length:** 13.3″ or 14.1″ overall.
Power: Spring, sidelever cocking.
Stocks: Walnut, stippled thumbrest; adjustable or fixed.
Sights: Front, interchangeable post element system, open rear, click adjustable for w. & e. and for sighting notch width. Scope mount avail.
Features: New shorter barrel for better balance and control. Cocking effort 9 lbs. Two-stage trigger, four adjustments. Quiet firing, 525 fps. Programs instantly for recoil or recoilless operation. Permanently lubricated. Steel piston ring. Special switch converts trigger from 17.6 oz. pull to 42 oz. let-off. Imported by Beeman.
Price: Right-hand . . . . $775.00 to $795.00
Price: Left-hand, 6.1″ barrel $825.00
Price: Model 65 Mk.I (7.5″ bbl.) . . . . $725.00 to $779.00

FWB 65 Mk. II

BEEMAN/WEIHRAUCH HW-70 AIR PISTOL
Caliber: 177, single shot.
Barrel: 6¼″, rifled.
Weight: 38 oz. **Length:** 12¾″ overall.
Power: Spring, barrel cocking.
Stocks: Plastic, with thumbrest.
Sights: Hooded post front, square notch rear adjustable for w. and e.
Features: Adjustable trigger, 24-lb. cocking effort, 410 fps MV; automatic barrel safety. Imported by Beeman.
Price: From Beeman $147.50

Beeman/Weihrauch HW-70

BENJAMIN 242/247 SINGLE SHOT PISTOLS
Caliber: 177 and 22.
Weight: 32 oz. **Length:** 11¾″ overall.
Power: Hand pumped.
Stocks: Walnut pump handle, optional walnut grips.
Sights: Blade front, open adjustable rear.
Features: Bolt action; fingertip safety; adjustable power.
Price: Model 242 (22 cal.) $86.95
Price: Model 247 (177 cal.) $86.95

Benjamin 242/247

CROSMAN MODEL 357 AIR PISTOL
Caliber: 177, 6- or 10-shot.
Barrel: 4″ (Model 357-4), 6″ (Model 357-6), rifled steel, 8″ (Model 357-8), rifled brass.
Weight: 32 oz. (6″). **Length:** 11⅜″ overall.
Power: CO_2 Powerlet.
Stock: Checkered wood-grain plastic.
Sights: Ramp front, fully adjustable rear.
Features: Average 430 fps (Model 357-6). Break-open barrel for easy loading. Single or double action. Vent. rib barrel. Wide, smooth trigger. Two speed loaders come with each gun. Model 357-8 has matte gray finish, black grips.
Price: 4″ or 6″, about $55.00
Price: 8″, about $62.00
Price: Model 1357 (as above, except shoots BBs, 6-shot clip), about . $55.00

Crosman Model 3357 Spot Marker
Same specs as 8″ Model 357 but shoots 50-cal. paint balls. Has break-open action for quick loading 6-shot clip of paint balls. CO_2 power allows repeater firing; hammer-block safety; adjustable rear sight, blade front.
Price: About $89.00

Crosman 357

CROSMAN MODEL SSP 250 PISTOL
Caliber: 177, 20, 22, single-shot.
Barrel: 9⅞″, rifled steel.
Weight: 3 lbs., 1 oz. **Length:** 14″ overall.
Power: CO_2 Powerlet.
Stocks: Composition; black, with checkering.
Sights: Hooded front, fully adjustable rear.
Features: Velocity about 460 fps. Interchangeable accessory barrels. Two-stage trigger. High/low power settings.
Price: About $47.00

CROSMAN 338 AUTO PISTOL
Caliber: BB, 20-shot magazine.
Barrel: 5″, steel.
Weight: 24 oz. **Length:** 8½″ overall.
Power: CO_2 Powerlet.
Stocks: Checkered plastic.
Sights: Patridge front, adjustable rear.
Features: Velocity about 370 fps. Replica of the Walther P-38 pistol. Semi-automatic repeater; thumb-operated lever safety. Introduced 1986.
Price: About $39.00

Crosman SSP 250

CROSMAN MODEL 1322 AIR PISTOL
Caliber: 22, single shot.
Barrel: 8″, button rifled.
Weight: 37 oz. **Length:** 13⅝″.
Power: Hand pumped.
Sights: Blade front, rear adjustable for w. and e.
Features: Moulded plastic grip, hand size pump forearm. Cross-bolt safety. Also available in 177/BB cal. as **Model 1377**.
Price: About **$50.00**
Price: 1377, about **$50.00**

Crosman 1322/1377

Crosman 1600

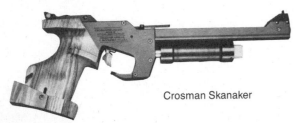

Crosman Skanaker

CROSMAN MODEL 1600 BB MATIC PISTOL
Caliber: BB, 17-shot magazine.
Barrel: 7¾″, smoothbore steel.
Weight: 29 oz.
Power: CO_2 Powerlet.
Stocks: Contoured wood-grain plastic with checkering.
Sights: Fixed front and rear.
Features: Velocity about 370 fps. Semi-auto repeater; positive slide-action safety.
Price: About **$35.00**

CROSMAN/SKANAKER MATCH AIR PISTOL
Caliber: 177.
Barrel: 9.94″.
Weight: 37 oz. **Length:** 16.38″ overall.
Power: Refillable CO_2 cylinders.
Stocks: Hardwood, adjustable for thickness; adjustable palm shelf.
Sights: Three-way adjustable post front, open rear with three interchangeable leaves.
Features: Velocity of 550 fps. Angled, adjustable match trigger can be aligned to fit the natural position of the trigger finger. Barrel is hinged near the muzzle for loading. Introduced 1987.
Price: About **$650.00**

DAISY MODEL 188 BB PISTOL
Caliber: BB.
Barrel: 9.9″, steel smoothbore.
Weight: 1.67 lbs. **Length:** 11.7″ overall.
Stocks: Die-cast metal; checkered with thumbrest.
Sights: Blade and ramp front, open fixed rear.
Features: 24-shot repeater. Spring action with under-barrel cocking lever. Grip and receiver of die-cast metal. Introduced 1979.
Price: About **$20.00**

DAISY/POWER LINE 717 PELLET PISTOL
Caliber: 177, single shot.
Barrel: 9.61″.
Weight: 2.8 lbs. **Length:** 13½″ overall.
Stocks: Moulded wood-grain plastic, with thumbrest.
Sights: Blade and ramp front, micro-adjustable notch rear.
Features: Single pump pneumatic pistol. Rifled steel barrel. Cross-bolt trigger block. Muzzle velocity 385 fps. From Daisy. Introduced 1979.
Price: About **$52.00**

DAISY POWER LINE MODEL 44 REVOLVER
Caliber: 177 pellets, 6-shot.
Barrel: 6″, rifled steel; interchangeable 4″ and 8″.
Weight: 2.7 lbs.
Power: CO_2.
Stocks: Moulded plastic with checkering.
Sights: Blade on ramp front, fully adjustable notch rear.
Features: Velocity up to 400 fps. Replica of 44 Magnum revolver. Has swing-out cylinder and interchangeable barrels. Introduced 1987. From Daisy.
Price: **$42.00**

DAISY/POWER LINE CO_2 1200 PISTOL
Caliber: BB, 177.
Barrel: 10½″, smooth.
Weight: 1.6 lbs. **Length:** 11.1″ overall.
Power: Daisy CO_2 cylinder.
Stocks: Contoured, checkered moulded wood-grain plastic.
Sights: Blade ramp front, fully adjustable square notch rear.
Features: 60-shot BB reservoir, gravity feed. Cross-bolt safety. Velocity of 420-450 fps for more than 100 shots. From Daisy.
Price: About **$29.00**

Daisy Model 188

Daisy/Power Line 747 Pistol
Similar to the 717 pistol except has a 12-groove rifled steel barrel by Lothar Walther. Velocity of 360 tps. Manual cross-bolt safety.
Price: About **$85.00**

Power Line 44

Daisy Power Line 92

DAISY/POWER LINE MATCH 777 PELLET PISTOL
Caliber: 177, single shot.
Barrel: 9.61″ rifled steel by Lothar Walther.
Weight: 32 oz. **Length:** 13½″ overall.
Power: Sidelever, single pump pneumatic.
Stocks: Smooth hardwood, fully contoured with palm and thumb rest.
Sights: Blade and ramp front, match-grade open rear with adjustable width notch, micro. click adjustments.
Features: Adjustable trigger; manual cross-bolt safety. MV of 385 fps. Comes with cleaning kit, adjustment tool and pellets. From Daisy.
Price: About **$180.00**

Daisy/Youth Line 1500

MARKSMAN #1010 REPEATER PISTOL
Caliber: 177, 18-shot repeater.
Barrel: 2½″, smoothbore.
Weight: 24 oz. **Length:** 8¼″ overall.
Power: Spring.
Features: Thumb safety. Black finish. Uses BBs, darts or pellets. Repeats with BBs only.
Price: Matte black finish **$22.50**
Price: Model 1010X (as above except nickel-plated) **$31.00**
Price: Model 1015 (brown finish with commemorative medallion) **$27.00**

MARKSMAN 17 AIR PISTOL
Caliber: 177, single shot.
Barrel: 7.5″.
Weight: 46 oz. **Length:** 14.5″ overall.
Power: Spring air, barrel-cocking.
Stocks: Checkered composition with right-hand thumb rest.
Sights: Tunnel front, fully adjustable rear.
Features: Velocity of 360-400 fps. Introduced 1986. Imported from Spain by Marksman Products.
Price: **$98.00**

MARKSMAN PLAINSMAN 1049 CO_2 PISTOL
Caliber: BB, 100-shot repeater.
Barrel: 5⅞″, smooth.
Weight: 28 oz. **Length:** 9½″ overall.
Stocks: Simulated walnut with thumbrest.
Power: 12-gram CO_2 cylinders.
Features: Velocity of 400 fps. Three-position power switch. Automatic ammunition feed. Positive safety.
Price: **$41.50**

DAISY POWER LINE MODEL 92 PISTOL
Caliber: 177 pellets, 10-shot magazine.
Barrel: Rifled steel.
Weight: 2.15 lbs. **Length:** 8.5″ overall.
Power: CO_2.
Stocks: Cast checkered metal.
Sights: Blade front, adjustable V-slot rear.
Features: Semi-automatic action; 400 fps. Replica of the official 9mm sidearm of the United States armed forces.
Price: About **$51.00**

Power Line 777

DAISY/YOUTH LINE MODEL 1500 PISTOL
Caliber: BB, 60-shot reservoir.
Barrel: 1.5″, smoothbore.
Weight: 22 oz. **Length:** 11.1″ overall.
Power: Daisy CO_2 cylinder.
Stocks: Moulded wood-grain plastic with checkering.
Sights: Blade on ramp front, fully adjustable notch rear.
Features: Velocity of 340 fps. Gravity feed magazine. Cross-bolt safety.
Price: About **$29.00**

"GAT" AIR PISTOL
Caliber: 177, single shot.
Barrel: 7½″ cocked, 9½″ extended.
Weight: 22 oz.
Power: Spring piston.
Stocks: Composition.
Sights: Fixed.
Features: Shoots pellets, corks or darts. Matte black finish. Imported from England by Stone Enterprises, Inc.
Price: **$31.95**

Marksman 1010

Marksman Model 17

CAUTION: PRICES CHANGE. CHECK AT GUNSHOP.

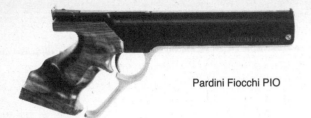

Pardini Fiocchi PIO

PARDINI FIOCCHI PIO MATCH AIR PISTOL
Caliber: 177.
Barrel: 7.7".
Weight: 37 oz. **Length:** 14" overall.
Power: Single stroke pneumatic.
Stocks: Stippled walnut with palm shelf.
Sights: Post front, fully adjustable open rear.
Features: Muzzle velocity of 425 fps. Cocking lever forms trigger guard. Imported from Italy by Fiocchi of America.
Price: **$375.00**

RECORD "JUMBO" DELUXE AIR PISTOL
Caliber: 177, single shot.
Barrel: 6", rifled.
Weight: 1.9 lbs. **Length:** 7.25" overall.
Power: Spring air, lever cocking.
Stocks: Smooth walnut.
Sights: Post front, fully adjustable open rear.
Features: Velocity of 322 fps. Thumb safety. Grip magazine compartment for extra pellet storage. Introduced 1983. Imported from West Germany by Great Lakes Airguns.
Price: **$87.50**

Record "Jumbo"

RECORD CHAMPION AIR PISTOL
Caliber: 177, 12-shot repeater.
Barrel: 7.6", rifled.
Weight: 2.8 lbs. **Length:** 10.2" overall.
Power: Spring air, sidelever cocking.
Stocks: Smooth hardwood. Contoured target-style available.
Sights: Post front, fully adjustable rear.
Features: Velocity of 420 fps. Magazine loads into bottom of grip. Ambidextrous grips. Introduced 1987. Imported from West Germany by Great Lakes Airguns.
Price: **$143.34**

> Consult our Directory pages for the location of firms mentioned.

RWS/DIANA MODEL 5G AIR PISTOL
Caliber: 177, single shot.
Barrel: 7".
Weight: 2³/₄ lbs. **Length:** 16" overall.
Power: Spring air, barrel cocking.
Stocks: Plastic, thumbrest design.
Sights: Tunnel front, micro-click open rear.
Features: Velocity of 410 fps. Two-stage trigger with automatic safety. Imported from West Germany by Dynamit Nobel-RWS, Inc.
Price: **$150.00**

RWS/Diana Model 5GS Air Pistol
Same as the Model 5G except comes with 1.5x15 pistol scope with ramp-style mount, muzzlebrake/weight. No open sights supplied. Introduced 1983.
Price: **$210.00**

Record Champion

RWS/DIANA MODEL 6M MATCH AIR PISTOL
Caliber: 177, single shot.
Barrel: 7".
Weight: 3 lbs. **Length:** 16" overall.
Power: Spring air, barrel cocking.
Stocks: Walnut-finished hardwood with thumbrest.
Sights: Adjustable front, micro. click open rear.
Features: Velocity of 410 fps. Recoilless double piston system, moveable barrel shroud to protect front sight during cocking. Imported from West Germany by Dynamit Nobel-RWS, Inc.
Price: Right-hand **$340.00**
Price: Left-hand **$360.00**

RWS Model 5G

RWS Model 10

RWS/Diana Model 10 Match Air Pistol
Refined version of the Model 6M. Has special adjustable match trigger, oil-finished and stippled match grips, barrel weight. Also available in left-hand version, and with fitted case.
Price: Model 10 . . . . **$610.00**
Price: Model 10, left-hand **$655.00**
Price: Model 10, with case **$640.00**
Price: Model 10, left-hand, with case **$685.00**

AIRGUNS — HANDGUNS

Sheridan Model HB

SHERIDAN MODEL HB PNEUMATIC PISTOL
Caliber: 5mm, single shot.
Barrel: 9³/₈″, rifled.
Weight: 36 oz. **Length:** 12″ overall.
Power: Under-lever pneumatic pump.
Stocks: Checkered simulated walnut; forend is walnut.
Sights: Blade front, fully adjustable rear.
Features: "Controller-Power" feature allows velocity and range control by varying the number of pumps—3 to 10. Maximum velocity of 400 fps. Introduced 1982. From Sheridan Products.
Price: **$86.95**

WALTHER CP CO₂ AIR PISTOL
Caliber: 177, single shot.
Barrel: 9″.
Weight: 40 oz. **Length:** 14³/₄″ overall.
Power: CO₂.
Stocks: Full target-type stippled wood with adjustable hand shelf.

Sights: Target post front, fully adjustable target rear.
Features: Velocity of 520 fps. CO₂ powered; target-quality trigger; comes with adaptor for charging with standard CO₂ air tanks, case, and accessories. Introduced 1983. Imported from West Germany by Interarms.
Price: **$900.00**
Price: Junior Model (modified grip, shorter gas cylinder) **$900.00**

AIRGUNS — LONG GUNS

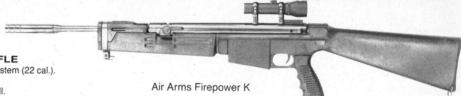

Air Arms Firepower K

AIR ARMS FIREPOWER AIR RIFLE
Caliber: 177, 20, 22, 35-shot Auto-Load system (22 cal.).
Barrel: 14³/₄″, Walther with 12 grooves.
Weight: 7 lbs., 8 oz. **Length:** 40¹/₂″ overall.
Power: Spring-air, sidelever.
Stock: Synthetic, military-style.
Sights: Blade on ramp front, adjustable aperture rear.
Features: Velocity of 936 fps (177), 681 fps (22). Adjustable trigger; removeable sights; receiver grooved for scope mounting. High polish blue finish; sling swivels. Introduced 1987. Imported from England by Great Lakes Airguns.
Price: **$293.27**

Air Arms Firepower K-Carbine Standard
Similar to the standard Firepower except has 11″ barrel, weighs 7.2 lbs., has 36.5″ overall length. Velocities are the same. Available in 177 and 22 cal. Introduced 1989.
Price: **$259.75**
Price: As above, Deluxe model (39″ o.a.l., comes with 1″, 2¹/₂x scope, no iron sights) **$407.18**

Air Arms Khamsin

AIR ARMS MODEL KHAMSIN
Caliber: 177, 22; single shot.
Barrel: 15″, rifled.
Weight: 8 lbs., 2 oz. **Length:** 39³/₄″ overall.
Power: Spring-air, sidelever cocking.
Stock: Oil-finished French walnut thumbhole-style, with cut checkering on p.g. and forend. Ventilated rubber buttplate and sling swivels.
Sights: None furnished. Comes with scope anti-slip block.

Features: Velocity up to 852 fps (177 cal.). Polished brass trigger and trigger guard. Introduced 1987. Imported from England by Great Lakes Airguns.
Price: Either caliber. **$544.50**
Price: With Auto-Load 34-pellet magazine **$579.85**

Air Arms Camargue

Air Arms Model Camargue
Basically the same as the Khamsin model except has a Tyrolean-style stock, post front sight with protective ears, micrometer-adjustable aperture rear. Velocity up to 871 fps (177 cal.). From Great Lakes Airguns.
Price: Either caliber. **$427.33**
Price: With Auto-Load 34-pellet magazine **$460.85**

Air Arms Model Mistral
Basically the same as the Model Camargue except has oil-finished beechwood stock with Monte Carlo. Velocity up to 859 fps (177 cal.). From Great Lakes Airguns.
Price: Either 177 or 22 caliber. **$293.27**
Price: With Auto-Load 34-pellet magazine **$328.78**

Air Arms Model Bora
Similar to the Mistral model except has 11″ barrel, weighs 7.7 lbs. and has 35.8″ overall length. Velocity up to 872 fps (177 cal.). Imported from England by Great Lakes Airguns.
Price: 177 or 22 . . . . **$293.27**
Price: With Auto-Load 34-pellet magazine **$328.78**

CAUTION: PRICES CHANGE. CHECK AT GUNSHOP.

Air Arms Shamal

AIR ARMS SHAMAL AIR RIFLE

Caliber: 177, 22, single shot.
Barrel: 23″, 12-groove rifling.
Weight: 7.72 lbs. **Length:** 41″ overall.
Power: Pneumatic.
Stock: Walnut with checkered grip and forend, high cheekpiece.
Sights: None supplied.
Features: Adjustable velocity. Uses pre-charged pneumatic reservoir filled from scuba tank, up to 3000 psi. Gives 80 to 100 shots per charge. Introduced 1989. Imported from England by Great Lakes Airguns.
Price: **$798.35**

AMERICAN ARMS JET AIR RIFLE

Caliber: 177, single shot.
Barrel: 19″.
Weight: 7 lbs. **Length:** 46″ overall.
Power: Spring-air, barrel cocking.
Stock: Hardwood.
Sights: Hooded post front, open fully adjustable rear.
Features: Velocity of 855 fps. Two-stage adjustable trigger, automatic safety. Grooved for scope mounting. Imported from Spain by American Arms, Inc.
Price: **$149.00**

AMERICAN ARMS JET JR. #56 AIR RIFLE

Caliber: 177, single shot.
Barrel: 16¼″.
Weight: 5 lbs. **Length:** 37½″ overall.
Power: Spring-air, barrel cocking.

Air Arms Shamal Match

Same as the standard Shamal except has fully adjustable walnut target stock with stippled grip and forend. Adjustable buttpad and comb. Introduced 1989.
Price: **$1,170.92**

AMERICAN ARMS COMMANDO AIR CARBINE

Caliber: 177, single shot.
Barrel: 16¼″.
Weight: 5 lbs. **Length:** 37¾″ overall.
Power: Spring-air, barrel cocking.
Stock: Retractable steel, camouflage painted forend.
Sights: Hooded post front, open rear adjustable for w. and e.
Features: Velocity of 540 fps. Blue finish. Comes with sling and swivels. Receiver grooved for scope mounting. Imported from Spain by American Arms, Inc.
Price: **$115.00**

Stock: Hardwood.
Sights: Adjustable.
Features: Velocity of 540 fps. Articulated trigger. Double safety. Receiver grooved for scope mounting. Imported from Spain by American Arms, Inc.
Price: **$86.00**

Anschutz 2001

ANSCHUTZ 2001 MATCH AIR RIFLE

Caliber: 177, single shot.
Barrel: 26″.
Weight: 10½ lbs. **Length:** 44½″ overall.
Stock: European hardwood; stippled grip and forend.

Sights: Globe front, #6824 Micro Peep rear.
Features: Balance, weight match the 1907 ISU smallbore rifle. Uses #5019 match trigger. Recoil and vibration free. Fully adjustable cheekpiece and buttplate. Introduced 1988. Imported from Germany by Precision Sales International.
Price: Right-hand **$1,355.00**
Price: Left-hand **$1,423.00**
Price: Model 2001 DRT (Running Target) **$1,445.00**

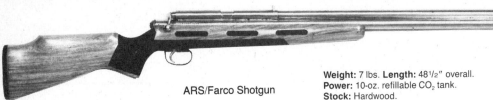

ARS/Farco Shotgun

ARS/FARCO CO₂ AIR SHOTGUN

Caliber: 51 (28 gauge).
Barrel: 30″.

Weight: 7 lbs. **Length:** 48½″ overall.
Power: 10-oz. refillable CO_2 tank.
Stock: Hardwood.
Sights: Bead front, fixed dovetail rear.
Features: Gives over 100 ft. lbs. energy for taking small game. Imported by Air Rifle Specialists.
Price: **$395.00**

Beeman/FWB 124

BEEMAN/FEINWERKBAU 124/127 MAGNUM

Caliber: 177 (FWB-124); 22 (FWB-127); single shot.
Barrel: 18.3″, 12-groove rifling.
Weight: 6.8 lbs. **Length:** 43½″ overall.
Power: Spring piston air; single stroke barrel cocking.
Stock: Walnut-finished hardwood.
Sights: Tunnel front; click-adjustable rear for w., slide-adj. for e.
Features: Velocity 680-820 fps, cocking effort of 18 lbs. Forged steel receiver; nylon non-drying piston and breech seals. Automatic safety, adjustable trigger. Hand-checkered p.g. and forend, high comb cheekpiece, and buttplate

with white spacer. Imported by Beeman.
Price: Deluxe model, right-hand **$399.98**
Price: As above, left-hand **$439.98**

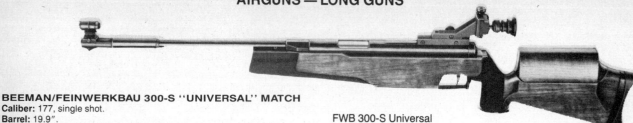

FWB 300-S Universal

BEEMAN/FEINWERKBAU 300-S "UNIVERSAL" MATCH

Caliber: 177, single shot.
Barrel: 19.9″.
Weight: 10.2 lbs. (without barrel sleeve). **Length:** 43.3″ overall.
Power: Spring piston, single stroke sidelever.
Stock: Walnut, stippled p.g. and forend. Detachable cheekpieces (one std., high for scope use.) Adjustable buttplate, accessory rail. Buttplate and grip cap spacers included.
Sights: Two globe fronts with interchangeable inserts. Rear is match aperture with rubber eyecup and sight visor. Front and rear sights move as a single unit.
Features: Recoilless, vibration free. Grooved for scope mounts. Steel piston ring. Cocking effort about 9½ lbs. Barrel sleeve optional. Left-hand model available. Introduced 1978. Imported by Beeman.
Price: Right-hand $998.00
Price: Left-hand $1,075.00

BEEMAN/FEINWERKBAU 300-S SERIES MATCH RIFLE

Caliber: 177, single shot.
Barrel: 19.9″, fixed solid with receiver.
Weight: Approx. 10 lbs. with optional bbl. sleeve. **Length:** 42.8″ overall.
Power: Single stroke sidelever, spring piston.
Stock: Match model—walnut, deep forend, adjustable buttplate.
Sights: Globe front with interchangeable inserts. Click micro. adjustable match aperture rear. Front and rear sights move as a single unit.
Features: Recoilless, vibration free. Five-way adjustable match trigger. Grooved for scope mounts. Permanent lubrication, steel piston. Cocking effort 9 lbs. Optional 10-oz. barrel sleeve. Available from Beeman.
Price: Right-hand $859.00
Price: Left-hand $930.00

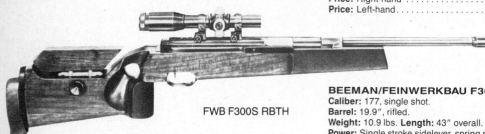

FWB F300S RBTH

BEEMAN/FEINWERKBAU F300-S RUNNING BOAR (TH)

Caliber: 177, single shot.
Barrel: 19.9″, rifled.
Weight: 10.9 lbs. **Length:** 43″ overall.
Power: Single stroke sidelever, spring piston.
Stock: Walnut with adjustable buttplate, grip cap and comb. Designed for fixed and moving target use.
Sights: None furnished; grooved for optional scope.
Features: Recoilless, vibration free. Permanent lubrication and seals. Barrel stabilizer weight included. Crisp single-stage trigger. Available from Beeman.
Price: Right-hand $910.00
Price: Left-hand $998.00

BEEMAN/FEINWERKBAU 300-S MINI-MATCH

Caliber: 177, single shot.
Barrel: 17⅛″.
Weight: 8.8 lbs. **Length:** 40″ overall.
Power: Spring piston, single stroke sidelever cocking.
Stock: Walnut. Stippled grip, adjustable buttplate. Scaled-down for youthful or slightly built shooters.
Sights: Globe front with interchangeable inserts, micro. adjustable rear. Front and rear sights move as a single unit.
Features: Recoilless, vibration free. Grooved for scope mounts. Steel piston ring. Cocking effort about 9½ lbs. Barrel sleeve optional. Left-hand model available. Introduced 1978.
Price: Right-hand $870.00
Price: Left-hand $879.00

Beeman/FWB 601 Running Target

Similar to the standard Model 601. Has 16.9″ barrel (33.7″ with barrel sleeve); special match trigger, short loading gate which allows scope mounting. No sights—built for scope use only. Introduced 1987.
Price: Right-hand $1,125.00
Price: Left-hand $1,255.00
Price: Running target scope mounts $134.95

BEEMAN/FEINWERKBAU MODEL 601 AIR RIFLE

Caliber: 177, single shot.
Barrel: 16.6″.
Weight: 10.8 lbs. **Length:** 43″ overall.
Power: Single stroke pneumatic.
Stock: Special laminated hardwoods and hard rubber for stability.
Sights: Tunnel front with interchangeable inserts, click micrometer match aperture rear.

Features: Recoilless action; double supported barrel; special, short rifled area frees pellet from barrel faster so shooter's motion has minimum effect on accuracy. Fully adjustable match trigger. Trigger and sights blocked when loading latch is open. Imported by Beeman. Introduced 1984.
Price: Right-hand $1,175.00
Price: Left-hand $1,295.00

Beeman/FWB C60

BEEMAN/FWB C60 CO₂ RIFLE

Caliber: 177.
Barrel: 16.9″. With barrel sleeve, 25.4″.
Weight: 10 lbs. **Length:** 42.6″ overall.
Stock: Laminated hardwood and hard rubber.
Sights: Tunnel front with interchangeable inserts, quick release micro. click match aperture rear.
Features: Similar features, performance as Beeman/FWB 601. Virtually no cocking effort. Right- or left-hand. Running target version available. Introduced 1987. Imported from Germany by Beeman.
Price: Right-hand $1,085.00
Price: Left-hand $1,185.00

Beeman/HW 55T

BEEMAN/HW 55 TARGET RIFLES

Model	55SM	55MM	55T
Caliber:	177	177	177
Barrel:	18¹/₂″	18¹/₂″	18¹/₂″
Length:	43¹/₂″	43¹/₂″	43¹/₂″
Wgt. lbs.:	7.8	7.8	7.8
Rear sight:	All aperture		
Front sight:	All with globe and 4 interchangeable inserts.		
Power:	All spring (barrel cocking). 660-700 fps.		
Price:	$389.50	$489.50	$539.50

Features: Trigger fully adj. and removable. Micrometer rear sight adj. for w. and e. in all. Pistol grip high comb stock with beavertail forend, walnut finish stock on 55SM. Walnut stock on 55MM, Tyrolean stock on 55T. Nylon piston seals in all. Imported by Beeman.

BEEMAN/HARPER AIRCANE

Caliber: 22 and 25, single shot.
Barrel: 31¹/₂″, rifled.
Weight: 1 lb. **Length:** 34″ overall.
Features: Walking cane also acts as an airgun. Solid walnut handle with polished brass ferrule. Available in various hand-carved models. Intricate deep engraving on the ferrule. Uses rechargeable air "cartridges" loaded with pellets. Kit includes separate pump, extra cartridges and fitted case. Introduced 1987. Imported by Beeman.
Price: Basic set $495.95
Price: Goose, Labrador, Spaniel sets $555.00

Beeman HW77

BEEMAN/HW77 AIR RIFLE & CARBINE

Caliber: 177, 20 or 22, single shot.
Barrel: 14.5″ or 18.5″, 12-groove rifling.
Weight: 8.9 lbs. **Length:** 39.7″ or 43.7″ overall.
Power: Spring-piston; under-lever cocking.
Stocks: Walnut-stained beech; rubber buttplate, cut checkering on grip; cheekpiece.
Sights: Blade front, open adjustable rear.
Features: Velocity 830 fps. Fixed-barrel with fully opening, direct loading breech. Extended under-lever gives good cocking leverage. Adjustable trigger. Grooved for scope mounting. Carbine has 14.5″ barrel, weighs 8.7 lbs., and is 39.7″ over-all. Imported by Beeman.

Price: Right-hand, 177, 22 . . . . $399.98
Price: Left-hand, 177, 22 . . . . $439.98
Price: Right-hand, 20 cal. $409.98
Price: Left-hand, 20 cal. $449.98

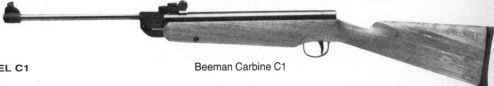

Beeman Carbine C1

BEEMAN CARBINE MODEL C1

Caliber: 177 or 22, single shot.
Barrel: 14″, 12-groove rifling.
Weight: 6¹/₄ lbs. **Length:** 38″ overall.
Power: Spring-piston, barrel cocking.
Stock: Walnut-stained beechwood with rubber buttpad.
Sights: Blade front, rear click-adjustable for windage and elevation.

Features: Velocity 830 fps. Adjustable trigger. Receiver grooved for scope mounting. Imported by Beeman.
Price: $199.95

BEEMAN/WEBLEY OMEGA AIR RIFLE

Caliber: 177 or 22, single shot.
Barrel: 19¹/₄″, rifled.
Weight: 7.8 lbs. **Length:** 43¹/₂″ overall.
Power: Spring-piston air; barrel cocking.
Stock: Walnut-stained beech with cut-checkered grip; cheekpiece; rubber buttpad.
Features: Special quick-snap barrel latch; self-lubricating piston seal; receiver grooved for scope mounting. Introduced 1985. Imported from England by Beeman.
Price: $349.50

Beeman/Webley Omega

BEEMAN/WEBLEY VULCAN II DELUXE

Caliber: 177 or 22, single shot.
Barrel: 17″, rifled.
Weight: 7.6 lbs. **Length:** 43.7″ overall.
Power: Spring-piston air, barrel cocking.
Stock: Walnut. Cut checkering, rubber buttpad, cheekpiece. Standard version has walnut-stained beech.
Sights: Hooded front, micrometer rear.
Features: Velocity of 830 fps (177), 675 fps (22). Single-stage adjustable trigger; receiver grooved for scope mounting. Self-lubricating piston seal. Introduced 1983. Imported by Beeman.
Price: Standard $199.95
Price: Deluxe $269.95

BEEMAN R1 AIR RIFLE

Caliber: 177, 20 or 22, single shot.
Barrel: 19.6″, 12-groove rifling.
Weight: 8.5 lbs. **Length:** 45.2″ overall.
Power: Spring-piston, barrel cocking.
Stock: Walnut-stained beech; cut-checkered pistol grip; Monte Carlo comb and cheekpiece; rubber buttpad.
Sights: Tunnel front with interchangeable inserts, open rear click adjustable for windage and elevation. Grooved for scope mounting.
Features: Velocity of 940-1050 fps (177), 860 fps (20), 800 fps (22). Non-drying nylon piston and breech seals. Adjustable metal trigger. Milled steel safety. Right- or left-hand stock. Custom and Super Laser versions available. Imported by Beeman.
Price: Right-hand $379.95
Price: Left-hand $419.95

Beeman R1 Carbine

BEEMAN R1 CARBINE

Caliber: 177, 20, 22, 25, single shot.
Barrel: 16.1″.
Weight: 8.6 lbs. **Length:** 41.7″ overall.
Power: Spring-piston, barrel cocking.
Stock: Stained beech; Monte Carlo comb and checkpiece; cut-checkered p.g.; rubber buttpad.
Sights: Tunnel front with interchangeable inserts, open adjustable rear; receiver grooved for scope mounting.
Features: Velocity up to 1,000 fps (177). Non-drying nylon piston and breech seals. Adjustable metal trigger. Right- or left-hand stock. Imported by Beeman.
Price: 177 or 22, right-hand $379.95
Price: 20 or 25 cal., right-hand $389.95

BEEMAN R1 LASER AIR RIFLE

Caliber: 177, 20, 22, 25, single shot.
Barrel: 16.1″ or 19.6″.
Weight: 8.4 lbs. **Length:** 41.7″ overall (16.1″ barrel).
Power: Spring-piston, barrel cocking.
Stock: Laminated wood with Monte Carlo comb and cheekpiece; checkered p.g. and forend; rubber buttpad.
Sights: Tunnel front with interchangeable inserts, open adjustable rear.
Features: Velocity up to 1050 fps (177). Receiver grooved for scope mounting. Imported by Beeman.
Price: 177 or 22 cal. $750.00
Price: 20 cal. $760.00
Price: 25 cal. $760.00

Beeman R8

BEEMAN R8 AIR RIFLE

Caliber: 177, single shot.
Barrel: 18.3″.
Weight: 7.2 lbs. **Length:** 43.1″ overall.
Power: Barrel cocking, spring-piston.
Stock: Walnut with Monte Carlo cheekpiece; checkered pistol grip.
Sights: Globe front, fully adjustable rear; interchangeable inserts.
Features: Velocity of 735 fps. Similar to the R1. Nylon piston and breech seals. Adjustable match-grade, two-stage, grooved metal trigger. Milled steel safety. Rubber buttpad. Imported by Beeman.
Price: $299.98

Beeman R7 Air Rifle

Similar to the R8 model except has lighter ambidextrous stock, match grade trigger block; velocity of 680-700 fps; barrel length 17″; weight 5.8 lbs. Milled steel safety. Imported by Beeman.
Price: $219.98

Beeman R10 Deluxe

BEEMAN R10 AIR RIFLES

Caliber: 177, 20, 22, single shot.
Barrel: 16.1″ and 19.7″; 12-groove rifling.
Weight: 7.9 lbs. **Length:** 46″ overall.
Power: Spring-piston, barrel cocking.
Stock: Standard—walnut-finished hardwood with M.C. comb, rubber buttplate; Deluxe has white spacers at grip cap, buttplate, checkered grip, cheekpiece, rubber buttplate.
Sights: Tunnel front with interchangeable inserts, open rear click adjustable for w. and e. Receiver grooved for scope mounting.

Features: Over 1000 fps in 177 cal. only; 26-lb. cocking effort; milled steel safety and body tube. Right- and left-hand models. Custom and Super Laser versions available. Introduced 1986. Imported by Beeman.
Price: . . . . $299.98 to $409.98

BEEMAN FX-1 AIR RIFLE

Caliber: 177, single shot.
Barrel: 18″, rifled.
Weight: 6.6 lbs. **Length:** 43″ overall.
Power: Spring-piston, barrel cocking.
Stock: Walnut-stained hardwood.
Sights: Tunnel front with interchangeable inserts; rear with rotating disc to give four sighting notches.
Features: Velocity 680 fps. Match-type adjustable trigger. Receiver grooved for scope mounting. Imported by Beeman.
Price: $149.50

Beeman FX-2 Air Rifle

Similar to the FX-1 except weighs 5.8 lbs., 41″ overall; front sight is hooded post on ramp, rear sight has two-way click adjustments. Adjustable trigger. Imported by Beeman.
Price: $79.50

CROSMAN MODEL 760 PUMPMASTER

Caliber: 177 pellets or BB, 200-shot.
Barrel: 19½″, rifled steel.
Weight: 3 lbs., 1 oz. **Length:** 36″ overall.
Power: Pneumatic, hand pump.
Features: Short stroke, power determined by number of strokes. Walnut-finished plastic checkered stock and forend. Post front sight and adjustable rear sight. Cross-bolt safety. Introduced 1983.
Price: About $30.00

Benjamin 342/347

BENJAMIN 342/347 AIR RIFLES

Caliber: 22 or 177, pellets or BB; single shot.

Barrel: 23″, rifled.
Weight: 6 lbs. **Length:** 35″ overall.
Power: Hand pumped.
Features: Bolt action, walnut Monte Carlo stock and pump handle. Ramp-type front sight, adjustable stepped leaf type rear. Push-pull safety.
Price: M342, 22 . . . . $104.05
Price: M347, 177 . . . . $104.05

CAUTION: PRICES CHANGE. CHECK AT GUNSHOP.

Crosman A*I*R* 17

CROSMAN A*I*R* 17
Caliber: BB and 177, 200-shot reservoir.
Barrel: 19 1/2", steel.
Weight: 3 lbs., 1 oz. **Length:** 36 3/4" overall.
Power: Pneumatic.
Stock: Black textured ABS plastic.
Features: Velocity of 450 fps (BB), 400 fps (pellet). Single-pump replica of the M-16 rifle. Comes with four-shot pellet clip. Storage compartment in stock. Introduced 1986.
Price: About $39.00

Crosman Model 84

CROSMAN MODEL 66 POWERMASTER
Caliber: 177 (single shot) or BB.
Barrel: 20", rifled, solid steel.
Weight: 3 lbs. **Length:** 38 1/2" overall.
Stock: Wood-grained plastic; checkered p.g. and forend.
Sights: Ramp front, fully adjustable open rear.
Features: Velocity about 675 fps. Bolt action, cross-bolt safety. Introduced 1983.
Price: About $42.00
Price: Model 664X (as above, with 4x scope) $47.00

CROSMAN MODEL 84 CO₂ MATCH RIFLE
Caliber: 177, single shot.
Barrel: 21". Barrel has a chrome shroud to give extra sight radius.
Weight: 9 lbs., 9 oz. **Length:** 45.5" overall.
Power: Refillable CO₂ cylinders.
Stock: Walnut; Olympic match design with stippled pistol grip and forend, adjustable buttplate and comb.
Sights: Match sights—globe front, micrometer adjustable rear.
Features: A CO₂ pressure regulated rifle with adjustable velocity up to 720 fps. Each CO₂ cylinder has more than enough power to complete a 60-shot Olympic match course. Each gun can be custom fitted to the shooter. Made in U.S.A. Introduced 1984.
Price: About $1,379.00

Crosman Backpacker

CROSMAN MODEL 781 SINGLE PUMP
Caliber: 177, BB, 4-shot pellet clip, 195-shot BB magazine.
Barrel: 19 1/2".
Weight: 2 lbs., 14 oz. **Length:** 34 3/4" overall.
Power: Pneumatic, single pump.
Stock: Wood-grained plastic; checkered p.g. and forend.
Sights: Blade front, open adjustable rear.
Features: Velocity of 350-400 fps (pellets). Uses only one pump. Hidden BB reservoir holds 195 shots; pellets loaded via 4-shot clip. Introduced 1984.
Price: About $29.00

CROSSMAN MODEL 1389 BACKPACKER RIFLE
Caliber: 177, single shot.
Barrel: 14", rifled steel.
Weight: 3 lbs., 3 oz. **Length:** 31" overall.
Power: Hand pump, pneumatic.
Stock: Composition, skeletal type.
Sights: Blade front, rear adjustable for windage and elevation.
Features: Velocity to 560 fps. Detachable stock. Receiver grooved for scope mounting. Metal parts blued.
Price: About $54.00

> Consult our Directory pages for the location of firms mentioned.

CROSMAN MODEL 2200 MAGNUM AIR RIFLE
Caliber: 22, single shot.
Barrel: 19", rifled steel.
Weight: 4 lbs., 12 oz. **Length:** 39" overall.
Stock: Full-size, wood-grained plastic with checkered p.g. and forend.
Sights: Ramp front, open step-adjustable rear.
Features: Variable pump power—three pumps give 395 fps, six pumps 530 fps, 10 pumps 620 fps (average). Full-size adult air rifle. Has white line spacers at pistol grip and buttplate. Introduced 1978.
Price: About $54.00

CROSMAN MODEL 788 BB SCOUT RIFLE
Caliber: BB only.
Barrel: 14", steel.
Weight: 2 lbs. 7 oz. **Length:** 31 1/2" overall.
Stock: Wood-grained ABS plastic, checkered p.g. and forend.
Sights: Blade on ramp front, open adjustable rear.
Features: Variable pump power—three pumps give MV of 330 fps, six pumps 437 fps, 10 pumps 500 fps (BBs, average). Steel barrel, cross-bolt safety. Introduced 1978.
Price: About $29.00

CROSMAN MODEL 3100 RIFLE
Caliber: 177, single shot.
Barrel: 16 7/16".
Weight: 6 lbs. **Length:** 39 3/4" overall.
Power: Spring-air, barrel cocking.
Stock: Hardwood with Monte Carlo.
Sights: Hooded front with three apertures, micro. adjustable rear.
Features: Velocity of 600 fps. Single-stroke cocking; adjustable trigger; thumb safety; rubber buttplate. Introduced 1986. Imported by Crosman.
Price: About $62.00

CROSMAN MODEL 2100 CLASSIC AIR RIFLE
Caliber: 177 pellets or BBs, 200-shot BB magazine.
Barrel: 21", rifled.
Weight: 4 lbs., 13 oz. **Length:** 39 3/4" overall.
Power: Pump-up, pneumatic.
Stock: Wood-grained checkered ABS plastic.
Features: Three pumps give about 450 fps, 10 pumps about 795 fps. Cross-bolt safety; concealed reservoir holds over 180 BBs.
Price: About $54.00

Daisy 753

DAISY/POWER LINE MODEL 753 TARGET RIFLE
Caliber: 177, single shot.
Barrel: 20.9", Lothar Walther.
Weight: 6.4 lbs. **Length:** 39.75" overall.
Power: Recoilless pneumatic, single pump.
Stock: Walnut with adjustable cheekpiece and buttplate.
Sights: Globe front with interchangeable inserts, diopter rear with mirco. click adjustments.
Features: Includes front sight reticle assortment, web shooting sling.
Price: About..$215.00

Daisy Model 840

DAISY/POWER LINE 856 PUMP-UP AIRGUN
Caliber: 177 (pellets), BB, 100-shot BB magazine.
Barrel: Rifled steel with shroud.
Weight: 2³/₄ lbs. **Length:** 37.4" overall.
Power: Pneumatic pump-up.
Stock: Moulded wood-grain plastic.
Sights: Ramp and blade front, open rear adjustable for e.
Features: Velocity from 315 fps (two pumps) to 650 fps (10 pumps). Finger grooved forend. Cross-bolt trigger-block safety. Introduced 1985. From Daisy.
Price: About..$29.00

DAISY MODEL 840
Caliber: 177 pellet (single shot) or BB (350-shot).
Barrel: 19", smoothbore, steel.
Weight: 2.7 lbs. **Length:** 36.8" overall.
Stock: Moulded wood-grain stock and forend.
Sights: Ramp front, open, adjustable rear.
Features: Single pump pneumatic rifle. Muzzle velocity 335 fps (BB), 300 fps (pellet). Steel buttplate; straight pull bolt action; cross-bolt safety. Forend forms pump lever. Introduced 1978.
Price: About......................................$29.00

Power Line Model 860

DAISY/POWER LINE 860 PUMP-UP AIRGUN
Caliber: 177 (pellets), BB, 100-shot BB magazine.
Barrel: Rifled steel with shroud.
Weight: 4.18 lbs. **Length:** 37.4" overall.
Power: Pneumatic pump-up.
Stock: Moulded wood-grain with Monte Carlo cheekpiece.
Sights: Ramp and blade front, open rear adjustable for e.
Features: Velocity from 315 fps (two pumps) to 650 fps (10 pumps). Shoots BBs or pellets. Heavy die-cast metal receiver. Cross-bolt trigger-block safety. Introduced 1984. From Daisy.
Price: About..$43.00

DAISY/POWER LINE 880 PUMP-UP AIRGUN
Caliber: 177 pellets, BB.
Barrel: Rifled steel with shroud.
Weight: 4.5 lbs. **Length:** 37³/₄" overall.
Power: Pneumatic pump-up.
Stock: Wood-grain moulded plastic with Monte Carlo cheekpiece.
Sights: Ramp front, open rear adjustable for e.
Features: Crafted by Daisy. Variable power (velocity and range) increase with pump strokes. 10 strokes for maximum power. 100-shot BB magazine. Cross-bolt trigger safety. Positive cocking valve.
Price: About......................................$45.00

DAISY/POWER LINE 900 PELLET REPEATER
Caliber: 177 pellets, 5-shot clip.
Barrel: Rifled steel.
Weight: 4.3 lbs. **Length:** 38.4" overall.
Power: Spring air.
Stock: Full-length moulded stock with checkering, cheekpiece, white spacers.
Sights: Blade and ramp front, V-slot rear fully adjustable for w. & e.
Features: Easy loading, automatic indexing five-shot clip. Heavy die-cast metal receiver, dovetail mount for scope, heavy die-cast pump lever. Single pump for 545 fps muzzle velocity.
Price: About..$54.00

Daisy Model 914

DAISY/POWER LINE MODEL 914
Caliber: BB or 177.
Barrel: 19", smoothbore.
Weight: 6 lbs. **Length:** 38.2" overall.
Power: Single-stroke pneumatic.
Stock: Moulded plastic.
Sights: Ramp front, peep rear.
Features: Velocity of 335 fps. Resembles a famous sporter rifle.
Price: About..$37.00

Daisy/Power Line Model 814
Similar to the Model 914 except has a detachable wire stock and pistol grip. Weight is 2.8 lbs.
Price: About......................................$40.00

DAISY/POWER LINE MODEL 922

Caliber: 22, 5-shot clip.
Barrel: Rifled steel with shroud.
Weight: 4.5 lbs. **Length:** 37³/₄″ overall.
Stock: Moulded wood-grained plastic with checkered p.g. and forend, Monte Carlo cheekpiece.
Sights: Ramp front, fully adjustable open rear.
Features: Muzzle velocity from 270 fps (two pumps) to 530 fps (10 pumps). Straight-pull bolt action. Separate buttplate and grip cap with white spacers. Introduced 1978.

Power Line Model 922

Price: About **$57.00**
Price: Models 970/920 (as above with hardwood stock and forend), about **$100.00**

Daisy Model 953

DAISY/POWER LINE 953

Caliber: 177 pellets.
Barrel: 20.9″; 12-groove rifling, high-grade solid steel by Lothar Walther℠, precision crowned; bore sized for precision match pellets.

Weight: 5.08 lbs. **Length:** 38.9″ overall.
Power: Single-pump pneumatic.
Stock: Full-length, select American hardwood, stained and finished; black buttplate with white spacers.
Sights: Globe front with four aperture inserts; precision micrometer adjustable rear peep sight mounted on a standard ³/₈″ dovetail receiver mount.
Features: Single shot.
Price: About **$130.00**

Daisy Red Ryder

DAISY 1938 RED RYDER CLASSIC

Caliber: BB, 650-shot repeating action.

Barrel: Smoothbore steel with shroud.
Weight: 2.2 lbs. **Length:** 35.4″ overall.
Stock: Wood stock burned with Red Ryder lariat signature.
Sights: Post front, adjustable V-slot rear.
Features: Wood forend. Saddle ring with leather thong. Lever cocking. Gravity feed. Controlled velocity. One of Daisy's most popular guns.
Price: About **$41.00**

Daisy Model 95

DAISY YOUTHLINE RIFLES

Model:	95	111	105
Caliber:	BB	BB	BB
Barrel:	18″	18″	13¹/₂″
Length:	35.2″	34.3″	29.8″
Power:	Spring	Spring	Spring
Capacity:	700	650	400
Price: About	**$28.00**	**$24.00**	**$19.00**

Features: Model 95 stock and forend are wood; 105 and 111 have plastic stocks.

FAMAS Air Rifle

FAMAS SEMI-AUTO AIR RIFLE

Caliber: 177, 10-shot magazine.
Barrel: 19.2″.
Weight: About 8 lbs. **Length:** 29.8″ overall.
Power: 12 gram CO_2.
Stock: Synthetic bullpup design.
Sights: Adjustable front, aperture rear.
Features: Velocity of 425 fps. Duplicates size, weight and feel of the centerfire MAS French military rifle in caliber 223. Introduced 1988. Imported from France by Century International Arms.
Price: **$432.95**

"GAT" AIR RIFLE

Caliber: 177, single shot.
Barrel: 17¹/₄″ cocked, 23¹/₄″ extended.
Weight: 3 lbs.
Power: Spring piston.
Stock: Composition.
Sights: Fixed.
Features: Velocity about 450 fps. Shoots pellets, darts, corks. Imported from England by Stone Enterprises, Inc.
Price: **$34.95**

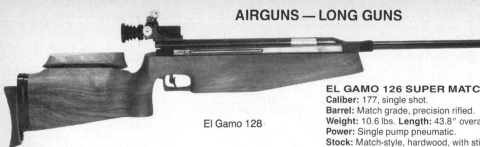

El Gamo 128

EL GAMO 126 SUPER MATCH TARGET RIFLE
Caliber: 177, single shot.
Barrel: Match grade, precision rifled.
Weight: 10.6 lbs. **Length:** 43.8″ overall.
Power: Single pump pneumatic.
Stock: Match-style, hardwood, with stippled grip and forend.
Sights: Hooded front with interchangeable elements, fully adjustable match rear.
Features: Velocity of 590 fps. Adjustable trigger; easy loading pellet port; adjustable buttpad. Introduced 1984. Imported from Spain by Daisy.
Price: About $325.00

MARKSMAN 28 INTERNATIONAL AIR RIFLE
Caliber: 177, single shot.
Barrel: 17″.
Weight: 5¾ lbs.
Power: Spring-air, barrel cocking.
Stock: Hardwood.
Sights: Hooded front, adjustable rear.
Features: Velocity of 580-620 fps. Introduced 1989. Imported from West Germany by Marksman Products.
Price: $198.00

MARKSMAN 29 AIR RIFLE
Caliber: 177 or 22, single shot.
Barrel: 18.5″.
Weight: 6 lbs. **Length:** 41.5″ overall.
Power: Spring air, barrel cocking.
Stock: Stained hardwood.
Sights: Blade front, open adjustable rear.
Features: Velocity of 610-640 fps (177), 610-640 fps (22). Introduced 1986. Imported from England by Marksman Products.
Price: Either caliber $232.00

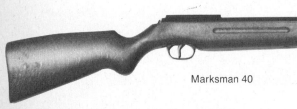

Marksman 40

MARKSMAN 40 INTERNATIONAL AIR RIFLE
Caliber: 177, single shot.
Barrel: 18⅜″.

Weight: 7⅓ lbs.
Power: Spring-air, barrel cocking.
Stock: Hardwood.
Sights: Hooded front, adjustable rear.
Features: Velocity of 700-720 fps. Introduced 1989. Imported from West Germany by Marksman Products.
Price: $237.00

Marksman 56-K

MARKSMAN 56-FTS FIELD TARGET RIFLE
Caliber: 177, single shot.
Barrel: 19⅝″.

Weight: 8.8 lbs.
Power: Spring-air, barrel cocking.
Stock: Hardwood with stippled grip; ambidextrous, with adjustable cheekpiece.
Sights: None furnished.
Features: Velocity of 910-940 fps. Rubber buttpad. Introduced 1989. Imported from West Germany by Marksman Products.
Price: $495.00
Price: Model 56-K, with scope and mount $708.00

Marksman 58-S

MARKSMAN 58-S SILHOUETTE RIFLE
Caliber: 177, single shot.
Barrel: 16″.

Weight: 8.5 lbs.
Power: Spring-air, barrel cocking.
Stock: Hardwood with stippled grip; ambidextrous.
Sights: None furnished.
Features: Velocity 910-940 fps. Adjustable trigger. Introduced 1989. Imported from West Germany by Marksman Products.
Price: $410.00
Price: Model 58-K with scope and mount $625.00

MARKSMAN 70 AIR RIFLE
Caliber: 177, 20 or 22, single shot.
Barrel: 19.75″.
Weight: 8 lbs. **Length:** 45.5″ overall.
Power: Spring air, barrel cocking.
Stock: Stained hardwood with M.C. cheekpiece, rubber buttpad, cut checkered p.g.
Sights: Hooded front, open fully adjustable rear.
Features: Velocity 910-940 fps (177), 810-840 fps (20), 740-780 fps (22); two-stage trigger. Introduced 1988. Imported from West Germany by Marksman Products.
Price: 177, 20 or 22 . . . . $290.00

Marksman 55 Air Rifle
Similar to the Model 70 except has uncheckered hardwood stock, no cheekpiece, plastic buttplate. Overall length is 45.25″, weight is 7½ lbs. Available in 177 caliber only.
Price: $249.00
Price: Model 59 (as above, carbine) $249.00

CAUTION: PRICES CHANGE. CHECK AT GUNSHOP.

Marksman Model 1740

MARKSMAN 1790 BIATHLON TRAINER
Caliber: 177, single shot.
Barrel: 15″, rifled.
Weight: 4.7 lbs.
Power: Spring-air, barrel cocking.
Stock: Synthetic.
Sights: Hooded front, match-style diopter rear.
Features: Velocity of 450 fps. Introduced 1989. From Marksman Products.
Price: $67.00

MARKSMAN 1740 AIR RIFLE
Caliber: 177 or 100-shot BB repeater.
Barrel: 15½″, smoothbore.
Weight: 5 lbs., 1 oz. **Length:** 36½″ overall.
Power: Spring, barrel cocking.
Stock: Moulded high-impact ABS plastic.
Sights: Ramp front, open rear adjustable for e.
Features: Automatic safety; fixed front, adjustable rear sight; shoots 177 cal. BBs, pellets and darts. Velocity about 475-500 fps.
Price: $40.00
Price: Model 1780 (shoots only pellets) $45.00

Mauser 300 SL

MAUSER MODEL 300 SL AIR RIFLE
Caliber: 177, single shot.
Barrel: 18.9″.
Weight: 8 lbs., 8 oz. **Length:** 43.7″ overall.
Power: Spring air, under-lever cocking.
Stock: Match style, hardwood, with stippled p.g., rubber buttpad.
Sights: Tunnel front, open adjustable rear.
Features: Velocity of 550-600 fps. Dovetail mount for diopter or scope. Automatic safety. Imported from West Germany by Marksman Products.
Price: $332.00
Price: With diopter sight $440.00

RWS/DIANA MODEL 36 AIR RIFLE
Caliber: 177, 22, single shot.
Barrel: 19″, rifled.
Weight: 8 lbs. **Length:** 45″ overall.
Power: Spring air, barrel cocking.
Stock: Beech.
Sights: Hooded front (interchangeable inserts avail.), adjustable rear.
Features: Velocity of 1000 fps (177-cal.). Comes with scope mount; two-stage adjustable trigger. Imported from West Germany by Dynamit Nobel-RWS, Inc.
Price: $275.00
Price: Model 38 (as above, walnut stock) $315.00

RWS/DIANA MODEL 52 AIR RIFLE
Caliber: 177, 22; single shot.
Barrel: 17″, rifled.
Weight: 8½ lbs. **Length:** 43″ overall.
Power: Spring air, sidelever cocking.
Stock: Beech.
Sights: Ramp front, adjustable rear.
Features: Velocity of 1100 fps (177). Blue finish. Solid rubber buttpad. Imported from West Germany by Dynamit Nobel-RWS, Inc.
Price: $355.00

RWS/DIANA MODEL 75T 01 MATCH AIR RIFLE
Caliber: 177, single shot.
Barrel: 19″.
Weight: 11 lbs. **Length:** 43.7″ overall.
Power: Spring air, sidelever cocking.
Stock: Oil-finished walnut with stippled grip, adjustable buttplate, accessory rail. Conforms to I.S.U. rules.
Sights: Globe front with five inserts, fully adjustable match peep rear.
Features: Velocity of 574 fps. Fully adjustable trigger. Model 75 HV has stippled forend, adjustable cheekpiece. Uses double opposing piston system for recoilless operation. Imported from West Germany by Dynamit Nobel-RWS, Inc.
Price: Model 75T 01 .... **$790.00**
Price: Model 75T 01 left-hand................... **$830.00**
Price: Model 75 UT 01, right-hand **$970.00**
Price: Model 75 U 01, left-hand................. **$1,010.00**

RWS/DIANA MODEL 24 AIR RIFLE
Caliber: 177, 22, single shot.
Barrel: 17″, rifled.
Weight: 6 lbs. **Length:** 42″ overall.
Power: Spring air, barrel cocking.
Stock: Beech.
Sights: Hooded front, adjustable rear.
Features: Velocity of 700 fps (177). Easy cocking effort; blue finish. Imported from West Germany by Dynamit Nobel-RWS, Inc.
Price: $150.00
Price: Model 34 (as above, except 19″ bbl., 7½ lbs., adj. trigger, synthetic seals). $225.00

Consult our Directory pages for the location of firms mentioned.

RWS/DIANA MODEL 45 AIR RIFLE
Caliber: 177, single shot.
Weight: 7¾ lbs. **Length:** 46″ overall.
Power: Spring air, barrel cocking.
Stock: Walnut-finished hardwood with rubber recoil pad.
Sights: Globe front with interchangeable inserts, micro. click open rear with four-way blade.
Features: Velocity of 820 fps. Dovetail base for either micrometer peep sight or scope mounting. Automatic safety. Imported from West Germany by Dynamit Nobel-RWS, Inc.
Features: 177
Price: Price: $240.00

RWS/DIANA Model 75KT 01 Running Boar Air Rifle
Similar to the Model 75 Match except has adjustable cheekpiece and buttplate, different stock, sandblasted barrel sleeve, detachable barrel weight, elevated-grip cocking lever, and a 240mm scope mount. Introduced 1983.
Price: Right-hand **$900.00**
Price: Left-hand............................... **$950.00**

Sheridan CO$_2$

SHERIDAN BLUE AND SILVER STREAK RIFLES

Caliber: 5mm (20 cal.), single shot.
Barrel: 18 1/2", rifled.
Weight: 5 lbs. **Length:** 37" overall.
Power: Hand pumped (swinging forend).
Features: Rustproof barrel and piston tube. Takedown. Thumb safety. Mannlicher-type walnut stock.
Price: Blue Streak $109.85
Price: Silver Streak $113.95

SHERIDAN CO$_2$ AIR RIFLES

Caliber: 5mm (20 cal.), single shot.
Barrel: 18 1/2", rifled.
Weight: 6 lbs. **Length:** 37" overall.
Power: Standard 12-gram CO$_2$ cylinder.
Stock: Walnut sporter.
Sights: Open, adjustable for w. and e. Optional Sheridan-Williams 5D-SH receiver sight or Weaver D4 scope.
Features: Bolt action single shot, CO$_2$ powered. Velocity approx. 514 fps, manual thumb safety. Blue or Silver finish.
Price: CO$_2$ Blue Streak $96.20
Price: CO$_2$ Silver Streak $100.55
Price: CO$_2$ Blue Streak with receiver sight $114.40
Price: CO$_2$ Blue Streak with scope $131.90

Sterling HR-83

THEOBEN SIROCCO CLASSIC AIR RIFLE

Caliber: 177 or 22.
Barrel: 15 1/2", Anschutz.
Weight: 7 3/4 lbs. **Length:** 44" overall.
Power: Gas-ram piston. Variable power.
Stock: Hand-checkered walnut.
Sights: None supplied. Comes with scope mount.
Features: Velocity 1100 fps (177), 900 fps (22). Adjustable recoil pad, barrel weight. Choked or unchoked barrel. Imported from England by Air Rifle Specialists.
Price: $860.00
Price: Grand Prix model (as above except thumbhole stock) $940.00

STERLING HR-81/HR-83 AIR RIFLE

Caliber: 177 or 22, single shot.
Barrel: 18 1/2".
Weight: 8 1/2 lbs. **Length:** 42 1/2" overall.
Power: Spring air (barrel cocking).
Stock: Stained hardwood, with cheekpiece, checkered pistol grip.
Sights: Tunnel-type front with four interchangeable elements, open adjustable V-type rear.
Features: Velocity of 700 fps (177), 600 fps (22). Bolt action with easily accessible loading port; adjustable single-stage match trigger; rubber recoil pad. Integral scope mount rails. Scope and mount optional. Introduced 1983. Made in U.S.A. by Benjamin Air Rifle Co.
Price: HR 81-7 (177 cal., standard walnut stock) $242.75
Price: HR 81-2 (as above, 22 cal.) $283.15
Price: HR 83-7 (177 cal., deluxe walnut stock) $386.65
Price: HR 83-2 (as above, 22 cal.) $391.40
Price: For 4x40 wide angle scope, add $82.35
Price: Scope mount $45.85

Theoben Prometheus

THEOBEN-PROMETHEUS SUPER SIROCCO

Caliber: 177 or 22; single shot.
Barrel: 15 3/4".
Weight: NA. **Length:** 44" overall.
Power: Gas-ram piston.
Stock: English walnut, checkered p.g. and forend.
Sights: None furnished; scope base and rings provided.
Features: Velocity 950-1200 fps. One-stroke cocking mechanism with captive gas-ram piston. Designed to shoot Prometheus and Titan Black pellets. Imported from England by Fisher Enterprises.
Price: Deluxe Super Sirocco $870.00
Price: Grand Prix $925.00
Price: Eliminator (thumbhole stock) $1,475.00

Theoben Sirocco Eliminator Air Rifle

Similar to the Sirocco Grand Prix except more powerful. Gives 1400 fps in 177 cal., 1100 fps in 22. Walnut thumbhole stock, adjustable recoil pad, scope mount. Variable power. Barrel weight, leather cobra sling, swivels. Choked barrel only.
Price: $1,450.00

Walther LGR Running Boar Air Rifle

Same basic specifications as standard LGR except has a high comb thumbhole stock. Has adjustable cheekpiece and buttplate, no sights. Introduced 1977.
Price: $1,050.00
Price: LGR Match $850.00

WALTHER CG90 AIR RIFLE

Caliber: 177, single shot.
Barrel: 18.9".
Weight: 10.2 lbs. **Length:** 44" overall.
Power: CO$_2$ cartridge.
Stock: Match type of European walnut; stippled grip.
Sights: Globe front, fully adjustable match rear.
Features: Uses tilting-block action. Introduced 1989. Imported from Germany by Interarms.
Price: $1,225.00

WALTHER LGR UNIVERSAL MATCH AIR RIFLE

Caliber: 177, single shot.
Barrel: 25.5".
Weight: 13 lbs. **Length:** 44 3/4" overall.
Power: Spring air, barrel cocking.
Stock: Walnut match design with stippled grip and forend, adjustable cheekpiece, rubber buttpad.
Features: Has the same weight and contours as the Walther U.I.T. rimfire target rifle. Comes complete with sights, accessories and muzzle weight. Imported from West Germany by Interarms.
Price: $1,175.00

Sporting Leaf and Open Sights

Wichita Multi Range rear (left) and front

BURRIS SPORTING REAR SIGHT
Made of spring steel, supplied with multi-step elevator for coarse adjustments and notch plate with lock screw for finer adjustments. Price **$14.95**

LYMAN No. 16
Middle sight for barrel dovetail slot mounting. Folds flat when scope or peep sight is used. Sight notch plate adjustable for e. White triangle for quick aiming. 3 heights: A — .400″ to .500″, B — .345″ to .445″, C — .500″ to .600″. Price. **$11.50**

MARBLE FALSE BASE #72, #73, #74
New screw-on base for most rifles replaces factory base. 3/8″ dovetail slot permits installation of any folding rear sight. Can be had in sweat-on models also. Price **$6.00**

MARBLE CONTOUR RAMP #14R
For late model Rem. 725, 740, 760, 742 rear sight mounting. 9/16″ between mounting screws. Accepts all sporting rear sights. Price **$12.25**

MARBLE FOLDING LEAF
Flat-top or semi-buckhorn style. Folds down when scope or peep sights are used. Reversible plate gives choice of "U" or "V" notch. Adjustable for elevation. Price **$11.25**
Also available with both w. and e. adjustment. **$13.00**

MARBLE SPORTING REAR
With white enamel diamond, gives choice of two "U" and two "V" notches of different sizes. Adjustment in height by means of double step elevator and sliding notch piece. For all rifles; screw or dovetail installation.
Price . . . . **$11.50-$13.00**

MARBLE #20 UNIVERSAL
New screw or sweat-on base. Both have .100″ elevation adjustment. In five base sizes. Three styles of U-notch, square notch, peep. Adjustable for w. and e.
Price: Screw-on **$18.50**
Price: Sweat-on **$17.00**

MILLETT RIFLE SIGHT
Open, fully adjustable rear sight fits standard 3/8″ dovetail cut in barrel. Choice of white outline or target rear blades, .360″. Front with white or orange bar, .343″, .400″, .430″, .460″, .500″, .540″.
Price: Rear sight **$52.95**
Price: Front sight **$11.75**

MILLETT SCOPE-SITE
Open, adjustable or fixed rear sights dovetail into a base integral with the top scope-mounting ring. Blaze orange front ramp sight is integral with the front ring half. Rear sights have white outline aperture. Provides fast, short radius, Patridge-type open sights on the top of the scope. Can be used with all Millett rings.
Price: Scope-Site ring set, adjustable **$77.95**
Price: As above, fixed **$44.95**
Price: Convertible Top Cap set, adjustable **$62.95**
Price: As above, fixed **$29.65**

WICHITA MULTI RANGE SIGHT SYSTEM
Designed for silhouette shooting. System allows you to adjust the rear sight to four repeatable range settings, once it is pre-set. Sight clicks to any of the settings by turning a serrated wheel. Front sight is adjustable for weather and light conditions with one adjustment. Specify gun when ordering.
Price: Rear sight **$88.00**
Price: Front sight **$66.00**

WILLIAMS DOVETAIL OPEN SIGHT
Open rear sight with w. and e. adjustment. Furnished with "U" notch or choice of blades. Slips into dovetail and locks with gib lock. Heights from .281″ to .531″. Price with blade **$13.00**
Price: Less Blade˙ **$8.55**

WILLIAMS GUIDE OPEN SIGHT
Open rear sight with w. and e. adjustment. Bases to fit most military and commercial barrels. Choice of square "U" or "V" notch blade, 3/16″, 1/4″, 5/16″, or 3/8″ high. Price with blade **$15.70**
Price: Extra blades, each **$4.45**
Price: Less blade **$11.25**

Micrometer Receiver Sights

Millett Ruger Mini-14

Millett AR-15

BEEMAN/WEIHRAUCH MATCH APERTURE SIGHT
Micrometer 1/4-minute click adjustment knobs with settings indicated on scales. Price **$79.95**

BEEMAN/FEINWERKBAU MATCH APERTURE SIGHTS
Locks into one of four eye-relief positions. Micrometer 1/4-minute click adjustments; may be set to zero at any range. Extra windage scale visible beside eyeshade. Primarily for use at 5 to 20 meters. Price **$159.95**

BEEMAN SPORT APERTURE SIGHT
Positive click micrometer adjustments. Standard units with flush surface screwdriver adjustments. Deluxe version has target knobs.
Price: Standard **$34.98**
Price: Deluxe **$39.98**

FREELAND TUBE SIGHT
Uses Unertl 1″ micrometer mounts. For 22-cal. target rifles, inc. 52 Win., 37, 40X Rem. and BSA Martini. Price **$150.00**

LYMAN No. 57
1/4-min. clicks. Stayset knobs. Quick release slide, adjustable zero scales. Made for almost all modern rifles. Price **$58.95**

LYMAN No. 66
Fits close to the rear of flat-sided receivers, furnished with Stayset knobs. Quick release slide, 1/4-min. adj. For most lever or slide action or flat-sided automatic rifles. Price **$58.95**

LYMAN No. 66U
Light weight, designed for most modern shotguns with a flat-sided, round-top receiver. 1/4-minute clicks. Requires drilling, taping. Not for Browning A-5, Rem. M11. Price **$58.95**

MILLETT ASSAULT RIFLE SIGHTS
Fully adjustable, heat-treated nickel steel peep aperture receiver sights for AR-15, Mini-14. AR-15 rear sight has w. & e. adjustments; non-glare replacement ramp-style front also available. Mini-14 sight has fine w. & e. adjustments; replaces original.
Price: Rear sight for above guns **$51.45**
Price: Front and rear combo for AR-15 . . . . **$62.65**
Price: Front sight for AR-15 . . . . **$12.25**
Price: Front and rear combo for Mini-14 . . . . **$68.25**
Price: Front sight for Mini-14 . . . . **$17.85**

WILLIAMS FP
Internal click adjustments. Positive locks. For virtually all rifles, T/C Contender, Heckler & Koch HK-91, Ruger Mini-14, plus Win., Rem. and Ithaca shotguns. Price, from. **$47.90**
Price: With Twilight Aperture **$49.37**
Price: With Target Knobs **$56.90**
Price: With Target Knobs & Twilight Aperture **$58.37**
Price: With Square Notched Blade **$50.42**
Price: With Target Knobs & Square Notched Blade **$59.53**
Price: FP-GR (for dovetail-grooved receivers, 22s and air guns) **$47.90**

WILLIAMS 5-D SIGHT
Low cost sight for shotguns, 22s and the more popular big game rifles. Adjustment for w. and e. Fits most guns without drilling or tapping. Also for Br. SMLE. Price. **$27.16**
Price: With Twilight Aperture **$28.63**
Price: With Shotgun Aperture **$27.16**

WILLIAMS GUIDE
Receiver sight for 30 M1 Car., M1903A3 Springfield, Savage 24s, Savage-Anschutz rifles and Wby. XXII. Utilizes military dovetail; no drilling. Double-dovetail w. adj., sliding dovetail adj. for e. Price **$25.79**
Price: With Twilight Aperture **$27.26**
Price: With Open Sight Blade **$23.69**

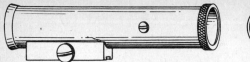

Freeland Superior with inserts

Lyman 17A

Lyman Screw-On Ramp

MMC M/85

Lyman Hunting Front

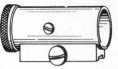

Freeland Military

Front Sights

LYMAN HUNTING SIGHTS
Made with gold or white beads 1/16″ to 3/32″ wide and in varying heights for most military and commercial rifles. Dovetail bases. Price **$7.95**

MARBLE STANDARD
Ivory, red, or gold bead. For all American-made rifles, 1/16″ wide bead with semi-flat face which does not reflect light. Specify type of rifle when ordering. Price **$7.00**

MARBLE-SHEARD "GOLD"
Shows up well even in darkest timber. Shows same color on different colored objects; sturdily built. Medium bead. Various models for different makes of rifles so specify type of rifle when ordering. Price **$8.75**

MARBLE CONTOURED
Same contour and shape as Marble-Sheard but uses standard 1/16″ or 3/32″ bead, ivory, red or gold. Specify rifle type. Price **$8.00**

MARBLE PATRIDGE
Gold-faced Patridge front sight is available in .250″ or .34″ widths and heights from .260″ to .538″. Price **$8.75**

POLY-CHOKE
Rifle front sights available in six heights and two widths. Model A designed to be inserted into the barrel dovetail; Model B is for use with standard .350″ ramp; both have standard 3/8″ dovetails. Gold or ivory color 1/16″ bead. From Marble Arms. Price **$5.50**

Globe Target Front Sights

FREELAND SUPERIOR
Furnished with six 1″ plastic apertures. Available in 4 1/2″-6 1/2″ lengths. Made for any target rifle. Price **$48.50**
Price: With six metal insert apertures **$51.60**
Price: Front base **$12.50**

FREELAND TWIN SET
Two Freeland Superior Front Sights, long or short, allow switching from 50 yd. to 100 yd. ranges and back again without changing rear sight adjustment. Sight adjustment compensation is built into the set; just interchange and you're "on" at either range. Set includes six plastic apertures.
Price: **$67.00**
Price: With six metal apertures **$70.00**

FREELAND MILITARY
Short model for use with high-powered rifles where sight must not extend beyond muzzle. Screw-on base; six plastic apertures. Price **$48.50**
Price: With six metal apertures **$51.60**
Price: Front base **$12.50**

LYMAN No. 17A TARGET
Includes seven interchangeable inserts: four apertures, one transparent amber and two posts .50″ and .100″ in width. Price **$24.95**

Ramp Sights

LYMAN SCREW-ON RAMP
Used with 8-40 screws but may also be brazed on. Heights from .10″ to .350″. Ramp without sight. Price **$14.95**

MARBLE FRONT RAMPS
Available in either screw-on or sweat-on style, five heights; 3/16″, 5/16″, 3/8″, 7/16″, 9/16″. Standard 3/8″ dovetail slot. Price **$14.00**
Hoods for above ramps. **$3.00**

WILLIAMS SHORTY RAMP
Companion to "Streamlined" ramp, about 1/2″ shorter. Screw-on or sweat-on. It is furnished in 1/8″, 3/16″, 9/32″, and 3/8″ heights without hood only. Price **$9.95**

WILLIAMS STREAMLINED RAMP
Hooded style in screw-on or sweat-on models. Furnished in 9/16″, 7/16″, 3/8″, 5/16″, 3/16″ heights. Price with hood **$17.80**
Price: Without hood **$14.70**

Handgun Sights

BO-MAR DE LUXE BMCS
Gives 3/8″ w. and e. adjustment at 50 yards on Colt Gov't 45, sight radius under 7″. For GM and Commander models only. Uses existing dovetail slot. Has shield-type rear blade. Price **$54.75**

BO-MAR LOW PROFILE RIB & ACCURACY TUNER
Streamlined rib with front and rear sights; 7 1/8″ sight radius. Brings sight line closer to the bore than standard or extended sight and ramp. Weighs 5 oz. Made for Colt Gov't 45, Super 38, and Gold Cup 45 and 38. Price **$89.00**

BO-MAR COMBAT RIB
For S&W Model 19 revolver with 4″ barrel. Sight radius 5 3/4″, weight 5 1/2 oz. Price. **$79.00**

BO-MAR FAST DRAW RIB
Streamlined full length rib with integral Bo-Mar micrometer sight and serrated fast draw sight. For Browning 9mm, S&W 39, Colt Commander 45, Super Auto and 9mm. Price **$79.00**

BO-MAR WINGED RIB
For S&W 4″ and 6″ length barrels—K-38, M10, HB 14 and 19. Weight for the 6″ model is about 7 1/4 oz. Price **$89.00**

BO-MAR COVER-UP RIB
Adj. rear sight, winged front guards. Fits right over revolver's original front sight. For S&W 4″ M-10HB, M-13, M-58, M-64 & 65, Ruger 4″ models SDA-34, SDA-84, SS-34, SS-84, GF-34, GF-84 Price **$85.00**

C-MORE SIGHTS
Replacement front sight blades offered in two types and five styles. Made of DuPont Acetal, they come in a set of five high-contrast colors: blue, green, pink, red and yellow. Easy to install. Patridge style for Colt Python (all barrels), Ruger Super Blackhawk (7 1/2″), Ruger Blackhawk (4 5/8″); Ramp style for Python (all barrels), Blackhawk (4 5/8″), Super Blackhawk (7 1/2″ and 10 1/2″). From Mag-na-port Int'l. Price, per set **$14.95**

MMC COMBAT FIXED REAR SIGHT (Colt 1911-Type Pistols)
This veteran MMC sight is well known to those who prefer a true combat sight for "carry" guns. Steel construction for long service. Choose from a wide variety of front sights.
Price: Combat Fixed Rear, plain **$18.45**
Price: As above, white outline **$23.65**
Price: Combat Front Sight for above, six styles, from **$5.15**

MMC M/85 ADJUSTABLE REAR SIGHT
Designed to be compatible with the Ruger P-85 front sight. Fully adjustable for windage and elevation.
Price: M/85 Adjustable Rear Sight, plain **$52.45**
Price: As above, white outline **$57.70**

CAUTION: PRICES CHANGE. CHECK AT GUNSHOP.

MMC Adjustable

Wichita Combat

Wichita Series 70/80

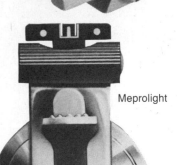
Meprolight

Millett Colt Lo-Profile, Ruger Standard Auto, S&W 400, 500, 600, Browning

MMC STANDARD ADJUSTABLE REAR SIGHT
Available for Colt 1911 type, Ruger Standard Auto, and now for S&W 469, and 659 pistols. No front sight change is necessary, as this sight will work with the original factory front sight.
Price: Standard Adjustable Rear Sight, plain leaf $46.05
Price: Standard Adjustable Rear Sight, white outline $51.15

MMC MINI-SIGHT
Miniature size for carrying, fully adjustable, for maximum accuracy with your pocket auto. MMC's Mini-Sight will work with the factory front sight. No machining is necessary, easy installation. Available for Walther PP, PPK, and PPK/S pistols. Will also fit fixed sight Browning Hi-Power (P-35).
Price: Mini-Sight, plain. $58.45
Price: Mini-Sight, white bar $63.45

MEPROLIGHT SIGHTS
Replacement open sights for popular handguns and Uzi carbine, AR-15/M-16 rifles. Both front and rear sights have tritium inserts for illumination in low-light conditions. Inserts give constant non-glare green light for 5 years, even in cold weather. Handguns: S&W 459, 659 (adjustable and non-adjustable), S&W 645, Beretta 92, Colt Gov't 45, Browning Hi-Power, Uzi carbine and mini, SIG-Sauer P226, Glock 17, Ruger P-85, universal front sight for revolvers. Also shotgun bead.
Price: Universal front for revolvers. $39.95
Price: Front and rear sights $79.95
Price: Shotgun bead. $24.95

MILLETT SERIES 100 ADJUSTABLE SIGHTS
Replacement sights for revolvers and auto pistols. Positive click adjustments for windage and elevation. Designed for accuracy and ruggedness. Made to fit S&W, Colt, Beretta, SIG Sauer P220, P225, P226, Ruger P-85, Ruger GP-100 (and others), Glock 17, CZ-75, TZ-75, Dan Wesson, Browning, AMT Hardballer. Rear blades are available in white outline or positive black target. All steel construction and easy to install.
Price . . . .$46.95 to $75.35

MILLETT MARK SERIES PISTOL SIGHTS
Mark I and Mark II replacement combat sights for government-type auto pistols, including H&K P7. Mark I is high profile, Mark II low profile. Both have horizontal light deflectors.
Price: Mark I, front and rear. $32.95
Price: Mark II, front and rear $46.95
Price: For H&K P7. . . . .$46.95

MILLETT REVOLVER FRONT SIGHTS
All-steel replacement front sights with either white or orange bar. Easy to install. For Ruger GP-100, Redhawk, Security-Six, Police-Six, Speed-Six, Colt Trooper, Diamondback, King Cobra, Peacemaker, Python, Dan Wesson 22 and 15-2. Price . . . .$12.95 to $15.25

MILLETT DUAL-CRIMP FRONT SIGHT
Replacement front sight for automatic pistols. Dual-Crimp uses an all-steel two-point hollow rivet system. Available in eight heights and four styles. Has a skirted base that covers the front sight pad. Easily installed with the Millett Installation Tool Set. Available in Blaze Orange Bar, White Bar, Serrated Ramp, Plain Post. Price $15.25

MILLETT STAKE-ON FRONT SIGHT
Replacement front sight for automatic pistols. Stake-On sights have skirted base that covers the front sight pad. Easily installed with the Millet Installation Tool Set. Available in seven heights and four styles—Blaze Orange Bar, White Bar, Serrated Ramp, Plain Post. Price $15.25

OMEGA OUTLINE SIGHT BLADES
Replacement rear sight blades for Colt and Ruger single action guns and the Interarms Virginian Dragoon. Standard Outline available in gold or white notch outline on blue metal. From Mag-na-port Int'l. Price $7.95

OMEGA MAVERICK SIGHT BLADES
Replacement "peep-sight" blades for Colt, Ruger SAs, Virginian Dragoon. Three models available—No. 1, Plain, No. 2, Single Bar, No. 3 Double Bar Rangefinder. From Mag-na-port Int'l. Price, each 6.95

TRIJICON SELF-LUMINOUS SIGHTS
Three-dot sighting system uses self luminous inserts in the sight blade and leaf. Tritium "lamps" are mounted in a metal cylinder and protected by a polished crystal sapphire. For most popular handguns, fixed or adjustable sights, and some rifles. From Armson, Inc.
Price . . . .$25.95 to $189.90

THOMPSON/CENTER "ULTIMATE" SIGHTS
Replacement front and rear sights for the T/C Contender. Front sight has four interchangeable blades (.060", .080", .100", .120"), rear sight has four notch widths of the same measurements for a possible 16 combinations. Rear sight can be used with existing soldered front sights.
Price: Front sight $30.00
Price: Rear sight $65.00

WICHITA SERIES 70/80 SIGHT
Provides click windage and elevation adjustments with precise repeatability of settings. Sight blade is grooved and angled back at the top to reduce glare. Available in Low Mount Combat or Low Mount Target styles for Colt 45s and their copies, S&W 645, Hi-Power, CZ 75 and others.
Price $62.50

WICHITA SIGHT SYSTEMS
For 45 auto pistols. Target and Combat styles available. Designed by Ron Power. All-steel construction, click adjustable. Each sight has two traverse pins, a large hinge pin and two elevation return springs. Sight blade is serrated and mounted on an angle to deflect light. Patridge front for target, ramp front for combat. Both are legal for ISPC and NRA competitions.
Price: Rear sight, target or combat $62.50
Price: Front sight, Patridge or ramp. $9.85

WICHITA GRAND MASTER DELUXE RIBS
Ventilated rib has wings machined into it for better sight acquisition. Made of stainless steel, sights blued. Uses Wichita Multi-Range rear sight, adjustable front sight. Made for revolvers with 6" barrel.
Price: Model 301 (adj. sight K-frames with custom bbl. of 1.000"-1.032" dia., L and N frames with 1.062"-1.100" bbl.) $143.00
Price: Model 302 (fixed sight K-frames; M10, 65, 13 with 1.000" bbl., N-frame with 1.062" bbl.). $143.00
Price: Model 303 (Model 29, 629 with factory bbl., adj. sight K, L, N frames) $143.00

WICHITA DOUBLE MASTER RIB
Ventilated rib has wings machined on either side of fixed front post sight for better acquisition and is relieved for Mag-na-ports. Milled to accept Weaver See-Thru-style rings. Made of blued steel. Has Wichita Multi-Range rear sight system. Made for Model 29/269 with factory barrel, and all adjustable-sight K, L and N frames.
Price: Model 403 . . . .$128.95

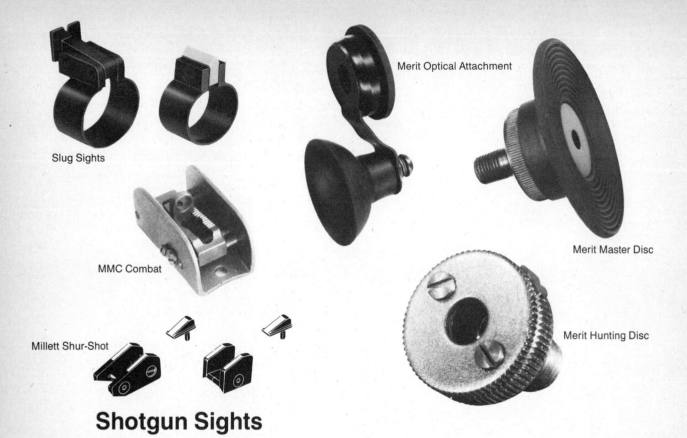

Slug Sights

MMC Combat

Millett Shur-Shot

Merit Optical Attachment

Merit Master Disc

Merit Hunting Disc

Shotgun Sights

ACCURA-SITE

For shooting shotgun slugs. Three models to fit most shotguns — "A" for vent. rib barrels, "B" for solid ribs, "C" for plain barrels. Rear sight has windage and elevation provisions. Easily removed and replaced. Includes front and rear sights. Price . . . . **$25.95 to $27.95**

LYMAN

Three sights of over-sized ivory beads. No. 10 Front (press fit) for double barrel or ribbed single barrel guns . . . **$3.50**; No. 10D Front (screw fit) for non-ribbed single barrel guns (comes with wrench) . . . **$4.50**; No. 11 Middle (press fit) for double and ribbed single barrel guns Price **$3.50**

MMC M&P COMBAT SHOTGUN SIGHT SET

A durable, protected ghost ring aperture, combat sight made of steel. Fully adjustable for windage and elevation.

Price: M&P Sight Set (front and rear) **$73.45**

Price: As above, installed **$83.95**

MARBLE

FOR DOUBLE BARREL SHOTGUNS (PRESS FIT)

Marble 214 — Ivory front bead, $^{11}/_{64}$" . . . **$3.55**; 215 — same with .080" rear bead and reamers . . . **$11.70**. Marble 220 — Bi-color (gold and ivory) front bead, $^{11}/_{64}$" and .080" rear bead, with reamers . . . **$13.50**; Marble 221 — front bead only . . . **$5.15**. Marble 223 — Ivory rear .080" . . . **$3.50**. Marble 224 — Front sight reamer for 214-221 beads . . . **$2.55**; Marble 226 — Rear sight reamer for 223. Price **$2.55**

MARBLE

FOR SINGLE OR DB SHOTGUNS (SCREW-ON FIT)

Marble 217 — Ivory front bead, $^{11}/_{64}$" . . . **$3.90**; Marble 216 . . . **$8.00**; Marble 218 — Bi-color front, $^{11}/_{64}$" . . . **$5.60**; Marble 219 . . . **$9.80**; Marble 223T — Ivory rear .080" Price **$5.30**

Marble Bradley type sights 223BT — $^1/_8$", $^5/_{64}$" and $^{11}/_{64}$" long. Gold, Ivory or Red bead **$3.50**

MILLETT SHURSHOT SHOTGUN SIGHT

A sight system for shotguns with ventilated rib. Rear sight attaches to the rib, front sight replaces the front bead. Front has an orange face, rear has two orange bars. For 870, 1100 or other models.

Price: Front and rear **$20.95**

Price: Adjustable front and rear **$27.40**

POLY-CHOKE

Replacement front shotgun sights in four styles — Xpert, Poly Bead, Xpert Mid Rib sights, and Bev-L-Block. Xpert Front available in 3x56, 6x48 thread, $^3/_{32}$" or $^5/_{32}$" shank length, gold, ivory (**$4.50**); or Sun Spot orange bead (**$4.50**); Poly Bead is standard replacement $^1/_8$" bead, 6x48 (**$2.40**); Xpert Mid Rib in tapered carrier (ivory only) or 3x56 threaded shank (gold only), **$3.50**; Hi and Lo Blok sights with 6x48 thread, gold or ivory (**$3.50**) or Sun Spot Orange (**$4.50**). From Marble Arms.

SLUG SIGHTS

Made of non-marring black nylon, front and rear sights stretch over and lock onto the barrel. Sights are low profile with blaze orange front blade. Adjustable for windage and elevation. For plain-barrel (non-ribbed) guns in 12, 16 and 20 gauge. From Innovision Ent.

Price: **$9.95**

WILLIAMS GUIDE BEAD SIGHT

Fits all shotguns, $^1/_8$" ivory, red or gold bead. Screws into existing sight hole. Various thread sizes and shank lengths. Price **$4.50**

Sight Attachments

FREELAND LENS ADAPTER

Fits $1^1/_8$" O.D. prescription ground lens to all standard tube and receiver sights for shooting without glasses. Price without lens **$66.50**

Clear lens ground to prescription **$24.00**

Yellow or green prescription lens **$24.00**

MERIT IRIS SHUTTER DISC

Eleven clicks gives 12 different apertures. No. 3 Disc (**$50.00**) and Master, primarily target types, 0.22" to .125"; No. 4, $^1/_2$" dia. hunting type, .025" to .155". Available for all popular sights. The Master Disc, with flexible rubber light shield, is particularly adapted to extension, scope height, and tang sights. All Merit Deluxe models have internal click springs; are hand fitted to minimum tolerance.

Master Deluxe **$60.00**

No. 4 Hunting Disc **$40.00**

MERIT LENS DISC

Similar to Merit Iris Shutter (Model 3 or Master) but incorporates provision for mounting prescription lens integrally. Lens may be obtained locally from your optician. Sight disc is $^7/_{16}$" wide (Mod. 3), or $^3/_4$" wide (Master). Model 3 Deluxe. Price **$63.00**

Master Deluxe **$74.00**

MERIT OPTICAL ATTACHMENT

For revolver and pistol shooters, instantly attached by rubber suction cup to regular or shooting glasses. Any aperture .020" to .156". Price, Deluxe (swings aside) **$60.00**

WILLIAMS APERTURES

Standard thread, fits most sights. Regular series $^3/_8$" to $^1/_2$" O.D., .050" to .125" hole. "Twilight" series has white reflector ring. .093" to .125" inner hole. Price, regular series . . . **$4.05**. Twilight series **$5.55**

Wide open $^5/_{16}$" aperture for shotguns fits 5-D and Foolproof sights. Price **$7.15**

Maker and Model	Magn.	Field at 100 Yds. (feet)	Relative Brightness	Eye Relief (in.)	Length (in.)	Tube Diam. (in.)	W&E Adjust.	Weight (ozs.)	Price	Other Data
Action Arms										
Micro-Dot										
1.5-4.5x LER	1.5-4.5	80-26	—	12-24	8.8	1	Int.	9.5	$265.00	Variable intensity LED red aiming dot. Average battery life up to 500 hours. Waterproof, nitrogen filled aluminum tube. Fits most standard 1" rings. [1]Also available in Pro V 45° for left or right-side positioning of battery pack. Same price.
1.5-4.5x	1.5-4.5	80-26	—	3	9.8	1	Int.	10.5	270.00	
2-7x	2-7	54-18	—	3	11	1	Int.	12.1	290.00	
3-9x	3-9	40-14	—	3	12.2	1	Int.	13.3	295.00	
Ultra-Dot	—	—	—	—	5.1	1	Int.	4.0	195.00	
ADCO										
Mark V	0	—	—	—	5	1	Int.	6	169.00	Mark V for rifles, handguns, shotguns. Projects red dot aiming point. Dot size 1 1/2" @ 100 yds. Pro V intended for handguns. Dot size less than 1 1/2" @ 100 yds. Both waterproof. Battery life 50-10,000 hours. Pro V Nickel—$209.00. All come with 1" extension tube for long or short action mounting. Imported by ADCO Int'l.
Pro V	0	—	—	—	4.5	1	Int.	3.9	199.00	
Aimpoint										
AP 1000[1]	0	—	—	—	6	—	Int.	7.8	179.95	Illuminates red dot in field of view. No parallax (dot does not need to be centered). Unlimited field of view and eye relief. On/off, adj. intensity. Dot covers 3" @ 100 yds. Mounts avail. for all sights and scopes. [1]Clamps to Weaver-type bases. Available in blue (AP1000-B) or stainless (AP1000-S) finish. 3x scope attachment (for rifles only), $94.95. [2]Requires 1" rings. Black or stainless finish. 3x scope attachment (for rifles only). $99.95. From Aimpoint. Made in Sweden.
Series 3000 Short[2]	0	—	—	—	5	1	Int.	5.5	229.95	
Series 2000 Long[2]	0	—	—	—	7.25	1	Int.	6	229.95	
Armson										
O.E.G.	0	—	—	—	5 1/8	1	Int.	4.3	159.90	Shows red dot aiming point. No batteries needed. Standard model fits 1" ring mounts (not incl.). Other models available for many popular shotguns, para-military rifles and carbines. [1]Daylight Only Sight with 3/8" dovetail mount for 22s. Does not contain tritium. Also avail. as 22 D/N (Day-Night) with tritium, $125.90. From Armson.
22 DOS[1]	0	—	—	—	3 3/4	—	Int.	3.0	91.95	
Armsport										
415	4	19	13.7	3.5	11.5	3/4	Int.	6	22.00	[1]Duplex reticle. Crosshair reticle, $90. 4x20, $79, 4x32, $82 (Duplex). [2]Parallax adjustment. [3]For blackpowder rifles. Polished brass tube with mounts. 4x32 W.A., 4x40 W.A., 6x40 W.A. also avail. Contact Armsport for full details.
3720	3-7	22.5-9.5	43.5-8.1	2.4	11	3/4	Int.	8.4	56.00	
2 1/2x32	2.5	32	163.8	3.7	12	1	Int.	9.3	86.00	
4x40[1]	4	29	100	3.5	12.5	1	Int.	9	97.00	
6x32	6	17.8	28	3.2	12	1	Int.	9	86.00	
1.5-4.5 x 32	1.5-4.5	55.1-20.4	707.6-64	4-3.1	11.8	1	Int.	14.1	124.00	
2-7x32	2-7	50-19	81-22	3.1-2.9	12.2	1	Int.	13.8	124.00	
3-9x40	3-9	35.8-12.7	176.9-19.4	3.1-2.9	13	1	Int.	15.2	131.00	
4-12x40 WA[2]	4-12	31-11	36-10.9	2.9-2.8	14.7	1	Int.	16.4	245.00	
4x15 BP-1[3]	4	19	13	3.5	32	3/4	Int.	44	110.00	
Bausch & Lomb										
2x Handgun	2	22.5	—	10-24	8.4	1	Int.	6.7	322.95	All except Target scopes have 1/4-minute click adjustments; Target scopes have 1/8-minute adjustments with standard turrets and expanded turret knobs. Target scopes come with sunshades, screw-on lens caps. Contact Bushnell for details.
4x Handgun	4	25	—	10-20	8.4	1	Int.	7.0	333.95	
4x Balfor Compact	4	25	—	3.3	10.0	1	Int.	10.0	356.95	
1.5-6x	1.5-6	75-18	294-18.4	3.3	10.6	1	Int.	10.5	533.95	
2-8x Balvar Compact	2-8	51-13	—	3.5	10.0	1	Int.	11.5	467.95	
3-9x40	3-9	36-12	—	3.2	13.0	1	Int.	16.2	500.95	
2.5-10x Balvar	2.5-10	43.5-11	—	3.3	13.8	1	Int.	13	556.95	
6-24x Varmint	6-24	18-4.5	66.1-4.2	3.1	16.6	1	Int.	20.1	600.95	
■ 6x-24x Target	6-24	18-4.5	—	3.3	16.9	1	Int.	20.1	733.95	
■ 12x-32x40	12-32	—	—	3.2	13.5	1	Int.	18.9	778.95	
■ 24x Target	24	4.7	—	3.2	15.2	1	Int.	15.7	722.95	
■ 36x Target	36	3.5	—	3.2	15.2	1	Int.	15.7	722.95	
Beeman										
Blue Ring 20[1]	1.5	14	150	11-16	8.3	3/4	Int.	3.6	49.95	All scopes have 5-pt. reticle, all glass, fully coated lenses. [1]Pistol scope; cast mounts included. [2]Pistol scope; silhouette knobs. [3]Rubber armor coating; built-in double adj. mount, parallax-free setting. [4]Objective focus; built-in double-adj. mount; matte finish. [5]Objective focus. [6]Has 8 lenses; objective focus; milled mounts included. [7]Includes cast mounts. [8]Objective focus; silhouette knobs; matte finish. [9]Has 9 lenses; objective focus. [10]Also in "L" models with reticle lighted by ambient light or tiny add-on illuminator. Lighted models slightly higher priced. Imported by Beeman.
Blue Ribbon 25[2]	2	19	150	10-24	9 1/16	1	Int.	7.4	129.95	
SS-1[3]	2.5	30	61	3.25	5 1/2	1	Int.	7	179.95	
SS-2[4,10]	3	34.5	74	3.5	6.8	1.38	Int.	13.6	225.00	
Blue Ribbon 50R[5]	2.5	33	245	3.5	12	1	Int.	11.8	169.98	
Blue Ring 35R[6]	3	25	67	2.5	11 1/4	3/4	Int.	5.1	69.98	
30A[7]	4	21	21	2	10.2	3/4	Int.	4.5	36.95	
Blue Ribbon 66R[8]	2-7	62-16	384-31	3	11.4	1	Int.	14.9	239.95	
Blue Ring 45R[9]	3-7	26-12	67-9	2.5	10 5/8	3/4	Int.	6	99.95	
Blue Ring 49R[5]	4	30	64	3	11.8	1	Int.	11.3	69.95	
MS-1	4	23	30	3.5	7.5	1	Int.	8	199.95	
SS-3[4]	1.5-4	44.6-24.6	172-24	3	5.75	7/8	Int.	8.5	250.00	
Blue Ribbon 67R[8]	3-9	435-15	265-29	3	14.4	1	Int.	15.2	349.00	
Blue Ribbon 68R[8]	4-12	30.5-11	150-13.5	3	14.4	1	Int.	15.2	379.95	
Blue Ribbon 54R[5]	4	29	96	3.5	12	1	Int.	12.3	169.98	
SS-2[4,10]	4	24.6	41	5	7	1.38	Int.	13.7	250.00	
Burrls										
Fullfield										
1 1/2x	1.6	62	—	3 1/4	10 1/4	1	Int.	9.0	187.95	All scopes avail. in Plex reticle. Steel-on-steel click adjustments. [1]Dot reticle $13 extra. [2]Post crosshair reticle $13 extra. [3]Matte satin finish $11 extra. [4]Available with parallax adjustment $28 extra (standard on 10x, 12x, 4-12x, 6-18x and 3-12x Signature). [5]Silver Safari finish $20 extra. [6]Avail. with Fine Plex reticle. [7]Sunshade avail. [8]Avail. with Fine Plex reticle. [9]Available with German three-post reticle. [10]Signature Series available in Silver Safari finish, except 3-
2 1/2x	2.5	55	—	3 1/4	10 1/4	1	Int.	9.0	197.95	
4x[1,2,3]	3.75	36	—	3 1/4	11 1/4	1	Int.	11.5	208.95	
6x[1,3]	5.8	23	—	3 1/4	13	1	Int.	12.0	225.95	
10x[1,4,6,7,8]	9.8	12	—	3 1/4	15	1	Int.	15	275.95	
12x[1,4,6,7,8]	11.8	10.5	—	3 1/4	15	1	Int.	15	282.95	
1 3/4-5x[1,2]	1.7-4.6	66-25	—	3 1/4	10 7/8	1	Int.	13	250.95	

Maker and Model	Magn.	Field at 100 Yds. (feet)	Relative Bright-ness	Eye Relief (in.)	Length (in.)	Tube Diam. (in.)	W&E Adjust-ments	Weight (ozs.)	Price	Other Data
Burris (cont'd.)										12x — 4x, **$332.95**, 6x, **$352.95**, 3-9x, **$405.95**. LER = Long Eye Relief; IER = Intermediate Eye Relief; XER = Extra Eye Relief. From Burris.
2-7x[1,2,3]	2.5-6.8	47-18	—	3 1/4	12	1	Int.	14	276.95	
3-9x[1,2,3]	3.3-8.7	38-15	—	3 1/4	12 5/8	1	Int.	15	291.95	
4-12x[1,4,8]	4.4-11.8	27-10	—	3 1/4	15	1	Int.	18	342.95	
6-18x[1,4,6,7,8]	6.5-17.6	16-7	—	3 1/4	15.8	1	Int.	18.5	355.95	
Mini Scopes										
4x[4,5]	3.6	24	—	3 3/4-5	8 1/4	1	Int.	7.8	165.95	
6x[1,4]	5.5	17	—	3 3/4-5	9	1	Int.	8.2	181.95	
2-7x	2.5-6.9	32-14	—	3 3/4-5	12	1	Int.	10.5	225.95	
3-9x[5]	3.6-8.8	25-11	—	3 3/4-5	12 5/8	1	Int.	11.5	230.95	
4-12x[1,4,6]	4.5-11.6	19-8	—	3 3/4-4	15	1	Int.	15	306.95	
Signature Series										
4x	4.0	30	—	3	12 1/8	1	Int.	14	324.95	
6x	6.0	20	—	3	12 1/8	1	Int.	14	339.95	
3-9x	3.3-8.8	36-14	—	3	12 7/8	1	Int.	15.5	392.95	
3-12x	3.3-11.7	34-9	—	3	14 1/4	1	Int.	21	491.95	
Handgun										
1 1/2-4x LER[1,5]	1.6-3.8	16-11	—	11-25	10 1/4	1	Int.	11	261.95	
2 1/2-7x LER[4,5]	2.7-6.7	12-7.5	—	11-28	12	1	Int.	12.5	275.95	
1x LER[1]	1.1	27	—	10-24	8 3/4	1	Int.	6.8	156.95	
2x LER[4,5,6]	1.7	21	—	10-24	8 3/4	1	Int.	6.8	163.95	
3x LER[4,6]	2.7	17	—	10-20	8 7/8	1	Int.	6.8	176.95	
4x LER[1,4,5,6]	3.7	11	—	10-22	9 5/8	1	Int.	9.0	184.95	
5x LER[1,4,6]	4.5	8.7	—	12-22	10 7/8	1	Int.	9.2	198.95	
7x IER[1,4,5,6]	6.5	6.5	—	10-16	11 1/4	1	Int.	10	213.95	
10x IER[1,4,6]	9.5	4	—	8-12	13 1/2	1	Int.	14	265.95	
Scout Scope										
1 1/2x XER[3,9]	1.5	22	—	7-18	9	1	Int.	7.3	165.95	
2 3/4x XER[3,9]	2.7	15	—	7-14	9 3/8	1	Int.	7.5	170.95	
Bushnell										
Armor Site 3-9x40	3-9	39-13	—	3.3	12	1	Int.	12.5	444.95	All Scope Chief, Banner and Custom models come with Multi-X reticle, with or without BDC (bullet drop compensator) that eliminates hold-over. Prismatic Rangefinder (PRF) on some models. Contact Bushnell for data on full line. Prices include BDC — deduct $5 if not wanted. Add $30 for PRF. BDC feature available in all Banner models, except 2.5x. [1]Has battery powered lighted reticle. [2]Also in 40mm. **Only selected models shown.** [3]For air rifle, silhouette shooting; range focus adj.; 1/4-MOA clicks. Contact Bushnell for complete details.
Scope Chief VI	4	29	96	3 1/2	12	1	Int.	9.3	189.95	
Scope Chief VI	3-9	35-12.6	267-30	3.3	12.6	1	Int.	14.3	296.95	
Scope Chief VI	3-9	39-13	241-26.5	3.3	12.1	1	Int.	13	369.95	
Scope Chief VI	2 1/2-8	45-14	247-96	3.3	11.2	1	Int.	12.1	262.95	
Scope Chief VI	1 1/2-4 1/2	73.7-24.5	267-30	3.5-3.5	9.6	1	Int.	9.5	258.95	
Scope Chief VI	4-12	29-10	150-17	3.2	13.5	1	Int.	17	367.95	
Sportview Rangemaster 3-9x	3-9	38-12	—	3.5	11.75	1	Int.	10	129.95	
■ Sportview Rangemaster 4-12x	4-12	27-9	—	3.2	13.5	1	Int.	14	153.95	
Sportview Standard 4x	4	28	—	4	11.75	1	Int.	9.5	67.95	
Sportview Standard 3-9x	3-9	38-12	—	3.5	11.75	1	Int.	10	92.95	
Banner 22 Rimfire 4x	4	28	—	3	11.9	1	Int.	8	78.95	
Banner 22 Rimfire 3-7x	3-7	29-13	—	2.5	10	3/4	Int.	6.5	89.95	
Banner 3-9x56	3-9	39-12.5	—	3.5	14.4	1	Int.	18.4	302.95	
Banner 10x[3]	10	12	—	3	14.7	1	Int.	14.3	289.95	
Banner Lite-Site 1.5-6x[1]	1.5-6	60-15	—	3.2	9.8	1	Int.	12.4	347.95	
Banner Lite-Site 3-9x[1]	3-9	36-12	—	3.3	13.6	1	Int.	14	347.95	
Banner Trophy WA 1.75-5x	1.75-5	68.5-24.5	—	3.2	10.4	1	Int.	10.2	167.95	
Banner Trophy WA 4x	4	34.2	—	3.4	12.4	1	Int.	11.9	144.95	
Banner Trophy WA 3-9x	3-9	39-13	—	3.3	11.8	1	Int.	12.9	173.95	
Banner Shotgun 2.5x	2.5	45	—	3.5	10.9	1	Int.	8	100.95	
Banner Standard 4x	4	29	—	3.5	12	1	Int.	10	136.95	
Banner Standard 6x[2]	6	19.5	—	3	13.5	1	Int.	11.5	189.95	
Banner Standard 3-9x	3-9	43-14	—	3	12.1	1	Int.	14	167.95	
Banner Standard 4-12x	4-12	29-10	—	3.2	13.5	1	Int.	15.5	269.95	
Charles Daly										
4x32	4	28	—	3.25	11.75	1	Int.	9.5	65.00	[1]For shotgun use. [2]Pistol scopes. From Outdoor Sports Headquarters.
4x40 WA	4	36	—	3.25	13	1	Int.	11.5	95.00	
6x40 WA	6	23	—	3	12.75	1	Int.	15	100.00	
2.5x32	2.5	47	—	3	12.25	1	Int.	10	75.00	
2-7x32 WA	2-7	56-17	—	3	11.5	1	Int.	12	119.00	
3-9x40	3-9	35-14	—	3	12.5	1	Int.	11.25	77.00	
3-9x40 WA	3-9	36-13	—	3	12.75	1	Int.	12.5	115.00	
4-16x40	4-16	25-7	—	3	14.25	1	Int.	16.75	130.00	
1-3.5x20[1]	1-3.5	91-31	—	3.5	9.75	1	Int.	16.25	158.00	
2x20[2]	2	16	—	16-25	8.75	1	Int.	6.5	105.00	
4x28[2]	4	6.5	—	16-25	9.3	1	Int.	8	105.00	
aus Jena										
ZF4x32-M	4	32	—	3.5	10.8	26mm	Int.	10	350.00	Fixed power scopes have 26mm alloy tubes, variables, 30mm alloy; rings avail. from importer. Also avail. with rail mount. Multi-coated lenses. Waterproof and fogproof. 1/3-min. clicks. Choice of nine reticles. Imported from E. Germany by Europtik, Ltd.
ZF6x42-M	6	22	—	3.5	12.6	26mm	Int.	13	410.00	
ZF8x56-M	8	17	—	3.5	14	26mm	Int.	17	470.00	
VZF1.5-6x42-M	1.5-6	67.8-22	—	3.5	12.6	30mm	Int.	14	595.00	
UZF3-12x56-M	3-12	30-11	—	3.5	15	30mm	Int.	18	665.00	
Kahles										
2.5x20[1]	2.5	61	—	3.25	9.6	1	Int.	12.7	450.00	[1]Steel only. [2]Lightweight model weighs 11 oz. [3]Aluminum only. [4]Lightweight model weighs 16 oz. [5]Lightweight model weighs 12.7 oz. [6]Lightweight model weighs 16 oz. [7]Lightweight model weighs 15.5 oz. [8]Lightweight model weighs 18 oz. Lightweight models priced slightly higher. Imported by Swarovski America, Ltd.
4x32[2]	4	33	—	3.25	11.3	1	Int.	15	465.00	
7x56[3]	7	20	—	3.25	14.4	1	Int.	16	610.00	
8x56[4]	8	17.1	—	3.25	14.4	1	Int.	23	595.00	
1.4-4.5x20[5]	1.1-4.5	79-29.5	—	3.25	10.5	30mm	Int.	15	560.00	

CAUTION: PRICES CHANGE. CHECK AT GUNSHOP.

Maker and Model	Magn.	Field at 100 Yds. (feet)	Relative Brightness	Eye Relief (in.)	Length (in.)	Tube Diam. (in.)	W&E Adjustments	Weight (ozs.)	Price	Other Data
Kahles (cont'd.)										
1.5-6x42[6]	1.5-6	61-21	—	3.25	12.6	30mm	Int.	20	625.00	
2.2-9x42[7]	2.2-9	39.5-15	—	3.25	13.3	30mm	Int.	20.4	765.00	
3-12x56[8]	3-12	30-11	—	3.25	15.25	30mm	Int.	25	835.00	
K-7FR4 (6x42)	6	23	—	3.25	15.5	1	Int.	17.5	860.00	
Kilham										
Hutson Handgunner II	1.7	8	—	—	5½	7/8	Int.	5.1	119.95	Unlimited eye relief; internal click adjustments; crosshair reticle. Fits Thompson/Center rail mounts, for S&W K, N, Ruger Blackhawk, Super, Super Single-Six, Contender.
Hutson Handgunner	3	8	—	10-12	6	7/8	Int.	5.3	119.95	
Laser Aim										
LA1	—	—	—	—	3.93	.812	Int.	4	298.00	Projects high intensity beam of laser light up to 300 yards. Dot size at 100 yards is 1". Adjustable for w. & e. Includes rings to mount on scope rail, battery charger plugs into cigarette lighter. Optional 110V charger, $19.95. From Emerging Technologies, Inc.
Laserscope										
FA-6	—	—	—	—	6.2	—	Int.	11	349.95	Projects high intensity beam of laser light onto target as an aiming point. Adj. for w. & e. FA-6 uses two 9V, others use eight AA batteries. Comes with rings, switch, fastener. From Laser Devices, Inc.
FA-9	—	—	—	—	12	—	Int.	16	399.95	
FA-9P	—	—	—	—	9	—	Int.	14	399.95	
Lasersight										
LS45	0	—	—	—	7.5	—	Int.	8.5	399.00	Projects a highly visible beam of concentrated laser light onto the target. Adjustable for w. & e. Visible up to 500 yds. at night. For handguns, rifles, shotguns. Uses two standard 9V batteries. From Imatronic Lasersight.
Leatherwood										
ART II	3.0-8.8	31-12	—	3.5	13.9	1	Int.	42	750.00	Compensates for bullet drop via external circular cam. Matte gray finish. Designed specifically for the M1A/M-14 rifle. Quick Detachable model for rifles with Weaver-type bases. From North American Specialties.
Leupold										
M8-2X EER[1]	1.8	22.0	—	12-24	8.1	1	Int.	6.8	194.15	Constantly centered reticles, choice of Duplex, tapered CPC, Leupoid Dot, Crosshair and Dot. CPC and Dot reticles extra. [1]2x and 4x scopes have from 12"-24" of eye relief and are suitable for handguns, top ejection arms and muzzleloaders. [2]3x9 Compact, 6x Compact, 12x, 3x9, 3.5x10 and 6.5x20 come with Adjustable Objective. [3]Target scopes have 1-min. divisions with ¼ min. clicks, and Adjustable Objectives. 50-ft. Focus Adaptor available for indoor target ranges, **$44.80**. Sunshade available for all Adjustable Objective scopes, **$13.05**. [4]Also available in matte finish for about **$20.00** extra. [5]Dot or Duplex; focused at 300 yds. with A.O. **$368.40**.
M8-2X EER Silver[1]	1.8	22.0	—	12-24	8.1	1	Int.	6.8	215.55	
M8-4X EER[1]	3.5	9.5	—	12-24	8.4	1	Int.	7.6	237.05	
M8-4X EER Silver[1]	3.5	9.5	—	12-24	8.4	1	Int.	8.5	258.50	
M8-2.5X Compact	2.3	42	—	4.3	8.5	1	Int.	7.4	218.00	
M8-4X Compact	3.6	26.5	—	4.1	10.3	1	Int.	8.5	242.20	
2-7x Compact	2.5-6.6	41.7-16.5	—	3.8-3.0	9.9	1	Int.	8.5	308.00	
6x Compact & A.O.	5.7	16	—	3.9	10.7	1	Int.	8.5	299.20	
3-9x Compact & A.O.	3.2-8.5	34.5-13.5	—	3.8-3.1	11	1	Int.	9.5	369.65	
M8-4X[4]	3.6	28	—	4.4	11.4	1	Int.	8.8	244.20	
M8-6X	5.9	18.0	—	4.3	11.4	1	Int.	9.9	260.70	
M8-8X[2]	7.8	14.5	—	4.0	12.5	1	Int.	13.0	347.60	
M8-8x36[5]	7.7	14	—	3.7	11.8	1	Int.	10	347.60	
M8-12X[2]	11.6	9.2	—	4.2	13.0	1	Int.	13.5	359.15	
6.5x20 Target AO	6.5-19.2	14.8-5.7	—	5.3-3.7	14.2	1	Int.	16	581.50	
M8-12X Target[3]	11.6	9.2	—	4.2	13.0	1	Int.	14.5	437.95	
M8-24X[3]	24.0	4.7	—	3.2	13.6	1	Int.	14.5	623.20	
M8-36X[3]	36.0	3.2	—	3.4	13.9	1	Int.	15.5	623.20	
Vari-X-II 2x7	2.5-6.6	44.0-19.0	—	4.1-3.7	10.7	1	Int.	10.4	317.15	
Vari-X-II 3x9[1,4]	3.5-9.0	32.0-13.5	—	4.1-3.7	12.3	1	Int.	14.5	340.70	
Vari-X-III 1.5x5	1.5-4.6	66.0-24.0	—	4.7-3.5	9.4	1	Int.	9.3	368.70	
Vari-X-III 2.5x8[4]	2.7-7.9	38.0-14.0	—	4.2-3.4	11.3	1	Int.	11.0	415.85	
Vari-X-III 3.5x10	3.4-9.9	29.5-10.5	—	4.6-3.6	12.4	1	Int.	13.0	435.05	
Vari-X-III 3.5x10[2]	3.4-9.9	29.5-10.5	—	4.6-3.6	12.4	1	Int.	14.4	472.50	
Vari-X-III 6.5x20[2]	6.5-19.2	14.8-5.7	—	5.3-3.7	14.2	1	Int.	16	515.25	
Mirador										
RXW 4x40[1]	4	37	—	3.8	12.4	1	Int.	12	179.95	[1]Wide Angle scope. Multi-coated objective lens. Nitrogen filled; waterproof; shockproof. From Mirador Optical Corp.
RXW 1.5-5x20[1]	1.5-5	46-17.4	—	4.3	11.1	1	Int.	10	188.95	
RXW 3-9x40	3-9	43-14.5	—	3.1	12.9	1	Int.	13.4	251.95	
Nikon										
4x40	4	26.7	—	3.5	11.7	1	Int.	11.7	263.00	Super multi-coated lenses and blackening of all internal metal parts for maximum light gathering capability; positive ¼ MOA; fogproof; waterproof; shockproof; lustre and matte finish. From Nikon Inc.
1.5-4.5x20	1.5-4.5	67.8-22.5	—	3.7-3.2	10.1	1	Int.	9.5	327.00	
2-7x32	2-7	46.7-13.7	—	3.9-3.3	11.3	1	Int.	11.3	374.00	
3-9x40	3-9	33.8-11.3	—	3.6-3.2	12.5	1	Int.	12.5	411.00	
4-12x40	4-12	25.7-8.6	—	3.6-3.2	14	1	Int.	16.6	512.00	
2x20 P	2	22	—	26.4	8.1	1	Int.	6.3	207.00	
Pentax										
1.5-5x	1.5-5	66-25	—	3-3¼	11	1	Int.	13	300.00	Multi-coated lenses, fogproof, waterproof, nitrogen filled. Penta-Plex reticle. Click ¼-MOA adjustments. Matte finish **$20.00** extra. Imported by Pentax Corp.
4x	4	35	—	3¼	11.6	1	Int.	12.2	260.00	
6x	6	20	—	3¼	13.4	1	Int.	13.5	300.00	
2-7x	2-7	42.5-17	—	3-3¼	12	1	Int.	14	355.00	
3-9x	3-9	33-13.5	—	3-3¼	13	1	Int.	15	370.00	
3-9x Mini	3-9	26.5-10.5	—	3¾	10.4	1	Int.	13	315.00	
Pistol										
2x LER	2	21	—	10-24	8¾	1	Int.	6.8	220.00	
1.5-4x LER	1.5-4	16-11	—	11-25	10	1	Int.	11	350.00	
RWS										
100S	4	—	—	8	10½	3/4	—	7	47.00	Air gun scopes. All have Dyna-Plex reticle. Imported from Japan by Dynamit Nobel of America.
150S	3-7	—	—	8	10½	3/4	—	8	60.00	
200S	4	—	—	8	11¾	7/8	—	11½	70.00	
250S	3-7	—	—	8	11¾	7/8	—	12	80.00	

CAUTION: PRICES CHANGE. CHECK AT GUNSHOP.

Maker and Model	Magn.	Field at 100 Yds. (feet)	Relative Brightness	Eye Relief (in.)	Length (in.)	Tube Diam. (in.)	W&E Adjustments	Weight (ozs.)	Price	Other Data
RWS (cont'd.)										
300	4	—	—	8	12¾	1		11	110.00	
350	4	—	—	8	10	1		10	95.00	
400	2-7	—	—	8	12¾	1		12	150.00	
800	1.5	—	—	28	8¾	1		6	100.00	
CS-10	2.5	—	—	8	5¾	1		7	100.00	
Redfield										
Ultimate Illuminator 4x	4.2	23	—	3-3.5	15.1	1	Int.	20	535.95	
Ultimate Illuminator 3-9x	3.4-9.1	27-9	—	3-3.5	15.1	1	Int.	20.5	625.95	
Ultimate Illuminator 3-12x[6]	2.9-11.7	27-10.5	—	3-3½	15.4	30mm	Int.	23	714.95	
Illuminator Trad. 3-9x	2.9-8.7	33-11	—	3½	12¾	1	Int.	17	435.95	
Illuminator Widefield 4x	4.2	28	—	3-3.5	11.7	1	Int.	13.5	375.95	
Illuminator Widefield 2-7x	2.0-6.8	56-17	—	3-3.5	11.7	1	Int.	13.5	428.95	
Illuminator Widefield 3-9x[*2]	2.9-8.7	38-13	—	3½	12¾	1	Int.	17	482.95	
Tracker 4x[3]	3.9	28.9	—	3½	11.02	1	Int.	9.8	141.95	
Tracker 2-7x[3]	2.3-6.9	36.6-12.2	—	3½	12.20	1	Int.	11.6	182.95	
Tracker 3-9x[3]	3.0-9.0	34.4-11.3	—	3½	14.96	1	Int.	13.4	204.95	
Traditional 4x ¾"	4	24½	27	3½	9⅜	¾	Int.	—	132.95	
Traditional 2½x	2½	43	64	3½	10¼	1	Int.	8½	165.95	
Golden Five Star 4x[4]	4	28.5	58	3.75	11.3	1	Int.	9.75	196.95	
Golden Five Star 6x[4]	6	18	40	3.75	12.2	1	Int.	11.5	215.95	
Golden Five Star 2-7x[4]	2.4-7.4	42-14	207-23	3-3.75	11.25	1	Int.	12	255.95	
Golden Five Star 3-9x[4]	3.0-9.1	34-11	163-18	3-3.75	12.50	1	Int.	13	272.95	
Golden Five Star 4-12xA.O.[*4]	3.9-11.4	27-9	112-14	3-3.75	13.8	1	Int.	16	351.95	
Golden Five Star 6-18xA.O.[*4]	6.1-18.1	18.6	50-6	3-3.75	14.3	1	Int.	18	371.95	
Compact Scopes										
Golden Five Star Compact 4x	3.8	28	—	3.5	9.75	1	Int.	8.8	192.95	
Golden Five Star Compact 6x	6.3	17.6	—	3.5	10.70	1	Int.	9.5	214.95	
Golden Five Star Compact 2-7x	2.4-7.1	40-16	—	3-3.5	9.75	1	Int.	9.8	254.95	
Golden Five Star Compact 3-9x	3.3-9.1	32-11.25	—	3-3.5	10.7	1	Int.	10.5	271.95	
Golden Five Star Compact 4-12x	4.1-12.4	22.4-8.3	—	3-3.5	12	1	Int.	13	342.95	
Pistol Scopes										
2½xMP[1]	2.5	9	64	14-19	9.8	1	Int.	10.5	204.95	
4xMP[1]	3.6	9	—	12-22	9¹¹⁄₁₆	1	Int.	11.1	215.95	
Golden Five Star 1-4x	1.3-4.0	80-26	—	3-3.75	9.50	1	Int.	10.25	244.95	
2-6x[5]	2-5.5	25-7	—	10-18	10.4	1	Int.	11	255.95	
Widefield										
Low Profile Compact										
Widefield 4xLP Compact	3.7	33	—	3.5	9.35	1	Int.	10	239.95	
Widefield 3-9x LP Compact	3.3-9	37.0-13.7	—	3-3.5	10.20	1	Int.	13	305.95	
Low Profile Scopes										
Widefield 2¾xLP	2¾	55½	69	3½	10½	1	Int.	8	222.95	
Widefield 4xLP	3.6	37½	84	3½	11½	1	Int.	10	249.95	
Widefield 6xLP	5.5	23	—	3½	12¾	1	Int.	11	271.95	
Widefield 1¾x5xLP	1¾-5	70-27	136-21	3½	10¾	1	Int.	11½	306.95	
Widefield 2x7xLP*	2-7	49-19	144-21	3½	11¾	1	Int.	13	371.95	
Widefield 3x-9xLP*	3-9	39-15	112-18	3½	12½	1	Int.	14	350.95	
Schmidt & Bender										
Vari-M 1¼-4x20[1]	1¼-4	96-16	—	3¼	10.4	30mm	Int.	12.3	625.00	
Vari-M 1½-6x42	1½-6	60-19.5	—	3¼	12.2	30mm	Int.	17.5	695.00	
Vari-M 2½-10x56	2½-10	37.5-12	—	3¼	14.6	30mm	Int.	21.9	825.00	
All Steel 1½x15[2]	1½	90	—	3¼	10	1	Int.	11.8	455.00	
All Steel 4x36[2]	4	30	—	3¼	11.4	1	Int.	14	490.00	
All Steel 6x42[2]	6	21	—	3¼	13.2	1	Int.	17.3	515.00	
All Steel 8x56[2]	8	16.5	—	3¼	14.8	1	Int.	21.9	580.00	
■ All Steel 12x42[3]	12	16.5	—	3¼	13	1	Int.	17.9	565.00	
All Steel 4-12x42	4-12	34.7-12	—	3¼	13.25	30mm	Int.	23	785.00	
Shepherd										
3940-E	3-9	43.5-15	178-20	3.3	13	1	Int.	17	444.00	
310-2[1]	3-10	35.3-11.6	178-16	3-3.75	12.8	1	Int.	18	376.00	
27-2[2]	2.5-7.5	42-14	164-18	2.5-3	11.6	1	Int.	16.3	349.00	
Simmons										
1001[3]	4	15	—	3.4	8.1	¾	Int.	3.5	32.25	
1002 Rimfire[1]	4	23	—	3	11.5	¾	Int.	6	11.75	
1004 Rimfire[2]	3-7	22.5-9.5	—	3	11	¾	Int.	8.4	39.00	
1013	1-4	63.1-15.7	—	3.5	9.8	1	Int.	8.8	136.25	
1022	4	36	—	3.5	11.6	1	Int.	10.0	83.00	

*Accutrac feature avail. on these scopes at extra cost. Traditionals have round lenses. 4-Plex reticle is standard. [1]"Magnum Proof." Specially designed for magnum and auto pistols. Uses "Double Dovetail" mounts. Also in brushed aluminum finish, 2½x **$211.95**, 4x **$222.95**. [2]With matte finish **$468.95**. [3]Also available with matte finish at extra cost. [4]All Golden Five Star scopes come with Butler Creek flip-up lens covers. [5]Black anodized finish. Also in nickel finish, **$277.95**. [6]56mm adj. objective; European #4 reticle; comes with 30mm steel rings with Rotary Dovetail System, hardwood box. ¼-min. click adj. Also in matte finish, **$723.95**.

[1]All steel. [2]Black chrome finish. [3]For silhouette and varmint shooting. Choice of nine reticles. 30-year warranty. All have ⅓-min. click adjustments, centered reticles, nitrogen filling. Most models avail. in aluminum with mounting rail. Imported from West Germany by Paul Jaeger, Inc.

[1]Also avail. as 310-MOA, 310-1, 310-E (**$376.00**) with ultra fine crosshair. [2]Also avail. as Model 27-4 for rimfires (**$345.00**). Reticle patterns set for shooter's choice of ballistics. Dual reticle system with instant range finder, bullet drop compensator. Waterproof, nitrogen filled, shockproof. From Shepherd Scope Ltd.

[1]With ring mount. [2]With ring mount. [3]With rings. [4]½-min. dot or Truplex; Truplex reticle also avail. with dot. Sunshade, screw-in lens covers. Parallax adj.; Silhouette knobs; graduated drums. Truplex reticle in all models. All scopes sealed, fogproof, with constantly centered reticles. Imported from Japan by Simmons Out-

CAUTION: PRICES CHANGE. CHECK AT GUNSHOP.

Maker and Model	Magn.	Field at 100 Yds. (feet)	Relative Brightness	Eye Relief (in.)	Length (in.)	Tube Diam. (in.)	W&E Adjustments	Weight (ozs.)	Price	Other Data
Simmons (cont'd.)										door Corp. **Partial listing.** Contact Simmons for complete details. Prices are approximate.
1025 W.A.	6	24.5	—	3	12.4	1	Int.	12	140.25	
1026 W.A.	1½-4½	86-28.9	—	3-3¼	10.6	1	Int.	13.2	152.50	
1027 W.A.	2-7	54.6-18.3	—	3-3¼	12	1	Int	12.8	176.25	
1028	3-9	42-14	—	3.1-2.5	13.1	1	Int.	14.3	141.25	
1044 W.A.	3-10	36.2-10.5	—	3.9-3.3	13.1	1	Int.	16.3	229.75	
1038 Mono Tube	3-9	42-14	—	3-3¼	13.3	1	Int.	13	208.50	
1040 Mono Tube	2-7	54-18	—	3-3¼	13.1	1	Int.	12.9	204.25	
1067	3-9	42-14	216-54	3.3	13	1	Int.	16.2	330.00	
1068	4-12	31-11	121-14	3.9-3.2	14.2	1	Int.	19.1	337.50	
1074	6½-20	18-6	—	3	15	1	Int.	16	259.50	
1075	6½-10	22-12	—	3	15	1	Int.	16	259.50	
1076	15	8	—	3	15	1	Int.	16	223.25	
1078	24	6	—	3	15	1	Int.	16	223.25	
1073 Sil. Airgun	2-7	54.6-18.3	—	3-3¼	12.1	1	Int.	15.7	180.75	
1080 Handgun	2	18	—	10-20	7.1	1	Int.	8.1	124.00	
1084 Handgun[4]	4	9	—	10-20	8.7	1	Int.	9.5	174.50	
1086 Handgun	1-3	37.2-12.1	—	13-27	10.7	1	Int.	10.5	238.25	
1087 Handgun	2-6	16-6	—	13-27	11	1	Int.	10.8	314.25	
1090 Shotgun	1.5	49.9	—	5	6.8	1	Int.	7.0	136.75	
21005 Shotgun	2.5	29	—	4.6	7.1	1	Int.	7.1	74.50	
WT01	4	29	—	3.7	12	1	Int.	9.1	80.25	
WT02	3-9	37-12.7	—	3.1-2.9	12.8	1	Int.	12.8	100.50	
Swarovski Habicht										All models offered in either steel or lightweight alloy tubes except 1.5x20, ZFM 6x42 and Co-
4x32	4	33	—	3¼	11.3	1	Int.	15	500.00	bras. Weights shown are for lightweight ver-
6x42	6	23	—	3¼	12.6	1	Int.	17.9	540.00	sions. Choice of nine constantly centered reti-
8x56	8	17	—	3¼	14.4	1	Int.	23	635.00	cles. Eyepiece recoil mechanism and rubber
1.5-4.5x20	1.5-4.5	74-25.5	—	3.5	9.5	1	Int.	11.3	590.00	ring shield to protect face. Cobra and ZFM also
1.5-6x42	1.5-6	61-21	—	3¼	12.6	30mm	Int.	16	685.00	available in NATO Stanag 2324 mounts. Im-
2.2-9x42	2.2-9	39.5-15	—	3¼	13.3	30mm	Int.	15.5	835.00	ported by Swarovski America Ltd.
3-9x36	3-9	39-13.5	—	3.4	11.9	1	Int.	13	655.00	
3-12x56	3-12	30-11	—	3¼	15.25	1	Int.	18	910.00	
ZFM 6x42	6	23	—	3¼	12.5	1	Int.	18	710.00	
Cobra 1.5-14	1.5	50	—	3.9	7.87	1	Int.	10	550.00	
AL Scopes										
4x32A	4	30	—	3.2	11.5	1	Int.	10.8	450.00	
6x36A	6	21	—	3.2	11.9	1	Int.	11.5	500.00	
3-9x36	3-9	39-13.5	—	3.3	11.9	1	Int.	13	655.00	
Swift										All Swift scopes, with the exception of the 4x15,
600 4x15	4	16.2	—	2.4	11	¾	Int.	4.7	19.75	have Quadraplex reticles and are fogproof and
601 3-7x20	3-7	25-12	—	3-2.9	11	1	Int.	5.6	48.50	waterproof. The 4x15 has crosshair reticle and
650 4x32	4	29	—	3.5	12	1	Int.	9	74.00	is non-waterproof. [1]Available in black or silver
653 4x40WA	4	35.5	—	3.75	12.25	1	Int.	12	96.50	finish — same price.
654 3-9x32	3-9	35.75-12.75	—	3	12.75	1	Int.	13.75	94.50	
656 3-9x40WA	3-9	42.5-13.5	—	2.75	12.75	1	Int.	14	103.50	
657 6x40	6	18	—	3.75	13	1	Int.	10	100.00	
660 4x20	4	25	—	4	11.8	1	Int.	9	79.50	
664 4-12x40	4-12	27-9	—	3-2.8	13.3	1	Int.	14.8	140.00	
665 1.5-4.5x21	1.5-4.5	69-24.5	—	3.5-3	10.9	1	Int.	9.6	102.75	
Pistol Scopes										
661 4x32	4	90	—	10-22	9.2	1	Int.	9.5	108.50	
662 2.5x32	2.5	14.3	—	9-22	8.9	1	Int.	9.3	102.50	
663 2x20[1]	2	18.3	—	9-21	7.2	1	Int.	8.4	103.50	
Tasco										[1]Water, fog & shockproof; fully coated optics;
WA 1-3.5x20 Wide Angle[1,3,10]	1-3½	115-31	400.0-32.4	3½	9¾	1	Int.	10.2	239.95	¼-min. click stops; haze filter caps; lifetime warranty. [2]30/30 range finding reticle. [3]World
WA 4x40 Wide Angle[1,3]	4	36	100.0	3¼	13	1	Int.	11.5	154.95	Class Wide Angle; Supercon multi-coated op-
WA 3-9x40 Wide Angle[1,3]	3-9	43½-15	176.8-19.3	3⅛	12¾	1	Int.	12.5	209.95	tics; Opti-Centered® 30/30 rangefinding reticle; lifetime warranty. [4]Shock-absorbing 30mm
WA 2-7x32 Wide Angle[1,3]	2-7	56-17	256.0-20.2	3¼	11½	1	Int.	12	209.95	tubes; 44 and 52mm objective lenses; Opti- Centered® 30/30 rangefinding reticle. [5]Selec-
WA 1.75-5x20 Wide Angle[1,3]	1¾-5	72-24	129.9-16.0	3	10⅝	1	Int.	9.8	239.95	tive Bi-reticle display — converts from 30/30 to lighted post reticle. [6]Illuminated Opti-Centered
W 3-12x40 MAG-IV[1,2,7]	3-12	33-11	176.8-10.8	3	12⅛	1	Int.	12	159.95	Post Reticle. [7]⅓ greater zoom range. [8]Trajec- tory compensating scopes, Opti-Centered sta-
W 4-16x40 MAG-IV[1,2,7]	4-16	25½-7	100.0-6.2	3	14¼	1	Int.	16.75	209.95	dia reticle. [9]Anodized finish. [10]True one-power scope. [11]Coated optics; crosshair reticle; ring
TR 4-16x40[1,2]	4-16	25½-7	100.0-6.2	3	14¼	1	Int.	16.75	304.95	mounts included to fit most 22, 10mm receiv- ers. [12]Fits Remington 870,110. [13]Electronic dot
W 4x32[1,2,9]	4	28	64.0	3	11¾	1	Int.	9.5	89.95	reticle with rheostat. Coated optics. Adj. for
W 3-9x32[1,2,9]	3-9	35.14	112.3-12.2	3¼	12¾	1	Int.	12.3	109.95	windage and elevation. Waterproof, shock- proof, fogproof. Lithium battery. 3x power
P1x22	1	65-24	—	8-28	7¾	1	Int.	8	209.95	booster avail. Matte black or matte alum. finish.
P2x22	2	26-18	—	10-24	7¾	1	Int.	7.6	209.95	Dot or T-3 reticle. **Contact Tasco for details on**
P4x30	4	7-6	—	12-24	9¾	1	Int.	12.1	279.95	**complete line.**
P6x40	6	5-5½	—	12-23	11	1	Int.	14.2	379.95	
RF 4x15[11]	4	21	13.6	2½	11	¾	Int.	4	18.45	
RF 4x20DS[11]	4	20	25.0	2½	10½	¾	Int.	3.8	27.95	
SG 2.5x32 with Shotgun Mount[1,12]	2½	42	163.8	3¼	11¾	1	Int.	15.7	159.95	
Propoint, II										
PDP1L[13]	1	25-12	—	—	5	30mm	Int.	5.5	349.95	
PDP2[13]	1	25-12	—	—	5	30mm	Int.	5.5	429.95	
Trijicon Spectrum										[1]Self-luminous low-light reticle glows in poor
4x40[1]	4	38	—	3.0	12.2	1	Int.	15.0	389.00	light; allows choice of red, amber or green via a
6x56[1]	6	24	—	3.0	14.1	1	Int.	20.3	439.00	selector ring on objective end. [2]Advanced Com-

CAUTION: PRICES CHANGE. CHECK AT GUNSHOP.

Maker and Model	Magn.	Field at 100 Yds. (feet)	Relative Brightness	Eye Relief (in.)	Length (in.)	Tube Diam. (in.)	W&E Adjustments	Weight (ozs.)	Price	Other Data
Trijicon (cont'd.)										bat Optical Gunsight for AR-15, M-16, with integral mount. [3]Reticle glows only red in poor light. From Armson, Inc.
1-3x20[1]	1-3	94-33	—	3.7-4.9	9.6	1	Int.	13.2	419.00	
3-9x40[1]	3-9	35-14	—	3.3-3.0	13.1	1	Int.	16.0	429.00	
3-9x56[1]	3-9	35-14	—	3.3-3.0	14.2	1	Int.	21.5	498.00	
ACOG[2]	4	37	—	1.5	5.8	—	Int.	9.7	695.00	
4x32 Red[3]	4	29	—	3.3	11.6	1	Int.	10.2	198.00	
Unertl										[1]Dural 1/4 MOA click mounts. Hard coated lenses. Non-rotating objective lens focusing. [2]1/4 MOA click mounts. [3]With target mounts. [4]With calibrated head. [5]Same as 1" Target but without objective lens focusing. [6]Price with 1/4 MOA click mounts. [7]With new Posa mounts. [8]Range focus unit near rear of tube. Price is with Posa mounts. Magnum clamp. With standard mounts and clamp ring $332.00.
■ 1" Target	6,8,10	16-10	17.6-6.25	2	21 1/2	3/4	Ext.	21	181.00	
■ 1 1/4" Target[1]	8,10,12,14	12-16	15.2-5	2	25	3/4	Ext.	21	244.00	
■ 1 1/2" Target	8,10,12,14 16,18,20	11.5-3.2	—	2 1/4	25 1/2	3/4	Ext.	31	275.00	
■ 2" Target[2]	8,10,12, 14,16,18, 24,30,36	8	22.6-2.5	2 1/4	26 1/4	1	Ext.	44	375.00	
■ Varmint, 1 1/4[3]	6,8,10,12	1-7	28-7.1	2 1/2	19 1/2	7/8	Ext.	26	242.00	
■ Ultra Varmint, 2"[4]	8,10 12,15	12.6-7	39.7-11	2 1/2	24	1	Ext.	34	351.00	
Unertl										
■ Small Game[5]	4,6	25-17	19.4-8.4	2 1/4	18	3/4	Ext.	16	138.00	
■ Vulture[6]	8	11.2	29	3-4	15 5/8	1	Ext.	15 1/2	270.00	
	10	10.9	18 1/2	—	16 1/8					
■ Programmer 200[7]	8,10,12, 14,16,18, 20,24,30,36	11.3-4	39-1.9	—	26 1/2	1	Ext.	45	465.00	
■ BV-20[8]	20	8	4.4	4.4	17 7/8	1	Ext.	21 1/4	332.00	
Weatherby										Lumiplex reticle in all models. Blue-black, non-glare finish.
Mark XXII	4	25	50	2.5-3.5	11 3/4	7/8	Int.	9.25	105.00	
Supreme 1 3/4-5x20	1.7-5	66.6-21.4	—	3.4	11	1	Int.	11	260.00	
Supreme 2-7x34	2.1-6.8	59-16	—	3.4	11 1/4	1	Int.	10.4	270.00	
Supreme 4x44	3.9	32	—	3	12 1/2	1	Int.	11.6	270.00	
Supreme 3-9x44	3.1-8.9	36-13	—	3.5	12.7	1	Int.	11.6	320.00	
Weaver										Micro-Trac adjustment system with 1/4-min. clicks on K2.5, K4, V3, V9, V10, RK4, RV7; 1/8-min. clicks on K6, KT15. All have Dual-X reticle. One-piece aluminum tube, gloss finish, nitrogen filled, multi-coated lenses, waterproof. From Weaver.
K2.5	2.5	35	—	3.7	10.2	1	Int.	8.5	112.55	
K4	4	30	—	3.3	11.8	1	Int.	10.8	122.10	
K6	6	20	—	3.6	13	1	Int.	11.2	132.98	
V3	1-3	95-35	—	3.9-3.7	9.5	1	Int.	9.5	147.93	
V9	2.9-8.7	37-13	—	3.5-3.4	13	1	Int.	11.2	159.29	
V10	1.9-9.3	46-11	—	3.3	12.6	1	Int.	12.8	169.16	
KT15	14.6	7.5	—	3.2	15.8	1	Int.	16.1	266.40	
RK4	3.8	25	—	3	10.8	7/8	Int.	7.7	103.34	
RV7	2.2-6.5	43-15	—	2.9-2.6	11.5	7/8	Int.	8.5	125.54	
Williams										TNT models
Twilight Crosshair TNT	1 1/2-5	57 3/4-21	177-16	3 1/2	10 3/4	1	Int.	10	196.30	
Twilight Crosshair TNT	2 1/2	32	64	3 3/4	11 1/4	1	Int.	8 1/2	138.95	
Twilight Crosshair TNT	4	29	64	3 1/2	11 3/4	1	Int.	9 1/2	145.25	
Twilight Crosshair TNT	2-6	45-17	256-28	3	11 1/2	1	Int.	11 1/2	196.30	
Twilight Crosshair TNT	3-9	36-13	161-18	3	12 3/4	1	Int.	13 1/2	206.30	
Pistol Scopes										
Twilight 1.5x TNT	1.5	19	177	18-25	8.2	1	Int	6.4	143.70	
Twilight 2x TNT	2	17.5	100	18-25	8.5	1	Int.	6.4	145.80	
Zeiss										All scopes have 1/4-minute click-stop adjustments. Choice of Z-Plex or fine crosshair reticles. Rubber armored objective bell, rubber eyepiece ring. Lenses have T-Star coating for highest light transmission. Z-Series scopes offered in non-rail tubes with duplex reticles only. Imported from West Germany by Carl Zeiss Optical, Inc.
Diatal C 4x32	4	30	—	3.5	10.6	1	Int.	11.3	525.00	
Diatal C 6x32	6	20	—	3.5	10.6	1	Int.	11.3	565.00	
Diatal C 10x36	10	12	—	3.5	12.7	1	Int.	14.1	675.00	
Diatal ZA 4x32	4	34.5	—	3.5	10.8	1.02 (26mm)	Int.	10.6	525.00	
Diatal ZA 6x42	6	22.9	—	3.5	12.7	1.02 (26mm)	Int.	13.4	620.00	
Diatal ZA 8x56	8	18	—	3.5	13.8	1.02 (26mm)	Int.	17.6	710.00	
Diavari C 1.5-4.5	1.5-4.5	72-27	—	3.5	11.8	1	Int.	13.4	725.00	
Diavari C 3-9x36	3-9	36-13	—	3.5	11.2	1	Int.	15.2	755.00	
Diavari ZA 1.5-6	1.5-6	65.5-22.9	—	3.5	12.4	1.18 (30mm)	Int.	18.5	870.00	
Diavari ZA 2.5-10	2.5-10	41-13.7	—	3.5	14.4	1.18 (30mm)	Int.	22.8	1,030.00	
Zero Mag										Has optional indirect lighting element to illuminate crosshairs (**$79.95**). For vent. rib, Rem. slug barrel, std. Weaver base, std. 22 dovetail, Hastings slug barrel mounts. From Autumn Tracker Design.
Zero Mag	0	—	—	—	5	—	Int.	7	59.95	

■ Signifies target and/or varmint scope. Hunting scopes in general are furnished with a choice of reticle—crosshairs, post with crosshairs, tapered or blunt post, or dot crosshairs, etc. The great majority of target and varmint scopes have medium or fine crosshairs but post or dot reticles may be ordered. W—Windage   E—Elevation   MOA-Minute of angle or 1" (approx.) at 100 yards, etc.

CAUTION: PRICES CHANGE. CHECK AT GUNSHOP.

Maker, Model, Type	Adjust.	Scopes	Price	Suitable for
Action Arms	No	1″ split rings.	From $32.00	For UZI, Ruger Mk. II, Mini-14, Win. 94, AR-15, Rem. 870, Ithaca 37, and many other popular rifles, handguns. From Action Arms.
Aimpoint	No	1″	36.95-79.95	Mounts/rings for all Aimpoint sights and 1″ scopes. For many popular revolvers, auto pistols, shotguns, military-style rifles/carbines, sporting rifles. Most require no gunsmithing. Contact Aimpoint for details.
Aimtech				
S&W K, L, N frame	No	1″	59.95	Mount scopes, lasers, electronic sights using Weaver-style base. All mounts allow use of iron sights; no gunsmithing. Available in satin black or satin stainless finish. From L&S Technologies, Inc.
Taurus revolvers	No	1″	59.95	
Rossi revolvers	No	1″	59.95	
Astra revolvers	No	1″	59.95	
Glock 17, 17L, 19	No	1″	59.95	
S&W 45, 9mm autos	No	1″	49.95	
Ruger Mk I, Mk II	No	1″	39.95	
AMT Auto Mag II, III	No	1″	49.95	
Gout. 45 Auto	No	1″	49.95	
Browning Hi-Power	No	1″	49.95	
Browning Buck Mark/Challenger II	No	1″	49.95	
Beretta/Taurus auto	No	1″	49.95	
S&W 422	No	1″	49.95	
A.R.M.S.				
Swan G-3	No	Weaver-type	145.00	[1]See-through mount. [2]Also FNC — $89.00 From A.R.M.S., Inc.
M16A1A2/AR-15[1]	No	Weaver-type rail	37.90	
FN FAL LAR	No	Weaver-type rail	95.00	
FN FAL LAR Para.[2]	No	—	120.00	
Beretta AR-70	No	—	59.00	
Armson				
AR-15[1]	No	O.E.G.	30.95	[1]Fastens with one nut. [2]Models 181, 182, 183, 184, etc. [3]Claw mount. [4]Claw mount, bolt cover still easily removable. From Armson, Inc.
Mini-14[2]	No	O.E.G.	42.95	
H&K[3]	No	O.E.G.	58.95	
UZI[4]	No	O.E.G.	58.95	
Armsport				
100 Series[1]	No	1″ rings. Low, med., high	10.50	[1]Weaver-type rings. [2]Weaver-type base; most popular rifles. Made in U.S. From Armsport.
104 22-cal.	No	1″	10.50	
201 See-Thru	No	1″	13.50	
1-Piece Base[2]	No		5.00	
2-Piece Base[2]	No		2.50	
B-Square				
Pistols				[1]Clamp-on, blue finish. Stainless finish $59.95. [2]For Bushnell Phantom only. [3]Blue finish; stainless finish $59.95. [4]Clamp-on, for Bushnell Phantom only, blue; stainless finish $49.95. [5]Requires drilling & tapping. [6]No gunsmithing, no sight removal; blue; stainless finish $79.95. [7]Weaver-style rings. Rings not included with Weaver-type bases. [8]NATO Stanag dovetail model, $99.50. [9]Blue; stainless $69.95. [10]Blue; stainless $49.95. [11]Handguard mounts. [12]Receiver mounts. **Partial listing of mounts shown here. Contact B-Square for more data.**
Beretta/Taurus 92/99[7]	—	1″	69.95	
Browning Buck Mark[7]	No	1″	29.95	
Colt 45 Auto	E only	1″	69.95	
Colt Python, King Cobra[1,7]	E	1″	49.95	
Daisy 717/722 Champion[2]	No	1″	19.95	
Dan Wesson Clamp-On[3,7]	E	1″	49.95	B-Square makes mounts for the following military rifles: AK47/AKS, Egyptian Hakim, French MAS 1936, M91 Argentine Mauser, Model 98 Brazilian and German Mausers, Model 93 Spanish Mauser (long and short), Model 1916 Mauser, Model 38 and 96 Swedish Mausers, Model 91 Russian (round and octagon receivers), Chinese SKS 56, SMLE No. 1, Mk. III, 1903 Springfield, U.S. 30-Cal. Carbine. Those following replace gun's rear sight: AK47/AKS, P14/1917 Enfield, FN49, M1 Garand, M1-A/M14 (no sight removal), SMLE No. 1, MK III/No. 4 & 5, MK I, 1903/1903-A3 Springfield, Beretta AR 70 (no sight removal).
Ruger 22 Auto Mono-Mount[4]	No	1″	39.95	
Ruger Single-Six[5]	No	1″	39.95	
Ruger Blackhawk, Super B'hwk[9]	W&E	1″	59.95	
Ruger GP-100[10]	No	1″	39.95	
Ruger Redhawk[9]	W&E	1″	59.95	
S&W 422[10]	No	1″	39.95	
Taurus 66[10]	No	1″	39.95	
S&W K, L, N frame[3,7]	No	1″	49.95	
T/C Contender	W&E	1″	49.95	
Rifles				
Charter AR-7	No	1″	19.95	
Mini-14[6,7]	W&E	1″	49.95	
M-94 Side Mount	W&E	1″	49.95	
RWS, Beeman/FWB Air Rifles	E only	—	49.95	
Ruger 77[7]	W&E	1″	49.95	
Ruger Ranch/Mini-30[7]	W&E	1″	49.95	
SMLE Side Mount	W&E	1″	49.95	
Rem. Model Seven, 600, 660, etc.[7]	No	1″ One piece base	9.95	
Military				
AK-47/AKM/AKS/SKS-56[11]	No	1″	39.95	
AK-47, SKS-56[12]	No	1″	59.95	
M1-A[8]	W&E	1″	59.95	
AR-15/16[8]	W&E	1″	49.95	
FN-LAR/FAL[7,8]	E only	1″	99.50	
HK-91/93/94[7,8]	E only	1″	69.95	
Shotguns[7]				
Browning A-5[7]	No	1″	49.95	
Franchi 48/AL[7]	No	1″	49.95	
Franchi Elite, Prestige, SPAS[7]	No	1″	49.95	
Ithaca 37[7]	No	1″	39.95	
Mossberg 500, 712, 5500[7]	No	1″	39.95	
Rem. 870/1100[7] (12 & 20 ga.)	No	1″	39.95	
Remington 870, 1100 (and L.H.)[7]	No	1″	39.95	
S&W 1000 P[7]	No	1″	39.95	

CAUTION: PRICES CHANGE. CHECK AT GUNSHOP.

Maker, Model, Type	Adjust.	Scopes	Price	Suitable for
Beeman				
Double Adjustable	W&E	1″	29.98	All grooved receivers and scope bases on all known
Deluxe Ring Mounts	No	1″	28.98	air rifles and 22-cal. rimfire rifles (1/2″ to 5/8″ — 6mm
Professional Mounts	W&E	1″	98.95	to 15mm). [1]Centerfire rifles. Scope detaches easily,
Professional Pivot[1]	W	1″	269.50	returns to zero.
Buehler				
One Piece (T)[1]	W only	1″ split rings, 3 heights.	Complete — 74.50	[1]Most popular models. [2]Sako dovetail receivers. [3]15
		1″ split rings, engraved	Rings only — 102.75	models. [4]No drilling & tapping. [5]Aircraft alloy, dyed
		26mm split rings, 2 heights	Rings only — 54.00	blue or to match stainless; for Colt Diamondback,
		30mm split rings, 1 height	Rings only — 65.00	Python, Trooper, Ruger Blackhawk, Single-Six, Se-
One Piece Micro Dial (T)[1]	W&E	1″ split rings.	Complete — 95.50	curity-Six, S&W K-frame, Dan Wesson.
Two Piece (T)[1]	W only	1″ split rings.	Complete — 74.50	
Two Piece Dovetail (T)[2]	W only	1″ split rings.	Complete — 91.75	
One Piece Pistol (T)[3]	W only	1″ split rings.	Complete — 74.50	
One Piece Pistol Stainless (T)[1]	W only	1″ stainless rings.	Complete — 96.50	
One Piece Ruger Mini-14 (T)[4]	W only	1″ split rings.	Complete — 91.75	
One Piece Pistol M83 Blue[4,5]	W only	1″ split rings.	Complete — 85.00	
One Piece Pistol M83 Silver[4,5]	W only	1″ stainless rings.	Complete — 98.75	
Burris				
Supreme One Piece (T)[1]	W only	1″ split rings, 3 heights.	1 piece base — 24.95	[1]Most popular rifles. Universal, rings, mounts fit
Trumount Two Piece (T)	W only	1″ split rings, 3 heights.	2 piece base — 22.95	Burris. Universal, Redfield, Leupold and Browning
Browning Auto Mount[2]	No	3/4″, 1″, split rings.	18.95	bases. Comparable prices. [2]Browning Standard 22
Rings Mounts[3]	No	3/4″, 1″, split rings.	1″ rings — 17.95	Auto rifle. [3]Grooved receivers. [4]Universal dovetail;
L.E.R. Mount Bases[4]	No	1″, split rings.	22.95	accept Burris, Universal, Redfield, Leupold scopes.
Extension Rings[5]	No	1″ scopes.	38.95	For Dan Wesson, S&W, Virginian, Ruger Black-
Ruger Ring Mount[6]	W only	1″ split rings.	43.95	hawk, Win. 94. [5]Medium standard front, extension
Std. 1″ Rings	—	Low, medium, high heights	31.95	rear, per pair. Low standard front, extension rear, per
Zee Rings	—	Fit Weaver bases; medium and high heights	26.95	pair. [6]Mini scopes, scopes with 2″ bell, for M77R. Selected rings and bases available with matte Safari finish.
Bushnell				
Detachable (T) mounts only[1]	W only	1″ split rings, uses Weaver base.	Rings — 19.95	[1]Most popular rifles. Includes windage adj.
22 mount	No	1″ only.	Rings — 9.95	
Clearview				
Universal Rings (T)[1]	No	1″ split rings.	19.95	[1]All popular rifles including Sav. 99. Uses Weaver
Mod 101, & 336[2]	No	1″ split rings.	19.95	bases. [2]Allows use of open sights. [3]For 22 rimfire
Broad-View[4]	No	1″	19.95	rifles, with grooved receivers or bases. [4]Fits 13
Model 22[3]	No	3/4″, 7/8″, 1″	11.95	models. Broadest view area of the type. [5]Side mount
94 Winchester[5]	No	1″	19.95	for both M94 and M94-375 Big Bore.
Conetrol				
Huntur[1]	W only	1″, 26mm, 26.5mm solid or split rings, 3 heights.	59.91	[1]All popular rifles, including metric-drilled foreign guns. Price shown for base, two rings. Matte finish.
Gunnur[2]	W only	1″, 26mm, 26.5mm solid or split rings, 3 heights.	74.91	[2]Gunnur grade has mirror-finished rings, satin-finished base. Price shown for base, two rings. [3]Custum
Custum[3]	W only	1″, 26mm, 26.5mm solid or split rings, 3 heights.	89.91	grade has mirror-finished rings and mirror-finished, streamlined base. Price shown for base, 2 rings.
One Piece Side Mount Base[4]	W only	1″, 26mm, 26.5mm solid or split rings, 3 heights.		[4]Win. 94, Krag, older split-bridge Mannlicher-Schoenauer, Mini-14, M1 Garand, etc. Prices same
Daptar Bases[5]	W only	1″, 26mm, 26.5mm solid or split rings, 3 heights.		as above. [5]For all popular guns with integral mounting provision, including Sako, BSA, Ithacagun, Ruger, H&K and many others. Also for grooved-re-
Pistol Bases, 2 or 3-ring[6]	W only	1″ scopes.		ceiver rimfires and air rifles. Prices same as above. [6]For XP-100, T/C Contender, Colt SAA, Ruger
Fluted Bases[7]	W only	Standard Conetrol rings	99.99	Blackhawk, S&W. [7]Sculptured 2-piece bases as
Ruger No. 1 Base[8]	W only	1″, 26mm, 26.5mm solid or split rings.	NA	found on fine custom rifles. Price shown is for base alone. Also available unfinished — **$74.91**. [8]Re-
30mm Rings[9]	W only	30mm	49.98-69.96	places Ruger rib, positions scope farther back. [9]30mm rings made in projectionless style, medium height only. Three-ring mount available for T/C Contender pistol, in Conetrol's three grades.
EAW				
Quick Detachable Top Mount[1]	W&E	1″/26mm	175.00-224.95	[1]Also 30mm rings to fit Redfield or Leupold-type
	W&E	1″/26mm with front extension ring.	175.00-224.95	bases, low and high, **$75**. Most popular rifles. Elevation adjusted with variable-height sub-bases for rear ring. Imported by Del Sports, Inc., Paul Jaeger, Inc.
	W&E	30mm	175.00-224.95	
	W&E	30mm with front extension ring.	175.00-224.95	
Griffin & Howe				
Standard Double Lever (S)	No	1″ or 26mm split rings.	305.00	All popular models (Garand **$215**). All rings **$75**. Top ejection rings available. Price installed for side mount.
Holden				
Wide Ironsighter ®	No	1″ split rings.	24.95	[1]Most popular rifles including Ruger Mini-14, H&R
Ironsighter Center Fire[1]	No	1″ split rings.	24.95	M700, and muzzleloaders. Rings have oval holes to
Ironsighter S-94	No	1″ split rings.	30.95	permit use of iron sights. [2]For 1″ dia. scopes. [3]For
Ironsighter 22 cal. rimfire				3/4″ or 7/8″ dia. scopes. [4]For 1″ dia. extended eye
Model #550[2]	No	1″ split rings.	13.95	relief scopes. Stainless finish **$32.95**. [5]702 —
Model #600[3]	No	7/8″ split rings also fits 3/4″.	13.95	Browning A-Bolt; 709 — Marlin 39A. [6]732 — Ruger
Series #700[5]	No	1″ split rings.	24.95	77/22 R&RS, No. 1 Ranch Rifle; 777 fits Ruger 77R, RS. Both 732, 777 fit Ruger integral bases. [7]Fits
Model 732, 777[6]	No	1″ split rings.	54.95	most popular blackpowder rifles; one model for
Ironsighter Handguns[4]	No	1″ split rings.	30.95	Holden Ironsighter mounts, one for Weaver rings.
Blackpowder Mount[7]	No	1″	16.00	Adj. rear sight is integral.
Jaeger				
QD, with windage (S)	W only	1″, 3 heights.	250.00	All popular models. From Paul Jaeger, Inc.
Kimber				
Deluxe[1]	No	1″ split rings.	59.50	[1]High rings and low rings. For either Kimber grooved
Double Lever Q.D.	No	1″ split rings.	89.00	receivers or other popular rifles using Kimber two-piece screw-on bases. Non-detachable. Vertically split rings. [2]One height for Kimber grooved receiver or other rifles using Kimber screw-on bases. Vertically split. Quick detachable.

CAUTION: PRICES CHANGE. CHECK AT GUNSHOP.

SCOPE MOUNTS

Maker, Model, Type	Adjust.	Scopes	Price	Suitable for
Kris Mounts				
Side-Saddle[1]	No	1″, 26mm split rings.	11.98	[1]One-piece mount for Win. 94. [2]Most popular rifles
Two Piece (T)[2]	No	1″, 26mm split rings.	7.98	and Ruger. [3]Blackhawk revolver. Mounts have oval
One Piece (T)[3]	No	1″, 26mm split rings.	11.98	hole to permit use of iron sights.
KWIK MOUNT				
Shotgun Mount	No	1″	49.95	Wrap-around design; no gunsmithing required. Models for Browning BPS, A-5 12 ga., Sweet 16, 20, Rem. 870/1100 (LTW and L.H.), S&W 916, Savage 67 12 ga., Mossberg 500, Ithaca 37 & 51 12 ga., S&W 1000/3000, Win. 1400. From KenPatable Ent.
Kwik-Site				
KS-See-Thru[1]	No	1″	22.95	[1]Most rifles. Allows use of iron sights. [2]22-cal. rifles
KS-22 See-Thru[2]	No	1″	19.95	with grooved receivers. Allows use of iron sights.
KS-W94[3]	Yes	1″	31.95	[3]Model 94, 94 Big Bore. No drilling or tapping. Also
KSM Bench Rest[4]	No	1″	31.95	in non-adjustable model $30.95. [4]Most rifles. One-
KS-WEV	No	1″	22.95	piece solid construction. Use on Weaver bases.
KS-WEV-HIGH	No	1″	22.95	32mm obj. lens or larger. [5]Non-see-through model;
KS-T22 1″[5]	No	1″	19.95	for grooved receivers. [6]Allows Mag Lite or C or D,
KS-FLM Flashlite[6]	No	Mini or C cell flashlight	49.95	Mini Mag Lites to be mounted atop See-Thru mounts. [7]Fits any Redfield, Tasco, Weaver or univer-
KS-T88[7]	No	1″, 30mm	9.95	sal-style dovetail base. Bright blue, black matte or satin finish. Standard, high heights.
Laserscope	No	Laserscope	37.95 to 99.50	Mounts Laserscope above or below barrel. For most popular military-type rifles, UZI, H&K submachine guns, Desert Eagle pistols. From Laser Devices, Inc.
Laser Aim	No	Laser Aim	37.00 to 133.35	Mounts Laser Aim above or below barrel. Avail. for most popular handguns, rifles, shotguns, including militaries. From Emerging Technologies, Inc.
Lasersight	No	LS45 only	$29.95 to 149.00	For the LS45 Lasersight. Allows LS45 to be mounted alongside any 1″ scope. Universal adapter attaches to any full-length Weaver-type base. For most popular military-type rifles, Mossberg, Rem. shotguns, Python, Desert Eagle, S&W N frame, Colt 45ACP. From Imatronic Lasersight.
Leupold				
STD Bases[1]	W only	One- or two-piece bases	22.10	[1]Rev. front and rear combinations. [2]Avail. polished,
STD Rings[2]		1″ Super low, low, medium, high	32.00	matte finish. [3]Base and two piece; Ruger, S&W, T/C;
STD Handgun mounts[3]	No		56.40	add $5.00 for silver finish. [4]Rem. 700, Win. 70-type
Dual Dovetail Bases[1,4]	No		22.10	actions. [5]For Ruger No. 1, 77/22; interchangeable
Dual Dovetail Rings		1″, Super low, low	32.00	with Ruger units. [6]For dovetailed rimfire rifles.
Ring Mounts[5,6,7]	No	1″	81.10	[7]Sako; medium, low. [8]Must be drilled, tapped for
Gunmaker Base[8]	W only	1″	14.60	each action. [9]Unfinished bottom, top completed;
Gunmaker Ring Blanks[9]		1″	21.10	sold singly.
Leatherwood				
Bridge Bases[1]	No	ART II or all dovetail rings	15.00	[1]Many popular bolt actions. Mounts accept Weaver
M1A/M-14 Q.D.	No	ART II or all dovetail rings	105.00	or dovetail-type rings. From North American Spe-
AR-15/M-16 Base	No	ART II or all dovetail rings	25.00	cialties.
FN-FAL Base	No	ART II or all dovetail rings	100.00	
FN Para. Base	No	ART II or all dovetail rings	110.00	
Steyr SSG Base	No	ART II or all dovetail rings	55.00	
Marlin				
One Piece QD (T)	No	1″ split rings	14.95	Most Marlin lever actions.
Millett				
Black Onyx Smooth		1″ Low, medium, high	29.65	Rem. 40X, 700, 722, 725, Ruger 77 (round top),
Chaparral Engraved		Engraved	43.95	Weatherby, etc. FN Mauser, FN Brownings, Colt 57,
Universal Two Piece Bases				Interarms, MkX, Parker-Hale, Sako (round receiver),
700 Series[1]	W only	Two-piece bases	23.95	many others. [1]Fits Win. M70, 70XTR, 670, Browning
FN Series[1]	W only	Two-piece bases	23.95	BBR, BAR, BLR, A-Bolt, Rem. 7400/7600, Four, Six,
70 Series[1]	W only	1″, two-piece bases	23.95	Marlin 336, Win. 94 A.E., Sav. 110. [2]To fit Weaver-
Angle-Loc[2] Rings	W only	1″, low, medium, high	30.65-44.95	type bases. Also for Colt, Dan Wesson, Ruger hand-
Ruger 77 Rings[3]	—	1″	44.95	guns—$44.95-$77.95. Avail. for Scope-Site (fixed,
Shotgun Rings[4]	—	1″	29.65	$44.95, or adjustable, $77.95). Universal Bases
Handgun Bases, Rings[5]	—	1″	32.95-61.35	also for Browning BAR, BLR, A-Bolt, Rem. 7400, 7600, Marlin 336, Win. 94 AE, Savage 110. [3]En- graved. Smooth $30.65. [4]For Rem. 870, 1100; smooth. [5]Two and three-ring sets for Colt Python, Trooper, Diamondback, Peacekeeper, Dan Wesson, Ruger Redhawk, Super Redhawk.
R.A.T.	No	1″	14.95	Allow mounting scopes, dot sights on vent. rib shot- guns. Also for Rem. and Hastings slug barrels ($19.95). From Autumn Tracker Design.
Redfield				
JR-SR(T)[1]	W only	3/4″, 1″, 26mm, 30mm	JR—20.95-50.95 SR—20.95-39.95	[1]Low, med & high, split rings. Reversible extension front rings for 1″. 2-piece bases for Sako. Colt Sauer
Ring (T)[2]	No	3/4″ and 1″		bases $39.85. [2]Split rings for grooved 22s. See-
Double Dovetail MP[3]	No	1″ split rings	58.95	Thru mounts $19.95. [3]Used with MP scopes for:
Midline Base & Rings[4]	No	1″	11.95	S&W K or N frame, XP-100, Colt J or I frame, T/C
Widefield See-Thru Mounts[4]	No	1″	19.95	Contender, Colt autos, blackpowder rifles. [4]One- and two-piece aluminum base; three ring heights.
Compact[5]	W only	1″	49.95	[5]For compact scopes on Browing A-Bolt long action,
Ruger Rings[6]	No	1″, med., high	32.95	Remington 700, Winchester 70A. [6]For Ruger Model
Ruger 30mm[7]	No	1″	43.95	77 rifles, medium and high; medium only for M/77/
Midline Ext. Rings	No	1″	18.95	22. [7]For Model 77. Also in matte finish, $44.95. [8]Fits
SR-AB Bases[8]	No	1	20.95	all Browning A-Bolt rifles, incl. 22, short and long- action, left and right.
S&K				
Insta-Mount (T) bases and rings[1]	W only	Use S&K rings only	25.00-99.00	[1]1903, A3, M1 Carbine, Lee Enfield #1, MK. III, #4,
Conventional rings and bases[2]	W only	1″ split rings	From 50.00	#5, M1917, M98 Mauser, FN Auto, AR-15, AR-180,
SKulptured Bases, Rings[2]	W only	1″, 26mm, 30mm	From 50.00	M-14, M-1. Ger. K-43, Mini-14, M1-A, Krag, AKM, AK-47, Win. 94, SKS Type 56, Daewoo, H&K. [2]Most popular rifles already drilled and tapped. Horizon- tally and vertically split rings, matte or high gloss.

Maker, Model, Type	Adjust.	Scopes	Price	Suitable for
SSK Industries				Custom installation using from two to four rings (included). For T/C Contender, most 22 auto pistols, Ruger and other S.A. revolvers, Ruger, Dan Wesson, S&W, Colt D.A. revolvers. Black or white finish. Uses Kimber rings in two- or three-rings sets. In blue or SSK Khrome. For T/C Contender or most popular revolvers. Standard, non-detachable model also available, from **$125.00**.
T'SOB	No	1″	55.00-145.00	
Quick Detachable	No	1″	From 160.00	
Sako				Sako, or any rifle using Sako action, 3 heights available, Stoeger, importer.
QD Dovetail	W only	1″ only	41.50-49.00	
Simmons				Weaver-type bases. #1401 (low) also in high style (#1404). #1406, 1408 for grooved receiver 22s. Bases avail. for most popular rifles; one- and two-piece styles. Most popular rifles. [1]For 22 RF rifles.
1401	No	1″	10.00	
1406	No	1″	10.00	
1408	No	1″	13.50	
Tasco				[1]Many popular rifles. [2]For 22s with grooved receivers. [3]Most popular rifles. [4]"Quick Peep" 1″ ring mount; fits all 22-cal. rifles with grooved receivers. [5]For Ruger Mini-14; also in brushed aluminum. [6]Side mount for Win. 94. [7]Side mount rings and base for Win. 94 in 30-30, 375 Win. [8]Avail. for most rifles. Steel or aluminum rings. Contact Tasco for details on complete line.
791 and 793 series[1]	No	1″, regular or high	12.95	
797[2]	No	Split rings	12.95	
799[4]	No	1″ only	12.95	
885 BK[7]	No	1″ only	19.95	
895[6]	No	1″ only	11.95	
896[5]	No	1″ only	54.95	
800L Series (with base)[3]	No	1″ only. Rings and base	15.95	
World Class[8]				
Steel Bases	Yes	1″, 26mm, 30mm	27.45-43.95	
Steel Rings	Yes	1″, 26mm	36.95	
Steel 30mm Rings	Yes	30mm	65.95	
Thompson/Center				[1]All Contenders except vent. rib. [2]T/C rail mount scopes; all Contenders except vent. rib. [3]All S&W K and Combat Masterpiece. Hi-Way Patrolman, Outdoorsman, 22 Jet, 45 Target 1955. Requires drilling, tapping. [4]Blackhawk, Super Blackhawk, Super Single-Six. Requires drilling, tapping. [5]45 or 50 cal.; replaces rear sight. [6]Rail mount scopes; 54-cal. Hawken, 50, 54, 56-cal. Renegade. Replaces rear sight. [7]Cherokee 32 or 45 cal., Seneca 36 or 45 cal. Replaces rear sight. Carbine mount #9743 for Short Tube scope #8640, **$11.50**.
Contender 9746[1]	No	T/C Lobo	15.50	
Contender 9741[2]	No	2½, 4 RP	15.50	
Contender 7410	No	Bushnell Phantom, 1.3, 2.5x	15.50	
S&W 9747[3]	No	Lobo or RP	15.50	
Ruger 9748[4]	No	Lobo or RP	15.50	
Hawken 9749[5]	No	Lobo or RP	15.50	
Hawken/Renegade 9754[6]	No	Lobo or RP	15.50	
Cherokee/Seneca 9756[7]	No	Lobo or RP	15.50	
New Englander 9757	No	Lobo or RP	15.50	
Unerti				[1]Unerti target or varmint scopes. [2]Any with regular dovetail scope bases.
Posa (T)[1]	Yes	¾″, 1″ scopes	Per set 70.00	
¼ Click (T)[2]	Yes	¾″, 1″ target scopes	Per set 100.00	
Weaver				[1]Nearly all modern rifles. Low, med., high. 1″ extension **$28.06**. 1″ med. stainless steel **$36.72**. [2]Nearly all modern rifles, shotguns. [3]Most modern big-bore rifles; std., high. [4]22s with ⅜″ grooved receivers. 1″ See-Thru extension **$28.06**. [6]Most modern big bore rifles. [7]No drilling, tapping. For Colt Python, Trooper, 357, Officer's Model, Ruger Blackhawk & Super, Mini-14, Security-Six, 22 auto pistols, Redhawk, Blackhawk SRM 357, S&W current K, L with adj. sights. [8]For Rem. 870/1100, Mossberg 500. No gunsmithing. [9]For some popular sporting rifles. [10]Dovetail design mount for Rem. 700, Win. 70, FN Mauser, low, med., high rings; std., extension bases. From Weaver.
Detachable Mounts				
Top Mount[1]	No	1″	24.02	
		⅞″	23.09	
Side Mount[2]	No	1″	25.40	
		1″ Long	30.01	
Pivot Mount[3]	No	1″	32.55	
Tip-Off Mount[4]	No	⅞″	18.47	
		1″	23.55	
See-Thru Mount				
Tip-Off[4]	No	⅞″	17.32	
		1″	24.02	
Detachable[5]	No	1″	24.02	
Integral[6]	No	1″	17.89	
Mount Base System[7]				
Blue Finish	No	1″	62.45	
Stainless Finish	No	1″	87.38	
Shotgun Mount System[8]	No	1″	62.45	
Rifle Mount System[9]	No	1″	27.71	
Imperial Mount Systems[10]				
Bases, pair	Yes	1″	21.47	
Rings, pair	No	1″	27.86	
Wideview				Models for many popular rifles — **$14.95**. Low ring, high ring and grooved receiver types. From Wideview Scope Mount Corp.
WSM-22	No	1″	14.95	
WSM-94	No	1″	24.95	
WSM-94AE	No	1″	22.95	
Premium See-Thru	No	1″	20.95	
22 Premium See-Thru	No	¾″, 1″	14.95	
Universal Ring Angle Cut	No	1″	22.95	
Universal Ring Straight Cut	No	1″	20.95	
Solid Mounts				
Lo Ring Solid	No	1″	14.95	
Hi Ring Solid	No	1″	14.95	
Williams				[1]Most rifles, Br. S.M.L.E. (round rec) $3.85 extra. [2]Same. [3]Most rifles including Win. 94 Big Bore. [4]Many modern rifles. [5]Most popular rifles.
Offset (S)[1]	No	⅞″, 1″, 26mm solid, split or extension rings	62.40	
QC(T)[2]	No	Same	45.00	
QC(S)[3]	No	Same	51.40	
Sight-Thru[4]	No	1″, ⅞″ sleeves $3.20.	21.00	
Streamline[5]	No	1″ (bases form rings).	21.00	
York				Centers scope over the action. No drilling, tapping or gunsmithing. Uses standard dovetail rings. From York M-1 Conversions.
M-1 Garand	Yes	1″	39.95	

(S) — Side Mount   (T) — Top Mount   22mm = .866″   25.4mm = 1.024″   26.5mm = 1.045″   30mm = 1.81″

CAUTION: PRICES CHANGE. CHECK AT GUNSHOP.

Directory of the Arms Trade

INDEX TO THE DIRECTORY

AMMUNITION (Commercial) 295
AMMUNITION (Custom) 295
AMMUNITION (Foreign) 296
AMMUNITION COMPONENTS — BULLETS, POWDER,
  PRIMERS 296
ANTIQUE ARMS DEALERS.....................297
APPRAISERS, GUNS, ETC.....................297
AUCTIONEERS, GUNS, ETC. 298
BOOKS (ARMS), Publishers and Dealers.............298
BULLET & CASE LUBRICANTS..................298
BULLET SWAGE DIES AND TOOLS 298
CARTRIDGES FOR COLLECTORS 298
CASES, CABINETS AND RACKS — GUN 299
CHOKE DEVICES,RECOIL ABSORBERS & RECOIL PADS 299
CHRONOGRAPHS AND PRESSURE TOOLS...........299
CLEANING & REFINISHING SUPPLIES 300
CUSTOM GUNSMITHS.........................300
CUSTOM METALSMITHS.......................303
DECOYS 304
ENGRAVERS, ENGRAVING TOOLS 304
GAME CALLS 305
GUN PARTS, U.S. AND FOREIGN................305
GUNS (Air) 307
GUNS (Foreign) 306
GUNS (U.S.-made) 305
GUNS & GUN PARTS, REPLICA AND ANTIQUE 308
GUNS, SURPLUS — PARTS AND AMMUNITION.......308
GUNSMITHS, CUSTOM (See Custom Gunsmiths) 300

GUNSMITHS, HANDGUN (see Pistolsmiths)..........314
GUNSMITH SCHOOLS........................308
GUNSMITH SUPPLIES, TOOLS, SERVICES...........308
HANDGUN ACCESSORIES 309
HANDGUN GRIPS..........................310
HEARING PROTECTORS 310
HOLSTERS & LEATHER GOODS 310
HUNTING AND CAMP GEAR, CLOTHING, ETC.........311
KNIVES AND KNIFEMAKER'S SUPPLIES —
  FACTORY and MAIL ORDER 311
LABELS, BOXES, CARTRIDGE HOLDERS 312
LOAD TESTING and PRODUCT TESTING,
  (CHRONOGRAPHING, BALLISTIC STUDIES) 312
MISCELLANEOUS 312
MUZZLE-LOADING GUNS, BARRELS or EQUIPMENT ...313
PISTOLSMITHS 314
REBORING AND RERIFLING 315
RELOADING TOOLS AND ACCESSORIES..........315
RESTS — BENCH, PORTABLE, ETC. 316
RIFLE BARREL MAKERS 317
SCOPES, MOUNTS, ACCESSORIES,
  OPTICAL EQUIPMENT......................317
SIGHTS, METALLIC........................318
STOCKS (Commercial and Custom)................318
TARGETS, BULLET & CLAYBIRD TRAPS...........320
TAXIDERMY.............................320
TRAP & SKEET SHOOTERS' EQUIPMENT.........320
TRIGGERS, RELATED EQUIPMENT 320

AMMUNITION (Commercial)

Activ Industries, Inc., P.O. Box F, 1000 Zigor Rd., Kearneysville, WV 25430/304-725-0451 (shotshells only)

Atlanta Discount Ammo, P.O. Box 627, Norcross, GA 30091/404-446-2429 (ctlg. $2)

Ballistic Research Industries (BRI), 2825 S. Rodeo Gulch Rd. #8, Soquel, CA 95073/408-476-7981

Cascade Cartridge Inc., (See Omark)

Dynamit Nobel-RWS Inc., 105 Stonehurst Court, Northvale, NJ 07647/201-767-1995 (RWS)

Eldorado Cartridge Corp., P.O. Box 308, Boulder City, NV 89005/702-294-0025

Elite Ammunition, P.O. Box 3251, Hinsdale, IL 60522/312-366-9006

Estate Cartridge Inc., P.O. Box 3702, Conroe, TX 77305/409-856-7277 (shotshell)

Federal Cartridge Co., 900 Ehlen Dr., Anoka, MN 55303/612-422-2840

Fisher Enterprises, 655 Main St. #305, Edmonds, WA 98020/206-776-4365 (Prometheus airgun pellets)

Frontier Cartridge Division-Hornady Mfg. Co., Box 1848, Grand Island, NE 68801/308-382-1390

Hansen Cartridge Co., 244 Old Post Rd., Southport, CT 06490/203-259-7337

ICI-America, P.O. Box 751, Wilmington, DE 19897/302-575-3000

Omark Industries, P.O. Box 856, Lewiston, ID 83501/208-746-2351

PMC-Eldorado Cartridge Corp., P.O. Box 308, Boulder City, NV 89005/702-294-0025

P.P.C. Corp., 625 E. 24th St., Paterson, NJ 07514

Palcher Ammunition, Techstar Engineering, Inc., 2239 S. Huron Ave., Santa Ana, CA 92705/714-556-7384

Precision Prods. of Wash., Inc., N. 311 Walnut Rd., Spokane, WA 99206/509-928-0604 (Exammo)

Prometheus/Titan Black (See Fisher Enterprises)

RWS (See Dynamit Nobel)

Remington Arms Co., 1077 Market St., Wilmington, DE 19898/302-773-5291

Southern Ammunition Co. Inc., Rte. 1, Box 6B, Latta, SC 29565/803-752-7751

3-D Ammunition & Bullets, 112 Plum St., Doniphan, NE 68832/402-845-2285

United States Ammunition Co. (USAC), Inc., 45500 - 15th St. East, Tacoma, WA 98424/206-922-7589

Weatherby's, 2781 E. Firestone Blvd., South Gate, CA 90280

Winchester, 427 N. Shamrock St., East Alton, IL 62024/618-258-2000

AMMUNITION (Custom)

A-Square Co., Inc., Rt. 4, Simmons Rd., Madison, IN 47250/812-273-3633

Accuracy Systems Inc., 15205 N. Cave Creek Rd., Phoenix, AZ 85032/602-971-1991

AFSCO Ammunition, 731 W. Third St., Owen, WI 54460/715-229-2516

Allred Bullet Co., 932 Evergreen Dr., Logan, UT 84321/801-752-6983

Atlanta Discount Ammo, P.O. Box 627, Norcross, GA 30091 (obsolete & wildcat calibers)

Beal's Bullets, 170 W. Marshall Rd., Lansdowne, PA 19050/215-259-1220 (Auto Mag Specialists)

Black Mountain Bullets, Rte.3, Box 297, Warrenton, VA 22186/703-347-1199

B.E.L.L. (See Eldorado Cartridge Corp.)

Russell Campbell Custom Loaded Ammo, 219 Leisure Dr., San Antonio, TX 78201/512-735-1183

Cartridges Unlimited, Rt. 1, Box 50, South Kent, CT 06785/203-927-3053 (British Express; metric; U.S.)

Cor-Bon Bullet Co., P.O. Box 10126, Detroit, MI 48210/313-894-2373

Cumberland Arms, Rt. 1, Box 1150, Shafer Rd., Blantons Chapel, Manchester, TN 37355

Custom Tackle & Ammo, P.O. Box 1886, Farmington, NM 87499/505-632-3539

Eldorado Cartridge Corp., P.O. Box 308, Boulder City, NV 89005/702-294-0025

Elko Arms, 28 rue Ecole Moderne, 7400 Soignies, Belgium/32-67.33.29.34

E.W. Ellis Sport Shop, RFD 1, Box 315, Corinth, NY 12822

Ellwood Epps Northern Ltd., 210 Worthington St. W., North Bay, Ont. PIB 3B4, Canada

Estate Cartridge Inc., P.O. Box 3702, Conroe, TX 77305/409-856-7277 (shotshell)

Jack First Distributors, Inc., 44633 Sierra Hwy., Lancaster, CA 93534/805-945-6981

Freedom Arms, P.O. Box 110, Freedom, WY 83120/307-883-2468

Ramon B. Gonzalez, P.O. Box 370, Monticello, NY 12701/914-794-4515

"Gramps" Antique Cartridges, Ellwood Epps, Box 341, Washago, Ont. L0K 2B0 Canada/705-689-5348

Hardin Specialty Distributors, P.O. Box 338, Radcliff, KY 40160/502-351-6649

Ace Hindman, 1880½ Upper Turtle Creek Rd., Kerrville, TX 78028/512-257-4290

Jett & Co. Inc., RR #3 Box 167-B, Litchfield, IL 62056/217-324-3779

R.H. Keeler, 817 "N" St., Port Angeles, WA 98362/206-457-4702

KTW Inc., 710 Foster Park Rd., Lorain, OH 44053/216-233-6919 (armor piercing for police and military only)

Lindsley Arms Cartridge Co., Inc., P.O. Box 757, 20 Crescent St., Henniker, NH 03242/603-428-3127 (inq. S.A.S.E.)

Lomont Precision Bullets, 4236 West 700 South, Poneto, IN 46781/219-694-6792 (custom cast bullets only)

McConnelistown Reloading & Cast Bullets, Inc., R.D. 3, Box 40, Huntingdon, PA 16652/814-627-5402

Mack's Sport Shop, Box 1155, Kodiak, AK 99615/907-486-4276

MagSafe Ammo, P.O. Box 5692, Olympia, WA 98503/206-456-4623

NAI/Ballistek, Box 535, Lake Havasu City, AZ 86403 (cases f. 25-20 Win. Single Shot)

North American Arms, 1800 North 300 West, Spanish Fork, UT 84660/801-798-7401

Patriot Mfg. & Sales, 2163 Oak Beach Blvd., P.O. Box 2041, Sebring, FL 33871/813-655-1798

Personal Protection Systems, Ltd., Aberdeen Rd., RD #5 Box 5027-A, Moscow, PA 18444/717-842-1766 (High-Performance handgun loads)

Precision Ammo Co., P.O. Box 63, Garnerville, NY 10923/914-947-2720

Precision Prods. of Wash., Inc., N. 311 Walnut Rd., Spokane, WA 99206/509-928-0604 (Exammo)

Anthony F. Sailer, see: AFSCO

Sanders Cust. Gun Serv., 2358 Tyler Lane, Louisville, KY 40205

George W. Spence, 115 Locust St., Steele, MO 63877/314-695-4926 (boxer-primed cartridges)

3-D Ammunition & Bullets, 112 Plum St., Doniphan, NE 68832/402-845-2285 (reloaded police ammo)

3-Ten Corp., P.O. Box 269, Feeding Hills, MA 01030/413-789-2086 (44 magnum bulleted shot loads; handgun)

Thunderbird Cartridge Co., Inc., P.O. Box 302, Phoenix, AZ 85001/602-237-3823

R. A. Wardrop, P.O. Box 245, Mechanicsburg, PA 17055/717-766-9663

Zero Ammunition Co., Inc., P.O. Box 1188, Cullman, AL 35056/205-739-1606

AMMUNITION (Foreign)

Action Arms Ltd., P.O. Box 9573, Philadelphia, PA 19124/215-744-0100

AFSCO Ammunition, 731 W. Third St., Owen, WI 54460/715-229-2516

Atlanta Discount Ammo, P.O. Box 627, Norcross, GA 30091/404-446-2429

Beeman Inc., 3440-GD Airway Dr., Santa Rosa, CA 95403/707-578-7900

Chinasports, Inc., P.O. Box 2566, Sante Fe Springs, CA 90670/213-942-2383

Dynamit Nobel-RWS, Inc., 105 Stonehurst Court, Northvale, NJ 07647/210-767-1995 (RWS, Geco, Rottweil)

Fiocchi of America, Inc., Rt. 2, Box 90-8, Ozark, MO 65721/417-725-4118

Gun South, Inc., P.O. Box 129, 108 Morrow Ave. Trussville, AL 35173/205-655-8299

Hansen Cartridge Co., 244 Old Post Rd., Southport, CT 06490/203-259-7337

Hirtenberger Patronen-, Zundhutchen- & Metallwarenfabrik, A.G., Leobersdorfer Str. 33, A2552 Hirtenberg, Austria

Hunters Specialty, Inc., 130 Orchard Dr., Pittsburgh, PA 15235/412-795-8885 (Hirtenberger)

Paul Jaeger, Inc., P.O. Box 449, 1 Madison Ave., Grand Junction, TN 38039/901-764-6909 (RWS centerfire ammo)

PMC-Eldorado Cartridge Co., P.O. Box 308, Boulder City, NV 89005/702-294-0025

PTK International, 6030 Hwy. 85, Suite 614, Riverdale, GA 30274/404-997-5811

RWS (Rheinische-Westfälische Sprengstoff) See Dynamit Nobel; Paul Jaeger, Inc.

AMMUNITION COMPONENTS — BULLETS, POWDER, PRIMERS

A-Square Co., Inc., Rt. 4, Simmons Rd., Madison, IN 47250/812-273-3633 (cust. bull.; brass)

Accurate Arms Co., Inc., (Propellents Div.), Rt. 1, Box 167, McEwen, TN, 37101/615-729-4207/4208 (powders)

Acme Custom Bullets, 2414 Clara Lane, San Antonio, TX 78213/512-680-4828

Alaska Bullet Works, P.O. Box 54, Douglas, AK 99824/907-789-1576 (Alaska copper-bond cust. bull; Kodiak bonded core bullets)

Allred Bullet Co., 932 Evergreen Dr., Logan, UT 84321/801-752-6983 (custom bullets)

American Bullets, P.O. Box 15313, Atlanta, GA 30333/404-482-4253

American Products Co., 14729 Spring Valley Rd., Morrison, IL 61270/815-772-3336 (12-ga. shot wad)

Ammo-O-Mart Ltd., P.O. Box 125, Hawkesbury, Ont., Canada K6A 2R8/613-632-9300 (Nobel powder)

Atlanta Discount Ammo, P.O. Box 627, Norcross, GA 30091/404-446-2429 (bulk brass, primers; ctlg. $2)

Ballistic Prods., Inc., Box 408, 2105 Daniels St., Long Lake, MN 55356/612-473-1550 (shotgun powders, primers)

Ballistic Research Industries (BRI), 2825 S. Rodeo Gulch Rd. #8, Soquel, CA 95073/408-476-7981 (Sabo shotgun slug; Gualandislug)

Barnes Bullets, Inc., P.O. Box 215, American Fork, UT 84003/801-756-4222

Bell's Gun & Sport Shop, 3309-19 Mannheim Rd., Franklin Pk., IL 60131/312-678-1900

Berger Bullets, 4234 N. 63rd Ave., Phoenix, AZ 85033/602-846-5791 (cust. 22, 6mm benchrest bull.)

Bergman and Williams, 2450 Losee Rd., Suite F, No. Las Vegas, NV 89030/702-642-1091 (copper tube 308 cust. bull.; lead wire l. all sizes)

Bitterroot Bullet Co., Box 412, Lewiston, ID 83501/208-743-5635 (Broch.:USA, Can. & Mexico $1 plus legal size env., intl. $2; lit. pkg.: USA, Can. & Mexico $7.75, intl. $10.75

Black Mountain Bullets, Rte. 3, Box 297, Warrenton, VA 22186/703-347-1199 (custom Fluid King match bullets)

B.E.L.L., (See Eldorado Cartridge Corp.)

Bruno Bullets, 10 Fifth St., Kelayres, PA 18231/717-929-1791 (22, 6mm benchrest bull.)

Buffalo Rock Shooters Supply, R. Rt. 1, Ottawa, IL 61350/815-433-2471

Bullet Swaging Supply, Inc., P.O. Box 1056, 303 McMillan Rd., West Monroe, LA 71219/318-387-7257

CCI, (See: Omark Industries)

CheVron Bullets, R.R. 1, Ottawa, IL 61350/815-433-2471

Colorado Sutlers Arsenal, Box 991, Granby, CO 80446/303-887-2813

Competition Bullets Inc., 9996-29 Ave., Edmonton, Alb. T6N 1A2, Canada/403-463-2817

Cooper-Woodward, 8073 Canyon Ferry Rd., Helena, MT 59601/406-375-3321

Corbin Mfg. & Supply, Inc., 600 Industrial Circle, P.O. Box 2659, White City, OR 97503/503-826-5211 (bullets)

Cor-Bon Custom Bullets, P.O. Box 10126, Detroit, MI 48210/313-894-2373 (375, 44, 45 solid brass partition bull.)

Creative Cartridge Co., 56 Morgan Rd., Canton, CT 06019/203-693-2[...]

DuPont, (See IMR Powder Co.)

Dynamit Nobel-RWS Inc., 105 Stonehurst Court, Northvale, NJ 07647/201-767-1995 (RWS percussion caps)

Eagle Bullet Works, P.O. Box 2104, White City, OR 97503/503-826-7143 (Div-Cor 375, 224, 257 cust. bull.)

Eldorado Cartridge Corp., P.O. Box 308, Boulder City, NV 89005/702-294-0025

Excaliber Wax, Inc., P.O. Box 432, Kenton, OH 43326/419-673-0512 (wax bullets)

Federal Cartridge Co., 900 Ehlen Dr., Anoka, MN 55303/612-422-2840 (primers)

Fiocchi of America, Inc., Rt. 2 Box 90-8, Ozark, MO 65721/417-725-4118 (primers; shotshell cases)

Fisher Enterprises, 655 Main St. #305, Edmonds, WA 98020/206-776-4365

Fowler Bullets, 3731 McKelvey St., Charlotte, NC 28215/704-568-7661 (benchrest bullets)

Glaser Safety Slug, P.O. Box 8223, Foster City, CA 94404/415-345-7677

GOEX, Inc., Belin Plant, 1002 Springbrook Ave., Moosic, PA 18507/717-457-6724 (blackpowder)

Golden Powder International Sales, Inc., 8300 Douglas Ave., Suite 729, Dallas, TX 75225/214-373-3350 (Golden Powder/blackpowder)

Green Bay Bullets, P.O. Box 10446, 1486 Servais St., Green Bay, WI 54307-54304/414-497-2949 (cast lead bullets)

Grizzly Bullets, 2137 Hwy. 200, Trout Creek, MT 59874/406-847-2627 (cust.)

GTM Co., George T. Mahaney, 15915B E. Main St., La Puente, CA 91744 (all brass shotshells)

Gun Unlimited, 212 West Main Ave., Bismarck, ND 58501/701-223-2304

Hardin Specialty Distr., P.O. Box 338, Radcliff, KY 40160/502-351-6649 (empty, primed cases)

Harrison Bullet Works, 6437 E. Hobart St., Mesa, AZ 85205/602-985-7844 (cust. swaged .41 Mag. bullets)

Robert W. Hart & Son, Inc. 401 Montgomery St., Nescopeck, PA 18635/717-752-3655

Hercules Inc., Hercules Plaza, Wilmington, DE 19894 (smokeless powder)

Hodgdon Powder Co. Inc., P.O. Box 2932, Shawnee Mission, KS 66201/913-362-9455 (smokeless, Pyrodex and black powder)

Hoffman New Ideas, Inc., 821 Northmoor Rd., Lake Forest, IL 60045/312-234-4075 (practice sub. vel. bullets)

Hornady Mfg. Co., P.O. Drawer 1848, Grand Island, NE 68802/308-382-1390

Hunters Specialty, Inc., 130 Orchard Dr., Pittsburgh, PA 15235/412-795-8885 (Hirtenberger bullets)

Huntington's, 601 Oro Dam Blvd., Oroville, CA 95965/916-534-1210

IMR Powder Co., Rt. 5 Box 247E, Plattsburgh, NY 12901/518-561-9530 (smokeless powders only)

Jaro Manuf., P.O. Box 6125, 206 E. Shaw, Pasadena, TX 77506/713-472-0417 (bullets)

Kodiak Custom Bullets, 8261 Henry Circle, Anchorage, AK 99507/907-349-2282

Lage Uniwad Co., 1814 21st St., Eldora, IA 50627/515-858-2634

Ljutic Ind., Inc., Box 2117, Yakima, WA 98907/509-248-0476 (Mono-wads)

Lomont Precision Bullets, 4236 West 700 South, Poneto, IN 46781/219-694-6792 (custom cast bullets)

Paul E. Low Jr., R.R. 1, Dunlap, IL 61525/309-685-1392 (jacketed 44- & 45-cal. bullets)

McConnellstown Reloading & Cast Bullets, Inc., R.D. 3, Box 40, Huntingdon, PA 16652/814-627-5402

Mack's Sport Shop, Box 1155, Kodiak, AK 99615/907-486-4276 (cust. bull.)

Magnus Bullet Co., Inc., P.O. Box 2225, Birmingham, AL 35201/205-785-3357

MagSafe Ammo, P.O. Box 5692, Olympia, WA 98503/206-456-4623 (Controlled core bullets f. reloading)

Marshall Enterprises, 792 Canyon Rd., Redwood City, CA 94062/415-356-1230

Mayville Engineering Co., 715 South St., Mayville, WI 53050/414-387-4500 (non-toxic steel shot kits)

Metallic Casting & Copper Corp. (MCC), 214 E. Third St., Mt. Vernon, NY 10550/914-664-1311 (cast bullets)

Michael's Antiques, Box 591, Waldoboro, ME 04572 (Balle Blondeau)

Midway Arms, Inc., 5875 W. Van Horn Tavern Rd., Columbia, MO 65203/314-445-2400

Miller Trading Co., 20 S. Front St., Wilmington, NC 28401/919-762-7107 (bullets)

Necromancer Industries, Inc., 14 Communications Way, West Newton, PA 15089/412-872-8722

NORMA (See Federal Cartridge Co.)

Nosler Bullets Inc., 107 S.W. Columbia, Bend, OR 97702/503-382-5108

Old Western Scrounger, 12924 Hwy A-12, Montague, CA 96064/916-459-5445

Omark Industries, P.O. Box 856, Lewiston, ID 83501/208-746-2351

PMC — Eldorado Cartridge Co., P.O. Box 308, Boulder City, NV 89005/702-294-0025

Patriot Manufacturing & Sales, 2163 Oak Beach Blvd., P.O. Box 2041, Sebring, FL 33871/813-655-1798 (cust. bullets)

Pattern Control, 114 No. 3rd St., Garland, TX 75040/214-494-3551 (plastic wads)

Polywad, Inc., P.O. Box 7916, Macon, GA 31209 (Spred-Rs for shotshells)

Pyrodex, See: Hodgdon Powder Co., Inc. (black powder substitute)

Robert Pomeroy, Morison Ave., East Corinth, ME 04427/207-285-7721 (formed cases, obsolete ammo, bullets)

Power Plus Enterprises, Inc., P.O. Box 6070, Colubmus, GA 31907/404-561-1717 (12-ga. shotguns slugs; 308, 45 ACP, 357 cust. bull.)

Precision Ammo Co., P.O. Drawer 86, Valley Cottage, NY 10989/914-947-2710

Professional Hunter Supplies, P.O. Box 608; 660 Berding St., Ferndale, CA 95536/707-786-4040 (408, 375, 308, 510 cust. bull.)

Prometheus/Titan Black (See Fisher Enterprises)

Reardon Products, P.O. Box 126, Morrison, IL 61270/815-772-3155 (dry-lube powder)

Redwood Bullet Works, 3559 Bay Rd., Redwood City, CA 94063/415-367-6741 (cust. bullets)

Remington Arms Co., 1007 Market St., Wilmington, DE 19898/302-773-5291

R.J. Renner Co., P.O. Box 3543, Glendale, CA 91221-0543/818-241-6488 (rubber bullets)

Rubright Bullets, 1008 S. Quince Rd., Walnutport, PA 18088/215-767-1239 (cust. 22 & 6mm benchrest bullets)

Sierra Bullets Inc., 10532 So. Painter Ave., Santa Fe Springs, CA 90670

Southern Ammunition Co., Inc., Rt. 1, Box 6B, Latta, SC 29565/803-752-7751

Speer Products, Box 856, Lewiston, ID 83501

Sport Flite, P.O. Box 1082, Bloomfield Hills, MI 48308/313-647-3747 (zinc bases, gas checks)

Swift Bullet Co., RR. 1, Box 140A, Quinter, KS 67752/913-754-3959 (375 big game, 224 cust.)

Taracorp Industries, 16th & Cleveland Blvd., Granite City, IL 62040/618-451-4400 (Lawrence Brand lead shot)

3-D Ammunition & Bullets, 112 Plum St., Doniphan, NE 68832/402-845-2285

Thunderbird Cartridge Co., P.O. Box 302, Phoenix, AZ 85001/602-237-3823 (powder)

Trophy Bonded Bullets, P.O. Box 262348, Houston, TX 77207/713-645-4499 (big game 458, 308, 375 bonded cust. bullets only)

U.S. Ammunition Co./USAC, 4500 15th Street E, Tacoma, WA 98424/206-922-7589 (bullets)

Vitt/Boos, 2178 Nichols Ave., Stratford, CT 06497/203-375-6859 (Aerodynamic shotgun slug, 12-ga. only)

Ed Watson, Trophy Match Bullets, 2404 Wade Hampton Blvd., Greenville, SC 29615/803-244-7948 (22, 6mm cust. benchrest bull.)

Winchester/Olin, 427 N. Shamrock St., East Alton, IL 62024/618-258-2000

Worthy Products, Inc., R.R.I. Box 213, Martville, NY 13111 (slug loads)

Zero Bullet Co. Inc., P.O. Box 1188, Cullman, AL 35056/205-739-1606

ANTIQUE ARMS DEALERS

AD Hominem, R.R. 3, Orillia, Ont., L3V 6H3, Canada/705-689-5303

Antique Arms Co., David F. Saunders, 1110 Cleveland, Monett, MO 65708/417-235-6501

Antique Gun Parts, Inc., 1118 S. Braddock Ave., Pittsburgh, PA 15218/412-241-1811

Beeman Precision Arms, Inc., 3440-GD Airway Dr., Santa Rosa, CA 95403/707-578-7900 (airguns only)

Wm. Boggs, 827 Copeland Rd., Columbus, OH 43212/614-486-6965

Can Am Enterprises, 350 Jones Rd., Fruitland, ON L0R 1L0, Canada/416-643-4357 (catalog $2)

Cape Outfitters, Rt. 2 Box 437C, Cape Girardeau, MO 62701/314-335-4103

Century Intl. Arms, Inc., 5 Federal St., St. Albans, VT 05478/802-527-1252

Chas. Clements, III, 1741 Dallas St., Aurora, CO 80010/303-364-0403

David Condon, Inc., P.O. Box 312, 14502-G Lee Rd., Chantilly, VA 22021/703-631-7748

Continental Kite & Key Co. (CONKKO), P.O. Box 40, Broomall, PA 19008/215-356-0711

John Corry, 628 Martin Lane, Deerfield, IL 60015/312-541-6250 (English guns)

Dixie Gun Works, Inc., P.O. Box 130, Gun Powder Lane, Union City, TN 38261/901-885-0561

Peter Dyson Ltd., 29-31 Church St., Honley, Huddersfield, W. Yorksh. HD7 2AH, England/0484-661062 (acc. f. ant. gun coll.; custom-and machine-made)

Ed's Gun House, Box 62, Rte. 1, Minnesota City, MN 55959/507-689-2925

Ellwood Epps Northern Ltd., 210 Worthington St. W., North Bay, Ont. PIB 3B4 Canada

William Fagan, Box 26100, Fraser, MI 48026/313-465-4637

Jack First Distributors, Inc., 44633 Sierra Hwy., Lancaster, CA 93534/805-945-6981

N. Flayderman & Co., P.O. Box 2446, Ft. Lauderdale, FL 33303/305-761-8855

The Flintlock Muzzle Loading Gun Shop, 1238 ''G'' So. Beach Blvd., Anaheim, CA 92804/714-821-6655

Chet Fulmer, P.O. Box 792, Rt. 2, Buffalo Lake, Detroit Lakes, MN 56501/218-847-7712

Robert S. Frielich, 396 Broome St., New York, NY 10013/212-254-3045

Garcia National Gun Traders, Inc., 225 S.W. 22nd Ave., Miami, FL 33135

Herb Glass, P.O. Box 25, Bullville, NY 10915/914-361-3021

James Goergen, Rte. 2, Box 182BB, Austin, MN 55912/507-433-9280

Griffin's Guns & Antiques, R.R. 4, Peterboro, Ont., Canada K9J 6X5/705-745-7022

Guncraft Sports, Inc., 125 E. Tyrone Rd., Oak Ridge, TN 37830/615-483-4024

Hallowell & Co., 340 West Putnam Ave., Greenwich, CT 06830/203-869-2190

Hansen & Company, 244 Old Post Rd., Southport, CT 06490/203-259-7337

Kelley's, Harold Kelley, Box 125, Woburn, MA 01801/617-935-3389

Krider's Gun Shop, 114 W. Eagle Rd., Havertown, PA 19083/215-789-7828

Lever Arms Serv. Ltd. 2131 Burrard St. Vancouver, B.C. Canada V6J 3H7/604-736-0004

Liberty Antique Gunworks, 19 Key St., P.O. Box 183GD, Eastport, ME 04631/207-853-2327

Log Cabin Sport Shop, 8010 Lafayette Rd., Lodi, OH 44254/216-948-1082

Lone Pine Trading Post, Jct. Highways 61 and 248, Minnesota City, MN 55959/507-689-2925

Arthur McKee, 121 Eaton's Neck Rd., Northport, L.I., NY 11768/516-757-8850 (Rem. double shotguns)

Michael's Antiques, Box 591, Waldoboro, ME 04572

Charles W. Moore, R.D. #1, Box 276, Schenevus, NY 12155/607-278-5721

Museum of Historical Arms, 1038 Alton Rd., Miami Beach, FL 33139/305-672-7480 (ctlg $5)

Muzzleloaders Etc. Inc., 9901 Lyndale Ave. So., Bloomington, MN 55420/612-884-1161

Navy Arms Co., 689 Bergen Blvd., Ridgefield, NJ 07657/201-945-2500

New Orleans Arms Co., 5001 Treasure St., New Orleans, LA 70186/504-944-3371

Old Western Scrounger, 12924 Hwy A-12, Montague, CA 96064/916-459-5445 (write for list; $2)

Pioneer Guns, 5228 Montgomery, (Cincinnati) Norwood, OH 45212/513-631-4871

Pony Express Sport Shop, Inc., 16606 Schoenborn St., Sepulveda, CA 91343/818-895-1231

Martin B. Retting, Inc., 11029 Washington, Culver City, CA 90232/213-837-2412

Rutgers Gun & Boat Center, 127 Raritan Ave., Highland Park, NJ 08904/201-545-4344

San Francisco Gun Exch., 124 Second St., San Francisco, CA 94105/415-982-6097

Charles Semmer, 7885 Cyd Dr., Denver, CO 80221/303-429-6947

S&S Firearms, 74-11 Myrtle Ave., Glendale, NY 11385/718-497-1100

Steves House of Guns, Rte. 1, Minnesota City, MN 55959/507-689-2573

Stott's Creek Armory Inc., R 1 Box 70, Morgantown, IN 46160/317-878-5489

James Wayne, 2608 N. Laurent, Victoria, TX 77901/512-578-1258

Ward & Van Valkenburg, 114-32nd Ave. N., Fargo, ND 58102

M.C. Wiest, 125 E. Tyrone Rd., Oak Ridge, TN 37830/615-483-4024

Lewis Yearout, 308 Riverview Dr. E., Great Falls, MT 59404

APPRAISERS, GUNS, ETC.

Ad Hominem, R.R. 3, Orillia, ON L3V 6H3, Canada/705-689-5303

Antique Gun Parts, Inc., 1118 So. Braddock Ave., Pittsburgh, PA 15218/412-241-1811

Ahiman's, Rt. 1, Box 20, Morristown, MN 55052/507-685-4244

Ammunition Consulting Serv., Inc., Richard Geer, P.O. Box 1303, St. Charles, IL 60174/312-377-4625

The Armoury Inc., Route 202, New Preston, CT 06777/203-868-0001

Beeman Precision Arms, Inc., 3440-GD Airway Dr., Santa Rosa, CA 95403/707-578-7900 (airguns only)

Gordon Bess, 708 River St., Canon City, CO 81212/303-275-1073

Butterfield & Butterfield, 220 San Bruno Ave., San Francisco, CA 94103/415-861-7500

Lou Camilli, 4700 Oahu Dr. N.E. Albuquerque, NM 87111/505-293-5259

Cape Outfitters, Rt. 2 Box 437C, Cape Girardeau, MO 63701/314-335-4103

Christie's-East, 219 E. 67th St., New York, NY 10021/212-606-0400

E. Christopher Firearms Co., Inc., Route 128 & Ferry St., Miamitown, OH 45041/513-353-1321

Chas. Clements, III, 1741 Dallas St., Aurora, CO 80010/303-364-0403

David Condon, Inc., P.O. Box 312, 14502-G Lee Rd., Chantilly, VA 22021/703-631-7748

John Corry, 628 Martin Lane, Deerfield, IL 60015/312-541-6250 (English guns)

Custom Tackle & Ammo, P.O. Box 1886, Farmington, NM 87499/505-632-3539

D.O.C. Specialists (Doc & Bud Ulrich), 2209 So. Central Ave., Cicero, IL 60650/312-652-3606

Ed's Gun House, Ed Kukowski, Route 1, Box 62, Minnesota City, MN 55952/507-689-2925

Ellwood Epps (Orillia) Ltd., R.R. 3, Hwy. 11 No., Orillia, Ont. L3V 6H3, Canada/705-689-5333

William Fagan & Co., 22952 E. 15 Mile Rd., Mt. Clemens, MI 48043/313-465-4637

N. Flayderman & Co., Inc., P.O. Box 2446, Ft. Lauderdale, FL 33303/305-761-8855

Valmore J. Forgett, Jr., 689 Bergen Blvd., Ridgefield, NJ 07657/201-945-2500

Frederick Gun Shop, Paul Frederick, 10 Elson Dr., Riverside, RI 02915/401-433-2805

James Goergen, Rte. 2, Box 182BB, Austin, MN 55912/507-433-9280

''Gramps'' Antique Cartridges, Ellwood Epps, Box 341, Washago, Ont. L0K 2B0 Canada/705-689-5348

Leon E. ''Bud'' Greenwald, 2553 S. Quitman St., Denver, CO 80219/303-935-3850

Griffin & Howe, 36 West 44th St., Suite 1011, New York, NY 10036/212-921-0980

Griffin & Howe, 33 Claremont Rd., Bernardsville, NJ 07924/201-766-2287

Guncraft Sports, Inc., 125 E. Tyrone Rd., Oak Ridge, TN 37830/615-483-4024

Hallowell & Co., 340 West Putnam Ave., Greenwich, CT 06830/203-869-2190

Hansen and Company, 244-246 Old Post Rd., Southport, CT 06490/203-259-7337

Lew Horton Sports Shop, 450 Waverly St., Framingham, MA 01772/617-485-3060

Idaho Ammunition Service, 2816 Mayfair Dr., Lewiston, ID 83501/208-743-0270 (ammunition)

Kelley's, Harold Kelley, Box 125, Woburn, MA 01801/617-935-3389

Kenneth Kogan, P.O. Box 130, Lafayette Hills, PA 19444/215-233-4509

Liberty Antique Gunworks, 19 Key St., P.O. Box 183GD, Eastport, ME 04631/207-853-2327
Lone Pine Trading Post, Jct. Highways 248 & 61, Minnesota City, MN 55959/ 507-689-2925
Elwyn H. Martin, 937 So. Sheridan Blvd., Lakewood, CO 80226/303-922-2184
Miller Trading Co., 20 So. Front St., Wilmington, NC 28401/919-762-7107
The Museum of Historical Arms, Inc., 1038 Alton Rd., Miami Beach, FL 33139/305-672-7480
New England Arms Co., Lawrence Lane, Kittery Point, ME 03905/207-439-0593
Orvis Co. Inc., 10 River Rd., Manchester, VT 05254/802-362-3622
Pioneer Guns, 5228 Montgomery Rd., Norwood, OH 45212/513-631-4871
Pony Express Sport Shop, Inc., 16606 Schoenborn St., Sepulveda, CA 91343/818-895-1231
John Richards, Rte. 2, Box 325, Bedford, KY 40006/502-255-7222
Silver Shields Inc., 4464-D Chinden Blvd., Boise, ID 83714/208-323-8991
Steel City Arms, Inc., P.O. Box 81926, Pittsburgh, PA 15217/412-461-3100
Dale A. Storey, DGS, Inc., 305 N. Jefferson, Casper, WY 82601/307-237-2414
James C. Tillinghast, P.O. Box 405GD, Hancock, NH 03449/603-525-66151
James Wayne, 2608 N. Laurent, Victoria, TX 77901/512-578-1258
R. A. Wells Ltd., 3452 1st Ave., Racine, WI 53402/414-639-5223
M. C. Wiest, 125 E. Tyrone Rd., Oak Ridge, TN 37830/615-483-4024
Lewis Yearout, 308 Riverview Dr. East, Great Falls, MT 59404/406-761-0589

AUCTIONEERS, GUNS, ETC.

Ammunition Consulting Serv., Inc., Richard Geer, P.O. Box 1303, St. Charles, IL 60174/312-377-4625
Richard A. Bourne & Co. Inc., Box 141, Hyannis Port, MA 02647/617-775-0797
Butterfield & Butterfield, 220 San Bruno Ave., San Francisco, CA 94103/ 415-861-7500
Christie's-East, 219 E. 67th St., New York, NY 10021/212-606-0400
William Fagan & Co., 22952 E. 15 Mile Rd., Mt. Clemens, MI 48043/313-465-4637
Kelley's, Harold Kelley, Box 125, Woburn, MA 01801/617-935-3389
"Little John's" Antique Arms, 777 S. Main St., Orange, CA 92668
Parke-Bernet (see Sotheby's)
Sotheby's, 1334 York Ave. at 72nd St., New York, NY 10021
James C. Tillinghast, Box 405GD, Hancock, NH 03449/603-525-6615

BOOKS (ARMS), Publishers and Dealers

Armory Publications, P.O. Box 4206, Oceanside, CA 92054/619-757-3930
Arms & Armour Press, Cassell TLC, Artillery House, Artillery Row, London SW1P 1RT England
Beeman Precision Arms Inc. 3440GD Airway Dr., Santa Rosa, CA 95403/ 707-578-7900 (airguns only)
Blacksmith Corp. P.O. Box 1752, Chino Valley, AZ 86323/602-636-4456
Blacktail Mountain Books, 42 First Ave., West Kalispell, MT 59901/406-257-5573
DBI Books, Inc., 4092 Commercial Ave., Northbrook, IL 60062/ 312-272-6310
Fortress Publications Inc., P.O. Box 9241, Stoney Creek, Ont. L8G 3X9, Canada/416-662-3505
Guncraft Books, Div. of Ridge Guncraft Sports, Inc., 125 E. Tyrone Rd., Oak Ridge, TN 37830/615-483-4024
Gun Hunter Books, Div. of Gun Hunter Trading Co., 5075 Heisig St., Beaumont, TX 77705/409-835-3006
The Gun Room Press, 127 Raritan Ave., Highland Park, NJ 08904/ 201-545-4344 (publisher)
Gunnerman Books, P.O. Box 4292, Auburn Hills, MI 48057/313-879-2779
Handgun Press, Box 406, Glenview, IL 60025/312-657-6500
Kopp Publishing Co., 1301 Franklin, Lexington, MO 64067/816-259-2636
Lyman, 147 West St., Middlefield, CT 06455/203-349-3421
David Madis, 2453 West Five Mile Pkwy., Dallas, TX 75233/214-330-7169
McKee Publications, 121 Eatons Neck Rd., Northport, NY 11768/ 516-575-5334
The Outdoorsman's Bookstore, Llangorse, Brecon, County Powys LD3 7UE, (England) U.K.
Paladin Press, P.O. Box 1307, Boulder, CO 80306/303-443-7250
Petersen Publishing Co., 84990 Sunset Blvd., Los Angeles, CA 99069
Gerald Pettinger Arms Books, Route 2, Russell, IA 50238/515-535-2239
Ray Riling Arms Books Co., 6844 Gorsten St., P.O. Box 18925, Philadelphia, PA 19119/215-438-2456
Rutgers Book Center, Mark Aziz, 127 Raritan Ave., Highland Park, NJ 08904/201-545-4344 (bookseller)
Stackpole Books, Cameron & Kelker Sts., Telegraph Press Bldg., Harrisburg, PA 17105
Stoeger Publishing Co., 55 Ruta Court, South Hackensack, NJ 07606
Tara Press, P.O. Box 17211, Tuscon, AZ 85731/602-296-5333
Ken Trotman Ltd., 135 Ditton Walk, Unit 11, Cambridge CB5 8QD, England
Paul Wahl Corp., P.O. Box 500, Bogota, NJ 07603-0500/201-261-9245
Winchester Press, 220 Old New Brunswick Rd., Piscataway, NJ 08854/201-981-0820
Wolfe Publishing Co., Inc., 6471 Air Park Dr., Prescott, AZ 86301/ 602-445-7810

BULLET & CASE LUBRICANTS

C-H Tool & Die Corp., 106 N. Harding St., Owen, WI 54460/715-229-2146
Cienzoil Corp., P.O. Box 1226, Sta. C, Canton, OH 44708/216-833-9758
Cooper-Woodward, 8073 Canyon Ferry Rd., Helena, MT 59601/ 406-475-3321 (Perfect Lube)
Corbin Mfg. & Supply Inc., 600 Industrial Circle, P.O. Box 2659, White City, OR 97503/503-826-5211
Dillon Precision Prods., Inc.. 7442 E. Butherus Dr., Scottsdale, AZ 85260/602-948-8009
Green Bay Bullets, 1486 Servais St., Green Bay, WI 54304/414-497-2949 (EZE-Size case lube)
Javelina Products, P.O. Box 337, San Bernadino, CA 92402/714-882-5847 (Alox beeswax)
Jet-Aer Corp., 100 Sixth Ave., Paterson, NJ 07524
LeClear Industries, 1126 Donald Ave., P.O. Box 484, Royal Oak, MI 48068/313-588-1025
Lee Precision, Inc., 4275 Hwy. U, Hartford, WI 53027/414-673-3075
Lyman Products Corp., 147 West St., Middlefield, CT 06455/203-349-3421 (Size-Ezy)
M&M Engineering, 10642 Arminta St., Sun Valley, CA 91352/818-842-8376 (case lubes)
Micro-Lube, P.O. Box 117, Mesilla Park, NM 88047/505-524-4215
Midway Arms, Inc., 5875 W. Van Horn Tavern Rd., Columbia, MO 65203/314-445-2400
M&N Bullet Lube, P.O. Box 495, 151 N.E. Jefferson St., Madras, OR 97741/ 503-475-2992
Northeast Industrial, Inc., 9330 N.E. Halsey, Portland, OR 97220/ 503-255-3750 (Ten X-Lube; NEI mold prep)
Pacific Tool Co., P.O. Box 2048, Ordnance Plant Rd., Grand Island, NE 68801/308-384-2308
Ponsness-Warren, P.O. Box 8, Rathdrum, ID 83858/208-687-2231 (case lubes)
Radix Research & Marketing, Box 247, Woodland Park, CO 80866/ 303-687-3182 (Magnum Dri-Lube)
Redding Inc., 1089 Starr Rd., Cortland, NY 13045/607-753-3331
Rooster Laboratories, P.O. Box 412514, Kansas City, MO 64141/ 816-474-1622 (Zambini and HVR bullet lubes; case lubes & polish)
SAECO (See Redding)
Sandia Die & Cartridge Co., Route 5, Box 5400, Albuquerque, NM 87123/505-298-5729
Shooters Accessory Supply (SAS) (See Corbin Mfg. & Supply)
Tamarack Prods., Inc., P.O. Box 625, Wauconda, IL 60084/312-526-9333 (Bullet lube)

BULLET SWAGE DIES AND TOOLS

Bullet Swaging Supply, Inc., P.O. Box 1056, 303 McMillan Rd., West Monroe, LA 71291/318-387-7257
C-H Tool & Die Corp., 106 N. Harding St., Owen, WI 54460/715-229-2146
J.A. Clerke Co., P.O. Box 627, Pearblossom, CA 93553/805-945-0713 (moulds)
Mrs. Lester Coats, 416 Simpson Ave., North Bend, OR 97459/503-756-6995 (lead wire core cutter)
Corbin Mfg. & Supply Inc., 600 Industrial Circle, P.O. Box 2659, White City, OR 97503/503-826-5211
Hanned Precision, P.O. Box 2888, Sacramento, CA 95812 (cast bullet tools)
Hollywood Loading Tools (See M&M Engineering)
Huntington Die Specialties, 601 Oro Dam Blvd., Oroville, CA 95965/ 916-534-1210
M&M Engineering, 10642 Arminta St., Sun Valley, CA 91352/818-842-8376
Necromancer Industries, Inc., 14 Communications Way, West Newton, PA 15089/412-872-8722
Rorschach Precision Products, P.O. Box 151613, Irving, TX 75015/ 214-790-3487
SAS Dies, (See Corbin Mfg. & Supply)
Seneca Run Iron Works Inc., dba "Swagease", P.O. Box 3032, Greeley, CO 80633/303-352-1452 (muzzle-loading round ball)
Sport Flite Mfg., Inc., 2520 Industrial Row. Troy. MI 48084/313-280-0648

CARTRIDGES FOR COLLECTORS

AD Hominem, R.R. 3, Orillia. Ont., Canada L3V 6H3/705-689-5303
Ammo-Mart Ltd., P.O. Box 125, Hawkesbury, ON, K6A 2R8 Canada/613-632-9300
Ammunition Consulting Serv., Inc., Richard Geer, P.O. Box 1303, St. Charles, IL 60174/312-377-4625
Ida I. Burgess, Sam's Gun Shop, 25 Squam Rd., Rockport, MA 01966/617-546-6839
Cameron's, 16690 W. 11th Ave., Golden CO 80401/303-279-7365
Cape Outfitters, Rt. 2 Box 437C, Cape Girardeau, MO 63701/314-335-4105
Cartridges Unlimited, R. 1, Box 50, South Kent, CT 06785/203-927-3053
Chas. E. Duffy, Williams Lane, West Hurley, NY 12419/914-679-2997
Tom M. Dunn, 1342 So. Poplar, Casper, WY 82601/307-237-3207
Eldorado Custom Shop, P.O. Box 308, Boulder City, NV 89005/702-294-0025 (antique brass)
Ellwood Epps (Orillia) Ltd., Hwy. 11 North, Orillia, Ont. L3V 6H3, Canada/ 705-689-5333
Excaliber Wax, Inc. P.O. Box 432, Kenton, OH 43326/419-673-0512
Fiocchi of America, Inc., Rt. 2 Box 90-8, Ozark, MO 65721/417-725-4118
Jack First Distributors, Inc., 44633 Sierra Hwy., Lancaster, CA 93534/805-945-6981
Furr Arms, 76 East 350 No., Orem, UT 84057/801-226-3877
GTM Co., Geo. T. Mahaney, 15915B East Main St., La Puente, CA 91744/ 818-768-5806

Glaser Safety Slug, Inc., P.O. Box 8223, Foster City, CA 94404/415-345-7677
''Gramps'' Antique Cartridges, Ellwood Epps, Box 341, Washago, Ont., Canada L0K 2B0
Griffin's Guns & Antiques, R.R. #4, Peterboro, Ont. K9J 6X5, Canada/705-745-7022
Gun Parts Corp., Box 2, West Hurley, NY 12491/914-679-2417
Hansen and Company, 244-246 Old Post Rd., Southport, CT 06490/203-259-7337
Idaho Ammunition Service, 2816 Mayfair Dr., Lewiston, ID 83501/208-743-0270 (ammunition)
Kelley's, Harold Kelley, Box 125, Woburn, MA 01801/617-935-3389
Metallic Casting & Copper Corp. (MCC), 214 E. Third St., Mt. Vernon, NY 10550/914-664-1311
Old Western Scrounger, 12924 Hwy. A-12, Montague, CA 96064/916-459-5445
PMC—Eldorado Cartridge Co., P.O. Box 308, Boulder City, NV 89005/702-294-0025
Jesse Ramos, P.O. Box 7105, La Puente, CA 91744/818-369-6384
San Francisco Gun Exchange, Inc., 124 Second St., San Francisco, CA 94105/415-982-6097
George W. Spence, 115 Locust St., Steele, MO 63877/314-695-4926
James C. Tillinghast, Box 405GD, Hancock, NH 03449/603-525-6615 (list $1)
Ward & VanValkenburg, 114-32nd Ave. No., Fargo, ND 58102/701-232-2351
Lewis Yearout, 308 Riverview Dr. E., Great Falls, MT 59404

CASES, CABINETS AND RACKS—GUN

API Outdoors Inc., P.O. Box 1432, Tallulah, LA 71284/318-574-4903 (racks)
Abel Safe & File Co., 105 North Fourth St., Fairbury, IL 61739/815-346-9280 (metal gun safes)
Alco Carrying Cases, 601 W. 26th St., New York, NY 10001/212-675-5820 (aluminum)
Bob Allen Co., 214 S.W. Jackson, Des Moines, IA 50315/515-283-2191/800-247-8048 (carrying)
The American Import Co., 1453 Mission St., San Francisco, CA 91403/415-863-1506
Art Jewel Ltd., Eagle Business Ctr., 460 Randy Rd., Carol Stream, IL 60188/312-260-0040 (cases)
Beeman Precision Arms, Inc., 3440-GDD Airway Dr., Santa Rosa, CA 95403/707-578-7900
Big Spring Enterprise ''Bore Stores'', P.O. Box 1115, Yellville, AR 72687/501-449-5297 (synthetic cases)
Boyt Co. Div. of Welsh Sportg. Gds., P.O. Drawer 668, Iowa Falls, IA 50126/515-648-4826
Browning, Rt. 4, Box 624-B, Arnold, MO 63010
Chipmunk (See Oregon Arms, Inc.)
Dara-Nes Inc., see: Nesci
Dart Mfg. Co., 4012, Bronze Way, Dallas, TX 75237/214-333-4221
Detroit-Armor Corp., 2233 No. Palmer Dr., Schaumburg, IL 60103/312-397-4070 (Saf-Gard steel gun safe)
Doskocil Mfg. Co., P.O. Box 1246, Arlington,TX 76004/817-467-5116 (Gun Guard carrying)
Ellwood Epps (Orillia) Ltd., R.R. 3, Hwy. 11 North, Orillia, Ont. L3V 6H3, Canada/705-689-5333 (custom gun cases)
Fort Knox Security Products, 1051 N. Industrial Park Rd., Orem, UT 84057/801-224-7233 (safes)
Gun Parts Corp., Box 2, West Hurley, NY 12491/914-679-2417 (cases)
Hansen and Hansen, 244 Old Post Rd., Southport, CT 06490/203-259-7337
Hogue Grips, P.O. Box 2038, Atascadero, CA 93423/805-466-6266
Marvin Huey Gun Cases, P.O. Box 22456, Kansas City, MO 64113/816-444-1637 (handbuilt leather cases)
Hugger Hooks Co., 3900 Easley Way, Golden, CO 80403/303-279-6160
Jumbo Sports Prod., P.O. Box 280-Airport Rd., Frederick, MD 21701
Kalispel Metal Prods. (KMP), P.O. Box 267, Cusick, WA 99119/509-445-1121 (aluminum boxes)
Kane Products Inc., 5572 Brecksville Rd., Cleveland, OH 44131/216-524-9962
Kolpin Mfg., Inc., Box 231, Berlin, WI 54923/414-361-0400
Bill McGuire, 1600 No. Eastmont Ave., East Wenatchee, WA 98802/509-884-6021 (custom)
Nesci Enterprises, Inc., P.O. Box 119, Summit St., East Hampton St., East Hampton, CT 06424/203-267-2588 (firearms security cases)
Oregon Arms, Inc., 164 Schulz Rd., Central Point, OR 97502/503-664-5586 (soft cases)
Paul-Reed, Inc., P.O. Box 227, Charlevoix, MI 49720
Penguin Industries, Inc., Airport Industrial Mall, Coatesville, PA 19320/215-384-6000
Protecto Plastics, Div. of Penguin Ind., Airport Industrial Mall, Coatesville, PA 19320/215-384-6000 (carrying cases)
Quality Arms, Inc., P.O. Box 19477, Houston, TX 77224/713-870-8377
Rahn Gun Works, Inc.,3700 Anders Rd., Hastings, MI 49058/616-945-9894 (leather trunk cases)
Red Head Inc., P.O. Box 7100, Springfield, MO 65801/417-864-5430
SSK Co., 220 N. Belvidere Ave., York, PA 17404/717-854-2897 (wooden cases)
San Angelo Co., 909 West 14th St., San Angelo, TX 76903/915-655-7126
Schulz Industries, 16247 Minnesota Ave., Paramount, CA 90723/213-439-5903 (carrying cases)
Security Gun Chest, (See Tread Corp.)

Sweet Home Inc., Subs. of Will-Burt., P.O. Box 250, Sweet Home, OR 97386/503-367-5185 (gun safes)
Tread Corp., P.O. Box 13207, Roanoke, VA 24032/703-982-6881 (security chest)
WAMCO, Inc., Mingo Loop, P.O. Box 337, Oquossoc, ME 04964-0337/207-864-3344 (wooden display cases)
Weather Shield Sports Equipm. Inc., Rte. #3, Peloskey Rd., Charlevoix, MI 49720
Wilson Case Co., 906 Juniata, Juniata, NE 68955/402-751-2145 (cases)

CHOKE DEVICES, RECOIL ABSORBERS & RECOIL PADS

Action Products Inc., 22 N. Mulberry St., Hagerstown, MD 21740/800-228-7763 (rec. shock eliminator)
Arms Ingenuity Co., Box 1; 51 Canal St., Weatogue, CT 06089/203-658-5624 (Jet-Away)
Armsport, Inc., 3590 N.W. 49th St., Miami, FL 33142/305-635-7850 (choke devices)
Baer Custom Guns, 1725 Minesite Rd., Allentown, PA 18103/215-398-2362 (compensator syst. f. 45 autos)
Stan Baker, 10000 Lake City Way, Seattle, WA 98125/206-522-4575 (shotgun specialist)
Briley Mfg. Co., 1085-B Gessner, Houston, TX 77055/713-932-6995 (choke tubes)
C&H Research, 155 Sunnyside Dr., Lewis, KS 67552/316-324-5445 (Mercury recoil suppressor)
Vito Cellini, Francesca Inc., 3115 Old Ranch Rd., San Antonio, TX 78217/512-826-2584 (recoil reducer; muzzle brake)
Clinton River Gun Serv. Inc., 30016 S. River Rd., Mt. Clemens, MI 48045 (Reed Choke)
Reggie Cubriel, 15610 Purple Sage, San Antonio, TX 78255/512-695-3364 (leather recoil pads)
Delta Vectors, Inc., 7113 W. 79th St., Overland Park, KS 66204/913-642-0307 (Techni-Port recoil compensation)
Edwards Recoil Reducer, 1104 Milton Rd., Alton, IL 62002/618-462-3257
Emsco Variable Shotgun Chokes, 101 Second Ave., S.E., Waseca, MN 56093/507-835-1779
Fabian Bros. Sptg. Goods, Inc., 1510 Morena Blvd., Suite ''I,'' San Diego, CA 92110/619-275-0816 (DTA Muzzle Mizer rec. abs.; MIL/brake)
Freshour Mfg., 1914-15th Ave. North, Texas City, TX 77590/713-945-7726 (muzzle brakes)
David Gentry Custom Gunmaker, 314 N. Hoffman, Belgrade, MT 59714/406-388-4867 (muzzle brakes)
Griggs Products, P.O. Box 789; 270 So. Main St., Suite 103, Bountiful, UT 84010/801-295-9696 (recoil director)
Gun Parts Corp., Box 2, West Hurley, NY 12491/914-679-2417
William E. Harper, The Great 870 Co., P.O. Box 6309, El Monte, CA 91734/213-579-3077
Hastings, P.O. Box 224, Clay Center, KS 67432/913-632-3169
I.N.C., Inc., P.O. Box 12767, Wichita, KS 67277/316-721-9570 (Sorbothane Kick-Eez recoil pad)
Intermountain Arms, 105 E. Idaho Ave., Meridian, ID 83642/208-888-4911 (Gunner's Choice muzzle brake)
KDF, Inc., 2485 Hwy. 46 N. Seguin, TX 78155/512-379-8141 (muzzle brake)
Lyman Products Corp., 147 West St., Middlefield, CT 06455/203-349-3421 (Cutts Comp.)
Mag-na-port International, Inc., 41302 Executive Drive, Mt. Clemens, MI 48045/313-469-6727 (muzzle-brake system)
Mag-Na-Port of Canada, 1861 Burrows Ave., Winnipeg, Manitoba R2X 2V6, Canada
Marble Arms Corp., 420 Industrial Park, Box 111, Gladstone, MI 49837/906-428-3710 (Poly-Choke)
Pachmayr Ltd., 1875 So. Mountain Ave., Monrovia, CA 91016/818-423-9704 (recoil pads)
P.A.S.T. Corp., 210 Park Ave., P.O. Box 7372, Columbia, MO 65205/314-449-7278 (recoil reducer shield)
Poly-Choke (See Marble Arms)
Pro-Port Ltd., 41302 Executive Dr., Mt. Clemens, MI 48045/313-469-7323
Protektor Model, 7 Ash St., Galeton, PA 16922/814-435-2442 (shoulder recoil pad)
Reed Choke (See Clinton River Gun Svc.)
Upper Missouri Trading Co., 304 Harold St., Crofton, NE 68730/402-388-4844
Walker Arms Co., Inc., Rte. 2, Box 73, Highway 80 West, Selma, AL 36701/205-872-6231

CHRONOGRAPHS AND PRESSURE TOOLS

Competition Electronics, Inc., 2542 Point O' Woods Dr., Rockford, IL 61111/815-877-3322
Custom Chronograph Inc., 5305 Reese Hill Rd., Sumas, WA 98295/206-988-7801
D&H Precision Tooling, 7522 Barnard Mill Rd., Ringwood, IL 60072/815-653-4011 (Pressure Testing Receiver)
H-S Precision, Inc., 112 N. Summit St., Prescott, AZ 86302/602-445-0607 (press. barrels)
Paul Jaeger, Inc., P.O. Box 449, 1 Madison Ave., Grand Junction, TN 38039
Oehler Research, Inc., P.O. Box 9135, Austin, TX 78766/512-327-6900
P.A.C.T. Inc., P.O. Box 531525, Grand Prairie, TX 75053/214-641-0049 (Precision chronogr.)
Quartz-Lok, 13137 N. 21st Lane, Phoenix, AZ 85029/602-863-2729
Tepeco, P.O. Box 342, Friendswood, TX 77546/713-482-2702 (Tepeco Speed-Meter)

CLEANING & REFINISHING SUPPLIES

Adco International, 1 Wyman St., Woburn, MA 01801/617-935-1799
The Alsa Corp., 7031 Marcelle, Paramount, CA 90723/213-531-4470 (ALLGUN Universal gun care kit)
American Gas & Chemical Co. Ltd., 220 Pegasus Ave., Northvale, NJ 07647/201-767-7300 (TSI gun lube)
Anderson Mfg. Co., P.O. Box 4218, Federal Way, WA 98063/206-838-4299 (stock finishes)
Armite Labs., 1845 Randolph St., Los Angeles, CA 90001/213-587-7744 (pen oiler)
Armoloy Co. of Ft. Worth, 204 E. Daggett St., Fort Worth, TX 76104/817-654-1751 (refinishing)
Beeman Precision Arms, Inc., 3440-GD Airway Dr., Santa Rosa, CA 95403/707-578-7900 (airguns only)
Belltung, Ltd., RR2, Box 69, Kent, CT 06757/203-354-5750 (gun cleaning cloth kit)
Birchwood-Casey, 7900 Fuller Rd., Eden Prairie, MN 55344/612-927-7933
Blacksmith Corp., P.O. Box 1752, Chino Valley, AZ 86323/602-636-4456 (Arctic Friction Free gun clg. equip.)
Blue and Gray Prods., Inc., R.D. #6, Box 362, Wellsboro, PA 16901/717-724-1383
Break-Free Corp., P.O. Box 25020, Santa Ana, CA 92799/714-953-1900 (lubricants)
Jim Brobst, 299 Poplar St., Hamburg, PA 19526/215-562-2103 (J-B Bore Cleaning Compound)
Brownells, Inc., 222 W. Liberty, Montezuma, IA 50171/515-623-5401
Browning Arms, Rt. 4, Box 624-B, Arnold, MO 63010
Chopie Mfg. Inc., 700 Copeland Ave., La Crosse, WI 54601/608-784-0926 (Black Solve gun cleaner)
Clenzoil Corp., Box 1226, Sta. C, Canton, OH 44708/216-833-9758
Crouse's Country Cover, P.O. Box 160, Storrs, CT 06268/203-429-3710 (Masking Gun Oil)
J. Dewey Mfg. Co., 186 Skyview Dr., Southbury, CT 06488/203-264-3064 (one-piece gun clg. rod)
Dri-Slide, Inc., 411 N. Darling, Fremont, MI 49412/616-924-3950
The Dutchman's Firearms Inc., 4143 Taylor Blvd., Louisville, KY 40215/502-366-0555
Eezox, Inc., P.O. Box 772, Waterford, CT 06385/203-447-8282 (cleaner, rust preventive)
Force 10, Inc., 3029 Fairfield Ave., Suite 223, Bridgeport, CT 06605/203-332-5901 (anti-rust protectant)
Forster Products, 82 E. Lanark Ave., Lanark, IL 61046/815-493-6360
Fountain Prods., 492 Prospect Ave., W. Springfield, MA 01089/413-781-4651
Forty-Five Ranch Enterpr., 119 S. Main St., Miami, OK 74354/918-542-9307
Grace Metal Products, Inc., P.O. Box 67, Elk Rapids, MI 49629/616-264-8133
Gun Parts Corp. (Successors to Numrich Arms Parts Div.), Box 2, West Hurley, NY 12491/914-679-2417 (gun blue)
Heller & Levin Associates, Inc., 88 Marlborough Court, Rockville Center, NY 11570/516-764-9349
Frank C. Hoppe Division, Penguin Ind., Inc., Airport Industrial Mall, Coatesville, PA 19320/215-384-6000
Hydrosorbent Products, Clayton Rd., Ashley Falls, MA 01222/413-229-2967 (silica gel dehumidifier)
J-B Bore Cleaner, 299 Poplar St., Hamburg, PA 19526/215-562-2103
Ken Jantz Supply, 222 E. Main, Davis, OK 73030/405-369-2316
Jet-Aer Corp., 100 Sixth Ave., Paterson, NJ 07524 (blues & oils)
Kellog's Professional Prods., Inc., 325 Pearl St., Sandusky, OH 44870/419-625-6551
Kleen-Bore, Inc., 20 Ladd Ave., Northampton, MA 01060/413-586-7240
K.W. Kleinendorst, R.D. #1, Box 113B, Hop Bottom, PA 18824/717-289-4687 (rifle cig. cables)
Terry K. Kopp, 1301 Franklin, Lexington, MO 64067/816-259-2636 (stock rubbing compound; rust preventative grease)
LPS Chemical Prods., Holt Lloyd Corp., 4647 Hugh Howell Rd., Box 3050, Tucker, GA 30084/404-934-7800
Mark Lee, 9901 France Court, Lakeville, MN, 55044/612-461-2114 (rust blue solution)
LEM Gun Specialties, P.O. Box 87031, College Park, GA 30337 (Lewis Lead Remover for handguns)
Lynx-Line, (see: Williams Shootin' Iron Service)
Marble Arms Co., 420 Industrial Park, Gladstone, MI 49837/906-428-3710
Mike Marsh, Croft Cottage, Main St., Elton, Derbyshire DE4 2BY, ENGLAND/062-988-669 (gun accessories)
Micro Sight Co., 242 Harbor Blvd., Belmont, CA 94002/415-591-0769 (stock bedding compound)
Nesci Enterprises, Inc., P.O. Box 119, Summit St., East Hampton, CT 06424/203-267-2588
Old World Oil Products, 3827 Queen Ave. No., Minneapolis, MN 55412/612-522-5037 (gun stock finish)
Omark Industries, P.O. Box 856, Lewiston, ID 83501/208-746-2351
Original Mink Oil, Inc., P.O. Box 20191, 11021 N.E. Beech St., Portland, OR 97220/503-255-2814
Outers Laboratories, Div. of Omark Industries, Route 2, Onalaska, WI 54650/608-781-5800
Ox-Yoke Originals, Inc., 34 W. Main St., Milo, ME 04463/207-943-2171 (dry lubrication patches)
Parker-Hale/Precision Sports, P.O. Box 5588, Cortland, NY 13045
Bob Pease Accuracy, P.O. Box 787, Zipp Rd., New Braunfels, TX 78131/512-625-1342
A.E. Pennebaker Co., Inc., P.O. Box 1386, Greenville, SC 29602/803-235-8016 (Pyro Dux)
Precision Sports, P.O. Box 708, 3736 Kellogg Rd., Cortland, NY 13045/607-756-2851 (Parker Hale)

R&S Industries Corp., 1312 Washington Ave., St. Louis, MO 63103/314-241-8464 (Miracle All Purpose polishing cloth)
RTI Research Ltd., P.O. Box 48300, Bental Three Tower, Vancouver, B.C. V7X 1A1, Canada/604-588-5141 (Accubore chemical bore cleaner)
Reardon Prod., P.O. Box 126, Morrison, IL 61270/815-772-3155 (Dry-Lube)
Red Star Target Co., 4519 Brisebois Dr. N.W., Calgary, AB T2L 2G3, Canada/403-289-7939
Rice Protective Gun Coatings, 235-30th St., West Palm Beach, FL 33407/407-848-7771
Richards Classic Oil Finish, John Richards, Rt. 2, Box 325, Bedford, KY 40006/502-255-7222 (gunstock oils, wax)
Rig Products, 87 Coney Island Dr., Sparks, NV 89431/702-331-5666
Rooster Laboratories, P.O. Box 412514, Kansas City, MO 64141/816-474-1622 (cartridge/case cleaner, polish, protectant)
Rusteprufe Labs., 1319 Jefferson Ave., Sparta, WI 54656/608-269-4144
Rust Guardit, see Kleen-Bore, Inc.
Tyler Scott, Inc., 313 Rugby Ave., Suite 162, Terrace Park, OH 45174/513-831-7603 (ML black solvent; patch lube)
Seacliff Inc., 2210 Santa Anita, So. El Monte, CA 91733/818-350-0515 (portable parts washer)
Shooter's Choice (See Venco Industries)
TDP Industries, Inc., 603 Airport Blvd., Doylestown, PA 18901/215-345-8687
Taylor & Robbins, Box 164, Rixford, PA 16745 (Throat Saver)
Texas Platers Supply Co., 2453 W. Five Mile Parkway, Dallas, TX 75233
Totally Dependable Products; See: TDP
Treso Inc., P.O. Box 4640, Pagosa Springs, CO 81157/303-731-2295 (mfg. Durango Gun Rod)
United States Products Co., 518 Melwood Ave., Pittsburgh, PA 15213/412-621-2130 (Gold Medallion bore cleaner/conditioner)
C. S. Van Gorden, 1815 Main St., Bloomer, WI 54724/715-568-2612 (Van's Instant Blue)
Venco Industries, Inc., 16770 Hilltop Park Pl., Chagrin Falls, OH 44022/216-543-8808 (Shooter's Choice bore cleaner & conditioner)
WD-40 Co., P.O. Box 80607, San Diego, CA 92138-9021/619-275-1400
J.C. Whitney & Co., 1917 Archer Ave., Chicago, IL 60680 (gunstock finish)
Williams Gun Sight, 7389 Lapeer Rd., Davison, MI 48423 (finish kit)
Williams Shootin' Iron Service, Rte. 1 Box 151A, Bennett Hill Rd., Central Lake, MI 49622/616-544-6615
Wisconsin Platers Supply Co., (See Texas Platters Supply Co.)
Z-Coat Co., 3915 U.S. Hwy. 98 S., Lakeland, FL 33801/813-665-1734 (Teflon coatings)
Zip Aerosol Prods., See Rig

CUSTOM GUNSMITHS

Accuracy Gun Shop, Lance Martini, 3651 University Ave., San Diego, CA 92104/619-282-8500
Accuracy Systems Inc., 15203 N. Cave Creek Rd., Phoenix, AZ 85032/602-971-1991
Accuracy Unlimited, 16036 N. 49 Ave., Glendale, AZ 85306/602-978-9089
Ahlman's Inc., R.R. 1, Box 20, Morristown, MN 55052/507-685-4244
Don Allen Inc., HC55, Box 326, Sturgis, SD 57785/605-347-5227
Alpine's Precision Gunsmithing, 2401 Government Way, Coeur d'Alene, ID 83814/208-765-3559
American Custom Gunmakers Guild, c/o Jan Meichert, Exec. Scy., 22 Division St., Northfield, MN 55057/507-645-8811
Amrine's Gun Shop, 937 Luna Ave., Ojai, CA 93023
Ann Arbor Rod and Gun Co., 1946 Packard Rd., Ann Arbor, MI 48104/313-769-7866
Antique Arms Co., D.F. Saunders, 1110 Cleveland Ave., Monett, MO 65708/417-235-6501
Armament Gunsmithing Co., Inc., 525 Route 22, Hillside, NJ 07205/201-686-0960
Arms Ingenuity Co., Box 1/51 Canal St., Weatogue, CT 06089/203-658-5624
Arms Services Corp., 33 Lockhouse Rd., Westfield, MA 01085/413-562-4196
Armurier Hiptmayer, P.O. Box 136, Eastman, Que. JOE 1P0, Canada/514-297-2492
Ed on Atzigen, The Custom Shop, 890 Cochrane Crescent, Peterborough, Ont., K9H 5N3 Canada/705-742-6693
Richard W. Baber, Alpine Gun Mill, 1507 W. Colorado Ave., Colorado Springs, CO 80904/303-634-4867
Baer Custom Guns, 1725 Minesite Rd., Allentown, PA 18103/215-398-2362 (rifles)
Bain & Davis Sptg. Gds., 307 E. Valley Blvd., San Gabriel, CA 91776/213-283-7449
Stan Baker, 10000 Lake City Way, Seattle, WA 98125/206-522-4575 (shotgun specialist)
Joe J. Balickie, 408 Trelawney Lane, Apex, NC 27502/919-362-5185
Barnes Custom Shop, dba Barnes Bullets Inc., P.O. Box 215, American Fork, UT 84003
Barta's Gunsmithing, 10231 US Hwy., #10, Cato, WI 54206/414-732-4472
Donald Bartlett, 31829-32nd Pl. S.W., Federal Way, WA 98023/206-927-0726
R.J. Beal, Jr., 170 W. Marshall Rd., Lansdowne, PA 19050/215-259-1220
Behlert Precision, RD 2 Box 63, Route 611 North, Pipersville, PA 18947/215-766-8681 (custom)
George Beitzinger, 116-20 Atlantic Ave., Richmond Hill, NY 11419/718-847-7661

Bell's Custom Shop, 3309 Mannheim Rd., Franklin Park, IL 60131/312-678-1900 (hadguns)

Bellm Contenders, P.O. Box 429, Cleveland, UT 84518

Bennett Gun Works, 561 Delaware Ave., Delmar, NY 12054/518-439-1862

Bergmann & Williams, 2450 Losee Rd., Suite F, No. Las Vegas, NV 89030, 702-642-1091

Gordon Bess, 708 Royal Gorge Blvd., Canon City, CO 81212/303-275-11073

Al Biesen, 5021 Rosewood, Spokane, WA 99208/509-328-9340

Roger Biesen, W. 2039 Sinto Ave., Spokane, WA 99201

Stephen L. Billeb, Box 1176, Big Piney, WY 83113/307-276-5627

Billingsley & Brownell, P.O. Box 25, Dayton, WY 82836/307-655-9344 (cust. rifles)

E.C. Bishop & Son Inc., 119 Main St., P.O. Box 7, Warsaw, MO 65355/816-438-5121

Duane Bolden, 1295 Lassen Dr., Hanford, CA 93230/209-582-6937 (rust bluing)

Charles Boswell, (Gunmakers), Div. of Saxon Arms Ltd., 615 Jasmine Ave., No., Unit J, Tarpon Springs, FL 34689/813-938-4882

Bowen Classic Arms Corp., P.O. Box 67, Louisville, TN 37777/615-984-3583

Kent Bowerly, Metolious Meadows Dr., H.O.R. Box 1903, Camp Sherman, OR 97730/503-595-6028

Larry D. Brace, 771 Blackfoot Ave., Eugene, OR 97404/503-688-1278

Brazos Arms Co., 17423 Autum Trails, Houston, TX 77084/713-463-0598 (gunsmithing)

Frank Brgoch, 1580 So. 1500 East, Bountiful, UT 84010/801-295-1885

A. Briganti, 475 Rt. 32, Highland Mills, NY 10930/914-928-9573

Brown Precision Inc., P.O. Box 270GD, 7786 Molinos Ave., Los Molinos, CA 96055/800-543-2506/916-384-2506 (rifles)

Ed Brown Products, Rte. 2 Box 2922, Perry, MO 63462/314-565-3261

Bruno Shooters Supply, 10 Fifth St., Lelayres, PA 18231/717-929-1791

David Budin, Main St., Margaretville, NY 12455/914-568-4103

Ida I. Burgess, Sam's Gun Shop, 25 Squam Rd., Rockport MA 01966/617-546-6839 (bluing repairs)

Leo Bustani, P.O. Box 8125, W. Palm Beach, FL 33407/305-622-2710

Cache La Poudre Rifleworks, 140 No. College Ave., Ft. Collins, CO 80524/303-482-6913 (cust. ML)

Cameron's Guns, 16690 W. 11th Ave., Golden, CO 80401

Lou Camilli, 4700 Oahu Dr. N.E., Albuquerque, NM 87111/505-293-5259 (ML)

Dick Campbell, 20000 Silver Ranch Rd., Conifer, CO 80433/303-697-0150

Ralph L. Carter, Carter's Gun Shop, 225 G St., Penrose, CO 81240/719-372-6240

Larry T. Caudill, 1025A Palomas Dr. S.E., Albuquerque, NM 87103/505-255-2515

Shane Caywood, P.O. Box 321, Minocqua, WI 54548/715-356-5414

Champlin Firearms, Inc., Box 3191, Woodring Airport, Enid, OK 73702/405-237-7388

R. MacDonald Champlin, P.O. Box 693, Manchester, NH 03105/603-483-8559 (ML rifles and pistols)

E. Christopher Firearms Co., Inc., Route 128 & Ferry St., Miamitown, OH 45041/513-353-1321

Classic Arms Corp., P.O. Box 8, Palo Alto, CA 94302/415-321-7243

Clinton River Gun Serv. Inc., 30016 S. River Rd., Mt. Clemens, MI 48045/313-468-1090

Charles H. Coffin, 3719 Scarlet Ave., Odessa, TX 79762/915-366-4729

Jim Coffin, 250 Country Club Lane, Albany, OR 97321/503-928-4391

David Costa, 94 Orient Ave., Arlington, MA 02174/617-643-9571

C. Ed Cox, 166 W. Wylie Ave., Washington, PA 15301/412-228-2932

Crocker, 1510 - 42nd St., Los Alamos, NM 87544 (rifles)

J. Lynn Crook, Rt. 6, Box 295-A, Lebanon, TN 37087/615-449-1930

Cumberland Arms, Rt. 1, Box 1150, Shafer Rd., Blantons Chapel, Manchester, TN 37355

Cumberland Knife & Gun Works, 5661 Bragg Blvd., Fayetteville, NC 28303/919-867-0009 (ML)

Custom Gun Guild, 2646 Church Dr., Doraville, GA 30340/404-455-0346

D&D Gun Shop, 383 Elmwood, Troy, MI 48083/313-583-1512

Homer L. Dangler, Box 254, Addison, MI 49220/517-547-6745 (Kentucky rifles; brochure $3)

Sterling Davenport, 9611 E. Walnut Tree Dr., Tucson, AZ 85715/602-749-5590

Davis Co., 2793 Del Monte St., West Sacramento, CA 95691/916-372-6789

Ed. Delorge, 2231 Hwy. 308, Thibodaux, LA 70301/504-447-1633

Jack Dever, 8520 N.W. 90, Oklahoma City, OK 73132/405-721-6393

R.H. Devereaux, D.D. Custom Rifles, 5240 Mule Deer Dr., Colorado Springs, CO 80919/719-548-8468

Dilliott Gunsmithing, Inc., Rt. 3, Box 340, Scarlett Rd., Dandridge, TN 37725/615-397-9204

Dominic DiStefano, 4303 Friar Lane, Colorado Springs, CO 80907

William Dixon, Buckhorn Gun Works, Rt. 4 Box 1230, Rapid City, SD 57702/605-787-6289

C.P. Donnelly-Siskiyou Gun Works, 45 Kubli Rd., Grants Pass, OR 97527/503-846-6604

Dowtin Gunworks (DGW), Rt. 4 Box 930A Flagstaff, AZ 86001/602-779-1898

Charles E. Duffy, Williams Lane, West Hurley, NY 12491/914-679-2997

Duncan's Gunworks Inc., 1619 Grand Ave., San Marcos, CA 92069/619-727-0515

D'Arcy A. Echols, 164 W. 580 S., Providence, UT 84332/801-753-2367

Jere Eggleston, P.O. Box 50238, Columbia, SC 29250/803-799-3402

Elko Arms, Dr. L. Kortz, 28 rue Ecole Moderne, B-7400 Soignies, H.T., Belgium

Bob Emmons, 11748 Robson Rd., Grafton, OH 44044/216-458-5890

Englishtown Sporting Goods, Inc., David J. Maxham, 38 Main St., Englishtown, NJ 07726/201-446-7717

Dennis Erhardt, P.O. Box 502, Canyon Creek, MT 59633/406-368-2298

Ken Eyster, Heritage Gunsmiths Inc., 6441 Bishop Rd., Centerburg, OH 43011/614-625-6131

Andy Fautheree, P.O. Box 4607, Pagosa Springs, CO 81157/303-731-5003 (cust ML; send SASE)

Ted Fellowes, Beaver Lodge, 9245-16th Ave., S.W., Seattle, WA 98106/206-763-1698 (muzzleloaders)

Ferlib, Via Costa 46, Gardone V.T., 25063, Italy

Ferris Firearms, Gregg Ferris, 1827 W. Hildebrand, San Antonio, TX 78201/512-734-0304

Fiberpro Inc., Robert Culbertson, 3636 California St., San Diego, CA 92101/619-295-7703 (rifles)

Jack First Distributors Inc., 44633 Sierra Highway, Lancaster, CA 93534/805-945-6981

Marshall F. Fish, Rt. 22 North, Box 2439, Westport, NY 12993/518-962-4897

Jerry A. Fisher, P.O. Box 652, 38 Buffalo Butte, Dubois, WY 82513/307-455-2722

Flaig's Inc., 2200 Evergreen Rd., Millvale, PA 15209/412-821-1717

Flint Creek Arms Co., David Demasi, P.O. Box 205, 136 Spring St., Phillipsburg, MT 59858 (bluing repairs)

Flynn's Cust. Guns, P.O. Box 7461, Alexandria, LA 71306/318-445-7130

James W. Fogle, RR 2, Box 258, Herrin, IL 62948/618-988-1795

Larry L. Forster, Box 212, 220-1st St., N.E., Gwinner, ND 58040/701-678-2475

Pete Forthofer's Gunsmithing, 711 Spokane Ave., Whitefish, MT 59937/406-862-2674

Forty-Niner Trading Co., P.O. Box 792, Manteca, CA 95336/209-823-7263

Fountain Products, 492 Prospect Ave., West Springfield, MA 01089/413-781-4651

Frank's Custom Rifles, 7521 E. Fairmount Pl., Tucson, AZ 85715/062-885-3901

Freeland's Scope Stands, 3737—14th Ave., Rock Island, IL 61201/309-788-7449

Fredrick Gun Shop, 10 Elson Drive, Riverside, RI 02915/401-433-2805

Karl J. Furr, 76 East 350 No., Orem, UT 84057/801-226-3877

Gander Mountain, Inc., P.O. Box 186, Wilmot, WI 53192/414-862-2344

Garcia Natl. Gun Traders, Inc., 225 S.W. 22nd Ave., Miami, FL 33135

Gator Guns & Repair, 6255 Spur Hwy., Kenai, AK 99611/907-283-7947

K. Genecco Gun Works, 10512 Lower Sacramento Rd., Stockton, CA 95210/209-951-0706

David Gentry Custom Gunmaker, 314 N. Hoffman, Belgrade, MT 59714-406-388-4867 (cust. Montana Mtn. Rifle)

Edwin Gillman, 33 Valley View Dr., Hanover, PA 17331/717-632-1662

Gilman-Mayfield, 1552 N. 1st, Fresno, CA 93703/209-237-2500

Dale Goens, Box 224, Cedar Crest, NM 87008

Ramon B. Gonzalez, P.O. Box 370, Monticello, NY 12701/914-794-4515

A.R. Goode, 4125 N.E. 28th Terr., Ocala, FL 32670/904-622-9575

Goodling's Gunsmithing, R.D. #1, Box 1097, Spring Grove, PA 17362/717-225-3350

Gordie's Gun Shop, Gordon Mulholland, 1401 Fulton St., Streator, IL 61364/815-672-7202

Charles E. Grace, 10144 Elk Lake Rd., Williamsburg, MI 49690/616-264-9483

Georges Granger, 66 cours Fauriel, 42100 Saint Etienne, France/77251473

Gene Graybill, 1035 Ironville Pike, Columbia, PA 17512/717-684-6220

Roger M. Green, P.O. Box 984, 435 East Birch, Glenrock, WY 82637/307-436-9804

Greg's Gunsmithing Repair, 3732 26th Ave. No., Robbinsdale, MN 55422/612-529-8103

Griffin & Howe, 36 W. 44th St., Suite 1011, New York, NY 10036/212-921-0980

Griffin & Howe, 33 Claremont Rd., Bernardsville, NJ 07924/201-766-2287

Guncraft, Inc., 117 W. Pipeline, Hurst, TX 76053/817-282-1464

Guncraft Sports, Inc., 125 E. Tyrone Rd., Oak Ridge, TN 37830/615-483-4024

Gunsite Gunsmithy, Box 451, Pauiden, AZ 86334/602-636-4104

The Gun Works, Joe Williams, 236 Main St., Springfield, OR 97477/503-741-4118 (ML)

H-S Precision, Inc., 112 N. Summit Ave., Prescott, AZ 86301/602-445-0607

Hagn Rifles & Actions, Martin Hagn, Box 444, Cranbrook, B.C. VIC 4H9, Canada/604-489-4861 (s.s. actions & rifles)

Fritz Hallberg, Inc., Gunsmithing, P.O. Box 322, Ontario, OR 97914/503-889-7052

Charles E. Hammans, P.O. Box 788, 2022 McCracken, Stuttgart, AR 72106/501-673-1388

Hammond Custom Guns, 619 S. Pandora, Gilbert, AZ 85234/602-892-3437

Dick Hanson, Hanson's Gun Center, 521 So. Circle Dr., Colorado Springs, CO 80910/719-634-4220

Harkrader's Cust. Gun Shop, 825 Radford St., Christiansburg, VA 24073

Rob't W. Hart & Son Inc., 401 Montgomery St., Nescopeck, PA 18635/717-752-3655 (actions, stocks)

Hartmann & Weiss GmbH, Rahistedter Bahnhofstr. 47, 2000 Hamburg 73, W. Germany/040-677-55-85

Hubert J. Hecht, Waffen-Hecht, P.O. Box 2635, Fair Oaks, CA 95628/916-966-1020

Stephen Heilmann, P.O. Box 657, Grass Valley, CA 95945/916-272-8758

Iver Henriksen, 1211 So. 2nd St. W, Missoula, MT 59801 (Rifles)

Darwin Hensley, P.O. Box 179, Brightwood, OR 97011/503-622-5411

Heppler's Gun Shop, 6000 B Soquel Ave., Santa Cruz, CA 95062/408-475-1235

High Bridge Arms Inc., 3185 Mission St., San Francisco, CA 94110/415-282-8358

Klaus Hiptmayer, P.O. Box 136, Eastman, PQ JOE 1PO, Canada/514-297-2492

Hoag Gun Works, 8523 Canoga Ave., Suite C, Canoga Park, CA 91304/818-998/1510

Wm. Hobaugh, The Rifle Shop, Box M, Phillipsburg, MT 59858/406-859-3515

Duane A. Hobbie Gunsmithing, 2412 Pattie Ave., Wichita, KS 67216/316-264-8266

Richard Hodgson, 9081 Tahoe Lane, Boulder, CO 80301

Hoenig and Rodman, 6521 Morton Dr., Boise, ID 83705/208-375-1116

Peter Hofer, F. Lang-Str. 13, A9170 Ferlach, Austria/0-42-27-3683 (cust.)

Dick Holland, 422 N.E. 6th St., Newport, OR 97365/503-265-7556

Hollis Gun Shop, 917 Rex St., Carlsbad, NM 88220/505-835-3782

Bill Holmes, Rt. 2, Box 242, Fayetteville, AR 72701/501-521-8958

Alan K. Horst, P.O. Box 68, 402 E. St., Albion, WA 99102/509-332-7109 (cust.)

Corey O. Huebner, 3604 S. 3rd W., Missoula, MT 59801/406-721-9647

Steven Dodd Hughes, P.O. Box 11455, Eugene, OR 97440/503-485-8869 (ML; ctlg. $3)

Al Hunkeler, Buckskin Machine Works, 3235 So. 358th St., Auburn, WA 98001/206-927-5412 (ML)

Hyper-Single Precision SS Rifles, 520 E. Beaver, Jenks, OK 74037/918-299-2391

Intermountain Arms, 105 E. Idaho Ave., Meridian, ID 83648/208-888-4911

Campbell H. Irwin, Hartland Blvd. (Rt. 20), Box 152, East Hartland, CT 06027/203-653-3901

Jackalope Gun Shop, 1048 S. 5th St., Douglas, WY 82633/307-358-3854

Paul Jaeger, Inc., P.O. Box 449, 1 Madison Ave., Grand Junction, TN 38039/901-764-6909

R.L. Jamison, Jr., Route 4, Box 200, Moses Lake, WA 98837/509-762-2659

Jarrett Rifles, Inc., Rt. 1 Box 411, Jackson SC 29831/803-471-3616 (rifles)

Jim's Gun Shop, James R. Spradlin, 113 Arthur, Pueblo, CO 81004/719-543-9462

Neal G. Johnson, Gunsmithing Inc., 111 Marvin Dr., Hampton, VA 23666/804-838-8091

Peter S. Johnson, The Orvis Co., Inc., 10 River Rd., Manchester, VT 05254/802-362-3622

Vern Juenke, 25 Bitterbush Rd., Reno, NV 89523/702-345-0225

L.E. Jurras & Assoc., Box 680, Washington, IN 47501/812-254-7698

Ken's Gun Specialties, K. Hunnell, Rt. 1 Box 147, Lakeview, AR 72642/501-431-5606

Kesseiring Gun Shop, 400 Pacific Hiway No., Burlington, WA 98233/206-724-3113

Benjamin Kilham, Kilham & Co., Main St., Box 37, Lyme, NH 03768/603-795-4112

Don Klein Custom Guns, Rt. 2, P.O. Box 277, Camp Douglas, WI 54618/608-427-6948

K.W. Kleinendorst, R.D. #1, Box 113B, Hop Bottom, PA 18824/717-289-4687

Terry K. Kopp, 1301 Franklin, Lexington, MO 64067/816-259-2636

J. Korzinek, R.D. #2, Box 73, Canton, PA 17724/717-673-8512 (riflesmith) (broch. $2)

Krider's Gun Shop, 114 W. Eagle Rd., Havertown, PA 19083/215-789-7828

Sam Lair, 520 E. Beaver, Jenks, OK 74037/918-299-2391 (single shots)

Maynard Lambert, Kamas, UT 84036

Ron Lampert, Rt. 1, Box 177, Guthrie, MN 56461/218-854-7345

Harry Lawson Co., 3328 N. Richey Blvd., Tucson, AZ 85716/602-326-1117

John G. Lawson, (The Sight Shop), 182 E. Columbia, Tacoma, WA 98404/206-474-5465

Mark Lee, 9901 France Court, Lakeville, MN 55044/612-461-2114

Frank LeFever & Sons, Inc., R.D. #1, Box 31, Lee Center, NY 13363/315-337-6722

Liberty Antique Gunworks, 19 Key St., P.O. Box 183GD, Eastport, ME 04631/207-853-2327

Lilja Precision Rifle Barrels, Inc., 245 Compass Creek Rd., P.O. Box 372, Plains, MT 59859/406-826-3084

Al Lind, 7821—76th Ave. S.W., Tacoma, WA 98498/206-584-6363

Ljutic Ind., Box 2117, Yakima, WA 98904 (shotguns)

James W. Lofland, 2275 Larkin Rd., Boothwyn, PA 19061/215-485-0391 (SS rifles)

Harry M. Logan, Box 745, Honokaa, HI 96727/808-776-1644

London Guns Ltd., P.O. Box 3750, Santa Barbara, CA 93130/805-683-4141

Long Island Gunsmith, Ltd., 573 Sunrise Hwy., West Babylon, NY 11704 (Carriage Trade Shotgun)

McCann's Muzzle-Gun Works, Tom McCann, 200 Federal City Rd., Pennington, NJ 08534/609-737-1707 (ML)

McCormick's Custom Gun Bluing, 609 N.E. 10th Ave., Vancouver, WA 98664/206-256-0579

Dennis McDonald, 8359 Brady St., Peosta, IA 52068/319-556-7940

Stan McFarland, 2221 Idella Ct., Grand Junction, CO 81506/303-243-4704 (cust. rifles)

Bill McGuire, 1600 N. Eastmont Ave., East Wenatchee, WA 98802/509-884-6021

MPI Stocks, 5655 N.W. St. Helens Rd., Portland, OR 97210/503-226-1215

Mag-na-port International, Inc., 41302 Executive Dr., Mt. Clemens, MI 48045/313-469-6727

Philip Bruce Mahony, 1-223 White Hollow Rd., Lime Rock, CT 06039/203-435-9341

Nick Makinson, R.R. #3, Komoka, Ont. N0L 1R0 Canada/519-471-5462 (English guns; repairs & renovations)

Monte Mandarino, 136 Fifth Ave. West, Kalispell, MT 59901/406-257-6208 (Penn. rifles)

Lowell Manley Shooting Supplies, 3684 Pine St., Deckerville, MI 48427/313-376-3665

Marquart Precision Co., P.O. Box 1740, Prescott, AZ 86302/602-445-5646

Elwyn H. Martin, Martin's Gun Shop, 937 S. Sheridan Blvd., Lakewood, CO 80226/303-922-2184

Maryland Gun Works, Ltd., TEC Bldg., 10097 Tyler Pl. #8, Ijamsville, MD 21754/301-831-8456

Seely Masker, Custom Rifles, 261 Washington Ave., Pleasantville, NY 10570/914-769-2627 (benchrest)

Geo. E. Matthews & Son Inc., 10224 S. Paramount Blvd., Downey, CA 90241

Maurer Arms, 2154-16th St., Akron, OH 44314/216-745-6864 (muzzleloaders)

John E. Maxson, 3507 Red Oak Lane, Plainview, TX 79072/806-293-9042 (high grade rifles)

Pete Mazur Restoration, 13083 Drummer Way, Grass Valley, CA 95949/916-268-2412 (double-bbld. rifles & shotguns)

R.M. Mercer, 216 S.Whitewater Ave., Jefferson, WI 53549/414-674-3839

Miller Arms, Inc., Dean E. Miller, P.O. Box 260,St. Onge, SD 57779/605-578-1790

S.A. Miller, Point Roberts Sports Ltd., P.O. Box 1053, 1440 Peltier Dr., Point Roberts, WA 98281/206-945-7014

Tom Miller, c/o Huntington's Sportsman's Store, 601 Oro Dam Blvd., Oroville, CA 95965/916-534-1210

Earl Milliron, 1249 N.E. 166th Ave., Portland, OR 97230/503-252-3725

Hugh B. Mills, Jr., 3615 Canterbury Rd., New Bern, NC 28560/919-637-4631

Monell Custom Guns, Red Mill Road, RD #2, Box 96, Pine Bush, NY 12566/914-744-3021

Wm. Larkin Moore & Co., 31360 Via Colinas, Suite 109, Westlake Village, CA 91361/818-889-4160

J.W. Morrison Custom Rifles, 4015 W. Sharon, Phoenix, AZ 85029/602-978-3754

Mitch Moschetti, P.O. Box 27065, Cromwell, CT 06416/203-632-2308

Mountain Bear Rifle Works, Inc., Wm. Scott Bickett, 100-B Ruritan Rd., Sterling, VA 22170/703-430-0420

Larry Mrock, R.F.D. 3, Box 207, Woodhill-Hooksett Rd., Bow, NH 03301/603-224-4096 (broch. $3)

William Neighbor, Bill's Gun Repair, 1007 Burlington St., Mendota, IL 61342/815-539-5786

Stephen E. Nelson, P.O. Box 1478, Albany, OR 97321/503-745-5232

Bruce A. Nettestad, R.R. 1, Box 140, Pelican Rapids, MN 56572/218-863-4301

New England Arms Co., Lawrence Lane, Kittery Point, ME 03905/207-439-0593

Newman Gunshop, 119 Miller Rd., Agency, IA 52530/515-937-5775 (ML)

Paul R. Nickels, P.O. Box 71043, Las Vegas, NV 89170/702-435-5318

Ted Nicklas, 5504 Hegel Rd., Goodrich, MI 48438/313-797-4493

William J. Nittler, 290 More Dr., Boulder Creek, CA 95006/408-338-3376 or 408-438-7731 (shotgun bbls. & actions; repairs)

Peter H. Noreen, Rt. 2 Box 49, Herman, MN 56248/612-677-2582

Jim Norman, Custom Gunstocks, 14281 Cane Rd., Valley Center, CA 92082/619-749-6252

Nu-Line Guns, 1053 Caulks Hill Rd., Harvester, MO 63303/314-441-4500

Eric Olson, 12711 E. 11th Ave., Spokane, WA 99216

Vic Olson, 5002 Countryside Dr., Imperial, MO 63052/314-296-8086

Oregon Trail Riflesmiths, Inc., P.O. Box 51, Mackay, ID 83251/208-588-2527

The Orvis Co., Inc., Peter S. Johnson, Rt. 7A, Manchester,VT 05254/802-362-3622

Maurice Ottmar, Box 657, 113 East Fir, Coulee City, WA 99115/509-632-5717

Pachmayr Ltd., 1875 So. Mountain Ave., Monrovia, CA 91016/818-357-7771

Jay A. Pagel, 1407 4th St. NW, Grand Rapids, MN 55744/218-326-3003 (cust. gunmaking & refinishing)

Pasadena Gun Center, 206 E. Shaw, Pasadena, TX 77506/713-472-0417

Paterson Gunsmithing, 438 Main St., Paterson, NJ 07502/201-345-4100

John T. Pell, KOGOT, 410 College Ave., Trinidad, CO 81082/719-846-9406

Pence Precision Barrels, RR #2 Box 179, So. Whitley, IN 46787/219-839-4745

Penrod Precision, 126 E. Main St., P.O. Box 307, No. Manchester, IN 46962/219-981-8385

A.W. Peterson Gun Shop, 1693 Old Hwy. 441, Mt. Dora, FL 32757 (ML)

Eugene T. Plante, Gene's Custom Guns, 3890 Hill Ave., White Bear Lake, MN 55110/612-429-5105

Precision Specialties, 131 Hendom Dr., Feeding Hills, MA 01030/413-786-3365

Professional Gunsmiths of America, 1301 Franklin, Lexington, MO 64067/816-259-2636

R&J Gunshop, Bob Kerr, 140 So. Redwood Hwy., Cave Junction OR 97523/503-592-2535

Rifle Shop, Box M, Philipsburg, MT 59858

J.J. Roberts, 166 Manassas Dr., Manassas Park, VA 22111/703-330-0448

Wm. A. Roberts, Jr., Rte. 4, Box 75, Athens, AL 35611/205-232-7027 (ML)

Don Robinson, Pennsylvania Hse., 36 Fairfaix Crescent, Southowram, Halifax, W. Yorkshire HX3 9SQ, England (airrifle stocks)

Rocky Mountain Rifle Works, Ltd., 1707 14th St., Boulder, CO 80302/303-443-9189

Bob Rogers Guns, P.O. Box 305, 344 S. Walnut St., Franklin Grove, IL 61031/815-456-2685

Royal Arms, 1210 Bert Acosta, El Cajon, CA 92020/619-448-5466

R.P.S. Gunshop, 11 So. Haskell, Central Point, OR 97502/503-664-5010

Russell's Rifle Shop, Route 5, Box 92, Georgetown, TX 78626/512-778-5338

Chad Ryan, RR 3 Box 72, Cresco, IA 52136

SSK Industries, 721 Woodvue Lane, Wintersville, OH 43952/614-264-0176

Sanders Custom Gun Serv., 2358 Tyler Lane, Louisville, KY 40205

Sandy's Custom Gunshop, Rte. #1, Box 4, Rockport, IL 62370/217-437-4241

Roy V. Schaefer, 965 W. Hilliard Lane, Eugene, OR 97404/503-688-4333

Schumaker's Gun Shop, Rte. 4, Box 500, Colville, WA 99114/509-684-4848

Schwartz Custom Guns, 9621 Coleman Rd., Hasiett, MI 48840/517-339-8939

David W. Schwartz Custom Guns, 2505 Waller St., Eau Claire, WI 54701/ 715-832-1735

Thad Scott Fine Guns Inc., P.O. Box 412, Indianola, MS 38751/601-887-5929

Shane's Gunsmithing, P.O. Box 321, Hwy. 51 So., Minocqua, WI 54548/715-356-7675

Shaw's Finest in Guns, 1201 La Mirada Ave., Escondido, CA 92026/619-746-2474

E.R. Shaw Inc., Small Arms Mfg. Co., Thomas Run Rd. & Prestley, Bridgeville, PA 15017/412-221-4343

Shell Shack, 113 E. Main, Laurel, MT 59044/406-628-8986 (ML)

Dan A. Sherk, 9701-17th St. Dawson Creek, B.C. V1G 4H7 Canada/604-782-5630

Shilen Rifles, Inc., 205 Metro Park Blvd., Ennis, TX 75119/214-875-5318

Shiloh Rifle Mfg. Co., Inc., P.O. Box 279; 20 Centennial Dr., Big Timber, MT 59011/406-932-4454

J.A. Shirley & Co. Riflemakers, 33 Malmers Well Rd., High Wycombe, Bucks. HP13 6PD, England/0494-446883

Harold H. Shockley, 204 E. Farmington Rd., Hanna City, IL 61536/309-565-4524 (hot bluing & plating)

Shootin' Shack, 1065 Silverbeach Rd. #1, Riviera Beach, FL 33403/407-842-0990 ('smithing services)

Shootist Supply, John Cook, 622 5th Ave., Belle Fourche, SD 57717/605-892-2811

Silver Shields Inc., 4464-D Chinden Blvd., Boise, ID 83714/208-323-8991

John E. Skinner, c/o Orvis Co., 10 River Rd., Manchester, VT 05254/802-362-3622

Steve Sklany, 566 Birch Grove Dr., Kalispell, MT 59901/406-755-4527 (Ferguson rifle)

Jerome F. Slezak, 1290 Marlowe, Lakewood (Cleveland), OH 44107/216-221-1668

Art Smith, 4124 Thrushwood Lane, Minnetonka, MN 55345/612-935-7829

John Smith, 912 Lincoln, Carpentersville, IL 60110

Jordan T. Smith, c/o Orvis Co., 10 River Rd., Manchester, VT 05254

Snapp's Gunshop, 6911 E. Washington Rd., Clare, MI 48617/517-386-9226

Fred D. Speiser, 2229 Dearborn, Missoula, MT 59801/406-549-8133

Spencer Reblue Service, 1820 Tupelo Trail, Holt, MI 48842/517-694-7474 (electroless nickel plating)

Sportsmen's Equip. Co., 915 W. Washington, San Diego, CA 92103/619-296-1501

Sportsmen's Exchange & Western Gun Traders, Inc., P.O. Box 111, 560 S. "C" St., Oxnard, CA 93030/805-483-1917

Ken Starnes, Rt. 1, Box 269, Scroggins, TX 75480/214-365-2312

Steelman's Gun Shop, 10465 Beers Rd., Swartz Creek, MI 48473/313-753-4884

Keith Stegall, Box 696, Gunnison, CO 81230

Dale Storey, 305 N. Jefferson, Casper, WY 82601/307-237-2414

Stott's Creek Armory Inc., R 1 Box 70, Morgantown, IN 46160/317-878-5489 (antique only)

Victor W. Strawbridge, 6 Pineview Dr., Dover Point, Dover, NH 03820/603-742-0013

W.C. Strutz, Rifle Barrels, Inc., P.O. Box 611, Eagle River, WI 54521/715-479-4766

Suter's House of Guns, 332 N. Tejon, Colorado Springs, CO 80902/303-635-1475

A.D. Swenson's 45 Shop, P.O. Box 606, Fallbrook, CA 92028

William G. Taimage, 451 Phantom Creek Lane, P.O. Box 512, Meadview, AZ 86444/602-564-2380

Target Airgun Supply, P.O. Box 428, South Gate, CA 90280/213-569-3417

Taylor & Robbins, Box 164, Rixford, PA 16745

James A. Tertin, c/o Gander Mountain, P.O. Box 128 - Hwy. W, Wilmot, WI 53192/414-862-2344

Larry R. Thompson, Larry's Gun Shop, 521 E. Lake Ave., Watsonville, CA 95076/408-724-5328

Daniel Titus, 872 Penn St., Bryn Mawr, PA 19010/215-525-8829

Tom's Gunshop, Tom Gillman, 4435 Central, Hot Springs, AR 71913/501-624-3856

Trapper Gun Inc., 18717 E. 14 Mile Rd., Fraser, MI 48026/313-792-0133

David Trevallion, R. 1, Box 39, Kittery Point, ME 03905/207-439-6822

Trinko's Gun Serv., 1406 E. Main, Watertown, WI 53094

James C. Tucker, 205 Trinity St., Woodland, CA 95695/916-662-0503

Dennis A. "Doc" & Bud Ulrich, D.O.C. Specialists, Inc., 2209 S. Central Ave., Cicero, IL 60650/312-652-3606

Upper Missouri Trading Co., Inc., Box 181, Crofton, MO 68730

Milton Van Epps, Rt. 69-A, Parish, NY 13131/313-625-7251

Gil Van Horn, P.O. Box 207, Llano, CA 93544

J.W. Van Patten, P.O. Box 145, Foster Hill, Milford, PA 18337/717-296-7069

John Vest, P.O. Box 1552, Susanville, CA 96130/916-257-7228

Vic's Gun Refinishing, 6 Pineview Dr., Dover, NH 03820/603-742-0013

Walker Arms Co., Inc., Rt. 2, Box 73, Hiwy 80 West, Selma, AL 36701/205-872-6231

R.D. Wallace, Star Rt. 1 Box 76, Grandin, MO 63943/314-593-4773

R.A. Wardrop, Box 245, 409 E. Marble St., Mechanicsburg, PA 17055

Weatherby's, 2781 Firestone Blvd., South Gate, CA 90280/213-569-7186

Weaver Arms Co., P.O. Box 8, Dexter, MO 63841/314-568-3800 (ambidextrous bolt action)

Chris Weber/Waffen-Weber, #6-1691 Powick Rd., Kelowna, BC V1X 4L1, Canada/604-762-7575

Cecil Weems, P.O. Box 657, Mineral Wells, TX 76067/817-325-1462

Wells Sport Store, Fed Wells, 110 N. Summit St., Prescott, AZ 86301/602-445-3655

R.A. Wells Ltd., 3452 N. 1st Ave., Racine, WI 53402/414-639-5223

Robert G. West, 3973 Pam St., Eugene, OR 97402/503-689-6610

Terry Werth, 1203 Woodlawn Rd., Lincoln, IL 62656/217-732-1300

Western Gunstocks Mfg. Co., 550 Valencia School Rd., Aptos, CA 95003

Duane Wiebe, P.O. Box 497, Lotus, CA 95651/916-626-6240

M.C. Wiest, 125 E. Tyrone Rd., Oak Ridge, TN 37830/615-483-4024

David W. Wills, 2776 Brevard Ave., Montgomery, AL 36109/205-272-8446

Williams Gun Sight Co., 7389 Lapeer Rd., Davison, MI 48423

Williamson-Pate Gunsmith Service, 117 W. Pipeline, Hurst, TX 76053/817-282-1464

Wilson's Gun Shop, P.O. Box 578, Rt. 3, Box 211-D, Berryville, AR 72616/501-545-3618

Robert M. Winter, R.R. 2, Box 484, Menno, SD 57045/605-387-5322

Wisner's Gun Shop, Inc., P.O. Box 58, Hiway 6, Adna, WA 98552/206-748-8942

Lester Womack, 512 Westwood Dr., Prescott, AZ 86301/602-778-9624

Mike Yee, 29927-56 Pl. S., Auburn, WA 98001/206-839-3991

Russ Zeeryp, 1601 Foard Dr., Lynn Ross Manor, Morristown, TN 37814

CUSTOM METALSMITHS

Accuracy Unlimited, Frank Glenn, 16036 N. 49th Ave., Glendale, AZ 85306/ 602-978-9089

Alley Supply Co., P.O. Box 848, Gardnerville, NV 89410/702-782-3800

Armament Gunsmithing Co., Inc., 525 Route 22, Hillside, NJ 07205/201-686-0960

Baer Custom Guns, 1725 Minesite Rd., Allentown, PA 18103/215-398-2362

Barta's Gunsmithing, 10231 US Hwy 10, Cato, WI 54206/414-732-4472

Behlert Precision, RD 2 Box 63, Rte. 611 North, Pipersville, PA 18497/215-766-8681

George Beitzinger, 116-20 Atlantic Ave., Richmond Hill, NY 11419/718-847-7661

Bellm Contenders, P.O. Box 429, Cleveland, UT 84518

Al Biesen & Assoc., West 2039 Sinto Ave., Spokane, WA 99201/509-328-6818

Ross Billingsley & Brownell, Box 25, Dayton, WY 82836/307-655-9344

E.C. Bishop & Son Inc., 119 Main St., P.O. Box 7, Warsaw, MO 65355/816-438-5121

Gregg Boeke, Rte. 2, Box 149, Cresco, IA 52136/319-547-3746

Larry D. Brace, 771 Blackfoot Ave., Eugene, OR 97404/503-688-1278

A. Briganti, 475 Rt. 32, Highland Mills, NY 10930/914-928-9573

Leo Bustani, P.O. 8125, W. Palm Beach, FL 33407/305-622-2710

Ralph L. Carter, 225 G St., Penrose, CO 81240/719-372-6240

Clinton River Gun Serv. Inc., 30016 S. River Rd., Mt. Clemens, MI 48045/ 313-468-1090

Condor Manufacturing, 418 W. Magnolia, Glendale, CA 91204/818-240-3173

Dave Cook, 5831-26th Lane, Brampton, MI 49837/906-428-1235

David Costa, 94 Orient Ave., Arlington, MA 02174/617-643-9571

Crandall Tool & Machine Co., 1545 N. Mitchell St., Cadillac, MI 49601/616-775-5562

Gordon D. Crocker, 1510 - 42nd St., Los Alamos, NM 87544/505-667-9117

Daniel Cullity Restorations, 209 Old County Rd., East Sandwich, MA 02537/ 508-888-1147

Custom Gun Guild, Frank Wood, 2646 Church Dr., Doraville, GA 30340/404-455-0346

D&D Gun Shop, 363 Elmwood, Troy, MI 48083/313-583-1512

D&H Precision Tooling, 7522 Barnard Mill Rd., Ringwood, IL 60072/815-653-4011

Jack Dever, 8520 N.W. 90th, Oklahoma City, OK 73132/405-721-6393

Dilliott Gunsmithing, Inc., Rte. 3 Box 340, Scarlett Rd., Dandridge, TN 37725/615-397-9204

Dominic DiStefano, 4304 Friar Lane, Colorado Springs, CO 80907/303-599-3366

D'Arcy A. Echols, 164 W. 580 S., Providence, UT 84332/801-753-2367

Ken Eyster Heritage Gunsmiths Inc., 6441 Bishop Rd., Centerburg, OH 43011/614-625-43031

Ferris Firearms, Gregg Ferris, 1827 W. Hildebrand, San Antonio, TX 78201/ 512-734-0304

Flaig's Inc., 2200 Evergreen Rd., Millvale, PA 15209/412-821-1717

Fountain Prods., 492 Prospect Ave., W. Springfield, MA 01089/413-781-4651

Frank's Custom Rifles, 7521 E. Fairmount Pl., Tucson, AZ 85715/602-885-3901

Fredrick Gun Shop, 10 Elson Dr., Riverside, RI 02915/401-433-2805 (engine turning)

Geo. M. Fullmer, 2499 Mavis st., Oakland, CA 94601/415-533-4193 (precise chambering — 300 cals.)

K. Genecco Gun Works, 10512 Lower Sacramento Rd., Stockton, CA 95210/209-951-0706

David Gentry Custom Gunmaker, 314 N. Hoffman, Belgrade, MT 59714/ 406-388-4867

Dale W. Goens, P.O. Box 224, Cedar Crest, NM 87008/505-281-5419

Gordie's Gun Shop, Gordon C. Mulholland, 1401 Fulton St., Streator, IL 61364/815-672-7202

Roger M. Green, P.O. Box 984, 435 East Birch, Glenrock, WY 82637/307-436-9804

Griffin & Howe, 36 West 44th St., Suite 1011, New York, NY 10036/212-921-0980

Griffin & Howe, 33 Claremont Rd., Bernardsville, NJ 07924/201-766-2287

Hagn Rifles & Actions, Martin Hagn, Box 444, Carnbrook, B.C. VIC 4H9, Canada/604-489-4861

Hammond Custom Guns, 619 S. Pandora, Gilbert, AZ 85234/602-892-3437

Harkrader's Custom Gun Shop, 825 Radford St., Christiansburg, VA 24073

Robert W. Hart & Son, Inc., 401 Montgomery St., Nescopeck, PA 18635/ 717-752-3655

Hartmann & Weiss GmbH, Rahlstedter Bahnhofstr. 47, 2000 Hamburg 73, West Germany/040-677-5585

Hubert J. Hecht, Waffen-Hecht, P.O. Box 2635, Fair Oaks, CA 95628/916-966-1020

Stephen Heilmann, P.O. Box 657, Grass Valley, CA 95945/916-272-8758

Heppler's Gun Shop, 6000 B Soquel AVe., Santa Cruz, CA 95062/408-475-1235

Klaus Hiptmayer, P.O. Box 136, R.R. 112 #750, Eastman, Que. JOE1P0, Canada/514-297-2492

Wm. H. Hobaugh, Box M, Phillipsburg, MT 59858/406-859-3515

Hollis Gun Shop, 917 Rex St., Carlsbad, NM 88220/505-885-3782

Intermountain Arms, 105 E. Idaho Ave., Meridian, ID 83642/208-888-4911

Paul Jaeger, Inc., P.O. Box 449, 1 Madison St., Grand Junction, TN 38039/901-764-6909

R. L. Jamison, Jr., Rt. 4, Box 200, Moses Lake, WA 98837/509-762-2659

Ken Jantz, 222 E. Main, Davis, OK 73030/405-369-2316

Neil A. Jones, RD #1, Box 483A, Saegertown, PA 16433/814-763-2769

L. E. Jurras & Assoc., Box 680, Washington, IN 47501/812-254-7698

Kennons Custom Rifles, 5408 Biffle Rd., Stone Mountain, GA 30088/404-469-9339

Benjamin Kilham, Kilham & Co., Main St., Box 37, Lyme, NH 03768/603-795-4112

Terry K. Kopp, 1301 Franklin, Lexington, MO 64067/816-259-2636

Ron Lampert, Rt. 1, Box 177, Guthrie, MN 56461/218-854-7345

Mark Lee, 9901 France Court, Lakeville, MN 55044/612-461-2114

Lija Precision Rifle Barrels, Inc., 245 Compass Creek Rd., P.O. Box 372, Plains, MT 59859/406-826-3084

Harry M. Logan, Box 745, Honokaa, HI 96727/808-776-1644

Pete Mazur Restoration, 13083 Drummer Way, Grass Valley, CA 94949/916-268-2412 (traditional metal finishing)

Stan McFarland, 2221 Idealla Ct., Grand Junction, CO 81505/303-243-4704

Miller Arms, Inc., P.O. Box 260, St. Onge, SD 57779/605-578-1790

J.W. Morrison Custom Rifles, 4015 W. Sharon, Phoenix, AZ 85029/602-978-3754

Mullis Guncraft, 3518 Lawyers Road East, Monroe, NC 28110/704-283-8789

Bruce A. Nettestad, Rt. 1, Box 140, Pelican Rapids, MN 56572/218-863-4301

Vic Olson, 5002 Countryside Dr., Imperial, MO 63052/314-296-8086

Pasadena Gun Center, 206 E. Shaw, Pasadena, TX 77506/713-472-0417

James Pearson, The Straight Shooter Gun Shop, 8132 County LS Rt. 2, Newton, WI 53063/414-726-4676

Penrod Precision, 126 E. Main St., P.O. Box 307, No. Manchester, IN 46962/219-982-8385

Precise Chambering Co., 2499 Mavis St., Oakland, CA 94601/415-533-4193

Precise Metalsmithing Enterprises, James L. Wisner, 146 Curtis Hill Rd., Chehalis, WA 98532/206-748-3743

Bob Rogers Gunsmithing, P.O. Box 305; 344 S. Walnut St., Franklin Grove, IL 61031/815-456-2685

J.A. Shirley & Co. Riflemakers, 33 Malmers Well Rd., High Wycombe, Bucks. HP13 6PD, England/0494-446883

Harold Shockley, 203 E. Farmington Rd., Hanna City, IL 61536/309-565-4524

Silver Shields Inc., 4464-D Chinden Blvd., Boise, ID 83714/208-323-8991

Snapp's Gunshop, 6911 E. Washington Rd., Calre, MI 48617/517-386-9226

Dale A. Storey, DGS, Inc., 305 N. Jefferson, Casper, WY 82601/307-237-2414

Dave Talley, P.O. Box 821, Glenrock, WY 82637/307-436-8724

J. W. Van Patten, P.O. Box 145, Foster Hill, Millford, PA 18337/717-296-7069

Vic's Gun Refinishing, 6 Pineview Dr., Dover, NH 03820/603-742-0013

Herman Waldron, Box 475, Pomeroy, WA 99347/509-843-1404

R. D. Wallace, Star Rt. 1 Box 76, Grandin, MO 63943/314-593-4773

Chris Weber/Waffen-Weber, #6-1691 Powick Rd., Kelowna, BC V1X 4L1, Canada/604-762-7575

Fred Wells, Wells Sport Store, 110 N. Summit St., Prescott, AZ 86301/602-445-3655

Terry Werth, 1203 Woodlawn Rd., Lincoln, IL 62656/217-732-9314

Robert G. West, 3973 Pam St., Eugene, OR 97402/503-689-6610

John Westrom, Precise Firearm Finishing, 25 N.W. 44th Ave., Des Moines, IA 50313/515-288-8680

DECOYS

Advance Scouts, Inc. 2741 Patton Rd., Roseville, MN 55113/612-639-1326 (goose getters)

Carry-Lite, Inc., 5203 W. Clinton Ave., Milwaukee, WI 53223/414-355-3520

Deer Me Products Co., Box 34, 1208 Park St., Anoka, MN 55303/612-421-8971 (Anchors)

Flambeau Prods. Corp., 15981 Valplast Rd., Middlefield, OH 44062/216-632-1631

Kenneth J. Klingler, P.O. Box 141; Thistle Hill, Cabot, VT 05647/802-426-3811

Penn's Woods Products, Inc., 19 W. Pittsburgh St., Delmont, PA 15626/412-468-8311

Royal Arms, 1210 Bert Acosta, El Cajon, CA 92020/619-448-5466 (wooden, duck)

Ron E. Skaggs, P.O. Box 34; 114 Miles Ct., Princeton, IL 61356/815-875-8207

ENGRAVERS, ENGRAVING TOOLS

John J. Adams, P.O. Box 167, Corinth, VT 04039/802-439-5904

Sam Alfano, 296 Henry Gaines Rd., Pearl River, LA 70452/504-863-3364

Gary Allard, Creek Side Metal & Woodcrafters, Fishers Hill, VA 22626/703-465-3903

Baron Technology, 62 Spring Hill Rd., Trumbull, CT 06611/203-452-0515

Billy R. Bates, 2905 Lynnwood Circle S.W., Decatur, AL 35603/205-355-3690

Sid Bell Originals Inc., R.D. 2, Box 219, Tully, NY 13159/607-842-6431

Weldon Bledsoe, 6812 Park Place Dr., Fort Worth, TX 76118/817-589-1704

C. Roger Blelle, 5040 Ralph Ave., Cincinnati, OH 45238/513-251-0249

Rudolph V. Bochenski, 11640 N. 51 Ave. #232, Glendale, AZ 85304/602-878-4327

Erich Boessler, Gun Engraving Intl., Am Vogeital 3, 8732 Munnerstadt, W. Germany/9733-9443

Ralph P. Bone, 718 N. Atlanta, Owasso, OK 74055/918-272-9745

Henry ''Hank'' Bonham, P.O. Box 242, Brownville, ME 04414/207-965-2891

Dan Bratcher, 311 Belle Air Pl., Carthage, MO 64836/417-358-1518

Frank Brgoch, 1580 So. 1500 East, Bountiful, UT 84010/801-295-1885

Dennis B. Brooker, Rt. 1, Box 12A, Derby, IA 50068/515-533-2103

Brownells, Inc., 222 W. Liberty, Montezuma, IA 50171/515-623-5401 (engraving tools)

Byron Burgess, 710 Bella Vista Dr., Morro Bay, CA 93442/805-772-3974

Brian V. Cannavaro, 480 Manning Rd., Kalispell, MT 59901/406-756-8851

E. Christopher Firearms Co., Inc., Route 128 & Ferry St., Miamitown, OH 45041/513-353-1321

Winston Churchill, Twenty Mile Stream Rd., RFD Box 29B, Proctorsville, VT 05153/802-226-7772

Clark Engravings, P.O. Box 80745, San Marino, CA 91108/818-287-1652

Frank Clark, 3714-27th St., Lubbock, TX 79410/806-799-1187

Crocker Engraving, 1510 - 42nd St., Los Alamos, NM 87544

Daniel Cullity, 209 Old County Rd., East Sandwich, MA 02537/508-888-1147

Ed Delorge, 2231 Hwy. 308, Thibodaux, LA 70301/504-447-1633

W. R. Dilling Engravers, Rod Dilling, 105 N. Ridgewood Dr., Sebring, FL 33870/813-385-0647

Mark Drain, S.E. 3211 Kamilche Point Rd., Shelton, WA 98584/206-426-5452

Michael W. Dubber, 5325 W. Mill Rd., Evansville, IN 47712/812-963-6156

Robert Evans, 332 Vine St., Oregon City, OR 97045/503-656-5693

Ken Eyster, Heritage Gunsmiths Inc., 6441 Bishop Rd., Centerburg, OH 43011/614-625-6131

John Fanzoi, P.O. Box 25, Ferlach, Austria 9170

Jacqueline Favre, 3111 So. Valley View Blvd., Suite B-214, Las Vegas, NV 89102/702-876-6278

Armi FERLIB, 46 Via Costa, 25063 Gardone V.T. (Brescia), Italy

Firearms Engravers Guild of America, Robert Evans, Secy., 332 Vine St., Oregon City, OR 97045/503-656-5693

Jeff W. Flannery Engraving Co., 11034 Riddles Run Rd., Union, KY 41091/606-384-3127 (color ctlg. $5)

James W. Fogle, RR 2, Box 258, Herrin, IL 62948/618-988-1795

Fountain Prods., 492 Prospect Ave., W. Springfield, MA 01089/413-781-4651

Henry Frank, Box 984, Whitefish, MT 59937/406-862-2681

Leonard Francolini, 56 Morgan Rd., Canton, CT 06019/203-693-2529

GRS Corp., (Glendo), P.O. Box 748, 900 Overlander St., Emporia, KS 66801/316-343-1084 (Gravermeister tool)

Jerome C. Glimm, 19 S. Maryland, Conrad, MT 59425/406-278-3574

Howard V. Grant, Hiawatha 153, Woodruff, WI 54568/715-356-7146

Griffin & Howe, 36 West 44th St., Suite 1011, New York, NY 10036/212-921-0980

Griffin & Howe, 33 Claremont Rd., Bernardsville, NJ 07924/201-766-2287

Gurney Engraving Method, #513-620 View St., Victoria, B.C. V8W 1J6 Canada/604-383-5243

John K. Gwilliam, 218 E. Geneva Dr., Tempe, AZ 85282/602-894-1739

Bryson J. Gwinnell, P.O. Box 998, Southwick, MA 01077

Hand Engravers Supply Co., 4348 Newberry Ct., Dayton, OH 45432/513-426-6762

Paul A. Harris Hand Engraving, 10630 Janet Lee, San Antonio, TX 78230/512-341-5121

Jack O. Harwood, 1191 S. Pendlebury Lane, Blackfoot, ID 83221/208-785-5368

Frank E. Hendricks, Master Engravers, Inc., Star Rt. 1A, Box 334, Dripping Springs, TX 78620/512-858-7828

Heidemarie Hiptmayer, R.R. 112, #750, P.O. Box 136, Eastman, Que., JOE 1PO, Canada/514-297-2492

Alan K. Horst, P.O. Box 68, 402 E. St. Albion, WA 99102/509-332-7109

Ken Hurst, P.O. Box 116, Estill, SC 29918/803-625-3070

Ralph W. Ingle, Master Engraver, #4 Missing Link, Rossville, GA 30741/404-866-5589 (color broch. $5)

Paul Jaeger, Inc., P.O. Box 449, 1 Madison Ave., Grand Junction, TN 38039/901-764-6909

Ken Jantz Supply, 222 E. Main, Davis, OK 73030/405-369-2316 (tools)

Bill Johns, 1113 Nightingale, McAllen, TX 78501/512-682-2971

Steven Kamyk, 9 Grandview Dr., Westfield, MA 01085/413-568-0457

Lance Kelly, 1824 Royal Palm Dr., Edgewater, FL 32032/904-423-4933

Jim Kelso, Rt. 1, Box 5300, Worcester, VT 05682/802-229-4254

E. J. Koevenig Engraving Service, P.O. Box 55, Rabbit Gulch, Hill City, SD 57745/605-574-2239

John Kudlas, 622-14th St. S.E., Rochester, MN 55904/507-288-5579

Nelson H. Largent, Silver Shield's Inc., 4464-D Chinden Blvd., Boise, ID 83714/208-323-8991

Leonard Leibowitz, 1025 Murrayhill Ave., Pittsburgh, PA 15217/412-361-5455 (etcher)

Franz Letschnig, Master-Engraver, 620 Cathcard, Rm. 422, Montreal, Queb. H3B 1M1, Canada/514-875-4989

Steve Lindsay, R.R.2 Cedar Hills, Kearney, NE 68847/308-236-7885

London Guns Ltd., P.O. Box 3750, Santa Barbara, CA 93130/805-683-4141

Dennis McDonald, 8359 Brady St., Peosta IA 52068/319-556-7940

Lynton S.M. McKenzie, 6940 N. Alvernon Way, Tucson, AZ 85718/602-299-5090

Wm. H. Mains, 3111 S. Valley View Blvd., Suite B-214, Las Vegas, NV 89102/702-876-6278

Robert E. Maki, School of Firearms Engraving, P.O. Box 947, Northbrook, IL 60065/312-724-8238

Laura Mandarino, 136 5th Ave. West, Kalispell, MT 59901/406-257-6208

George Marek, P.O. Box 213, Westfield, MA 01086/413-568-9816

Frank Mele, Longdale Rd., Mahopac, NY 10541/914-225-8872

Frank Mittermeier, 3577 E. Tremont Ave., New York, NY 10465/212-828-3843 (tool)

Mitch Moschetti, P.O. Box 27065, Denver, CO 80227/303-936-1184

Gary K. Nelson, 975 Terrace Dr., Oakdale, CA 95361/209-847-4590

NgraveR Co., 879 Raymond Hill Rd., Oakdale, CT 06370/203-848-8031 (MagnaGraver tool)

New Orleans Arms Co., P.O. Box 26087, New Orleans, LA 70186/504-944-3371

New Orleans Jewelers Supply, 206 Chartres St., New Orleans, LA 70130/504-523-3839 (engr. tool)

Oker's Engraving, 365 Bell Rd., Bellford Mtn. Hts., P.O. Box 126, Shawnee, CO 80475/303-838-6062

Old Dominion Engravers, Rt. 2 Box 54, Goode, VA 24556/703-586-5402

Pachmayr Ltd., 1875 So. Mountain Ave., Monrovia, CA 91016/818-357-7771

C. R. Pedersen & Son, 2717 S. Pere Marquette, Ludington, MI 49431/616-843-2061

E. Larry Peters, c/o Kimber, 9039 SE Janssen Rd., Clackamas, OR 97015/503-656-6016

Scott Pilkington, P.O. Box 125, Dunlap, TN 37237/615-592-3786

Paul R. Piquette, 80 Bradford Dr., Feeding Hills, MA 01030/413-786-5811

Eugene T. Plante, Gene's Custom Guns, 3890 Hill AVe., P.O. Box 10534, White Bear Lake, MN 55110/612-429-5105

Jeremy W. Potts, 1680 So. Granby, Aurora, CO 80012/303-752-2528

Wayne E. Potts, 912 Poplar St., Denver, CO 80220/303-355-5462

Ed Pranger, 1414-7th St., Anacortes, WA 98221/206-293-3488

E. C. Prudhomme, #426 Lane Building, 610 Marshall St., Shreveport, LA 71101/318-425-8421

Leonard Puccinelli Design, 3790 Via De LaValle, Suite 204, Del Mar, CA 92104/619-259-7978

Martin Rabeno, Spook Hollow Trading Co., Box 37F, RD #1, Ellenville, NY 12428/914-647-4567

Jim Riggs, 206 Azalea, Boerne, TX 78006/512-249-8567 (handguns)

J. J. Roberts, 166 Manassas Dr., Manassas Park, VA 22111/703-330-0448

John R. and Hans Rohner, 710 Sunshine Canyon, Boulder, CO 80302/303-444-3841

Bob Rosser, 142 Ramsey Dr., Albertville, AL 35950/205-878-5388

Joe Rundell, 6198 Frances Rd., Clio, MI 48420/313-687-0559

Robert P. Runge, 94 Grove St., Ilion, NY 13357/315-894-3036

Shaw's "Finest In Guns," 1201 LaMirada Ave., Escondido, CA 92026/619-746-2474

George Sherwood, Box 735, Winchester, OR 97495/503-672-3159

Ben Shostle, The Gun Room, 1201 Burlington Dr., Muncie, IN 47302/317-282-9073

W. P. Sinclair, 46 Westbury Rd., Edington, Wiltshire BA13 4PG, England

Ron Skaggs, P.O. Box 34, 114 Miles Ct., Princeton, IL 61356/815-875-8207

Mark A. Smith, 200 N. 9th Sinclair, WY 82334/307-324-7929

Ron Smith, 5869 Straley, Ft. Worth, TX 76114/817-732-6768

Terry Theis, P.O. Box 535, Fredericksburg, TX 78624/512-997-6778

George W. Thiewes, 1846 Allen Lane, St. Charles, IL 60174/312-584-1383

Denise Thirion, Box 408, Graton, CA 95444/707-829-1876

Robert B. Valade, 931-3rd. Ave., Seaside, OR 97138/503-738-7672

John Vest, P.O. Box 1552, Susanville, CA 96130/916-257-7228

Ray Viramontez, 4348 Newberry Ct., Dayton, OH 45432/513-426-6762

Vernon G. Wagoner, 2325 E. Encanto, Mesa, AZ 85203/602-835-1307

R. D. Wallace, Star Rt. 1 Box 76, Grandin, MO 63943/314-593-4773

Terry Wallace, 385 San Marino, Vallejo, CA 94589/707-642-7041

Floyd E. Warren, 1273 State Rt. 305 N.E., Cortland, OH 44410/216-638-4219

Kenneth W. Warren, Mountain States Engraving, P.O. Box 4631, Scottsdale, AZ 85261/602-991-5035

Rachel Wells, 110 N. Summit St., Prescott, AZ 86301/602-445-3655

Sam Welch, CVSR Box 2110, Moab, UT 84532/801-259-7620

Claus Willig, Siedlerweg 17, 8720 Schweinfurt, West Germany/09721-41446

Bernie Wolfe, 900 Tony Lama, El Paso, TX 79915 (engraving, plating, scrimshawing)

Mel Wood, P.O. Box 1255, Sierra Vista, AZ 85636/602-455-5541

GAME CALLS

Burnham Bros., Box 669, 912 Main St., Marble Falls, TX 78654/512-693-3112

Joe Hall's Shooting Products, Inc., 443 Wells Rd., Doylestown, PA 18901/215-345-6354

Hunter's Specialties, Inc., 5285 Rockwell Dr. N.E., Cedar Rapids, IA 52402/319-395-0321

Lohman Mfg. Co., P.O. Box 220, Neosho, MO 64850/417-451-4438

Mallardtone Game Calls, 2901 16th St., Moline, IL 61265/309-762-8089

Phil. S. Olt Co., Box 550, Pekin, IL 61554/309-348-3633

Quaker Boy Inc., 6426 West Quaker St., Orchard Parks, NY 14127/16-662-3979

Penn's Woods Products, Inc., 19 W. Pittsburgh St., Delmont, PA 15626

Pete Rickard, Inc., RD1 Box 292, Cobleskill, NY 12043/518-234-2731

Scotch Game Call Co., Inc., 6619 Oak Orchard Rd., Elba, NY 14058/716-757-9958

Johnny Stewart Game Calls, Inc., Box 7954, 5100 Fort Ave., Waco, TX 76714/817-772-3261

Tink's Safariland Hunting Corp., P.O. Box 69, Trappe, MD 21673/301-820-9797

GUN PARTS, U.S. AND FOREIGN

AMT (Arcadia Machine & Tool, Inc.), 6226 Santos Diaz, Irwindale, CA 91702/818-334-6629

Armes de Chasse, P.O. Box 827, Chadds Ford, PA 19317/215-388-1146

Armsport, Inc., 3590 N.W. 49th St., Miami, FL 33142/305-635-7850

Aztec International Ltd., P.O. Box 1888, Norcross, GA 30091/404-446-2304 (cartridge magazines)

Badger Shooter's Supply, 106 So. Harding, Owen, WI54460/715-229-2101

Behlert Custom Guns, Inc., RD 2, Box 36C, Route 611 North, Pipersville, PA 18947/215-766-8681 (handgun parts)

Can Am Enterprises, 350 Jones Rd., Fruitland, ON LOR 1L0, Canada/416-643-4357 (catalog $2)

Caspian Arms, 14 No. Main St., Hardwick, VT 05843/802-472-6454

Cherokee Gun Accessories, 4127 Bay St. Suite 226, Fremont, CA 94538/415-471-5770

D&E Magazines Mfg., P.O. Box 4876-D, Sylmar, CA 91342

Charles E. Duffy, Williams Lane, West Hurley, NY 12491

Eagle International, Inc., 5195 W. 58th Ave., Suite 300, Arvada, CO 80002/303-426-8100

Essex Arms, Box 345, Island Pond, VT 05846/802-723-4313 (.45 1911A1 frames & slides)

Federal Ordnance Inc., 1443 Potrero Ave., So. El Monte, CA 91733/213-350-4161

Jack First Distributors Inc., 44633 Sierra Highway, Lancaster, CA 93534/805-945-6981

Gun Parts Corp., Box 2, West Hurley, NY 12491/914-679-2417

Gun-Tec, P.O. Box 8125, W. Palm Beach, FL 33407 (Win. mag. tubing; Win. 92 conversion parts; SASE f. reply)

Hansen and Co., 244 Old Post Rd., Southport, CT 06490/203-259-7337

Hastings, P.O. Box 224, Clay Center, KS 67432/913-632-3169

Heller & Levin Associates, Inc., 88 Marlborough Court, Rockville Center, NY 11570/516-764-9349

Liberty Antique Gunworks, 19 Key St., P.O. Box 183GD, Eastport, ME 04631/207-853-2327 (S&W only; ctlg. $5)

Walter H. Lodewick, 2816 N.E. Halsey, Portland, OR 97232/503-284-2554 (Winchester parts)

Arthur McKee, 121 Eaton's Neck Rd., Northport, L.I., NY 11768/516-757-8850 (micrometer rec. sights)

John V. Martz, 8060 Lakeview Lane, Lincoln, CA 95648/916-645-2250 (parts for Luger and P-38s)

Olympic Arms Inc. dba SGW, 624 Old Pacific Hwy. S.E., Olympia, WA 98503/206-456-3471

Pacific Intl. Merch. Corp., 2215 "J" St., Sacramento, CA 95816/916-446-2737 (Vega 45 Colt mag.)

Para-Ordnance Mfg. Inc., 3411 McNicoll Ave., Unit #14, Scarborough, ON M1V 2V6, Canada/416-297-7855 (frames only)

Pre-64 Winchester Parts Co., P.O. Box 8125, West Palm Beach, FL 33407 (send stamped env. w. requ. list)

Quality Parts Co., 999 Roosevelt Trail, Windham, ME 04062/800-556-SWAT

Martin B. Retting, Inc., 11029 Washington Blvd., Culver City, CA 90232/213-837-2412

Royal Ordnance Works Ltd., P.O. Box 3245, Wilson, NC 27893/919-237-0515

Sarco, Inc., 323 Union St., Stirling, NJ 07980/201-647-3800

Sherwood Intl. Export Corp., 18714 Parthenia St., Northridge, CA 91324

Clifford L. Smires, R.D. 1, Box 100, Columbus, NJ 08022/609-298-3158 (Mauser rifle parts)

Springfield Sporters Inc., R.D. 1, Penn Run, PA 15765/412-254-2626

Triple-K Mfg. Co., 2222 Commercial St., San Diego, CA 92113/619-232-2066 (magazines, gun parts)

U.S.F.S. (United States Frame Specialists), P.O. Box 7762, Milwaukee, WI 53207/414-643-6387 (SA frames; back straps)

GUNS (U.S.-made)

A.A. Arms, Inc., P.O. Box 25610-272, Mint Hill, NC 28227/704-545-5565 (AP-9 auto pistol)

AMAC (American Military Arms Corp.), 2202 Redmond Rd., Jacksonville, AR 72076/501-982-1633

AMT (Arcadia Machine & Tool, Inc.), 6226 Santos Diaz, Irwindale, CA 91702/818-334-6629

Accuracy Systems, Inc., 15205 N. Cave Creek Rd., Phoenix, AZ 85032/602-971-1991

American Arms, Inc., P.O. Box 27163, Salt Lake City, UT 84127/801-971-5006

American Derringer Corp., 127 N. Lacy Dr., Waco, TX 76705/817-799-9111

American Industries, 8700 Brookpark Rd., Cleveland, OH 44129/216-398-8300

Armitage International, Ltd., P.O. Box 1099, Seneca, SC 29679/803-882-5900 (Scarab Skorpion 9mm pistol)

Armes de Chasse, 3000 Valley Forge Circle, King of Prussia, PA 19406/215-783-6133

A-Square Co., Inc., Rt. 4, Simmons, Rd., Madison, IN 47250/812-273-3633

Auto-Ordnance Corp., Williams Lane, West Hurley, NY 12491/914-679-7225

BF Arms, 1123 So. Locust, Grand Island, NE 68801/308-382-1121 (single shot pistol)

BJT, 445 Putman Ave., Hamden, CT 06517 (stainless double derringer)

Ballistic Research Industries (BRI), 2825 S. Rodeo Gulch Rd. #8, Soquel, CA 95073/408-476-7981

Barrett Firearms Mfg., Inc., P.O. Box 1077, Murfreesboro, TN 37133/615-896-2938 (Light Fifty)

Beretta U.S.A., 17601 Beretta Dr., Accokeek, MD 20607/301-283-2191

Browning (Gen. Offices), Rt. 1, Morgan, UT 84050/801-876-2711

Browning (Parts & Service), Rt. 4, Box 624-B, Arnold, MO 63010/314-287-6800

Bryco Arms (Distributed by Jennings Firearms)

Bushmaster Firearms Co., 999 Roosevelt Trail, Bldg. #3, Windham, ME 04062 (police handgun)

Calico (California Instrument Co.), 405 E. 19th St., Bakersfield, CA 93305/805-323-1327

Century Gun Dist., Inc., 1467 Jason Rd., Greenfield, IN 46140/317-462-4524 (Century Model 100 SA rev.)

Charter Arms Corp., 430 Sniffens Ln., Stratford, CT 06497/203-377-8080

Cheney Firearms Co., P.O. Box 321, Woods Cross, UT 84087/801-295-4396 (ML rifles)

Chipmunk (See Oregon Arms, Inc.)

Colt Firearms, P.O. Box 1868, Hartford CT 06101/203-236-6311

Competition Limited, 1664 S. Research Loop Rd., Tucson, AZ 85710/602-722-6455

Coonan Arms, Inc., 830 Hampden Ave., St. Paul, MN 55114/612-646-6672 (357 Mag. Autom.)

Daisy Manufacturing Co., Inc., P.O. Box 220, Rogers, AR 72756/501-636-1200

Dakota Arms, Inc., HC 55 Box 326, Sturgis, SD 57785/605-347-4686 (B.A. rifles)

Davis Industries, 15150 Sierra Bonita Lane, Chino, CA 91710/714-591-4726 (derringers; 32 auto pistol)

Detonics Mfg. Corp., 13456 S.E. 27th Pl., Bellevue, WA 98005/206-747-2100 (auto pistol)

DuBiel Arms Co., 1724 Baker Rd., Sherman, TX 75090/214-893-7313

E.M.F. Co. Inc., 1900 East Warner Ave. 1-D, Santa Ana, CA 92705/714-261-6611

Encom America, Inc., P.O. Box 5314, Atlanta, GA 30307/404-525-2801

Excam, Inc., 4480 East 11th Ave., Hialeah, FL 33013/305-681-4661

F.I.E. Corp. (See Firearms Import & Export Corp.)

Falling Block Works, P.O. Box 3087, Fairfax, VA 22038/703-476-0043

Feather Industries, 2500 Central Ave., Boulder, CO 80301/303-442-7021

Federal Eng. Corp., 2335 So. Michigan Ave., Chicago, IL 60616/312-842-1063

Firearms Imp. & Exp. Corp., P.O. Box 4866, Hialeah Lakes, Hialeah, FL 33014/305-685-5966 (FIE)

Freedom Arms Co., P.O. Box 1776, Freedom, WY 83120 (mini revolver, Ca-sull rev.)

Freedom Arms Marketing (See: L.A.R. Mfg. Co.)

Gilbert Equipment Co., Inc., P.O. Box 9846, Mobile, AL 36609

Göncz Co., 11526 Burbank Blvd., #18, No. Hollywood, CA 91601/818-505-0408

Gonic Arms Inc., 134 Flagg Rd., Gonic, NH 03867/603-332-8456 (ML)

Grendel, Inc., P.O. Box 908, Rockledge, FL 32955/305-636-1211

Hatfield Rifle Works, 2020 Calhoun, St. Joseph, MO 64501/816-279-8688 (squirrel rifle)

Holmes Firearms Corp., Rte. 6, Box 242, Fayetteville, AR 72703

Lew Horton Dist. Co. Inc., 15 Walkup Dr., Westboro, MA 01581/508-366-7400 (sporting firearms wholesaler)

Hyper-Single Precision SS Rifles, 520 E. Beaver, Jenks, OK 74037

IAI/Irwindale Arms, Inc., 6226 Santos Diaz St., Irwindale, CA 91702/818-334-1200

Interarms Ltd., 10 Prince St., Alexandria, VA 22323/703-548-1400

Intratec, 12405 S.W. 130th St., Miami, FL 33186/305-232-1821

Ithaca Gun, Route 34B, King Ferry, NY 13081/607-273-0200

Jennings Firearms, Inc., 3656 Research Way, Unit 33, Carson City, NV 89706/702-882-4007

Iver Johnson, see: AMAC

Kimber of Oregon, Inc., 9039 S.E. Jannsen Rd., Clackamas, OR 97015/503-656-1704

Kimel Industries, Box 335, Matthews, NC 28105/704-821-7663

L.A.R. Manufacturing Co., 4133 West Farm Rd., West Jordan, UT 84084/801-255-7106 (Grizzly Win Mag pistol)

Ljutic Ind. Inc., P.O. Box 2117, 732 N 16th Ave., Yakima, WA 98907/509-248-0476 (Mono-Gun)

Lorcin Engineering Co., Inc., 6471 Mission Blvd., Riverside, CA 92509/714-682-7374 (L-25 pistol)

Magnum Research, Inc., P.O. Box 32221, Minneapolis, MN 55432/612-574-1868

Marlin Firearms Co., 100 Kenna Drive, New Haven, CT 06473

Maverick Arms, Inc., Industrial Blvd., P.O. Box 586, Eagle Pass, TX 78853/512-773-9007

Merrill Pistol (See RPM)

M.O.A. Corp., 7996 Brookville-Salem Rd., Brookville, OH 45309/513-833-5559 (Maximum pistol)

Modern Muzzleloading, Inc., Hwy. 136 East, P.O. Box 130, Lancaster, MO 63548/816-457-2125 (ML Knight rifles)

O.F. Mossberg & Sons, Inc., 7 Grasso St., No. Haven, CT 06473

Navy Arms Co., 689 Bergen Blvd., Ridgefield, NJ 07657

New England Firearms Co., Inc., Industrial Rowe, Gardner, MA 01440/508-632-9393

North American Arms, 1800 North 300 West, Spanish Fork, UT 84660/801-798-7401

North American Specialists, 25422 Trabuco Rd. #105-328, El Toro, CA 92630/714-979-4867

Olympic Arms (See SGW/Safari Arms)

Oregon Arms, Inc., 165 Schulz Rd., Central Point, OR 97502/503-664-5586

Oregon Trail Riflesmiths, Inc., P.O. Box 51, Mackay, ID 83251/208-588-2527 (ML)

Pachmayr, Ltd., 1875 So. Mountain Ave., Monrovia, CA 91016/818-357-7771

Patriot Distribution Co., 2872 So. Wentworth Ave., Milwaukee, WI 53207/414-769-0760 (Avenger pistol)

E. F. Phelps Mfg., Inc. P.O. Box 2266, Evansville, IN 47714/812-423-2599 (Heritage I in 45-70)

Precision Small Parts, Inc., 155 Carlton Rd., Charlottesville, VA 22901/804-293-6124

RPM (R&R Sporting Arms, Inc.), 150 Viking Ave., Brea, CA 92621/714-990-2444 (XL pistol; formerly Merrill)

Rahn Gun Works, Inc., 3700 Anders Rd., Hastings, MI 49058/616-945-9894

Raven Arms, 1300 Bixby Dr., Industry, CA 91745/818-961-2511 (P-25 pistols)

Remington Arms Co., 1007 Market St., Wilmington, DE 19898/302-773-5291

Ruger (See Sturm, Ruger & Co.)

SAM Inc., see: Special Service Arms Mfg. Inc.

SGW/Safari Arms, Inc., 624 Pacific Hwy SE, Olympia, WA 98503/206-456-3471

S/S Sales of Georgia, P.O. Box 94168, Atlanta, GA 94168/404-355-5986

Savage Industries, Inc., Springdale Rd., Westfield, MA 01085/413-562-2361

Sedco Industries Inc., 506 Spring St., Unit E, Lake Elsinore, CA 92330/714-674-5957 (SP-22 pistol)

L.W. Seecamp Co., Inc., P.O. Box 255, New Haven, CT 06502/203-877-3429

C. Sharps Arms Co., Inc., P.O. Box 885, Big Timber, MT 59011/406-932-4353

Shiloh Rifle Mfg. Co., Inc., P.O. Box 279; 201 Centennial Dr., Big Timber, MT 59011/406-932-4454

Smith & Wesson, Inc., 2100 Roosevelt Ave., Springfield, MA 01101

Sokolovsky Corp., P.O. Box 70113, Sunnyvale, CA 94086/408-245-9268 (45 Automaster pistol)

Special Service Arms Mfg. Inc., 405 Rabbit Trail, Edgefield, SC 29824/803-637-1200

Sporting Arms Mfg., P.O. Box 191, Littlefield, TX 79339/806-385-5665 (Night Charmer/Snake Charmer II)

Springfield Armory, Inc., 420 W. Main St., Geneseo, IL 61254/309-944-5631

Steel City Arms, Inc., P.O. Box 81926, Pittsburgh, PA 15217/412-461-3100 (d.a. "Double Deuce" pistol)

Sturm, Ruger & Co., Inc., Lacey Place, Southport, CT 06490/203-259-7843

Sundance Industries, Inc., 8216 Lankershim Blvd., #11, North Hollywood, CA 91605/818-768-1083 (Model A-25 pistol)

Super Six Limited, P.O. Box 54, Mequon, WI 53092/414-723-5058

TMI Products, 1010 S. Plumer Ave., Tucson, AZ 85719/602-792-1075

Texas Longhorn Arms, Inc., P.O. Box 703, Richmond, TX 77469/713-341-0775 (S.A. sixgun)

Thompson/Center Arms, Farmington Rd., P.O. Box 5002, Rochester, NH 03867/603-332-2394

Trail Guns Armoury, 1422 E. Main St., League City, TX 77573/713-332-5833 (muzzleloaders)

Ultra Light Arms Co., P.O. Box 1270; 214 Price St., Granville, WV 26534/304-599-5687

United States Frame Specialists, Inc. (U.S.F.S.), P.O. Box 7762, Milwaukee, WI 53207/414-643-6387

U.S. Repeating Arms Co., P.O. Box 30-300, New Haven, CT 06511/203-789-5000

Varner Sporting Arms, Inc., 100-F N. Cobb Pkwy., Marietta, GA 30062/404-422-5468

Weatherby's, 2781 E. Firestone Blvd., South Gate, CA 90280

Weaver Arms Corp., 6265 Greenwich Dr., Suite 201, San Diego, CA 92122/619-452-2551

Dan Wesson Arms, 293 Main St., Monson, MA 01057/413-267-4081

Wichita Arms, 444 Ellis, Wichita, KS 67211/316-265-0661

Wildey Inc., P.O. Box 475, Brookfield, CT 06804/203-355-9000

Wilkinson Arms, 26884 Pearl Rd., Parma, ID 83660/208-722-6771

Winchester, (See U.S. Repeating Arms)

Wyoming Armory, Inc., Forest Pl., Bedford, WY 83112/307-883-2151

GUNS (Foreign)

Action Arms, P.O. Box 9573, Philadelphia, PA 19124/215-744-0100

American Arms, Inc., 715 E. Armour Rd., N. Kansas City, MO 64116/816-474-3161

Anschutz (See PSI — Precision Sales)

Armes de Chasse, P.O. Box 827, Chadds Ford, PA 19317/215-388-1146 (Merkel, Mauser pistols)

Armscor Precision, 1175 Chess Dr., Suite 204, Foster City, CA 94404/415-349-3592

GUNS (Foreign) — cont'd.

Armscorp of America, Inc., 4424 John Ave., Baltimore, MD 21227/301-247-6200

Arms Corp. of the Philippines (See: Armscor Precision)

Armoport, Inc., 3500 N.W. 10th Ct., Miami, FL 00142/005-005-7050

Autumn Sales Inc., 1320 Lake St., Fort Worth, TX 76102/817-335-1634

BRI (See Ballistic Research Industries)

Ballistic Research Industries, 2825 S. Rodeo Gulch Rd. #8, Soquel, CA 95073/408-476-7981

Beeman Precision Arms, Inc., 3440-GD Airway Dr., Santa Rosa, CA 95403/707-578-7900 (FWB, Weihrauch, Unique, Cork, Hammerli firearms)

Benelli Armi, S.p.A. (See: Sile Distributors — handguns/ Heckler & Koch — Shotguns)

Beretta U.S.A., 17601 Beretta Dr., Accokeek, MD 20607/301-283-2191

Charles Boswell (Gunmakers), Div. of Saxon Arms Ltd., 615 Jasmine Ave. N., Unit J, Tarpon Springs, FL 34689/813-938-4882

Bretton, 19, rue Victor Grignard, Z.I. Montreynaud, 42-St. Etienne, France

BRNO (See T.D. Arms)

Browning (Gen. Offices), Rt. 1, Morgan, UT 84050/801-876-2711

Browning, (parts & service), Rt. 4, Box 624-B, Arnold, MO 63010/314-287-6800

Cape Outfitters, Rt. 2 Box 437C, Cape Girardeau, MO 63701/314-335-4103

Century Intl. Arms Inc., 5 Federal St., St. Albans, VT 05478/802-527-1252

Chapuis Armes, 23, rue de Montorcier, BP15, 42380 St. Bonnet-Le-Chateau, France/(33)77.50.06.96

China Sports, Inc., 11805 E. Smith Ave., Santa Fe Springs, CA 90670/213-942-2383

Cimarron Arms, 9439 Katy Freeway, Houston, TX 77024 (Uberti)

Classic Doubles Intl., Inc., 1982 Innerbelt Business Center Dr., St. Louis, MO 63111/314-423-6191 (shotguns)

Connecticut Valley Arms Co., 5988 Peachtree Corners East, Norcross, GA 30071/404-449-4687 (CVA)

Charles Daly (See Outdoor Sports HQ)

Dixie Gun Works, Inc., Hwy 51, South, Union City, TN 38261/901-885-0561 (ML guns)

Dynamit Nobel-RWS Inc., 105 Stonehurst Court, Northvale, NJ 07647/201-767-1995 (Rottweil)

E.M.F. Co. Inc. (Early & Modern Firearms), 1900 E. Warner Ave. 1-D, Santa Ana, CA 92705/714-261-6611

Eagle Imports Inc., 1907 Highway #35, Ocean, NJ 07712/201-531-8375

Elko Arms, 28 rue Ecole Moderne, 7400 Soignes, Belgium

Euroarms of America, Inc., P.O. Box 3277, 1501 Lenoir Dr., Winchester, VA 22601/703-662-1863 (ML)

Excam Inc., 4480 E. 11 Ave., P.O. Box 3483, Hialeah, FL 33013/305-681-4661

F.I.E. Corp. (See Firearms Import & Export Corp.)

J. Fanzoj, P.O. Box 25, Ferlach, Austria 9170

Armi FERLIB di Libero Ferraglio, 46 Via Costa, 25063 Gardone V.T. (Brescia), Italy

Fiocchi of America, Inc., Rt. 2, Box 90-8, Ozark, MO 65721/417-725-4118

Firearms Imp. & Exp. Corp., (F.I.E.), P.O. Box 4866, Hialeah Lakes, Hialeah, FL 33014/305-685-5966

Auguste Francotte & Cie, S.A., rue de Trois Juin 109, 4400 Herstal-Liege, Belgium

Frankonia Jagd, Hofmann & Co., Postfach 6780, D-8700 Wurzburg 1, West Germany

Frigon Guns, 627 W. Crawford, Clay Center, KS 67432/913-632-5607 (cust.-made)

Galaxy Imports, Ltd., Inc., P.O. Box 3361, Victoria, TX 77903/512-573-4867

Renato Gamba, S.p.A., P.O. Box 48, I-25063 Gardone V.T. (Brescia), Italy

Armas Garbi, Urki #12, Eibar (Guipuzcoa) Spain (shotguns, See W. L. Moore)

Glock, Inc., 6000 Highlands Pkwy., Smyrna, GA 30082/404-432-1202

Griffin & Howe, 36 West 44th St., Suite 1011, New York, NY 10036/212-921-0980 (Purdey, Holland & Holland)

Griffin & Howe, 33 Claremont Rd., Bernardsville, NJ 07924/201-766-2287

Gun South, Inc., P.O. Box 129, 108 Morrow Ave., Trussville, AL 35173/205-655-8299 (Steyr, FN, Mannlicher)

Hallowell & Co., 340 West Putnam Ave., Greenwich, CT 06830/203-869-2190 (Agents for John Rigby & Co.)

Heckler & Koch Inc., 21480 Pacific Blvd., Sterling, VA 22170/703-450-1900

Heym America, Inc., 1426 East Tillman St., Ft. Wayne, IN 46816/219-447-4708

Incor, Inc., P.O. Box 132, Addison, TX 75001/214-931-3500 (Cosmi auto shotg.)

Interarmco, See Interarms (Walther)

Interarms Ltd., 10 Prince St., Alexandria, VA 22313/703-548-1400

Paul Jaeger Inc., P.O. Box 449, 1 Madison Ave., Grand Junction, TN 38039/901-764-6909

KDF, Inc., 2485 Hwy 46 No., Seguin, TX 78155/512-379-8141 (Mauser rifles)

Kimel Industries, Box 335, Matthews, NC 28105/704-821-7663

Krieghoff International, Inc., P.O. Box 549, Ottsville, PA 18942/215-847-5173

Laurona shotguns (See Galaxy Imports)

Llama (See Stoeger)

Magnum Research, Inc., P.O. Box 32221, Minneapolis, MN 55432/612-574-1868 (Desert Eagle)

Mandall Shooting Supplies, Inc., 3616 N. Scottsdale Rd., Scottsdale, AZ 85252/602-945-2553

Mannlicher (See Gun South)

Mauser-Werke Oberndorf, P.O. Box 1349, 7238 Oberndorf/Neckar, West Germany

Merkuria, FTC, Argentinska 38, 17000 Prague 7, Czechoslovakia (BRNO)

Midwest Gun Sport, 1108 Herbert Dr., Zebulon, NC 27597/919-269-5570 (E. Dumoulin)

Mitchell Arms, Inc., 3411 Lake Center Dr., Santa Ana, CA 92704/714-957-5711

Wm. Larkin Moore & Co., 31360 Via Colinas, Suite 109, Westlake Village, CA 91361/818-889-4160 (Garbi, Ferlib, Piotti, Perugini Visini)

Navy Arms Co., 689 Bergen Blvd., Ridgefield, NJ 07657

Norinco (See China Sports, Inc.)

Outdoor Sports Headquarters, Inc., 967 Watertower Lane, Dayton, OH 45449/513-865-5855 (Charles Daly shotguns)

PTK International, Inc., 6030 Hwy. 85, Suite 614, Riverdale, GA 30274/404-997-5811

Pachmayr Gun Works, 1875 So. Mountain Ave., Monrovia, CA 91016/818-357-7771

Pacific Intl. Merch. Corp., 2215 "J" St., Sacramento, CA 95816/916-446-2737

Parker Reproductions, 124 River Rd., Middlesex, NJ 08846/201-469-0100

Parker-Hale, Bisleyworks, Golden Hillock Rd., Sparbrook, Birmingham B11 2PZ, England

Perazzi U.S.A. Inc., 1207 S. Shamrock Ave., Monrovia, CA 91016/818-303-0068

Poly Technologies, Inc. (See PTK International, Inc.)

Precision Sales Intl. Inc., PSI, P.O. Box 1776, Westfield, MA 01086/413-562-5055 (Anschutz)

Precision Sports, P.O. Box 708, Kellogg Rd., Cortland, NY 13045/607-756-2851 (Parker-Hale)

Quality Arms, Inc., Box 19477, Houston, TX 77224/713-870-8377 (Bernardelli; Ferlib; Bretton shotguns)

Quantetics Corp., Imp.-Exp. Div., 582 Somerset St. W., Ottawa, Ont. K1R 5K2 Canada/613-237-0242 (Unique pistols-Can. only)

Rahn Gun Works, Inc., 3700 Anders Rd., Hastings, MI 49058/616-945-9894

Rottweil, (See Dynamit Nobel)

The New SKB Gun Co., RD #8 Box 145, Manheim, PA 17545/717-664-4040

Samco Enterprises, Inc., 6995 N.W. 43rd St., Miami, FL 33166/305-593-9782

Sauer (See Sigarms)

Thad Scott, P.O. Box 412; Hwy 82 West, Indianola, MS 38751/601-887-5929 (Perugini Visini; Bertuzzi; Mario Beschi shotguns)

Sigarms Inc., 470 Spring Park Pl., Unit 900, Herndon, VA 22070/703-481-6660

Sile Distributors, 7 Centre Market Pl., New York, NY 10013/212-925-4111

Ernie Simmons Enterprises, see: New SKB Gun Company

Franz Sodia Jagdgewehrfabrik, Schulhausgasse 14, 9170 Ferlach, (Karnten) Austria

Sportarms of Florida, 5555 N.W. 36 Ave., Miami, FL 33142/305-635-2411

Springfield Armory, 420 W. Main St., Geneseo, IL 61254/309-944-5631

Steyr-Daimler-Puch, Gun South, Inc., Box 6607, 7605 Eastwood Mall, Birmingham, AL 35210/800-821-3021 (rifles)

Stoeger Industries, 55 Ruta Ct., S. Hackensack, NJ 07606/201-440-2700

T.D. Arms, 32464#2 23 Mile Rd., New Baltimore, MI 48047/313-949-1890

Taurus International Mfg. Inc., P.O. Box 558567, Ludlam Br., Miami, FL 33155/305-662-2529

Tradewinds, Inc., P.O. Box 1191, Tacoma, WA 98401

Uberti USA, Inc., 41 Church St., New Milford, CT 06776/203-355-8827

Ignacio Ugartechea, Apartado 21, Eibar, Spain

Valmet (See Stoeger)

Verney-Carron, B.P. 72, 54 Boulevard Thiers, 42002 St. Etienne Cedex, France/33-77.79.15.00

Perugini Visini & Co. s.r.l., Via Camprelle, 126, 25080 Nuvolera (Bs.), Italy

Waffen-Frankonia, see: Frankonia Jagd

Weatherby's, 2781 Firestone Blvd., So. Gate, CA 90280/213-569-7186

Zavodi Crvena Zastava (See Interarms)

Antonio Zoli USA Inc., P.O. Box 6190, Fort Wayne, IN 46896/219-447-4603

GUNS (Air)

Air Rifle Specialists, 311 East Water St., Elmira, NY 14901/607-734-7340

Beeman Precision Arms, Inc., 3440-GD Airway Dr., Santa Rosa, CA 95403/707-578-7900 (Feinwerkbau, Weihrauch, Webley)

Benjamin Air Rifle, 2600 Chicory Rd., Racine, WI 53403/414-554-7900

Brass Eagle Inc., 3876 Midhurst Lane, Mississauga, Ont. L4Z 1C7, Canada/416-848-4844 (paint ball guns)

China Sports, Inc., 11805 E. Smith Ave., Santa Fe Springs, CA 90670/213-942-2383

The Command Post, Inc., P.O. Box 1500, Crestview, FL 32536/904-682-2492 (airsoft, paintball marking guns)

Component Concepts, Inc., 20955 S. W. Regal Court, Aloha, OR 97006/503-642-3967

Crosman Airguns, a Coleman Co., Routes 5 and 20, E. Bloomfield, NY 14443/716-657-6161

Daisy Mfg. Co., P.O. Box 220, Rogers, AR 72756/501-636-1200

Dynamit Nobel-RWS Inc., 105 Stonehurst Ct., Northvale, NJ 07647/201-767-1995 (Dianawerk)

Fiocchi of America, Inc., Rt. 2 Box 90-8, Ozark, MO 65721/417-725-4118

Fisher Enterprises, 655 Main St. #305, Edmonds, WA 98020/206-776-4365

Great Lakes Airguns, 6175 So. Park Ave., Hamburg, NY 14075/716-648-6666

Gil Hebard Guns, Box 1, Knoxville, IL 61448

Interarms, 10 Prince, Alexandria, VA 22313 (Walther)

Marksman Products, 5622 Engineer Dr., Huntington Beach, CA 92649/714-898-7535

McMurray & Son, 13972 Van Ness Ave., Gardena, CA 90249/213-327-3582 (custom airguns)

National Survival Game, Inc., Box 1439, Main St., New London, NH 03257/603-735-5151 (paintball guns)

Phoenix Arms Co., Hy-Score Works, 40 Stonar Industrial Estate, Sandwich, Kent CT13 9LN, England (Jackal)

Power Line (See Daisy Mfg. Co.)
Precision Sales International, Inc., P.O. Box 1776, Westfield, MA 01086
Pursuit Marketing, Inc. (PMI), 1980 Raymond Dr., Northbrook, IL 60062/
312-272-4765 (paintball)
Sheridan Products, Inc., 2600 Chicory Rd., Racine, WI 53403/414-554-
7900
Stone Enterprises Ltd., Rt. 609, P.O. Box 335, Wicomico Church, VA 22579/
804-580-5114
Target Airgun Supply, P.O. Box 428, South Gate, CA 90280/213-569-3417
Tippman Pneumatics, Inc., 4402 New Haven Ave., Fort Wayne, IN 46803/
219-422-6448

GUNS & GUN PARTS, REPLICA AND ANTIQUE

Antique Arms Co., David E. Saunders, 1110 Cleveland, Monett, MO 65708/
417-235-6501
Antique Gun Parts, Inc., 1118 S. Braddock Ave., Pittsburgh, PA 15218/412-
241-1811 (ML)
Armsport, Inc., 3590 N.W. 49th St., Miami, FL 33142
Beeman Precision Arms, Inc., 3440-GDD Airway Dr., Santa Rosa, CA
95403/707-578-7900
Border Gun & Leather, Box 1423, Deming, NM 88031/505-546-2151
Cache La Poudre Rifleworks, 140 No. College Ave., Fort Collins, CO 80524/
303-482-6913
Leonard Day & Sons, Inc., One Cottage St., P.O. Box 723, East Hampton,
MA 01027/413-527-7990
Dixie Gun Works, Inc., Hwy 51, South, Union City, TN 38261/901-885-0561
Dan Dwyer, 915 W. Washington St., San Diego, CA 92103/619-296-1501
(manufacture of obsolete & antique parts)
Andy Fautheree, P.O. Box 4607, Pagosa Springs, CO 81157/303-731-5003
Federal Ordnance Inc., 1443 Portrero Ave., So. El Monte, CA 91733/213-
350-4161
Jack First Distributors, Inc., 44633 Sierra Hwy., Lancaster, CA 93534/805-
945-6981
Fred Goodwin, Goodwin's Gun Shop, Silver Ridge, Sherman Mills, ME
04776/207-365-4451 (Winchester rings & studs)
Gun Parts Corp., Box 2, West Hurley, NY 12491/914-679-2417
Hansen and Company, 244 Old Post Rd., Southport, CT 06490/203-259-
7337
Hopkins & Allen (parts only), P.O. Box 217, Hawthorne, NJ 07507
Terry K. Kopp, 1301 Franklin, Lexington, MO 64067/816-259-2636 (restora-
tion & pts. 1890 & 1906 Winch.)
The House of Muskets, Inc., P.O. Box 4640, Pagosa Springs, CO 81157/
303-731-2295 (ML supplies; catalog $3)
Liberty Antique Gunworks, 19 Key St., P.O. Box 183GD, Eastport, ME
04631/207-853-2327 (S&W only; ctlg. $5)
Log Cabin Sport Shop, 8010 Lafayette Rd., Lodi, OH 44254/216-948-1082
(ctlg. $3)
Edw. E. Lucas, 32 Garfield Ave., East Brunswick, NJ 08816/201-251-5526
(45/70 Springfield parts; some Sharps, Spencer parts)
Lyman Products Corp., Middlefield, CT 06455
Arthur McKee, 121 Eatons Neck Rd., Northport, NY 11768/516-757-8850
Tommy Munsch Gunsmithing, Rt. 2, Box 248, Little Falls, MN 56345/612-
632-6695 (Winchester obsolete and Marlin parts only; list $2.00; oth. inq.
SASE)
Precise Metalsmithing Ent., James L. Wisner, 146 Curtis Hill Rd., Chehalis,
WA 98532/206-748-3743 (pre '64-M70 Winchester)
Ram Line, Inc., 15611 W. 6th Ave., Golden, CO 80401/303-279-0886
S&S Firearms, 88-21 Aubrey Ave., Glendale, NY 11385/718-497-1100
Sarco, Inc., 323 Union St., Stirling, NJ 07980/201-647-3800
Shiloh Rifle Mfg., Co., Inc., P.O. Box 279; 201 Centennial Dr., Big Timber,
MT 59011/406-932-4454 (Sharps)
South Bend Replicas, Inc., 61650 Oak Rd., South Bend, IN 46614/219-289-
4500 (ctlg. $6)
C. H. Stoppler, 1426 Walton Ave., New York, NY 10452 (miniature guns)
Stott's Creek Armory Inc., R 1 Box 70, Morgantown, IN 46160/317-878-5489
Uberti USA, Inc., 41 Church St., New Milford, CT 06776/203-355-8827
Upper Missouri Trading Co., 304 Harold St., Crofton, NE 68730/402-388-
4844
Weisz Antique Gun Parts, P.O. Box 311, Arlington, VA 22210/703-243-9161
W. H. Wescombe, P.O. Box 488, Glencoe, CA 95232 (Rem. R.B. parts)

GUNS, SURPLUS—PARTS AND AMMUNITION

Aztec International Ltd., P.O. Box 1888, Norcross, GA 30091/404-446-2304
(ctlg. $2)
M. Braun, 32, rue Notre-Dame, 2440 Luxembourg, Luxembourg
Can Am Enterprises, 350 Jones Rd., Fruitland, Ont. LOR ILO, Canada/416-
643-4357 (Enfield rifles; catalog $2)
Century Intl. Arms, Inc., 5 Federal St., St. Albans, VT 05478/802-527-1252
Federal Ordnance, Inc., 1443 Potrero Ave., So. El Monte, CA 91733/818-
350-4161
Garcia National Gun Traders, 225 S.W. 22nd, Miami, FL 33135
Gun Parts Corp., Box 2, West Hurley, NY 12491/914-679-2417
Hansen and Company, 244 Old Post Rd., Southport, CT 06490/203-259-
6222

Lever Arms Service Ltd., 2131 Burrard St., Vancouver, B.C., Canada V6J
3H7/604-736-0004
Paragon Sales & Services, Inc., P.O. Box 2022, Joliet, IL 60434 (ammuni-
tion)
Raida Intertraders S.A., Raida House, 1-G Ave. de la Couronne, B1050
Brussels, Belgium (surplus guns)
Sarco, Inc., 323 Union St., Stirling, NJ 07980/201-647-3800 (military surpl.
ammo)
Sherwood Intl. Export Corp., 18714 Parthenia St., Northridge, CA 91324/
818-349-7600
Southern Ammunition Co., Inc., Rte. 1, Box 6B, Latta, SC 29565/803-752-
7751
Southern Armory, P.O. Box 879, Hillsville, VA 24343/703-236-7835 (modern
military parts)
Springfield Sporters, Inc., R.D. 1, Penn Run, PA 15765/412-254-2626

GUNSMITHS, CUSTOM (see Custom Gunsmiths)

GUNSMITHS, Handgun (see Pistolsmiths)

GUNSMITH SCHOOLS

Colorado School of Trades, 1575 Hoyt, Lakewood, CO 80215/303-233-4697
Lassen Community College, P.O. Box 3000, Hiway 139, Susanville, CA
96130/916-257-6181
Robert E. Maki, School of Engraving, P.O. Box 947, Northbrook, IL 60065/
312-724-8238 (firearms engraving ONLY)
Modern Gun Repair School, 2538 No. 8th St., Phoenix, AZ 85006/602-990-
8346 (home study)
Montgomery Technical College, P.O. Box 787, Troy, NC 27371/919-572-
3691 (also 1-yr. engraving school)
Murray State College, Gunsmithing Program, 100 Faculty Dr., Tishomingo,
OK 73460/405-371-2371
North American Correspondence Schools, The Gun Pro School, Oak &
Pawnee St., Scranton, PA 18515/717-342-7701
Penn. Gunsmith School, 812 Ohio River Blvd., Avalon, Pittsburgh, PA
15202/412-766-1812
Piedmont Technical College, P.O. Box 1197, Roxboro, NC 27573/919-599-
1181
Pine Technical Institute, 1100 Fourth St., Pine City, MN 55063/612-629-
6764
Professional Gunsmiths of America, 1301 Franklin, Lexington, MO, 64067/
816-259-2636
Shenandoah School of Gunsmithing, P.O. Box 300, Bentonville, VA 22610/
703-743-5494
Southeastern Community College—North Campus, 1015 Gear Ave., P.O.
Drawer F, West Burlington, IA 52655/319-752-2731
Trinidad State Junior College, 600 Prospect, Trinidad, CO 81082/719-846-
5631
Yavapai College, 1100 East Sheldon St., Prescott, AZ 86301/602-445-7300

GUNSMITH SUPPLIES, TOOLS, SERVICES

Don Allen, Inc., HC55, Box 326, Sturgis, SD 57785/605-347-5227 (stock
duplicating machine)
Alley Supply Co., Carson Valley Industrial Park, P.O. Box 848, Gardnerville,
NV 89410/702-782-3800 (JET line lathes, mills, etc.; Sweany Site-A-Line
Optical bore collimator)
Anderson Mfg. Co., P.O. Box 4218, Federal Way, WA 98063/206-838-4299
(tang safe)
Armite Labs., 1845 Randolph St., Los Angeles, CA 90001/213-587-7744
(pen oiler)
B-Square Co., Box 11281, Ft. Worth, TX 76110/817-923-0964
Jim Baiar, 490 Halfmoon Rd., Columbia Falls, MT 59912 (hex screws)
Baron Technology, 62 Spring Hill Rd., Trumbull, CT 06611/203-452-0515
(chemical etching, plating)
Behlert Custom Guns, Inc., RD 2 Box 36C, Route 611 North, Pipersville, PA
18947/215-766-8680
Bell Design Gun Services, 718 South 2nd, Atwood, KS 67730/913-626-3270
(Accusorb bedding system)
Belim Contenders, P.O. Box 429, Cleveland, UT 84518 (rifles only)
Al Biesen, W. 2039 Sinto Ave., Spokane, WA 99201 (grip caps, buttplates)
Roger Biesen, 5021 W. Rosewood, Spokane, WA 99208/509-328-9340
Blue Ridge Machinery and Tools, Inc., P.O. Box 536-GD, 2806 Putnam Ave.,
Hurricane, WV 25526/304-562-3538/800-872-6500 (gunsmithing lathe,
mills & shop suppl.)
Briganti Custom Gun-Smithing, P.O. Box 56, 475-Route 32, Highland Mills,
NY 10930/914-928-9573 (cold rust bluing, hand polishing, metal work)
Brownells, Inc. 222 W. Liberty, Montezuma, IA 50171/515-623-5401
W.E. Brownell Checkering Tools, 3356 Moraga Place, San Diego, CA 92117/
619-276-6146
Buehler Scope Mounts, 17 Orinda Way, Orinda, CA 94563/415-254-3201
Burgess Vibrocrafters, Inc. (BVI), Rte. 83, Grayslake, IL 60030
M.H. Canjar, 500 E. 45th, Denver, CO 80216/303-295-2638 (triggers, etc.)
Chapman Mfg. Co., P.O. Box 250, Rte. 17 at Saw Mill Rd., Durham, CT
06422/203-349-9228
Chicago Wheel & Mfg. Co., 1101 W. Monroe St., Chicago, IL 60607/312-
226-8155 (Handee grinders)

Chopie Mfg., Inc., 700 Copeland Ave., LaCrosse, WI 54603/608-784-0926

Classic Arms Corp., P.O. Box 8, Palo Alto, CA 94302/415-321-7243 (floor-plates, grip caps)

Clymer Mfg. Co., Inc., 1645 W. Hamlin Rd., Rochester Hills, MI 48309-3368/313-853-5555 (reamers)

Dave Cook, 720 Hancock Ave., Hancock, MI 49930 (metalsmithing only)

Crouse's Country Cover, P.O. Box 160, Storrs, CT 06268/203-429-3720 (Masking Gun Oil)

Dayton Traister Co., 4778 N. Monkey Hill Rd., Oak Harbor, WA 98277/206-675-3421 (triggers; safeties)

Dem-Bart Hand Checkering Tools, Inc., 6807 Hiway #2, Snohomish, WA 98290/206-568-7356

Dremel Mfg. Co., 4915-21st St., Racine, WI 53406 (grinders)

Chas. E. Duffy, Williams Lane, West Hurley, NY 12491

The Dutchman's Firearms Inc., 4143 Taylor Blvd., Louisville, KY 40215/502-366-0555

Peter Dyson Ltd., 29-31 Church St., Honley, Huddersfield, West Yorksh. HD7 2AH, England/0484-661062 (accessories f. antique gun coil.)

Edmund Scientific Co., 101 E. Gloucester Pike, Barrington, NJ 08033/609-573-6250

Jack First Distributors, Inc., 44633 Sierra Hwy., Lancaster, CA 93534/805-945-6981

Jerry A. Fisher, P.O. Box 652, 38 Buffalo Butte, Dubois, WY 82513/307-455-2722

Forster Products, Inc., 82 E. Lanark Ave., Lanark, IL 60146/815-493-6360

G.R.S. Corp. (Glendo), P.O. Box 748, 900 Overlander St., Emporia, KS 66801/316-343-1084 (Gravermeister; Grave Max tools)

Garrett Accur-Lt. D.F.S. Co., P.O. Box 8675, Ft. Collins, CO 80524/303-224-3067

Grace Metal Prod., 115 Ames St., Elk Rapids, MI 49629/616-264-8133 (screw drivers, drifts)

Gunline Tools, 2970 Saturn ST., Brea, CA 92621/714-993-5100

Gun Parts Corp., Box 2, West Hurley, NY 12491/914-679-2417

Gun-Tec, P.O. Box 8125, W. Palm Beach, FL 33407 (files; SASE f. reply)

Half Moon Rifle Shop, 490 Halfmoon Rd., Columbia Falls, MT 59912/406-892-4409 (hex screws)

Henriksen Tool Co., Inc., 8515 Wagner Creek Rd., Talent, OR 97540/503-535-2309 (reamers)

Huey Gun Cases (Marvin Huey), P.O. Box 22456, Kansas City, MO 64113/816-444-1637 (high grade English ebony tools)

Ken Jantz Supply, 222 E. Main, Davis, OK 73030/405-369-2316

JGS Precision Tool Mfg., 1141 S. Sumner Rd., Coos Bay, OR 97420/503-267-4331

Jeffredo Gunsight Co., 1629 Via Monserate, Fallbrook, CA 92028 (trap buttplate)

Jim's Gun Shop, James R. Spradlin, 113 Arthur, Pueblo, CO 81004/719-543-9462 (''Belgian Blue'' rust blues; stock fillers)

Kasenit Co., Inc., P.O. Box 726, 3 King St., Mahwah, NJ 07430/201-529-3663 (surface hardening compound)

Terry K. Kopp, 1301 Franklin, Lexington, MO 64067/816-259-2636 (stock rubbing compound; rust preventive grease)

J. Korzinek, RD#2, Box 73, Canton, PA 17724/717-673-8512 (stainl. steel bluing; broch. $2)

John G. Lawson, (The Sight Shop) 1802 E. Columbia Ave., Tacoma, WA 98404/206-474-5465

Lea. Mfg. Co., 237 E. Aurora St., Waterbury, CT 06720/203-753-5116

Mark Lee Supplies, 9901 France Court, Lakeville, MN 55044/612-461-2114

Liberty Antique Gunworks, 19 Key St., P.O. Box 183GD, Eastport, ME 04631/207-853-2327 (spl. S&W tools)

Lock's Phila. Gun Exch., 6700 Rowland Ave., Philadelphia, PA 19149/215-332-6225

McMillan Rifle Barrels, U.S. International, P.O. Box 3427, Bryan, TX 77805/409-846-3990 (services)

Mike Marsh, Croft Cottage, Main St., Elton, Derbyshire DE4 2BY, England/062-988-6699 (gun accessories)

Meier Works, Steve Hines, Box 328, 2102-2nd Ave., Canyon, TX 79015/806-655-7806 (European accessories)

Metalife Industries, Box 53, Mong Ave., Reno, PA 16343/814-436-7747 (Metalife refinishing services)

Michaels of Oregon Co., P.O. Box 13010, Portland, OR 97213/503-255-6890

Miller Single Trigger Mfg. Co., R.D. 1, Box 99, Millersburg, PA 17061/717-692-3704 (selective or non-selective f. shotguns)

Miniature Machine Co. (MMC), 210 E. Poplar St., Deming, NM 88030/505-546-2151 (screwdriver grinding fixtures)

Frank Mittermeier, 3577 E. Tremont, New York, NY 10465/212-828-3843

N&J Sales Co., Lime Kiln Rd., Northford, CT 06472/203-484-0247 (screw-drivers)

Nitex, Ed House, P.O. Box 1706, Uvalde,TX 78801/512-278-8843 (cust. metal finish)

Palmgren Steel Prods., Chicago Tool & Engineering Co., 8383 South Chicago Ave., Chicago, IL 60617/312-721-9675 (vises, etc.)

Panavise Prods., Inc., 2850 E. 29th St., Long Beach, CA 90806/213-595-7621

Pilkington Gun Co., P.O. Box 1296, Muskogee, OK 74402/918-683-9418 (Q.D. scope mt.)

Redman's Rifling & Reboring, Route 3, Box 330A, Omak, WA 98841/509-826-5512 (22 RF liners)

Roto/Carve, 6509 Indian Hills Rd., Minneapolis, MN 55435/612-944-5150 (tool)

A.G. Russell Co., 1705 Hiway 471 North, Springdale, AR 71764/501-751-7341 (Arkansas oilstones)

Rusteprufe Labs, 1319 Jefferson Ave., Sparta, WI 54656/608-269-4144

Seacliff International Inc., 2210 Santa Anita, So. El Monte, CA 91733/818-350-0515 (portable parts washer)

Shaws, 1201 La Mirada Ave., Escondido, CA 92026/619-746-2474

L.S. Starrett Co., 121 Crescent St., Athol, MA 01331/617-249-3551

Stuart Products, Inc., P.O. Box 1587, Easley, SC 29641/803-859-9360 (Sight-Vise)

Texas Platers Supply Co., 2453 W. Five Mile Parkway, Dallas, TX 75233 (plating kit)

Timney Mfg. Inc., 3065 W. Fairmount Ave., Phoenix, AZ 85017/602-274-2999 (triggers)

Stan de Treville, Box 33021, San Diego, CA 92103/619-298-3393 (checkering patterns)

Walker Arms Co., Inc., Rt. 2, Box 73, Hwy. 80 W, Selma, AL 36701/205-872-6231 (tools)

Washita Mountain Whetstone Co., P.O. Box 378, Lake Hamilton, AR 71951/501-525-3914

Weaver Arms Co., P.O. Box 8, Dexter, MO 63841/314-568-3800 (action wrenches & transfer punches)

Chris Weber/Waffen-Weber, #6-1691 Powick Rd., Kelowna, BC V1X 4L1, Canada/604-762-7575

Will-Burt Co., 169 So. Main, Orrville, OH 44667 (vises)

Williams Gun Sight Co., 7389 Lapeer Rd., Davison, MI 48423

Wilson Arms Co., 63 Leetes Island Rd., Branford, CT 06405/203-488-7297

W.C. Wolff Co., P.O. Box 232, Ardmore, PA 19003/215-896-7500 (springs)

HANDGUN ACCESSORIES

AMT (Arcadia Machine & Tool, Inc.), 6226 Santos Diaz St., Irwindale, CA 91702/818-334-6629

Adco International, 1 Wyman St., Woburn, MA 01801/617-935-1799

Ajax Custom Grips, Inc., Div. of A. Jack Rosenberg & Sons, 11311 Stemmons, Suite #5, Dallas, TX 75229/214-241-6302

Bob Allen Companies, 214 S.W. Jackson St., Des Moines, IA 50302/515-283-2191

American Gas & Chemical Co., Ltd., 220 Pegasus Ave., Northvale, NJ 07647/201-767-7300 (clg. lube)

Armsport, Inc., 3590 N.W. 49th St., Miami, FL 33142/305-635-7850

Baramie Corp., 6250 E. 7 Mile Rd., Detroit, MI 48234 (Hip-Grip)

Bar-Sto Precision Machine, 73377 Sullivan Rd., P.O. Box 1838, Twentynine Palms, CA 92277/619-367-2747 (barrels)

Behlert Precision, RD 2 Box 63, Route 611 North, Pipersville, PA 18947/215-766-8681

Brauer Bros. Mfg. Co., 2020 Delmar Blvd., St. Louis, MO 63103/314-231-2864

Ed Brown Products, Rte. 2, Box 2922, Perry, MO 63462/314-565-3261

Centaur Systems, Inc., 15127 NE 24th, C-3, Suite 114, Redmond, WA 98052/206-392-8472 (Quadra-Lok bbls.)

Central Specialties Co., 200 Lexington Dr., Buffalo Grove, IL 60089/312-537-3300 (trigger locks only)

Clymer Mfg. Co., Inc., 1645 W. Hamlin Rd., Rochester Hills, MI 48309/313-853-5555

D&E Magazines Mfg., P.O. Box 4876-D, Sylmar, CA 91342 (clips)

Detonics Firearms Industries, 13456 SE 27th Pl., Bellevue, WA 98005/206-747-2100

Doskocil Mfg. Co., Inc., P.O. Box 1246, Arlington, TX 76004/817-467-5116 (Gun Guard cases)

Eagle International, Inc., 5195 W. 58th Ave., Suite 300, Arvada, CO 80002/303-426-8100

Essex Arms, Box 345, Island Pond, VT 05846/802-723-4313 (45 Auto frames)

Frielich Police Equipment, 396 Broome St., New York, NY 10013/212-254-3045 (cases)

R. S. Frielich, 211 East 21st St., New York, NY 10010/212-777-4477 (cases)

Glock, Inc. 6000 Highlands Parkway, Smyrna, GA 30082/404-432-1202

Gun Parts Corp., Box 2, West Hurley, NY 12491/914-679-2417

Gil Hebard Guns, 125-129 Public Square, Knoxville, IL 61448

Intratec, 12405 S.W. 130th St., Miami, FL 33186/305-232-1821

Jett & Co. Inc., RR #3 Box 167-B, Litchfield, IL 62056/217-324-3779

Art Jewel Ent., 460 Randy Rd., Carol Stream, IL 60188/312-260-6144 (Eagle Grips)

K&K Ammo Wrist Band, R.D. #1, Box 448-CA18, Lewistown, PA 17044/717-242-2329

King's Gun Works, 1837 W. Glenoaks Blvd., Glendale, CA 91201/818-956-6010

Terry K. Kopp, 1301 Franklin, Lexington, MO 64067/816-259-2636

Lee's Red Ramps, 7252 E. Ave. U-3, Littlerock, CA 93543/805-944-4487 (ramp insert kits; spring kits)

Lee Precision Inc., 4275 Hwy. U, Hartford, WI 53027 (pistol rest holders)

Liberty Antique Gunworks, 19 Key St., P.O. Box 183GD, Eastport, ME 04631/207-853-2327 (shims f. S&W revs.)

Kent Lomont, 4236 West 700 South, Poneto, IN46781 (Auto Mag only)

Lone Star Gunleather, 1301 Brushy Bend Dr., Round Rock, TX 78681/512-255-1805

Los Gatos Grip & Specialty Co., P.O. Box 1850, Los Gatos, CA 95030 (custom-made)

M.A.M. Products, Inc., 153 B Cross Slope Court, Englishtown, NJ 07726/201-536-7268 (free standing brass catcher f. all auto pistols and/or semi-auto rifles)

MTM Molded Prods. Co., P.O. Box 14117, Dayton, OH 45414/513-890-7461

Magnum Research, Inc., P.O. Box 32221, Minneapolis, MN 55432/612-574-1868

Mag-Pack, P.O. Box 846, Chesterland, OH 44026

Millet Industries, 16131 Gothard St., Huntington Beach, CA 92647/714-842-5575

No-Sho Mfg. Co., 10727 Glenfield Ct., Houston, TX 77096/713-723-5332

Jim Noble Co., 1305 Columbia St., Vancouver, WA 98660/206-695-1309

Omega Sales, Inc., P.O. Box 1066, Mt. Clemens, MI 48403/313-469-6727
Harry Owen (See Sport Specialties)
Pachmayr Ltd., 1875 So. Mountain Ave., Monrovia, CA 91016/818-357-7771 (cases)
Pacific Intl. Mchdsg. Corp., 2215 "J" St., Sacramento, CA 95818/916-446-2737 (Vega 45 Colt. comb. mag.)
Poly-Choke Div., Marble Arms Corp., 420 Industrial Park, Gladstone, MI 49827/906-428-3710 (handgun ribs)
Ranch Products, P.O. Box 145, Malinta, OH 43535/313-277-3118 (third-moon clips)
Ransom Intl. Corp., 1040 Sandretto Dr., Suite J, Prescott, AZ 86302/602-778-7899
SSK Industries, 721 Woodvue Lane, Wintersville, OH 43952/614-264-0176
Safariland Ltd., Inc., 1941 S. Walker, Monrovia, CA 91016/818-357-7902
Sile Distributors, 7 Centre Market Pl., New York, NY 10013
Robert Sonderman, 735 W. Kenton, Charleston, IL 61920/217-345-5429 (solid walnut fitted handgun cases; other woods)
Sport Specialties, (Harry Owen), Box 5337, Hacienda Hts., CA 91745/213-968-5806 (.22 rimfire adapters; .22 insert bbls. f. T/C Contender, autom. pistols)
Sportsmen's Equipment Co., 415 W. Washington, San Diego, CA 92103/619-296-1501
Turkey Creek Enterprises, Rt. 1, Box 10, Red Oak, CA 74563/918-754-2884 (wood handgun cases)
Melvin Tyler Mfg.-Dist., 1326 W Britton, Oklahoma City, OK 73114/405-842-8044 (grip adaptor)
Wardell Precision Handguns Ltd., Box 4132 New River Stage 1, New River, AZ 85029/602-242-0186
Whitney Sales, P.O. Box 875, Reseda, CA 91335/818-345-4212
Wilson's Gun Shop, P.O. Box 578, Rt. 3, Box 211-D, Berryville, AR 72616/501-545-3618

HANDGUN GRIPS

Action Products Inc., 22 N. Mulberry St., Hagerstown, MD 21740/301-797-1414
Ajax Custom Grips, Inc., Div. of A. Jack Rosenberg & Sons, 11311 Stemmons, Suite #5, Dallas, TX 75229/214-241-6302
Altamont Mfg. Co., 510 N. Commercial St., P.O. Box 309, Thomasboro, IL 61878/217-643-3125
Art Jewel Enterprises Ltd., Eagle Business Ctr., 460 Randy Rd., Carol Stream, IL 60188/312-260-0040 (Eagle grips)
Barami Corp., 6250 East 7 Mile Rd., Detroit, MI 48234/313-891-2536
Bear Hug Grips, Inc., P.O. Box 25944, Colorado Springs, CO 80936/719-598-5675 (cust.)
Beeman Precision Arms, Inc., 3440-GD Airway Dr., Santa Rosa, CA 95403/707-578-7900 (airguns only)
Behlert Precision, RD 2 Box 63, Route 611 North, Pipersville, PA 18947/215-766-8681
Boone's Custom Ivory Grips, Inc., 562 Coyote Rd., Brinnon, WA 98320/206-796-4330
Fab-U-Grip, An-Lin Enterprises, Inc., P.O. BOX 550, Vineland, NJ 08360/609-652-1089
Fitz Pistol Grip Co., P.O. Box 171, Douglas City, CA 96024/916-778-3136
Gun Parts Corp., Box 2, West Hurley, NY 12491/914-679-2417
Herrett's, Box 741, Twin Falls, ID 83303/208-733-1498
Hogue Grips, P.O. Box 2038, Atascadero, CA 93423/805-466-6266 (Monogrip)
Paul Jones Munitions Systems, (See Fitz Co.)
Logan Security Products, Box 16206, Columbus, OH 43216 ("Streetloader" f. K & L frame S&Ws)
Russ Maloni (See Russwood)
Monogrip, (See Hogue)
Monte Kristo Pistol Grip Co., Box 171, Douglas City, CA 96024/916-778-3136
Mustang Custom Pistol Grips, see: R.J. Renner Co.
Nygord Precision Products, P.O. Box 8394, La Crescenta, CA 91214/818-352-3027
Pachmayr Ltd., 1875 So. Mountain Ave., Monrovia, CA 91016/818-357-7771
Robert H. Newell, 55 Coyote, Los Alamos, NM 87544/505-662-7135 (custom stocks)
Olympic Arms Inc. dba SGW, 624 Old Pacific Hwy. S.E., Olympia, WA 98503/206-456-3471
R.J. Renner Co., P.O. Box 3543, Glendale, CA 91221-0543/818-241-6488
A. Jack Rosenberg & Sons, 12229 Cox Lane, Dallas, TX 75234/214-241-6302 (Ajax)
Royal Ordnance Works Ltd., P.O. Box 3254, Wilson, NC 27893/919-237-0515
Russwood Custom Pistol Grips, P.O. Box 460, East Aurora, NY 14052/716-842-6012 (cust. exotic woods)
Jean St. Henri, 6525 Dume Dr., Malibu, CA 90265/213-457-7211 (custom)
Ben Shostle, The Gun Room, 1121 Burlington, Muncie, IN 47302/317-282-9073 (custom)
Sile Dist., 7 Centre Market Pl., New York, NY 10013/212-925-4111
Craig Spegel, P.O. Box 1334, Hillsboro, OR 97123/503-628-1631
Sports Inc., P.O. Box 683, Park Ridge, IL 60068/312-825-8952 (Franzite)
R. D. Wallace, Star Rte. 1 Box 76, Grandin, MO 63943/314-593-4773 (cust. only)
Wayland Prec. Wood Prods., Box 1142, Mill Valley, CA 94942/415-381-3543
Wilson's Gun Shop, P.O. Box 578, Rt. 3, Box 211-D, Berryville, AR 72616/501-545-3618

HEARING PROTECTORS

AO Safety Prods., Div. of American Optical Corp., 14 Mechanic St., Southbridge, MA 01550/617-765-9711 (ear valves, ear muffs)
Bausch & Lomb, 635 St. Paul St., Rochester, NY 14602
Bilsom Interntl., Inc., 109 Carpenter Dr., Sterling, VA 22170/703-834-1070 (ear plugs, muffs)
David Clark Co., Inc., 360 Franklin St., P.O. Box 15054, Worcester, MA 01615/508-756-6216
Gun Parts Corp., Box 2, West Hurley, NY 12491/914-679-2417
Marble Arms Corp., 420 Industrial Park, Box 111, Gladstone, MI 49837/906-428-3710
North Consumer Prods. Div., 2664-B Saturn St., Brea, CA 92621/714-524-1665 (Lee Sonic ear valves)
Safety Direct, 56 Coney Island Dr., Sparks, NV 89431/702-354-4451 (Silencio)
Smith & Wesson, 2100 Roosevelt Ave., Springfield, MA 01101
Willson Safety Prods. Div., P.O. Box 622, Reading, PA 19603 (Ray-O-Vac)

HOLSTERS & LEATHER GOODS

Alessi Holsters, Inc., 2465 Niagara Falls Blvd., Tonawanda, NY 14150/716-691-5615
Bob Allen Companies, 214 S.W. Jackson, Des Moines, IA 50315/515-283-2191
American Enterprises, 649 Herbert, El Cajon, CA 92020/619-588-1222
American Sales & Mfg. Co., P.O. Box 677, Laredo, TX 78042/512-723-6893
Andy Arratoonian, The Cottage, Sharow, Ripon HG4 5BP, England (0765)-5858
Rick M. Bachman (see Old West Reproductions)
Bang-Bang Boutique, 720 N. Flagler Dr., Fort Lauderdale, FL 33304/305-463-7910
Barami Corp., 6250 East 7 Mile Rd., Detroit, MI 48234/313-891-2536
Beeman Precision Arms, Inc., 3440-GD Airway Dr., Santa Rosa, CA 95403/707-578-7900 (airguns only)
Behlert Precision, RD 2 Box 63, Route 611 North, Pipersville, PA 18947/215-766-8681
Bianchi International Inc., 100 Calle Cortez, Temecula, CA 92390/714-676-5621
Ted Blocker's Custom Holsters, 409 West Bonita Ave. San Dimas, CA 91773/714-599-4415
Border Guns & Leather, Box 1423, Deming, NM 88031/505-546-2151 (Old West cust.)
Boyt Co., Div. of Welsh Sptg., P.O. Box 220, Iowa Falls, IA 51026/515-648-4626
Brauer Bros. Mfg. Co., 2020 Delmar, St. Louis, MO 63103/314-231-2864
Browning, Rt. 4, Box 624-B, Arnold, MO 63010
J.M. Bucheimer Co., P.O. Box 280, Airport Rd., Frederick, MD 21701/301-662-5101
Buffalo Leather Goods, Inc., 100 E. Church St., El Dorado, AR 71730
Cathey Enterprises, Inc., 3423 Milam Dr., P.O. Box 2202, Brownwood, TX 76804/915-643-2553
Cattle Baron Leather Co., Dept. GD, P.O. Box 100724, San Antonio, TX 78201/512-697-8900 (ctlg. $3)
Chace Leather Prods., Longhorn Div., 507 Alden St., Fall River, MA 02722/508-678-7556
Cherokee Gun Accessories, 4127 Bay St., Suite 226, Fremont, CA 94538/415-471-5770
Chas. Clements, Handicrafts Unltd., 1741 Dallas St., Aurora, CO 80010/303-364-0403
Dart Manufacturing Co., 4012 Bronze Way, Dallas, TX 75237/214-333-4221
Davis Leather Co., G. Wm. Davis, 3930 Valley Blvd., Unit F, Walnut, CA 91789/714-598-5620
DeSantis Holster & Leather Co., 140 Denton Ave., New Hyde Park, NY 11040/516-354-8000
El Paso Saddlery, P.O. Box 27194, El Paso, TX 79926/915-544-2233
Ellwood Epps Northern Ltd., 210 Worthington ST. W., North Bay, Ont. P1B 3B4, Canada (custom made)
GALCO International, Ltd., 2019 West Quail Ave., Phoenix, AZ 85027/602-233-0956 (ctlg. $5)
Glock, Inc., 6000 Highlands Pkwy. Smyrna, GA 30082/404-432-1202 (holsters)
Gould & Goodrich Leather Inc., 709 E. McNeil St.; P.O. Box 1479, Lillington, NC 27546/919-893-2071 (licensed mfgr. of S&W leather products)
Gun Parts Corp., Box 2, West Hurley, NY 12491/914-679-2417
High North Products, P.O. Box 2, Antigo, WI 54409/715-623-5117 (1-oz. Mongoose gun sling)
Holster Outpost, 649 Herbert St., El Cajon, CA 92020/619-588-1222
Horseshoe Leather Prods., (See Andy Arratoonian)
Hoyt Holster Co., P.O. Box 69, Coupeville, WA 98239/20-6-678-6640
Don Hume, Box 351, Miami, OK 74355/918-542-6604
Hunter Corp., 3300 W. 71st Ave., Westminster, CO 80030/303-427-4626
John's Custom Leather, 525 S. Liberty St., Blairsville, PA 15717/412-459-6802
Jumbo Sports Prods., P.O. Box 280, Airport Rd., Frederick, MD 21701
Kane Leather Products, Inc., 5572 Brecksville Rd., Cleveland, OH 44131/216-524-9962 (GunChaps)
Kirkpatrick Leather Co., P.O. Box 3150, Laredo, TX 78044/512-723-6631
Kolpin Mfg. Inc., P.O. Box 231, Berlin, WI 54923/414-361-0400
L.A.R. Manufacturing, Inc., 4133 West Farm Rd., West Jordan, UT 84088/801-255-7106
Lawrence Leather Co., 1435 N.W. Northrup, Portland, OR 97209/503-228-8244
Lone Star Gunleather, 1301 Brushy Bend Dr., Round Rock, TX 78681/512-255-1805
Michael's of Oregon, Co., P.O. Box 13010, Portland, OR 97213/503-255-6890 (Uncle Mike's)

No-Sho Mfg. Co., 10727 Glenfield Ct., Houston, TX 77096/713-723-5332
Jim Noble Co., 1305 Columbia St., Vancouver, WA 98660/206-695-1309 (Supreme quick-draw shoulder holster, etc.)
Kenneth L. Null-Custom Concealment Holsters, R.D. #5, Box 197, Hanover, PA 17331
Old West Reproductions, R. M. Bachman, 1840 Stag Lane, Kalispell, MT 59901/406-755-6902 (ctlg. $3)
Orient-Western, P.O. Box 27573, San Francisco, CA 94127
Pony Express Sport Shop Inc., 1606 Schoenborn St., Sepulveda, CA 91343/818-895-1231
Red Head Inc., P.O. Box 7100, Springfield, MO 65801/417-864-5430
Rogers Holsters Co., Inc., 1736 St. Johns Bluff Rd., Jacksonville, FL 32216/904-641-9434
Safariland Leather Products, 1941 So. Walker Ave., Monrovia, CA 91016/818-357-7902
Safety Speed Holster, Inc., 910 So. Vail, Montebello, CA 90640/213-723-4140
Schulz Industries, 16247 Minnesota Ave., Paramount, CA 90723/213-439-5903
Sile Distr., 7 Centre Market Pl., New York NY 10013/212-925-4111
Silhouette Leathers, H.R. Brown, P.O. Box 241645, Memphis, TN 38124/901-327-0528 (cust. holst.)
Smith & Wesson Leather (See Gould & Goodrich)
Milt Sparks, Box 187, Idaho City, ID 83631/208-392-6695 (broch. $2)
Strong Holster Co., 105 Maplewood Ave., Gloucester, MA 01930/508-281-3300
Torel, Inc., 1053 N. South St., P.O. Box 592, Yoakum, TX 77995/512-293-2341 (gun slings)
Triple-K Mfg. Co., 2222 Commercial St., San Diego, CA 92113/619-232-2066
Uncle Mike's (See Michaels of Oregon)
Viking Leathercraft, Inc., 1579A Jayken Way, Chula Vista, CA 92011/619-429-8050
Walt Whinnery, 1947 Meadow Creek Dr., Louisville, KY 40218/502-458-4361
Wild Bill Cleaver, Rt. 4, Box 462, Vashon, WA 98070 (antique holstermaker)
Zeus International, P.O. Box 953, Tarpon Springs, FL 33589/813-5029 (all leather shotshell belt)

HUNTING AND CAMP GEAR, CLOTHING, ETC.

API Outdoors Inc., 602 Kimbrough Dr., Tallulah, LA 71282/318-574-4903
Bob Allen Co., 214 S.W. Jackson, Des Moines, IA 50315/515-283-2191/800-247-8048
Eddie Bauer, 15010 NE 36th St., Redmond, WA 98052
L. L. Bean, Freeport, ME 04032
Bear Archery, R.R. 4, 4600 Southwest 41st Blvd., Gainesville, FL 32601/904-376-2327 (Himalayan backpack)
Big Beam, Teledyne Co., 290 E. Prairie St., Crystal Lake, IL 60014 (lamp)
Browning, Rte. 1, Morgan, UT 84050
Challanger Mfg. Co., Box 550, Jamaica, NY 11431 (glow safe)
Chippewa Shoe Co., P.O. Box 2521, Ft. Worth, TX 76113/817-332-4385 (boots)
Coleman Co., Inc., 250 N. St. Francis, Wichita, KS 67201
Danner Shoe Mfg. Co., P.O. Box 22204, Portland, OR 97222/503-653-2920 (boots)
DEER-ME Prod. Co., Box 34, Anoka, MN 55303/612-421-8971 (tree steps)
Dunham Co., P.O. Box 813, Brattleboro, VT 05301/802-254-2316 (boots)
Durango Boot, see: Northlake
Frankonia Jagd, Hofmann & Co., Postfach 6780, D-8700 Wurzburg 1, West Germany
Game-Winner, Inc., 2625 Cumberland Parkway, Suite 220, Atlanta, GA 30339/404-434-9210 (camouflage suits; orange vests)
Gander Mountain, Inc., P.O. Box 128, Hwy. ''W'', Wilmot, WI 53192/414-862-2344
Gun Club Sportswear, Box 477, Des Moines, IA 50302
Bob Hinman Outfitters, 1217 W. Glen, Peoria, IL 61614
Hunter's Specialties, Inc., 5285 Rockwell Dr. N.E., Cedar Rapids, IA 52402/319-395-0321
Kenko Intl. Inc., 8141 West I-70 Frontage Rd. No., Arvada, CO 80002/303-425-1200 (footwear & socks)
Langenberg Hat Co., P.O. Box 1860, Washington, MO 63090/314-239-1860
Liberty Trouser Co., 2301 First Ave. North, Birmingham, AL 35203/205-251-9143
Marathon Rubber Prods. Co. Inc., 510 Sherman St., Wausau, WI 54401/715-845-6255 (rain gear)
Marble Arms Corp., 420 Industrial Park, Gladstone, MI 49837
Northlake Boot Co., 1810 Columbia Ave., Franklin, TN 37064/615-794-1556
The Orvis Co., 10 River Rd., Manchester, VT 05254/802-362-3622 (fishing gear; clothing)
P.A.S.T. (Precision Action Sports Technologies), 210 Park Ave., Columbia, MO 65203/314-449-7278 (shooting shirts)
Pendleton Woolen Mills, 218 S.W. Jefferson St., Portland, OR 97201/503-226-4801 (OutdoorsMan cloth.)
Precise International, 3 Chestnut St., Suffern, NY 10901/914-357-6200
Pyramid, Inc., 625 Ellis St., Suite 209, Mountain View, CA 94043/415-964-6991 (portable camp stove)
Ranger Mfg. Co., Inc., 1536 Crescent Dr., Augusta GA 30919/404-738-3469 (camouflage suits)
Ranger Rubber Co., 1100 E. Main St., Endicott, NY 13760/607-757-4260 (boots)

Red Ball, 100 Factory St., Nashua, NH 03060/603-881-4420 (boots)
Red Head Inc., P.O. Box 7100, Springfield, MO 65801/417-864-5430
Refrigiwear, Inc., 71 Inip Dr., Inwood, Long Island, NY 11696
Re-Heater Inc., 96302 S. Western Ave. #5, Lomita, CA 90717 (re-usable portable heat pack)
Remington Footwear Co., 1810 Columbia Ave., Franklin, TN 37064/800-332-2688 (boots)
SanLar Co., N3784 Liberty St., Sullivan, WI 53170/414-500-0000 (hunty. sweatsuits, camouflage clothing)
Servus Rubber Co., 1136 2nd St., P.O. Box 3610 Rock Island, IL 61204 (footwear)
Teledyne Co., Big Beam, 290 E. Prairie St., Crystal Lake, IL 60014
10-X Mfg. Products Group, 2828 Forest Lane, Suite 1107, Dallas, TX 75234/214-243-4016
Thermos Div., KST Co., Norwich, CT 06361 (Pop Tent)
Norm Thompson, 18905 N.W. Thurman St., Portland, OR 97209
Tink's Safariland Hunting Corp., P.O. Box 69, Trappe, MD 21673/301-820-9797 (camouflage rain gear)
Utica Duxbak Corp., 1745 S. Acoma St., Denver, CO 80223/303-778-0324
Waffen-Frankonia, see: Frankonia Jagd
Walker Shoe Co., P.O. Box 1167, Asheboro, NC 27203-1167/919-625-1380 (boots)
Wolverine Boots & Shoes Div., Wolverine World Wide, 9341 Courtland Dr., Rockford, MI 49351/616-866-1561 (footwear)
Woolrich Woolen Mills, Mill St., Woolrich, PA 17779/717-769-6464
Wyoming Knife Corp., 101 Commerce Dr., Ft. Collins, CO 80524/303-224-3454 (saw)

KNIVES AND KNIFEMAKER'S SUPPLIES—FACTORY and MAIL ORDER

Alcas Cutlery Corp., 1116 E. State St., Olean, NY 14760/716-372-3111 (Cutco)
Atlanta Cutlery Corp., 2143 Geesmill Rd., Conyers, GA 30208/404-922-3700 (mail order, supplies)
L.L. Bean, 386 Main St., Freeport, ME 040032/207-865-3111 (mail order)
Benchmark Knives (See Gerber)
Blackjack Knives, 7210 Jordan Ave., #D72, Canoga Park, CA 91303/818-902-9853
Boker USA, Inc., 14818 West 6th Ave., Suite #17A, Golden, CO 80401/303-279-5997
Bowen Knife Co., P.O. Box 590, Blackshear, GA 31516/912-449-4794
Browning, Rt. 1, Morgan, UT 84050/801-876-2711
Buck Knives, Inc., P.O. Box 1267; 1900 Weld Blvd., El Cajon, CA 92022/619-449-1100 or 800-854-2557
Camillus Cutlery Co., 52-54 W. Genesee St., Camillus, NY 13031/315-672-8111 (Sword Brand)
W. R. Case & Sons Cutlery Co., Owens Way, Bradford, PA 16701/814-368-4123
Cattle Baron Leather Co., P.O. Box 100724, Dept. GD, San Antonio, TX 78201/512-697-8900 (ctlg. $3)
Charter Arms Corp., 430 Sniffens Lane, Stratford, CT 06497/203-377-8080 (Skatchet)
Chicago Cutlery Co., 5420 N. County Rd., 18, Minneapolis, MN 55428/612-533-0472
E. Christopher Firearms Co., Inc., Route 128 & Ferry St., Miamitown, OH 45041/513-353-1321 (supplies)
Chas. Clements, Handicraft Unltd., 1741 Dallas St., Aurora, CO 80010/303-364-0403 (exotic sheaths)
Collins Brothers Div. (belt buckle knife), See Bowen Knife Co.
Colonial Knife Co. P.O. Box 3327, Providence, RI 02909/401-421-1600 (Master Brand)
Compass Industries, Inc., 1054 East 25th St., New York, NY 10010/212-473-2614
Crosman Blades™, The Coleman Co., 250 N. St. Francis, Wichita, KS 67201
Custom Knifemaker's Supply (Bob Schrimsher), P.O. Box 308, Emory, TX 75440/214-473-3330
Damascus-USA, P.O. Box 220, Howard, CO 81233/719-942-3527
Dixie Gun Works, Inc., P.O. Box 130, Union City, TN 38261/901-885-0700 (supplies)
Eze-Lap Diamond Prods., Box 2229, 15164 Weststate St., Westminster, CA 92683/714-847-1555 (knife sharpeners)
Gerber Legendary Blades, 14200 S.W. 72nd Ave., Portland, OR 99223/503-639-6161
Gutmann Cutlery Co., Inc., 120 S. Columbus Ave., Mt. Vernon, NY 10553/914-699-4044
H & B Forge Co., Rte. 2 Geisinger Rd., Shiloh, OH 44878/419-895-1856 (throwing knives, tomahawks)
Russell Harrington Cutlery, Inc., Subs. of Hyde Mfg. Co., 44 River St., Southbridge, MA 01550/617-765-0201 (Dexter, Green River Works)
J. A. Henckels Zwillingswerk, Inc., 9 Skyline Dr., Hawthorne, NY 10532/914-592-7370
Indian Ridge Traders (See Koval Knives)
Ken Jantz Supply, 222 E. Main, Davis, OK 73030/405-369-2316 (supplies)
Jet-Aer Corp., 100 Sixth Ave., Paterson, NJ 07524/201-278-8300
Art Jewel Ent., 460 Randy Rd., Carol Stream, IL 60188/312-260-0486
KA-BAR Cutlery, Div. of American Consumer Prods. Inc., 31100 Solon Rd., Solon, OH 44139/216-248-7000
KA-BAR Knives, Collectors Division, 434 No. 9th St., Olean, NY 14760/716-372-5611
Kershaw Knives/Kai Cutlery USA Ltd., Stafford Bus. Pk., 25300 SW Parkway, Wilsonville, OR 97070/503-636-0111
Koval Knives/IRT, P.O. Box 26155, Columbus, OH 43226/614-888-6486 (supplies)

Lamson & Goodnow Mfg. Co., 45 Conway St., Shelburne Falls, MA 03170/413-625-6331

Lansky Sharpeners, P.O. Box 800, Buffalo, NY 14221/716-634-6333 (sharpening devices)

Linder Solingen Knives, 4401 Sentry Dr., Tucker, GA 30084/404-939-6915

Al Mar Knives, Inc., P.O. Box 1626, 5755 SW Jean Rd., Suite 101, Lake Oswego, OR 97034/503-635-9229

Matthews Cutlery, 4401 Sentry Dr.,Tucker, GA 30084/404-939-6915 (mail order)

R. Murphy Co., Inc., 13 Groton-Harvard Rd., P.O. Box 376, Ayer, MA 01432/617-772-3481 (StaySharp)

Normark Corp., 1710 E. 78th St., Minneapolis, MN 55423/612-869-3291

Ontario Knife, Queen Cutlery Co., P.O. Box 500, Franklinville, NY 14737/716-676-5527 (Old Hickory)

Parker Cutlery, 6928 Lee Highway, Chattanooga, TN 37415/615-894-1782

Phoenix Arms Co. Ltd., Hy-Score Works, 40 Stonar Industrial Estate, Sandwich, Kent CT13 9LN, England/0304-61 12 21

Plaza Cutlery Inc., 3333 Bristol, #161, South Coast Plaza, Costa Mesa, CA 92626/714-549-3932 (mail order)

Precise International, 3 Chestnut St., Suffern, NY 10901/914-357-6200

Queen Cutlery Co., 507 Chestnut St., Titusville, PA 16354/800-222-5233

R & C Knives and Such, P.O. Box 1047, Manteca, CA 95336/209-239-3722 (mail order; ctlg. $2)

Randall-Made Knives, Box 1988, Orlando, FL 32802/407-855-8075 (ctlg. $1)

A. G. Russell Co., 1705 Hiwy. 471 No., Springdale, AR 72764/501-751-7341

Bob Sanders, 2358 Tyler Lane, Louisville, KY 40205/502-454-3338 (Swedish Bahco steel)

Schrade Cutlery Corp., 1776 Broadway, New York, NY 10019/212-757-1814

Sheffield Knifemakers Supply, P.O. Box 141, Deland, FL 32721/904-775-6453

Smith & Wesson, 2100 Roosevelt Ave., Springfield, MA 01101/413-781-8300

Jesse W. Smith Saddlery, N. 1325 Division, Spokane, WA 99202/509-534-3229 (sheathmakers)

Swiss Army Knives, Inc., P.O. Box 846, Shelton, CT 06484/203-929-6391

Tekna, 1075 Old County Rd., Belmont, CA 94002/415-592-4070

Thompson/Center, P.O. Box 2426, Rochester, NH 03867/603-332-2394

Tru-Balance Knife Co., 2155 Tremont Blvd., N.W., Grand Rapids, MI 49504/616-453-3679

Utica Cutlery Co., 820 Noyes St., Utica, NY 13503/315-733-4663 (Kutmaster)

Valor Corp., 5555 N.W. 36th Ave., Miami, FL 33142/305-633-0127

Washita Mountain Whetstone Co., P.O. Box 378, Lake Hamilton, AR 71951/501-525-3914

Wenoka Cutlery, P.O. Box 8238, West Palm Beach, FL 33407/305-845-6155

Western Cutlery Co., 1800 Pike Rd., Longmont, CO 80501/303-772-5900

Walt Whinnery, Walts Cust. Leather, 1947 Meadow Creek Dr., Louisville, KY 40218/502-458-4361 (sheathmaker)

Wyoming Knife Co., 101 Commerce Dr., Ft. Collins, CO 80524/303-224-3454

LABELS, BOXES, CARTRIDGE HOLDERS

Corbin Mfg. & Supply, Inc., P.O. Box 2659, White City, OR 97503/503-826-5211

Del Rey Products, P.O. Box 91561, Los Angeles, CA 90009/213-823-0494

E-Z Loader, Del Rey Products, P.O. Box 91561, Los Angeles, CA 90009

Flambeau Products Corp., 15981 Valplast Rd., Middlefield OH 44062/216-632-1631

Hunter Co., Inc., 3300 W. 71st Ave., Westminster, CO 80030/303-472-4626

Peterson Label Co., P.O. Box 186, 23 Sullivan Dr., Redding Ridge, CT 06876/203-938-2349 (cartridge box labels; Targ-Dots)

LOAD TESTING and PRODUCT TESTING, (CHRONOGRAPHING, BALLISTICS STUDIES)

Accuracy Systems Inc., 15205 N. Cave Creek Rd., Phoenix, AZ 85032/602-971-1991

Ballistic Research, Tom Armbrust, 1108 W. May Ave., McHenry, IL 60050/815-385-0037 (ballistic studies, pressure & velocity)

Ballistics Research Group, Kayusoft Intl. Star Route, Spray, OR 97874/503-462-3934 (computer software "Computer Shooter", ballistic studies)

W.W. Blackwell, 9826 Sagedale, Houston, TX 77089/713-484-0935 (computer program f. internal ball. f. rifle cartridges; "Load from a Disk")

Corbin Applied Technology, P.O. Box 2171, White City, OR 97503/503-826-5211

D&H Precision Tooling, 7522 Barnard Mill Rd., Ringwood, IL 60072/815-653-4011 (Pressure testing equipment)

H-S Precision, Inc., 112 N. Summit Ave., Prescott, AZ 86301/602-445-0607

Hutton Rifle Ranch, P.O. Box 45236, Boise, ID 83711/208-384-5461 (ballistic studies)

Kent Lomont, 4236 West 700 South, Poneto, IN 45781/219-694-6792 (handguns, handgun ammunition)

Plum City Ballistics Range, Norman E. Johnson, Rte. 1, Box 29A, Plum City, WI 54761/715-647-2539

Quartz-Lok, 13137 N. 21st Lane, Phoenix, AZ 85029/602-863-2729

Russell's Rifle Shop, Rte. 5, Box 92, Georgetown, TX 78626/512-778-5338 (load testing and chronographing to 300 yds.)

H. P. White Laboratory Inc., 3114 Scarboro Rd., Street, MD 21154/301-838-6550

MISCELLANEOUS

Action, Left-Hand, David Gentry Custom Gunmaker, 314 N. Hoffman, Belgrade, MT 59714/406-388-4867

Action, Mauser-style only, Crandall Tool & Machine Co., 1545 N. Mitchell St., Cadillac, MI 49601/616-775-5562

Action, Rifle, Hall Mfg., 1801 Yellow Leaf Rd., Clanton, AL 35045/205-755-4094 (stainless steel)

Action, Single Shot, Miller Arms, Inc., P.O. Box 260 St. Onge, SD 57779 (de-Haas-Miller)

Activator, B.M.F. Activator, Inc., P.O. Box 262364, Houston, TX 77207/713-477-8442

Adapters for Subcalibers, Harry Owen, P.O. Box 5337, Hacienda Hts., CA 917245/818-968-5806

Airgun Accessories, Beeman Precision Arms, Inc., 3440-GD Airway Dr., Santa Rosa, CA 95403/707-578-7900 (Beeman Pell seat, Pell-Size, etc.)

Archery, Bear, R.R. 4, 4600 Southwest 41st Blvd., Gainesville, FL 32601/904-376-2327

Arms Restoration, Pete Mazur, 13083 Drummer Way, Grass Valley, CA 95949/916-268-2412

Assault Rifle Accessories, Cherokee Gun Accessories, 4127 Bay St. Suite 226, Fremont, CA 94538/415-471-5770

Assault Rifle Accessories, Feather Industries, 2500 Central Ave., Boulder, CO 80301/303-442-7021

Assault Rifle Accessories, Ram-Line, Inc., 15611 W. 6th Ave., Golden, CO 80401/303-279-0886 (folding stock)

Bedding Kit, Fenwal, Inc., Resins Systems Div., 400 Main St., Ashland, MA 01721/508-881-2000, Ext. 2372 (Tru-Set)

Belt-Buckles, Herrett's Stocks, Inc., Box 741, Twin Falls, ID 83303/208-733-1498 (laser engr. hardwood)

Belt Buckles, Just Brass Inc., 121 Henry St., P.O. Box 112, Freeport, NY 11520/516-378-8588

Belt Buckles, Pilgrim Pewter Inc., R.D. 2, Tully, NY 13159/607-842-6431

Benchrest & Accuracy Shooters Equipment, Bob Pease Accuracy, P.O. Box 787, Zipp Road, New Braunfels, TX 78130/512-625-1342

Benchrest Rifles & Accessories, Robert W. Hart & Son Inc., 401 Montgomery St., Nescopeck, PA 18635/717-752-3655

Bore Collimator, Alley Supply Co., P.O. Box 848, Gardnerville, NV 89410/702-782-3800 (Sweany Site-A-Line optical collimator)

Brass Catcher, M.A.M. Products, Inc., 153 B Cross Slope Court, Englishtown, NJ 07726/201-536-7268 (free standing f. all auto pistols and/or semi-auto rifles)

Brass Shotgun Shells, GTM Co., T. Mahaney, 15915B East Main St., La Puente, CA 91744/818-968-5806

Bull-Pup Conversion Kits, Bull-Pup Industries Inc., P.O. Box 187, Pioneertown, CA 92268/619-228-1949

Cannons, South Bend Replicas Inc., 61650 Oak Rd., S. Bend, IN 44614/219-289-4500 (ctlg. $6)

Cartridge Adapters, Sport Specialties, Harry Owen, Box 5337, Hacienda Hts., CA 91745/213-968-5806 (ctlg. $3)

Case Gauge, Plum City Ballistics Range, Rte. 1, Box 29A, Plum City, WI 54761/715-647-2539

Cased, high-grade English tools, Marvin Huey Gun Cases, P.O. Box 22456, Kansas City, MO 64113/816-444-1637 (ebony, horn, ivory handles)

Clips, D&E Magazines Mfg., P.O. Box 4876-D, Sylmar, CA 91342 (handgun and rifle)

Computer & PSI Calculator, Hutton Rifle Ranch, P.O. Box 45236, Boise, ID 83711/208-384-5461

Computer Systems, Corbin Applied Technology, P.O. Box 2171, White City, OR 97503/503-826-5211 (software, books f. ballistic research)

Convert-A-Pell, Jett & Co., Inc., RR#3 Box 167-B, Litchfield, IL 62056/217-324-3779

Crossbows, Barnett International, 1967 Gunn Highway, Odessa, FL 33552/813-920-2241

Damascus Steel, Damascus-USA, P.O. Box 220, Howard, CO 81233/719-942-3527

Deer Drag, D&H Prods. Co., Inc., 465 Denny Rd., Valencia, PA 16059/412-898-2840

Dehumidifiers, Buenger Enterprises, P.O. Box 5286, Oxnard, CA 93030/805-985-0541

Dehumidifiers, Hydrosorbent Products, Clayton Rd., Ashley Falls, MA 01222/413-229-2967 (silica gel dehumidifier)

Dryer, Thermo-Electric, Golden-Rod, Buenger Enterprises, Box 5286, Oxnard, CA 93030/805-985-0541

Dummy Rounds, Duds Ammo & Supply Co., P.O. Box 393, Barton, VT 05822/802-525-3835

E-Z Loader, Del Rey Prod., P.O. Box 91561, Los Angeles, CA 90009/213-823-04494 (f. 22-cal. rifles)

Ear-Valve, North Consumer Prods. Div., 2664-B Saturn St., Brea, CA 92621/714-524-1655

Farrsight, Farr Studio, 1231 Robinhood Rd., Greenville, TN 37743/615-638-8825 (sighting aids for handgunners—clip on aperture)

Firearms Training, Ballistics Research Group, Kayusoft Intl., Star Route, Spray, OR 97874/503-462-3934 (computer software "Computer Shooter")

Flares, Aztec International Ltd., P.O. Box 1888, Norcross, GA 30091/404-446-2304 (ctlg. $2)

Game Hoist, Cam Gear Ind., P.O. Box 1002, Kalispell, MT 59901 (Sportsmaster 500 pocket hoist)

Game Scent, Buck Stop Lure Co., Inc., 3600 Grow Rd., Box 636, Stanton, MI 48888/517-762-5091

Game Scent, Pete Rickard, Inc., RD1 Box 292, Cobleskill, NY 12043/518-234-2731 (Indian Buck lure)

Game Scent, Tink's Safariland Hunting Corp., P.O. Box 69, Trappe, MD 21673/301-820-9707 (buck lure)

Gas Pistol, Penguin Ind., Inc., Airport Industrial Mall, Coatesville, PA 19320/215-384-6000

Grip Caps, Classic Arms Corp., P.O. Box 8, Palo Alto, CA 94301/415-321-7243

Gun Bedding Kit, Fenwal, Inc., Resins System Div., 400 Main St., Ashland, MA 01721/508-881-2000. Ext. 2372

Gun Covers, E. Christopher Firearms Co., Inc., Route 128 & Ferry St. Miamitown, OH 45041/513-353-1321 (Gunnysox)

Gun Jewelry, Sid Bell Originals, R.D. 2, Box 219, Tully, NY 13159/607-842-6431 (jewelry for sportsmen)

Gun Jewelry, Pilgrim Pewter Inc., R.D. 2, Box 219, Tully, NY 13159/607-842-6431

Gun Jewelry, Sports Style Assoc., 148 Hendricks Ave., Lynbrook, NY 11563

Gun photographer, Mustafa Bilal, 5429 Russell Ave. NW, Suite 202, Seattle, WA 98107/206-782-4164

Gun photographer, John Hanusin, 3306 Commercial, Northbrook, IL 60062/312-564-2706

Gun photographer, Intl. Photographic Assoc., Inc. 4500 E. Speedway, Suite 90, Tucson, AZ 85712/602-326-2941

Gun photographer, Charles Semmer, 7885 Cyd Dr., Denver, CO 80221/303-429-6947

Gun photographer, Weyer International, 333-14th St., Toledo, OH 43624/419-241-5454

Gun photographer, Steve White, 1920 Raymond Dr., Northbrook, IL 60062/312-564-2720

Gun Safes, Abel Safe & File Co., 104 North Fourth St., Fairbury, IL 61739/815-346-9280

Gun Safety, Gun Alert Covers, Master Products, Inc., P.O. Box 8474, Van Nuys, CA 91409/818-365-0864

Gun Slings, Torel, Inc., 1053 N. South St., Yoakum, TX 77995

Gun Vise, Pflumm Gun Mfg. Co., 6139 Melrose Lane, Shawnee, KS 66203/913-268-3105

Hand Exerciser, Action Products, Inc., 22 No. Mulberry St., Hagerstown, MD 21740/301-797-1414

Horsepac, Yellowstone Wilderness Supply, P.O. 129, West Yellowstone, MT 59758/406-646-7613

Horsepacking Equipment/Saddle Trees, Ralide West, P.O. Box 998, 299 Firehole Ave., West Yellowstone, WY 59758/406-646-7612

Hugger Hooks Co., 3900 Easley Way, Golden, CO 80403/303-279-6160

Insect Repellent, Armor, Div. of Buck Stop, Inc., 3015 Grow Rd., Stanton, MI 48888

Insert Chambers, GTM Co., Geo T. Mahaney, 15915B E. Main St., La Puente, CA 91744 (rifles, shotguns)

Insert Barrels and Cartridge Adapters, Sport Specialties, Harry Owen, Box 5337, Hacienda Hts., CA 91745/213-968-5806 (ctlg. $3)

Knife Sharpeners, Lansky Sharpeners, P.O. Box 800, Buffalo, NY 14221/716-634-6333

Laser Aim, Laser Aim, Inc., 100 S. Main St., Box 581, Little Rock, AR 72203

Laser Aim, Laser Devices, Inc., 2880 Research Park Dr., Soquel, CA 95073/408-476-8300

Locks, Gun Bor-Lok Prods., 105 5th St., Arbuckle, CA 95912

Locks, Gun, Master Lock Co., 2600 N. 32nd St., Milwaukee, WI 53245/414-444-2800

Lugheads, Floorplate Overlays, Sid Bell Originals, Inc., RD2, Box 219, Tully, NY 13159/607-842-6431

Lug Recess Insert, P.P.C. Corp., 625 E. 24th St. Paterson, NJ 07514

Magazines, Mitchell Arms Inc., 3411 Lake Center Dr., Santa Ana, CA 92704/714-957-5711 (stainless steel)

Magazines, Ram-Line, Inc., 15611 W. 6th Ave., Golden, CO 80401/303-279-0886

Miniature Cannons, Karl J. Furr, 76 East 350 North, Orem, UT 84057/801-226-3877 (replicas; Gatling guns)

Monte Carlo Pad, Hoppe Division, Penguin Ind., Airport Industrial Mall, Coatesville, PA 19320/215-384-6000

Old Gun Industry Art, Hansen and Company, 244 Old Post Rd., Southport, CT 06490/203-259-7337

Police Batons & Accessories, Armament Systems and Procedures, Inc., P.O. Box 1794, Appleton, WI 54913/414-731-7075

Powderhorns, Frontier, 2910 San Bernadino, Laredo, TX 78040/512-723-5409

Powderhorns, Tennessee Valley Mfg., P.O. Box 1175, Corinth, MS 38834/601-286-5014

Practice Ammunition, Hoffman New Ideas Inc., 821 Northmoor Rd., Lake Forest, IL 60045/312-234-4075

Practice Wax Bullets, Brazos Arms Co., 17423 Autumn Trails, Houston, TX 77084/713-463-0598

Ram Line, Inc., 15611 W. 6th Ave., Golden, CO 80401/303-279-0886 (accessories)

Ransom Handgun Rests, Ransom Intl. Corp., P.O. Box 3845, Prescott, AZ 86302/602-778-7899

Rifle Magazines, Butler Creek Corp., 290 Arden Dr., Belgrade, MT 59714/406-388-1356 (30-rd. Mini-14)

Rifle Magazines, Condor Mfg., 418 W. Magnolia Ave., Glendale, CA 91204/818-240-3173 (25-rd. 22-cal.)

Rifle Magazines, S.A. Miller, P.O. Box 1053, 1440 Peltier Dr., Point Roberts, WA 98281/206-945-7014 (30-cal. M1 15&30-round)

Rifle Slings, Bianchi International, 100 Calle Cortez, Temecula, CA 92390/714-676-5621

Rifle Slings, Butler Creek Corp., 290 Arden Dr., Belgrade, MT 59714/406-388-1356

Rifle Slings, Chace Leather Prods., Longhorn Div., 507 Alden St. Fall River, MA 02722/508-678-7556

Rifle Slings, High North Products, P.O. Box 2, Antigo, WI 54409/715-623-5117 (1-oz. Mongoose gun sling)

Rifle Slings, John's Cust. Leather, 525 S. Liberty St., Blairsville, PA 15717/412-459-6802

Rifle Slings, Kirkpatrick Leather Co., P.O. Box 3150, Laredo, TX 78044/512-723-6631

Rifle Slings, Schulz Industr., 16247 Minnesota Ave., Paramount, CA 90723/213-439-5903

RIG, NRA Scoring Plug, Rig Products, 87 Coney Island Dr., Sparks, NV 89431/702-331-5666

Rubber Cheekpiece, W.H. Lodewick, 2816 N.E. Halsey, Portland, OR 97232/503-284-2554

Rust Prevention, Rusteprufe Laboratories, 1319 Jefferson Ave., Sparta, WI 54656/608-269-4144

Saddle Rings, Studs, Fred Goodwin, Sherman Mills, ME 04776

Safeties, William E. Harper, The Great 870 Co., P.O. Box 6309, El Monte, CA 91734/213-579-3077 (f. Rem. 870P)

Safeties, Williams Gun Sight Co., 7389 Lapeer Rd., Davison, MI 48423

Safety Slug, Glaser Safety Slug, P.O. Box 8223, Foster City, CA 94404/415-345-7677

Sav-Bore, Saunders Sptg. Gds., 338 Somerset St., N. Plainfield, NJ 07060

Scrimshaw, Henry "Hank" Bonham, P.O. Box 242, Brownsville, ME 04414/207-965-2891

Scrimshaw, Boone Trading Co., 562 Coyote Rd., Brinnon, WA 98320/206-796-4330

Scrimshaw, G. Marek, P.O. Box 213, Westfield, MA 01086/413-568-9816

Scrimshaw, George Sherwood, 46 No. River Dr., Roseburg, OR 97470/503-672-3159

Scrimshaw, Twyla Taylor, P.O. Box 252; #2 Engress Rd., Oracle, AZ 85623/602-896-2860 (handgun grips-ivory or Micarta)

Sharpening Stones, A.G. Russell Co., 1705 Hiway 471 North, Springdale, AR 72764/501-751-7341 (Arkansas Oilstones)

Shell Catcher, Condor Mfg., 418 W. Magnolia Ave., Glendale, CA 91204/818-240-3173

Shooting Coats, 10-X Products Group, 2828 Forest Lane, Suite 1107, Dallas, TX 75234/214-243-4016

Shooting Glasses, American Optical Corp., 14 Mechanic St., Southbridge, MA 01550/617-765-9711

Shooting Glasses, Bausch & Lomb, Inc., 42 East Ave., Rochester, NY 14603/800-828-5423 (Ray Ban®)

Shooting Glasses, Bilsom Intl., Inc., 109 Carpenter Dr., Sterling, VA 22170/703-834-1070

Shooting Glasses, Willson Safety Prods. Division, P.O. Box 622, Reading, PA 19603

Shooting Gloves, James Churchill Glove Co., Box 298, Centralia, WA 98531 (singles only, right or left)

Shooting Range Equipment, Caswell Internatl. Corp., 1221 Marshall St. N.E., Minneapolis, MN 55413/612-379-2000

Shotgun bore, Custom Shootg. Prods., 8505 K St., Omaha, NE 68127

Shotgun Ribs, Poly-Choke Div., Marble Arms Corp., 420 Industrial Park, Gladstone, MI 49837/906-428-3710

Shotgun Sight, bi-ocular, Trius Prod., Box 25, Cleves, OH 45002

Shotgun Specialist, Moneymaker Guncraft, 1420 Military Ave., Omaha, NE 68131/402-556-0226 (ventilated, free-floating ribs)

Shotshell Adapter, PC Co., 5942 Secor Rd., Toledo, OH 43623/419-472-6222 (Plummer 410 converter)

Shotshell Adapter, Jesse Ramos, P.O. Box 7105, La Puente, CA 91744/818-369-6384 (12 ga./410 converter)

Sight-Vise, Stuart Products, Inc., P.O. Box 1587, Easley, SC 29641/803-859-9360

Snap Caps, Armsport, Inc., 3950 N.W. 49th St., Miami, FL 33142/305-635-7850

Snap Caps, Edwards Recoil Reducer, 1104 Milton Rd., Alton, IL 62002/618-462-3257

Springs, W.C. Wolff Co., P.O. Box 232, Ardmore, PA 19003/215-896-7500

Stock Duplicating Machine, Don Allen, Inc., HC55, Box 326, Sturgis, SD 47785/605-347-5227

Supersound, Edmund Scientific Co., 101 E. Gloucester Pike, Barrington, NJ 08033/609-573-6250 (safety device)

Swivels, Michaels, P.O. Box 13010, Portland, OR 97213/503-255-6890

Swivels, Sile Dist., 7 Centre Market Pl., New York, NY 10013/212-925-4111

Swivels, Williams Gun Sight Co., 7389 Lapeer Rd., Davision, MI 48423

Tomahawks, H&B Forge Co., Rt. 2, Shiloh, OH 44878/419-896-2075

Tree Stand, Climbing, API Outdoors Inc., P.O. Box 1432, Tallulah, LA 71284/318-574-4903

Tree Steps, Deer Me Products Co., Box 34, 1208 Park St., Anoka, MN 55303/612-421-8971

Trophies, V.H. Blackinton & Co., P.O. Box 1300, 221 John L. Dietsch Blvd., Attleboro Falls, MA 02763/617-699-4436

Trophies, F. H. Noble & Co., 888 Tower Rd., Mundelein, IL 60060

Warning Signs, Delta Ltd., P.O. Box 777, Mt. Ida, AR 71957

World Hunting Info., J/B Adventures & Safaris, Inc., 6312 S. Fiddlers Green Circle, Suite 330N, Englewood CO 80111/303-771-0977

MUZZLE-LOADING GUNS, BARRELS or EQUIPMENT

Luther Adkins, Box 281, Shelbyville, IN 46176/317-392-3795 (breech plugs)

Allen Firearms Co., 2679 All Trades Rd., Santa Fe, NM 87501/505-471-6090

Anderson Mfg. Co., P.O. Box 4218, Federal Way, WA 98063/206-838-4299 (Flame-N-Go fusil; Accra-Shot)

Antique Gun Parts, Inc., 1118 S. Braddock Ave., Pittsburgh, PA 15218/412-241-1811 (parts)

Armoury, Inc., Rte. 202, New Preston, CT 06777

Armsport, Inc., 3590 N.W. 49th St., Miami, FL 33142/305-635-7850

B-Square Co., P.O. Box 11281, Ft. Worth, TX 76109/817-923-0964

Beaver Lodge, 9245 16th Ave. S.W., Seattle, WA 98106/206-763-1698 (cust. ML)

Beeman Precision Arms, Inc., 3440-GDD Airway Dr., Santa Rosa, CA 95403/707-578-7900

Blackhawk East, Box 2274, Loves Park, IL 61131 (blackpowder)

Blackhawk Mtn., Box 210, Conifer, CO 80433 (blackpowder)

Blackhawk West, Box 285, Hiawatha, KS 66434 (blackpowder)

Blue and Gray Prods., Inc. RD #6, Box 362, Wellsboro, PA 16901/717-724-1383 (equipment)

Brazos Arms Co., 17423 Autumn Trails, Houston, TX 77084/713-463-0598

Butler Creek Corp., 290 Arden Dr., Belgrade, MT 59714/406-388-1356 (poly & maxi patch)

Cache La Poudre Rifleworks, 140 N. College, Ft. Collins, CO 80524/303-482-6913 (custom muzzleloaders)

R. MacDonald Champlin, P.O. Box 693, Manchester, NH 03105/603-483-8557 (custom muzzleloaders)

Cheney Firearms Co., P.O. Box 321, Woods Cross, UT 84087/801-295-4396 (rifles)

Chopie Mfg. Inc., 700 Copeland Ave., LaCrosse, WI 54601/608-784-0926 (nipple wrenches)

Connecticut Valley Arms Co. (CVA), 5988 Peachtree East, Norcross, GA 30071/404-449-4687 (kits also)

Cumberland Knife & Gun Works, 5661 Bragg Blvd., Fayetteville, NC 28303/919-867-0009

Earl T. Cureton, Rte. 2, Box 388, Willoughby Rd., Bulls Gap, TN 37711/615-235-2854 (powder horns)

Homer L. Dangler, Box 254, Addison, MI 49220/517-547-6745

Leonard Day & Sons, Inc., One Cottage St., P.O. Box 723, East Hampton, MA 01027/413-527-7990

Denver Arms, Ltd., P.O. Box 4640, Pagosa Springs, CO 81157/303-731-2295 (S.A.S.E.)

Des Moines River Trading Co., 503 Clinton St., Boone, IA 50036

Dixie Gun Works, Inc., P.O. Box 130, Union City, TN 38261

Peter Dyson Ltd., 29-31 Church St., Honley, Huddersfield, W. Yorksh. HD7 2AH, England/0484-661062 (acc. f. ML shooter replicas)

EMF Co., Inc., 1900 E. Warner Ave. 1-D, Santa Ana, CA 92705/714-261-6611

Euroarms of America, Inc., P.O. Box 3277, 1501 Lenoir Dr., Winchester, VA 22601/703-662-1863

F.P.F. Co., P.O. Box 211, Van Wert, OH 45891 (black powder accessories)

Andy Fautheree, P.O. Box 4607, Pagosa Springs, CO 81157/303-731-5003 (cust. ML guns; must send SASE)

Ted Fellowes, Beaver Lodge, 9245 16th Ave. S.W., Seattle, WA 98106/206-763-1698 (cust. ML)

Marshall F. Fish, Rt. 22 N., Box 2439, Westport, NY 12993/518-962-4897 (antique ML repairs)

The Flintlock Muzzle Loading Gun Shop, 1238 "G" So. Beach Blvd., Anaheim, CA 92804/714-821-6655

Forster Prods., 82 E. Lanark Ave., Lanark, IL 61046/815-493-6360

Frontier, 2910 San Bernardo, Laredo, TX 78040/512-723-5409 (powderhorns)

Getz Barrel Co., Box 88, Beavertown, PA 17813/717-658-7263 (barrels)

GOEX, Inc., Belin Plant, Moosic, PA 18507/717-457-6724 (black powder)

Gonic Arms Inc., 134 Flagg Rd., Gonic, NH 03867/603-332-8456

A.R. Goode, 4125 N.E. 28th Terr., Ocala, FL 32670/904-622-9575 (ML rifle barrels)

Guncraft Inc., 117 W. Pipeline, Hurst, TX 76053/817-282-1464

Gun Parts Corp., Box 2, West Hurley, NY 12491/914-679-2417

The Gun Works, 236 Main St., Springfield, OR 97477/503-741-4118 (supplies)

Hatfield Rifle Works, 2020 Calhoun, St. Joseph, MO 64501/816-279-8688 (squirrel rifle)

Hopkins & Allen, P.O. Box 217, Hawthorne, NJ 7507 (parts only)

The House of Muskets, Inc., P.O. Box 4640, Pagosa Springs, CO 81157/303-731-2295 (ML bbls. & supplies; catalog $3)

Steven Dodd Hughes, P.O. Box 11455, Eugene, OR 97440/503-485-8869 (cust. guns; ctlg. $3)

A. Hunkeler, Buckskin Machine Works, 3235 So. 358th St., Auburn, WA 98001/206-927-5412 (ML guns)

Wm. Large Gun & Mach. Shop, James W. McKenzie, R.R. 1, Box 188, Ironton, OH 45638/614-532-5298

Lever Arms Serv. Ltd., 2131 Burrard St., Vancouver, BC V6J 3H7/604-736-0004, Canada

Log Cabin Sport Shop, 8010 Lafayette Rd., Lodi, OH 44254/216-948-1082 (ctlg. $3)

Lyman Products Corp., 147 West St., Middlefield, CT 06455/203-349-3421

McCann's Muzzle-Gun Works, 200 Federal City Rd., Pennington, NJ 08534/609-737-1707

Maurer Arms, 2154-16th St., Akron, OH 44314/216-745-6864 (cust. muzzleloaders)

Modern Muzzleloading, Inc., Highway 136 East, P.O. Box 130, Lancaster, MO 63548/816-457-2125

Mountain State Muzzleloading Supplies, Inc., Box 154-1, Rt. #2 Williamstown, WV 26187/304-375-7842

Muzzleload Magnum Products (MMP), Rt. 6 Box 384, Harrison, AR 72601/501-741-5019

Muzzleloaders Etc., Inc., Jim Westberg, 9901 Lyndale Ave., S., Bloomington, MN 55420/612-884-1161

Navy Arms Co., 689 Bergen Blvd., Ridgefield, NJ 07657/201-945-2500

Newman Gunshop, 119 Miller Rd., Agency, IA 52530/515-937-5775 (custom ML rifles)

October Country, P.O. Box 969, Hayden Lake, ID 83835/208-772-2068

Oregon Trail Riflesmiths, Inc., P.O. Box 51, Mackay, ID 83251/208-588-2527

Ox-Yoke Originals Inc., 34 W. Main St., Milo, ME 04463/207-943-2171 (dry lubr. patches)

A.W. Peterson Gun Shop, 1693 Old Hwy. 441 N., Mt. Dora, FL 32757

Phyl-Mac, 609 N.E. 104th Ave., Vancouver, WA 98664/206-256-0579

R.V.I., P.O. Box 1439 Stn. A, Vancouver, B.C. V6C 1A0, Canada/604-524-3214 (high grade BP acc.)

Richland Arms, 321 W. Adrian St., Blissfield, MI 49228

Rooster Laboratories, P.O. Box 412514, Kansas City, MO 64141/816-474-1622 (Patch & ball bullet lubricants)

H.M. Schoeller, 569 So. Braddock Ave., Pittsburgh, PA 15221

Tyler Scott, Inc., 313 Rugby Ave., Suite 162, Terrace Park, OH 45174/513-831-7603 (Shooter's choice black solvent; patch lube)

C. Sharps Arms Co., Inc., P.O. Box 885, Big Timber, MT 59011/406-932-4353

Sile Distributors, 7 Centre Market Pl., New York, NY 10013/213-925-4111

C.E. Siler Locks, 7 Acton Woods Rd., Candler, NC 28715/704-667-9991 (flint locks)

South Bend Replicas, Inc., 61650 Oak Rd., South Bend, IN 46614/219-289-4500 (ctlg. $6)

Dale A. Storey, DGS, Inc., 305 N. Jefferson, Casper, WY 82601/307-237-2414

The Swampfire Shop, 1693 Old Hwy. 441 N., Mt. Dora, FL 32757/904-383-0595

Tennessee Valley Mfg., P.O. Box 1125, Corinth, MS 38834 (powderhorns)

Ten-Ring Precision, Inc., 1449 Blue Crest Lane, San Antonio, TX 78232/512-494-3063

Traditions, Inc., 452 Main St.; P.O. Box 235, Deep River, CT 06417/203-526-9555 (guns, kits, accessories)

Trail Guns Armory, 1422 E. Main, League City, TX 77573/713-332-5833

Uberti USA, Inc., 41 Church St., New Milford, CT 06776/203-355-8827

Upper Missouri Trading Co., 304 Harold St., Crofton, NE 68730/402-388-4844

Warren Muzzle Loading, Hwy. 21, Ozone, AR 72854 (black powder accessories)

Fred Wells, Wells Sport Store, 110 N. Summit St., Prescott, AZ 86301/602-445-3655

W.H. Wescomb, P.O. Box 488, Glencoe, CA 95232/209-293-7010 (parts)

Williamson-Pate Gunsmith Serv., 117 W. Pipeline, Hurst, TX 76053/817-282-1464

Winchester Sutler, HC 38 Box 1000, Winchester, VA 22601/703-888-3595 (haversacks)

Winter & Associates, 239 Hillary Dr., Verona, PA 15147/412-795-4124 (Olde Pennsylvania ML accessories)

PISTOLSMITHS

Accuracy Gun Shop, Lance Martini, 3651 University Ave., San Diego, CA 92104/619-282-8500

Accuracy Systems, Inc., 15205 N. Cave Creek Rd., Phoenix, AZ 85032/602-971-1991

Accuracy Unlimited, 16036 N. 49 Ave., Glendale, AZ 85306/602-978-9089

Ahlman's Inc., R.R. #1 Box 20, Morristown, MN 55052/507-685-4243

Alpha Precision, Inc., Rte. 1, Box 35-1, Preston Rd., Good Hope, GA 30641/404-267-6163

American Pistolsmiths Guild, Rt. 1, Della Dr., Bloomingdale, OH 43910/614-264-0176

Ann Arbor Rod and Gun Co., 1946 Packard Rd., Ann Arbor, MI 48104/313-769-7866

Armament Gunsmithing Co., Inc., 525 Route 22, Hillside, NJ 07205/201-686-0960

Richard W. Baber, Alpine Gun Mill, 1507 W. Colorado Ave., Colorado Springs, CO 80904/303-634-4867

Baer Custom Guns, 1725 Minesite Rd., Allentown, PA 18103/215-398-2362 (accurizing 45 autos and Comp II Syst.; cust. XP100s, P.P.C. rev.)

Bain & Davis Sptg. Gds., 307 E. Valley Blvd., San Gabriel, CA 91776/213-573-4241

Bar-Sto Precision Machine, 73377 Sullivan Rd., P.O. Box 1838, Twentynine Palms, CA 92277/619-367-2747 (S.S. bbls. f. 45 ACP and others)

Barta's Gunsmithing, 10231 US Hwy. #10, Cato, WI 54206/414-732-4472

R.J. Beal, Jr., 170 W. Marshall Rd., Lansdowne, PA 19050/215-259-1220 (conversions, SASE f. inquiry)

Behlert Precision, RD 2 Box 63, Route 611 North, Pipersville, PA 18947/215-766-8681 (short actions)

Bell's Custom Shop, 3309 Mannheim Rd., Franklin Park, IL 60131/312-678-1900

Bowen Classic Arms Corp., P.O. Box 67, Louisville, TN 37777/615-984-3583

C.T. Brian, 1101 Indiana Ct., Decatur, IL 62521/217-429-2290

Ed Brown Products, Rte. 2 Box 2922, Perry, MO 63462/314-565-3261

Leo Bustani, P.O. Box 8125, W. Palm Beach, FL 33407/305-622-2710

Dick Campbell, 20000 Silver Ranch Rd., Conifer, CO 80433/303-697-0150 (PPC guns; custom)

Cellini's, Francesca Inc., 3115 Old Ranch Rd., San Antonio, TX 78217/512-826-2584

Clark Custom Guns, Inc., James E. Clark, Rt. 2 Box 22A, Keithville, LA 71047/318-915-0836

The Competitive Pistol Shop, John Henderson, 5233 Palmer Dr., Ft. Worth, TX 76117/817-834-8479

Custom Gun Guild, 2646 Church Dr., Doraville, GA 30340/404-455-0346

D&D Gun Shop, 363 Elmwood, Troy, MI 48083/313-583-1512

Davis Co., 2793 Del Monte St., West Sacramento, CA 95691/916-372-6789

Leonard Day & Sons, Inc., One Cottage St., P.O. Box 723, East Hampton, MA 01027/413-527-7990

Dilliott Gunsmithing, Inc., Rte. 3, Box 340, Dandridge, TN 37725

Dominic DiStefano, 4303 Friar Lane, Colorado Springs, CO 80907/303-599-3366 (accurizing)

Duncan's Gunworks Inc., 1619 Grand Ave., San Marcos, CA 92069/619-727-0515

Dan Dwyer, 915 W. Washington, San Diego, CA 92103/619-296-1501

Peter Dyson Ltd., 29-31 Church St., Honley, Huddersfield, Yorksh. HD7 2AH, ENGLAND

Englishtown Sptg. Gds. Co., Inc., David J. Maxham, 38 Main St., Englishtown, NJ 07726/201-446-7717

Ferris Firearms, Gregg Ferris, 1827 W. Hildebrand, San Antonio, TX 78201/512-734-0304

Jack First Distributors, Inc., 44633 Sierra Hwy., Lancaster, CA 93534/805-945-6981

Fountain Prods., 492 Prospect Ave., W. Springfield, MA 01089/413-781-4651

Frielich Police Equipment, 396 Broome St., New York, NY 10013/212-254-3045

K. Genecco Gun Works, 10512 Lower Sacramento Rd., Stockton, CA 95210/209-951-0706

Gilman-Mayfield, 1552 N. 1st, Fresno, CA 93703/209-237-2500

Gunsite Gunsmithy, P.O. Box 451, Paulden, AZ 86334/602-636-4104

Fritz Hallberg, 240 No. Oregon St., P.O. Box 322, Ontario, OR 97914/503-889-7052

Keith Hamilton, P.O. Box 871, Gridley, CA 95948/916-846-2361

Hanson's Gun Center, 521 So. Circle Dr., Colorado Springs, CO 80910/719-634-4220

Gil Hebard Guns, Box 1, Knoxville, IL 61448

Richard Heinie, 821 E. Adams, Havana, IL 62644/309-543-4535

High Bridge Arms Inc., 3185 Mission St., San Francisco, CA 94110/415-282-8358

James W. Hoag, 8523 Canoga Ave., Suite C, Canoga Park, CA 91304/818-998-1510

Campbell H. Irwin, Hartland Blvd. (Rt. 20), Box 152, East Hartland, CT 06027/203-653-3901

Paul Jaeger, Inc., P.O. Box 449, 1 Madison Ave., Grand Junction, TN 38039/901-764-6909

J.D. Jones, 721 Woodvue Lane, Wintersville, OH 43952/614-264-0176

Reeves C. Jungkind, 5805 N. Lamar Blvd., Austin, TX 78752/512-442-1094

L.E. Jurras & Assoc., P.O. Box 680, Washington, IN 47501/812-254-7698

Ken's Gun Specialties, Rt. 1, Box 147, Lakeview, AR 72642/501-431-5606

Benjamin Kilham, Kilham & Co., Main St., Box 37, Lyme, NH 03768/603-795-4112

Terry K. Kopp, 1301 Franklin, Lexington, MO 64067/816-259-2636 (rebblg., conversions)

LaFrance Specialties, P.O. Box 178211, San Diego, CA 92117/619-293-3373

Nelson H. Largent, Silver Shield's Inc., 4464-D Chinden Blvd., Boise, ID 83714

William R. Laughridge, Cylinder & Slide Shop, 515 E. Military Ave., Fremont, NE 68025/402-721-4277

John G. Lawson, The Sight Shop, 1802 E. Columbia Ave., Tacoma, WA 98404/206-474-5465

Kent Lomont, 4236 West South, Poneto, In 46781/219-694-6792 (Auto Mag only)

George F. Long, 1500 Rougue River Hwy., Ste. F, Grants Pass, OR 97527/503-476-7552

Mac's .45 Shop, Box 2028, Seal Beach, CA 90740/213-438-5046

Mag-na-port International, Inc., 41302 Executive Drive, Mt. Clemens, MI 48045/313-469-6727

Robert A. McGrew, 3315 Michigan Ave., Colorado Springs, CO 80910/303-636-1940

Philip Bruce Mahony, 1-223 White Hollow Rd., Lime Rock, CT06039/203-435-9341

Rudolf Marent, 9711 Tiltree, Houston, TX 77075/713-946-7028 (Hammerli)

Elwyn H. Martin, Martin's Gun Shop, 937 So. Sheridan Blvd., Lakewood, CO 80226/303-922-2184

John V. Martz, 8060 Lakeview Lane, Lincoln, CA 95648/916-645-2250 (cust. German Lugers & P-38s)

Alan C. Marvel, 3922 Madonna Rd., Jarretsville, MD 21084/301-557-6545

Maryland Gun Works, Ltd., TEC Bldg., 10097 Tyler Pl. #8, Ijamsville, MD 21754/301-831-8456

Mountain Bear Rifle Works, Inc., Wm. Scott Bickett, 100-B Ruritan Rd., Sterling, VA 22170/703-430-0420

Mullis Guncraft, 3518 Lawyers Road East, Monroe, NC 28110/704-283-8789

Nastoff's 45 Shop, Steve Nastoff, 1057 Laverne Ave., Younstown, OH 44511/216-799-8870 (1911 conversions)

William Neighbor, Bill's Gun Repair, 1007 Burlington St., Mendota, IL 61342/815-539-5786

Wayne Novak, 1206½ 30th St., Parkersburg, WV 26101/304-467-2086

Nu-Line Guns, 1053 Caulks Hill Rd., Harvester, MO 63303/314-441-4501

Nygord Precision Products, P.O. Box 8394, La Crescenta, CA 91214/818-352-3027

Pachmayr Ltd., 1875 So. Mountain Ave., Monrovia, CA 91016/818-357-7771

Frank J. Paris, 13945 Minock Dr., Redford, MI 48239/313-255-0888

Paterson Gunsmithing, 438 Main St., Paterson, NJ 07502/201-345-4100

Phillips & Bailey, Inc., 815A Yorkshire St., Houston, TX 77022/713-699-4288

J. Michael Plaxco, Rt. 1, Box 203, Roland, AR 72135/501-868-9787

Power Custom, Inc., R Rt. 2 Box 756AB, Gravois Mills, MO 65037/314-372-5684

Precision Specialties, 131 Hendom Dr., Feeding Hills, MA 01030/413-786-3365

RPS Gunshop, 11 So. Haskell St., Central Point, OR 97502/503-664-5010

Roberts Custom Guns (Dayton Traister Co.), 4778 N. Monkey Hill Rd., Oak Harbor, WA 98277/206-675-3421

Bob Rogers Gunsmithing, P.O. Box 305; 344 S. Walnut St., Franklin Grove, IL 61?/815-456-2685 (custom)

SSK Industries (See: J.D. Jones)

L.W. Seecamp Co., Inc., Box 255, New Haven, CT 06502/203-877-3429

Harold H. Shockley, 204 E. Farmington Rd., Hanna City, IL 61536/309-565-4524

Hank Shows, dba The Best, 1078 Alice Ave., Ukiah, CA 95482/707-462-9060

Spokhandguns Inc., Vern D. Ewer, P.O. Box 370, 1206 Fig St., Benton City, WA 99320/509-588-5255

Sportsmens Equipmt. Co., 915 W. Washington, San Diego, CA 92103/619-296-1501 (specialty limiting trigger motion in autos)

James R. Steger, 1131 Dorsey Pl., Plainfield, NJ 07062

Irving O. Stone, Jr., 7337 Sullivan Rd., P.O. Box 1838, Twentynine Palms, CA 92277/619-367-2747

Victor W. Strawbridge, 6 Pineview Dr., Dover Pt., Dover, NH 03820

A.D. Swenson's 45 Shop, P.O. Box 606, Fallbrook, CA 92028

Ten-Ring Precision, Inc., Alex B. Hamilton, 1449 Blue Crest Ln., San Antonio, TX 78232/512-494-3063

Randall Thompson, Highline Machine Co., 654 Lela Pl., Grand Junction, CO 81504/303-434-4971

"300" Gunsmith Service, 4655 Washington St., Denver, CO 80216/303-295-2437

Timney Mfg. Co., 3065 W. Fairmount Ave., Phoenix, AZ 85017/602-274-2999

Trapper Gun, Inc., 18717 East 14 Mile Rd., Fraser, MI 48026/313-792-0134

Dennis A. "Doc" & Bud Ulrich, D.O.C. Specialists, 2209 So. Central Ave., Cicero, IL 60650/312-652-3606

Vic's Gun Refinishing, 6 Pineview Dr., Dover, NH 03820/603-742-0013

Walters Industries, 6226 Park Lane, Dallas, TX 75225/214-691-6973

Wardell Precision Handguns Ltd., Box 4132 New River Stage 1, New River, AZ 85029/602-242-0186

Wilson's Gun Shop, P.O. Box 578, Rt. 3, Box 211-D, Berryville, AR 72616/501-545-3618

Wisner's Gun Shop, Inc., P.O. Box 58; Hiway 6, Adna, WA 98552/206-748-8942

REBORING AND RERIFLING

P.O. Ackley (See Belim Contenders)

Barnes Custom Shop, dba Barnes Bullets Inc., P.O. Box 215, American Fork, UT 84003

Belim Contenders, P.O. Box 429, Cleveland, UT 84518 (price list $3; rifle only)

A.R. Goode, 4125 N.E. 28th Terr., Ocala, FL 32760/904-622-9575

Terry K. Kopp, 1301 Franklin, Lexington, MO 64067/816-259-2636 (invis-A-Line bbl.; relining)

LaBounty Precision Reboring, P.O. Box 186, 7968 Silver Lk. Rd., Maple Falls, WA 98266/206-559-2047

Wm. Large Machine Shop, James W. McKenzie, RR #1, Ironton, OH 45638/614-532-8465

Matco, Inc., 1003-2nd St., No. Manchester, IN 46962/219-982-8282

Nu-Line Guns, 1053 Caulks Hill Rd., Harvester, MO 63303/314-441-4500

Redman's Reboring & Rerifling, Route 3, Box 330A, Omak, WA 98841/509-826-5102

Ridgetop Sporting Goods, P.O. Box 306; 42907 Hilligoss Ln. East, Eatonville, WA 98328/206-832-6422

Siegrist Gun Shop, 8752 Turtle Rd., Whittemore, MI 48770/517-873-3929

Silver Shields Inc., 4464-D Chinden Blvd., Boise, ID 83714/208-323-8991

Snapp's Gunshop, 6911 E. Washington Rd., Clare, MI 48617

J.W. Van Patten, P.O. Box 145, Foster Hill, Milford, PA 18337/717-296-7069

Robt. G. West, 3973 Pam St., Eugene, OR 97402/503-689-6610 (barrel relining)

RELOADING TOOLS AND ACCESSORIES

AMT (Arcadia Machine & Tool, Inc.), 6226 Santos Diaz, Irwindale, CA 91702/818-334-6629

ASI, 6226 Santos Diaz St., Irwindale, CA 91702/818-334-6629 (Autoscale)

Activ Industries, Inc., P.O. Box F, 1000 Zigor Rd., Kearneysville, WV 25430/304-725-0451 (plastic hulls, wads)

Advance Car Mover Co., Inc., Rowell Div., P.O. Box 1181, 112 N. Outagamie St., Appleton, WI 54912/414-734-1878 (bottom pour lead casting ladles)

Alpine's Precision Gunsmithing, 2401 Government Way, Coeur d'Alene, ID 83814/208-765-3559 (heavy-duty, large-caliber loading press)

American Products Co., 14729 Spring Valley Rd., Morrison, IL 61270/815-772-3336 (12-ga. shot wad)

Ammo Load Inc., 1560 E. Edinger, Suite G, Santa Ana, CA 92705/714-558-5816

Balaance Co., 340-39 Ave. S.E.. Box 505, Calgary, AB T2G 1X6, Canada/403-279-0334 (Adjust. bar f. Lee Auto-Disk meas.)

Ballistic Products, Inc., P.O. Box 408, 2105 Daniels St., Long Lake, MN 55356/612-473-1550 (f. shotguns)

Benson Ballistics, Box 3796, Mission Viejo, CA 92690

Colorado Sutlers Arsenal, Box 991, Granby, CO 80446/303-887-2813

B-Square Eng. Co., Box 11281, Ft. Worth, TX 76110/817-923-0964

Ballistic Prods., P.O. Box 488, 2015 Shaughnessy Circle, Long Lake, MN 55356/612-473-1550

Ballistic Research Industries (BRI), 2825 S. Rodeo Gulch Rd. #8, Soquel, CA 95073/408-476-7981 (shotgun slugs)

Belding & Mull, Inc., P.O. Box 428, 100 N. 4th St., Phillipsburg, PA 16866/814-342-0607

Berdon Machine Co., P.O. Box 9457, Yakima, WA 98909/509-453-0374 (metallic press)
Bonanza (See: Forster Products)
C-H Tool & Die Corp., 106 N. Harding St., Owen, WI 54460/715-229-2146
Camdex, Inc., 2330 Alger, Troy, MI 48083/313-528-2300
Carbide Die & Mfg. Co., Inc., 15615 E. Arrow Hwy., Covina, CA 91706/818-337-2518
Carter Gun Works, 2211 Jefferson Pk. Ave., Charlottesville, VA 22903
Cascade Cartridge, Inc., (See: Omark)
Cascade Shooters, 63990 Deschutes Mkt. Rd., Bend, OR 97701/503-382-1257 (bull. seating depth gauge)
Chevron Case Master, R.R. 1, Ottawa, IL 61350
Chu Tani Industries, Inc., Box 3782, Chula Vista, CA 92011 (lube-sizer adapter mts. on C- or O-type press)
Mrs. Lester Coats, 416 Simpson Ave., No. Bend, OR 97459/503-756-6995 (lead wire core cutter)
Colorado Shooter's Supply, P.O. Box 132, Fruita, CO 81521/303-858-9191 (Hoch cust. bull. moulds)
Colorado Sutlers Arsenal, Box 991, Granby, CO 80446/303-887-2813
Container Development Corp., 424 Montgomery St., Watertown, WI 53094
Continental Kite & Key Co., (CONKKO) P.O. Box 40, Broomall, PA 19008/215-356-0711 (primer pocket cleaner)
Cooper-Woodward, 8073 Canyon Ferry Rd., Helena, MT 59601/406-475-3321 (Perfect Lube)
Corbin Mfg. & Supply Inc., 600 Industrial Circle, P.O. Box 2659, White City, OR 97503/503-826-5211
Custom Products, RD #1, Box 483A, Saegertown, PA 16443/814-763-2769 (decapping tool, dies, etc.)
J. Dewey Mfg. Co., 186 Skyview Dr., Southbury, CT 06488/203-264-3064
Dillon Precision Prods., Inc., 7442 E. Butherus Dr., Scottsdale, AZ 85260/602-948-8009
Efemes Enterprises, Box 691, Colchester, VT 05446 (Berdan decapper)
Fitz, Box 171, Douglas City, CA 96024 (Fitz Flipper)
Flambeau Prods. Corp., 15981 Valplast Rd., Middlefield, OH 44062/216-632-1631
Forster Products Inc., 82 E. Lanark Ave., Lanark IL 61046/815-493-6360
Francis Tool Co., P.O. Box 7861, Eugene, OR 97401/503-345-7457 (powder measure)
Geo. M. Fullmer, 2499 Mavis St., Oakland, CA 94601/415-533-4193 (seating die)
Hanned Precision, P.O. Box 2888, Sacramento, CA 95812 (22-SGB tool)
Hart Products, Rob W. Hart & Son Inc., 401 Montgomery St., Nescopeck, PA 18635/717-752-3655
Hensley & Gibbs, P.O. Box 10, Murphy, OR 97533 (bullet moulds)
Ace Hindman, 1880½ Upper Turtle Creek Rd., Kerrville, TX 78028/512-257-4290 (Reloader's Logbook)
Hoffman New Ideas Inc., 821 Northmoor Rd., Lake Forest, IL 60045/312-234-4075 (spl. gallery load press)
Hollywood Loading Tools (See M & M Engineering)
Hornady Mfg. Co., P.O. Drawer 1848, Grand Island, NE 68802/308-382-1390
Hulme see: Marshall Enterprises (Star case feeder)
Huntington, 601 Oro Dam Blvd., Oroville, CA 95965/916-534-1210 (Compact Press)
JACO Precision Co., 11803 Indian Head Dr., Austin, TX 78753/512-836-44180 (JACO precision neck turner)
Javelina Products, Box 337, San Bernardino, CA 92402 (Alox beeswax)
Neil Jones, RD #1, Box 483A, Saegertown, PA 16433/814-763-2769 (decapping tool, dies)
Paul Jones Munitions Systems (See Fitz Co.)
King & Co., Edw. R. King, Box 1242, Bloomington, IL 61701
Lage Uniwad Co., 1814 21st St., Eldora, IA 50627/515-858-2364 (Universal Shotshell Wad)
Lee Precision, Inc., 4275 Hwy. U, Hartford, WI 53027/414-673-3075
J.F. Littleton, 22 Service St., Oroville, CA 95966/916-533-6084 (shotmaker)
Ljutic Industries Inc., P.O. Box 2117, 732 N. 16th Ave., Yakima, WA 98907/509-248-0476 (plastic wads)
Lock's Phila. Gun Exch., 6700 Rowland, Philadelphia, PA 19149/215-332-6225
Lyman Products Corp., 147 West St., Middlefield, CT 06455/203-349-3421
McKillen & Heyer Inc., 37603 Arlington Dr., Box 627, Willoughby, OH 44094/216-942-2491 (case gauge)
MEC, Inc. (See Mayville Eng. Co.)
M&M Engineering, 10642 Arminta St., Sun Valley, CA 91352/818-842-8376
MMP, R.R. 6 Box 384, Harrison, AR 72601/501-741-5019 (Tri-Cut trimmer; Power powder trickler)
MTM Molded Products Co., P.O. Box 14117, Dayton, OH 45414/513-890-7461
Magma Eng. Co., P.O. Box 161, Queen Creek, AZ 85242/602-987-9008
Marquart Precision Co., P.O. Box 1740, Prescott, AZ 86302/602-445-5646 (precision case-neck turning tool)
Marshall Enterprises, 792 Canyon Rd., Redwood City, CA 94062/415-365-1230 (Hulme autom. case feeder f. Star rel.)
Mayville Eng. Co., 715 South St., Mayville, WI 53050/414-387-4500 (shotshell loader; steel shot kits)
Metallic Casting & Copper Corp. (MCC), 214 E. Third St., Mt. Vernon, NY 10550/914-664-1311
Midway Arms Inc., 7450 Old Highway 40 West, Columbia, MO 65201/314-445-9521 (cartridge boxes)
Mo's Competitor Supplies, (MCS, Inc.), 34 Delmar Dr., Brookfield, CT 06804 (neck turning tool)
Muzzleload Magnum Products (MMP), RR 6, Box 384, Harrison, AR 72601/501-741-5019

Necromancer Industries, Inc., 14 Communications Way, West Newton, PA 15089/412-872-8722 (Compucaster automated bull. casting machine)
Normington Co., Box 6, Rathdrum, ID 83858 (powder baffles)
Northeast Industrial Inc., N.E.I., 9330 N.E. Halsey, Portland, OR 97220/503-255-3750 (bullet mould)
Ohaus Scale, (See RCBS)
Old Western Scrounger, 12924 Hwy. A-12, Montague, CA 96064/916-459-5445 (press f. 50-cal. B.M.G round)
Omark Industries, Box 856, Lewiston, ID 83501/208-746-2351
P&P Tool Co., 125 W. Market St., Morrison, IL 61270/815-772-7618 (12-ga. shot wad)
Pacific Tool Co., P.O. Box 2048, Ordnance Plant Rd., Grand Island, NE 68801/308-384-2308
Pak-Tool, Roberts Products, 25238 S. E. 32nd, Issaquah, WA 98027/206-392-8172
Pflumm Gun Mfg., 6139 Melrose Ln., Shawnee, KS 66203/913-268-3105 (Drawer Vise)
Pitzer Tool Co., RR #3, Box 50, Winterset, IA 50273/515-462-4268 (bullet lubricator & sizer)
Plum City Ballistics Range, Norman E. Johnson, Rte. 1, Box 29A, Plum City, WI 54761/715-647-2539
Ponsness-Warren, P.O. Box 8, Rathdrum, ID 83858/208-687-2231
Quinetics Corp., P.O. Box 29007, San Antonio, TX 78229/516-684-8561 (kinetic bullet puller)
RCBS (See Omark Industries)
R.D.P. Tool Co., Inc., 49162 McCoy Ave., East Liverpool, OH 43920/216-385-5129 (progressive loader)
Ransom Intl. Corp., P.O. Box 3845, 1040 Sandretto Dr., Suite J. Prescott, AZ 86302/602-778-7899 (Grandmaster progr. loader)
Redding Inc., 1089 Starr Rd., Cortland, NY 13045/607-753-3331
Rochester Lead Works, 76 Anderson Ave., Rochester, NY 146077/716-442-8500 (leadwire)
Rooster Laboratories, P.O. Box 412514, Kansas City, MO 64141/816-474-1622 (Universal Heater f. lubricator-sizers)
Rorschach Precision Prods., P.O. Box 151613, Irving, TX 75015/214-790-3487 (carboloy bull. dies)
SAECO (See Redding)
SSK Industries, 721 Woodvue Lane, Wintersville, OH 43952/614-264-0176
Sandia Die & Cartridge Co., Rte. 5, Box 5400, Albuquerque, NM 87123/505-298-5729
Vernon C. Seeley, Box 6, Osage, WY 82723/307-465-2264 (Osage arbor press)
Shooters Accessory Supply, (See Corbin Mfg. & Supply)
Jerry Simmons, 715 Middlebury St., Goshen, IN 46526/219-533-8546 (Pope de- & recapper)
Sinclair International, Inc., 718 Broadway, New Haven, IN 46774/219-493-1858
J.A. Somers Co., P.O. Box 49751, Los Angeles, CA 90049 (Jasco)
Sport Flite Mfg., Inc., P.O. Box 1082, Bloomfield Hills, MI 48303/313-647-3747 (swaging dies)
Star Machine Works, 418 10th Ave., San Diego, CA 92101/619-232-3216
Stuart Products, Inc., P.O. Box 1587, Easley, SC 29641/803-859-9360 (sight vise)
Trammco, Inc., P.O. Box 1258, Bellflower, CA 90706/213-428-5250 (Electra-Jacket bullet plater)
Tru Square Metal Products, 640 First St. S.W., P.O. Box 585, Auburn, WA 98002/206-833-2310 (Thumler's tumbler case polishers; Ultra Vibe 18)
Vibra-Tek Co., 1844 Arroya Rd., Colorado Springs, CO 80906/719-634-8611 (brass polisher; Brite Rouge)
Weatherby, Inc., 2781 Firestone Blvd., South Gate, CA 90280/213-569-7186
Weaver Arms Ltd., P.O. Box 3316, Escondido, CA 92025/619-746-2440 (progr. loader)
Webster Scale Mfg. Co., P.O. Box 188, Sebring, FL 33870/813-385-6362
Whitetail Design & Engineering Ltd., 9421 E. Mannsiding Rd., Clare, MI 48617/517-386-3932 (Match Prep primer pocket tool)
Whits Shooting Stuff, P.O. Box 1340, Cody, WY 82414
L. E. Wilson, Inc. P.O. Box 324, 404 Pioneer Ave., Cashmere, WA 98815/509-782-1328

RESTS — BENCH, PORTABLE, ETC.

Armor Metal Products, P.O. Box 4609, Helena, MT 59604/406-442-5560 (portable shooting bench)
B-Square Co., P.O. Box 11281, Ft. Worth, TX 76110/817-923-0964
Butler Creek Corp., 290 Arden Dr., Belgrade, MT 59714/496-388-1356
Cravener's Gun Shop, 1627 - 5th Ave., Ford City, PA 16226/412-763-8312
Decker Shooting Products, 1729 Laguna Ave., Schofield, WI 54476/715-359-5873 (rifle rests)
The Gun Case, 11035 Maplefield, El Monte, CA 91733
Joe Hall's Shooting Products, Inc., 443 Wells Rd., Doylestown, PA 18901/215-345-6354 (adj. portable)
Harris Engineering, Inc., Barlow, KY 42024/502-334-3633 (bipods)
Rob W. Hart & Son, 401 Montgomery St., Nescopeck, PA 18635
Tony Hidalgo, 12701 S.W. 9th Pl., Davie, FL 33325/305-476-7645 (adj. shooting seat)
J. B. Holden Co., 295 W. Pearl, P.O. Box 320, Plymouth, MI 48170/313-455-4850
Hoppe's Div., Penguin Industries, Inc., Airport Industrial Mall, Coatesville, PA 19320/215-384-6000 (bench rests and bags)
Metro Straight-Shooter, 38 Livonia Ave., Brooklyn, NY 11212/800-443-7734 (shooting bench)
Protektor Model Co., 7 Ash St., Galeton, PA 16922/814-435-2442 (sandbags)

Ransom Intl. Corp., 1040 Sandretto Dr., Suite J, P.O. Box 3845, Prescott, AZ 86302/602-778-7899 (handgun rest)

San Angelo Mfg. Co., 909 West 14th St., San Angelo, TX 76903/915-655-7126

Sharpshooter's Rest, Box 70, Cleveland, MO 64734/816-331-5113 (portable)

Suter's, Inc., House of Guns, 332 N. Tejon, Colorado Springs, CO 80902/303-635-1475

Turkey Creek Enterprises, Rt. 1, Box 65, Red Oak, OK 74563/918-754-2884 (portable shooting rest)

Wichita Arms, 444 Ellis, Wichita, KS 67211/316-265-06612

RIFLE BARREL MAKERS

P.O. Ackley Rifle Barrels (See Bellm Contenders)

Jim Baiar, 490 Halfmoon Rd., Columbia Falls, MT 59912/406-892-4409

Bellm Contenders, P.O. Box 429, Cleveland, UT 84518; price list $3 (new rifle bbls., incl. special & obsolete)

Leo Bustani, P.O. Box 8125, West Palm Beach, FL 33407/305-622-2710 (Win.92 take-down; Trapper 357-44 mag. bbls.: SASE f. reply)

Ralph L. Carter, Carter's Gun Shop, 225 G St., Penrose, CO 81240/719-372-6240

J. A. Clerke Co., P.O. Box 627, Pearblossom, CA 93553/805-945-0713

Competition Limited, 1664 S. Research Loop Rd., Tucson, AZ 85710/602-722-6455

Charles P. Donnelly & Son, Siskiyou Gun Works, 405 Kubli Rd., Grants Pass, OR 97527/503-846-6604

Douglas Barrels, Inc., 5504 Big Tyler Rd., Charleston, WV 25313/304-776-1341

David Gentry Custom Gunmaker, 314 N. Hoffman, Belgrade, MT 59714/406-388-4867

Getz Barrel Co., Box 88, Beavertown, PA 17813/717-658-7263

A. R. Goode, 4125 N.E. 28th Terr., Oscala, FL 32670/904-622-9575

H-S Precision, Inc., 112 N. Summit Ave., Prescott, AZ 86301/602-445-0607

Half Moon Rifle Shop, 490 Halfmoon Rd., Columbia Falls, MT 59912/406-892-4409

Hart Rifle Barrels, Inc., RD 2, Lafayette, NY 13084/315-677-9841

Hastings, P.O. Box 224, Clay Center, KS 67432/913-632-3169 (shotguns ONLY)

Jackalope Gun Shop, 1048 S. 5th St., Douglas, WY 82633/307-358-3441

Terry K. Kopp, 1301 Franklin, Lexington, MO 64067/816-259-2636 (22-cal. blanks)

Krieger Barrels, Inc., N114 W18697 Clinton Dr., Germantown, WI 53022/414-255-9593

Lija Precision Rifle Barrels, Inc., 245 Compass Creek Rd., P.O. Box 372, Plains, MT 59859/406-826-3084

Marquart Precision Co., P.O. Box 1740, Prescott, AZ 86302/602-445-5646

Matco, Inc., 1003-2nd St., No Manchester, IN 46962/219-982-8282

McGowen Rifle Barrels, Route 3, St. Anne, IL 60964/815-937-9816

McMillan Rifle Barrels U.S. International, P.O. Box 3427, Bryan, TX 77805/409-846-3990

Nu-Line Guns, 1053 Caulks Hill Rd., Harvester, MO 63303/314-441-4500

Olympic Arms Inc. dba SGW, 624 Old Pacific Hwy. S.E., Olympia, WA 98503/206-456-3471

John T. Pell Octagon Barrels, (KOGOT), 410 College Ave., Trinidad, CO 81082/719-846-9406

Pence Precision Barrels, RR #2 Box 179, So. Whitley, IN 46787/219-839-4745

Redman's Rifling & Reboring, Rt. 3, Box 330A, Omak, WA 98841/509-826-5512

Rocky Mountain Rifle Works, Ltd., 1707 14th St., Boulder, CO 80302/303-449-9189

Sanders Cust. Gun Serv., 2358 Tyler Lane, Louisville, KY 40205

Gary Schneider, 12202 N. 62nd Pl., Scottsdale, AZ 85254/602-948-2525

SGW, Inc., D. A. Schuetz, 624 Old Pacific Hwy. S.E., Olympia, WA 98503/206-456-3471

E. R. Shaw, dba Small Arms Mfg. Co., Thoms Run Rd. & Prestley, Bridgeville, PA 15017/412-221-4343 (also shotgun bbls.)

Shilen Rifles, Inc., 205 Metro Park Blvd., Ennis, TX 75119/214-875-5318

Shiloh Rifle Mfg. Co., Inc., P.O. Box 279; 201 Centennial Dr., Big Timber, MT 59011/406-932-4454

W. C. Strutz, Rifle Barrels, Inc., P.O. Box 611, Eagle River, WI 54521/715-479-4766

Fred Wells, Wells Sport Store, 110 N. Summit St., Prescott, AZ 86301/602-445-3655

Bob Williams, P.O. Box 143, Boonsboro, MD 21713

Wilson Arms, 63 Leetes Island Rd., Branford, CT 06405/203-488-7297

Wiseman, (see: McMillan Rifle Barrels)

SCOPES, MOUNTS, ACCESSORIES, OPTICAL EQUIPMENT

A.R.M.S., Inc. (Atlantic Research Marketing Systems), 375 West St., West Bridgewater, MA 02379/508-584-7816 (mounts)

Action Arms Ltd., P.O. Box 9573, Philadelphia, PA 19124/215-744-0100

Adco International, 1 Wyman St., Woburn, MA 01801/617-935-1799 (Inter-Aims Mark V sight)

Aimpoint U.S.A., 203 Elden St., Suite 302, Herndon, VA 22070/703-471-6828 (electronic sight)

Aimtech (See L&S Technologies)

Alley Suppl. Co., P.O. Box 848, Gardnerville, NV 89410/702-782-3800

American Arms, Inc., P.O. Box 27163, Salt Lake City, UT 84127/801-972-5006

The American Import Co., 1453 Mission, San Francisco, CA 94103/415-863-1506

Anderson Mfg. Co., P.O. Box 4218, Federal Way, WA 98063/206-838-4299 (lens cap)

Armsport, Inc., 3590 N.W. 49th St., Miami, FL 33122/305-635-7850

Armson, Inc. (See: Trijicon, Inc.)

Autumn Tracker Design, 7600-166th Ave., N.W., Anoka, MN 55303/612-753-4433 (Zero Mag, R.A.T. mounts)

B-Square Co., Box 11281, Ft. Worth, TX 76110/800-433-2909 (Mini-14 mount)

Bausch & Lomb Inc., 42 East Ave., Rochester, NY 14603/800-828-5423

Beeman Precision Arms, Inc., 3440-GD Airway Dr., Santa Rosa, CA 95403/707-578-7900 (airguns only)

Bennett, 561 Delaware, Delmar, NY 12054/518-439-1862 (mounting wrench)

Browning Arms, Rt. 4, Box 624-B, Arnold, MO 63010

Buehler Scope Mounts, 17 Orinda Highway, Orinda, CA 94563/415-254-3201

Burris Co. Inc., 331 E. 8th St., Box 1747, Greeley, CO 80632/303-356-1670

Bushnell, 300 N. Lone Hill Ave., San Dimas, CA 91773/714-592-8000

Butler Creek Corp., 290 Arden Dr., Belgrade, MT 59714/406-388-1356 (lens caps)

Clear View Mfg. Co., Inc., 413 So. Oakley St., Fordyce, AR 71742/501-352-8557 (SEE-THR mounts)

Colt Firearms, P.O. Box 1868, Hartford, CT 06101/203-236-6311

Compass Instr. & Optical Co., Inc., 104 E. 25th St., New York, NY 10010

Conetrol Scope Mounts, Hwy 123 South, Seguin, TX 78155

Cougar Optics, P.O. Box 115, Groton, NY 13073/607-898-5747

D&H Prods. Co., Inc., 465 Denny Rd., Valencia, PA 16059/412-898-2840 (lens covers)

Del-Sports Inc., Main St., Margaretville, NY 12455/914-586-4103 (EAW mts.)

Dickson (See American Import Co.)

Dynamit Nobel-RWS, Inc., 105 Stonehurst Court, Northvale, NJ 07647/201-767-1995

Emerging Technologies, Inc., P.O. Box 581, Little Rock, AR 72203/501-375-2227 (Laser sight & mounts)

Europtik, Ltd., P.O. Box 319, Dunmore, PA 18512/717-347-6049

Flaig's, Babcock Blvd., Millvale, PA 15209

Freeland's Scope Stands, Inc., 3737 14th, Rock Island, IL 61201/309-788-7449

GSI, 108 Morrow Ave., P.O. Box 129, Trussville, AL 35173/205-655-8299 (Bock mounts)

Griffin & Howe, Inc., 36 West 44th St., Suite 1011, New York, NY 10036/212-921-0980

Griffin & Howe, 33 Claremont Rd., Bernardsville, NJ 07924/201-766-2287

Gun Parts Corp., Box 2, West Hurley, NY 12491/914-679-2419

Gun South, Inc., P.O. Box 129, Trussville, AL 35173/205-655-8299 (KSM mounts)

Heckler & Koch, Inc., 21480 Pacific Blvd., Sterling, VA 22170/703-450-1900

H.J. Hermann Leather Co., Rt. 1, P.O. Box 525, Skiatook, OK 74070/918-396-1226 (lens caps)

J.B. Holden Co., 975 Arthur, P.O. Box 320, Plymouth, MI 48170/313-455-4850 (mounts)

Imatronic Lasersight, 1275 Paramount Pkwy., P.O. Box 520, Batavia, IL 60510/312-406-1920 (Laser Sights)

Interarms, 10 Prince St., Alexandria, VA 22313

Paul Jaeger, Inc., P.O. Box 449, 1 Madison Ave., Grand Junction, TN 38039/901-764-6909 (Schmidt & Bender; EAW mts., Noble)

Jason Empire Inc., 9200 Cody, P.O. Box 14930, Overland Park, KS 66214/913-888-0220

Kenko Intl. Inc., 8141 West I-70 Frontage Rd. No., Arvada, CO 80002/303-425-1200 (optical equipment)

KenPatable Ent. Inc., P.O. Box 19422, Louisville, KY 40219/502-239-5447

Kilham & Co., Main St., Box 37, Lyme, NY 03768/603-795-4112 (Hutson handgun scopes)

Kowa Optimed, Inc., 20001 S. Vermont Ave., Torrance, CA 90502/213-327-1913

Kris Mounts, 108 Lehigh St., Johnstown, PA 15905

Kwik Mount (See KenPatable)

Kwik-Site, 5555 Treadwell, Wayne, MI 48184/313-326-1500

L&S Technologies, Inc., P.O. Box 223, Thomasville, GA 31799/912-226-4313 (mount system f. handguns)

Laser Devices, Inc., 2880 Research Park Dr., Soquel, CA 95073/408-476-8300 (Laser Sight)

Leica USA, 156 Ludlow Ave., Northvale, NJ 07647/201-767-7500 (binoculars)

Leitz (See: Leica USA)

Leupold & Stevens Inc., P.O. Box 688, Beaverton, OR 97075/503-646-9171

Jake Levin and Son, Inc., 9200 Cody, Overland Park, KS 66214

W.H. Lodewick, 2816 N.E. Halsey, Portland OR 97232/503-284-2554 (scope safeties)

Lyman Products Corp., 147 West St., Middlefield, CT 06455/203-349-3421

Mandall Shooting Supplies, 7150 E. 4th St., Scottsdale, AZ 85252

Marble Arms Co., 420 Industrial Park, Gladstone, MI 49837/906-428-3710

Marlin Firearms Co., 100 Kenna Dr., New Haven, CO 06473

Michaels of Oregon, P.O. Box 13101, Portland, OR 97213 (QD scope covers)

Military Armament Corp., P.O. Drawer 111, Mt. Zion Rd., Lingleville, TX 76461/817-965-3077 (Leatherwood)

Millett Industries, 16131 Gothard St., Huntington Beach, CA 92647/714-842-5575 (mounts)

Mirador Optical Corp., P.O. Box 11614, Marina Del Rey, CA 90295/213-821-5587

Mitchell Arms, Inc., 3411 Lake Center Dr., Santa Ana, CA 92704/714-957-5711

Nikon Inc., 623 Stewart Ave., Garden City, NY 11530/516-222-0200

North American Specialties, 25422 Trabuco Rd. #105-328, El Toro, CA 92630/714-979-4867 (Leatherwood scopes)

Olympic Arms Inc. dba SGW, 624 Old Pacific Hwy. S.E., Olympia, WA 98503/206-456-3471 (mounts)
Omark Industries (See Weaver)
Orchard Park Enterprise, P.O. Box 563, Orchard Park, NY 14127/716-662-0356 (Saddleproof mounts only)
Pachmayr Ltd., 1875 So. Mountain Ave., Monrovia, CA 91016/818-357-7771
PaycheX Industries, 520 Moore St., Albion, NY 14411/716-589-7787 (mounts)
Pentax Corp., 35 Inverness Dr. E., Englewood CO 80112/303-799-8000 (riflescopes)
Pilkington Gun Co., P.O. Box 1296, Muskogee, OK 74402/918-693-9418 (Q. D. mt.)
Pioneer Marketing & Research Inc., 216 Haddon Ave. Suite 522, Westmont, NJ 08108/609-854-2424 (German Steiner binoculars; scopes)
Precision Sport Optics, 7340 Firestone Blvd., Suite 222, Downey, CA 90241/213-937-7990
Ram Line, Inc., 15611 W. 6th Ave., Golden, CO 80401/303-279-0886 (see-thru mt. f. Mini-14)
Ranging, Inc., Routes 5 & 2, East Bloomfield, NY 14443/716-657-6161
Ray-O-Vac, Willson Prod. Div., P.O. Box 622, Reading, PA 19603 (shooting glasses)
Redfield Gun Sight Co., 5800 E. Jewell Ave., Denver, CO 80224/303-757-6411
S & K Mfg. Co., Box 247, Pittsfield, PA 16340/814-563-7808 (Insta-Mount)
SSK Industries, 721 Woodvue Lane, Wintersville, OH 43952/614-264-0176 (bases)
Sanders Cust. Gun Serv., 2358 Tyler Lane, Louisville, KY 40205 (MSW)
Schmidt & Bender, see: Paul Jaeger, Inc.
Seattle Binocular & Scope Repair Co., P.O. Box 46094, Seattle, WA 98146
Shepherd Scope Ltd., Box 189, Waterloo, NE 68069/402-779-2424
Sherwood Intl. Export Corp., 18714 Parthenia St., Northridge, CA 91324/818-349-7600 (mounts)
Shooters Supply, 1120 Tieton Dr., Yakima, WA 98902/509-452-1181 (mount f. M14/M1A rifles)
W.H. Siebert, 22720 S.E. 56th St., Issaquah, WA 98027
Simmons Outdoor Corp., 14530 S.W. 119 Ave., Miami, FL 33186/305-252-0477
Spacetron Inc., Box 84, Broadview, IL 60155 (bore lamp)
Springfield Armory, Inc., 420 W. Main St., Genesco, IL 61254/309-944-5631
Steiner binoculars (See Pioneer Marketing & Research)
Stoeger Industries, 55 Ruta Ct., S. Hackensack, NJ 07606/201-440-2700
Supreme Lens Covers, (See Butler Creek) (lens caps)
Swarovski America Ltd., 2 Slater Rd., Cranston, RI 02920/401-463-3000
Swift Instruments, Inc., 952 Dorchester Ave., Boston, MA 02125
Tasco Sales, Inc., 7600 N.W. 26th St., Miami, FL 33122/305-591-3670
Tele-Optics, 5514 W. Lawrence Ave., Chicago, IL 60630/312-283-7757 (optical equipment repair services only; binoculars)
Tele-Optics Inc., P.O. Box 176, 219 E. Higgins Rd., Gilberts, IL 60136/312-426-7444 (spotting scopes)
Thompson/Center Arms, Farmington Rd., P.O. Box 5002, Rochester, NH 03867/603-332-2394 (handgun scope)
Tradewinds, Inc., Box 1191, Tacoma, WA 98401
Trijicon, Inc., P.O. Box 2130, Farmington Hills, MI 48018/313-553-4960 (rifle scopes)
John Unerti Optical Co., 1224 Freedom Rd., Mars, PA 16046/412-776-9700
United Binocular Co., 9043 S. Western Ave., Chicago, IL 60620
Wasp Shooting Systems, Box 241, Lakeview, AR 72642/501-431-4506 (mtg. system f. Ruger Mini-14 only)
Weatherby's, 2781 Firestone, South Gate, CA 90280/213-569-7186
Weaver, Omark Industries, Box 856, Lewiston, ID 83501/208-746-2351
Weaver Scope Repair Service, 1121 Larry Mahan Dr., Suite B, El Paso, TX 79925/915-593-1005
Wide View Scope Mount Corp., 26110 Michigan Ave., Inkster, MI 48141/313-274-1238
Williams Gun Sight Co., 7389 Lapeer Rd., Davison, MI 48423
Boyd Williams Inc., 8701-14 Mile Rd. (M-57), Cedar Springs, MI 49319 (BR)
York M-1 Conversions, P.O. Box 262364, Houston, TX 77217/800-527-2881
Carl Zeiss Optical Inc., Consumer Prods. Div., Box 2010, 1015 Commerce St., Petersburg, VA 23803/804-861-0033

SIGHTS, METALLIC

Accura-Site, All's, The Jim J. Tembells Co., Inc., 280 E. Fernau Ave., Oshkosh, WI 54901/800-562-6688/414-426-1080 (shotgun)
Alley Supply Co., P.O. Box 848, Gardnerville, NV 89410/702-782-3800
Armson, Inc. (See: Trijicon, Inc.)
Autumn Tracker Design, 7600-166th Ave. N.W., Anoka, MN 55303/612-753-4433 (Electronic slug sight aids)
Beeman Precision Arms, Inc., 3440-GDD Airway Dr., Santa Rose, CA 95403/707-578-7900
Behlert Precision, RD 2 Box 63, Route 611 North, Pipersville, PA 18947/215-766-8681
Bo-Mar Tool & Mfg. Co., Rt. 12, Box 405, Longview, TX 75605/214-759-4784
Burris Co., Inc., 331-8th St., P.O. Box 1747, Greeley, CO 80632/303-356-1670
Cherokee Gun Accessories, 4127 Bay St., Suite 226, Fremont, CA 94538/415-471-5770 (Tritium Tacsight)
J.A. Clerke Co., P.O. Box 627, Pearblossom, CA 93553/805-945-0713
Farr Studo, 1231 Robinhood Rd., Greeneville, TN 37743/615-638-8825 (sighting aids — clip-on aperture; the Farr Sight; the Concentrator)
Andy Fautheree, P.O. Box 4607, Pagosa Springs, CO 81157/303-731-5003 ("Calif. Sight" f. ML; must send SASE)
Freeland's Scope Stands, Inc., 3734-14th Ave., Rock Island, IL 61201/309-788-7449

Gun Parts Corp., Box 2, West Hurley, NY 12491/914-679-2417
Paul Jaeger, Inc., P.O. Box 449, 1 Madison Ave., Grand Junction, TN 38039/901-764-6909
James W. Lofland, 2275 Larkin Rd., Boothwyn, PA 19061/215-485-0391 (single shot replica)
Innovision Enterprises, 728 Skinner Dr., Kalamazoo, MI 49001/616-382-1681 (Slug Sights)
Lyman Products Corp., 147 West St., Middlefield, CT 06455/203-349-3421
MMC Co., Inc., 210 E. Poplar, Deming, NM 88030
Marble Arms Corp., 420 Industrial Park, Box 111, Gladstone, MI 49837/906-428-3710
Meprolight, 2821 Greenville Rd., LaGrange, GA 30240/404-884-7967
Merit Corp., Dept. GD, P.O. Box 9044, Schenectady, NY 12309/518-346-1420
Millett Ind., 16131 Gothard St., Huntington Beach, CA 92647/714-842-5575
Miniature Mach. Co., 210 E. Poplar, Deming, NM 88030/505-546-2151 (MMC)
Omega Sales, Inc., P.O. Box 1066, Mt. Clemens, MI 48043/313-469-6727
Poly Choke Div., Marble Arms Corp., 420 Industrial Park, Gladstone MI 49837/906-428-3710
Redfield Gun Sight Co., 5800 E. Jewell St., Denver, CO 80224/303-757-6411
Slug Site Co., Ozark Wilds, Versailles, MO 65084/314-378-6430
Tradewinds, Inc., Box 1191, Tacoma, WA 98401
Trijicon, Inc., P.O. Box 2130, Farmington Hills, MI 48333/313-553-4960
Wichita Arms, 444 Ellis, Wichita, KS 67211/316-265-0661
Williams Gun Sight Co., 7389 Lapeer Rd., Davison, MI 48423

STOCKS (Commercial and Custom)

Ahlman's Inc., R.R. 1, Box 20, Morristown, MN 55052
Don Allen Inc., HC55, Box 326, Sturgis, SD 57785/605-347-5227
Angelo & Little Custom Gun Stock Wood, N 4026 Sargent St., Spokane, WA 99212/509-926-0794 (blanks only)
Ann Arbor Rod and Gun Co., 1946 Packard Rd., Ann Arbor, MI 48104/313-769-7866
Bain & Davis Sporting Goods, Walter H. Little, 307 E. Valley Blvd., San Gabriel, CA 91776/213-283-7449 (cust.)
Joe J. Balickie, Custom Stocks, 408 Trelawney Lane, Apex, NC 27502/919-362-5185
Bartas Gunsmithing, 10231 U.S.H. #10, Cato, WI 54206/414-732-4472
Donald Bartlett, 31829-32nd Pl. S.W., Federal Way, WA 98023/206-927-0726
Beeman Precision Arms, Inc., 3440GD Airway Dr., Santa Rosa, CA 95403/707-578-7900 (airguns only)
Bell & Carlson, Inc., 509 N. 5th St., Atwood, KS 67730/913-626-3204 (coml.)
Belim Contenders, P.O. Box 429, Cleveland, UT 84518
Al Biesen, West 2039 Sinto Ave., Spokane, WA 99201
Roger Biesen, 5021 W. Rosewood, Spokane, WA 99208/509-328-9340
Stephen L. Billeb, Box 1176, Big Piney, WY 83113/307-276-5627
E.C. Bishop & Son Inc., 119 Main St., Box 7, Warsaw, MO 65355/816-438-5121
Gregg Boeke, Rte. 2, Box 149, Cresco, IA 52136/319-547-3746 (cust.)
John M. Boltin, P.O. Box 644, Estill, SC 29918/803-625-4111
Kent Bowerly, Metolious Meadows Dr., H.C.R. Box 1903, Camp Sherman, OR 97730/503-595-6028 (custom)
Larry D. Brace, 771 Blackfoot Ave., Eugene, OR 97404/503-688-1278
Frank Brgoch, #1580 South 1500 East, Bountiful, UT 84010/801-295-1885
A. Briganti, 475 Rt. 32, Highland Mills, NY 10930/914-928-9573
Brown Precision Co., P.O. Box 270GD; 7786 Molinos Ave., Los Molinos, CA 96055/916-384-2506
Jack Burres, 10333 San Fernando Road, Pacoima, CA 91331/818-899-8000 (English, Claro, Bastogne Paradox walnut blanks only)
Calico Hardwood, Inc., 1648 Airport Blvd., Windsor, CA 95492/707-546-4045 (blanks)
Lou Camilli, 4700 Oahu Dr. N.E., Albuquerque, NM 87111/505-293-5259
Dick Campbell, 20000 Silver Ranch Rd., Conifer, CO 80433/303-697-0150 (custom)
Larry T. Caudill, 1025A Palomas Dr. S.E., Albuquerque, NM 87108/505-255-2515 (custom)
Shane Caywood, P.O. Box 321, Minocqua, WI 54548/715-356-5414 (cust.)
Winston Churchill, Twenty Mile Stream Rd., RFD, Box 29B, Proctorsville, VT 05153
J.A. Clerke Co., P.O. Box 627, Pearblossom, CA 93553/805-945-0713
Clinton River Gun Serv., Inc., 30016 S. River Rd., Mt. Clemens, MI 48045/313-468-1090
Charles H. Coffin, 3719 Scarlet Ave., Odessa, TX 79762/915-366-4729
Jim Coffin, 250 Country Club Lane, Albany, OR 97321/503-928-4391
David Costa, 94 Orient Ave., Arlington, MA 02174/617-643-9571 (cust.)
Reggie Cubriel, 15610 Purple Sage, San Antonio, TX 78255/512-695-3364 (cust. stockm.)
Custom Gun Guild, 2646 Church Dr., Doraville, GA 30340/404-455-0346
D&D Gun Shop, 363 Elmwood, Troy, MI 48083/313-583-1512 (cust.)
Dahl's Custom Stocks, Rt. 4, Box 558, Lake Geneva, WI 53147/414-248-2464
Dakota Arms, Inc., HC 55, Box 326, Sturgis, SD 57785/605-347-4686
Homer L. Dangler, Box 254, Addison, MI 49220/517-547-6745
Sterling Davenport, 9611 E. Walnut Tree Dr., Tucson, AZ 85715/602-749-5590
Jack Dever, 8520 N.W. 90, Oklahoma City, OK 73132/405-721-6393
R.H. "Dick" Devereaux, D.D. Custom Rifles, 5240 Mule Deer Dr., Colorado Springs, CO 80919/719-548-8468
William Dixon, Buckhorn Gun Works, Rte. 4 Box 1230, Rapid City, SD 57702/605-787-6289
Dowtin Gunworks (DGW), Rt. 4 Box 930A, Flagstaff, AZ 86001/602-779-1898 (custom; blanks)

Duncan's Gunworks Inc., 1619 Grand Ave., San Marcos, CA 92069/619-727-0515 (cust.)

D'Arcy A. Echols, 164 W. 580 S., Providence, UT 84332/801-753-2367 (cust.)

Jere Eggleston, P.O. Box 50238, Columbia, SC 29250/803-799-3402 (cust.)

Bob Emmons, 11748 Robson Road, Grafton, OH 44044 (custom)

Englishtown Sporting Goods Co., Inc., David J. Maxham, 38 Main St., Englishtown, NJ 07726/201-446-7717 (custom)

Dennis Erhardt, P.O. Box 502, Canyon Creek, MT 59633/406-368-2298 (cust.)

Ken Eyster Heritage Gunsmiths Inc., 6441 Bishop Rd., Centerburg, OH 43011/614-625-6131 (cust.)

Reinhart Fajen Inc., 1000 Red Bud Dr., P.O. Box 338, Warsaw, MO 65355/816-438-5111

Ted Fellowes, Beaver Lodge, 9245 16th Ave. S.W., Seattle, WA 98106/206-763-1698 (cust. ML)

Fiberpro Inc., 3636 California St., San Diego, Ca 92101/619-295-7703 (blanks; fiberglass; Kevlar)

Jerry A. Fisher, P.O. Box 652, 38 Buffalo Butte, Dubois, WY 82513/307-455-2722

Flaig's Inc., 2200 Evergreen Rd., Millvale, PA 15209/412-821-1717

Flynn's Cust. Guns, P.O. Box 7461, Alexandria, LA 71301/318-455-7130

Donald E. Folks, 205 W. Lincoln St., Pontiac, IL 61764/815-844-7901 (custom trap, Skeet, livebird stocks)

Larry L. Forster, Box 212, 220 First St., N.E., Gwinner, ND 58040/701-678-2475

Fountain Prods., 492 Prospect Ave., W. Springfield, MA 01089 (cust.)

Frank's Custom Rifles, 7521 E. Fairmount Pl., Tucson, AZ 85715/602-885-3901

Freeland's Scope Stands, Inc., 3737 14th Ave., Rock Island, IL 61201/309-788-7449

Game Haven Gunstocks, 13750 Shire Rd., Wolverine, MI 49799/616-525-8238 (Keviar riflestocks)

Garrett Accur-Lt. D.F.S. Co., P.O. Box 8675, Fort Collins, CO 80524/303-224-3067 (fiberglass)

K Genecco Gun Works, 10512 Lower Sacramento Rd., Stockton, CA 95210/209-951-0706

Dale Goens, Box 224, Cedar Crest, NM 87008

Goodling's Gunsmithing, R.D. #1, Box 1007, Spring Grove, PA 17632/717-225-3350 (cust.)

Gordie's Gun Shop, Gordon Mulholland, 1401 Fulton St., Streator, IL 61364/815-672-7202 (cust.)

Gary Goudy, 263 Hedge Rd., Menlo Park, CA 94025/415-322-1338 (cust.)

Charles E. Grace, 10144 Elk Lake Rd., Williamsburg, MI 49690/616-264-9483

Roger M. Green, 435 E. Birch, P.O. Box 984, Glenrock, WY 82637/307-436-9804 (Teyssler French walnut blanks)

Greene's Machine Carving, 17200 W. 57th Ave., Golden, CO 80403/303-279-2383 (gunstock duplicating & machining serv.; custom)

Michael L. Greene, 17200 W. 57th Ave., Golden, CO 80403/303-279-2383 (English walnut blanks)

Griffin & Howe, 36 West 44th St., Suite 1011, New York, NY 10036/212-921-0980

Griffin & Howe, 33 Claremont Rd., Bernardsville, NJ 07924/201-766-2287

Guncraft, Inc. 117 W. Pipeline, Hurst, TX 76053/817-282-1464

Gun Parts Corp., Box 2, West Hurley, NY 12491/914-679-2417 (commercial)

H-S Precision, Inc., 112 N. Summit Ave., Prescott, AZ 86301 (Fiberglass)

Hanson's Gun Center, 521 So. Circle Dr., Colorado Springs, CO 80910/719-634-4220

Harper's Custom Stocks, 928 Lombrano St., San Antonio, TX 78207/512-732-5780

Robert W. Hart & Son, Inc., 401 Montgomery St., Nescopeck, PA 18635/717-752-3655 (cust.)

Hubert J. Hecht, Waffen-Hecht, P.O. Box 2635, Fair Oaks, CA 95628/916-966-1020

Darwin Hensley, P.O. Box 179, Brightwood, OR 97011/503-622-5411 (cust.)

Heppler's Gun Shop, 6000 B Soquel Ave., Santa Cruz, CA 95062/408-475-1235

Keith M. Heppler, 540 Banyan Circle, Walnut Creek, CA 94598/415-934-3509 (cust. rifle)

Warren Heydenberk, 1059 W. Sawmill Rd., Quakertown, PA 18951/215-538-2682

Paul D. Hillmer Custom Gunstocks, 7251 Hudson Heights, Hudson, IA 50643/319-988-3941

Klaus Hiptmayer, P.O. Box 136, Eastman, Que., J0E 1P0 Canada/514-297-2492

Hoenig & Rodman, 6521 Morton Dr., Boise, ID 83705/208-375-1116 (stock duplicating machine)

Hollis Gun Shop, 917 Rex St., Carlsbad, NM 88220

Corey O. Huebner, 3604 S. 3rd W., Missoula, MT 59801/406-721-9647 (cust.)

Intermountain Arms, 105 E. Idaho Ave., Meridian, ID 83649/208-888-4911 (cust.)

Paul Jaeger, Inc., P.O. Box 449, 1 Madison Ave., Grand Junction, TN 38039/901-764-6909

Robert L. Jamison, Rt. 4, Box 200, Moses Lake, WA 98837/509-762-2659 (cust. target)

Jarrett Rifles, Inc., Rt. 1 Box 411, Jackson, SC 29831/803-471-3616 (cust.)

Jim's Gun Shop, James R. Spradlin, 113 Arthur, Pueblo, CO 81004/719-543-9462 (cust.)

Johnson Wood Products, I.D. Johnson & Sons, Rte. #1, Strawberry Point, IA 52076/319-933-4930 (blanks only)

Neal G. Johnson, Gunsmithing, Inc., 111 Marvin Dr., Hampton, VA 23666/804-838-8091

Peter S. Johnson, c/o Orvis Co., 10 River Rd., Manchester, VT 05254/802-362-3622, Ext. 283 (cust.)

David Kartak, SRS Box 3042, South Beach, OR 97366/503-867-4951 (custom)

Ken's Rifle Blanks, Ken McCullough, Rt. 2 Box 85B, Weston, OR 97886/503-566-3879

Don Klein, Rt. 2, Box 277, Camp Douglas, WI 54618/608-427-6948 (cust.)

Kenneth J. Klingler, P.O. Box 141; Thistle Hill, Cabot, VT 05647/802-426-3811 (carving only)

Richard Knippel, 825 Stoddard Ave., Modesto, CA 95350/209-529-6205 (cust.)

Harry Lawson Co., 3328 N. Richey Blvd., Tucson, AZ 85716/602-326-1117

Frank LeFever Arms & Sons, Inc., R.D. #1, Box 31, Lee Center, NY 13363/315-337-6722

Al Lind, 7821 76th Ave. S.W., Tacoma, WA 98498/206-584-6361 (cust.)

Howard M. Logan, Box 745, Honokaa, HI 96727/808-776-1644 (cust.)

MPI Stocks, P.O. Box 03266, Portland, OR 97203/503-289-8025 (fiberglass)

Monte Mandarino, 136 Fifth Ave. West, Kalispell, MT 59901/406-257-6208

Lowell Manley Shooting Supplies, 3684 Pine St., Deckerville, MI 48427/313-376-3665

Peter Mazur Restoration, 13083 Drummer Way, Grass Valley, CA 95949/916-268-2412 (cust.)

Dennis McDonald, 8359 Brady St., Peosta, IA 52068/319-556-7940 (cust.)

Stan McFarland, 2221 Idella Ct., Grand Junction, CO 81505/303-243-4704

Bill McGuire, 1600 N. Eastmont Ave., East Wenatchee, WA 98802/509-884-6021 (custom)

George E. Mathews & Son, Inc., 10224 S. Paramount Blvd., Downey, CA 90241/213-862-6719

John E. Maxson, 3507 Red Oak Lane, Plainview, TX 79072/806-293-9042

Meadow Industries, P.O. Box 450, Marlton, NJ 08053/609-953-0922

R.M. Mercer, 216 S. Whitewater Ave., Jefferson, WI 53549/414-674-3839

Robt. U. Milhoan & Son, Rt. 3, Elizabeth, WV 26143

Miller Arms, Inc., D.E. Miller, P.O. Box 260, St. Onge, SD 57779/605-578-1790

S.A. Miller, Point Roberts Sports Ltd., P.O. Box 1053, 1440 Peltier Dr., Point Roberts, WA 98281/206-945-7014 (gunwood)

Earl Milliron Custom Guns & Stocks, 1249 N.E. 166th Ave., Portland, OR 97230/503-252-3725

Mitchell Arms, Inc., 3411 Lake Center Dr., Santa Ana, CA 92704/714-957-5711

Monell Custom Guns, Red Mill Road, RD #2, Box 96, Pine Bush, NY 12566/914-744-3021 (custom)

J.W. Morrison Custom Rifles, 4015 W. Sharon, Phoenix, AZ 85029

Stephen E. Nelson, P.O. Box 1478, Albany, OR 97321/503-745-5232 (cust.)

New England Arms Co., Lawrence Lane, Kittery Point, ME 03905/207-439-0593

Paul R. Nickels, P.O. Box 71043, Las Vegas, NV 89170/702-435-5318 (cust.)

Ted Nicklas, 5504 Hegel Rd., Goodrich, MI 48438/313-797-4493 (custom)

Jim Norman, Custom Gunstocks, 14281 Cane Rd., Valley Center, CA 92082/619-749-6252

Vic Olson, 5002 Countryside Dr., Imperial, MO 63052/314-296-8086 (custom)

Maurice Ottmar, Box 657, 113 E. Fir, Coulee City, WA 99115/509-632-5717

Pachmayr Gun Works, 406 So. Lake Ave., Pasadena, CA 99101 (blanks and custom jobs)

Pasadena Gun Center, 206 E. Shaw, Pasadena, TX 77506/713-472-0417

Paulsen Gunstocks, Rte. 71, Box 11, Chinook, MT 59523/406-357-3403 (blanks)

R&J Gunshop, Bob Kerr, 140 So. Redwood Hwy., Cave Junction, OR 97523/503-592-2535 (cust.)

Wallace E. Reiswig, Claro Walnut Gunstock Co., 1235 Stanley Ave., Chico, CA 95928/916-342-5188 (California walnut blanks)

Richards Micro-Fit Gunstocks, P.O. Box 1066, Sun Valley, CA 91352/818-767-6097 (thumbhole)

Don Robinson, Pennsylvania Hse., 36 Fairfax Crescent, Southowram, Halifax, W. Yorksh. HX3 9SW, England (blanks only)

Bob Rogers Gunsmithing, P.O. Box 305, 344 S. Walnut St., Franklin Grove, IL 61031/815-456-2685

Royal Arms, 1210 Bert Acosta, El Cajon, CA 92020/619-448-5466

Chad Ryan, RR 3 Box 72, Cresco, IA 52136 (cust.)

Sanders Cust. Gun Serv., 2358 Tyler Lane, Louisville, KY 40205 (blanks)

Roy Schaefer, 965 W. Hilliard Lane, Eugene, OR 97404/503-688-4333 (commercial blanks)

Curt Schiffman, 12237 Powhatan Trail, Conifer, CO 80433/303-838-7128 (cust.)

Norman H. Schiffman, 12237 Powhatan Trail, Conifer, CO 80433/303-838-7128 (cust.)

Schwartz Custom Guns, 9621 Coleman Rd., Haslett, MI 48840/517-339-8939

David W. Schwartz, 2505 Waller St., Eau Claire, WI 54701/715-832-1735

Shaw's, The Finest in Guns, 1201 LaMirada Ave., Escondido, CA 92026/619-746-2474 (custom only)

Dan A. Sherk, 9701-17th St., Dawson Creek, B.C. V1G 4H7, Canada/604-782-5630 (custom)

Hank Shows, The Best, 1078 Alice Ave., Ukiah, CA 95482/707-462-9060

Sile Dist., 7 Centre Market Pl., New York, NY 10013/212-925-4111

Sinclair International, Inc., 718 Broadway, New Haven, IN 46774/219-493-1858

Six Enterprises, 6564 Hidden Creek Dr., San Jose, CA 95120/408-268-8296 (fiberglass)

Ed Sowers, 8331 DeCelis Pl., Unit C, Sepulveda, CA 91343/818-893-1233 (custom hydro-coil gunstocks)

Fred D. Speiser, 2229 Dearborn, Missoula, MT 59801/406-549-8133

Sport Serv. Ctr., 2364 N. Neva, Chicago, IL 60635/312-889-1114 (custom)

Sportsmen's Equip. Co., 915 W. Washington, San Diego, CA 92103/714-296-1501 (carbine conversions)

Keith Stegall, Box 696, Gunnison. CO 81230

William G. Talmage, 451 Phantom Creek Lane, P.O. Box 512, Meadview, AZ 86444/602-564-2380

Tiger-Hunt, Michael D. Barton, P.O. Box 214, Jerome, PA 15937/814-479-2215 (curly maple stock blanks)

Trevallion Gunstocks, R. 1, Box 39, Kittery Point, ME 03905/207-439-6822 (custom)

Trinko's Gun Service, 1406 E. Main St., Watertown, WI 53094/414-261-5175

James C. Tucker, 205 Trinity St., Woodland, CA 95695/916-662-0503 (cust.)

Milton Van Epps, Rt. 69-A, Parish, NY 13131/315-625-7251

Gil Van Horn, P.O. Box 207, Llano, CA 93544

John Vest, P.O. Box 1552, Susanville, CA 96130/916-257-7228 (classic rifles)

Vic's Gun Refinishing, 6 Pineview Dr., Dover, NH 03820/603-742-0013

Ed von Atzigen, The Custom Shop, 890 Cochrane Cres., Peterborough, Ont. K9H 5N3, Canada/705-742-6693 (cust.)

R.D. Wallace, Star Rt. 1, Box 76, Grandin, MO 63943/314-593-4773 (cust.)

Weatherby's, 2781 Firestone, South Gate, CA 90280/213-569-7186

Chris Weber/Waffen-Weber, #6-1691 Powick Rd., Kelowna, BC V1X 4L1, Canada/604-762-7575

Cecil Weems, P.O. Box 657, Mineral Wells, TX 76067/817-325-1462

Fred Wells, 110 N. Summit St., Prescott, AZ 86301/602-445-3655

Terry Werth, 1203 Woodlawn Rd., Lincoln, IL 62656/217-732-1300 (cust.)

Robert G. West, 3973 Pam St., Eugene, OR 97402/503-689-6610

Western Gunstocks Mfg. Co., 550 Valencia School Rd., Aptos, CA 95003

Duane Wiebe, P.O. Box 497, Lotus, CA 95651

Bob Williams, P.O. Box 143, Boonsboro, MD 21713

Williamson-Pate Gunsmith Service, 117 W. Pipeline, Hurst, TX 76053/817-282-1464

Jim Windish, 2510 Dawn Dr., Alexandria, VA 22306/703-765-1994 (walnut blanks)

David W. Wills, 2776 Brevard Ave., Montgomery, AL 36109/305-272-8446

Robert M. Winter, R.R. 2, Box 484, Menno, SD 57045/605-387-5322

Wisner's Gun Shop Inc., P.O. Box 58, Hiway 6, Adna, WA 98552/206-748-8942

Mike Yee, 29927-56 Pl. S., Auburn, WA 98001/206-839-3991

Russel R. Zeeryp, 1601 Foard Dr., Lynn Ross Manor, Morristown, TN 37814

Dean A. Zollinger, Rt. 2, Box 135-A, Rexburg, ID 83440/208-356-6167

TARGETS, BULLETS & CLAYBIRD TRAPS

Aztec International Ltd., P.O. Box 1888, Norcross, GA 30091/404-446-2304 (Exploding Bullseye targets)

Beeman Precision Arms, Inc., 3440-GD Airway Dr., Santa Rosa, CA 95043/707-578-7900 (airguns only)

Birchwood-Casey, 7900 Fuller Rd., Eden Prairie, MN 55344/612-937-7933

Caswell International Corp. Inc., 1221 Marshall St. N.E., Minneapolis, MN 55413/612-379-2000 (target carriers; commercial shooting ranges)

J.G. Dapkus Co., P.O. Box 180, Cromwell, CT 06416/203-632-2308 (live bullseye targets)

Data-Targ, (See Rocky Mountain Target Co.)

Detroit-Armor Corp., Detroit Bullet Trap Div., 2233 N. Palmer Dr., Schaumburg, IL 60103/312-397-4070 (Shooting Ranges)

The Dutchman's Firearms Inc., 4143 Taylor Blvd., Lousville, KY 40215/502-366-0555

Ellwood Epps Northern Ltd., 210 Worthington St., W., North Bay, Ont. P1B 3B4, Canada (hand traps)

Hunterjohn, P.O. Box 477, St. Louis, MO 63166 (shotgun patterning target)

Jaro Manuf., 206 E. Shaw, Pasadena, TX 77506/713-472-0417 (paper targets)

MTM Molded Prods. Co., P.O. Box 14117, Dayton, OH 45414/513-890-7461

Maki Industries, 26-10th St. S.E., Medicine Hat, AB T1A 1P7, Canada/403-526-7997 (X-Spand Target System)

Outers Laboratories, Div. of Omark Industries, Rte. 2, Onalaska, WI 54650/608-783-1515 (claybird traps)

Peterson Instant Targets, Inc., P.O. Box 755, Bethel, CT 06801/203-791-0456 (paste-ons; Targ-Dots)

Phillips Enterprises, Inc., 3600 Sunset Ave., Ocean, NJ 07712/201-493-3191 (portable target holder)

Red Star Target Co., 4519 Brisebois Dr. N.W., Calgary, AB T2L 2G3, Canada/403-289-7939

Remington Arms Co., 1007 Market St., Wilmington, DE 19898/302-773-5291 (claybird traps)

Rocky Mountain Target Co., P.O. Box 700, Black Hawk, SD 57718/605-787-5946 (Data-Targ)

Julio Santiago, P.O. Box O, Rosemount, NM 55068/612-890-7631 (targets)

Sheridan Products, Inc., 2600 Chicory Rd., Racine, WI 54303/414-554-7900 (traps)

Trius Prod. Inc., P.O. Box 25, Cleves, OH 45002/513-914-5682 (claybird, can thrower)

Winchester, Olin Corp., 427 N. Shamrock St., East Alton, IL 62024 (claybird traps)

TAXIDERMY

Jack Atcheson & Sons, Inc., 3210 Ottawa St., Butte, MT 59701

Dough's Taxidermy Studio, Doug Domedion, 5112 Edwards Rd., Medina, NY 14103/716-798-4022 (deer head specialist)

Jonas Bros. Denver, Inc., 1037 Broadway, Denver, CO 80203/303-534-7400 (catlg. $2)

Kulls Freeze-Dry Taxidermy, 725 Broadway Ave., Bedford, OH 44146

Mark D. Parker, 1240 Florida Ave. #7, Longmont, CO 80501/303-772-0214

TRAP & SKEET SHOOTERS EQUIP.

The American Import Co., 1453 Mission St., San Francisco, CA 94103/415-863-1506 (Targetthrower; claybird traps)

Briley Mfg. Co., 1085-B Gessner, Houston, TX 77055/713-932-6995 (choke tubes)

C&H Research, 115 Sunnyside Dr., Lewis, KS 67552/316-324-5445 (Mercury recoil suppressor)

Caswell International Corp., 1221 Marshall St. N.E., Minneapolis, MN 55413/612-379-2000

Clymer Mfg. Co., Inc., 1645 W. Hamlin Rd., Rochester Hills, MI 48309/313-853-5555

D&H Prods. Co., Inc., 465 Denny Rd., Valencia, PA 16059/412-898-2840 (snap shell)

Euroarms of America, Inc., 1501 Lenoir Dr.; P.O. Box 3277, Winchester, VA 22601/703-662-1863

Frigon Guns, 627 W. Crawford, Clay Center, KS 67432/913-632-5607

Griggs Products, P.O. Box 789; 270 S. Main St., Suite 103, Bountiful, UT 84010/801-295-9696 (recoil redirector)

Ken Eyster Heritage Gunsmiths, Inc., 6441 Bishop Rd., Centerburg, OH 43011/614-625-6131 (shotgun competition choking)

William E. Harper, The Great 870 Co., P.O. Box 6309, El Monte, CA 91734/213-579-3077

Hastings, P.O. Box 224, Clay Center, KS 67432/913-632-3169

Hoppe Division, Penguin Inds. Inc., Airport Mall, Coatesville, PA 19320/215-384-6000 (Monte Carlo pad)

Hunter Co., Inc., 3300 W. 71st Ave., Westminster, CO 80030/303-427-4626

Krieghoff International, Inc., P.O. Box 549, Ottsville, PA 18942/215-847-5173

Ljutic Industries Inc., P.O. Box 2117; 732 N 16th Ave., Yakima, WA 98907/509-248-0476

MTM Molded Products, P.O. Box 14117, Dayton, OH 45414/513-890-7461 (claybird thrower)

Magnum Research, Inc., P.O. Box 32221, Minneapolis, MN 55432/612-574-1868

Meadow Industries, P.O. Box 450, Marlton, NJ 08053/609-953-0922 (stock pad, variable; muzzle rest)

Wm. J. Mittler, 290 Moore Dr., Boulder Creek, CA 95006/408-338-3376 or 408-438-7331 (shotgun choke specialists)

Moneymaker Guncraft, 1420 Military Ave., Omaha, NE 68131/402-556-0226 (free-floating, ventilated ribs)

William J. Nittler, 111 Bean Creek Rd., Scotts Valley, CA 95066/408-438-7331 (shotgun barrel repairs)

Jim Noble Co., 1305 Columbia St., Vancouver, WA 98660/206-695-1309

Outers Laboratories, Div. of Omark Industries, Route 2, Onalaska, WI 54650/608-783-1515 (trap, claybird)

Protektor Model Co., 7 Ash St., Galeton, PA 16922/814-435-2442

Remington Arms Co., 1007 Market St., Wilmington, DE 19898 (trap, claybird)

Daniel Titus, Shooting Specialties, 872 Penn St., Bryn Mawr, PA 19010/215-525-8829 (hullbag)

Trius Products Inc., P.O. Box 25, Cleves, OH 45002/513-941-5682 (can thrower; trap, claybird)

Winchester Div., Olin Corp., 427 N. Shamrock St., East Alton, IL 62024 (trap, claybird)

Zeus International, P.O. Box 953, Tarpon Springs, FL 34688/813-863-5029

TRIGGERS, RELATED EQUIP.

Bell Design Corp., 718 So. 2nd/P.O. Box 64, Atwood, KS 67730/913-626-3270 (rifle triggers)

Brownells, Inc., 222 W. Liberty, Montezuma, IA 50171/515-623-5401

M.H. Canjar Co., 500 E. 45th Ave., Denver, CO 80216/303-295-2638 (triggers)

Central Specialties Co., 200 Lexington Dr., Buffalo Grove, IL 60089/312-537-3300 (trigger locks only)

Custom Products, Neil A. Jones, RD #1, Box 483A, Saegertown, PA 16433/814-763-2769 (trigger guard)

Cycle Dynamics Inc., 74 Garden St., Feeding Hills, MA 01030/413-786-0141

Dayton-Traister/MKII Co., 4778 N. Monkey Hill Rd., Oak Harbor, WA 98277/206-675-3421 (triggers)

Electronic Trigger Systems, 4124 Thrushwood Lane, Minnetonka, MN 55345/612-935-7929

Flaig's, 2200 Evergreen Rd., Millvale, PA 15209/412-821-1717 (trigger shoes)

Gun Parts Corp., Box 2, West Hurley, NY 12491/914-679-2419

Hastings, P.O. Box 224, Clay Center, KS 67432/913-632-3169

Bill Holmes, Rt. 2, Box 242, Fayetteville, AR 72701/501-521-8958 (trigger release)

Neil A. Jones, see: Custom Products

Meier Works, Steve Hines, Box 328, Canyon, TX 79015/806-655-7806 (shotgun trigger guard)

Miller Single Trigger Mfg. Co., R.D. 1, Box 99, Millersburg, PA 17061/717-692-3704 (selective or non-selective f. shotguns)

Bruce A. Nettestad, Rt. 1, Box 140, Pelican Rapids, MN 56572/218-863-4301 (trigger guards)

Pachmayr Ltd., 1875 So. Mountain Ave., Monrovia, CA 91016/818-357-7771 (trigger shoe)

Pacific Tool Co., P.O. Box 2048, Ordnance Plant Rd., Grand Island, NE 68801 (trigger shoe)

Serrifie Inc., P.O. Box 508, Littlerock, CA 93543/805-945-0713

Timney Mfg. Co., 3065 W. Fairmount Ave., Phoenix, AZ 85017/602-274-2999 (triggers)

Melvin Tyler Mfg.-Dist., 1326 W. Britton Rd., Oklahoma City, OK 73114/405-842-8044 (trigger shoe)

U.S.F.S. (Untied States Frame Specialists), P.O. Box 7762, Milwaukee, WI 53207/414-643-6387

Williams Gun Sight Co., 7389 Lapeer Rd., Davison, MI 48423 (trigger shoe)